NOTES

ON THE

OLD TESTAMENT

EXPLANATORY AND PRACTICAL

BY

ALBERT BARNES

ENLARGED TYPE EDITION

EDITED BY
ROBERT FREW, D.D.

DANIEL
VOL. I

BAKER BOOK HOUSE
GRAND RAPIDS, MICHIGAN

ISBN: 0-8010-0562-0

First Printing, July 1950
Second Printing, July 1957
Third Printing, May 1959
Fourth Printing, November 1961
Fifth Printing, May 1964
Sixth Printing, September 1966
Seventh Printing, December 1968
Eighth Printing, June 1970
Ninth Printing, November 1971
Tenth Printing, August 1973

PHOTOLITHOPRINTED BY CUSHING - MALLOY, INC.
ANN ARBOR, MICHIGAN, UNITED STATES OF AMERICA
1973

AUTHOR'S PREFACE.

A VERY remarkable resemblance has always been observed between the Book of Daniel and the Book of Revelation. Whatever view may be taken of the proper interpretation of these books, it is difficult to write a Commentary on one of them without carefully studying the other, and without practically furnishing to a considerable extent an exposition of the other. There is no evidence, indeed, that John, in the Book of Revelation, intended to imitate Daniel, and yet there is so strong a resemblance in the manner in which the Divine disclosures respecting the future were made to the two writers; there is so clear a reference to the same great events in the history of the world; there is so much similarity in the symbols employed, that no commentator can well write on the one without discussing many points, and making use of many illustrations, which would be equally appropriate in an exposition of the other.

The following Notes on the Book of Daniel were mostly written before I commenced the preparation of Notes on the Book of Revelation, though the latter book is published first. It has thus happened that many inquiries have been started, and many subjects discussed, in connection with this book, which would otherwise have found a place in the Notes on the Book of Revelation, and that in the exposition of the latter, I have, in many places, to avoid needless repetition, done little more than refer to corresponding places in the Notes on Daniel. While I have endeavoured to make each work a complete exposition in itself, it is nevertheless true that the two are designed, in some measure, to go together, and that the one is necessary to the full understanding of the other.

PHILADELPHIA, *December* 26, 1851.

EDITOR'S PREFACE.

WE send forth these volumes on Daniel, in perfect confidence that they will be hailed with acceptance by the author's numerous admirers in this country.

The book of Daniel possesses charms alike for the susceptible mind of youth, and the mature mind of the advanced student. Who has not hung with delight in the days of his childhood over the wondrous stories of the captive prophet, regarding the judgment of God on the haughty Nebuchadnezzar, Belshazzar's impious feast and awful doom, the three children in the burning fiery furnace, and Daniel in the lions' den? No Eastern tales, no *Arabian Nights' Entertainments*, have so fascinated us as these. Here, assuredly, truth is more wonderful than fiction. And what student of Scripture has not been arrested and detained by the sublime visions of Daniel, and has not felt all his powers tasked in the interpretation of them? The vision of the colossal statue; of the four beasts from the sea; of the ram and the he-goat; of the seventy weeks, and the final resurrection scene, presenting a kind of epitomized history of the successive empires of the world, and of the varying condition of the church, as existing in them, or affected by them, have all along excited deep interest, and formed the subject of prolonged inquiry to the most gifted minds. Sir Isaac Newton was as anxious to penetrate into these prophetic depths, as into those depths of heaven, where he sought the starry worlds, whose laws he expounded.

Of the Author's commentary the reader will judge for himself. It seems to us to be characterized by his usual thoroughness of research, and solidity of judgment. We do not say that we can accord with him on all points, or that his book is likely to satisfy any student of prophecy on all points; but inasmuch as what may be called the Protestant scheme of exposition is presented with more clearness and fulness, and with more advantages from the new lights of modern history and research, than in any other English work of the kind, we should anticipate for it a very high, if not the highest place, among English commentaries on Daniel.   We doubt not a brief outline or analysis of the exposition will be acceptable to our readers.   We shall, therefore, present it here, noting, when it may seem necessary, the points where our author diverges from the usual course of exposition, or differs from those who have been regarded as authorities.

We say nothing of the historical part, but pass at once to the prophetic.   The vision of the colossal statue (chap. ii.) is interpreted in the usual way of the four great monarchies ; and "the stone cut out of the mountain without hands," is the kingdom of the Messiah, superhuman in its origin, feeble in its beginnings, but ultimately supplanting all other kingdoms, and filling the earth.   The vision of the four beasts, the lion, the bear, the leopard, and the nondescript animal, "dreadful and terrible," (chap. vii.) presents the four monarchies again, under another form or different set of symbols.   The ten horns in the head of this last monster (which represents the Roman empire) are the ten kingdoms into which the Western empire was divided ; and the little horn springing up among the ten, and destroying three of them, the horn with "eyes of man, and mouth speaking great things," is the Papacy, not Antiochus Epiphanes, as Eichhorn, Bertholdt, Bleek, Stuart, and others, maintain.   The Author's defence (vol. ii. p. 76–82), of this interpretation, seems to us not only able, but triumphant.   The time of this little horn, or Papal power (vii. 25), is $3\frac{1}{2}$ prophetic years, or 1260 prophetic days, that is, years, beginning, A.D. 752 (vol. ii. p. 96), when Pepin, king of France, gave a grant to Pope Stephen of the exarchate of Ravenna, and the Pentapolis.   The year A.D. 2012 is, of course, the termination of the period.

We have next the vision of the ram and the he-goat, interpreted of the Medo-Persian and Greek empires, of which these animals were respectively the well-known emblems (chap. viii.)   The "notable horn" (ver. 5) of the goat is Alexander the Great.   The "four notable ones" that come up afterwards are his successors ; and the "little horn out of one of them" is Antiochus Epiphanes.   The time in this vision is 2300 days, which our author interprets literally of a period of six years and 110 days ; and applies to the whole period of the Antiochian persecution, from B.C. December, 25, 165, when the sanctuary was cleansed under Judas Maccabeus, and the persecution of course ended, backwards to B.C. August 5, 171, when the aggressions on the part of Antiochus began. It may not be practicable to make out the precise number of days, but this calculation brings us to the year which is necessary to make out the 2300 days. So Mr. Barnes. The two Newtons, on the other hand, in strict consistency with their Year-day principle, expound the little horn of Rome, and calculate the time from B.C. 334, the date of Alexander's invasion of Asia, or from the vision of the he-goat, and thus they make it end with the world's sixth millennium. Scott, following Faber, expounds of the Mahometan delusion, and dates from somewhere in the time of the ram or Persian empire; that is, somewhere between B.C. 536 and B.C. 330, and maintains, of course, the Year-day principle.

Next we have the famous vision of the seventy weeks. This general period, explained of 490 years, is calculated by our author from the 20th of Artaxerxes Longimanus, that is, from B.C. 454: it is divided into three parts; first, a period of seven weeks or forty-nine years to the rebuilding of the city, which, counting from the *terminus a quo* as above, brings us to B.C. 405, the time when Nehemiah had completely finished his undertaking (vol. ii. p. 175); second, a period of sixty-two weeks, or 434 years, *after* which Messiah would appear and be cut off, which brings us to A.D. 29; and third, a period of one week, or seven years, which was occupied in confirming the covenant with many, through the ministry of Christ and his apostles; in the midst of this week Jesus, in accordance with the prediction, died, and the sacrifice and oblation for ever ceased! (vol. ii. p. 182). A more remarkable prophecy, and one whose fulfilment can be more distinctly traced, never was uttered; and our author's full and lucid exposition, after his happiest manner, makes this one of the most interesting portions of his book.

The prophecy next passes, at chap. xi., to the wars between the kings of the north and the south, that is, between Syria and Egypt, or the Seleucidæ and the Ptolemies. The introductory part (vers. 1-4) presents an epitome of previous history—noticing the three successors of Cyrus, viz., Cambyses, Smerdis, and Darius Hystaspis; also the fourth and rich king, viz., Xerxes; and the mighty king, whose kingdom should be divided to the four winds of heaven, viz., Alexander the Great and his four generals, who, at his death, partitioned the kingdom among them.

After this introductory part, the wars between the north and the south,
or the long succession of hostilities between two parts of Alexander's
dominions, Syria, and Egypt, immediately follow (vers. 5-20).   At this
place (ver. 21) Antiochus Epiphanes, king of Syria, is again introduced,
under the character of a "vile person."   Mr. Barnes applies the whole
chapter, from this verse onwards to the end, to him alone.   There is,
however, difference of opinion among interpreters in regard to the
passage beginning at verse 31, where, according to many, the Romans
or Antichrist must be understood.   See the application to this last
power ably defended in Elliott's *Horæ Apoc.*, vol. iv. p. 7, 4th edition.
The argument of Birks, Elliott, and others, in favour of a change of
subject at verse 31, from the translation of the first clause, "arms
shall stand up *from* or *after* him," seemingly indicating some *new* prince
or power, has been overlooked by our author; and on other grounds
the entire application to Antiochus seems not very tenable, though
argued with very great learning and ingenuity.   At verse 40 occurs
another indication of change of subject.   Certain events are said to
take place at "the time of the end," that is, of the period to which
the vision refers.   But as no such events as those described happened
towards the *close* of the reign of Antiochus, Mr. Barnes has recourse
to a theory of recapitulation on the part of the prophet, which, to say
the best of it, is but an ingenious conjecture.   This enables him to
find events in the history of Antiochus corresponding with the prophetic description.

   The prophecy concludes with a sublime vision of the resurrection
(ch. xii.), which is indeed but a continuation of the vision commenced
in ch. x.   According to our author, the primary reference is to the
restoration of the temple worship, and deliverance of the Jews by Judas
Maccabeus and his compatriots; while the mind of the prophet is supposed to rest ultimately, by the law of prophetic association, on the
general resurrection at the last day.   The various notices of time in
this chapter are thus treated; the 1260 (verse 7) has a primary
reference to the three and a half years' persecution under Antiochus,
and an ultimate reference to the downfall of the Papacy, as in vii. 25 ;
the 1290 and the 1335 are not to be known till the event, and conjecture is useless.   Newton, Scott, and the school to which they
belong, suppose that, when at the close of the well-known 1260, Anti-

christ shall be subverted—thirty years more may be occupied in *totally* extirpating that power, while forty-five years more still may serve to completely introduce the millennium.

Such is a very brief sketch of our author's work on Daniel. We add a sentence or two on his mode of interpreting the Danielic times. It will be seen, from the above analysis, that he does not rigidly adhere to the Year-day principle. He seems very much to adopt or reject it as the exigency of the particular passage under consideration may require. The time, times, and dividing of a time, in ch. vii. 25, is interpreted on that principle, and accordingly is explained of the 1260 years of Antichrist; while the 2300 days of ch. viii. 13, 14, are interpreted on the Literal-day principle, and explained of the duration of the Antiochian persecution. Again, the Year-day theory is adopted in the vision of the seventy weeks in ch. ix.; while in ch. xii. 7, the three-and a half years, are both literal and prophetic, in order to answer the primary reference to Antiochus, and the ultimate one to Antichrist. Possibly, this varying principle of interpretation may be the true one. It *may* be, that in many cases the shorter period is typical of the longer, and that, therefore both may be understood in the same passages. Yet if this be so in many passages, or in any, why not in all? We could wish to see all interpretations of prophetic times preceded by some *clear* observations on the *principles* by which the author professes to be guided. We confess, therefore, a strong partiality for that system of interpretation which carries the Year-day principle consistently out; of course the merit of consistency belongs equally to those who carry out any other well-understood principle. In the author's note on ch. vii. 25, and other places where notices of time occur, very able defences of the Year-day principle may be found, to which, as the Notes on Daniel were written first, there is constant reference in the Notes on the times of the Apocalypse; and we have only to regret the want of some hints to guide us in regard to the mode of its application.

To do justice to the author and to himself, the reader, moreover, must remember that the Commentary on Daniel, and that on the Apocalypse, form together but one work. The author, in an advertisement, informs us, that the two may, without impropriety, be considered as parts of one whole. The two books, according to the views taken in the exposition, refer to a considerable extent to the same events;

and the intention was, that they should be published as nearly simultaneously as possible. Many important points, therefore, which are merely glanced at in the Commentary on Revelation, will be found more fully elucidated in the Notes on Daniel, which, though last in point of publication, were first composed.

Of the general character of these volumes, we must say again, that we cannot speak too highly. They form, we think, take them all in all, our best English Commentary on Daniel. The author has made himself familiar with the more ancient expositions; with the rich stores of Germany—of Eichhorn, Bertholdt, and Hengstenberg, from whom he has drawn with that nice discrimination which the admixture of good and bad in these works required at his hands; with the views of his own great countrymen, Stuart and Bush; and with those of our own Newtons and Wintles; and, in fine, with all that has been written worthily on the subject—and the result is a most satisfying fulness. Another result of the author's labours will be to confirm public confidence more completely in that system of interpretation of prophecy which has so long prevailed amongst us, and to destroy which so many attempts have recently been made. The cry against it originating in Germany, and echoed in America by Professor Moses Stuart, has been adopted and defended by eminent scholars at home. But in the author of the Notes on Daniel and the Apocalypse, we have a man of no mean learning and research adhering to the old, though much maligned principles, and willing to hazard his reputation by following such a guide as the despised Bishop Newton. When we read such sneering assaults as the following, from the pen of one who may be styled the chief of the New School, we will be better able to appreciate the boldness with which our author, in spite of it, has taken up his position. We introduce the quotation by simply remarking that Bishop Newton has long maintained his place, and is likely to maintain it for a long while to come; and that something more is necessary to an expounder of the Word of God, than a knowledge of historico-grammatical interpretation. The profoundest scholars may prove the poorest exegetes, as witness Grotius and the great man who writes:—

"As to the book of Daniel itself, I believe that no other of the scriptural books, the Apocalypse excepted, has called forth such a variety of discrepant opinions and interpretations. How can I agree with all of them? And yet the great mass of readers are ready to say, each one for himself, that I ought to agree with him. But why? my friend. You take the liberty to differ from others; and why should you refuse the same liberty to me? Besides, I have to ask, On what grounds have you based your opinion? Have you studied the book in its original languages; sought for light on every side, from history, and from antiquities; and above all, have you thoroughly and simply applied to it, irrespective of any favourite and preconceived notions about it, the established principles of historico-grammatical exegesis? And do you even know, with any certainty, what those principles are? If not, how much is your opinion worth, even in your own eyes, when you look candidly at such a difficult matter as the interpretation of the book before us?

"If here and there a self-complacent critic of my Commentary on the Apocalypse, had asked himself such questions, before he sat down to write his *diatribe,* the public would have been spared a deal of *à priori* interpretation and spider-web theories. Some had written their book, on the same work of John, and mine disagreed with it. *Hinc illae lacrymae.* Some had read that *profound* work of Bishop Newton on the Prophecies; and because I did not agree with him, I must be in the wrong. The most confident of my condemning judges were, of course, those who could not read a word of the original, and would not be able to form any idea what one means, who talks about historico-grammatical interpretation. I have no defence to make against any such assailants."

In taking leave of this latest work of our author, we must not omit to advert to the reappearance of an admirable feature in his earliest publications. We have very full and pointed practical reflections at the close of each chapter, onward to the sixth inclusive. In the remaining portions of the work, such reflections are more sparingly introduced.

Of this edition we can only say, that the text has been subjected to careful revision; that very many errors have been corrected; and that the illustrations have everywhere been greatly improved, while in some instances the original ones have been rejected, and others more appropriate substituted in their room. We had intended to enlarge the Essay on the Year-day principle which is prefixed to our edition of the author's Notes on the Apocalypse, with the view of giving it a place here.　But the rapidity with which the work has gone through the press, allowed no time for the necessary labour.　We can, therefore, in the meantime, only refer to that Essay in the imperfect form in which it already exists.　In the first volume will be found one or two Appendices, from the Commentary of Professor Stuart, on such points as his learning and scholarship eminently qualified him to discuss.　In the second volume there is an Appendix, consisting of part of the first and second books of the Maccabees, which we were induced to insert from a conviction that in an exposition of a prophecy, where Antiochus Epiphanes and the Maccabees figure so conspicuously, it would be for the reader's convenience to have the original history at hand, to which reference is made in almost every page.

N.B.—The copyright of the Notes on Daniel for Great Britain and Ireland, has been assigned by the author to Messrs. Knight and Hawkes; and this edition is now published under arrangement with them.

DANIEL.

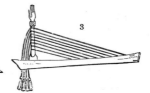

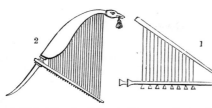

1, Ancient Egyptian Triangular Harp.   2, Persian *Chang*.
From Persian MS. 410 years old.

3, Assyrian Dulcimer.
Sculptures, British Museum.

Large Egyptian Harps.—From Rosellini.

Assyrian Lyre.
Sculptures, British Mus.

Egyptian Double Pipe, and clapping
hands.—British Museum.

[DANIEL vol. i. p. 209.]

Assyrian Drums.
Sculptures, British Mus.

INTRODUCTION.

OF Daniel little more is known, or can now be ascertained, than is recorded in this book. There are two other persons of this name mentioned in the Bible — a son of David (1 Chron. iii. 1); and a Levite of the race of Ithamar (Ezra viii. 2; Neh. x. 6). The latter has been sometimes confounded with the prophet, as he is in the apocryphal addenda to the Septuagint.

Daniel, supposed commonly to be the same person as the author of this book, is twice mentioned by Ezekiel, once as deserving to be ranked with Noah and Job, and once as eminent for wisdom. "Though these three men, Noah, Daniel, and Job, were in it, they should deliver but their own souls by their righteousness, saith the Lord God" (Ezek. xiv. 14). "Behold, thou art wiser than Daniel; there is no secret that they can hide from thee" (Ezek. xxviii. 3). Whether this is the Daniel who is the author of this book, however, or whether this was some ancient patriarch whose name had been handed down by tradition, and whose name was *assumed* by the author of this book in later times, has been a question among recent critics, and will properly come up for examination under the next section in this Introduction.

Assuming now that the book is genuine, and that it was written by him whose name it bears, all that is known of Daniel is substantially as follows :—

He was descended from one of the highest families in Judah, if not one of royal blood (Notes on ch. i. 3; Josephus' *Ant.* b. x. ch. x. § 1). His birthplace was probably Jerusalem (comp. ch. ix. 24), though it is not absolutely certain that this passage would demonstrate it.

Of his first years nothing is recorded. At an early age we find him in Babylon, among the captive Hebrews whom Nebuchadnezzar had carried away at the first deportation of the people of Judah, in the fourth year of Jehoiakim. He is mentioned in connection with three

A

other youths, apparently of the same rank, Hananiah, Mishael, and
Azariah, who, with him, were selected for the purpose of being
instructed in the language and literature of the Chaldeans, with a
view to their being employed in the service of the court (Dan. i. 3, 4).
His age at that time it is impossible to determine with accuracy, but
it is not improbable that it was somewhere about twelve or fifteen
years.   In ch. i. 4, he and his three friends are called "children"
(יְלָדִים).   "This word properly denotes the period from the age of
childhood up to manhood, and might be translated *boys*, *lads*, or
youth."—(Professor Stuart on Daniel, p. 373).   Ignatius (*Ep. ad
Magn.*) says that Daniel was twelve years of age when he went into
exile; Chrysostom says that he was eighteen (*Opp.* vi. p. 423);
Epiphanius says, ἔτι νήπιος ὤν; Jerome calls him *admodum puer*.
These are, of course, mere conjectures, or traditions, but they are
probably not far from the truth.   Such was the age at which persons
would be most *likely* to be selected for the training here referred to.
The design of this selection and training is not mentioned, but in the
circumstances of the case it is perhaps not difficult to conjecture it.
The Hebrews were a captive people.   It was natural to suppose that
they would be restless, and perhaps insubordinate, in their condition,
and it was a matter of policy to do all that could be done to conciliate them.   Nothing would better tend to this than to select some
of their own number who were of their most distinguished families;
to place them at court; to provide for them from the royal bounty;
to give them the advantages of the best education that the capital
afforded; to make an arrangement that contemplated their future
employment in the service of the state, and to furnish them every
opportunity of promotion.   Besides, in the intercourse of the government with the captive Hebrews, of which, from the nature of the case,
there would be frequent occasion, it would be an advantage to have
native-born Hebrews in the confidence of the government, who could
be employed to conduct that intercourse.

In this situation, and with this view, Daniel received that thorough
education which Oriental etiquette makes indispensable in a courtier
(comp. Plato, *Alcib.* § 37), and was more especially instructed in the
science of the Chaldeans, and in speaking and writing their language.
He had before evidently been carefully trained in the Hebrew learning,
and in the knowledge of the institutions of his country, and was
thoroughly imbued with the principles of the religion of his fathers.
An opportunity soon occurred of putting his principles to the test.
Trained in strict religious principles, and in the sternest rules of temperance in eating and drinking, and fearing the effect of the luxurious
living provided for him and his companions by the royal bounty, he
resolved, with them, to avoid at once the danger of conforming to the
habits of idolaters; of "polluting" himself by customs forbidden by
his religion, and of jeoparding his own health and life by intemperate

indulgence. He aimed, also, to secure the utmost vigour of body, and the utmost clearness of mind, by a course of strict and conscientious temperance. He obtained permission, therefore, to abstain from the food provided for him, and to make an experiment of the most temperate mode of living (ch. i. 8–14). "His prudent proceedings, wise bearing, and absolute refusal to comply with such customs, were crowned with the Divine blessing, and had the most splendid results."

After the lapse of three years spent in this course of discipline, Daniel passed the examination which was necessary to admit him to the royal favour, and was received into connection with the government, to be employed in the purposes which had been contemplated in this preparatory training (ch. i. 18–20). One of his first acts was an interpretation of a dream of Nebuchadnezzar, which none of the Chaldeans had been able to interpret, the result of which was that he was raised at once to that important office, the governorship of the province of Babylon, and the head inspectorship of the sacerdotal caste (ch. ii.)

Considerably later in the reign of Nebuchadnezzar, we find Daniel interpreting another dream of his, to the effect that, in consequence of his pride, he would be deprived for a time of his reason and his throne, and would be suffered to wander from the abodes of men, and to live among wild beasts, but that after a time he would be again restored. The record which we have of this is found in a proclamation of the king himself, which is preserved by Daniel (ch. iv.) In the interpretation of this remarkable dream, and in stating to the king—the most proud and absolute monarch of the earth at that time —what would come upon him, Daniel displays the most touching anxiety, love, and loyalty for the prince, and shows that he was led to this interpretation only by the conviction of the truth. In view of a calamity so great, he exhorted the monarch yet to humble himself and to repent of his sins, and to perform acts of charity, with the hope that God might be merciful, and avert from him a doom so humiliating—so much to be dreaded (ch. iv. 19–27).

Under the immediate successor of Nebuchadnezzar—Evil-Merodach —Daniel appears to have been forgotten, and his talents and his former services seem to have passed away from the recollection of those in power. His situation at court appears to have been confined to an inferior office (ch. viii. 27), and it would seem also that this led him occasionally, if not regularly, away from Babylon to some of the provinces to attend to business there. (Comp. Notes on ch. viii. 2). This was not strange. On the death of a monarch, it was not unusual to discharge the officers who had been employed in the government, as, at the present time, on the death of a king, or a change of dynasty, the members of the cabinet are changed; or as the same thing happens in our own country when a change occurs in the chief magistracy of the nation.* Sir John Chardin, in his MS. Notes on Persia, says that, in his time, on the death of a Shah or king, all the soothsayers and physicians attached to the court were at once dismissed from office; the former because they did not *predict* his death, and the latter because they did not *prevent* it. It is to be remembered also, that Daniel was raised to power by the will of Nebuchadnezzar alone, and that the offices which he held were, in part, in consequence of the service which he had rendered that prince; and it is not strange, therefore, that on a change of the government, he, with perhaps the other favourites of the former sovereign, should be suffered to retire. We find consequently no mention made of Daniel during the reign of Evil-Merodach, or in the short reign of his successor; we lose sight of him until the reign of Belshazzar, the last king of Babylon, and then he is mentioned only in connection with the closing scene of his life (ch. v.) In consequence of a remarkable vision which Belshazzar had of a handwriting on the wall, and of the inability of any of the wise men of the Chaldeans to read and interpret it, Daniel, at the instance of the queen-mother, who remembered his former services at court, was called in, and read the writing, and announced to the king the impending destiny of himself and his empire. For this service he was again restored to honour, and the purpose was formed to raise him to an exalted rank at court—a purpose which was, however, frustrated by the fact that Babylon was that very night taken, and that the government passed into the hands of the Medes and Persians. It was under this king, however, that Daniel had two of his most remarkable visions (ch. vii., viii.) respecting future events— visions which, perhaps, more definitely than any other in the Scriptures, disclose what is to occur in the ages to come.

After the conquest of Babylon by the united arms of the Medes and Persians, under the reign of Darius or Cyaxares, Daniel was raised again to an exalted station. The whole kingdom was divided into one hundred and twenty provinces, and over these three presidents or chief governors were appointed, and of these Daniel had the first rank (ch. vi. 1—3). The *reasons* of this appointment are not stated, but they were doubtless found in such circumstances as the following : that it was desirable for Darius to employ some one who was familiar with the affairs of the Babylonian empire; that Daniel probably had know-ledge on that subject equal or superior to any other one that could be found; that he had long been employed at court, and was familiar with the laws, usages, and customs that prevailed there; that he knew better

---

* Since this was written, a remarkable illustration of what is here said has occurred in our own country (United States), on the death of the late president, General Zachary Taylor. It will be recollected that on the very night of his death, all the members of the cabinet tendered their resignation to his constitutional successor, and all of them in fact ceased to hold office, and retired to private life.

than any one else, perhaps, what would secure the tranquillity of that portion of the empire ; that, being himself a foreigner, it might be supposed better to employ him than it would be a native Chaldean, for it might be presumed that he would be less inimical to a foreign dominion. Under these circumstances he was again raised to a high rank among the officers of the government; but his elevation was not beheld without malice and envy. Those who might have expected this office for themselves, or who were dissatisfied that a foreigner should be thus exalted, resolved, if possible, to bring him into such a situation as would ruin him (ch. vi. 4). To do this, they determined to take advantage of a principle in the government of the Medes and Persians, that a law having once received the royal sanction could not be changed ; and by securing the passing of such a law as they knew Daniel would not obey, they hoped to humble and ruin him. They, therefore, under plausible pretences, secured the passing of a law that no one in the realm should be allowed for a certain time to offer any petition to any God or man, except the king, on penalty of being thrown into a den of lions. Daniel, as they anticipated, was the first to disregard this law, by continuing his regular habit of worshipping God, praying, as he had been accustomed, three times a-day, with his window open. The consequence was, that the king, there being no way to prevent the execution of the law, allowed it to be executed. Daniel was cast into the den of lions, but was miraculously preserved ; and this new proof of his integrity, and of the Divine favour, was the means of his being raised to more exalted honour (ch. vi.)

In this situation at court, and with these advantages for promoting the interests of his people, he employed himself in seriously and diligently securing the return of the exiles to their own country, though it does not appear that he himself returned, or that he contemplated a return. It is probable that he supposed that at his time of life it would not be wise to attempt such a journey; or that he supposed he could be of more use to his countrymen in Babylon in favouring their return than he could by accompanying them to their own land. His position at the court of the Medo-Persian government gave him an opportunity of rendering material aid to his people, and it is not improbable that it was through his instrumentality that the decree was obtained from Cyrus which allowed them to return. One of the designs of Providence in raising him up was, doubtless, that he might exert that influence at court, and that he might thus be the means of restoring the exiles. He had at last the happiness to see his most ardent wishes accomplished in this respect.

In the third year of Cyrus, he had a vision, or a series of visions (ch. x.—xii.), containing minute details respecting the history and sufferings of his nation to the time of Antiochus Epiphanes, concluding with a more general representation (ch. xii.) of what would occur in the last days of the world's history.

Beyond this, nothing certain is known of Daniel. The accounts respecting him are vague, confused, and strange. How long he lived, and when and where he died, are points on which no certain information can now be obtained. Josephus gives no account of his latter days, or of his death, though he says respecting him, " he was so happy as to have strange revelations made to him, and those as to one of the greatest of the prophets, insomuch that while he was alive he had the esteem and applause both of kings and of the multitude ; and now he is dead, he retains a remembrance that will never fail." (*Ant.* b. x. ch. xi). It is commonly believed that he died in Chaldea, having been detained there by his employments in the Persian empire. Epiphanius says that he died in Babylon, and this has been the commonly received opinion of historians. This opinion, however, has not been universal. Some suppose that he died at Shushan or Susa. Josephus (*Ant.* b. x. ch. xi.) says that, " on account of the opinion which men had that he was beloved of God, he built a tower at Ecbatana in Media, which was a most elegant building and wonderfully made," and that it was still remaining in his day. Benjamin of Tudela says that his monument was shown at Chuzestan, which is the ancient Susa. As Benjamin of Tudela professes to record what he saw and heard, and as his *Itinerary* is a book which has been more frequently transcribed and translated than almost any other book, except the *Travels* of Maundeville, it may be of some interest to copy what he has said of the tomb of Daniel. It is a record of the traditions of the East—the country where Daniel lived and died, and it is not improbably founded in essential truth. At any rate, it will show what has been the current tradition in the East respecting Daniel, and is all that can now be known respecting the place of his death and burial. Benjamin of Tudela was a Jewish Rabbi of Spain, who travelled through Europe, Asia, and Africa, from Spain to China, between A.D. 1160 and 1173. His *Itinerary* was first printed in 1543. It was a work in wide circulation in the thirteenth, fourteenth, and fifteenth centuries, and has been translated from the original Hebrew into Latin, English, French, Dutch, and Jewish German, and in these languages has passed through not less than twenty-two editions. I quote from the London and Berlin edition of 1840. " Four miles from hence begins Khuzestan, Elam of Scripture, a large province which, however, is but partially inhabited, a portion of it lying in ruins. Among the latter are the remains of Shushan, the metropolis and palace of king Achashverosh, which still contains very large and handsome buildings of ancient date. Its seven thousand Jewish inhabitants possess fourteen synagogues, in front of one of which is the tomb of Daniel, who rests in peace. The river Ulai divides the parts of the city, which are connected with a bridge ; that portion of it which is inhabited by the Jews contains the markets ; to it all trade is confined, and there dwell all the rich ; on the other side of the river they are poor, because they are deprived of the above-named advantages, and have even no gardens nor orchards. These circumstances gave rise to jealousy, which was fostered by the belief that all honour and riches originated from the possession of the remains of the prophet Daniel, who rests in peace, and who was buried on their side. A request was made *by the poor* for permission to remove the sepulchre to the other side, but it was rejected; upon which a war arose, and was carried on between the two parties for a length of time. This strife lasted 'until their souls became loath' (Numb. xxi. 4, 5; Judg. xvi. 16), and they came to a mutual agreement, by which it was stipulated that the coffin which contained Daniel's bones should be deposited alternately every year on either side. Both parties faithfully adhered to this arrangement, which was, however. interrupted by the interference of Sanjar Shah Ben Shah, who governs all Persia, and holds supreme power over forty-five of its kings.

"When this great emperor Sanjar, king of Persia, came to Shushan, and saw that the coffin of Daniel was removed from side to side, he crossed the bridge with a very numerous retinue, and accompanied by Jews and Mahometans, inquired into the nature of these proceedings. Upon being told what we have related above, he declared that it was derogatory to the honour of Daniel, and recommended that the distance between the two banks should be exactly measured; that Daniel's coffin should be deposited in another coffin, made of glass, and that it should be suspended from the very middle of the bridge, fastened by chains of iron. A place of public worship was erected on the very spot, open to every one who desired to say his prayers, whether he be Jew or Gentile, and the coffin of Daniel is suspended from the bridge unto this very day."—(Vol. i. pp. 117—120).

This story, trifling as it is in some of its details, may be admitted as evidence of a tradition in the East that Daniel died and was buried at Shushan. This tradition, moreover, is very ancient. In a note on this passage (vol. ii. p. 152), A. Asher, the publisher of the *Itinerary* of Benjamin, says: "Aasim of Cufah, a venerable historian, who preceded Ibn Haukel by two hundred years (for he died 735), mentions the discovery of Daniel's coffin at Sus. Ibn Haukel, who travelled in the tenth century, speaks of it, and ascribes to the possession of the bones of Daniel the virtue of dispelling all sorts of distress, particularly that of famine from want of rain." It has been a matter of much controversy whether the place now known as Chouck, Chouz, or Sous is the ancient Shushan (lat. 31° 55', long. 83° 40'), or the place now called Shuster (lat. 31° 30', long. 84° 30'). The former opinion is maintained by Rennel, Ouseley, Barbié du Bocage, Kinneir, and Hoek; the latter by d'Herbelot, d'Anville, Vincent, Mannert, and Hammer. Major Rawlinson, who has furnished the most recent account of this place, maintains that "Shushan the palace" is the present Susan on the Kulan or Eulaeus, the Ulai of Scripture. (See vol. ix. of the *Journal of the Royal Geographical Society*).

§ II.—GENUINENESS AND AUTHENTICITY OF THE BOOK OF DANIEL.

Consideration of Objections.

Until a comparatively recent period, with some slight exceptions, the genuineness and authenticity of the book of Daniel have been regarded as settled, and its canonical authority was as little doubted as that of any other portion of the Bible. The ancient Hebrews never called its genuineness or authenticity in question (Lengerke, *Das Buch Daniel*, Königsberg, 1835, p. 6; Hengstenberg, *Die Authentie des Daniel*, Berlin, 1831, p. 1). It is true that in the *Talmud* (*Tract. Baba Bathra*, Fol. 15, Ed. Venet.) it is said that "the men of the Great Synagogue wrote—כתבו the כנגד K. D. N. G.—that is, portions (eleven chapters) of the book of Ezekiel, the prophet Daniel, and the book of Esther;" but this, as Lengerke has remarked (p. v.), does not mean that they had introduced this book into the canon, as Bertholdt supposes, but that, partly by tradition, and partly by inspiration, they revised it anew. But whatever may be the truth in regard to this, it does not prove that the ancient Jews did not consider it canonical. It is true that much has been said about the fact that the Jews did not class this book among the prophets, but placed it in the *Hagiographa* or *Kethubim*, כתובים. It has been inferred from this, that they believed that it was composed a considerable time after the other prophetic books, and that they did not deem it worthy of a place among their prophetic books in general. But, even if this were so, it would not prove that they did not regard it as a genuine production of Daniel; and the fact that it was not placed among the prophetic books may be accounted for without the supposition that they did not regard it as genuine. The usual statement on that subject is, that they placed the book there because they say that Daniel lived the life of a courtier in Babylon, rather than the life of a prophet; and the Jews further assert that, though he received Divine communications, they were only by dreams and visions of the night, which they regard as the most imperfect kind of revelations.—(Horne, *Intro.* iv. 188). The place which Daniel should occupy in the Sacred Writings probably became a matter of discussion among the Hebrews only after the coming of the Saviour, when Christians urged so zealously his plain prophecies (ch. ix. 24–27) in proof of the Messiahship of the Lord Jesus.

The first open and avowed adversary to the genuineness and authenticity of the book of Daniel was Porphyry, a learned adversary of the Christian faith in the third century. He wrote fifteen books against Christianity, all of which are lost, except some fragments preserved by Eusebius, Jerome, and others. His objections against Daniel were made in his twelfth book, and all that we have of these objections has been preserved by Jerome in his commentary on the book of Daniel. A full account of Porphyry, and of his objections against the Christians and the sacred books of the Old and New Testament, so far as can now be known, may be seen in Lardner, *Jewish and Heathen Testimonies*, vol. vii. pp. 390–470, of his works, Ed. London, 1829. In regard to the book of Daniel, he maintained, according to Jerome (*Pr.* and *Explan.* in Daniel), "that the book was not written by him whose name it bears, but by another who lived in Judea in the time of Antiochus, surnamed Epiphanes; and that the book of Daniel does not foretell things to come, but relates what had already happened. In a word, whatever it contains to the time of Antiochus is true history; if there is anything relating to after-times it is falsehood; forasmuch as the writer could not see things future, but at the most only could make some conjectures about them. To him several of our authors have given answers of great labour and diligence—in particular, Eusebius, bishop of Cæsarea, in three volumes, the 18th, the 19th, and the 20th; Apollinarius, also, in one large book, that is, the 26th; and before them, in part, Methodius. 'As it is not my design,' says Jerome, 'to confute the objections of the adversary, which would require a long discourse; but only to explain the prophet to our own people, that is, to Christians, I shall just observe that none of the prophets have spoken so clearly of Christ as Daniel, for he not only foretells his coming, as do others likewise, but he also teaches the time when he will come, and mentions in order the princes of the intermediate space, and the number of the years, and the signs of his appearance. And because Porphyry saw all these things to have been fulfilled, and could not deny that they had actually come to pass, he was compelled to say as he did; and because of some similitude of circumstances, he asserted that the things foretold as to be fulfilled in Antichrist at the end of the world happened in the time of Antiochus Epiphanes:—which kind of opposition is a testimony of truth; for such is the plain interpretation of the words, that to incredulous men the prophet seems not to foretell things to come, but to relate things already past; and though, as before said, it is not my intention to confute all his objections, I shall, as occasion offers, take notice of some of his weak arguments. And it may be proper for us, among other things, to observe now, that Porphyry argued that the book of Daniel was not genuine, because it was written in Greek, and, therefore, was not the work of any Jew, but the forgery of some Greek writer. This he argued from some Greek words which are in the fable of Susanna, to which both Eusebius and Apollinarius returned the same answer, that the fabulous stories of Susanna, and Bel and the Dragon, are not in the Hebrew, but are said to have been composed by a person of the tribe of Levi; whereas the sacred Scriptures assure us that Daniel and the three children, his companions, were of the tribe of Judah. And they said they were not accountable for what was not received by the Jews, nor was a part of the sacred Scriptures.' " A few of the objections which Porphyry makes to the credibility of certain parts of Daniel, Jerome has quoted in his commentary on the particular passages referred to. These have been collected by Dr. Lardner, and may be seen in his works, vol. vii. pp. 402–415. It is not necessary to transcribe them here, as they will come up for consideration in the notes on the particular chapters.

Dr. Lardner (vol. vii. p. 401) remarks respecting Porphyry, "that Porphyry's work against the Christians was much laboured, and that in this argument he displayed all his learning, which was very considerable. Hence we can perceive the difficulty of undertaking an answer to him, for which very few were fully qualified; in which none of the apologists for Christianity seem to have answered expectations." We cannot now form a correct opinion of the argument of Porphyry, for we have only the few fragments of his work which Jerome and others have seen proper to preserve. We are in danger, therefore, of doing injustice to what may have been the real force of his argument, for it *may* have been stronger than would be indicated by those fragments that remain. It is impossible to recover his main objections; and all that can now be said is, that, as far as is known, he did not make any converts to his opinions, and that his objections produced no change in the faith of the Christian world.

No further attack on the genuineness and authenticity of Daniel seems to have been made, and no further doubt entertained, until the time of Spinoza. Spinoza was by birth a Jew; was born at Amsterdam in 1632; became professedly converted to Christianity in consequence of supposing that his life was in danger among the Jews, but was probably indifferent to all religions. He gave himself up to philosophical inquiries, and is commonly understood to have been a pantheist. He maintained (*Tractat. Theol. Politicus*, c. 10, t. i. p. 308, Ed. Paulus), that the last five chapters of Daniel were written by Daniel himself, but that the seven previous chapters were collected about the time of the Maccabees from the chronological writings of the Chaldeans, and that the whole was arranged by some unknown hand. Edward Wells, who lived in the first part of the eighteenth century, maintained that the work was composed by some one soon after the death of Daniel. Antony Collins, one of the British Deists, maintained also that it was not written by Daniel. In more recent times, the genuineness of the book has been doubted or denied, in whole or in part, by Corrodi, Gesenius, Lüderwald, Dereser, Scholl, Lengerke, Eichhorn, De Wette, Griesenger, Bertholdt, Bleek, Ewald, Hitzig, and Kirms; it has been defended by the English writers generally, and among the Germans by Staudlin, Beckhaus, Jahn, Hävernick, Hengstenberg, and others. The general ground taken by those who have denied its genuineness and authenticity is, that the book was written, at or about the time of the Maccabees, by some Jew, who, in order to give greater authority and importance to his work, wrote under the assumed name of Daniel, and laid the scene in Babylon in the time of the captivity.

The various arguments urged against the genuineness of the book may be seen in Bertholdt, Eichhorn, Lengerke, Kirms (*Commentatio*

Historico Critica, Jenae, 1828), and De Wette. The best defence of its authenticity, probably, is the work of Hengstenberg (*Die Authentie des Daniel*, Berlin, 1831). The examination of the objections alleged against the particular chapters, and particular portions of chapters, it will be most convenient to examine in the introductions to the respective chapters. I propose, in this general Introduction, merely to examine the objections of a general character which have been made to the work. These have been concisely arranged and stated by De Wette (*Lehrbuch der Historisch-kritischen, Einleitung*, &c., Berlin, 1845, pp. 382-389), and in the examination of the objections I shall consider them in the order in which he has stated them.

The view which De Wette entertains of the book is stated in the following manner:—"That in the time of Antiochus Epiphanes, when the spirit of prophecy among the Jews had been a long time extinct, a Jewish friend of his country endeavoured to encourage and strengthen his contemporary sufferers, and those who were contending for their liberty, through these apocalyptic prophecies respecting the future ascendency of the theocratic principle, which, in order to give the work greater reputation and authority, he ascribed to an ancient Seer of the name of Daniel, of whom probably something had been handed down by tradition. Designedly he suffered the promises to extend to a great length of time, in order to make them appear the more certain. After the manner of the ancient prophets also, he inwove much that was historical, and especially such as would be fitted to excite and arouse the martyr spirit of his own people."—(*Lehrbuch*, p. 390).

I. The first objection which is urged against the genuineness of the book is derived from what is denominated *the fabulous contents*— Mährchenhaften Inhalte—*of its narrative parts*. This objection, in the words of De Wette, is, that "the book is full of improbabilities (ii. 3, ff. 46, f. iii. 1, 5, f. 20, 22, 28, f. 31, ff. iv. 31, f. v. 11, f. 18, ff. 29, vi. 8, ff. 26, ff.); of wonders (ii. 28, iii. 23, ff. v. 5, vi. 23, 25); its historical inaccuracies are such as are found in no prophetic book of the Old Testament, and are founded on the same type (comp. ii. 2-11, with iv. 4, v. 8; iii. 4-12, 26-30, with vi. 8-18, 21-24).* This seeking after wonders and strange things, and the religious fanaticism nourished through these persecutions, which it breathes, place the book in the same condition as the second book of the Maccabees, as a production of the time of Antiochus Epiphanes, and the similarity of the former of the two books betrays the fictitious character (*Dichtung*) of the book."—(*Lehrbuch*, pp. 382, 383).

In reference to this objection, which turns on the marvellous character of the book, and the improbable historical statements in it, the following remarks may be made :—

---

* These references of De Wette's are according to the chapters and verses of the Hebrew Bible.

(*a*) These objections are noticed in detail in the introductions to the respective chapters where the historical events here objected to are stated, and the question whether they are fabulous, or are in accordance with true history, is there fully considered. This will make it needless to notice them here particularly. In the introduction to the respective chapters, I have noticed, and have endeavoured to answer, all the objections which I have found of this character in the works of Eichhorn, Bertholdt, Bleek, and Lengerke. This will make it the less necessary to dwell on this point in this general Introduction.

(*b*) But as to the alleged contradiction between Daniel and the historical accounts which we have of the affairs to which he refers, it may be proper to observe in general—(1.) That, for anything that appears, Daniel may be as accurate an historian as any of the heathen writers of those times. There is, in the nature of the case, no reason why we should put implicit confidence in Berosus, Abydenus, Xenophon, and Herodotus, and distrust Daniel; nor why, if a statement is omitted by them, we should conclude at once that, if mentioned by Daniel, it is false. It is an unhappy circumstance, that there are many persons who suppose that the fact that a thing is mentioned by a profane historian is presumptive evidence of its truth; if mentioned by a sacred writer, it is presumptive evidence of its falsehood. Under the influence of the same feeling, it is inferred, that if an event is mentioned by a sacred writer which is omitted by a profane historian, it is regarded as demonstrative that the work in which it is found is fabulous. It is unnecessary to show that this feeling exists in many minds; and yet nothing can be more unjust—for the mere fact that an author writes on sacred subjects, or is the professed friend of a certain religion, *should not* be allowed to cast a suspicion on his testimony. That testimony must depend, in regard to its value, on his credibility as a historian, and not on the subject on which he writes. In the nature of things, there is no more reason why a writer on sacred subjects should be unworthy of belief, than one who is recording the ordinary events of history. (2.) Daniel, according to the account which we have of him, had opportunities of ascertaining the truth of the facts which he narrates, which no profane historian had. He spent the greater part of a long life in Babylon, in the very midst of the scenes which he describes; he was intimately acquainted with the affairs of the government; he enjoyed, in a remarkable degree, the confidence of those in authority, and he was himself deeply concerned in most of these transactions, and could have adopted the language of Æneas—*et quorum magna pars fui.* (3.) It is to be remembered, also, in regard to these events and times, that we have few fragments of history remaining. We have fragments of the writings of Berosus, a Chaldean, indeed, who wrote in Greece; and of Abydenus, a Greek, who wrote in Chaldea; we have some historical statements in Xenophon, and a few in Herodotus: but the Chaldean history, if ever written, is lost; the public documents are destroyed; the means of an accurate and full knowledge of the Chaldean or Babylonish power in the time when Daniel lived, have disappeared for ever. Under these circumstances, it would not be strange if we should not be able to clear up all the difficulties of a historical nature that may be suggested respecting these fragmentary accounts, or be able to verify the statements which we find in the sacred books by the explicit testimony of contemporary writers.

(c) As a matter of fact, the investigations of history, as far as they can be made, go to confirm the authority of Daniel. Instances of this will occur in the examination of the particular chapters in this book, and all that can now be done is merely to refer to them, particularly to the introductions to ch. i., iv.–vi. In general, it may be said here, that none of the historical authorities *contradict* what is stated by Daniel, and that the few fragments which we have go to confirm what he has said, or at least to make it probable.

(d) As to the objections of De Wette and others, derived from the miraculous and marvellous character of the book, it may be observed further, that the same objection would lie against most of the books of the Bible, and that it is, therefore, not necessary to notice it particularly in considering the book of Daniel. The Bible is a book full of miracles and marvels; and he who would have any proper understanding of it must regard and treat it as such. It is impossible to understand or explain it without admitting the possibility and the reality of miraculous events; and in a book which *claims* to be founded on miracles, it does not prove that it is not authentic or genuine simply to say that it assumes that miracles are possible. To destroy the credibility of the book, it is necessary to show that *all* claims of a miraculous character are unfounded, and *all* miracles impossible and absurd; and this objection would not lie against the book of Daniel peculiarly, but equally against the whole Bible. Two remarks here may be made, however, of a more particular character: (1), that the statements in Daniel are not more marvellous than those which occur in other parts of the Bible, and if *they* may be believed, those occurring in Daniel may be also; and (2), that it would rather be an argument against the genuineness and authenticity of the book if *no* miraculous and marvellous statements were found in it. It would be *so* unlike the other books of the Bible, where miracles abound, that we should feel that there was wanting in its favour the evidence of this nature, which would show that it had the same origin as the other portions of the volume. The particular objections in regard to the statements in Daniel of this nature are considered in the notes on the book.

II. A second objection to the genuineness of the book of Daniel relates to the *prophecies* which are found in it. This objection is derived from the peculiar character of these prophecies; from the minuteness of the detail; the exact designation of the order of events;

the fact that they seem to be a summary of history written *after* the events occurred; and that in these respects they are essentially unlike the other prophecies in the Bible. This objection, we have seen, is as old as Porphyry; and this was, in fact, with him the *principal* argument against the authenticity of the book. This objection is summed up and stated by De Wette in the following manner (§ 255 *b*, pp. 384, 385): "The ungenuineness (Unächtheit) appears further from the prophetic contents of the same, which is to a remarkable extent different from that of all the remaining prophetic books, (*a*) through its apocalyptic character, or through this—that the coming of the kingdom of the Messiah is mentioned and determined according to certain definite periods of time, or specified periods, and that the representation of it occurs so much in the form of visions; (*b*) that the circumstances of the distant future, and the fortune of the kingdoms which were not yet in existence, even down to the time of Antiochus Epiphanes, are described with so much particularity and accuracy (viii. 14, ix. 25, ff. xii. 11, ff.) that the account must have been written after the event; (*c*) and that, if Daniel was a prophet, he must have lived in the times of Ezekiel and Zechariah, and we must suppose that his prophecies would have borne the general character of the prophecies of those times, but that in fact we find in them the spirit of a later age—the spirit that ultimately developed itself in the Sibylline books, to which these prophecies bear a strong resemblance."

In reply to this it may be remarked:—

(1.) That all that is said in Daniel is *possible:* that is, it is possible that prophetic intimations of the future should be given with as much particularity as are found in Daniel. No one can demonstrate, or even affirm, that God could not, if he chose, inspire a prophet to predict in detail the occurrences of the most remote times, and the fall of kingdoms not yet in being. All this knowledge must be with him; and for anything that appears, it would be as easy to inspire a prophet to predict *these* events as any other. The sole inquiry, therefore, is in regard to a fact; and this is to be settled by an examination of the evidence, that the prophet lived and prophesied *before* the events predicted occurred.

(2.) The prophecies in Daniel are not, in their structure and character, *so* unlike those whose genuineness is undisputed as to make it certain, or even probable, that the latter are genuine and those of Daniel not. Dreams and visions were common methods of communicating the Divine will to the prophets — see Introduction to Isaiah, § 7, (2), (4)—and who will undertake from any internal evidence to determine between those of Isaiah, Jeremiah, Ezekiel, and Daniel?

(3.) As to the allegation respecting the details in Daniel of future events—the particularity with which he describes them—all is to be admitted that is affirmed on the subject. It *is* a fact that there is such particularity and minuteness of detail as could be founded only on truth, and that the delineations of Alexander and his conquests, and the statements of the events that would succeed his reign down to the time of Antiochus Epiphanes (ch. xi.), are drawn with as much accuracy of detail as they would be by one writing after the events had occurred. No one can doubt this who attentively examines these remarkable prophecies. Porphyry was undoubtedly right in affirming, that in regard to their minuteness and accuracy, these prophecies appeared to be written *after* the events; and if it can be shown, therefore, that they were written *before* the events referred to, the testimony of Porphyry is a strong evidence of the fact that Daniel was inspired; for no one will maintain that man, by any natural sagacity, could describe events before they occur with the exactness of detail and the minute accuracy which is found in this part of Daniel.

But is not what is here said of Daniel as to the accuracy and minuteness of detail true also, in the main, of other prophecies in the Old Testament? Are there not many prophecies that are as accurate, and in some respects as minute, as they would have been if they were written after the events referred to? Is not this true of the predictions respecting the destruction of Tyre and of Babylon, and the carrying away of the Jews into captivity? Is not Cyrus expressly mentioned by Isaiah, and is not the work which he would perform in the conquest of Babylon drawn out in exact detail? (See Isa. xlv. 1, *seq.*) So in Jeremiah (l., li.), there is a prophetic account of the destruction of Babylon, as minute in many respects as the predictions of Daniel, and as exact and minute as it would have been if written after the events had occurred, and the author had been making a historical record instead of uttering a prediction. But on this point I must content myself with referring to the argument of Hengstenberg, *Authentie des Daniel*, pp. 173–195. It may be added, however, that it is on this accuracy of detail in Daniel that we ground one of the strong arguments for his inspiration. It will be admitted on all hands—it cannot be denied —that no one could foresee those events, and describe them with such accuracy of detail, by any natural sagacity; but no one who believes in the fact of inspiration at all, can doubt that it would be as easy for the Divine Spirit to present future events in this accuracy of detail as in a more general manner. At all events, this accuracy and minuteness of detail removes the prophecies from the region of conjecture, and is an answer to the usual objections that they are obscure and ambiguous. No one can pretend this of the writings of Daniel; and if it can be shown that the book was written before the events occurred, the conclusion cannot be avoided that the author was inspired.

III. A third objection to the genuineness and authenticity of the book of Daniel is thus stated by De Wette (§ 255, b. 3, p. 385): "Grounds of objection lie further in the repeated mention of Daniel himself in so honourable a manner (ch. i. 17, 19, f. v. 11, f. vi. 4, ix. 23, x. 11, *et al.*)"

This objection cannot be regarded as having any great degree of force, or as contributing much to set aside the direct evidence of the authority of the book:—for (*a*) it is possible that all these honours were conferred on him. This is, in itself, no more incredible or remarkable than that Joseph should have reached the honours in Egypt, which are attributed to him in Genesis; and no one can show that if the account had been written by another, it would have been unworthy of belief. (*b*) If it were a fact that he was thus honoured, it was not improper to state it. If Daniel was the historian of those times, and kept the records of the events of his own life, and actually obtained those honours, there was no impropriety in his making a record of those things. He has done no more than what Cæsar did in the mention of himself, his plans, his conquests, his triumphs. In the record of Daniel there is no unseemly parading of his wisdom, or the honours conferred on him; there is no praise for the mere sake of praise; there is no language of panegyric on account of his eminent piety. The account is a mere record of facts as they are said to have occurred—that Daniel was successful in his early studies, and his preparation for the examination through which he and his companions were to pass (ch. i.); that on more than one occasion he succeeded in interpreting a dream or vision which no one of the Chaldeans could do; that in consequence of this he was raised to an exalted rank; that he was enabled to maintain his integrity in the midst of extraordinary temptations; and that he was favoured with the Divine protection when in extraordinary danger. I presume that no one who has read the book of Daniel with an unprejudiced mind ever received an impression that there was any want of modesty in Daniel in these records, or that there was any unseemly or unnecessary parading of his own virtues and honours before the world.

IV. A fourth objection which has been urged against the genuineness of Daniel is derived from the *language* in which it is written. This objection, as stated by De Wette (§ 235, b. 4, p. 385), is founded on "the corrupt Hebrew and Chaldee, and the intermingling of Greek words in the composition." The objection is urged more at length in Bertholdt (p. 24, *seq.*), and by Bleek, Kirms, and others. The objection, as derived from the language of the book, is properly divided into three parts:—(*a*) that it is written in Hebrew and Chaldee; (*b*) that in each part of it there is a want of purity of style, indicating a later age than the time of the captivity; and (*c*) that there is an intermingling of Greek words, such as it cannot be presumed that one who wrote in the time of the exile, and in Babylon, would have employed, and such as were probably introduced into common use only by a later intercourse with the Greeks, and particularly by the Macedonian conquest.

(*a*) As to the first of these, little stress can be laid on it, and indeed it is rather an argument *for* the genuineness of the work than against it. It is well known that from the fourth verse of the second chapter to the end of the seventh chapter, the work is written in the Chaldee language, while the remainder is pure Hebrew. The only way in which this fact could be regarded as an objection to the genuineness of the book, would be that it is an indication that it is the production of two different authors. But this would be an objection only on the supposition that the author could write and speak only one language, or that, supposing he was acquainted with two, there were no circumstances which could account for the use of both. But neither of these suppositions applies here. There is every reason to believe that Daniel was acquainted with both the Hebrew and the Chaldee; and there is no improbability in the supposition that he wrote in both with equal ease. And, on the other hand, it may be remarked, that the very circumstance here referred to is a confirmation of the genuineness of the book; for (1.) it accords with all that is known of Daniel. He was a youth when he left his native country, and there is every probability that he was familiar with the Hebrew in early life, and that he would never forget it, though it might be true that he would ordinarily use the language of Chaldea. He was still familiar with the Hebrew books, and it is to be presumed that the language used by the Hebrews in exile was their native tongue. In all his intercourse with his own countrymen, therefore, it is every way probable that he would use his native language, and would thus through life retain his knowledge of it. (2.) It is equally clear that he was familiar with the Chaldee language. He was early, in connection with three other Hebrew youths (ch. i. 3, 4), placed under the best instruction in Babylon, for the express purpose of acquiring, with other branches of learning, a knowledge of the "tongue of the Chaldeans;" and he speedily made such acquisitions as to pass with honour the examination appointed before he was admitted to public employment (ch. i. 18–20). He was, moreover, employed at court during a considerable part of his long life, and no one, therefore, can doubt that he was entirely familiar with the language used in Babylon, and that he could compose in it with ease. (3.) It is evident that the work must, if it is the production of one author, have been composed by some person who was, in this respect, in the circumstances of Daniel; that is, by one who was familiar with both the languages: and the circumstances bear on their face evidence that the work was written by one in the condition in which Daniel was known to be; that is, one who had been early trained in the Hebrew, and who had lived in Chaldea. No native-born Hebrew who had not lived in Chaldea would be likely to be so well acquainted with the two languages that he could use either with equal facility; and it may be presumed that no native-born Chaldean could evince so intimate an acquaintance with the Hebrew. The direct evidence that it *is* the production of one author will be adduced in another part of this Introduction. (4.) It is by no means probable that one who lived so late as the time of Antiochus Epiphanes *could* have written the book as it is written; that is, that he would have been so familiar with the two languages, Hebrew and Chaldee, that he could use them with equal ease. It is an uncommon thing for a man to write in two different languages in the same work, and he never does it without some special design—a design for which there would not be likely to be occasion if one were writing in the time of Antiochus Epiphanes. It was perfectly *natural* that Daniel should write in this manner, and perfectly *unnatural* that any one should do it in a later age, and in different circumstances. If the book had been forged by a Hebrew in the time of Antiochus Epiphanes, there is every reason to believe that he would have been careful to write it in as pure Hebrew as possible, for that was the language in which the canonical books were written, and if he had endeavoured to gain credit for the book as one of Divine authority, he would not have intermingled so much of a foreign language. If he were a Chaldean, and could write Hebrew at all, as it is certain that the author of this book could, then, for the reason just given, he would have been careful to write the whole book in as pure Hebrew as possible, and would not have jeoparded its credit by so large an infusion of a foreign tongue. (5.) This reasoning is conclusive, unless it be supposed that the author *meant* to represent it as a composition of some Hebrew in the time of the exile, and that in order to give it the greater verisimilitude he adopted this device— to make it *appear* as if written by one who was a native Hebrew, but who had become familiar with a foreign language. But this device would be too refined to be likely to occur, and, for the reasons given above, would be difficult of execution if it should occur. Even in such a case, the writer would be much more likely to represent its author as writing in the sacred language of the prophets, in order to procure for himself the credit of employing the language used in all the Divine communications to men. The language in which the book is written, therefore, is just such as it would be on the supposition that it is genuine, and just such as it would *not* be on the supposition that it is a forgery of a later age.

(*b*) As to the statement that the language is *corrupt* Hebrew and Chaldee—in der Verderbten sowohl Hebräischen als Chaldäishen Sprache (De Wette)—it may be remarked that this position has never been satisfactorily made out, nor has it been shown that it is not such as might be employed, or would be employed, by one who resided in Babylon in the time of the exile. That the language would not be the purest kind of Hebrew, or the purest Chaldee, might be possible, in the circumstances of the case; but it could be shown that it was not such as might be employed there, in case there are words and forms of speech which did not come into use until a later period of the world. This has not been shown. It is true that there are Persian words ; but this is not unnatural in the circumstances of the case—bordering as Chaldea did on Persia, and during a part of the time referred to in the book, being actually subject to Persia. It is true that there are Greek words; but under the next specification I shall endeavour to show that this does not militate against the supposition that the book may have been written in Babylon in the time of the exile. It is true that there are words and forms of speech which were not in use in the earlier periods of Hebrew literature, but which became common in the later periods of their literature ; but this does not prove that they may not have been in use as early as the exile. A specimen of the words referred to—indeed all on which the argument is founded—may be seen in De Wette, p. 385, note (e). They are few in number, and in respect to none of these can it be *proved* that they were not in existence in the time of Daniel. They are of Persian, of Syriac, or of Chaldee origin, and are such words as would be *likely* to come into use in the circumstances of the case. In regard to this objection it may be added, that it has been abandoned by some of the objectors to the genuineness of the book of Daniel themselves. Bleek is candid enough to give it up entirely. He says : " We have, in general, too few remains of the different centuries after the exile to draw any conclusions as to the gradual depreciation of the language, and to determine with any certainty to what particular period any writer belongs."—(*Zeitschr.* p. 213). " Daniel," says Prof. Stuart, " in the judgment of Gesenius (*Geschich. Heb. Sprach.* p. 35), has decidedly a purer diction than Ezekiel ; in which opinion," says he, " as far as I am able to judge, after much time spent upon the book, and examining minutely every word and phrase in it many times over, I should entirely coincide."—(*Com.* p. 465).

(c) A more material objection is derived from the use of *Greek* words in the composition of the book. That there *are* such words is undeniable, though they are by no means numerous. Bertholdt (pp. 24, 25) has enumerated *ten* such words ; De Wette has referred to *four* (p. 386). The words enumerated by Bertholdt are פרתמים—πρότιμοι ; פהגם — φθέγμα ; כרוזא — κήρυξ ; כרז —κηρύσσειν ; קיתרוס.—κιθαρις ; סבכא — סמבוכה ; כיסבניא — συμφωνία.; פסנתר—ψαλτήριον ; פטיש—πέτασος ; נבזבה—νόμισμα.

In regard to this objection, it may be remarked, in general, that it does not assert that the structure of the book of Daniel is fashioned after the Greek manner, or that the Greek style pervades it ; it asserts only that a few Greek words have been incorporated into the book. The question then is, whether even all these words are of Greek origin; and whether, if they are, or if only a part of them are, their use in the book can be accounted for on the supposition that it was written in the time of the captivity, or rather, whether their occurrence in the book is a proof that the book could not have been written at that time.

The first point is the question, whether these words are of undoubted Greek origin ; and this question will require us to examine them in detail.

(1.) The first word specified is פַּרְתְּמִים *partemim*, rendered *princes* (ch. i. 3), which it is alleged is the same as the Greek πρότιμοι, *protimoi*. The word used by Daniel occurs only in two other places in the

Old Testament (Esth. i. 3, vi. 9), where it is rendered *nobles*, and *most noble ;* and it is obvious to remark, that the fact that it is found in Esther *might* be urged in proof that the book of Daniel was written at the time in which it is commonly believed to have been, since the antiquity and genuineness of the book of Esther is not called in question. But apart from this, there is no evidence that the word is of Greek origin. Gesenius, who may be considered as impartial authority on the subject, says, "It is of Persian origin, 1—9. Pehlvi, *pardom*, the first, see Anquetil du perron Zendavesta, ii. p. 468. Comp. Sanscr. *prathama* the first. In the Zend dialect the form is *peoerim*. Comp. Sanscr. *pura* prius, antea, purâna, antiquus. From the former comes the Greek πρῶτος, and from the latter the Latin *primus*."—(*Lex.*) The same account of the origin of the word is given by Jahn, De Wette, Bleek, and Kirms. This word, then, may be set aside. It is, indeed, objected by Bertholdt, that, though the word had a Persian origin, yet there is no evidence that it would be used in Babylon in the time of the exile. But this objection can have no force. Babylon and Persia were neighbouring kingdoms, and there is no presumption that Persian words might not find their way to Babylon, and as a matter of fact such words occur in Jeremiah, and probably in Isaiah, and in Nahum. (See Hengstenberg, pp. 11, 12). The truth was, that the Assyrians and the Medo-Persians were originally all of the same stem or stock, and there is no presumption against the supposition that the same words might be found in each of the languages spoken by them.

(2.) The next word referred to is פִּתְגָּם *pithgham* (Dan. iii. 16, iv. 17, rendered *matter*), which it is alleged is the same as the Greek φθεγμα, *phthegma*. The word occurs, besides these places in Daniel, in Ezra iv. 17, v. 11, rendered *answer ;* v. 7, rendered *letter ;* and vi. 11, rendered *word*. In Hebrew it occurs in Esth. i. 20, rendered *decree*, and in Eccles. viii. 11, rendered *sentence*. In respect to this word, also, Gesenius says, "The origin of the word is to be sought in the Persian, in which *pedam* is *word, edict, mandate*."—(*Lex.*) The fact, also, it may be added, that it is found in Esther, in Ezra, and the book of Ecclesiastes, is sufficient to destroy the objection that its use proves that the book of Daniel was written later than the time of the exile. It was brought, probably, into the Greek language from the common origin of the Persian and the Greek.

(3, 4.) The next words referred to, are כָּרוֹז *kâhroz* (a herald), ch. iii. 4, and כָּרַז *kârăz*, to cry out, to make proclamation, which it is alleged are the same as the Greek κηρυξ, *kerux*, and κηρυσσειν, *kerussein*. Of these words, also, Gesenius remarks, "The root is widely diffused in the Indo-European languages, *e.g.* Sansc. *krus*, to cry out ; Zenda. *khresio*, crying out, a herald ; Pers. to cry out; Gr. κηρύσσω, also κρίζω, κραζω ; Germ. *kreischen, kreissen ;* Eng. to cry."—(*Lex.*) Among the Christian Arabs, Gesenius remarks, it means to preach. Jahn and Dereser say that the word is related to the Zendish word *khresio,* which means to tread behind, and to scream out, to screech, *kreischen.* Hengstenberg (p. 13) remarks of this word, that its use is spread abroad not only in Chaldee, but in Syriac, and that this circumstance makes it probable that it had a Semitish origin. The probability is, that this word and the Greek had a common origin, but its use is so far spread in the world that it cannot be argued that the fact of its being found in the book of Daniel, demonstrates that the book had a later origin than the period of the exile.

(5.) The next word mentioned as of Greek origin is קִיתָרֹם *kitharos* (ch. iii. 5, 7, 10, 15), *cithara, harp, lyre* (rendered in each place *harp*), which it is said is the same as the Greek κιθαρις, *citharis.* In regard to this word, which is the name of a musical instrument, it is to be admitted that it is the same as the Greek word. It occurs nowhere else in the Old Testament, and its origin is unknown. *As* a Greek word, it will be considered in connection with the three others of the same class, in the sequel. It cannot be affirmed, indeed, that it has a Greek *origin,* but its origin cannot be found in the Chaldee, Persian, or Sanscrit languages. But, although it is admitted that it is a Greek word, and denotes an instrument that was well known in Greece, this does not *demonstrate* that it is of Greek *origin.* It is admitted on all hands, that the names of Greek instruments of music were mostly of foreign derivation; and there is nothing to lead to the supposition that this was of *Greek* origin, unless it be that the word κιθάρα, or κιθάρος, means, in the Doric dialect, the *breast,* and that this instrument *might* have received its name either because it was played by being placed against the breast, like the violin with us, or because its form resembled the human breast. This is the opinion of Isidorus, Origg. i. 2, 21. But there is great uncertainty in regard to this.

(6.) The next word specified is סַבְּכָא *sabbeka* (ch. iii. 5), and the similar word, שַׂבְּכָא (ch. iii. 7, 10, 15), in each case rendered *sackbut.* Of this word it is alleged that it is the same as the Greek σαμβύκη, *sambuca,* a stringed instrument well known in Greece. But in regard to this word, also, the remark of Gesenius may be quoted : " Strabo affirms," says he, " that the Greek word σαμβύκη (*sambuca*) is of barbarian, *i. e.,* of Oriental origin, and if so, the name might have allusion to the interweaving of the strings—from the root סָבַךְ"—*to interweave, to entwine, to plait.* Gesenius, however, remarks that in this place it is joined with a word (symphony) which is manifestly of Greek origin ; and he *seems* to infer that this word also may have had a Greek origin. The direct affirmation of Strabo is (lib. x.) that the names of the Greek instruments of music were of foreign origin ; and in reference to this particular instrument, Athenæus (i. iv.) affirms that it was of *Syrian* origin. So Clemens Alex. expressly declares that the sambuca had a foreign origin.—(*Strom.* lib. i. p. 307). Even Bleek admits this in regard to this particular instrument. (See Hengstenberg, p. 15).

(7.) The next word for which a Greek origin is claimed is סִימְפֹנְיָא

symphony, Greek συμφωνια (ch. iii. 5, 10, 15), rendered in the text, in each place, *dulcimer*, and in the margin *symphony*, or *singing*. Gesenius remarks, in regard to this word, that "it is the Greek word adopted into the Chaldee tongue, just as at the present day the same instrument is called in Italy *zampogna*, and in Asia Minor *zambouja*." It cannot be denied that the word is the same as the Greek word, though it is to be remarked that among the Greeks it was not used to denote the name of an instrument of music; yet, as it is compounded of two Greek words—σύν and φωνή—its Greek origin cannot well be doubted. With the Greeks, the word meant properly harmony, or concert of sounds (*Passow*); and it was then readily given to an instrument that was fitted to produce harmony, or that was distinguished for its sweet sounds. The word is found in Syriac, as applied to a musical instrument; but the evidence seems to be strong that the *word* had a Greek origin, though there is no evidence that the Greeks ever applied it to a musical instrument.

(8.) The next word for which a Greek origin is claimed is פְּסַנְתֵּרִין and פְּסַנְתֵּרִין *pesanterin* (ch. iii. 7, 5, 10, 15), rendered *psaltery* in each place), which, it is said, is the same as the Greek ψαλτήριον, *psaltery*. "This word," says Gesenius (*Lex.*), "was adopted from the Greek into Chaldee, ל and נ being interchanged." The origin of the word is, however, wholly uncertain. That it is found in Greek is undoubtedly true; but, as has been before remarked, as it is admitted that the names of the Greek instruments of music had mostly a foreign origin, it is impossible to demonstrate that this may not have been true in regard to this word. Baxtorf (*Lex. Chald.*) says, that it is a word "corrupted from the Greek."

(9.) The next word is פַּטִּישׁ *pattish* (ch. iii. 21, rendered *hosen*), which it is said is the same as the Greek πετασος, *petasos*. But there is no reason to believe that this word had an original Greek origin. It is found in Syriac, and the root פַּטַשׁ *patash*, Gesenius remarks, "is widely found in the Indo-European languages. The primary form," says he, "is *batt, patt*, whence later Lat. *battere;* French, *battre;* Dutch, *bot;* Swed. *batsch*," &c. The Greek word has undoubtedly had the same origin, and it cannot be maintained that the Chaldee word is *derived* from the Greek.

(10.) The remaining word, which is alleged to be of Greek origin, is נְבִזְבָּה *nebizbah* (ch. ii. 6, v. 17), rendered in both cases in the text *rewards*, and in the margin *fee*. It does not elsewhere occur in the Old Testament. It is maintained by Bertholdt and others, that this is the same word as the Greek νόμισμα, *money*. But there is no evidence that the word is of Greek origin. Gesenius says (*Lex.*) that the word *may* have a Chaldee origin, though he prefers to assign to it a Persian origin, and he says that the idea of *money* (implied in the Greek word) is foreign to the context here. Bohlen, Winer, and Hengstenberg agree in assigning the word to a Persian origin. (See Hengs. *Authen.* p. 12).

The result, then, to which we have come in regard to the objection that words of Greek origin, and indicating an age later than the time of the exile, are found in Daniel, is, that the number alleged to be of such an origin is very few at best, and that of those which have been referred to, there are not *more* than four (marked 5, 6, 7, and 8, in the enumeration above) to which the objection can be supposed to apply with any degree of probability. These are the words actually selected by De Wette (p. 386) as those on which he relies.

In regard to these *four* words, then, we may make the following general observations :—

(*a*) They are all names of musical instruments said to have been used in Babylon.

(*b*) The general remark of Strabo above referred to may be called to recollection here, that the names of musical instruments among the Greeks were mostly of foreign origin. In itself considered, therefore, there is no improbability in the supposition that the same words should be applied to musical instruments in Greece and in Chaldea.

(*c*) The languages in which these words are found belong to the same great family of languages—the Indo-European; that is, the Persian, the Greek, the Latin, &c. They had a common origin, and it is not strange if we find the same words spread extensively through these languages.

(*d*) There was sufficient intercourse between Persia, Chaldea, Asia Minor, and Greece, before and at the time of the Hebrew captivity, to make it not improbable that the names of musical instruments, and the instruments themselves, should be borne from one to the other. There is, therefore, no improbability in supposing that such instruments may have been carried to Babylon from Greece, and may have retained their Greek names in Babylon. Curtius (b. iv. c. 12) says, that in the Persian host that came out to meet Alexander the Great, there were many persons found of Greek origin who had become subject to the authority of Media. For further historical proofs on this subject, see Hengs. *Authen.* pp. 16, 17. Indeed, little proof is needed. It is known that the Greeks were in the habit of visiting foreign lands, and particularly of travelling into the region of the East, for the purpose of obtaining knowledge; and nothing is, in itself, more probable than that in this way the names of a few musical instruments, in common use among themselves, should have been made known to the people among whom they travelled, and that those names should have been incorporated into the languages spoken there.

V. A fifth objection, or *class* of objections, is derived from the alleged reference to usages, opinions, and customs, *later* than the time of the exile. This objection, which embraces several subordinate points, is thus summed up by De Wette : "The remarkable later representations on the subject of angels (der Angelologie, iv. 14, ix. 21, x. 13, 21; of Christology, vii. 13, f. xii. 1-3; of dogmatics [or doctrines, Dogmatik],

xii. 2, f.; of morals [Sittenlehre] or customs, iv. 24, comp. Tobit, iv. 11,
xii. 9; and of asceticism [Askese], i. 8–16, comp. Apoc. Esth. iv. 17,
2 Mac. v. 27, vi. 11, furnish at least an additional argument [einen
Hülfsbeweis] against the genuineness of the book."—§ 255, c. (5.)

This objection, it will be observed, divides itself into several parts
or portions, though coming under the same *general* description. The
general statement is, that there is an allusion to customs and opinions
which were found among the Jews *only at a later period* than the
captivity, and that, therefore, the book could not have been composed
at the time alleged. The specifications relate to angelology, or the
representations respecting angels; to Christology, or the views of the
Messiah; to the doctrines stated, particularly to those respecting the
resurrection of the dead and the final judgment; to the customs that
prevailed, and to the ascetic views expressed, particularly on the effect
of abstinence from rich kinds of diet. It will be convenient to notice
them in their order, so far as to furnish a *general* answer. Most of
them will be noticed more particularly in the notes on the passages as
they occur; and for a full and complete answer the reader may be
referred, in general, to Hengstenberg, *Authentie des Daniel*, pp.
137–173.

A. The first specification is derived from the statements which occur
respecting angels, ch. iv. 17; ix. 21; x. 13, 21. These, it is affirmed,
indicate a state of opinion which prevailed among the Hebrews *only* at
a later age than the time of the exile, and consequently the book could
not have been written at that time. This objection, as urged by
Bertholdt and others, refers to two points: first, that the statements
respecting the opinions of the Chaldeans on the subject are not in
accordance with the opinions in the time when the book is said to have
been written; and, secondly, that the statements respecting angels,
considered as Hebrew opinions, are those which belong to a later age.
It will be proper to notice these in their order.

I. The first is, that the statements which occur as representing the
opinions of the Chaldeans express sentiments which did not prevail
among them. The objections on this point relate to two statements
in the book: one, that the Son of God, or *a* Son of God, is spoken of
by Nebuchadnezzar; the other, to what is said (ch. iv. 17) of the
"decree of *the Watchers.*"

The former objection is thus stated by Bertholdt:—In ch. iii. 25,
"Nebuchadnezzar speaks of a Son of God ['and the form of the fourth
is like the Son of God']; and although the Chaldeans, and most of the
dwellers in Upper Asia were polytheists, yet there is no evidence that
anything was known at the time of the views which prevailed among
the Greeks on this subject, but that such views became known in the
time of Seleucus Nicator" (p. 29). It is hence inferred that the book
could not have been written before the time of Seleucus.

In regard to the *objection*, it may be observed, in addition to what is said in the notes on the passage (ch. iii. 25) where the expression occurs, that the objection is so vague and indefinite that it scarcely needs a reply. The opinions which prevailed in the East on the subject of the gods is so little known now, that it is impossible to demonstrate that such an opinion as this might not have existed in the time of Nebuchadnezzar, and impossible to prove that such views as would have suggested this expression did *not* prevail before the time of Seleucus Nicator. Indeed, it is not easy to show that such language as is here ascribed to Nebuchadnezzar would have been more likely to have been suggested by the views of mythology that prevailed in Greece, and that were spread abroad in consequence of the diffusion of Greek opinions in the East, than by the views which prevailed in Babylon in the time of the exile. But it may be more particularly observed in reply to the objection,

(*a*) That according to Gesenius (*Thes.* p. 237), this language, as used by Nebuchadnezzar, is such as would properly denote merely *one* of the gods, or one in the form of the gods ; that is, one who resembled the gods—in the same way as the phrase "son of man" denotes a man, or one in the form and appearance of a man. Perhaps this was all that was meant by Nebuchadnezzar ; at least, that is all that can be demonstrated to have been his meaning, or all that is necessarily implied in his words. See notes on the passage. But,

(*b*) There were opinions which prevailed in Chaldea on the subject of the gods which would fully justify the use of such language. That they regarded one portion of the gods as descended from another, or as begotten by another ; that they looked upon them as constituting *families*, in a way similar to the Greeks, and, particularly, that they regarded Bel, their supreme god, always accompanied by the goddess Mylitta, as the father of the gods, has been abundantly demonstrated. On this point, see Gesenius, *Com. zu.* Isa. ii. 332, *seq.* (Beylage § 2, *Gottheiten der Chaldäer*), and Creuzer, *Symbolik,* on the word *Mylitta,* vol. i. p. 231; vol. ii. pp. 331, 333, 350, 460. The idea of derivation, descent, or birth among the gods, was one that was quite familiar to the Chaldeans, perhaps as much so as to the Greeks : in fact, this has been so common an opinion among all polytheists, that it is rather to be presumed that it would be found everywhere among the heathen than otherwise.

The other objection on this point is derived from what is said of the Watchers, ch. iv. 13, 17. The objection is, that there are betrayed here traces of a later Parsish-Jewish representation ; that is, that this indicates that the book was composed in later times.

In regard to the *meaning* of this language, see notes on ch. iv. 13. Perhaps a reference to this note, where the probability that such a term would be used in Babylon is shown, is all that is necessary in answering the objection. But, in addition to this, an observation of Diodorus Siculus may be introduced here. I copy it as I find it in Gesenius,

Com. zu. Isa. vol. ii., pp. 333, 334. Diodorus is speaking of the sun, moon, and five planets as adored by the Chaldeans, and adds, "To the course of these stars there are, as they say, thirty others that are subordinate, which are represented as *divine counsellors* (θεοὶ βουλαίοι —*consulting gods*, as we would say), of whom one-half has the supervision of the regions under the earth; the other half has the supervision of things on the earth, among men, and in heaven. Every ten days is one of them sent as a messenger of the stars from those above to those below, and from those below to those above." This quotation will render it unnecessary to say anything more as to the question whether it is improbable that such language would be used by one residing in Babylon in the time of the exile. It is to be remembered that this is language which is represented in *a dream* as having been addressed to Nebuchadnezzar; and the quotation proves that it is such language as would be likely to occur to the king of Babylon in the visions of the night. It was such language as he must have been accustomed to; and so far is the use of this language from being an *objection* to the genuineness of Daniel, that it might rather have been urged as a *proof* of it, since it is not probable that it would have been used by one who was not familiar with the customary ideas of the Chaldeans.

(2.) The other form of the objection derived from the statements respecting the *angels* in the book of Daniel, refers to the opinions held among the Hebrews themselves. The general objection is, that these are representations respecting the ranks, and orders, and names of the angels which pertain only to later times in the history of Jewish opinions, and which did not exist in the period of the exile. This objection divides itself into several specifications, which it may be proper to notice briefly in their order.

(*a*) One is, that there is in the book, and particularly in ch. viii. 16, an allusion to the Persian doctrine of the seven Amhaspands, or angels that stand before God, and that this idea is found only in times later than the exile.—Bertholdt, p. 528.

To this the answer is obvious : (1.) That there is no *manifest* allusion to that Persian doctrine in the book, and no statement which would not as readily have been made if that doctrine had no existence—since it is a mere representation of angels with certain names, and with no particular reference to the number seven ; and (2.) if this were so, it is certain that this representation occurs in the Zendavesta, and the Zendavesta was composed in a distant antiquity, probably long before the time of the exile, and certainly before the time of Alexander the Great. See Creuzer, *Symbolik*, i. 183, *seq.*, and the authorities there referred to. This, then, if it were true that the doctrine of the seven Amhaspands is found in the book of Daniel, and was derived from the Zendavesta, or the Persian, would remove the objection so far as to show that the book was composed *before* the time of Alexander the Great, or at least that there is no reason, from this quarter, to suppose that it was written *afterwards*. But the truth is, that the doctrine respecting angels and intermediate beings was so prevalent a doctrine all over the East, that this objection can have no solid foundation.

(*b*) It is objected, that there are found in this book representations of the angels, in reference to their ranks and orders, which are opinions of the Jews of a later age, and which did not exist in the time of the exile; and that, therefore, the book had a later origin than the captivity. —Bertholdt.

To this it is sufficient to reply, (1,) that such a representation of ranks and orders of angels is implied in Isa. vi. 1, *seq.*, in the account of the Seraphim, a representation which supposes that there are angels of exalted rank and names ; (2,) that there are traces of such an opinion in much earlier ages, as in Psal. ciii. 20 ; lxviii. 17 ; (3,) that this. representation of differences in the ranks of angels is one that *prevails* in the Old Testament ; and (4,) that, for anything that appears, all that is implied in Daniel may have been a matter of common belief in his time. There is nothing in the book which would indicate any very definite arrangement of the angels into orders, though it is evidently implied that there *are* different degrees in the ranks of the angelic hosts (ch. x. 5, 13 ; xii. 1) ; but this was a common opinion in the East, and indeed has been a common sentiment where a belief in the existence of angels has prevailed at all.

(*c*) It is objected that *names* are given to the angels—the name of *Gabriel* and *Michael*—and that this is indicative of a later age. To this, also, it may be replied (1,) that long before this we find the name *Satan* given to the leader of evil angels (Job i. 6), and there is no presumption against the belief that names may have been given to good angels also ; (2,) that even if the practice had *not* prevailed before, no reason can be assigned why the angels who appeared to Daniel may not have assumed names, or been mentioned under appropriate titles to designate them as well as those who appeared in after times ; and (3,) that, for anything that appears, the fact that names were given to the angels among the Jews of later times may have had its origin in the time of Daniel, or may have occurred from the fact that he actually mentioned them under specific names.

(*d*) A similar objection is, that the statement in ch. vii. 10, that "thousand thousands ministered unto him, and ten thousand times ten thousand stood before him," is also a statement that had its origin in the representation of a Persian court—in the numbers that stood round the throne of a Persian monarch, and that *this* indicates a later age, or a Persian origin. To this objection it is sufficient to refer to Isa. vi., and to the notes on this passage. But we have other representations of the same kind abounding in the Scriptures, in which God is described as a magnificent monarch, attended and surrounded by hosts of angels, and the same objection would lie against them which is urged against the account in Daniel. See particularly Deut. xxxiii. 2; 1 Kings xxii. 19–22; Job ii. 1; Psal. lxviii. 17.

(e) Another objection, from the representations of the angels, is derived from what is said of their interposition in human affairs, and their appearing particularly as the guardians and protectors of nations, in ch. x. 12–20; xii. 1; which it is said indicates opinions of a later age. In reply to this, all that is necessary is to refer to the copious notes on these passages, where the foundation of that opinion is examined, and to add that no one can demonstrate that that opinion may not have had an existence as early as the time of the exile: indeed it was a common opinion in ancient times—an opinion whose origin no one now can determine—an opinion whose correctness no one can disprove. That this was a *prevailing* opinion in ancient times is admitted by Bertholdt himself, pp. 32, 33, 705–707.

In general, therefore, it may be remarked respecting the objections derived from the angelology of the book of Daniel, (*a*) that there *may* be things occurring in the book which were suggested by opinions prevailing in Babylon and the East; (*b*) that the statements in Daniel— the revelations made to him as an eminent prophet—may have been the *germ* of the opinions which prevailed among the Jews in later times, developments of which we have in the books of the Apocrypha, and in the later Rabbinical writings: if so, the objection derived from the angelology of the book is entirely unfounded.

B. The second objection derived from the alleged reference to later customs and opinions, is founded on the *Christology* of the book, or the doctrine relating to the Messiah. The objection is, that the opinions which are found in the book belong to a later age; or that in the time of the exile no such views exist in the genuine writings of the prophets, and that consequently the book must have been composed when those later views had come to prevail. The views referred to as the ground of the objection are found in ch. vii. 13, 14, and xii. 1-3. This objection, thus stated by De Wette, has been expanded by Bertholdt and others, and properly embraces, as stated by them, *four* specifications which it will be convenient to notice in their order.

(1.) The first is, that in the time of the exile, the doctrine of the Messiah had not become so developed that it was expected that he would appear in glory and majesty, and set up a kingdom upon the earth, as is implied in ch. vii. 13, 14. See Bertholdt, p. 31.

In reply to this, all that is necessary to be said is, to refer to the prophecies in the other portions of the Old Testament, whose antiquity and genuineness are undoubted. In the prophecies of Isaiah, there are predictions of the Messiah as clear, as definite, as distinct, as any that occur in Daniel; and no one can compare the prophecies found in other parts of the Old Testament with those found in Daniel, and determine, by any internal evidence, that one class must have been written before, and another after, the time of the exile. Besides, why may not the predictions, under the Spirit of inspiration, have been more clearly communicated to one prophet than to another—to Daniel than to Isaiah? And why may not some circumstances respecting the Messiah and his reign have been made to one rather than to another? If it be admitted that all that occurs in the first part of Isaiah (ch. i.–xxxix.) was actually revealed to him, and recorded by him, previous to the exile, there can be no difficulty in admitting that what is found in Daniel may have been communicated and recorded *at* the time of the exile. In proof of what is here said, it is only necessary to refer to Hengstensberg's *Christology*, vol. i. The Messianic prophecies there collected and illustrated, Gen. iii. 14, 15; ix. 26, 27; xlix. 10; Num. xxiv. 17; Deut. xviii. 15–18; Psal. ii., xvi., xxii., xlv., cx.; Isa. ii.–iv., vii., xi., xii., furnish statements *as* clear, in many respects, respecting the Messiah as anything in Daniel, and of many of these statements it might as well be alleged that they are couched in the language of later times, as anything that occurs in the book before us.

(2.) It is alleged further, of the Christology of Daniel, that the ideas respecting the kingdom of the Messiah are stated in the language of later times.—Bertholdt, p. 31. In proof of this, Bertholdt refers to ch. ii. 44; vii. 13, *seq.*

This is the same objection in another form. The reply to it is obvious : (*a*) If Daniel is admitted to be a true prophet, there is no presumption against the supposition that some ideas may have been imparted to him which might not be found in other prophets—any more than that circumstances respecting the power and kingdom of the Messiah may have been communicated to Isaiah which were not to the earlier prophets ; and (*b*) as a matter of fact, as before stated, many of the prophecies of Isaiah are as minute and as clear in regard to the kingdom of the Messiah as those in Daniel. Comp. Isa. ix. 6, 7. No one could place *that* prediction by the side of the prediction in Daniel vii. 13, 14, and determine from any internal evidence that the one was written before the exile, and that the other was couched in the language of later times.

(3.) It is objected (Bertholdt, p. 31), that the sentiment found in Daniel (ch. xii. 1), that the setting up of the kingdom of the Messiah would be preceded by times of trouble, is a doctrine of the Rabbinical writings of later times, and savours of a later origin than the times of the exile. To this, also, the reply is obvious. (*a*) It is to be admitted that this idea occurs in the Rabbinical writings, and that it was a common doctrine among the Jews ; but can any one demonstrate that the doctrine had not its origin in this very passage in Daniel? It is quite *as* philosophical to suppose that this language may have been found in the genuine language of the prophets, and that the doctrine may have sprung up from that cause, as to suppose that it was first originated by uninspired men among the Jews, and then embodied in a pretended prophecy. (*b*) It was natural that Daniel, if a real prophet, should connect the two things together not *in time*, but *in the range of vision*. See Intro. to Isa. § 7, iii. (5). Placing himself in prophetic vision in the midst of foreseen trouble coming upon his country, it was natural that the mind should be directed to brighter days, and that he should endeavour to cheer his own heart, and to comfort his afflicted countrymen, by dwelling on happier scenes when, under the Messiah, these troubles would cease. (c) As a matter of fact, the same thing elsewhere occurs. Thus Isaiah (ch. xl. and onward) describes the coming of the kingdom of the Messiah, by connecting it with the deliverance from the calamities that would come upon the Jewish people in the time of their captivity. He seeks to comfort them in their troubles by the assurance of better days ; and in describing their return to their own land, the mind of the prophet insensibly glides on to the coming of the Messiah—to the happier times that would occur under him—to the deliverance from the bondage of sin, and to the setting up of a kingdom of peace and truth in the world ; and the description which *began* with the troubles of the exile, and the return to their own land, *ends* with a sublime and glorious view of the times of the Messiah, and of the happiness of the world under his reign. And it may be added, that this is in accordance with a general principle laid down in the Bible : "But the Lord shall judge his people, and repent himself for his servants, when he seeth that their power is gone, and there is none shut up, or left" (Deut. xxxii. 36). Comp. Isa. xi. 11, and the Notes of Gesenius on that place. See also Hos. iii. 5 ; Amos ix. 14, 15 ; Mic. iv. 6, 7 ; Joel iii. 16, 17 ; Zeph. iii. 19, 20´; Jer. xxiii. 8 ; xxxiii. 7 ; Ezek. xxxvi. 36.

(4.) A fourth specification respecting the Christology in the book of Daniel, is derived from the reference to the doctrine of the resurrection (chap. xii. 2). It is objected that this is a doctrine of later times, and that it could not have been known in the age when Daniel is said to have lived.

That the doctrine of the resurrection of the dead is referred to in that passage, or that what is there said is *based* on the belief of that doctrine, and implies that the doctrine was so commonly believed as to make it proper to refer to it as such, seems plain from the passage itself. See notes on the passage.

But in regard to the objection derived from this fact, it may be remarked :—

(a) That there is evidence elsewhere that the doctrine *was* known as early as the time of the exile, and was assumed to be true in the same manner in which it is here. Thus in Isa. xxvi. 19, it is referred to in the same manner, for the remark of the prophet is *based* on that, and cannot be explained except on the supposition that this was an article of common belief. See notes on that passage. See also Gesenius, who says, "that this place actually contains the doctrine of the resurrection of the dead, and that in these words the doctrine of the resurrection is undoubtedly implied." The same thing seems also to be true in the vision of the valley of dry bones (Ezek. xxxvii. 1-14). Though that passage does not refer *primarily* to the resurrection of the dead, and is not intended directly to teach it, yet it is difficult, if not impossible, to explain it, except on the supposition that this doctrine was understood, and was believed to be true. It is just such an illustration as would be used now in a community where that doctrine is understood and believed.

(*b*) It is undoubtedly true that, in the passage under consideration (Dan. xii. 2), the design is not directly to *teach* the doctrine of the resurrection of the dead, but that it refers, as the primary thought, to the restoration and recovery of the Jewish people, *as if* they were raised from the dead ; but still, as in the passages in Isaiah and Ezekiel above referred to, the doctrine of the resurrection is assumed, and the illustration is derived from that, and, as Jerome has remarked on the passage, such an illustration would not be employed unless the doctrine were believed, for "no one would attempt to confirm an uncertain or doubtful thing by that which had no existence." But the same design exists in each of the cases in Daniel, Isaiah, and Ezekiel. The doctrine is alluded to in the same manner, and in each case is assumed to be true in the same way—as a doctrine that was known, and that might be employed for *illustration*. This is one of the best proofs that there could be that it was a common article of belief ; and as it is used by these three writers in the same manner, if it proves that one of them lived in a later age, it proves the same of all. But as the genuineness of that portion of Isaiah where the passage occurs, and of Ezekiel is not called in question, it follows that the objection has no force as alleged against the genuineness of Daniel.

(*c*) It may be added, that on the supposition that there *is* no allusion to this doctrine in any of the prophets that lived in the time of the exile, or before it, that would furnish no evidence that it might not be found in a book written by Daniel. The belief undoubtedly sprang up at *some* time among the Jews, for it is admitted by those who object to the genuineness of Daniel on this account, that it *did* exist in the time in which they allege that the book was written—in the time of Antiochus Epiphanes; and it undoubtedly *somehow* gained so much currency among the Jews as to lay the foundation of the peculiar belief of the Pharisees on the subject. But no one can show that this doctrine could not have had its origin in Daniel himself; or that *he*, living in the time of the exile, might not have made such statements on the subject as to lay the foundation for the general belief of the doctrine in later times. Even on the supposition that he was not inspired, this might have been ; much more on the supposition that he *was* inspired —for he was one of the latest of the prophets of the Old Testament, and one of those who were most eminently favoured of God. In itself considered, there is no improbability in supposing that God might have honoured Daniel, by making him the instrument of first distinctly announcing the doctrines of the resurrection and the future judgment of the world.

C. A third objection, from the alleged reference to later customs and opinions in the book of Daniel, is derived from the fact stated in ch. vi. 10, that Daniel in his prayer is said to have turned his face towards Jerusalem. This objection as urged by Bertholdt and others, is, that the custom of turning the face towards Jerusalem in prayer was one that was originated after the building of the second temple, and that no traces of it are found while the first temple was standing. It is admitted, indeed, that the custom of turning the face towards a temple or place of worship prevailed extensively in Oriental countries —as among the Mahometans at present—but it is alleged that this had its origin among the Jews *after* the captivity, and after the second temple was built. It is further added that it is improbable that Daniel would turn his face towards *Jerusalem* on that occasion, for the city and temple were destroyed, and the Shekinah, the symbol of the divine presence there, had disappeared. See Bertholdt, p. 30.

To this objection the following remarks may be made in reply :—

(1.) The custom of turning the face in worship towards a temple or shrine, was one that existed early in the world, and has prevailed in almost all countries. It is one that would naturally spring up, even if there were no positive commands on the subject, for this would seem to be demanded by respect for the god who was worshipped, and who was supposed to have his residence in a particular temple. If Jehovah, therefore, was supposed to have his dwelling in the temple; if the symbols of his presence were believed to be there; if that was his *house*, just in proportion as that was believed would the custom be likely to prevail of turning the face towards that place in worship, just as we now naturally turn the face towards heaven, which we regard as the peculiar place of his abode. It would have been unnatural, therefore, if Daniel had *not* turned his face towards Jerusalem in his devotions.

(2.) The custom is, in fact, far-spread in the East, and goes back, in its origin, beyond any period we can now assign to it. It prevails everywhere among the Mahometans; it was found by Mungo Park among the negroes in Africa (Rosenmüller, *Morgenland*, iv. 361); and it may be said to be the general custom of the East. No one can determine its origin, and probably, for the reason above stated, it existed in the first periods of the history of the world.

(3.) The custom is mentioned in the Psalms as existing *before* the time of Daniel. Thus, in Psal. v. 7, "As for me, I will come into thy house in the multitude of thy mercy; and in thy fear will I worship toward thy holy temple." Psal. cxxxviii. 2, "I will worship toward thy holy temple," &c. Comp. Psal. cxxi. 1. So Psal. xxviii. 2, "Hear the voice of my supplications—when I lift up my hands toward thy holy oracle."

(4.) The custom was sanctioned by what Solomon said at the dedication of the temple. In his prayer, on that occasion, it is implied that the custom *would* prevail, and what was said at that time could not but be regarded as giving a sanction to it. Thus, in the prayer offered at the dedication of the temple, he seems to have supposed just such a case as that before us: "If they sin against thee, and thou be angry with them, and deliver them to the enemy, so that they carry them away captive unto the land of the enemy, far or near; if they shall bethink themselves in the land whither they were carried captives, and repent, and pray unto thee toward their land which thou gavest unto their fathers, the city which thou hast chosen, and the house which I have built for thy name, then hear thou their prayer," &c. (1 Kings viii. 44–49. Comp. also vers. 33, 35, 38, 42).

(5.) It may be added, that nothing was more natural than for Daniel to do this. It is not said that he turned his face toward the "*temple*," but toward "Jerusalem." It was true that the temple was in ruins; true that the ark was removed, and that the Shekinah had disappeared. It was true also that Jerusalem was in ruins. But it is to be remembered that Jerusalem had been long regarded as the city of God, and his dwelling-place on the earth; that this was the place where his worship had been celebrated for ages, and where he had manifested himself by visible symbols; that this was the place where the ancestors of Daniel had lived and worshipped, and where he believed the temple of God would be built again, and where God would again dwell—a place sacred in the recollections of the past and in the anticipations of the future— a place where Daniel had himself been taught to worship God when a child, and where he anticipated that they who should be delivered from the long captivity would again offer sacrifice and praise; and nothing, therefore, was more natural than for him, in his prayer, to turn his face to a spot hallowed by so many sacred associations.

D. A fourth objection designed to show that the book betrays a later origin than the time of the captivity is, that Daniel is represented (ch. vi. 10), as entering into his chamber, or "upper room" ($\hat{v}\pi\epsilon\rho\tilde{\omega}ov$), when he prayed, and that the custom of setting apart a chamber in a house for private devotion sprang up in a later age among the Jews, as one of the results of formalism and ostentation in religion.—(*Bertholdt*, p. 30.)

In regard to this custom among the later Jews, see the notes on the passage referred to. But there are two remarks to be made, showing conclusively that this objection has no force :—

(*a*) There is no evidence that it was such an "upper room" ($\hat{v}\pi\epsilon\rho\tilde{\omega}ov$), as is here referred to. All that is fairly implied in the word in this passage (עֲלִיּתֵהּ) might be applied to any house, and at any time. It denotes, indeed, an upper room, upper story, or loft; but not necessarily *such* an upper room as was built by the Jews in later times, and designated by the word $\hat{v}\pi\epsilon\rho\tilde{\omega}ov$. It is not improbable that Daniel would retire to such a part of his house to pray, but it is not neces-

sarily implied in this word that the chamber referred to had been
specifically constructed *as* a place of prayer.

(*b*) But even supposing that this was the case, it is impossible to
prove that such a custom may not have prevailed in the time of the
captivity. We cannot now trace the origin of that custom among the
Jews; and though it undoubtedly prevailed in a later age, yet no one
can demonstrate that it did not exist also at a time as early as that of
the exile. Indeed, there is some evidence that it *did* prevail at an
earlier period among the Hebrews. Thus, in 2 Sam. xviii. 33, it is
said of David on the death of Absalom, "And the king was much moved,
and went up to *the chamber over the gate*, and wept," &c. So in the
case of the prophet Elijah, during his residence with the widow of
Zarephath, an upper chamber or loft was assigned the prophet (1 Kings
xvii. 19), called "a *loft* where he abode"—עֲלִיָּה—the very word which
is used in Daniel. The same word occurs again in Judg. iii. 20, 23,
24, 25, in each case rendered *parlour*, and referring to a private room
where one might retire, and, as the word implies, to an *upper room*,
doubtless a small room built on the flat roof of the house, as being more
retired and cool. And again, in 2 Kings i. 2, it is said of Ahaziah
that "he fell down through a lattice in his *upper chamber* that was in
Samaria." And again, in 2 Kings iv. 10, the Shunamitess proposes to
her husband to make for the prophet Elisha "a little *chamber* on the
wall"—עֲלִיַּת־קִיר—a place of retirement for him. These passages show
that the custom of constructing a chamber, or upper room for the purpose of retirement or devotion, prevailed long before the time of Daniel;
and, therefore, the fact that he is represented as having such a place in
his house in Babylon, if that *be* the fact referred to here, cannot be
alleged as evidence that the book was written at a later period than the
captivity.

E. It is alleged, as an evidence that the book was written at a period
later than the exile, that Daniel is represented (in the same passage,
ch. vi. 10) as praying three times a-day, a custom, it is said, which
originated in later times.

But the reply to this is obvious. (*a*) The custom of praying three
times a-day in sacred devotion is one of which there are traces in earlier
times. Thus the Psalmist (Psa. lv. 17), "Evening, and morning, and at
noon, will I pray, and cry aloud: and he shall hear my voice." (*b*) Daniel
may have had such a custom, without supposing that he derived it
from any one. (*c*) These are the *natural* times of prayer; times that
devout persons will be *likely* to select as seasons of devotion; the morning, when one just enters upon the duties and trials of the day, when it
is appropriate to give thanks for preservation, and to ask of God that
he will guide, direct, and sustain us; the evening, when, having finished
the toils of the day, it is appropriate to render thanksgiving, to pray
for the remission of the sins of the day, and to seek the blessing and
protection of God as we lie down to rest; and noon, when we feel the

propriety of dividing the labours of the day by an interval of rest and devotion; thus keeping up, amidst the cares of the world, the life of religion in the soul. (*d*) There is no certain evidence that this became a regular and settled usage in later times among the Jews, any more than that it was of a former age.

F. It is alleged that what is said in ch. iv. 27, of the efficacy of almsgiving in averting the judgments of God, is an opinion that had its origin in later times, and proves that the book must have been written at a period subsequent to the captivity. The passage is, "Let my counsel be acceptable unto thee, and break off thy sins by righteousness, *and thine iniquities by showing mercy to the poor ;* it may be a lengthening of thy tranquillity." This, it is said, could have been written only at a time when great merit was attributed to almsgiving, and when such acts, it was supposed, would avert Divine vengeance from the guilty; and this opinion, it is alleged, sprang up at a period subsequent to the captivity. That the sentiment here adverted to prevailed in later times there can be no doubt, but there is no proof that it is used in the passage before us in the sense in which it prevailed in the time when the books of the Apocrypha were written; and, in reference to the objection here urged, all that is necessary, it seems to me, is to refer to the notes on the passage, where its true meaning is fully considered. The short answer is, that the passage does not teach any such peculiar doctrine on the subject of almsgiving, as prevailed in later times among the Jews, but only the *general* doctrine, which is found everywhere in the Bible, and which accords with all just notions on the subject, that if a sinner will abandon the error of his ways, and perform acts of righteousness, it will conduce to his happiness, and, in all probability, to the lengthening out of his days.

G. One other objection, under the general head now under consideration, remains. It is derived from what are called the *ascetic* customs referred to in the book. On this point De Wette refers to ch. i. 8–16, as compared with 2 Macc. v. 27, and with the apocryphal portion of the book of Esther.

In regard to this objection, also, perhaps all that is necessary is to refer to the notes on the passage. The reason which Daniel gave for not partaking of the food and wine furnished by the king of Babylon, is not such as would be derived from any ascetic or monastic opinions, but such as would be given by any Jew of that age who was conscientious. It was "that he might not defile himself with the portion of the king's meat, nor with the wine which he drank " (ch. i. 8); that is, he purposed to keep himself clear from all participation in idolatry, and to save himself from the temptations to which one would be exposed if he indulged freely in the luxuries in eating and drinking which were practised at the royal table. As this solution explains the passage on principles that would be likely to influence a pious Jew, and which would be proper in young men everywhere, it is unnecessary to seek any other, and improper to suppose that there is an allusion here to superstitious customs which prevailed among the Jews in later times.

VI. A sixth objection to the authenticity and genuineness of the book is derived from the place assigned it in the canon. This objection is urged by Bertholdt, Bleek, Eichhorn, Kirms, and De Wette, and is substantially this, as stated by Bertholdt:—It is well known that the Jews, in the time when the *Talmud* was composed, divided their sacred books into three parts—the Law, the Prophets, and the Hagiographa. The latter class embraced the Psalms, Job, Proverbs, Song of Solomon, Ruth, Lamentations, Ecclesiastes, Esther, Daniel, Ezra, Nehemiah, and the two books of the Chronicles. This classification also existed in the time of Jerome, who obtained it evidently from the Jews in Palestine. The objection is, that in collecting and arranging the books of the Old Testament, Daniel was assigned to this latter class, and was not placed among the Prophets. The book professes to be, in a great part, prophetical, and if genuine, its true place, it is argued, would be among the prophets; and, it is said, it would have been placed in that class if it had been in existence at the time when the collection of the sacred books was made. It is argued, therefore, that it must have had a later origin, and that when it was written it was assigned a place in that *general* collection of writings where all those books were arranged which could not be placed with either of the other classes. This objection is summarily stated by Prof. Stuart (*Critical History and Defence of the Old Testament Canon*, p. 266) in the following words :—" The argument runs thus : ' No reason can be assigned, except the *lateness* of the composition, why Daniel and the Chronicles should be placed among the Kethubim or Hagiographa, since the first belongs to the class of the later prophets, and the second, like Samuel, Kings, &c., to the class of the former prophets. The fact, then, that Daniel and the Chronicles are joined with the Kethubim, shows that they were written after the second class of the Scriptural books, viz., the Prophets, was fully defined and completed; now, as this class comprises Haggai, Zechariah, and Malachi, so we have conclusive evidence that Daniel and Chronicles must have been composed, or at all events introduced into the canon, at a period subsequent to Nehemiah and Malachi, which was about 430–420 B.C.' "

In reference to this objection, perhaps all that would be necessary for me would be to refer to the very full and satisfactory argument of Prof. Stuart on the Canon in the work just named, § 9-13, pp. 214-298. A few remarks, however, on two or three points, seem to be demanded to show the results which have been reached by a careful investigation of the subject, and how entirely without foundation is the objection.

A. The objection, then, takes for granted the following things, which it is impossible now to prove: (1.) That the division of the books of the Old Testament found in the *Talmud*, and prevailing among the Jews in the time of Jerome, in which Daniel is placed in the third class, the

Kethubim, or Hagiographa, is the ancient and original division; for if this is not so, then Daniel *may* have been placed among the prophets, and of course the objection would not then exist. There is the strongest reason to believe that this was *not* the arrangement that prevailed at an earlier period, but that it was made long after the time of Josephus; at any rate it cannot be *proved* to have been the original arrangement. (2.) It takes for granted that the main reason for inserting Daniel and the books of the Chronicles in the Hagiographa was the *recent* origin of these books, or the fact that they were composed *after* the second class —the Prophets—was completed and collected together, for the whole weight of the objection rests on this. If any of these books in the Hagiographa were in fact written at an earlier period than some in the second class—the Prophets—or if any other reason existed for referring them to the class of the Hagiographa than the *lateness* of their composition, then the objection would have no force. But this difficulty of itself would be fatal to the objection, for there is every reason to suppose that the lateness of the composition was *not* the reason why these books were placed in the Hagiographa, and that this was never supposed or implied by those who made the arrangement; for, not to speak of the book of Job, which is found in that class, and which is probably one of the oldest compositions in the Bible, if not the very oldest, what shall we say of the Psalms, and the book of Proverbs, and the book of Ecclesiastes, and the Canticles, which are also found in that class? Assuredly it could not have been pretended that these writings belonged to the Maccabean age, and that they were inserted in the Hagiographa because they were supposed to have had a *later* origin than the Prophets; for, in all ages, the Jews have regarded the book of Proverbs, the book of Ecclesiastes, and the Canticles, as the genuine productions of Solomon. Why, then, were they put into the Hagiographa?—for there the Psalms, and the book of Proverbs, and Ecclesiastes, and the Song of Solomon, have always been, in every triplex division of the books of the Old Testament which has ever been made. (3.) The objection takes for granted that the two classes, the Prophets and the Hagiographa, have been fixed and uniform, like the first, the Law, as to the number of books in each, ever since the division was made; that the same number of books, and the same arrangement, has been found which existed in the time of Josephus; and that no causes have ever operated since to produce a change in the arrangement; for if this is not so, it would be fatal to the objection. But this can never be shown to be true; indeed, there is every reason to believe that the contrary is true—and if it cannot be demonstrated to be true, the objection is without force. But,

B. There are strong positive arguments to show that the fact that Daniel, in the later divisions of the Hebrew books, is placed in the list of the Hagiographa or Kethubim, is no argument against the genuineness and authenticity of the book.

(1.) There is every presumption that in the earliest arrangement of the books of the Old Testament, the book of Daniel, with several that now occupy the same place in the Talmudical arrangement, was ranked with the *second* class—the Prophets. This presumption is founded, mainly, on what is said of the division of the books of the Old Testament by Josephus. It is true that he has not enumerated the books of the Old Testament, but he has mentioned the division of the books in his time, and, of course, in earlier times, in such a way as to make it morally certain that Daniel was not in the third class, but in the second class—the Prophets. His account of this division (*Against Apion*, b. 1, § 8) is as follows : " We have not a countless number of books, discordant and arranged against each other, but only two and twenty books, containing the history of every age, which are justly accredited as Divine [the old editions of Josephus read merely, 'which are justly accredited'—θεῖα (divine) comes from Eusebius' translation of Josephus, in *Ecc. Hist.* iii. 10] ; and of these, five belong to Moses, which contain both his laws and the history of the generations of men until his death. This period lacks but little of 3000 years. From the death of Moses, moreover, until the reign of Artaxerxes, king of the Persians after Xerxes, the prophets who followed Moses have described the things which were done during the age of each one respectively, in *thirteen* books. The remaining *four* contain hymns to God and rules of life for men. From the time of Artaxerxes, moreover, till our present period, all occurrences have been written down ; but they are not regarded as entitled to the like credit with those which precede them, because there was no certain succession of prophets. Fact has shown what confidence we place in our own writings ; for, although so many ages have passed away, no one has dared to add to them, nor to take anything from them, nor to make alterations. In all Jews it is implanted, even from their birth, to regard them as being the instructions of God, and to abide steadfastly by them, and, if it be necessary, to die gladly for them." —(Prof. Stuart's translation, *ut supra*, pp. 430, 431).

Now, in this extract from Josephus, stating the number and order of the sacred books in his time, it is *necessarily* implied that the book of Daniel was then included in the *second* part, or among the "Prophets." For (*a*) it is clear that it was not in the third division, or the Hagiographa. Of that division Josephus says, " The remaining *four* contain hymns to God, and rules of life for men." Now, we are not able to determine with exact certainty, indeed, what these four books were, for Josephus has not mentioned their names ; but we can determine with certainty that Daniel was *not* of the number, for his book does not come under the description of " hymns to God," or " rules of life for men." If we *cannot*, therefore, make out what these books were, the argument would be complete on that point ; but although Josephus has not enumerated them, they *can* be made out with a good degree of probability. That the " hymns to God " would embrace the Psalms there can be no doubt; and there can be as little doubt that, in the books containing "rules of life for men," the Proverbs would be included. The other books that would more properly come under this designation than any other are Ecclesiastes and the Song of Solomon (see the full evidence of this in Prof. Stuart, *ut supra*, pp. 256–264); at all events, it is clear that *Daniel* would not be included in that number. (*b*) There is evidence, then, that Daniel *was* included at that time in the second division—that of the Prophets. Josephus says that that division comprised "*thirteen* books," and that Daniel was included among them is evident from the rank which Josephus gives to him as one of the greatest of the prophets. Thus he says of him (*Ant.* b. x. chap. xi.) : "He was so happy as to have strange revelations made to him, and those as to one of the greatest of the prophets ; insomuch that while he was alive he had the esteem and applause both of kings and of the multitude, and now he is dead he retains a remembrance that will never fail. For the several books that he wrote and left behind him are still read by us till this time, and from them we believe that he conversed with God ; for he not only prophesied of future events, as did the other prophets, but he also determined the time of their accomplishment. And while prophets used to foretell misfortunes, and on that account were disagreeable both to the kings and the multitude, Daniel was to them a prophet of good things, and this to such a degree, that, by the agreeable nature of his predictions, he procured the good-will of all men ; and by the accomplishment of them he procured the belief of their truth, and the opinion of a sort of divinity for himself among the multitude. He also wrote and left behind him what evinced the accuracy and the undeniable veracity of his predictions." From this it is clear that Josephus regarded Daniel as worthy to be ranked among the greatest of the prophets, and that he considered his writings as worthy to be classed with those of the other eminent prophets of his country. This is such language as would be used in speaking of *any* ancient prophet ; and, as we have seen that the book of Daniel could not have been of the number mentioned by him in the third class— those containing "hymns to God and rules of life for men"—it follows that it must have been ranked by Josephus in the second division—that of *the prophets*. It does not seem easy to suppose that there could be clearer proof than this, short of direct affirmation. The proof that he regarded Daniel as belonging to this division of the books, is as clear as can be made out from his writings in favour of Isaiah, Jeremiah, or Ezekiel.

(2.) If Daniel had this rank in the time of Josephus, then it would follow that, in the division of the books of the Old Testament, as referred to by the Saviour (Luke xxiv. 44), he must have had this rank also. There can be no doubt that Josephus expresses not his own private judgment in the matter, but the prevailing opinion of his countrymen on the subject. Josephus was born A.D. 37, and consequently he must have uttered what was the general sentiment in the time of the Saviour and the apostles—for it cannot be supposed that any change had occurred in that short time among the Jews, by which Daniel had been transferred from the *third* division to the *second*. If *any* change had occurred in the arrangement of the books, it would have been, for reasons which are obvious, just the reverse—since the predictions of Daniel were at this time much relied on by Christians, in their arguments against the Jews, to prove that Jesus was the Messiah. We may regard it as morally certain, therefore, that in the time of the Saviour, Daniel was ranked among the prophets. It may be added here, also, that if Daniel had this rank in the estimation of Josephus, it may be presumed that he had the same rank when the division of the sacred books is referred to in the only other two instances among the Jews, previous to the composition of the *Talmud*. In both these cases there is mention of the *triplex* division; in neither are the *names* of the books recorded. One occurs in the " Prologue of the Wisdom of Jesus, the Son of Sirach," in the Apocrypha. This Prologue was probably written about 130 B.C.; the book itself probably about 180 B.C. In this Prologue the writer mentions the divisions of the sacred books three times in this manner : " Since so many and important things have been imparted to us by *the Law, the Prophets, and other [works] of the like kind* which have followed, for which one must needs praise Israel on account of learning and wisdom ; and inasmuch as not only those who read ought to be well-informed, but those who are devoted to learning should be able to profit, both in the way of speaking and writing, such as are foreigners, my grandfather, Jesus, having devoted himself very much to the reading of *the Law, the Prophets, and the other books of his country*, and having acquired a great degree of experience in these things, was himself led on to compose something pertaining to instruction and wisdom, so that those desirous of learning, being in possession of these things, might grow much more by a life conformed to the law. Ye are invited, therefore, with good will and strict attention to make the perusal, and to take notice whenever we may seem to lack ability, in respect to any of the words which we have laboured to translate. Not only so, but *the Law itself, and the Prophets, and the remaining books*, exhibit no small diversity among themselves as to the modes of expression."

The other reference of the same kind occurs in Philo Judæus. He flourished about A.D. 40, and in praising a contemplative life, and giving examples of it, he comes at last to the *Therapeutæ*, or *Essenes*, and in speaking of their devotional practices, he uses this language : " In every house is a sanctuary, which is called *sacred place* or *monastery*, in which, being alone, they perform the mysteries of a holy life ; introducing nothing into it, neither drink, nor bread-corn, nor any of the other things which are necessary for the wants of the body, but *the Laws, and Oracles predicted by the prophets, and Hymns, and other writings, by*

which knowledge and piety are increased and perfected." There can be
no reasonable doubt that precisely the same division of the books of the
Old Testament is referred to in each of these cases which is mentioned
by Josephus. If so, then Daniel was at that time reckoned among the
prophets.

(3.) He certainly had this rank among the early Christians, alike in
their estimation of him, and in the order of the sacred books. It happens that, although Josephus, the Son of Sirach, and Philo have given
no *list* of the names and order of the sacred books, yet the early Christians *have*, and from these lists it is easy to ascertain the rank which
they assigned to Daniel. " Melito places Daniel among the Prophets,
and *before* Ezekiel. The same does Origen. The Council of Laodicea
places Daniel next ,after Ezekiel, and, of course, among the Prophets.
The same do the *Canones Apostol.*, Cyrill of Jerusalem, Gregory
Nazianzen, Athanasius, *Synopsis Scripturæ in Athan.* The Council of
Hippo, like Melito and Origen, place it *before* Ezekiel, as also does
Hilary; and Rufinus places it next after Ezekiel. Jerome alone, in
giving an account of the Rabbinical usage in his day, puts Daniel among
the Hagiographa; and after it he puts Chronicles, Ezra (with Nehemiah),
and Esther."—(Prof. Stuart, *ut supra*, p. 284).* The *Talmud* thus stands
alone, with the exception of Jerome, in placing Daniel among the books
constituting the Hagiographa; and Jerome, in doing this, merely gives
an account of what was customary in his time among the Jewish
Rabbins, without expressing any opinion of his own on the subject.
These testimonies are sufficient to show that Daniel was *never* placed in
the division composing the Hagiographa, so far as can be proved by
the Son of Sirach, by Philo, by Josephus, by the Jews in the time of
the Saviour, or by the Christian writers of the first four centuries ; and
of course, until it can be demonstrated that he *was* thus classified, this
objection must fall to the ground. But,

(4.) The fact that Daniel occupied this place in the divisions made
of the books by the later Jews can be accounted for in a way perfectly
consistent with the supposition that he wrote at the time when the book
is commonly believed to have been composed. For,

(*a*) The reason which they themselves give for this arrangement is,
not that his writings were of later *date*, but some fanciful view which
they had about the *degrees* of inspiration of the prophets. They say
that the books of Moses take the precedence above all others, because
God spake with him mouth to mouth ; that the prophets who came
after him were such as, whether sleeping or waking when they received
revelations, were deprived of all the use of their senses, and were spoken
to by a voice, or saw prophetic visions in ecstasy ; and that the third
and lowest class of writers were those who, preserving the use of their

---

* The lists of the books, as given by these writers and councils, may be seen
at length in Prof. Stuart, *ut supra*, Appendix, pp. 431–452.

senses, spake like other men, and yet in such a way that, although not favoured with dreams or visions in ecstacy, they still perceived a Divine influence resting upon them, at whose suggestion they spake or wrote what they made public. For the proof of this, see Prof. Stuart, *ut supra,* p. 269.   Agreeably to this fanciful opinion, they made the arrangement of the sacred books which is found in the *Talmud;* and on this principle they placed Daniel in the list of the Hagiographa.   But assuredly this fanciful opinion, and the mistake of the Jews consequent on it, can be no reason for supposing that the book of Daniel was written in the time of the Maccabees; and especially as they who made this arrangement never pretended this, and never could have made the arrangement on this ground.   And,

(*b*) There is great reason for supposing, after all, that Daniel was not assigned to the place which he has in the Talmudic divisions of the sacred books, on the ground that he was properly classed there, even on their arbitrary and fanciful opinion as to the degrees of inspiration among the prophets, but because, in the disputes between Christians and Jews about the Messiah, in the first three and a half centuries, the Jews felt themselves to be so pressed by the prediction in Dan. ix., respecting the seventy weeks, that they sought to give the book a lower place than it had occupied before, and thus to remove it somewhat from an association with the other prophets, and to diminish the force of the argument in proof that Jesus of Nazareth was the Christ.

(5.) To all this it may be added, that it would have been impossible to have foisted a book into the canon that was composed in the time of the Maccabees, and that was not regarded as of Divine inspiration. We have, as above, the express testimony of Josephus, that for some four hundred years before his time they had no prophets who wrote inspired books, or who could be regarded as sacred writers.   The canon, according to him, was closed at the time of Artaxerxes, and afterward they had books in which " all occurrences were written down; but these were not regarded as of like credit with those that preceded them, because there was no certain succession of prophets;" that is, the canon of inspired books was then closed, in the apprehension of the Jews, or they had a definite number which they regarded as of Divine origin, and as distinguished from all others.

Now, supposing this to have been, as no doubt it was, a prevailing opinion among the Jews, it would have been impossible to have foisted in a book written in the time of the Maccabees—or after the time of Antiochus Epiphanes, as the objection supposes the book of Daniel to have been—in such a way that it would be regarded as entitled to a place among the sacred writings. If this book was written at that time, it must have been known that it was not the genuine production of the Daniel of the captivity; and by whom could it be introduced into the canon?   On what pretence could it be done?   What claim could have been urged for a spurious book of this kind to a place by the side of Isaiah and Ezekiel? It is well known that the Hebrews have been, in all ages, most careful of their sacred books; that they have transcribed them with the greatest possible attention; that they have counted the words and the letters; that they have marked and preserved every variety, irregularity, and anomaly, even every unusual shape and position of a letter in the manuscript; and it may be asked with emphasis, In what way it would be possible to introduce a book which was known and admitted to be spurious—a book falsely ascribed to one who was said to have lived long before—among those which they regarded as of Divine origin, and whose purity they guarded with so much care? Scarcely any greater literary absurdity can be imagined than this.

VII. A seventh objection which has been urged to the genuineness of the book of Daniel is derived from the silence of the Son of Sirach in regard to it. This objection is urged by De Wette, Bleek, Eichhorn, Kirms, and Bretschneider, and is substantially this:—That in the book of Ecclesiasticus (ch. xlix.), the author of that book, Jesus, the Son of Sirach, undertakes to give a list of the personages in the Jewish history who had been eminent for virtue, piety, and patriotism; and that the circumstances of the case are such that it is to be presumed that if he had known anything of Daniel and his writings, he would have been mentioned among them. Thus he mentions David, Hezekiah, Josiah, Jeremiah, Ezekiel, the twelve Prophets, Zorobabel, Jesus the son of Josedec, Nehemiah, Enoch, Joseph, Shem, Seth, and Adam. The particular *point*, however, of the objection seems to be, that he mentions men who were eminent in securing the return of the Hebrews to their own country, as Nehemiah and Zorobabel, and that if Daniel had lived then in Babylon, and had had the important agency in effecting the return of the captives which is ascribed to him in this book, or had had the influence at the court of Persia attributed to him, it is unaccountable that his name was not mentioned.

To this objection we may reply: (1.) That the *argumentum a silentio* is admitted not to be a conclusive kind of reasoning. So long as there *may* have been other reasons why the name was omitted in such a list, it is unfair and inconclusive to infer that he had not then an existence, or that there was no such man. It is necessary, in order that this reasoning should have any force, to show that this is the *only* cause which could have led to this omission, or that this *alone* could account for it. But it is easy to conceive that there may have been many reasons why the name was omitted in this rapid enumeration, consistently with the belief that Daniel then lived in Babylon, and that he occupied the position, and rendered the services, which it may be supposed from the account in this book he would render. In such a rapid enumeration, it cannot be supposed that the writer mentioned all the eminent men among the Hebrews, and therefore it is in no way remarkable that the name of Daniel should have been omitted. This is conceded even by Kirms. (See his work, *Commentatio Historico-Critica*, &c., p. 9.) (2.) The objection, if of any value, would prove that no such person as Daniel existed at that time, or even at any time previous to the age of the Son of Sirach; for he did not mention these persons as authors of books, but as eminent persons—as distinguished not by their *writings*, but by their *lives*. But the existence of Daniel, as a historical personage, is as clear as that of any of the eminent men mentioned in the Jewish history, and is even conceded by the objectors themselves. (See § I. of this Introduction.) 3. As a matter of fact, the Son of Sirach has omitted the names of others whom he would be at least as *likely* to refer to as the name of Daniel. He has wholly omitted the name of Ezra. Would not his agency be as likely to occur to such a writer as that of Daniel? He has omitted the names of Mordecai and Esther—personages whose agency would be as likely to be remembered in such a connection as that of Daniel. He has omitted also the whole of the minor prophets; for the passage in ch. xlix. 10, which in the common version makes mention of them, is shown by Bretschneider (*in loc.*) to be clearly spurious, it having been copied verbatim from ch. xlvi. 12, with merely the substitution of the words "the twelve prophets" for the word "their." (See Prof. Stuart, *Com.* p. 463.) How can such an omission be accounted for, if the objection derived from the omission of the name of Daniel has any force? And if the mere *silence* of the Son of Sirach be allowed to be an argument against the existence of prominent persons in the Jewish history, and the genuineness of the books which they wrote, who will determine the limit to which the objection will go? How small a portion of the patriarchs and prophets—how small a portion of the writings of the Old Testament would be spared! And, after all, why should so much weight be allowed to the mere silence of the Son of Sirach—an author comparatively unknown—as to set aside the positive testimony of all antiquity, and change the faith of the world?

§ III.—CONTINUATION OF THE ARGUMENT FOR THE GENUINENESS AND AUTHENTICITY OF THE BOOK OF DANIEL.

B. *Positive Proofs of its Genuineness and Authenticity.*

Having thus examined at length the objections which have been made to the genuineness and authenticity of the book of Daniel, I proceed now to notice the positive proofs that it was written at the time when it is alleged to have been, and by the author whose name it bears. This need not detain us long; for if the objections which are made to the genuineness of the book are not well founded, there will be little difficulty in showing that the common sentiment in the church in regard to its authorship and authenticity is correct. It has undeniably for a long time had a place in the sacred canon; it has been received by the Christian church at all times as a sacred book, on the same level with the other inspired books; it has had a place among the books regarded by the Jews as inspired; and if it cannot be *displaced* from the position which it has so long occupied, the conclusion would seem to be fair that that is its proper position. We have seen, in the previous discussion, that it was ranked by Josephus among the prophetic books; that it was held in high estimation among the Jews as one of their sacred books; that the canon of Scripture was closed some four hundred years before the time of the Saviour; and that, from the nature of the case, it would have been impossible to foist a book of doubtful origin, or an acknowledged fiction, into that canon in a later age.

In looking now at the *positive* evidence of the genuineness and canonical authority of the book, the only points that are really necessary to be made out are two : that it is the work of one author, and that that author was the Daniel of the captivity. If these two points can be established, its right to a place in the canon will be easily demonstrated. My object, then, will be to establish these two points, and then to show how, if these points are admitted, it follows that the book is inspired, and has a right to a place in the canon.

I. It is the work of one author. That is, it is not made up of fragments from different hands, and composed at different times. It is a book by itself, every part of which is entitled to credit if any part of it is, and entitled to the same credit on the ground of being the composition of the same author.

The *evidence* of this lies in such circumstances as the following :—

(1.) It is apparent on the face of the book that the design is to represent it as the production of one author. If the book is a forgery, this was no doubt the intention of its author; if it is genuine, it was of course the design. No one, on reading the book, it is presumed, could fail to perceive that the design of the author was to leave the impression that it is the work of one hand, and that it was intended to represent what occurred in the lifetime of one man, and that one man had committed it to writing. This is apparent, because the same name occurs throughout; because there is substantially one series of transactions; because the transactions are referred to as occurring in one place—Babylon; and because the same languages, customs, usages, and times are referred to. All the *internal* marks which can go to demonstrate that any work is by one hand would be found to be applicable to this; and all the *external* marks will be found also to agree with this supposition.

There are two things, indeed, to be admitted, which have been relied on by some to prove that the work is the composition of different authors.

(*a*) The one is, that it is divided into two parts : the one (ch. i.–vi.), in the main historical; the other (ch. vii.–xii.), in the main prophetical. But this is no argument against the identity of the authorship, for the same intermingling of history with prophecy occurs in most of the prophetic books; and it is no objection that these occur in separate continuous portions, instead of being irregularly intermingled. In fact, the same thing occurs in Isaiah, where the first part (ch. i.–xxxix.), is made up, in a considerable degree, of historic allusions mingled with prophecy; and where the second part (ch. xl.–lxvi.), is wholly prophetic. Besides, any one must admit, that on the supposition that Daniel was the sole author of the book, nothing would be more natural than this very arrangement. What objection could there be to the supposition that one part of his book might relate to historic incidents mainly— though even these have a strong prophetic character—and that the other should be composed of prophecies? What would there be in his condition or character that would forbid such a supposition?

(b) The other circumstance is, that, between these two parts, there is a change in the *person* of the writer; that in the first portion (ch. i.–vi.), he uses the third person when speaking of Daniel, and in the other (ch. vii.–xii.), the first person. This is, in the main, true, though it is true also that in the second part the third person is sometimes used when speaking of himself, ch. vii. 1; x. 1. But in regard to this it may be observed (1.) That it is no uncommon thing for an author to speak of himself in the third person. This is uniformly done by Cæsar in his *Commentaries*, and this fact is never urged now as an argument against the genuineness of his work. (2.) This is often done by the prophets. See Isa. ii. 1; vii. 3; xiii. 1; Ezek. i. 3. So Hosea, throughout the first chapter of his book, speaks uniformly of himself in the third person, and in ch. ii. and iii. in the first person; and so Amos, ch. vii. 1, 2, 4, 5, 7, 8, speaks of himself in the first person, and again, vers. 12, 14, in the third person. It may be added that it is the uniform method, also, of the evangelist John, to speak of himself in the third person; and, in fact, this is so common in authors that it can constitute no argument against the genuineness of any particular book.

It may be observed also that, in general, those who have denied the genuineness and authenticity of the book of Daniel have admitted that it is the work of one author. This is expressly admitted by Lengerke, p. ci., who says, " The identity of the author appears from the uniformity of the plan, and the relations which the different parts bear to each other; that the historical and prophetic parts are related to each other; that there is a certain uniform gradation (Stufenfolge) of the oracles from the uncertain to the certain; that there is a remarkable similarity of ideas, images, and forms of speech; and that, in the respective parts of the Hebrew and Chaldee, there is great similarity of style." The same opinion is maintained by Dereser, Gesenius, Bleek, De Wette, Kirms, Hoffmann, and Hengstenberg; though nearly all of these authors suppose that it was written in the time of the Maccabees. They admit, however, that it is the work of a single author. Eichhorn and Bertholdt appear to have been the only authors of distinction who have denied it.

(2.) The identity of the book appears from the manner in which it is written in respect to language. We have already seen that a part of it is written in Hebrew, and a part in Chaldee. From the beginning to ch. ii. 4 it is Hebrew, then from ch. ii. 4 to the end of ch. vii. it is Chaldee, and the remainder (ch. viii.–xii.), is Hebrew. Now, it may be admitted, that if the historical part (ch. i.–vi.) had been wholly in either of these languages, and the prophetical part (ch. vii.–xii.) had been wholly in the other, it *might* have constituted a plausible argument against the identity of the book. But the present arrangement is one that furnishes no such argument. It cannot well be conceived that, if the work were the production of two authors, one would begin his portion in one language and end it in another, and that the other would just reverse the process in regard to languages. Such an arrangement would not be likely to occur in two independent compositions professedly treating of the same general subjects, and intended to be palmed off as the work of one author. As it is, the arrangement is natural, and easy to be accounted for; but the other supposition would imply an artifice in composition which would not be likely to occur, and which would be wholly unnecessary for any purpose which can be imagined.

(3.) The identity of the book appears from the fact that it refers to the same series of subjects; that the same great design is pursued through the whole. Thus, in the two parts, though the first is mainly historical and the last prophetical, there is a remarkable parallelism between the predictions in ch. ii. and in ch. vii. The same great series of events is referred to, though in different forms; and so throughout the book, as remarked above in the quotation from Lengerke, we meet with the same ideas, the same modes of speech, the same symbols, the same imagery, the operations of the same mind, and the manifestation of the same character in the authors. The Daniel of the first part is the Daniel of the last; and, in this respect, the similarity is so great as to leave the irresistible impression on the mind that he is *the* personage of the whole book, and that his own hand is apparent throughout.

(4.) The identity of the book appears from the fact that the objections made to it pertain alike to every part of it, and in reference to the different parts are substantially the same. By referring to the objections which have, in the previous section, been examined at length, it will be seen that they all suppose the identity of the book, or that they are drawn from the book considered as a whole, and not from any particular part. Whatever difficulty there is in regard to the book pertains to it as a whole, and difficulties of precisely the same kind lie scattered through the entire volume. This fact proves that the book has such an identity as appertains to one and the same author; and this fact would not be likely to occur in a book that was made up of the productions of different authors.

(5.) It may be added, that whenever Daniel is spoken of by Josephus, by the Saviour, or by the early Christian writers, it is always done as if the book was the production of one author. Just such language is used as would be used on the supposition that the book is the composition of one man; nor is there an intimation that there were two Daniels, or that there was even any doubt about the identity of the authorship. The fact that the book of Daniel is the production of one author may be regarded as established; indeed, there is no ancient work, concerning which, the evidence is more direct and clear.

II. The second point to be made out is, that the author was the Daniel of the captivity. The evidences on this point will be adduced in the order, not of *time*, but of what seems due to them in value and importance.

(1.) I refer, first, to the testimony of the writer himself. In ch. vii. 28; viii. 1, 15, 27; ix. 2; x. 2; xii. 5, the writer speaks of himself as "*I Daniel;*" that is, the same Daniel whose history is given in ch. i. This cannot be, indeed, regarded as conclusive evidence; for the forger of a book might insert the name of another person as the author, and be constant in maintaining it to be so. All that is affirmed is, that this is *primâ facie* evidence, and is good evidence until it is set aside by substantial reasons. We assume this in regard to any book, and the evidence should be admitted unless there are satisfactory reasons for supposing that the name is assumed for purposes of deception. It cannot be doubted that the book bears on its face the *appearance* and the *claim* of having been written by the Daniel of the captivity, and that, in this respect, it is altogether such as it would be on that supposition. There is certainly an air of simplicity, honesty, and sincerity about it which we expect to find in a genuine production.

(2.) I refer, secondly, to the fact that the book of Daniel was received into the canon of the Old Testament as an authentic work of the Daniel of the captivity, and as entitled to a place among the inspired books of Scripture.

(*a*) It has been shown above, that the canon of Scripture was regarded as complete long before the time of the Maccabees; or that, according to the testimony of Josephus, there were three classes of books among the Hebrews, all regarded as *sacred* books, and all, in this respect, differing from certain *other* books which they had, as containing the record of affairs subsequent to the time of Artaxerxes. These classes of books were known as the Law, the Prophets, and the "Kethubim"—the "other writings," or the "Hagiographa;" and these books together constituted what, in the New Testament, are called *the Scriptures*, or *Scripture:* the *Scripture* in Mark xii. 10; xv. 28; Luke iv. 21; John ii. 22; vii. 38, 42; x. 35; xix. 37; Rom. iv. 3; ix. 17; Gal. iii. 8, 22; 2 Tim. iii. 16; 1 Pet. ii. 6; 2 Pet. i. 20;—the *Scriptures* in Matt. xxi. 42; xxii. 29; xxvi. 54; Luke xxiv. 27, 32, 45; John v. 39; Acts xvii. 2, 11; xviii. 24, 28; Rom. i. 2; xv. 4; xvi. 26; 1 Cor. xv. 3, 4; 2 Tim. iii. 15; 2 Pet. iii. 16. These constituted a *collection* of writings which were distinct from all others, and the use of the word

Scripture, or *Scriptures,* at once suggested them, and no others, to the mind.

(*b*) The book of Daniel was found in *that* list of writings, and would be suggested by that term as belonging to the general collection; that is, in order to adduce his authority, or to mention a prophecy *in* that book, it would be done as readily as a part of the Scriptures, and would be as well understood as in quoting a declaration of Moses or Isaiah. This is apparent (1) from the fact seen above, that Josephus must have regarded Daniel as having a rank among the Prophets; and (2), mainly, from the fact that Daniel has *always,* from the earliest knowledge which we have of the book, had a place in the canon. The book has *never,* so far as we have any knowledge, been placed among the apocryphal writings. It was evidently regarded by Josephus, speaking the common sentiment of his countrymen, as having a place in the canonical writings; it was *certainly* so regarded by the authors of the *Talmud,* though they assigned it a place in the third division, or Kethubim; it is expressly so mentioned by Jerome, by Melito, bishop of Sardis (A.D. 170), by Origen, by the Council of Laodicea (A.D. 360–364), by Cyril of Jerusalem (A.D. 350), by Gregory Nazianzen (A.D. 370), by Athanasius of Alexandria (A.D. 326), and by the author of the *Synopsis Scripturæ Sacræ,* who lived in the time of Athanasius. See Prof. Stuart on the Old Testament, Appendix. From that time onward it is needless to show that the book of Daniel has *always* had a place in the canon of Scripture, and been regarded as on a level with the other writings of the sacred volume: indeed, it has never had, so far as we have any historical information, any *other* place than that, but wherever known, and wherever mentioned, it has always been as a portion of the sacred writings.

(*c*) It is morally certain that it could not have been introduced into that canon if it was the work of a later age, and if it was not believed, at the time when the canon of the Old Testament was completed, or when the books of the Old Testament were collected and arranged, by whomsoever this was done, to have been the genuine work of Daniel. This point has been considered already. The Jews were the most cautious of all people in regard to their sacred books, and at an early period of their history the contending sects of the Pharisees and Sadducees arose, and from the very nature of their opinions, and the vigilance of the one against the other, it was impossible that a book could be introduced into the sacred canon which was not universally regarded as genuine and authentic. The exact period, indeed, when these sects arose has not been determined, and cannot now be; but it is put beyond a doubt that it was before the time of the Maccabees. Josephus first mentions them (*Ant.* xiii. 5, 9) under the high priest Jonathan (B.C. 159–144); but he mentions them, together with the Essenes, as sects already fully and definitely formed. Winer thinks that the spirit of Judaism, soon after the return from the exile, gave rise to a feeling which led to the formation of the party of the Pharisees; and that this very naturally called forth an opposition, which embodied itself in the party of the Sadducees. In the time of John Hyrcanus, nephew of Judas Maccabæus, Josephus speaks of the Pharisees as having such influence with the common people that "they would be believed even if they uttered anything against the king or high priest." The Sadducees were always opposed to them; always watched all their movements, opinions, and aims with jealousy; always contended with them for power, and always embodied in their own ranks no small part of the learning, the wealth, and the influence of the nation. The main subject of division between them was one that pertains to the very point before us. It was not the question about the existence of angel or spirit, or the question of predestination, as has been sometimes said, but it was *whether the Scriptures are to be regarded as the only rule of faith and practice.* The Pharisees insisted on the authority of tradition, and claimed that the oral or unwritten law was of equal authority with the written ; while the Sadducees rejected all traditions and ordinances of men not expressly sanctioned by the Scriptures. So Josephus says expressly : "Their custom was to regard nothing except the Laws [that is, the written Laws—the Old Testament]; for they reckon it as a virtue to dispute against the doctors in favour of the wisdom (σοφίας) which they follow."—*Ant.* xviii. 1, 4. Again, in *Ant.* xiii. 10, 6, he says, "The Pharisees inculcated many rules upon the people, received from the fathers, which are not written in the Law of Moses ; and on this account the sect of the Sadducees reject them, alleging that those things are to be regarded as rules which are written" [in the Scriptures], "but that the traditions of the fathers are not to be observed."

The rise of these contending sects must, at all events, be referred to a time which preceded the Maccabees—the time when it is pretended by objectors that the book of Daniel was composed. But the moment when these two parties were formed, the *extent* of the Jewish Scriptures was, of course, a matter that was fully and permanently decided. It is impossible to suppose that the Sadducees would concede to their antagonists the right to introduce new books into the canon, or that a new book could be introduced without producing controversy. This would have been giving up the very point in dispute. No book could be introduced, or could be recognised as entitled to a place there, which was not acknowledged by both parties as having been written by a true prophet, and as being believed to be Divinely inspired. If the book of Daniel, then, was the work of that age, and was falsely attributed to the Daniel of the exile, it is impossible that it could have been introduced into the canon.

(*d*) It may be asked, in addition, why, if the book of Daniel was written in the time of the Maccabees, and was then introduced into the canon, the book of Ecclesiasticus, and other books of the Apocrypha, were not also introduced ? If the book of Daniel was spurious, what was there that should entitle *that* to a place in the canon which could not have been urged in favour of the *Book of Wisdom*, or of some of the other books of the Apocrypha? Yet these books never found a place in the canon, and were never regarded as belonging to it; and there was, therefore, some reason why Daniel had a place there which could not be applied to them. The only reason must have been that the book of Daniel was regarded as the genuine work of the Daniel of the exile, and therefore written by a prophet before the times of inspiration ceased.

(3.) I refer, thirdly, in proof of the genuineness and authenticity of the book of Daniel, to the New Testament.

Daniel is *expressly* mentioned in the New Testament but once, and that is by the Saviour, in Matt. xxiv. 15, and in the parallel passage in Mark xiii. 14. In the former passage the Saviour says, "When ye, therefore, shall see the abomination of desolation, spoken of by Daniel the prophet, stand in the holy place (whoso readeth let him understand), then let them which be in Judea flee into the mountains." In the latter place—the same passage reported by another writer—"But when ye shall see the abomination of desolation spoken of by Daniel the prophet, standing where it ought not (let him that readeth understand), then let them which be in Judea," &c.

These, it must be admitted, are the only places in the New Testament where Daniel is directly quoted, though it cannot be denied that there are others which seem to imply that the book was known, and that it was intended to be referred to. Compare the argument in Hengstenberg, *Authentie des Daniel*, pp. 273-277. The passages of this nature referred to by De Wette, § 255, (3), and commonly relied on, are the following :—

 1 Pet. i. 10, seq., compared with Dan. xii. 8, seq.
 2 Thess. ii. 3.   „   „   vii. 8, 25.
 1 Cor. vi. 2.   „   „   vii. 22.
 Heb. xi. 33.   „   „   vi.

In regard to these passages, however, it may be doubted of some of them (2 Thess. ii. 3; 1 Cor. vi. 2) whether there is in them any designed allusion to *any* prophet of the Old Testament; and of 1 Pet. i. 10, that the allusion is so general that it cannot be demonstrated that Peter had his eye on Daniel rather than on the other prophets, or that he necessarily included Daniel in the number; and of the other passage (Heb. xi. 33), "Stopped the mouths of lions," that, from anything that appears in the passage, it cannot be demonstrated that Paul meant to refer to Daniel, or, if he did, all that is there implied *may* have been founded on a traditional report of Daniel, and it cannot be adduced as proof that he meant to refer to the *book* of Daniel. It cannot be denied that there is, in some respects, a very strong resemblance between the book of Daniel and the book of Revelation, and that the book of Daniel was familiar to the author of the Apocalypse; but still, as Daniel is not expressly quoted or referred to, it cannot be demonstrated with certainty that John meant to recognise the book as inspired. The argument, then, rests mainly, if not exclusively, on the testimony of the Saviour.

And here it is proper to say that, in this country, we may lay out of view, as not worthy of attention, the remark of De Wette, that " Christ neither *would* (*wollte*) nor *could* (*konnte*), from the nature of the case, be *a critical authority*," § 255, (3). In this argument it must be assumed, that if a book of the Old Testament can be shown to have *his* sanction, it is to be regarded as belonging to the inspired canon. Or, to state the proposition in a form which cannot, on any account, be regarded as objectionable, the point of inquiry is, to ascertain whether Christ did, or did not, regard the book of Daniel as belonging to the canon of the inspired writings, and as coming within the class which he, in John v. 39, and elsewhere, calls "the Scriptures."

Now, in regard to this reference to Daniel by the Saviour, considered as an argument for the genuineness and authenticity of the book, the following remarks may be made :—

(*a*) There is a distinct recognition of Daniel as an historical personage—as a man. This is plain on the face of the quotation, for he refers to him as he would to Moses, Isaiah, or Jeremiah. No one can believe that he regarded Daniel as a fictitious or fabulous personage, or that, in this respect, he meant to speak of him as different from the most eminent of the ancient prophets. Indeed, in all the doubts that have been expressed about the genuineness of the book of Daniel, it has never been maintained that the Lord Jesus did not mean to be understood as referring to Daniel as a real historical personage.

(*b*) He refers to him as a prophet : " When ye shall see the abomination of desolation, spoken of by Daniel *the prophet*"—τοῦ προφήτου. This word he uses evidently, in its ordinary signification, as meaning one who predicted future events, and as entitled to a rank among the true prophets. It is the very word which Josephus, in a passage quoted above, employs in relation to Daniel, and is manifestly used in the same sense. The Saviour assigns him no inferior place among the prophets; regards him as having uttered a true prediction, or a prediction which was to be fulfilled at a period subsequent to the time when he was then speaking ; and refers to him, in this respect, as he would have done to any one of the ancient inspired writers.

(*c*) He refers to him as the author of *a book*, and, by his manner of speaking of him, and by the quotation which he makes, gives his sanction to some well-known book of which he regarded Daniel as the author. This, which if true settles the question about the testimony of the Saviour, is apparent from the following considerations :—(1.) From the very use of the word *prophet* here, it is evident, on the face of the passage, that he refers to him in the use of this word, not as having *spoken* the prediction, but as having *recorded* it ; that the language is used as it would have been of any other of the "prophets," or of those who had this appellation *because* they had made a record predicting future events. It is clear that the word among the Jews had so far a technical signification, that this would at once be suggested on its use. (2.) Because he quotes the *language* found in the book of Daniel—βδέλυγμα τῆς ἐρημώσεως. This very phrase occurs in the Greek translation, in ch. xii. 11, and a similar expression (βδέλυγμα τῶν ἐρημώσεων) occurs in ch. ix. 27 ; and another similar expression (βδέλυγμα ἠφανισμένον) occurs in ch. xi. 31. The phrase, therefore, may be regarded as belonging to Daniel, not only by the express mention of his name, but by the fact that it does not elsewhere occur in the sacred Scriptures. (3.) The same thing is apparent from the parenthetical expression, " Whoso readeth, let him understand." The point of this remark is in the word " *readeth,*" as referring to some written record. There has been, indeed, much difference of opinion in regard to this phrase, whether it is to be considered as the command of the Saviour that they who read the words of Daniel should pay attention to its meaning ; or whether it is the remark of the evangelist, designed to call attention to the meaning of the prophecy, and to the words of the Saviour. In my notes on the passage in Matt. xxiv. 15, the opinion is expressed that these are the words of the evangelist. It is proper now to say, that on a more careful consideration of that passage, this seems to me to be very doubtful ; but whether correct or not, it would only vary the force of the argument by making Matthew the speaker instead of the Saviour. It would still be an inspired testimony that, at the time when Matthew wrote, there was a book which was understood to be the production of Daniel, and that it was the intention of the evangelist to rank him among the prophets, and to call particular attention to what he had *written.* The interpretation of the parenthesis, it must be admitted, however, is so uncertain that no argument can be founded on it to demonstrate that *Christ* meant to call attention to the words of Daniel ; but the passage does prove that such words to be " *read*" were found in the book, and that in order to determine their exact sense there was need of close attention. Olshausen agrees with the interpretation of the parenthesis expressed in my notes on Matthew, regarding it as the declaration of the evangelist. The older expositors generally regard the parenthesis as the words of the Saviour ; more recent ones generally as the words of the evangelist. The former opinion is defended by Hengstenberg.—*Authen.* pp. 259, 260.

Whichever interpretation is adopted, it seems clear, from the above remarks, that the Saviour meant to refer to Daniel as a real historical personage, and to a well-known book bearing his name, as a genuine production of the Daniel of the exile. If so, then the testimony of Christ is expressly in favour of its canonical authority.

(4.) I refer, fourthly, in proof of the genuineness and authenticity of the book, or in proof that it was written by the Daniel of the captivity, to the fact that it had an existence *before* the times of the Maccabees, and was referred to then as among the books having a Divine authority. This might, indeed, be regarded as already demonstrated, if it had a place in the canon of Scripture, as I have endeavoured to show that it had ; but there is other proof of this that will go further to confirm the point. It will be recollected that one of the main positions of those who deny its genuineness is, that it was written in the time of the Maccabees by some one who assumed the name of Daniel. The point now to be made out is, that there is direct evidence that it had an existence *before* that time.   In proof of this, I refer,

(*a*) To the testimony of Josephus.   His statement is found in his *Antiquities*, b. xi. ch. viii., in the account which he gives of the interview between Alexander and the high-priest Jaddua, in Jerusalem : "And when he went up into the temple he offered sacrifices to God, according to the high-priest's directions ; and magnificently treated both the high-priest and the priests.   And when the book of Daniel was shown to him, wherein Daniel declared that one of the Greeks should destroy the empire of the Persians, he supposed that himself was the person intended.   And as he was then glad, he dismissed the multitude for the present ; but the next day he called them to him, and bade them ask what favours they pleased of him."   The genuineness of this narrative has been examined at length by Hengstenberg, *Authen.* pp. 277-288.   In reference to that testimony the following remarks may be made :—(1.) The authority of Josephus is entitled to great credit, and his testimony may be regarded as good proof of a historical fact. (2.) There is here express mention of " the book of Daniel " as a book existing in the time of Alexander, and as shown to him, in which he was so manifestly referred to that he at once recognised the allusion. The passages referred to are the following : ch. vii. 6 ; viii. 3–8, 21, 22 ; xi. 3, 4.   For the evidence that these passages relate to Alexander, the reader is referred to the notes on them respectively.   It is clear that if they were read to Alexander, and if he regarded them as applying to himself, he could not doubt that his victory over the Persians would be certain.   (3.) There is every probability in the circumstances of the case, that, if the Jewish high-priest was in possession of the book of Daniel at that time, with so clear a reference to a Grecian conqueror, he would show those passages to him, for nothing would be more likely to appease his wrath, and to obtain protection for the Jews in Jerusalem, and for those who were scattered in the lands where it was manifest that he purposed to extend his conquests.   And (4) it may be presumed that, as a consequence of this, Alexander would grant to the Jews all that Josephus says that he did.   The best way of accounting for the favour which Josephus says he did show to the Jews, is the fact which he states, that these predictions were read to him announcing his success in his projected wars.   Thus Josephus says, as a consequence of these predictions being shown to him (*Ant. ut supra*), "And as he was then glad, he dismissed the multitude for the present; but the next day he called them to him, and bade them ask what favours they pleased of him. Accordingly the high-priest desired that they might enjoy the laws of their forefathers, and might pay no tribute the seventh year. This was readily granted. And when they entreated that he would permit the Jews in Babylon and Media to enjoy their own laws also, he willingly promised to do hereafter what they desired. And when he said to the multitude, that if any of them would enlist themselves in his. army, on the condition that they should continue under the laws of their forefathers, and live according to them, he was willing to take them with him, many were ready to accompany him in his wars."

There is intrinsic probability that this account in Josephus is true, and the main historical facts, as stated by Josephus, are vouched for by other writers. "That Alexander was personally in Judea, Pliny testifies, *Hist. Nat.* xii. 26. That Palestine voluntarily surrendered to him is testified in Arrian's *History of Alexander*, ii. 25. That he was met by the high-priest and his brethren dressed in turbans, is testified by Justin (xi. 10), who says: Obvios cum *infulis* multos orientis regis habuit."—(See Stuart on Daniel, p. 408.)

There is, therefore, the highest degree of probability that this narrative of Josephus is true; and if this is a correct historical narrative, then it is clear that the book of Daniel, containing, in respect to the conquests of Alexander, the same passages that are now applied to him, was in existence long before the time of the Maccabees. This occurred in 332 B.C.; and if this account is correct, then "the book of Daniel, as it now exists, was current among the Jews as a sacred book at least some 168-170 years before the time when, according to the critics of the sceptical school, the book could be written."

(*b*) The same thing may be inferred from a passage in the Apocrypha. In 1 Macc. ii. 49-68, the dying Mattathias is said, in an exhortation to his sons to be "zealous for the law, and to give their lives for the covenant of their fathers," to have referred to the ancient examples of piety and fortitude among the Hebrews, mentioning, among others, Abraham, "found faithful in temptation;" Joseph, who "in a time of distress kept the commandments, and was made lord of Egypt;" Joshua, who, "for fulfilling the word was made a judge in Israel; Caleb, who for "bearing witness before the congregation received the heritage of the land;" David, Elias, Ananias, Azarias, and Misael, and then (ver. 60) he mentions Daniel in these words: "Daniel, for his innocency, was delivered from the mouth of lions. Here is an evident reference to the history of Daniel as we have it (ch. vi.); and although it is true that such an account *might* be handed down by tradition, and that such a reference as this might be made if there were nothing more than mere tradition, yet it is also true that this is such a reference as would be made if the book were in existence then as it is now, and true also that the other references are, mostly at least, to written accounts of the worthies who are there mentioned. If there were no positive evidence to the contrary, the *primâ facie* proof in this quotation would be, that Mattathias referred to some well-known written record of Daniel.

(*c*) The fact of the existence of the book before the time of the Maccabees, may be inferred from its translation by the authors of the Septuagint. The fact that the book was translated with the other Hebrew and Chaldee books of the Old Testament, is a proof that it had an existence at an early period, and that it was worthy, in the estimation of the translators, of a place among the sacred books of the Jews.

(5.) I refer, fifthly, in proof of the genuineness and authenticity of the book, to the *language* in which it is written. We have already seen that it is written partly in Hebrew and partly in Chaldee. The argument to which I refer from this fact, in proof of the genuineness of the book, consists of the following things :—

(*a*) The language is such as it might be expected it *would* be on the supposition that Daniel was the real author. Daniel was by birth a Hebrew. He was probably born in Jerusalem, and remained there until he was about twelve or fifteen years of age (see § i.), when he was removed to Babylon. In his youth, therefore, he had used the Hebrew language, and his early education had been in that language. In Babylon he was instructed in the language and literature of the Chaldeans, and probably became as familiar with the language of the Chaldeans, as he was with his native tongue. Both these languages he undoubtedly spoke familiarly, and probably used· them with the same degree of ease. That the book, therefore, is written in both these languages accords with this representation ; and, if written by one man, it must have been composed by one who was thus familiar with both. It is true that the fact that Daniel could thus speak the two languages is in itself no proof that *he* was the author, but the fact that it was so written accords with the circumstances of the case. His early training, and the fact that the book is written in the two languages with which it is known he was familiar, furnish a coincidence, such as would occur on the supposition that he was the author ; and a coincidence, like those adverted to by Dr. Paley in his argument in favour of the genuineness of the New Testament (*Horæ Paulinæ*), the more valuable because it is clear that it was undesigned.

But *why* the book was written in two languages is a question that is not so easily solved, and which it is not necessary to solve. No reason is given in the book itself ; none appears from anything in the design of the portions written respectively in Hebrew and Chaldee. There is nothing apparent in these portions of the book which would lead us to suppose that one was designed to be read by the Hebrews and the other by the Chaldeans, or, as it is often affirmed (comp. Horne, *Introduction*, vol. iv. p. 193), that one portion "treats of the Chaldean or Babylonish affairs." There is no particular "treatment" of the Chaldean or Babylonish affairs, for example, in the seventh chapter, where the Chaldean portion ends, any more than in the eighth, where the Hebrew is resumed, and, in fact, no internal reason can be assigned why one of those chapters should have been written in Chaldee or Hebrew rather than the other or both. The same remark is applicable to the first and second chapters, and indeed to every portion of the book; and the reason which induced the author to write different portions of it in different languages must be for ever unknown. This does not, however, affect the force of the argument which I am suggesting.

(*b*) The circumstance now adverted to may be regarded as of some force in showing that it is not probable that the book was forged, and especially that it was not forged in the time of the Maccabees. It is an unusual thing for a man to attempt to forge a book in two languages; and though cases have occurred in great numbers where a man could so familiarly write in two languages that he could do this, yet this would not be likely to occur in the time of the Maccabees. It was probably a very uncommon thing at that time that a man was so familiar with the two languages that he could write readily in each, for there are no writings extant in either of these languages in that age; and it is well known that the Hebrew language became greatly adulterated by foreign admixtures soon after the return from the exile, and never regained the purity which it had in the early periods of its history.

(*c*) To these considerations it may be added, that if the book was written in the times of the Maccabees, or at a later period, there is every reason to suppose that it would have been written in the *Greek* language. This appears from the fact that all the books which we have of that age are written in Greek, and that the Greek at that time had become so prevalent that it would be natural that it should be used. Thus all the books of the Apocrypha, and those parts which profess to be additions to the book of Daniel, as the Song of the Three Holy Children, the History of Susanna, and the Destruction of Bel and the Dragon, are found only in Greek, and there is no evidence that they were ever written in Hebrew or Chaldee. (See § IV. of this Introduction.) If the book of Daniel itself was written in that age, why was not it also written in Greek? Or why should the book, as we have it now, if it were a forged book, have been written in Hebrew and Chaldee, and those other portions, which the author seems to have designed should be regarded as belonging to the book, have been written in Greek? There are none of the books of the Apocrypha of which there is any evidence that they were written in Hebrew or Chaldee. The only one of those books for which such a claim has been set up is the book of Ecclesiasticus. That is affirmed by the Son of Sirach (see the Prologue) to have been written originally by his grandfather in Hebrew, and to have been translated by himself into Greek. But the Hebrew original is not in existence; nor is there any certain evidence that it ever was. It is an additional circumstance, showing that a book of the Maccabæan age would have been written in Greek, that even Berosus, who was himself a Chaldean, wrote his history of Chaldea in Greek. (See Intro. to ch. iv. § 1.)

To all these considerations, which seem to me of themselves to settle the question, I may be permitted to add a very ingenious argument of Prof. Stuart, in his own words; an argument which, I think, no one can answer. (*Com. on Daniel,* pp. 438–449) :—

"The accurate knowledge which the writer of the book of Daniel displays, of ancient history, manners, and customs, and Oriental Babylonish peculiarities, shows that he must have lived at or near the time and place when and where the book leads us to suppose that he lived.

"A great variety of particulars might be adduced to illustrate and confirm this proposition; but I aim only to introduce the leading and more striking ones.

"(*a*) In drawing the character of Nebuchadnezzar, and giving some brighter spots to it, Daniel agrees with hints of the like nature in Jer. xlii. 12 ; xxxix. 11. If a writer in the Maccabæan age had undertaken, as is asserted, to symbolize Antiochus Epiphanes by drawing the character of Nebuchadnezzar, it would be difficult to conceive how he would have been persuaded to throw into the picture these mellower tints.

"(*b*) In drawing the portrait of Belshazzar, the last king of Babylon, Daniel agrees very strikingly with Xenophon. In this latter writer, he appears as a debauched, pleasure-loving, cruel, and impious monarch. *Cyrop.* (iv. v.) represents him as killing the son of Gobryas, one of his nobles, because he had anticipated him, while hunting, in striking down the game. When the father remonstrated, he replied, that he was sorry only that he had not killed him also. In lib. v. 2, he is styled *haughty* and *abusive.* One of his concubines spoke in praise of Gadates, a courtier, as a handsome man. The king invited him to a banquet, and there caused him to be seized and unmanned. It is all in keeping with this, when he appears in Dan. v. In his intoxication and pride, he orders the sacred vessels of the Jerusalem temple to be profaned; and Daniel is so disgusted with his behaviour, that he does not, as in the case of Nebuchadnezzar (ch. iv.) disclose any strong sympathy for him, but denounces unqualified destruction. Xenophon calls this king ανόσιος.

"(*c*) Cyaxares (*Darius the Mede*) in Dan. is drawn by Xenophon as devoted to wine and women (*Cyrop..* iv.) In Dan. vi. 18, it is mentioned of Darius, as an extraordinary thing, that after he saw the supposed ruin of Daniel, he neither approached his table nor his harem. Xenophon speaks of him as indolent, averse to business, of small understanding, vain, without self-restraint, and easily thrown into tears ; and then, moreover, as subject to violent outbursts of passion (iv. v.) In Daniel he appears as wholly governed by his courtiers; they flatter his vanity, and obtain the decree intended to destroy Daniel. Daniel's supposed impending fate throws him into lamentation, and he betakes himself to fasting and vigils; and when he learns the safety of his Hebrew servant, he sentences his accusers, with all their wives and children, to be thrown into the lions' den, vi. 18-24.

"Now as there was no history of these times and kings among the Hebrews, and none among the Greeks that gave any minute particulars, in what way did a *late* writer of the book of Daniel obtain his knowledge?

"(*d*) When in Dan. i. 21, it is stated that Daniel continued until the *first year of Cyrus*, without any specification when this was, the writer seems plainly to suppose his readers to be familiar with this period. It is true, that from the book of Ezra a knowledge of that time, the period of Jewish liberation, might be gained; but the familiar manner of the reference to it indicates that the writer feels himself to be addressing those who were cognizant of matters pertaining to the period.

"(*e*) In ch. i. and ii. we are told that *king* Nebuchadnezzar besieged Jerusalem, took it, and sent Daniel and his companions to Babylon. There they were taken under the care and instruction of learned men among the Chaldees, and trained up for the personal service of the king. The period of training was *three* years. At the close of this, they were examined and approved by the king; and soon after this occurred Nebuchadnezzar's first dream, which Daniel was summoned to interpret. This dream is said to be in the *second* year of Nebuchadnezzar's reign. Here, then, is an apparent *parachronism*. How could Daniel have been taken and sent into exile by *king* Nebuchadnezzar, educated *three* years, and then be called to interpret a dream in the *second* year of Nebuchadnezzar's reign? The solution of this difficulty I have already exhibited in an *Exc.* at the end of the commentary on ch. i. I need not repeat the process here. It amounts simply to this, viz., that Nebuchadnezzar is called *king* in Dan. i. 1, *by way of anticipation;* a usage followed by Kings, Chronicles, and Jeremiah. Before he quitted Judea he became actual king by the death of his father; and the Jews, in speaking of him as commanding the invading army, always called him *king*. But in Dan ii. 1, Nebuchadnezzar is spoken of in the Chaldee mode of reference to his actual reign. This leaves some *four* years for Daniel's discipline and service. But to those who were not familiar with the Jewish mode of speaking in respect to Nebuchadnezzar, it would naturally and inevitably appear like a parachronism, or even a downright contradiction of dates. Yet the writer has not a word of explanation to make. He evidently feels as if all were plain to his readers (as doubtless it was). But a writer of the Maccabæan age would plainly have seen and avoided the difficulty.

"(*f*) In Dan. v. 30, it is stated that Belshazzar was slain; but not a word is said descriptive of the manner in which this was brought about, nor even that the city of Babylon was taken. The next verse simply mentions that Darius the Mede took the kingdom. All this brevity seems to imply, that the writer supposed those whom he was addressing to be cognizant of the whole matter. Had he lived in the Maccabæan age, would he have written thus respecting events so interesting and important? In like manner Daniel (x. 1, *seq.*) tells us, that in the third year of Cyrus, Daniel mourned and fasted three weeks. But not a word is said to explain the occasion of this peculiar and extraordinary humiliation. If we turn now to Ezra iv. 1-5, we shall find an account of a combination among the enemies of the Jews to hinder the building of the city walls, which was successful, and which took place in the *third* year of Cyrus' reign, *i.e.*, the same year with Daniel's mourning. There can scarcely be a doubt that this was the occasion of that mourning; for certainly it was no ritual, legal, or ordinary fast. The manner now in which ch. x. is written plainly imports that the writer feels no need of giving explanations. He takes it for granted that his readers will at once perceive the whole extent of the matter. But how, in the Maccabæan age, could a writer suppose this knowledge within the grasp of his readers?

"(*g*) In Dan. ii., the dream is interpreted as indicating the destruction of the Babylonish empire by the Medo-Persians. Abydenus, in his singular account of Nebuchadnezzar's last hours (given on p. 122 above), represents this king as wrapped into a kind of prophetic ecstasy, and in this state as declaring his fearful anticipations of the Medo-Persian conquest. How came such a coincidence?

"(*h*) In Dan. iv. 30, Nebuchadnezzar is introduced as saying, Is not this *great* Babylon which I have built? Recent critics allege this to be a mistake. 'Ctesias,' they tell us, 'attributes the building of Babylon to Semiramis (*Bähr Ctes.* p. 397, *seq.*), and Herodotus (i. 181, *seq.*) ascribes it to Semiramis and Nitocris.' My answer is, that Ctesias follows the Assyrian tradition, and Herodotus the Persian. But Berosus and Abydenus give us the *Babylonian* account; which is, that Nebuchadnezzar added much to the old town, built a magnificent royal palace, surrounded the city with new walls, and adorned it with a vast number of buildings. Well and truly might he say that he had built it, meaning (as he plainly did) its magnificent structures. It was not any falsehood in his declaration which was visited with speedy chastisement, but the pride and vain-glory of his boasting gave offence to Heaven. But how came a writer of the *Maccabæan* period to know of all this matter? No Greek writer has told anything about Nebuchadnezzar or his doings. To Berosus and Abydenus, a writer of the Maccabæan age could hardly have had access. Herodotus and Ctesias told another and different story. Whence, then, did he get his knowledge of the part which Nebuchadnezzar had acted in the building of the city? And yet the account of it in Daniel accords entirely with both Berosus and Abydenus. Even the account of Nebuchadnezzar's madness is virtually adverted to in these writers: see above, p. 122, *seq.*

"(*i*) In Dan. v. 10-12 is introduced a personage styled the *queen,* not because she was Belshazzar's wife, for the latter was already in the banqueting-room (v. 3, 23), but probably because she was a queen-mother. Not improbably this was the Nitocris of Herodotus; and Berosus, *Diod. Sic.* (ii. 10), and Alex. Polyhist (in *Chron. Armen.*), all say that Nitocris was a wife of Nebuchadnezzar. If so, she might have had much to do with ornamenting the city both before and after Nebuchadnezzar's death; and this will account for the great deference paid to her by Belshazzar, as related in ch. v. 10–12. It is one of those accidental circumstances which speaks much for the accordance of Daniel with the narrations of history. It is, moreover, a circumstance about which a writer of the Maccabæan age cannot well be supposed to have known anything.

"And since we are now examining ch. v., it may be proper to note another circumstance. We have seen, that at *Babylon* the wives and concubines of the king were, without any scruple, present at the feast. But in Esth. i. we have an account of the positive refusal of queen Vashti to enter the guest-chamber of Ahasuerus. In other words, this was, and is, against the general custom of the East. How came a writer of the Maccabæan period to know this distinction between the customs of Babylon and of Persia? The author of the Sept. Version, a contemporary of this period, knows so little of such a matter that he even leaves out the passage respecting the presence of women at the feast. Why? Plainly because he thought this matter would be deemed incredible by his readers. In Xen. *Cyrop.* (v. 2, 28,) is an account of a feast of Belshazzar, where his concubines are represented as being present. Not only so, but we have elsewhere, in Greek and Roman writers, abundant testimony to usages of this kind, in their accounts of the Babylonish excesses. But how comes it about, that the forger of the book of Daniel, whose familiarity with those writings is not credible, should know so much more of Babylonish customs than the Sept. translator?

"(j) Of the manner in which Babylon was taken, and Belshazzar slain, Daniel has not given us any minute particulars. But he has told us that the *Medes* and *Persians* acquired the dominion of Babylon (v. 28), and that *Darius the Mede* succeeded Belshazzar. The manner in which he announces the slaying of Belshazzar (v. 30) shows that the event was altogether sudden and unexpected. Now Herodotus (I. 190) and Xenophon (*Cyrop.* VII.) have told us, that Cyrus diverted the waters of the Euphrates, and marched in its channel into the heart of Babylon, and took the city in a single night. They tell us that the Babylonians were in the midst of feast-rioting that night, and were unprepared to meet the enemy, who were not expected in the city. How entirely all this harmonizes with Daniel is quite plain. Gesenius himself acknowledges that this is *sehr auffallend, i.e.*, very striking. He has even acknowledged, in a moment of more than usual candour and concession, that Isa. xliv. 27 has a definite reference to the stratagem of Cyrus in taking the city. In connection with a prediction concerning Cyrus, Jehovah is here represented as saying to the deep, '*Be dry; yea, I will dry up thy rivers.*' So in Jer. l. 38, 'A drought is upon her waters, and they shall be dried up;' and again, li. 36, 'I will dry up her sea [river], and make her springs dry.' If the book of Daniel is to be cast out as a late production, and as spurious, because it seems to predict the sudden capture of Babylon in one night, by the Medes and Persians, what is to be done with these passages of Isaiah and Jeremiah? Even the Neologists, although they maintain a later composition in respect to those parts of the prophets which have just been cited, still do not venture to place that composition *post eventum*. If not, then there is *prediction;* and this, too, of a strange event, and one so minute and specific, that *guessing* is out of question. If, then, Isaiah and Jeremiah *predicted*, why might not a Daniel also *predict?*

"Another circumstance there is also in which all three of these prophets are agreed. According to Dan. v., Babylon was feasting and carousing on the night of its capture. In Isa. xxi. 5, we have the like: 'Prepare the table. . . . . Eat, drink; arise, ye princes, and anoint the shield,' *i.e.*, rise up from your feast-table, and make ready for assault. So Jer. li. 39, 'I will prepare their feasts, and I will make them drunken, that they may rejoice, and sleep a perpetual sleep, and not wake, saith the Lord.'

"If now a writer of the Maccabæan period had undertaken to write the story of the capture of Babylon, is there any probability that he would have hit upon all these circumstances, so peculiar and so concordant? Conversant with the native Greek historians we cannot well suppose him to have been; for Greek literature was regarded as reproachful by the Jews of that period, and even down to the time of Josephus, who speaks strongly on this subject.

"(*k*) Daniel (v. 30) relates the *violent death* of Belshazzar when the city was taken. In this particular he is vouched for by Xenophon, *Cyrop.* VII. v. 24, 30. So do Isa. xiv. 18—20 ; xxi. 2—9 ; Jer. l. 29—35 ; li. 57, declare the same thing. But here Berosus and Abydenus dissent, both of them representing the Babylonish king as surrendering, and as being treated humanely by Cyrus. How comes it, if the forger of the book of Daniel wrote about B.C. 160, that he did not consult those authors on Babylonish affairs? Or if (as was surely the fact in regard to most Jewish writers at that period) he had no familiarity with Greek authors, then where did he obtain his views about the death of Belshazzar? For a full discussion of this matter, see p. 147, *seq.*, above. There can scarcely be a doubt that the account of Daniel and Xenophon is the true one.

"Xenophon relates, that the party which assailed the palace, who were led on by Gobryas and Gadates, fell upon the guards who were carousing, πρὸς φῶς πολύ, *i.e., at broad daylight* :* (*Cyrop.* VII. 5, 27). In other words, the Persians did not accomplish their onset upon the palace until the night was far spent, and daylight was dawning. How now are matters presented in the book of Daniel? First, there is the feast (of course in the evening); then the quaffing of wine; then the handwriting on the wall; then the assembling of all the Magi to interpret it; then the introduction of Daniel, whose interpretation was followed by his being clothed with the *insignia* of nobility, and being proclaimed the third ruler in the kingdom. All this must of course have taken up most of the night. Here, then, one writer confirms and illustrates the other. A pseudo-Daniel would not have risked such a statement as the true one has made ; for, at first view, the matter seems incredible, and it is charged upon the book as such. But Xenophon has freed it from all difficulties.

"Daniel (v.) also declares that Belshazzar was a son, *i.e.*, a descendant, of Nebuchadnezzar. An appeal is made to Berosus and Megasthenes, to show that this was not true. Yet they do not so testify, but only that Belshazzar was *not .of the regular line* of heirs of the throne. He might still have been a younger son of Nebuchadnezzar, or a son of Nebuchadnezzar's daughter. Now Herodotus agrees with Daniel, i. 188, i. 74. So does Xenophon. And as the other authors have not in reality contradicted this, what reason is there for refusing to believe? See the discussion of this topic at large, p. 144, *seq.*

" It certainly deserves to be noted, that, in part, the book of Daniel is on the side of the Greek writers, and against Berosus and Abydenus, where the representations of the latter may be justly regarded as designed to save the honour and credit of the Babylonians ; in part also is Daniel on the side of the latter, and against the Greek writers, *i.e.*, in cases where there is no reason to suppose the native historians to be partial. The *media via* appears in this case to be hit upon, by the simple pursuit of historical truth in the narratives of the book before us.

"Again, in Dan. v. 31, we have an assurance that *Darius* the *Mede* assumed the throne of Babylon. Here Herodotus and Ctesias are silent ; but here Xenophon fully confirms the account given by Daniel. Herodotus himself states (i. 95) that there were two other modes of telling the story of Cyrus besides that which he follows ; and that of Xenophon and Daniel is probably one of these. This is confirmed by Isa. xiii. 17, where the *Mede* is declared to be the leading nation in destroying Babylon, and the same is also said in Jer. li. 11, 28. In Isa. xxi. 2, both Media and Persia are mentioned. The *silence* of Herodotus and

---

* " Singular, that in a critical edition and commentary on Xenophon, now before me, this is rendered *before a good fire*. First, the Greek words do not allow this. Secondly, the Babylonians need and have no fires for warmth. Thirdly, Cyrus would not have drained the Euphrates, and marched his army in its channel, at a time when fires were needed for warmth."

Ctesias cannot disprove a matter of this kind. See a full discussion of the topic, p. 148, *seq.*

"Daniel (vi. 1) states that Darius set over his kingdom 120 satraps. Xenophon (*Cyrop.* VIII. 6, 1, *seq.*) relates that satraps were set over all the conquered nations, when Cyrus was in Babylon. He speaks of the appointments as made by Cyrus; and doubtless they were, since he was the only *acting* governor of Babylon, and *vicegerent* of the king. No less true is it, that to Darius also, as supreme, may the appointment be attributed. How came the alleged *late* writer of Daniel to know this? Xenophon mentions no express number. The book of Esther (i. 1) mentions 127 satraps. Why did not our late writer copy that number in order to remove suspicion as to so great a number of those high officers? And how is it that 120 in Daniel is objected to as an incredible number, when the empire was actually as large at the time of their appointment, as it was in the time of Xerxes, as exhibited in Esth. i. 1? The Septuagint translator of Daniel, who belonged to the Maccabæan age, did not venture to write 120, as it seems, but 127 (so in *Cod. Chis.*), thus according with Esth. i. 1, and leaning upon that passage. He seems evidently to have felt that the story of so many satrapies must be supported by the book of Esther, in order to be believed. He even, in his ignorance of history, translates ver. 31 thus: 'And Artaxerxes, the Mede, took the kingdom,' probably meaning the Persian Artaxerxes Longimanus.

"(*l*) It is worthy of remark, that the order of the two nations, *Medes and Persians*, is to be found in strict accordance with the idiom of the times. Thus in vi. 8, 12, 15, we have the *Medes and Persians;* but after Cyrus comes to the throne, the order is invariably *Persians and Medes.* So in the book of Esther, *the law of the Persians and Medes* shows the same change of *usus loquendi.* Would a Pseudo-Daniel have been likely to note such a small circumstance?

"It is also noted (Dan. 5. 31), that when Darius took the kingdom, he was threescore and two years old. From his history, his reign, and his descent from Ahasuerus (ix. 1), this seems altogether probable. But no other author states his age. The fact that it is done in Daniel betokens a familiarity of the writer with the *minutiæ* of his history. So does the mention that in the *first* year of his reign Daniel took into most serious consideration the prophecy of Jeremiah respecting the seventy years' exile of the Hebrews.

"Thus far, then, all is well. All seems to be in conformity with true history, so far as we can ascertain it. It is not upon one or two particulars that we would lay stress. We acknowledge that these might have been traditionally known, and accurately reported. It is on the *tout ensemble* of the historical matters contained in the book that stress is to be laid. And certainly it would be very singular if all these circumstances should be true and consistent, and yet the book be written in the Maccabæan period.

" How is it with the best historical books of that period? The first book of the Maccabees is, in the main, a trustworthy and veracious book. But how easy it is to detect errors in it, both in respect to geography and history! In viii. 7, it is related that the Romans took Antiochus the Great prisoner alive. But this never happened. They gained a great victory over him, and took away many of his provinces; but he himself escaped their grasp. In viii. 8, it is said that they took from him the land of *India, Media,* and Lydia. But neither India nor Media ever belonged to him. The efforts to show that Mysia was originally written instead of Media, are of course but mere guesses; and if true, *India* still remains. More likely is it that the author himself put Media for Mysia, and if so, then this does not mend the matter. In viii. 9, 10, it is related, that 'the Greeks resolved to send an army to Rome and destroy it; but that the Romans learning this, sent forth an army, who slew many, carried away numerous captives of their women and children, laid hold of their strong places, and took possession of their lands, and reduced the people of Syria to servitude *unto this day.*' Now nothing of all this ever happened. There was indeed a fracas between the Ætolians and the Romans at that period; but it was soon made up, without any ravages of war, or any servitude. Further, the author, in viii. 15, represents the Roman Senate as consisting of 320 members, continually administering the government. He goes on to state (ver. 16), that they choose a ruler annually, and that all obey this one. Every tyro in Roman history knows how unfounded all this is. And what shall we say of the very first sentence in the book, which tells us that Alexander, the son of Philip, smote Darius, king of the Persians and Medes, and then reigned *in his stead* over Greece? In i. 6, he states that the same Alexander, about to die, made a partition of his empire among his chiefs—a thing that took place some considerable time afterwards, partly by mutual agreement, and partly by force. In vi. 1, he makes Elymais a *town* instead of a province.

" Such are some of the specimens of this writer's errors in geography and history. That he was a grave, enlightened, and veracious writer, in the main, is conceded by all. But if in things so plain, and transactions so recent, he commits so many errors as have been specified, what would he have done if the scene had been shifted from near countries to the remote places where the book of Daniel finds its circle of action?

" As to the *second* book of the Maccabees, it is so notorious for errors and mistakes, that very little credit has been attached to it on the part of intelligent critics. It is not once to be named in comparison with the book of Daniel. It must have been written when a knowledge of historical events was confused, and at a very low ebb. The book of Tobit, which originated in or near the Maccabæan period, exhibits not only a romantic, and, as it were, fairy tale, but contains historical and geographical difficulties incapable of solution; also physical pheno-

mena are brought to view which are incredible.   It is needless to
specificate them here.   De Wette's *Einleit.* presents them, § 309.
    "We have dwelt hitherto, under our 5th head, mainly on things
of a *historical* nature, *i.e.*, events and occurrences.   Let us now
examine a number of things that are of a miscellaneous nature, which
it would be somewhat difficult, if not useless, to classify throughout, but
most of which are connected with manners, customs, demeanour, &c.
    " (*m*) Daniel makes no mention in his book of prostration before the
king in addressing him.   *O king, live for ever!* was the usual greeting.
Arrian (iv.) testifies that the story in the East was, that Cyrus was the
first before whom prostration was practised.   It is easy to see how this
came about.   With the Persians, the king was regarded as the *repre-
sentative of Ormusd,* and therefore entitled to adoration.   Nebuchadnezzar was high enough in claims to submission and honour ; but not a
word of exacting adoration from those who addressed him.   How could
a Pseudo-Daniel know of this nice distinction, when all the Oriental
sovereigns of whom he had any knowledge had, at least for four centuries,
exacted prostration from all who approached them ?
    "(*n*) In mere prose (Dan. i. 2) Babylon is called by the old name,
Shinar (Gen. xi. 2 ; xiv. 1) ; and as an old name, it is poetically used
once by Isaiah (xi. 11), and once by Zechariah (v. 11).   Now *Shinar*
was the vernacular name of what foreigners called *Babylonia ;* and it
was easy and natural for Daniel to call it so.   But *how* or *why* came a
Pseudo-Daniel to such a use of the word?   *Babylon* he would naturally,
and almost with certainty, call it.
    " (*o*) Daniel (i. 5) tells us that the Hebrew lads were to be fed from
the king's table.   Such a custom, even in respect to royal prisoners,
Jeremiah (lii. 33, 34) discloses.   Among the Persians this was notorious,
and extended to the whole *corps d'elites* of the soldiery.   Ctesias tells
us that the king of Persia daily fed 15,000 men.   How came the *late*
writer of Daniel to be acquainted with a minute circumstance of the
nature of that before us ?
    " (*p*) Daniel and his companions received Chaldee names, some of
which are compounded of the names of their false gods.   In 2 Kings
xxiv. 17, Nebuchadnezzar is reported to have changed the name of king
Mattaniah into *Zedekiah.*   How did the late forger of the book come
by the notion of assigning to his Hebrew heroes the names of idol-gods?
The rigorous attachment to all that was Jewish, and the hearty hatred
of heathenism by all the pious in the time of the Maccabees, makes it
difficult to account for his course.
    " (*q*) In Dan. ii. 1, the Babylonish mode of reckoning time is intro-
duced, viz., the second year of Nebuchadnezzar.   Where else, unless in
Ezek. i. 1, is this employed ?   How came the late interpolator of the
sacred books to betake himself to this mode of reckoning, and especially
since it apparently contradicts i. 1, and ver. 18 ?   See the solution of
the difficulty, in *Exc.* I. [See App. I. to this Vol.]

" (*r*) In Dan. ii. 5, and iii. 29, one part of the threatened punishment is, that the houses of the transgressors should be turned into a *dung-hill*, or rather a *morass-heap*. Here an intimate acquaintance with the Babylonish mode of building is developed. The houses were mostly constructed of *sun-baked* bricks, or with those slightly burned ; and when once demolished, the rain and dew would soon dissolve the whole mass, and make them sink down, in that wet land near the river, into a miry place of clay, whenever the weather was wet.

" (*s*) In Dan. iii. 1, the plain of *Dura* is mentioned ; a name found nowhere else, yet mentioned here as a place familiar to the original readers of the book, inasmuch as no explanation is added. Whence did the *Pseudo-Daniel* derive this name ?

" (*t*) In Dan. ii. 5, and iii. 6, we find the punishment of hewing to pieces and burning in ovens mentioned. Testimony to such modes of punishment may be found in Ezek. xvi. 40; xxiii. 25 ; and Jer. xxix. 22. But such a mode of punishment could not exist among the Persians, who were *fire-worshippers;* and accordingly, in ch. vi. we find casting into a den of lions as substituted for it.

" (*u*) In Dan. iii. we find not only a huge idol (in keeping with the Babylonish taste), but also a great variety of musical instruments employed at the dedication of it. Quintus Curtius has told us, that when Alexander the Great entered Babylon, 'there were in the procession singing Magi...and artists playing on stringed instruments of a peculiar kind, accustomed to chant the praises of the king' (lib. v. 3).

" (*v*) According to Herod. I. 195, the Babylonish costume consisted of three parts—first, the wide and long pantaloons for the lower part of the person ; secondly, a woollen shirt ; and, thirdly, a large mantle with a girdle round it. On the cylinder rolls found at Babylon, Münter (*Relig. d. Bab.* s. 96) discovered the same costume. In Dan. iii. 21, the same three leading and principal articles of dress are particularized. Other parts of clothing are merely referred to, but not specificated; but these garments being large and loose, and made of delicate material, are mentioned in order to show how powerless the furnace was, since they were not even singed. How did a Pseudo-Daniel obtain such particulars as these ?

" (*w*) Daniel (v. 16) shows that the regal token of honour bestowed was a collet or golden chain put round the neck. Brissonius, in his work on the Persian dominion, has shown the same custom among the Persian kings, who, not improbably, borrowed it from the Babylonians.

" (*x*) In Dan. vi. 8, 'the laws of the Medes which change not' are mentioned. In Esth. i. 19, and viii. 8, we have repeated mention of this same peculiar custom. The reason of this probably was, that the king was regarded as the impersonation of Ormusd, and therefore as infallible.

" (*y*) In Dan. vii. 9, we have a description of the Divine throne as placed upon *movable wheels*. The same we find in Ezek. i. and x.;

which renders it quite probable that the Babylonian throne was constructed in this way, so that the monarch might move in processions, with all the insignia of royalty about him.

" (z) It deserves special remark, that Daniel has given individual classifications of priests and civilians, such as are nowhere else given in Scripture, and the knowledge of which must have been acquired from intimate acquaintance with the state of things in Babylon. In Dan. ii. 2, 10, 27, the various classes of diviners and literati are named. In Dan. iii. 2, 3, the different classes of magistrates, civilians, and rulers are specifically named. On this whole subject, I must refer the reader to *Exc.* III. *on the Chaldees* [See App. III. to this Vol.] Whence a *Maccabæan* writer could have derived such knowledge it would be difficult to say. It is one of those circumstances which could not well be feigned. Several of the names occur nowhere else in the Heb. Bible, and some of them are evidently derivates of the Parsi or Median language ; *e.g.*, פַרְדְּכִין in Dan. vi. 3, a name unknown in the Semitic. On the other hand, several of them are exclusively Chaldean; *e.g.*, Dan. iii. 3, אֲדַרְגָּזְרַיָּא, תִּפְתָּיֵא —of which no profane writer has given the least hint. How came the Pseudo-Daniel to a knowledge of such officers ? "

The evidence that the book is a genuine production of the Daniel of the captivity may be summed up now in few words. There is (1), on the face of the book, the testimony of the writer himself to his own authorship—good evidence in itself, unless there is some reason for calling it in question or setting it aside. There is (2) the fact that it was early received into the canon as a part of the inspired Scriptures, and that it has always been, both by Jews and Christians, regarded as entitled to a place there. There is (3) the express testimony of the Saviour that Daniel was a prophet, and a clear reference to a part of the prophecy by him, as we have it now in the book of Daniel. There is (4) express testimony that the book was in existence before the time of the Maccabees, and was then regarded as a genuine production of Daniel, particularly (a) the testimony of Josephus ; (b) of the author of the book of *Maccabees*, and (c) of the authors of the Septuagint translation. There is (5) the fact that the book was so written in two different languages that we cannot well attribute it to a writer of the Maccabæan period. And there is (6) "the accurate knowledge which the writer of the book of Daniel displays of ancient history, manners, and customs, and Oriental-Babylonish peculiarities, which shows that he must have lived at or near the time and place when and where the book leads us to suppose that he lived." For the genuineness and authenticity of what other book can more clear and decisive testimony be brought ? These considerations seem to make it clear that the book could not have been a forgery of the time of the Maccabees, and that every circumstance combines to confirm the common belief that it was written in the time of the exile, and by the author whose name it bears. But if this is so, then its canonical authority is established : for we have

all that can be urged in favour of the canonical authority of any of the
books of the Old Testament. Its place in the canon from the earliest
period; the testimony of Christ; the testimony of Josephus and the
Jews in all ages to its canonical authority; the testimony of the early
Christian fathers; its prophetic character; and the strong internal probabilities that it was written at the time and in the manner in which it
professes to have been, all go to confirm the opinion that it is a genuine
production of the Daniel of the captivity, and worthy to be received
and accredited as a part of the inspired oracles of truth. On *one* of
these points, which has not been insisted on in this Introduction—its
prophetic character—the evidence can be appreciated only by an examination of the particular prophecies; and that will be seen as the result
of the exposition of those parts of the book which refer to future events.
It may be said in general, however, that if it is proved to have been
written in the time of the captivity, there will be no hesitation in
admitting its inspiration. Porphyry maintained, as we have seen, that
the pretended prophecies were so clear that they *must* have been written
after the events; and this, as we have seen also, is one of the leading
objections urged against the book in more modern times. If this is so,
then, apart from all the evidence which will be furnished of the fulfilment of the prophecies of Daniel in the course of the exposition, it may
be properly inferred, that if the book was written in the time in which
it professes to have been, it furnishes the highest evidence of inspiration,
for no one can pretend that the predictions occurring in it, pertaining
to future events, are the results of any mere natural sagacity.

§ IV.—NATURE, DESIGN, AND GENERAL CHARACTER OF THE BOOK OF
DANIEL.

The book of Daniel is not properly a *history* either of the Jews or
Babylonians, nor is it a biography of the writer himself. It is not continuous in its structure, nor does it appear to have been written at one
time. Though the work, as we have seen, of one author, it is made up
of portions, written evidently on different occasions, in two different
languages, and having, to a considerable extent, different objects in
view. Though the author was a Jewish exile, and surrounded by his
own countrymen as exiles, yet there is almost no reference to the past
history of these people, or to the causes of their having been carried
into captivity, and no description of their condition, struggles, and sufferings in their exile; and though written by one who resided through
the greatest part of a very long life in a land of strangers, and having
every opportunity of obtaining information, there is no distinct reference
to *their* history, and no description of their manners and customs. And
although his own career while there was eventful, yet the allusions to
himself are very few; and of the largest portion of that long life in
Babylon—probably embracing more than seventy years—we have no

information whatever. In the book there are few or no allusions to the condition of the exiles there; but two of the native kings that reigned there during that long period are even mentioned; one of those—Nebuchadnezzar—only when Daniel interpreted two of his dreams, and when the colossal idol was set up on the plain of Dura; and the other—Belshazzar—only on the last day of his life. The book is not regular in its structure, but consists of an intermixture of history and prophecy, apparently composed as occasion demanded, and then united in a single volume. Yet it has a unity of authorship and design, as we have seen, and is evidently the production of a single individual.

In considering the nature, design, and general character of the book, the attention may be properly directed to the following points:—

I. The portions containing incidents in the life of the author, and of his companions in Babylon, of permanent value.

II. The prophetic portions.

III. The language and style of the book.

I. The portions containing incidents in the life of the author, and of his companions in Babylon, of permanent value.

As already remarked, the allusions to his own life, and to the circumstances of his companions in exile, are few in number; and it may be added, that where there are such allusions they are made apparently rather to illustrate their principles, and the nature of their religion, than to create an interest in them personally. We could make out but little respecting their biography from this volume, though that little is sufficient to give us decided views of their *character*, and of the value and power of the religion which they professed.

The few personal incidents which we have relate to such points as the following:—The selection of Daniel, and three other captives, when young, with a view to their being trained in the language and science of the Chaldeans, that they might be employed in the service of the government, ch. i.; the fact that Daniel was called, when all the skill of the Chaldeans failed, to interpret a dream of Nebuchadnezzar, and that he was enabled to give an explanation that was so satisfactory that the king promoted him to exalted honour, ch. ii.; the narrative respecting the three friends of Daniel—Shadrach, Meshach, and Abednego—who refused to fall down and adore the golden image that Nebuchadnezzar erected in the plain of Dura, and who for their disobedience were cast into the fiery furnace, ch. iii.; Daniel's interpretation of a second dream of Nebuchadnezzar, and the fulfilment of the interpretation of that dream on the monarch, ch. iv.; his interpretation of the handwriting on the wall at the feast of Belshazzar, ch. v.; and the attempt of the enemies of Daniel to destroy his influence and his life by taking advantage of his known piety, and the firmness of his attachment to God, ch. vi.

These must have been but a few of the incidents that occurred to

Daniel in the course of a long life spent in Babylon, and they were probably selected as furnishing valuable illustrations of character; as evincing the nature of true piety; as proofs of Divine inspiration; and as showing that God has control over kings and nations. .All that is here stated occurred at distant intervals in a long life, and this fact should be remembered in reading the book. For the practical lessons taught by these portions of the book, I may be permitted to refer to the remarks at the close of ch. i., ii., iii., vi.

II. The prophetic portions of the book.

The prophecies of the book of Daniel may be arranged under two great classes :—those relating to the Babylonian monarchs; and those of more general interest pertaining to the future history of the world.

(A.) The former are confined to the calamities that would come upon the two monarchs who are mentioned in the book—Nebuchadnezzar and Belshazzar. Of the former of these kings, Nebuchadnezzar, his derangement as a judgment of heaven, on account of his pride, is predicted, ch. iv. ; and of the latter, Belshazzar, the termination of his reign, and the taking of his kingdom, are predicted on account of his impiety, ch. v. The object did not seem to be to state what farther would occur to the kingdom of the Chaldeans, except as it should be lost in the great kingdom of the Medes and Persians, in which it would be absorbed.

(B.) Those of general interest pertaining to future times. Of these there are several classes :—

(a) The prospective history of the revolutions in the great kingdoms of the world; or a *general glance* at what would happen in relation to the empires that were then playing their part in human affairs, and of those which would grow out of the kingdoms existing in the time of Daniel.

These may be arranged under the following general heads :—

(1.) A description of the great kingdoms or empires that would properly grow out of the Babylonian or Chaldean monarchy, ch. ii. That kingdom was, in the time of Daniel, the great, and almost the single, sovereignty of the earth; for, in the time of Nebuchadnezzar, this had absorbed all others. From this, however, were to spring other great dynasties that were to rule over the world, and that might properly, in some sense, be represented as the successors of this. These great revolutions are represented in the dream of Nebuchadnezzar respecting the golden image, ch. ii., and they are described by Daniel as (a) the great monarchy of which Nebuchadnezzar was the head—Babylon—represented in the image by the head of gold (ch. ii. 38) ; (b) as another kingdom inferior to this, represented in the image by the breast and arms of silver (ch. ii. 32, 39)—the Medo-Persian empire, that would succeed that of Babylon ; (c) as a third kingdom that would succeed this, represented in the image by the belly and the thighs of brass, (ch. ii. 32, 39) ; (d) as a fourth kingdom more mighty than either, subduing all nations under it, and crushing the powers of the earth, yet made of discordant materials, so as never firmly to adhere as one—represented by the legs of iron, and the feet and toes partly of iron and partly of clay in the image (ch. ii. 33, 41–43), denoting the mighty Roman power ; and (e) as another kingdom that would spring up under this fourth kingdom, and that would ultimately supplant it, and become the permanent kingdom on the earth (ch. ii. 44, 45).

Substantially the same representation occurs again in ch. vii., under the image of a succession of formidable beasts that were seen by Daniel in a dream.   These four great kingdoms, represented successively by a lion, by a bear, by a leopard, and by a nondescript monster, were also succeeded by a great and permanent kingdom on the earth—the reign of God.   In this representation, Daniel goes more into detail in respect to the last great empire than he does in interpreting the dream of Nebuchadnezzar. Indeed, the design of this latter representation seems to be, to give a more full account of the changes which would occur in this last great kingdom on the earth—the kingdom of the saints—than had been before given.

(2.) A particular prophecy of the conquests of the king of Grecia—Alexander the Great—extending down to the time of Antiochus Epiphanes, and to the calamities and desolations which he would bring upon the holy land (ch. viii).   This occurs in a vision which Daniel had at Shushan, in the province of Elam, and consisted of a representation of a ram with two horns, " pushing" in every direction, as if to extend its conquests everywhere.   From the West, however, there came a goat, with a single horn between its eyes, that attacked and overcame the ram.   This single horn on the head of the goat is subsequently represented as broken, and in its place there came up four other horns, and out of one of them a little horn that became great, and that magnified itself particularly against " the prince of the host," and that took away the daily sacrifice, or that closed the sacred services of religion in the temple.

A part of this is explained by Gabriel, as referring to the king of Grecia ; and there can be no difficulty in understanding that Alexander the Great is referred to, and that by the four horns that sprang up out of the one that was broken, the four kingdoms into which that of Alexander was divided at his death are meant, and that by the little horn that sprang up Antiochus Epiphanes is designated.

(3.) A particular and minute prophecy respecting the wars between two of the kingdoms that sprang out of the empire of Alexander—Syria and Egypt—so far especially as they affected the holy land, and the services in the sanctuary of God (ch. x., xi).   This vision occurred in the third year of the reign of Cyrus, and on an occasion when Daniel had been fasting three full weeks.   The prediction was imparted to him by an angel that appeared to him by the river Hiddekel, or Tigris, and contains a detailed account of what would occur for a long period in the conflicts which would exist between the sovereigns of Syria and Egypt. In these wars the Hebrew people were to be deeply interested, for their country lay between the two contending kingdoms; their land would be taken and re-taken in those conflicts; not a few of the great battles that would be fought in these conflicts would be fought on their territory; and deep and permanent disasters would occur to them in consequence of the manner in which the Hebrew people would regard and treat one or both of the contending parties. This prophetic history is conducted onward, with great particularity, to the death of Antiochus Epiphanes, the most formidable enemy that the Hebrew people would have to encounter in the future, and then (ch. xii.) the vision terminates with a few unconnected *hints* of what would occur in future periods, to the end of the world.

It was from this portion of the book particularly that Porphyry argued that the whole work must have been written *after* the events had occurred, and that, therefore, it must be a forgery of a later age than the time of the exile in Babylon.

(4.) A particular and minute prophecy respecting the time when the Messiah would appear (ch. ix). This was imparted to Daniel when, anxious about the close of the long captivity of his countrymen, and supposing that the predicted time of the return to the land of their fathers drew on, he gave himself to an earnest and careful study of the books of Jeremiah. At the close of the solemn prayer which he offered on that occasion (ch. ix. 4–19), the angel Gabriel appeared to him (ch. ix. 20, 21) to assure him that his prayer was heard, and to make an important communication to him respecting future times (ch. ix. 22, 23). He then proceeded to inform him how long a period was determined, in respect to the holy city, before the great work should be accomplished of making an end of sin, and of making reconciliation for iniquity, and of bringing in everlasting righteousness; when, that great work having been accomplished, the oblations at the temple would cease, and the overspreading of abomination would occur, and desolation would come upon the temple and city (ch. ix. 24–27). This celebrated prophecy of the "seventy weeks" is among the most important, and, in some respects, among the most difficult parts of the sacred volume. If the common interpretation [and the one that is adopted in these Notes] is correct, it is the most definite prediction of the time when the Messiah would appear to be found in the Old Testament.

(5.) Particular prophecies respecting events that would occur *after* the coming of the Messiah. These relate to two points:—

A. Prophecies relating to the church (ch. vii. 7–27).

(*a*) The rise of ten kingdoms out of the great fourth monarchy which would succeed the Babylonian, the Medo-Persian, and the Macedonian —to wit, the *Roman* power (ch. vii. 24).

(*b*) The rise of another power after them, springing out of them, and subduing three of those powers—to wit the *Papal* power (ch. vii. 24).

(c) The characteristics of that new power—as arrogant, and perse-cuting, and claiming supreme legislation over the world (ch. vii. 25).

(d) The duration of this power (ch. vii. 25).

(e) The manner in which it would be terminated (ch. vii. 26).

(f) The permanent establishment of the kingdom of the saints on the earth (ch. vii. 27).

B. Prophecies relating to the final judgment and the end of all things (ch. xii).

This portion (ch. xii.) is made up of *hints* and *fragments*—broken thoughts and suggestions, which there was no occasion to fill up. What is said is not communicated in a direct form *as* a revelation of new truths, but is rather based *on* certain truths as already known, and employed here for the illustration of others. It is *assumed* that there will be a resurrection of the dead and a judgment, and the writer employs the language based on this assumption to illustrate the point immediately before him (ch. xii. 2–4, 9, 13). There is also a very obscure reference to the times when certain great events were to occur in the future (ch. xii. 11, 12); but there is nothing, in this respect, that can enable us certainly to determine when these events will take place.

In reference to these prophetic portions of the book of Daniel, a few illustrative remarks may now be made :—

(1.) They relate to most momentous events in the history of the world. If the views taken of these portions of the book are correct, then the eye of the prophet rested on those events in the future which would enter most deeply into the character of coming ages, and which would do more than any other to determine the final condition of the world.

(2.) The prophecies in Daniel are more *minute* than any others in the Bible. This is particularly the case in respect to the four great kingdoms which would arise; to the conquests of Alexander the Great; to the kingdoms which would spring out of the one great empire that would be founded by him; to the wars that would exist between two of those sovereignties; to the time when the Messiah would appear; to the manner in which he would be cut off; to the final destruction of the holy city; and to the rise, character, and destiny of the Papacy. Of these great events there are no other so minute connected descrip-tions anywhere else in the Old Testament; and even, on many of these points, the more full disclosures of the New Testament receive important light from the prophecies of Daniel.

(3.) There is a remarkable resemblance between many of the predic-tions in Daniel and in the book of Revelation. No one can peruse the two books without being satisfied that, in many respects, they were designed to refer to the same periods in the history of the world, and to the same events, and especially where *time* is mentioned. There is, indeed—as is remarked in the Preface to these Notes—no express allu-sion in the Apocalypse to Daniel. There is no direct quotation from the book. There is no certain evidence that the author of the Apocalypse ever saw the book of Daniel, though no one can doubt that he did. There is nothing in the Apocalypse which might not have been written if the book of Daniel had not been written, or if it had been entirely unknown to John. Perhaps it may be added, that there is nothing in the book of Revelation which might not have been as easily explained if the book of Daniel had not been written. And yet it is manifest, that in most important respects the authors of the two books refer to the same great events in history; describe the same important changes in human affairs; refer to the same periods of duration; and have in their eye the same termination of things on the earth. No other two books in the Bible have the same relation to each other; nor are there any other two in which a commentary on the one will introduce so many topics which must be considered in the other, or where the explanations in the one will throw so much light on the other.

III. The language and style of the book.

(1.) The language of the book of Daniel is nearly half Chaldee and half Hebrew. In ch. i. ii. 1–3, it is Hebrew; from ch. ii. 4, to the end of ch. vii., it is Chaldee; and the remainder of the book is Hebrew. The book of Ezra also contains several chapters of Chaldee, exhibiting the same characteristics as the part of the book of Daniel written in that language.

As Daniel was early trained in his own country in the knowledge of the Hebrew, and as he was carefully instructed, after being carried to Babylon, in the language and literature of the Chaldees (see § 1.), it is certain that he was capable of writing in either language; and it is probable that he would use either, as there might be occasion, in his intercourse with his own countrymen, or with the Chaldeans. There is the highest probability that the captive Hebrews would retain the knowledge of their own language in a great degree of purity, during their long captivity in Babylon, and that this would be the language which Daniel would employ in his intercourse with his own countrymen; while from his own situation at court, and the necessity of his intercourse with the Chaldeans, it may be presumed that the language which he would perhaps most frequently employ would be the Chaldean.

That there were reasons why one portion of this book was written in Chaldee, and another in Hebrew, there can be no doubt, but it is now utterly impossible to ascertain what those reasons were. The use of one language or the other *seems* to be perfectly arbitrary. The portions written in Hebrew have no more relation to the Jews, and would have no more interest to them, than those written in Chaldee; and, on the other hand, the portions written in Chaldee have no special relation to the Chaldeans. But while the reasons for this change must for ever remain a secret, there are two obvious suggestions which have often been made in regard to it, and which have already been incidentally adverted to, as bearing on the question of the authorship of the book.

(1.) The first is, that this fact accords with the account which we have of the education of the author, as being instructed in both these languages—furnishing thus an undesigned proof of the authenticity of the book ; and (2) the other is, that this would not have occurred if the work was a forgery of a later age ; for (*a*) it is doubtful whether, in the age of the Maccabees, there were any who could write with equal ease in both languages, or could write both languages with purity ; (*b*) if it could be done, the device would not be one that would be likely to occur to the author, and he would have been likely to betray the design if it had existed ; and (*c*) as the apocryphal additions to Daniel (see § v.) were written in Greek, the presumption is, that if the book had been forged in that age it would have been wholly written in that language. At all events, the *facts* of the case, in regard to the languages in which the book was written, accord with all that we know of Daniel.

(2.) The book abounds with symbols and visions. In this respect it resembles very closely the writings of Ezekiel and Zechariah. One of these was his cotemporary, and the other lived but little after him, and it may be presumed that this style of writing prevailed much in that age. All these writers, not improbably, "formed their style, and their manner of thinking and expression, in a foreign land, where symbol, and imagery, and vision, and dreams, were greatly relished and admired. The ruins of the Oriental cities recently brought to the light of day, as well as those which have ever remained exposed to view, are replete with symbolic forms and images, which once gave a play and a delight to the fancy."—Prof. Stuart on Daniel, p. 393. Perhaps none of the other sacred writers abound so much in symbols and visions as Daniel, except John in the book of Revelation ; and in these two, as before suggested, the resemblance is remarkable. The interpretation of either of these books involves the necessity of studying the nature of symbolic language ; and on the views taken of that language must depend, in a great degree, the views of the truths disclosed in these books.

(3.) The book of Daniel, though not written in the *style* of poetry, yet abounds much with the *spirit* of poetry—as the book of Revelation does. Indeed, the Apocalypse may be regarded as, on the whole, the most *poetic* book in the Bible. We miss, indeed, in both these books, the usual *forms* of Hebrew poetry ; we miss the *parallelism* (comp. Intro. to Job, § v.); but the *spirit* of poetry pervades both the book of Daniel and the book of Revelation, and the latter, especially if it were a mere human production, would be ranked among the highest creations of genius. Much of Daniel, indeed, is simple prose—alike in structure and in form ; but much also in his visions deserves to be classed among the works of imagination. Throughout the book there are frequent bursts of feeling of a high order (comp. ch. ii. 19–23); there are many passages that are sublime (comp. ch. ii. 27–45 ; **iv.** 19–27 ; v. 17–28); there is a spirit of unshaken fidelity and boldness— as in the passages just referred to ; there is true grandeur in the prophetic portions (comp. ch. vii. 9–14; x. 5–9; xi. 41–45; xii. 1–3, 5–8; and there is, throughout the book, a spirit of humble, sincere, firm, and devoted piety, characterizing the author as a man eminently prudent and wise, respectful in his intercourse with others, faithful in every trust, unceasing in the discharge of his duties to God; a man who preferred to lose the highest offices which kings could confer, and to subject himself to shame and to death, rather than shrink, in the slightest degree, from the discharge of the proper duties of religion.

§ V.—THE APOCRYPHAL ADDITIONS TO THE BOOK OF DANIEL.

These additions are three in number:—

(1.) "The Song of the Three Holy Children;" that is, the song of Shadrach, Meshach, and Abednego, who were cast into the burning furnace by Nebuchadnezzar (ch. iii). This "Song," as it is called, is inserted in the Greek copies, in ch. iii., between the twenty-third and twenty-fourth verses, and contains sixty-eight verses, making the whole chapter, in the Greek, to contain an hundred verses. The "Song" consists properly of three parts : I. A hymn of "Azariah," or of "Ananiah, Azariah, and Misael"—Ανανίας καὶ Αζαρίας και Μισαήλ—of whom Azariah is the speaker, in which praise is given to God, and a prayer is offered that they may be accepted, preserved, and delivered (vers. 1–22). These are the *Hebrew* names of the three persons that were cast into the fiery furnace (Dan. i. 6, 7), but why these names are inserted here rather than the names given them in Babylon by the "prince of the eunuchs" (ch. i. 7), and which are used in the Chaldee in this chapter, is not known; and the circumstance that they *are* so used furnishes a strong presumption that this addition in Greek is spurious, since, in the other portions of the chapter (vers. 12–14, 16, 19, marked in *Codex Chisian.* in brackets), the same names occur which are found in the original Chaldee. II. A statement, that the king's servants added fuel to the flame, or kept up the intensity of the heat by putting in rosin, pitch, tow, and small wood, making the furnace so hot that the flame rose above it to the height of forty-nine cubits, and so hot as to consume the Chaldeans that stood around it, but that the angel of the Lord came down, and smote the flame of fire out of the oven, and made the midst of the furnace like a moist, whistling wind, so that the three "children" were safe (vers. 23–27). III. A hymn of praise, calling on all things to praise God, uttered by "the three, as out of one mouth," (vers. 28–68). The narrative then proceeds, in the Greek translation, as it is in the Chaldee, and as it now stands in our common translation of the book of Daniel.

(2.) The second addition is what is called *The History of Susanna.* This is a story the design of which is to honour Daniel. A man in Babylon, of great wealth, by the name of Joacim, marries Susanna, a Jewess, who had been brought up in the fear of the Lord. The house of Joacim was a place of much resort, and particularly by two men of advanced life, who were appointed judges of the people. Susanna was a woman of great beauty, and each one of the two judges, ignorant of the feelings of the other, fell violently in love with her. They both observed that at a certain time of the day she walked in the garden, and both, unknown to each other, resolved to follow her into the garden. They proposed, therefore, to each other to return to their own homes; and both, after having gone away, returned again, and then, surprised at this, they each declared their love for Susanna, and agreed to watch for the time when she should enter the garden, and then to accomplish their purpose. She entered the garden as usual for the purpose of bathing, and the elders, having hid themselves, suddenly came upon her, and threatened her with death if she would not gratify their desires. She, rather than yield, calmly made up her mind to die, but gave the alarm by crying aloud, and the elders, to save themselves, declared that they found a young man with her in the garden, and the matter coming before the people, she was condemned to death, and was led forth to be executed. At this juncture, Daniel appeared, who proposed to examine the elders anew, and to do it separately. In this examination, one of them testified that what he had seen occurred under a mastick or lentisk tree, the other that it was under a holm tree. The consequence was, that Susanna was discharged, and the two elders themselves put to death.

This story is said, in the common version of the Apocrypha, to be "set apart from the beginning of Daniel because it is not in the Hebrew." It is found only in the Apocrypha, and is not incorporated in the Greek translation of Daniel.

(3.) The third addition is what is called "The History of the Destruction of Bel and the Dragon, cut off from the end of Daniel." This is a story in two parts. The first relates to Bel, the idolgod of the Babylonians. A large quantity of food was daily placed before the idol in the temple, which it was supposed the idol consumed. The inquiry was made of Daniel by Cyrus, king of Persia, why he did not worship the idol. Daniel replied that he was permitted by his religion to worship only the living God. Cyrus asked him whether Bel was not a living God; and, in proof of it, appealed to the large quantity of food which he daily consumed. Daniel smiled at the simplicity of the king, and affirmed that the god was only brass and clay, and could devour nothing. The king, enraged, called for the priests of Bel, and insisted on being informed who ate the large quantity of food that was daily placed before the idol. They, of course, affirmed that it was the idol, and proposed that a test should be applied by placing the food before him, as usual, and by having the temple carefully closed and sealed with the signet of the king. Under the table they had, however, made a private entrance, and in order to detect them, Daniel caused ashes to be sprinkled on the floor, which, on the following day, revealed the footprints of men, women, and children, who had secretly entered the temple, and consumed the food. The consequence was, that they were put to death, and Bel and his temple were delivered to Daniel, who destroyed them both.

The other part of the story relates to a great dragon which was worshipped in Babylon. The king said that it could not be affirmed that this dragon was made of brass, or that he was not a living being, and required Daniel to worship him. Daniel still declared that he would worship only the living God, and proposed to put the dragon to death. This he did by making a ball of pitch, and fat, and hair, and putting it into the mouth of the dragon, so that he burst asunder. A tumult, in consequence of the destruction of Bel and the Dragon, was excited against the king, and the mob came and demanded Daniel, who had been the cause of this. Daniel was delivered to them, and was thrown into the den of lions, where he remained six days; and, in order that the lions might at once devour him, their appetites had been sharpened by having been fed each day with "two carcasses"—in the margin, "two slaves" — and two sheep. At this juncture, it is said that there was in Jewry a prophet, by the name of Habbacuc, who had made pottage, and was going with it into a field to carry it to the reapers. He was directed by an angel of the Lord to take it to Babylon to Daniel, who was in the lions' den. The prophet answered that he never saw Babylon, and knew not where the den was. So the angel of the Lord took him by the crown, and bare him by the hair of his head, and placed him in Babylon over the den. He gave Daniel the food, and was immediately restored to his own place in Judea. On the seventh day the king went to bewail Daniel; found him alive; drew him out, and threw in those who had caused him to be placed there, who were, of course, at once devoured.

This foolish story is said, in the title, in the common version of the Apocrypha, to have been "cut off from the end of Daniel." Like the Prayer of the Three Children, and the History of Susanna, it is found only in Greek, in which language it was undoubtedly written.

In respect to these additions to the book of Daniel, and the question whether they are entitled to be regarded as a part of his genuine work, and to have a place in the inspired writings, the following remarks may now be made :—

(*a*) Neither of them, and no portion of them, is found in the Hebrew or the Chaldee, nor is there the slightest evidence that they had a Hebrew or Chaldee original. There is no historical proof that they ever existed in either of these languages, and, of course, no proof that they ever formed a part of the genuine work of Daniel. If they were written originally in Greek, and if the evidence above adduced that the book of Daniel was written in the time of the exile is conclusive, then it is clear that these additions were *not* written by Daniel himself, and of course that they are not entitled to a place among the inspired records.   For the Greek language was not understood in Babylon to any considerable extent, if at all, until the time of Alexander the Great, and his conquests in the East; and it is every way certain, that a book written in Babylon in the time of the exile would *not* have been written in Greek.   The evidence is conclusive that these additions were never any part of the genuine book of Daniel; and, of course, that they have no claim to a place in the canon.   Moreover, as they constituted no part of that book, *none* of the evidence urged in favour of the canonical authority of that book can be urged in behalf of these stories, and any claim that they may have must rest on their own merits.

(*b*) They have no claim, on their own account, to a place in the canon.   Their authors are unknown.   The time of their composition is unknown.   They were never recognised by the Jews as canonical, and never had the sanction of the Saviour and the apostles, as they are never quoted or alluded to in the New Testament.   And they have no internal evidence that they are of Divine origin.   There is no evidence which could be urged in favour of their claims to a place in the canonical Scriptures which could not be urged in favour of the whole of the Apocrypha, or which could not be urged in favour of *any* anonymous writings of antiquity.   The only ground of claim which *could* be urged for the admission of these stories into the sacred canon would be, that they were a part of the genuine book of Daniel ; but this claim *never* can be made out by any possibility.

(*c*) In common with the other books of the Apocrypha, these books were rejected by the early Christian writers, and were not admitted into the canon of Scripture during the first four centuries of the Christian church. (See Horne's *Introduction*, i. 628.)   Some of the books of the Apocrypha were indeed quoted by some of the fathers with respect (Lardner, iv. 331), particularly by Ambrose (who lived A. D. 340–397), but they are referred to by Jerome only to be censured and condemned (Lardner, iv. 424, 440, 466–472), and are mentioned only with contempt by Augustine (Lardner, iv. 499).

It is seldom that these additions to Daniel in the Apocrypha are quoted or alluded to at all by the early Christian writers, but when they are it is only that they may be condemned.   Origen, indeed, refers to the story of Susanna as a true history, and, in a letter to Africanus, says of it, " That the story of Susanna being dishonourable to the Jewish elders, it was suppressed by their great men; and that there were many things kept, as much as might be, from the knowledge of the people, some of which, nevertheless, were preserved in some apocryphal books." —Lardner, ii. 466.   Origen, indeed, in the words of Dr. Lardner, "Says all he can think of to prove the history [of Susanna] true and genuine, and affirms that it was made use of in Greek by all the churches of Christ among the Gentiles ; yet he owns that it was not received by the Jews, nor to be found in their copies of the book of Daniel."— Lardner, ii. 541, 542. (Comp. also Dupin, *Dissertation Préliminaire sur la Bible,* Liv. i. ch. i. § 5, p. 15, note (*e*). To the arguments of Origen on the subject, Africanus replies, that he " wondered that he did not know that the book was spurious, and says it was a piece lately forged." —Lardner, ii. 541. The other books, the Prayer of the Three Children, and the Story of Bel and the Dragon—we do not find, from Lardner, to have been quoted or referred to at all by the early Christian writers.

(*d*) The foolishness and manifest fabulousness of the Story of Bel and the Dragon may be referred to as a proof that that cannot be a part of the genuine book of Daniel, or entitled to a place among books claiming to be inspired. It has every mark of being a fable, and is wholly unworthy a place in any volume claiming to be of Divine origin, or any volume of respectable authorship whatever.

(*e*) Little is known of the origin of these books, and little importance can be attached to them ; but it may be of some use to know the place which they have commonly occupied in the Bible by those who have received them as a part of the canon, and the place where they are commonly found in the version of the Scriptures.

" The Song of the Three Children" is placed in the Greek version of Daniel, and also in the Latin Vulgate, between the twenty-third and twenty-fourth verses of the third chapter. "It has always been admired," says Horne (*Intro.* iv. 217, 218), " for the piety of its sentiments, but it was never admitted to be canonical, until it was recognised by the Council of Trent. The fifteenth verse ['Neither is there at this time prince, or prophet, or leader, or burnt-offering, or sacrifice, or oblation, or incense, or place to sacrifice before thee, and to find mercy'] contains a direct falsehood; for it asserts that there was no prophet at that time, when it is well known that Daniel and Ezekiel both exercised the prophetic ministry in Babylon. This apocryphal fragment is, therefore, most probably the production of a Hellenistic Jew. The Hymn (ver. 29, *seq.*) resembles the hundred and forty-eighth Psalm, and was so approved of by the compilers of the Liturgy, that in the first Common Prayer Book of Edward VI. they appointed it to be used instead of the *Te Deum* during Lent."

" The History of Susanna has always been treated with some respect, but has never been considered as canonical, though the Council of Trent admitted it into the number of the sacred books. It is evidently the work of some Hellenistic Jew, and in the Vulgate version it forms the thirteenth chapter of the book of Daniel. In the Septuagint version it is placed at the beginning of that book."—Horne, iv. 218.

" The History of the Destruction of Bel and the Dragon was always rejected by the Jewish church; it is not extant either in the Hebrew or the Chaldee language. Jerome gives it no better title than The Fable of Bel and the Dragon ; nor has it obtained more credit with posterity, except with the fathers of the Council of Trent, who determined it to be a part of the canonical Scriptures. This book forms the fourteenth chapter of the book of Daniel in the Latin Vulgate ; in the Greek, it

was called the Prophecy of Habakkuk, the son of Jesus, of the tribe of
Levi.   There are two Greek texts of this fragment—that of the Septuagint, and that found in Theodotion's Greek version of Daniel.   The
former is the most ancient, and has been translated into Syriac.   The
Latin and Arabic versions, together with another Syriac translation,
have been made from the text of Theodotion."—Horne, iv. 218.   These
additions to Daniel may be found in Greek, Arabic, Syriac, and Latin,
in Walton's *Polyglott*, tom. iv.

§ VI.—THE ANCIENT VERSIONS OF THE BOOK OF DANIEL.

(1.) Of these, the oldest, of course, is the Septuagint.   For a general
account of this version, see Intro. to Isaiah, § VIII. I. (1.) Of the *author*
of that portion of the Septuagint version which comprised the book
of Daniel—for no one can doubt that the Septuagint was the work of
different authors—we have now no information.   The translation of
Daniel was among the least faithful, and was the most erroneous, of the
whole collection; and, indeed, it was so imperfect that its use in the
church was early superseded by the version of Theodotion—the version
which is now found in the editions of the Septuagint.

The Septuagint translation of the book of Daniel was for a long time
supposed to be lost, and it is only at a comparatively recent period that
it has been recovered and published.   For a considerable period before
the time of Jerome, the version by the LXX. had been superseded by
that of Theodotion, doubtless on account of the great imperfection of
the former, though it is probable that its disuse was gradual.   Jerome,
in his Preface to the Book of Daniel, says, indeed, that it was not known
to him on what ground this happened—"Danielem prophetam juxta
LXX. interpretes ecclesiæ non legunt, *et hoc cur acciderit, nescio*,"—but
it is in every way probable that it was on account of the great imperfection of the translation; for Jerome himself says, "Hoc unum affirmare,
quod multum a veritate discordet et recto judicio repudiata sit."   He
adds, therefore, that though Theodotion was understood to be an *unbeliever*—"post adventum Christi incredulus fuit"—yet that his translation was preferred to that of the LXX. "Illud quoque lectorem admoneo,
Danielem non juxta LXX. interpretes, sed juxta Theodotionem eccle-
sias legere, qui utique post adventum Christi incredulus fuit.   Unde
judicio magistrorum ecclesiæ editio eorum in hoc volumine repudiata
est, et Theodotionis vulgo legitur, quæ et Hebræo et ceteris transla-
toribus congruit."

From this cause it happened that the translation of Daniel by the
LXX. went into entire disuse, and was for a long time supposed to have
been destroyed.   It has, however, been recovered and published, though
it has not been substituted in the editions of the Septuagint in the
place of the version by Theodotion.   A copy of the old version by the
LXX. was found in the Chisian library at Rome, in a single manuscript

(Codex Chisianus), and was published in Rome, in folio, in the year 1772, under the title, Daniel Secundum LXX. ex tetraplis Origenis nunc primum editus e singulari Chisiano Codice annorum supra DCCC.—*Romæ*, 1772. fol. This was republished at Gœttingen, in 1773, and again in 1774. These editions were prepared by J. D. Michaelis, the former containing the text only, the latter with the text of the LXX., the version of Theodotion, the interpretation of Hippolytus, a Latin version, and the annotations of the Roman editor.

These editions were published from one manuscript, and without any attempt to correct the text by a comparison with other versions. The text is supposed to have been corrupted, so that, as Hahn says, no one can believe that this codex exhibits it as it was when the version was made. "This corruption," says he, "exists not only in particular words and phrases, but in the general disarrangement and disorder of the whole text, so that those parts are separated which ought to be united, and those parts united which ought to be kept distinct. Besides this, there was entire inattention to the *signs* which Origen had used in his edition of the Septuagint."—Pref. to Daniel, κατα τους Εβδομηκοντα. As there was but one manuscript, all hope of correcting the text in the way in which it has been done in the other parts of the Septuagint, and in other versions, by a comparison of manuscripts, was, of course, out of the question.

After four editions of the work had been published, it happened that, in the Ambrosian Library at Milan, Cajetan Bugati discovered a Syriac Hexaplar manuscript, written in the year 616 or 617, after Christ, which embraced the Hagiographa and the prophetic books, and, among others, "Daniel, according to the Septuagint translation." The title of this Syriac version, as translated by Hahn, is as follows : "Explicit liber Danielis prophetæ, qui conversus est ex traditione *τῶν* Septuaginta, duorum, qui in diebus Ptolemæi regis Ægypti ante adventum Christi annis centum plus minus verterunt libros sanctos de lingua Hebræorum, in Græcum, in Alexandria civitate magna. Versus est autem liber iste etiam de Græco in Syriacum, in Alexandria civitate mense Canun posteriori anni nongentesimi vicesimi octavi Alexandri indictione quinta (*i.e.* a 617, p. ch.)." This professes, therefore, to be a Syriac translation of the Septuagint version of Daniel. This version was found to be in good preservation, and the signs adopted by Origen to determine the value of the text were preserved, and a new edition of the Greek translation was published, corrected by this, under the title, "Daniel secundum editionem LXX. interpretum ex tetraplis desumptum. Rom., 1788." This Syriac version enabled the editor to correct many places that were defective, and to do much towards furnishing a more perfect text. Still the work was, in many respects, imperfect ; and, from all the aids within his reach, and probably all that can now be hoped for, Hahn published a new edition of the work, corrected in many more places (see them enumerated in his Preface, p. ix.), under the following title, " ΔΑΝΙΗΛ κατα τους Εβδομηκοιτα. E Codice Chisiano post Segaarium edidit secundum versionem Syriaco-Hexaplarem recognovit annotationibus criticis et philologicis illustravit Henricus Augustus Hahn, Philosophiæ Doctor et Theologiæ candidatus. Lipsiæ, CIƆIƆCCCXLV." This is now the most perfect edition of the Septuagint version of Daniel, but still it cannot be regarded as of great critical value in the interpretation of the book. It has been used in the preparation of this commentary. An account of the instances in which it departs from the Hebrew and Chaldee original may be seen at length in Lengerke, Das Buch Daniel, Einleitung, pp. cix.-cxiv. It has the Prayer of the Three Children, inserted in the usual place (ch. iii. 23, 24), and the History of Susanna, and the Destruction of Bel and the Dragon, as separate pieces, at the end.

(2.) The translation of Theodotion. That is, that which has been substituted in the Septuagint for the version above referred to, and which is found in the various editions of the Septuagint, and in the Polyglott Bibles. Theodotion was a native of Ephesus, and is termed by Eusebius an Ebionite, or semi-Christian. Jerome, as we have seen above, regarded him as an unbeliever—post adventum Christi incredulus fuit: that is, he *remained* an unbeliever after the coming of Christ ; probably meaning that he was a Jew by birth, and remained unconvinced that Jesus was the Messiah. He was nearly contemporary with Aquila, who was the author of a Greek translation of the Old Testament, and who was also of Jewish descent. The Jews were dissatisfied with the Septuagint version as being too paraphrastic, and Aquila undertook to make a literal version, but without any regard to the genius of the Greek language. We have only some fragments of the version by Aquila. The version of Theodotion is less literal than that of Aquila —holding a middle rank between the servile closeness of Aquila, and the freedom of Symmachus. This version is cited by Justin Martyr, in his *Dialogue with Tryphon the Jew*, which was composed about the year 160. The version of Theodotion is a kind of revision of the Septuagint, and supplies some deficiencies in the Septuagint, but the author shows that he was indifferently skilled in Hebrew. It is evident, that in his translation Theodotion made great use of both the previous versions, that by the LXX. and that of Aquila ; that he followed sometimes the diction of the one, and sometimes that of the other ; that he often mingled them together in the compass of the same verse ; and that he adapted the quotations from the two versions to his own style. As his style was similar to that of the LXX., Origen, in his *Hexapla*, perhaps for the sake of uniformity, supplied the additions which he inserted in his work chiefly from this version. There are but few fragments of these versions now remaining. See Horne, *Intro.* iv. 171-176. Lengerke supposes that Theodotion was a Christian, p. cxv. From this translation of Theodotion, a version was made in Arabic, in the tenth century, Lengerke, p. cxv.

(3.) The Syriac versions. For the general character of these versions, see Intro. to Isaiah, § viii. (3.) There is nothing remarkable in these versions of Daniel. For an account of a later Syriac version of the Septuagint, see the remarks above. " As Daniel has no Targum or Chaldee version, the Syriac version performs a valuable service in the explanation of Hebrew words."—Stuart, p. 491.

(4.) The Latin Vulgate. For the general character of this, see Intro. to Isaiah, § viii. (2.) As this contains the apocryphal portions, the Prayer of the Three Children, the History of Susanna, and the Destruction of Bel and the Dragon, and as the Latin Vulgate was declared canonical by the Council of Trent, of course those fragments have received the sanction of the Roman Catholic church as a part of the inspired records. This version, as a whole, is superior to any of the other ancient versions, and shows a more thorough knowledge than any of them of the tenor and nature of the book. " An invaluable service has Jerome done, by the translation of Daniel, and by his commentary on the book."—Prof. Stuart, p. 491.

(5.) The Arabic version. For an account of the Arabic versions, see Intro. to Isaiah, § viii. (4.) There is nothing peculiar in the Arabic version of Daniel.

§ VII.—EXEGETICAL HELPS TO THE BOOK OF DANIEL.

Besides the versions above referred to, I have made use of the following exegetical helps to the book of Daniel, in the preparation of these Notes. The order in which they are mentioned is not designed to express anything in regard to their value, but is adopted merely for the sake of convenience :—

Critici Sacri. Tom. iv.

Calvin, Prælectiones in Daniel. Works, vol. v., ed. Amsterdam, 1667.

Jerome, Commentary on Daniel. Works, tom. iv., ed. Paris, 1623.

The Pictorial Bible (Dr. Kitto). London, 1836.

Bush's Illustrations of Scripture. Brattleboro, 1836.

Dr. Gill, Commentaries. Vol. vi., ed. Philadelphia, 1819.

Hengstenberg's Christology, translated by the Rev. Reuel Keith, D.D. Alexandria, 1836.

Newton on the Prophecies. London, 1832.

Einleitung in das Alte Testament. Von Johann Gottfried Eichhorn, Vierter Band, § 612–619.

Daniel aus dem Hebräisch-Aramäischen neu übersetzt und erklärt mit einer vollständigen Einleitung, und einigen historischen und exegetischen Excursen, Von Leonhard Bertholdt. Erlangen, 1806.

Das Buch Daniel Verdeutscht und Ausleget Von Dr. Cæsar von Lengerke, Professor der Theologie zu Königsburg in Pr. Königsberg, 1835.

Commentarius Grammaticus in Vetus Testamentum in usum maxime

Gymnasiorum et Academiarum adornatus. Scripsit Franc. Jos. Valent. Dominic. Maurer. Phil. Doct. Soc. Historico-Theol. Lips. Sod. Ord. Volumen Secundum. Lipsiæ, 1838.

Isaaci Newtoni ad Danielis Profetæ Vaticinia. Opuscula, tom. iii. 1744.

Lehrbuch der Historisch-Kritischen Einleitung in die kanonischen und Apokryphischen Bücher des Alten Testamentes. Von Wilhelm Martin Leberecht De Wette, § 253–259. Berlin, 1845.

In Danielem Prophetam Commentarius editus a Philippo Melanthone, Anno MDXLIII. Corpus Reformatorum, Bretschneider, vol. xiii., 1846.

Ueber Verfasser und Zweck des Buches Daniel. Theologische Zeitschrift. Drittes Heft. Berlin, 1822, pp. 181–294. By Dr. Fried. Lücke.

Commentatio Historico-Critica Exhibens descriptionem et censuram recentium de Danielis Libro Opinionum, Auctore Henrico Godofredo Kirmss, Saxone Seminarii Theologici Sodali. Jenæ, 1828.

Die Authentie des Daniel. Von Ernst Wilhelm Hengstenberg. Berlin, 1831.

The Season and Time, or an Exposition of the Prophecies which relate to the two periods of Daniel subsequent to the 1260 years now recently expired. By W. Ettrick, A.M. London, 1816.

An Essay towards an Interpretation of the Prophecies of Daniel. By Richard Amner. London, 1776.

Neue Kritische Untersuchungen über des Buch Daniel. Von Heinrich Hävernick, der Theologie Doctor und A. O. Professor an der Universität Rostock. Hamburgh, 1838.

An Exposition of such of the Prophecies of Daniel as receive their accomplishment under the New Testament. By the late Rev. Magnus Frederic Roos, A.M., Superintendent and Prelate in Lustnau and Anhausen. Translated from the German, by Ebenezer Henderson. Edinburgh, 1811.

A Description accompanying an Hieroglyphical Print of Daniel's Great Image. London.

Daniel, his Chaldie Visions and his Ebrew : both translated after the original, and expounded both, by the reduction of heathen most famous stories, with the exact proprietie of his wordes (which is the surest certaintie what he must meane) : and joining all the Bible and learned tongues to the frame of his Worke. London, 1596. By Hugh Broughton.

Observations intended to point out the application of Prophecy in the eleventh chapter of Daniel to the French Power. London, 1800. Author unknown.

An Apologie in Briefe Assertions defending that our Lord died in the time properly foretold to Daniel. For satisfaction to some studentes in both Universities. By H. Broughton. London, 1592.

An Essay in Scripture Prophecy, wherein it is endeavoured to explain the three periods contained in the twelfth chapter of the Prophet Daniel, with some arguments to make it probable that the *first* of the *periods* did expire in the year 1715. Printed in the year 1715. Author and place unknown.

Daniel, an improved Version Attempted, with a Preliminary Dissertation, and Notes, critical, historical, and explanatory. By Thomas Wintle, B.D., Rector of Brightwall, in Berkshire, and Fellow of Pembroke College. Oxford, 1792.

Hermanni Venema Commentarius, ad Danielis cap. xi. 4-45, et xii. 1-3. Leovardiæ, 1752.

A Chronological Treatise upon the Seventy Weeks of Daniel. By Benjamin Marshall, M.A., Rector of Naunton, in Gloucestershire. London, 1725.

The Times of Daniel, Chronological and Prophetical, examined with relation to the point of contact between Sacred and Profane Chronology. By George, Duke of Manchester. London, 1845.

Prof. Stuart's Commentary on Daniel (Boston, 1850) was not published until after the "Notes" or Commentary in this work had been written. I have consulted it carefully in revising the manuscript for the press.

Besides these works, which I have consulted freely, in proportion to what seemed to me their respective worth, and such collateral exegetical helps in addition as I have access to in my own library, the following works are referred to by De Wette, Lehrbuch, pp. 378, 379, as valuable aids in interpreting Daniel:—

Ephræm, d. S. Ausleg. des Proph. Daniel, Opp. ii. 203, *seq.*

Theodoret, Comment. in Visiones Dan. Proph. Opp. ed. Sculz. ii. 1053, *seq.*

Paraph. Josephi Jachidæ in Dan. c. Vers. et Annotatt. Const. l'Empereur. Amst. 1633.

Prælectt. Acad. in Dan. Proph. habitæ a Mart. Geir. Lips. 1667, ed. corr. 84.

H. Venem. Dissertatt. ad Vatice.'Danielis, c. ii. vii. et viii. Leov. 1745.

Chr. B. Michæl. Annotatt. in Dan. in J. H. Michæl. Ueberr. Annotatt. in Hagiogr. iii. 1, *seq.*

Rosenmüller schol.

THE BOOK OF DANIEL.

CHAPTER I.

§ I.—AUTHENTICITY OF THE CHAPTER.

FOR the general argument in favour of the genuineness and authenticity of the book of Daniel, see Intro. §§ II., III. To the genuineness and authenticity of each particular chapter in detail, however, objections, derived from something peculiar in each chapter, have been urged, which it is proper to meet, and which I propose to consider in a particular introduction to the respective chapters. These objections it is proper to consider, not so much because they have been urged by distinguished German critics — De Wette, Bertholdt, Bleek, Eichhorn, and others —for their writings will probably fall into the hands of few persons who will read these Notes—but (a) because it may be presumed that men of so much learning, industry, acuteness, and ingenuity, have urged all the objections which can, with any appearance of plausibility, be alleged against the book ; and (b) because the objections which they have urged may be presumed to be felt, to a greater or less degree, by those who read the book, though they might not be able to express them with so much clearness and force. There are numerous objections to various portions of the Scriptures floating in the minds of the readers of the Bible, and many difficulties which occur to such readers, which are not expressed, and which it would be desirable to re-move, and which it is the duty of an expositor of the Bible, if he can, to remove. Sceptical critics, in general, but collect and embody in a plausible form difficulties which are felt by most readers of the Scriptures. It is for this reason, and with a view to remove what *seems* to furnish plausible arguments against the different portions of this book, that the objections which have been urged, principally by the authors above referred to, will be noticed in special sections preceding the exposition of each chapter.

The only objection to the genuineness and authenticity of the first chapter which it seems necessary to notice is, that the account of Daniel in the chapter is inconsistent with the mention of Daniel by Ezekiel. The objection substantially is, that it is improbable that the Daniel who is mentioned by Ezekiel should be one who was a cotemporary with himself, and who at that time lived in Babylon. Daniel is three times mentioned in Ezekiel, and in each case as a man of eminent piety and integrity ; as one so distinguished by his virtues as to deserve to be classed with the most eminent of the patriarchs. Thus in Ezek. xiv. 14, "Though these three men, Noah, Daniel, and Job, were in it, they should deliver but their own souls by their righteousness, saith the Lord God." So again, ver. 20, "Though Noah, Daniel, and Job, were in it, as I live, saith the Lord God, they shall deliver neither son nor daughter, they shall deliver but their own souls by their righteousness." And again, ch. xxviii. 3, speaking of the prince of Tyre, "Behold thou art wiser than Daniel." The objection urged in respect to the mention of Daniel in these passages is substantially this—that if the account in the book of Daniel is true, he must have been a cotemporary with Ezekiel, and must have been, when Ezekiel prophesied, a young man; that it is incredible that he should have gained a degree of reputation which would entitle him to be ranked with Noah and Job; that he could not have been so well known as to make it natural or proper to refer to him in the same connection with those eminent men; and *especially* that he could not have been thus known to the prince of Tyre, as is supposed of those mentioned by Ezekiel in the passages referred to, for it cannot be presumed that a man so young had acquired such a fame abroad as to make it proper to refer to him in this manner in an address to a heathen prince. This objection was urged by Bernstein (über das Buch Hiob, in den Analekten von Keil und Tzschirner, i. 3, p. 10), and it is found also in Bleek, p. 284, and De Wette, *Einl.* p. 380. De Wette says that it is probable that the author of the book of Daniel used the name of "an ancient mythic or poetic person falsely," in order to illustrate his work.

Now, in regard to this objection, it may be remarked (*a*) that, according to all the accounts which we have in the Bible, Ezekiel and Daniel *were* cotemporary, and were in Babylon at the same time. As Daniel, however, lived a long time in Babylon after this, it is to be admitted, also, that at the period referred to by Ezekiel, he must have been comparatively a young man. But it does not follow that he might

not then have had a well-known character for piety and integrity, which would make it proper to mention his name in connection with the most eminent saints of ancient times. If the account in the book of Daniel *itself* is a correct account of him, this will not be doubted, for he soon attracted attention in Babylon; he soon evinced that extraordinary piety which made him so eminent as a man of God, and that extraordinary wisdom which raised him to the highest rank as an officer of state in Babylon. It was very soon after he was taken to Babylon that the purpose was formed to train him, and the three other selected youths, in the learning of the Chaldeans (ch. i. 1–4), and that Daniel showed that he was qualified to pass the examination, preparatory to his occupying an honourable place in the court (ch. i. 18–21); and it was only in the second year of the reign of Nebuchadnezzar that the remarkable dream occurred, the interpretation of which gave to Daniel so much celebrity (ch. ii.). According to a computation of Hengstenberg (*Authentie des Daniel*, p. 71), Daniel was taken to Babylon full ten years before the prophecy of Ezekiel, in which the first mention of him was made; and if so, there can be no real ground for the objection referred to. In that time, if the account of his extraordinary wisdom is true; if he evinced the character which it is said that he did evince—and against this there is no intrinsic improbability; and if he was exalted to office and rank, as it is stated that he was, there can be no improbability in what Ezekiel says of him, that he had a character which made it proper that he should be classed with the most eminent men of the Jewish nation. (*b*) As to the objection that the name of Daniel could not have been known to the king of Tyre, as would seem to be implied in Ezek. xxviii. 3, it may be remarked, that it is not necessary to suppose that these prophecies were ever known to the king of Tyre, or that they were ever designed to influence him. The prophecies which were directed against the ancient heathen kings were uttered and published among the Hebrew people, primarily for *their* guidance, and were designed to furnish to them, and to others in future times, arguments for the truth of religion, though they assumed the form of direct addresses to the kings themselves. Such an imaginary appeal may have been made in this case by Ezekiel to the king of Tyre; and, in speaking of him, and of his boasted wisdom, Ezekiel may have made the comparison which would then naturally occur to him, by mentioning him in connection with the most eminent man for wisdom of that age. But it should be said, also, that there can be no certain evidence that the name of Daniel was *not* known to the king of Tyre, and no intrinsic improbability in the supposition that it was. If Daniel had at that time evinced the remarkable wisdom at the court of Babylon which it is said in this book that he had; if he had been raised to that high rank which it is affirmed he had reached, there is no improbability in supposing that so remarkable a circumstance should have been made known to the king of Tyre. Tyre was taken by Nebuchadnezzar, B.C. 572, after a siege of thirteen years, and it is in no way improbable that the king of Tyre would be made acquainted with what occurred at the court of the Chaldeans. The prophecy in Ezekiel, where Daniel is mentioned (ch. xxviii. 3), could not have been uttered long before Tyre was taken, and, in referring to what was to occur, it was not unnatural to mention the

man most distinguished for wisdom at the court of Babylon, and in the councils of Nebuchadnezzar, with the presumption that his name and celebrity would not be unknown to the king of Tyre. (c) As to the objection of Bernstein, that it would be improbable, if Daniel lived there, and if he was comparatively a young man, that his name would be placed *between* that of Noah and Job (Ezek. xiv. 14), as if he had lived *before* Job, it may be remarked, that there might be a greater similarity between the circumstances of Noah and Daniel than between Noah and Job, and that it was proper to refer to them in this order. But the mere circumstance of the *order* in which the names are mentioned cannot be adduced as a proof that one of the persons named did not exist at that time. They may have occurred in this order to Ezekiel, because in his apprehension, that was the order in which the degree of their piety was to be estimated.

To this objection thus considered, that the mention of Daniel in connection with Noah and Job, proves that Ezekiel referred to some one of ancient times, it may be further replied, that, if this were so, it is impossible to account for the fact that no such person is mentioned by any of the earlier prophets and writers. How came his name to be known to Ezekiel? And if there had been a patriarch so eminent as to be ranked with Noah and Job, how is it to be accounted for that all the sacred writers, up to the time of Ezekiel, are wholly silent in regard to him? And why is it that, when *he* mentions him, he does it as of one who was well known? The mere mention of his name in this manner by Ezekiel, proves that his character was well known to those for whom he wrote. Noah and Job were thus known by the ancient records; but how was *Daniel* thus known? He is nowhere mentioned in the ancient writings of the Hebrews ; and if he was so well known that he could be referred to in the same way as Noah and Job, it must be either because there was some *tradition* in regard to him, or because he was then living, and his character was well understood by those for whom Ezekiel wrote. But there is no evidence that there was any such tradition, and no probability that there was ; and the conclusion, then, is inevitable, that he was then so well known to the Hebrews in exile, that it was proper for Ezekiel to mention him just as he did Noah and Job. If so, this furnishes the highest evidence that he actually lived in the time of Ezekiel ; that is, in the time when this book purports to have been written.

§ II.— ANALYSIS OF THE CHAPTER.

This chapter is entirely historical, the prophetic portions of the book commencing with the second chapter. The *object* of this chapter seems to be to state the way in which Daniel, who subsequently acted so important a part in Babylon, was raised to so distinguished favour with the king and court. It was remarkable that a Jewish captive, and a young man, should be so honoured ; that he should be admitted as one of the principal counsellors of the king, and that he should ultimately become the prime-minister of the realm ; and there was a propriety that there should be a preliminary statement of the steps of this extraordinary promotion. This chapter contains a record of the way in which the future premier and prophet was introduced to the notice of the reigning monarch, and by which his wonderful genius and sagacity were discovered. It is a chapter, therefore, that may be full of interest and instruction to all, and especially to young men. The chapter contains the record

of the following points, or steps, which led to the promotion of Daniel :—

I. The history of the Jewish captivity, as explanatory of the reason why those who are subsequently referred to were in Babylon. They were exiles, having been conveyed as captives to a foreign land, vers. 1, 2.

II. The purpose of the king, Nebuchadnezzar, to bring forward the principal talent to be found among the Jewish captives, and to put it under a process of training, that it might be employed at the court, vers. 3, 4. In carrying out this purpose, a confidential officer of the court, Ashpenaz, was directed to search out among the captives the most promising youths, whether by birth or talent, and to put them under a process of training, that they might become fully instructed in the science of the Chaldeans. What were the reasons which led to this cannot be known with certainty. They may have been such as these : (1.) The Chaldeans had devoted themselves to science, especially to those sciences which promised any information respecting future events, the secrets of the unseen world, &c. Hence they either originated or adopted the science of astrology ; they practised the arts of magic; they studied to interpret dreams ; and, in general, they made use of all the means which it was then supposed could be employed to unlock the secrets of the invisible world, and to disclose the future. (2.) They could not have been ignorant of the fact, that the Hebrews claimed to have communications with God. They had doubtless heard of their prophets, and of their being able to foretell what was to occur. This kind of knowledge would fall in with the objects at which the Chaldeans aimed, and if they could avail themselves of it, it would enable them to secure what they so ardently sought. It is probable that they considered this as a sort of *permanent* power which the Hebrew prophets had, and supposed that at all times, and on all subjects, they could interpret dreams, and solve the various questions about which their own magicians were so much engaged. It is not to be presumed that they had any very accurate knowledge of the exact character of the Hebrew prophecies, or the nature of the communication which the prophets had with God; but it was not unnatural for them to suppose that this spirit of prophecy or divination would be possessed by the most noble and the most talented of the land. Hence Ashpenaz was instructed to select those of the royal family, and those in whom there was no blemish, and who were handsome, and who were distinguished for knowledge, and to prepare them, by a suitable course, for being presented to the king. (3.) It may have been the purpose of the Chaldean monarch to bring forward all the talent of the realm, whether native or foreign, to be employed in the service of the government. There is no reason to suppose that there was any jealousy of foreign talent, or any reluctance to employ it in any proper way, in promoting the interests of the kingdom. As the Chaldean monarch had now in his possession the Hebrew royal family, and all the principal men that had been distinguished in Judea, it was not unnatural to suppose that there might be valuable talent among them of which he might avail himself, and which would add to the splendour of his own court and cabinet. It might have been naturally supposed, also, that it would tend much to conciliate the captives themselves, and repress any existing impatience, or insubordination, to select the most noble and the most gifted of them, and to employ them in the service of the government; and in any questions that

might arise between the government and the captive nation, it would be an advantage for the government to be able to employ native-born Hebrews in making known the wishes and purposes of the government. It was, moreover, in accordance with the proud spirit of Nebuchadnezzar (see ch. iv.) to surround himself with all that would impart splendour to his own reign.

III. The method by which this talent was to be brought forward, vers. 5–7. This was by a course of living in the manner of the royal household, with the presumption that at the end of three years, in personal appearance, and in the knowledge of the language of the Chaldeans (ver. 4), they would be prepared to appear at court, and to be employed in the service to which they might be appointed.

IV. The resolution of Daniel not to corrupt himself with the viands which had been appointed for him and his brethren, ver. 8. He had heretofore been strictly temperate; he had avoided all luxurious living; he had abstained from wine; and, though now having all the means of luxurious indulgence at command, and being unexpectedly thrown into the temptations of a splendid Oriental court, he resolved to adhere stedfastly to his principles.

V. The apprehension of the prince of the eunuchs that this would be a ground of offence with his master, the king, and that he would himself be held responsible, vers. 9, 10. This was a very natural apprehension, as the command seems to have been positive, and as an Oriental monarch was entirely despotic. It was not unreasonable for him to suppose that a failure on his part to accomplish what he had been directed to do would be followed by a loss of place or life.

VI. The experiment, and the result,

CHAPTER I.

IN the third year of the reign of Jehoiakim king of Judah came

a Nebuchadnezzar king of Babylon unto Jerusalem, and besieged it.

a 2 Ki. 24. 1, 2; 2 Chr. 36. 6, 7.

vers. 11–17. Daniel asked that a trial might be made of the effects of temperance in preparing him and his companions for presentation at court. He requested that they might be permitted, even for a brief time, yet long enough to make a fair experiment, to abstain from wine, and the other luxuries of the royal table, and that then it might be determined whether they should be allowed to continue the experiment. The result was as he had anticipated. At the end of ten days, on a fair comparison with those who had indulged in luxurious living, the benefit of their course was apparent, and they were permitted to continue this strict abstinence during the remainder of the time which was deemed necessary for their preparation to appear at court.

VII. The presentation at court, vers. 18–21. At the end of the time appointed for preparation, Daniel and his selected companions were brought into the royal presence, and met with the most favourable reception which could have been hoped for. They were distinguished, it would seem, for beauty and manly vigour, and as much distinguished for wisdom as they were for the beauty and healthfulness of their bodily appearance. They at once took an honourable station, greatly surpassing in true wisdom and knowledge those at the court who were regarded as skilled in the arts of divination and astrology. These years of preparation we are not to suppose were spent in merely cultivating the beauty of their personal appearance, but they were doubtless employed, under all the advantages of instruction which could be afforded them, in the careful cultivation of their mental powers, and in the acquisition

of all the knowledge which could be obtained under the best masters at the court of the Chaldeans. Comp. ver. 4.

1. *In the third year of the reign of Jehoiakim king of Judah came Nebuchadnezzar king of Babylon unto Jerusalem.* This event occurred, according to Jahn (*History of the Hebrew Commonwealth*), in the year 607 B.C., and in the 368th year after the revolt of the ten tribes. According to Usher, it was in the 369th year of the revolt, and 606 B.C. The computation of Usher is the one generally received, but the difference of a year in the reckoning is not material. Comp. Michaelis, Anmerkung, zu 2 Kön. xxiv. 1. Jehoiakim was a son of Josiah, a prince who was distinguished for his piety, 2 Ki. xxii. 2 ; 2 Chron. xxxv. 1–7. After the death of Josiah, the people raised to the throne of Judah Jehoahaz, the youngest son of Josiah, probably because he appeared better qualified to reign than his elder brother, 2 Ki. xxiii. 30 ; 2 Chron. xxxvi. 1. He was a wicked prince, and after he had been on the throne three months, he was removed by Pharaoh-nechoh, king of Egypt, who returned to Jerusalem from the conquest of Phœnicia, and placed his elder brother, Eliakim, to whom he gave the name of Jehoiakim, on the throne, 2 Ki. xxiii. 34 ; 2 Chron. xxxvi. 4. Jehoahaz was first imprisoned in Riblah, 2 Ki. xxiii. 33, and was afterwards removed to Egypt, 2 Chron. xxxvi. 4. Jehoiakim, an unworthy son of Josiah, was, in reality, as he is represented by Jeremiah, one of the worst kings who reigned over Judah. His reign continued eleven years, and as he came to the throne B.C. 611, his reign continued to the year 600 B.C. In the third year of his reign, after the battle of Megiddo, Pharaoh-nechoh undertook a second expedition against Nabopolassar, king of Babylon, with a numerous army, drawn in part from Western Africa, Lybia, and Ethiopia.—Jahn's *Hist.*

2 And the Lord gave Jehoiakim king of Judah into his hand, with part of the vessels of the house of God, which he carried into the land

---

Heb. Commonwealth, p. 134. This Nabopolassar, who is also called Nebuchadnezzar I., was at this time, as Berosus relates, aged and infirm. He therefore gave up a part of his army to his son Nebuchadnezzar, who defeated the Egyptian host at Carchemish (Circesium) on the Euphrates, and drove Nechoh out of Asia. The victorious prince marched directly to Jerusalem, which was then under the sovereignty of Egypt. After a short siege Jehoiakim surrendered, and was again placed on the throne by the Babylonian prince. Nebuchadnezzar took part of the furniture of the temple as booty, and carried back with him to Babylon several young men, the sons of the principal Hebrew nobles, among whom were Daniel and his three friends referred to in this chapter. It is not improbable that one object in conveying them to Babylon was that they might be hostages for the submission and good order of the Hebrews in their own land. It is at this time that the Babylonian sovereignty over Judah commences, commonly called the Babylonian captivity, which, according to the prophecy of Jeremiah, (xxv. 1–14 ; xxix. 10), was to continue seventy years. In Jer. xxv. 1, and xlvi. 2, it is said that this was in the *fourth* year of Jehoiakim ; in the passage before us it is said that it was the *third* year. This difference, says Jahn, arises from a different mode of computation : " Jehoiakim came to the throne at the end of the year, which Jeremiah reckons as the first (and such a mode of reckoning is not uncommon), but Daniel, neglecting the incomplete year, numbers one less." For a more full and complete examination of the objection to the genuineness of Daniel from this passage, I would refer to Prof. Stuart on Daniel, *Excursus* I. [See App. I. to this Vol.] ¶ *And besieged it.* Jerusalem was a strongly-fortified place, and it was not easy to take it, except as the result of a siege. It was, perhaps, never carried by direct and immediate assault. Comp. 2 Ki. xxv. 1–3, for an account of a siege of Jerusalem a second time

by Nebuchadnezzar. At that time the city was besieged about a year and a half. How long the siege here referred to continued is not specified.

2. *And the Lord gave Jehoiakim king of Judah into his hand.* Jehoiakim was taken captive, and it would seem that there was an intention to convey him to Babylon (2 Chron. xxxvi. 6), but that for some cause he was not removed there, but died at Jerusalem (2 Ki. xxiv. 5, 6), though he was not honourably buried there, Jer. xxii. 19 ; xxxvi. 30. In the second book of Chronicles (xxxvi. 6), it is said that " Nebuchadnezzar king of Babylon came up, and bound Jehoiakim in fetters, to take him to Babylon." Jahn supposes that an error has crept into the text in the book of Chronicles, as there is no evidence that Jehoiakim was taken to Babylon, but it appears from 2 Ki. xxiv. 1, 2, that Jehoiakim was continued in authority at Jerusalem under Nebuchadnezzar three years, and then rebelled against him, and that then Nebuchadnezzar sent against him " bands of the Chaldees, and bands of the Syrians, and bands of the Moabites, and bands of the children of Ammon, and sent them against Judah to destroy it." There is no necessity of supposing an error in the text in the account in the book of Chronicles. It is probable that Jehoiakim was taken, and that the *intention* was to take him to Babylon, according to the account in Chronicles, but that, from some cause not mentioned, the purpose of the Chaldean monarch was changed, and that he was placed again over Judah, under Nebuchadnezzar, according to the account in the book of Kings, and that he remained in this condition for three years till he rebelled, and that then the bands of Chaldeans, &c., were sent against him. It is probable that at this time, perhaps while the siege was going on, he died, and that the Chaldeans dragged his dead body out of the gates of the city, and left it unburied, as Jeremiah had predicted, Jer. xxii. 19 ; xxxvi. 30. ¶ *With part of the vessels of the house of God.* 2 Chron. xxxvi. 7. Another portion of the

of Shinar, to the house of his god ;
and he brought the vessels into the
treasure-house of his god.

3 ¶ And the king spake unto

Ashpenaz the master of his eunuchs,
that he should bring *certain* of the
children *a* of Israel, and of the king's
seed, and of the princes ;

a Foretold, 2 Ki. 20. 17, 18; Is. 39. 7.

vessels of the temple at Jerusalem was
taken away by Nebuchadnezzar, in the
time of Jehoiachin, the successor of Jehoiakim, 2 Chron. xxxvi. 10. On the
third invasion of Palestine, the same
thing was repeated on a more extensive scale, 2 Ki. xxiv. 13. At the fourth
and final invasion, under Zedekiah,
when the temple was destroyed, all its
treasures were carried away, 2 Ki. xxv.
6–20. A part of these treasures were
brought back under Cyrus, Ezra i. 7 ;
the rest under Darius, Ezra vi. 5. Why
they were not *all* taken away at first
does not appear, but perhaps Nebuchadnezzar did not then intend wholly
to overthrow the Hebrew nation, but
meant to keep them tributary to him
as a people. The temple was not at
that time destroyed, but probably he
allowed the worship of Jehovah to be
celebrated there still, and he would
naturally leave such vessels as were absolutely necessary to keep up the services of public worship. ¶ *Which he
carried into the land of Shinar.* The
region around Babylon. The exact
limits of this country are unknown,
but it probably embraced the region
known as Mesopotamia—the country
between the rivers Tigris and Euphrates. The derivation of the name
Shinar is unknown. It occurs only in
Gen. x. 10 ; xi. 2 ; xiv. 1, 9 ; Josh. vii.
21 ; Isa. xi. 11 ; Dan. i. 2 ; Zech. v. 11.
¶ *To the house of his god.* To the
temple of Bel, at Babylon. This was
a temple of great magnificence, and the
worship of Bel was celebrated there
with great splendour. For a description of this temple, and of the god
which was worshipped there, see Notes
on Isa. xlvi. 1. These vessels were subsequently brought out at the command
of Belshazzar, at his celebrated feast,
and employed in the conviviality and
revelry of that occasion. See Dan. v. 3.
¶ *And he brought the vessels into the
treasure-house of his god.* It would
seem rom this that the vessels had been
taken to the temple of Bel, or Belus, in

Babylon, not to be used in the worship
of the idol, but to be laid up among
the valuable treasures there. As the
temples of the gods were sacred, and
were regarded as inviolable, it would
be natural to make them the repository of valuable spoils and treasures.
Many of the spoils of the Romans were
suspended around the walls of the
temples of their gods, particularly in
the temple of Victory. Compare Es-
chenberg, *Manual of Class. Lit.* pt. iii.
§ 149, 150.

3. *And the king spake unto Ashpenaz
the master of his eunuchs.* On the
general reasons which may have influenced the king to make the selection
of the youths here mentioned, see the
analysis of the chapter. Of Ashpenaz,
nothing more is known than is stated
here. Eunuchs were then, as they are
now, in constant employ in the harems
of the East, and they often rose to
great influence and power. A large
portion of the slaves employed at the
courts in the East, and in the houses
of the wealthy, are eunuchs. Comp.
Burckhardt's *Travels in Nubia,* pp.
294, 295. They are regarded as the
guardians of the female virtue of the
harem, but their situation gives them
great influence, and they often rise
high in the favour of their employers,
and often become the principal officers of the court. "The chief of the
black eunuchs is yet, at the court of
the Sultan, which is arranged much in
accordance with the ancient court of
Persia, an officer of the highest dignity.
He is called Kislar-Aga, the overseer
of the women, and is the chief of the
black eunuchs, who guard the harem,
or the apartments of the females. The
Kislar-Aga enjoys, through his situation, a vast influence, especially in
regard to the offices of the court, the
principal Agas deriving their situations
through him." See Jos. von Hammers
des Osmanischen Reichs Staatsverwalt,
Th. i. s. 71, as quoted in Rosenmüller's
Alte und neue Morgenland, ii. 357, 358.

[The figures in the annexed engravings are from the Nimroud sculptures, and represent two *eunuchs* holding high official rank in the royal

household of the Assyrian monarch. The one is the royal sceptre-bearer, and the other the

royal cup-bearer, the office of each being designated by the insignia he bears.]

That it is common in the East to desire that those employed in public service should have vigorous bodies, and beauty of form, and to train them for this, will be apparent from the following extract: —"Curtius says, that in all barbarous

or uncivilized countries, the stateliness of the body is held in great veneration ; nor do they think him capable of great services or action to whom nature has not vouchsafed to give a beautiful form and aspect. It has always been the custom of eastern nations to choose such for their principal officers, or to wait on princes and great personages. Sir Paul Ricaut observes, 'That the youths that are designed for the great offices of the Turkish empire must be of admirable features and looks, well shaped in their bodies, and without any defect of nature ; for it is conceived that a corrupt and sordid soul can scarcely inhabit in a serene and ingenuous aspect ; and I have observed, not only in the seraglio, but also in the courts of great men, their personal attendants have been of comely lusty youths, well habited, deporting themselves with singular modesty and respect in the presence of their masters ; so that when a Pascha Aga Spahi travels, he is always attended with a comely equipage, followed by flourishing youths, well clothed, and mounted, in great numbers.' "—Burder. This may serve to explain the reason of the arrangement made in respect to these Hebrew youths. ¶ *That he should bring certain of the children of Israel.* Heb., "of the *sons* of Israel." Nothing can with certainty be determined respecting their *age* by the use of this expression, for the phrase means merely the descendants of Jacob, or Israel, that is, *Jews*, and it would be applied to them at any time of life. It would seem, however, from subsequent statements, that those who were selected were young men. It is evident that young men would be better qualified for the object contemplated — to be *trained* in the language and the sciences of the Chaldeans (ver. 4)— than those who were at a more advanced period of life. ¶ *And of the king's seed, and of the princes.* That the most illustrious, and the most promising of them were to be selected ; those who would be most adapted to accomplish the object which he had in view. Compare the analysis of the chapter. It is probable that the king presumed, that among the royal youths

4 Children in whom *was* no blemish, but well-favoured, and skilful | in all wisdom, and cunning in knowledge, and understanding science,

who had been made captive there would be found those of most talent, and of course those best qualified to impart dignity and honour to his government, as well as those who would be most likely to be qualified to make known future events by the interpretation of dreams, and by the prophetic intimations of the Divine will.

4. *Children in whom* was *no blemish.* The word rendered *children* in this place (וְלָדִים) is different from that which is rendered *children* in ver. 3—בָּנִים. That word denotes merely that they were *sons,* or *descendants,* of Israel, without implying anything in regard to their age ; the word here used would be appropriate only to those who were at an early period of life, and makes it certain that the king meant that those who were selected should be youths. Comp. Gen. iv. 23, where the word is rendered "a young man." It is sometimes, indeed, used to denote a son, without reference to age, and is then synonymous with בֵּן *bēn, a son.* But it properly means *one born ;* that is, *recently born ;* a child, Gen. xxi. 8 ; Exod. i. 17 ; ii. 3 ; and then one in early life. There can be no doubt that the monarch meant to designate youths. So the Vulgate, *pueros,* and the Greek, νεανισκους, and so the Syriac. All these words would be applicable to those who were in early life, or to young men. Compare Intro. to Daniel, § I. The word *blemish* refers to bodily defect or imperfection. The object was to select those who were most perfect in form, perhaps partly because it was supposed that beautiful youths would most grace the court, and partly because it was supposed that such would be likely to have the brightest intellectual endowments. It was regarded as essential to personal beauty to be without blemish, 2 Sam. xiv. 25 : "But in all Israel there was none to be so much praised as Absalom for beauty ; from the sole of his foot even to the crown of his head there was no blemish in him." Canticles iv. 7 : "Thou art all fair, my love ; there is no spot in thee."

The word is sometimes used in a moral sense, to denote corruption of heart or life (Deut. xxxii. 5 ; Job xi. 15 ; xxxi. 7), but that is not the meaning here. ¶ *But well-favoured.* Heb., "good of appearance ;" that is, beautiful. ¶ *And skilful in all wisdom.* Intelligent, wise—that is, in all that was esteemed wise in their own country. The object was to bring forward the most talented and intelligent, as well as the most beautiful, among the Hebrew captives. ¶ *And cunning in knowledge.* In all that could be known. The distinction between the word here rendered *knowledge* (דַּעַת) and the word rendered *science* (מַדָּע) is not apparent. Both come from the word יָדַע *to know,* and would be applicable to any kind of knowledge. The word rendered *cunning* is also derived from the same root, and means *knowing,* or *skilled in.* We more commonly apply the word to a particular kind of knowledge, meaning artful, shrewd, astute, sly, crafty, designing. But this was not the meaning of the word when the translation of the Bible was made, and it is not employed in that sense in the Scriptures. It is always used in a good sense, meaning intelligent, skilful, experienced, well-instructed. Comp. Gen. xxv. 27 ; Exod. xxvi. 1 ; xxviii. 15 ; xxxviii. 23 ; 1 Sam. xvi. 16 ; 1 Chron. xxv. 7 ; Psal. cxxxvii. 5 ; Isa. iii. 3. ¶ *And understanding science.* That is, the sciences which prevailed among the Hebrews. They were not a nation distinguished for *science,* in the sense in which that term is now commonly understood — embracing astronomy, chemistry, geology, mathematics, electricity, &c. ; but their science extended chiefly to music, architecture, natural history, agriculture, morals, theology, war, and the knowledge of future events ; in all which they occupied an honourable distinction among the nations. In many of these respects they were, doubtless, far in advance of the Chaldeans ; and it was probably the purpose of the Chaldean monarch to avail himself of what they knew.

and such as *had* ability in them to stand in the king's palace, and whom | they might teach the learning and the tongue of the Chaldeans.

¶ *And such as* had *ability in them to stand in the king's palace.* Heb., "had *strength* " — כֹּחַ. Properly meaning, who had strength of body for the service which would be required of them in attending on the court. " A firm constitution of body is required for those protracted services of standing in the hall of the royal presence."— Grotius. The word *palace* here (הֵיכָל) is commonly used to denote the temple (2 Kings xxiv. 13 ; 2 Chron. iii. 17 ; Jer. l. 28 ; Hag. ii. 15. Its proper and primitive signification, however, is a large and magnificent building—a palace—and it was given to the temple as *the palace* of Jehovah, the abode where he dwelt as king of his people. ¶ *And whom they might teach.* That they might be better qualified for the duties to which they might be called. The purpose was, doubtless (see analysis), to bring forward their talent, that it might contribute to the splendour of the Chaldean court ; but as they were, doubtless, ignorant to a great extent of the language of the Chaldeans, and as there were sciences in which the Chaldeans were supposed to excel, it seemed desirable that they should have all the advantage which could be derived from a careful training under the best masters. ¶ *The learning* — סֵפֶר. Literally, *writing* (Isa. xxix. 11, 12). Gesenius supposes that this means the *writing* of the Chaldeans ; or that they might be able to read the language of the Chaldeans. But it, doubtless, included *the knowledge* of what was written, as well as the ability *to read* what was written ; that is, the purpose was to instruct them in the sciences which were understood among the Chaldeans. They were distinguished chiefly for such sciences as these : (1.) Astronomy. This science is commonly supposed to have had its origin on the plains of Babylon, and it was early carried there to as high a degree of perfection as it attained in any of the ancient nations. Their mild climate, and their employment as shepherds, leading them to pass much

of their time at night under the open heavens, gave them the opportunity of observing the stars, and they amused themselves in marking their positions and their changes, and in mapping out the heavens in a variety of fanciful figures, now called constellations. (2.) Astrology. This was at first a branch of astronomy, or was almost identical with it, for the stars were studied principally to endeavour to ascertain what influence they exerted over the fates of men, and especially what might be predicted from their position, on the birth of an individual, as to his future life. Astrology was then deemed a science whose laws were to be ascertained in the same way as the laws of any other science ; and the world has been slow to disabuse itself of the notion that the stars exert an influence over the fates of men. Even Lord Bacon held that it was a science to be *"reformed,"* not wholly rejected. (3.) Magic ; soothsaying ; divination ; or whatever would contribute to lay open the future, or disclose the secrets of the invisible world. Hence they applied themselves to the interpretation of dreams ; they made use of magical arts, probably employing, as magicians do, some of the ascertained results of science in producing optical illusions, impressing the vulgar with the belief that they were familiar with the secrets of the invisible world ; and hence the name *Chaldean* and *magician* became almost synonymous terms (Dan. ii. 2 ; iv. 7 ; v. 7. (4.) It is not improbable that they had made advances in other sciences, but of this we have little knowledge. They knew little of the true laws of astronomy, geology, chemistry, electricity, mathematics ; and in these, and in kindred departments of science, they may be supposed to have been almost wholly ignorant. ¶ *And the tongue of the Chaldeans.* In regard to the *Chaldeans*, see Notes on Job i. 17 ; and Isa. xxiii. 13. The kingdom of Babylon was composed mainly of Chaldeans, and that kingdom was called " the realm of the Chaldeans " (Dan. ix. 1). Of that realm, or kingdom, Babylon was the capital. The origin of the Chaldeans has been a subject of great perplexity, on which there is still a considerable variety of opinions. According to Heeren, they came from the North ; by Gesenius they are supposed to have come from the mountains of Kurdistan ; and by Michaelis, from the steppes of Scythia. They seem to have been an extended race, and probably occupied the whole of the region adjacent to what became Babylonia. Heeren expresses his opinion as to their origin in the following language : "It cannot be doubted that, at some remote period, antecedent to the commencement of historical records, *one mighty race* possessed these vast plains, varying in character according to the country which they inhabited ; in the deserts of Arabia, pursuing a nomad life ; in Syria, applying themselves to agriculture, and taking up settled abodes ; in Babylonia, erecting the most magnificent cities of ancient times ; and in Phœnicia, opening the earliest ports, and constructing fleets, which secured to them the commerce of the known world." There exists at the present time, in the vicinity of the Bahrein Islands, and along the Persian Gulf, in the neighbourhood of the Astan River, an Arab tribe, of the name of the *Beni Khaled,* who are probably the same people as the *Gens Chaldei* of Pliny, and doubtless the descendants of the ancient race of the Chaldeans. On the question when they became a kingdom, or realm, making Babylon their capital, see Notes on Isa. xxiii. 13. Compare, for an interesting discussion of the subject, Forster's *Historical Geography of Arabia,* vol. i. pp. 49–56. The language of the Chaldeans, in which a considerable part of the book of Daniel is written (see the Intro. § IV., III.), differed from the Hebrew, though it was a branch of the same Aramean family of languages. It was, indeed, very closely allied to the Hebrew, but was so different that those who were acquainted with only one of the two languages could not understand the other. Compare Neh. viii. 8. Both were the offspring of the original Shemitish language. This original language may be properly reduced to three great branches : (1.) The Aramean, which prevailed in Syria, Babylonia, and Mesopotamia ; and which may, therefore, be divided into the Syriac or West-Aramean, and the Chaldee or East-Aramean, called after the Babylonish Aramean. (2.) The Hebrew, with which the fragments of the Phœnician coincide. (3.) The Arabic, under which belongs the Ethiopic as a dialect. The Aramean, which, after the return from the Babylonish captivity, was introduced into Palestine, and which prevailed in the time of the Saviour, is commonly called the Syro-Chaldaic, because it was a mixture of the Eastern and Western dialects. The Chaldee, or East Aramean, and the Hebrew, had in general the same stock of original words, but they differed in several respects, such as the following : (a) Many words of the old primitive language which had remained in one dialect had been lost in the other. (b) The same word was current in both dialects, but in different significations, because in the one it retained the primitive signification, while in the other it had acquired a different meaning. (c) The Babylonian dialect had borrowed expressions from the Northern Chaldeans, who had made various irruptions into the country. These expressions were foreign to the Shemitish dialects, and belonged to the Japhetian language, which prevailed among the Armenians, the Medes, the Persians, and the Chaldeans, who were probaby related to these. Traces of these foreign words are found in the names of the officers of state, and in expressions having reference to the government. (d) The Babylonian pronunciation was more easy and more sonorous than the Hebrew. It exchanged the frequent sibilants of the Hebrew, and the other consonants which were hard to pronounce, for others which were less difficult : it dropped the long vowels which were not essential to the forms of words ; it preferred the more sonorous *a* to the long *o,* and assumed at the end of nouns, in order to lighten the pronunciation, a prolonged auxiliary vowel (the so-called emphatic א) ; it admitted

5 And the king appointed them a daily provision of the king's meat, and of the wine [1] which he drank ;

1 *Of his drink.*

so nourishing them three years, that at the end thereof they might stand before the king.

6 Now among these were of the

contractions in pronouncing many words, and must have been, as the language of common life, far better adapted to the sluggish Orientals than the harsher Hebrew. See an article "On the Prevalence of the Aramean Language in Palestine in the age of Christ and the Apostles," by Henry F. Pfannkuche, in the *Biblical Repository*, vol. i. pp. 318, 319. On this verse also, comp. Notes on Isa. xxxix. 7.

5. *And the king appointed them.* Calvin supposes that this arrangement was resorted to in order to render them effeminate, and, by a course of luxurious living, to induce them gradually to forget their own country, and that with the same view their names were changed. But there is no evidence that this was the object. The purpose was manifestly to train them in the manner in which it was supposed they would be best fitted, in bodily health, in personal beauty, and in intellectual attainments, to appear at court; and it was presumed that the best style of living which the realm furnished would conduce to this end. That the design was not to make them effeminate, is apparent from ver. 15. ¶ *A daily provision.* Heb., "The thing of a day in his day ;" that is, he assigned to them each day a portion of what had been prepared for the royal meal. It was not a permanent provision, but one which was made each day. The word rendered " provision "—פַּת *path* —means *a bit, crumb, morsel,* Gen. xviii. 5 ; Judg. xix. 5 ; Psa. cxlvii. 17. ¶ *Of the king's meat.* The word *meat* here means *food*, as it does uniformly in the Bible, the old English word having this signification when the translation was made, and not being limited then, as it is now, to animal food. The word in the original— בַּג *bág* —is of Persian origin, meaning *food*. The two words are frequently compounded —פַּתְבַּג *path-bag* (Dan. i. 5, 8, 13, 15, 16 ; xi. 26) ; and the compound means delicate food, dainties ; literally, food

of the father, *i.e.*, the king ; or, according to Lorsbach, in *Archiv. f. Morgcnl. Litt.* II. 313, food for idols, or the gods ; — in either case denoting delicate food ; luxurious living.—Gesenius, *Lex.* ¶ *And of the wine which he drank.* Marg., *of his drink.* Such wine as the king was accustomed to drink. It may be presumed that this was the best kind of wine. From anything that appears, this was furnished to them in abundance ; and with the leisure which they had, they could hardly be thrown into stronger temptation to excessive indulgence. ¶ *So nourishing them three years.* As long as was supposed to be necessary in order to develop their physical beauty and strength, and to make them well acquainted with the language and learning of the Chaldeans. The object was to prepare them to give as much dignity and ornament to the court as possible. ¶ *That at the end thereof they might stand before the king.* Notes, ver. 4. On the arrangements made to bring forward these youths, the editor of the *Pictorial Bible* makes the following remarks, showing the correspondence between these arrangements and what usually occurs in the East :— "There is not a single intimation which may not be illustrated from the customs of the Turkish seraglio, till some alterations were made in this, as in other matters, by the present sultan [Mahmoud]. The pages of the seraglio, and officers of the court, as well as the greater part of the public functionaries and governors of provinces, were originally Christian boys, taken captive in war, or bought or stolen in time of peace. The finest and most capable of these were sent to the palace, and, if accepted, were placed under the charge of the chief of the white eunuchs. The lads did not themselves become eunuchs ; which we notice, because it has been erroneously inferred, that Daniel and the other Hebrew youths *must* have been made eunuchs, *because* they were committed to the care of the

children of Judah, Daniel, Hananiah, Mishael, and Azariah ;

chief eunuch. The accepted lads were
brought up in the religion of their masters ; and there were schools in the
palace where they received such complete instruction in Turkish learning
and science as it was the lot of few
others to obtain. Among their accomplishments we find it mentioned, that
the greatest pains were taken to teach
them to speak the Turkish language (a
foreign one to them) with the greatest
purity, as spoken at court. Compare
this with ' Teach them the learning and
tongue of the Chaldeans.' The lads
were clothed very neatly, and well, but
temperately dieted. They slept in large
chambers, where there were rows of
beds. Every one slept separately ;
and between every third or fourth bed
lay a white eunuch, who served as a
sort of guard, and was bound to keep
a careful eye upon the lads near him,
and report his observations to his superior. When any of them arrived at
a proper age, they were instructed in
military exercises, and pains taken to
make them active, robust, and brave.
Every one, also, according to the custom of the country, was taught some
mechanical or liberal art, to serve him
as a resource in adversity. When their
education was completed in all its
branches, those who had displayed the
most capacity and valour were employed about the person of the king,
and the rest given to the service of
the treasury, and the other offices of
the extensive establishment to which
they belonged. In due time the more
talented or successful young men got
promoted to the various high court
offices which gave them access to the
private apartments of the seraglio, so
that they at almost any time could see
and speak to their great master. This
advantage soon paved the way for their
promotion to the government of provinces, and to military commands ; and
it has often happened that favourite
court officers have stepped at once into
the post of grand vizier, or chief minister, and other high offices of state,
without having previously been abroad
in the world as pashas and military

7 Unto whom the prince of the
eunuchs gave names : for he gave

commanders. How well this agrees to,
and illustrates the usage of the Babylonian court, will clearly appear to the
reader without particular indication.
See Habesci's *Ottoman Empire;* Taver-
nier's *Relation de l'Intérieur du Sérail
du Grand Seigneur.*"

6. *Now among these were of the children of Judah.* That is, these were a
part of those who were selected. They
are mentioned because they became so
prominent in the transactions which
are subsequently recorded in this book,
and because they evinced such extraordinary virtue in the development of
the principles in which they had been
trained, and in the remarkable trials
through which they were called to pass.
It does not appear that they are mentioned here particularly on account of
any distinction of birth or rank ; for
though they were among the noble and
promising youth of the land, yet it is
clear that others of the same rank and
promise also were selected, ver. 3. The
phrase "the children of Judah" is only
another term to denote that they were
Hebrews. They belonged to the tribe,
or the kingdom of Judah. ¶ *Daniel.*
This name (דָּנִיֵּאל) means properly *judge
of God;* that is, one who acts as judge
in the name of God. Why this name
was given to him is not known. We
cannot, however, fail to be struck with
its appropriateness, as the events of his
life showed. Nor is it known whether
he belonged to the royal family, or to
the nobles of the land, but as the selection was made from that class it is probable. Those who were at first carried
into captivity were selected exclusively
from the more elevated classes of society, and there is every reason to believe that Daniel belonged to a family
of rank and consequence. The Jews
say that he was of the royal family,
and was descended from Hezekiah, and
cite his history in confirmation of the
prophecy addressed by Isaiah to that
monarch, " Of thy sons which shall
issue from thee, which thou shalt beget,
shall they take away ; and they shall be
eunuchs in the palace of the king of

unto Daniel *the name* of Belteshazzar ; *a* and to Hananiah, of Sha-

drach ; and to Mishael, of Meshach ;
and to Azariah, of Abed-nego.

a ch. 4. 8; 5. 12.

Babylon," Isa. xxxix. 7.   Comp. Intro.
§ I.   ¶ *Hananiah, Mishael, and Aza-*
riah.   Of the rank and early history of
these young men nothing is known.
They became celebrated for their refusal to worship the golden image set up
by Nebuchadnezzar, ch. iii. 12, *seq.*
7. *Unto whom the prince of the*
eunuchs gave names. This practice is
common in Oriental courts.   "The
captive youths referred to in the notes
on ver. 5, in the Turkish court also
receive new names, that is, Mahometan
names, their former names being Christian."—*Pict. Bible.*   It is *possible* that
this changing of their names may have
been designed to make them forget
their country, and their religion, and
to lead them more entirely to identify
themselves with the people in whose
service they were now to be employed,
though nothing of this is intimated
in the history.   Such a change, it is
easy to conceive, might do much to
make them feel that they were identified with the people among whom they
were adopted, and to make them forget
the customs and opinions of their own
country.   It is a circumstance which
may give some additional probability
to this supposition, that it is quite a
common thing now at missionary stations to give new names to the children who are taken into the boarding-
schools, and especially the names of
the Christian benefactors at whose ex-
pense they are supported.   Compare
also Gen. xli. 45.   Another reason, of
the same general character, for this
change of names may have been, that
the name of the true God constituted
a part of their own names, and that
thus they were constantly reminded of
him and his worship.   In the new
names given them, the appellation of
some of the idols worshipped in Babylon was incorporated, and this might
serve as remembrancers of the divinities
to whose service it was doubtless the
intention to win them.   ¶ *For he gave*
unto Daniel the name *of Belteshazzar.*
The name Belteshazzar (בֵּלְטְשַׁאצַּר) is
compounded of two words, and means,

according to Gesenius, *Bel's prince ;*
that is, he whom Bel favours.   *Bel* was
the principal divinity worshipped at
Babylon (Notes, Isa. xlvi. 1), and this
name would, therefore, be likely to
impress the youthful Daniel with the
idea that he was a favourite of this
divinity, and to attract him to his service.   It was a flattering distinction
that he was one of the favourites of
the principal god worshipped in Babylon, and this was not improbably designed to turn his attention from the
God whose name had been incorporated
in his own.   The giving of this name
seemed to imply, in the apprehension
of Nebuchadnezzar, that the spirit of
the gods was in him on whom it was
conferred.   See ch. iv. 8, 9.   ¶ *And*
to Hananiah, of Shadrach.   The name
Hananiah (חֲנַנְיָה) means, "whom Jehovah has graciously given," and is
the same with Ananias (Gr., Ἀνανίας),
and would serve to remind its possessor
of the name of *Jehovah,* and of his
mercy.   The name *Shadrach* (שַׁדְרַךְ),
according to Lorsbach, means *young*
friend of the king ; according to Bohlen, it means *rejoicing in the way,* and
this last signification is the one which
Gesenius prefers.   In either signification it would contribute to a forgetfulness of the interesting significancy of
the former name, and tend to obliterate
the remembrance of the early training
in the service of Jehovah.   ¶ *And*
to Mishael, of Meshach.   The name
Mishael (מִישָׁאֵל) means, *who is what*
God is ?—from מִי *who,* שׁ *what,* and אֵל
God. It would thus be a remembrancer
of the greatness of God ; of his supremacy over all his creatures, and of his
incomparable exaltation over the universe.   The signification of the name
Meshach (מֵישַׁךְ) is less known.   The
Persian word means *ovicula,* a little
sheep (Gesenius), but why this name
was given we are not informed.   Might
it have been on account of his beauty,
his gentleness, his lamb-like disposition?   If so, nothing perhaps would be
better fitted to turn away the thoughts

8 ¶ But Daniel purposed in his heart that he would not defile him- self with the portion *a* of the king's

from the great God and his service to himself. ¶ *And to Azariah, of Abed- nego.* The name *Azariah* (עֲזַרְיָה) means, *whom Jehovah helps,* from עָזַר *to help,* and יָהּ, the same as *Jehovah.* This name, therefore, had a striking significancy, and would be a constant remembrancer of the true God, and of the value of his favour and protection. The name *Abed-nego* (עֲבֵד נְגוֹ) means, *a servant of Nego,* or perhaps of *Nebo* —נְבוֹ. This word *Nebo,* among the Chaldeans, probably denoted the planet Mercury. This planet was worshipped by them, and by the Arabs, as the celestial scribe or writer. See Notes on Isa. xlvi. 1. The Divine worship paid to this planet by the Chaldeans is attested, says Gesenius, by the many compound proper names of which this name forms a part ; as Nebuchadnezzar, Nebushasban, and others mentioned in classic writers ; as Nabonedus, Nabo- nassar, Nabonabus, &c. This change of name, therefore, was designed to denote a consecration to the service of this idol-god, and the change was emi- nently adapted to make him to whom it was given forget the true God, to whom, in earlier days, he had been devoted. It was only extraordinary grace which could have kept these youths in the paths of their early train- ing, and in the faithful service of that God to whom they had been early consecrated, amidst the temptations by which they were now surrounded in a foreign land, and the influences which were employed to alienate them from the God of their fathers.

8. *But Daniel purposed in his heart.* Evidently in concurrence with the youths who had been selected with him. See vers. 11-13. Daniel, it seems, formed this as a *decided* purpose, and *meant* to carry it into effect, as a mat- ter of principle, though he designed to secure his object, if possible, by making a request that he might be *allowed* to pursue that course (ver. 12), and wished not to give offence, or to provoke op- position. What would have been the result if he had not obtained permission

we know not ; but the probability is, that he would have thrown himself upon the protection of God, as he after- wards did (ch. vi.), and would have done what he considered to be duty, regardless of consequences. The course which he took saved him from the trial, for the prince of the eunuchs was will- ing to allow him to make the experi- ment, ver. 14. It is always better, even where there is decided principle, and a settled purpose in a matter, to obtain an object by a peaceful request, than to attempt to secure it by violence. ¶ *That he would not defile himself with the portion of the king's meat.* Notes, ver. 5. The word which is rendered *defile himself*—רִֽתְגָּאַל from גָּאַל—is com- monly used in connection with *redemp- tion,* its first and usual meaning being to redeem, to ransom. In later Hebrew, however, it means, to be defiled ; to be polluted, to be unclean. The *connection* between these significations of the word is not apparent, unless, as redemption was accomplished with the shedding of blood, rendering the place where it was shed defiled, the idea came to be per- manently attached to the word. The defilement here referred to in the case of Daniel probably was, that by partak- ing of this food he might, in some way, be regarded as countenancing idolatry, or as lending his sanction to a mode of living which was inconsistent with his principles, and which was perilous to his health and morals. The Syriac renders this simply, *that he would not eat,* without implying that there would be defilement. ¶ *Nor with the wine which he drank.* As being contrary to his principles, and perilous to his morals and happiness. ¶ *Therefore he requested of the prince of the eunuchs that he might not defile himself.* That he might be permitted to abstain from the luxu- ries set before him. It would seem from this, that he represented to the prince of the eunuchs the real danger which he apprehended, or the real cause why he wished to abstain—that he would regard the use of these viands as con- trary to the habits which he had formed, as a violation of the principles of his

meat, nor with the wine which he drank : therefore he requested of the prince of the eunuchs that he might not defile himself.

religion ; and as, in his circumstances, wrong as well as perilous. This he presented as a *request*. He asked it, therefore, as a favour, preferring to use mild and gentle means for securing the object, rather than to put himself in the attitude of open resistance to the wishes of the monarch. What *reasons* influenced him to choose this course, and to ask to be permitted to live on a more temperate and abstemious diet, we are not informed. Assuming, however, what is apparent from the whole narrative, that he had been educated in the doctrines of the true religion, and in the principles of temperance, it is not difficult to conceive what reasons *would* influence a virtuous youth in such circumstances, and we cannot be in much danger of error in suggesting the following : (1.) It is not improbable that the food which was offered him had been, in some way, connected with idolatry, and that his participation in it would be construed as countenancing the worship of idols.—Calvin. It is known that a part of the animals offered in sacrifice was sold in the market ; and known, also, that splendid entertainments were often made in honour of particular idols, and on the sacrifices which had been offered to them. Compare 1 Cor. viii. Doubtless, also, a considerable part of the food which was served up at the royal table consisted of articles which, by the Jewish law, were prohibited as unclean. It was represented by the prophets, as one part of the evils of a captivity in a foreign land, that the people would be under a necessity of eating that which was regarded as unclean. Thus, in Ezek. iv. 13 : "And the Lord said, Even thus shall the children of Israel eat their defiled bread among the Gentiles, whither I will drive them." Hos. ix. 3 : "They shall not dwell in the Lord's land, but Ephraim shall return to Egypt ; and shall eat unclean things in Assyria." Rosenmüller remarks on this passage (*Alte u. neue Morgenland*, 1076), "It was customary among the ancients to bring a portion of that which was eaten and drank as an offering to the gods, as a sign of thankful recognition that all which men enjoy is their gift. Among the Romans these gifts were called *libamina*, so that with each meal there was connected an act of offering. Hence Daniel and his friends regarded that which was brought from the royal table as food which had been offered to the gods, and therefore as impure." (2.) Daniel and his friends were, doubtless, restrained from partaking of the food and drink offered to them by a regard to the principles of temperance in which they had been educated, and by a fear of the consequences which would follow from indulgence. They had evidently been trained in the ways of strict temperance. But now new scenes opened to them, and new temptations were before them. They were among strangers. They were noticed and flattered. They had an opportunity of indulging in the pleasures of the table, such as captive youth rarely enjoyed. This opportunity, there can be no doubt, they regarded as a temptation to their virtue, and as in the highest degree perilous to their principles, and they, therefore, sought to resist the temptation. They were captives—exiles from their country—in circumstances of great depression and humiliation, and they did not wish to forget that circumstance.— Calvin. Their land was in ruins ; the temple where they and their fathers had worshipped had been desecrated and plundered ; their kindred and countrymen were pining in exile ; everything called them to a mode of life which would be in accordance with these melancholy facts, and they, doubtless, felt that it would be in every way inappropriate for them to indulge in luxurious living, and revel in the pleasures of a banquet. But they were also, doubtless, restrained from these indulgences by a reference to the dangers which would follow. It required not great penetration or experience, indeed, to perceive, that in their circumstances —young men as they were, suddenly noticed and honoured — compliance would be perilous to their virtue ; but

9 Now God had brought Daniel into favour *a* and tender love with the prince of the eunuchs.

10 And the prince of the eunuchs

it did require uncommon strength of principle to meet the temptation. Rare has been the stern virtue among young men which could resist so strong allurements ; seldom, comparatively, have those who have been unexpectedly thrown, in the course of events, into the temptations of a great city in a foreign land, and flattered by the attention of those in the higher walks of life, been sufficiently firm in principle to assert the early principles of temperance and virtue in which they may have been trained. Rare has it been that a youth in such circumstances would form the steady purpose not to "defile himself" by the tempting allurements set before him, and that, at all hazards, he would adhere to the principles in which he had been educated.

9. *Now God had brought Daniel into favour.* Comp. Gen. xxxix. 21 ; Prov. xvi. 7. By what means this had been done is not mentioned. It may be presumed, however, that it was by the attractiveness of his person and manners, and by the evidence of promising talent which he had evinced. Whatever were the means, however, two things are worthy of notice : (1.) The effect of this on the subsequent fortunes of Daniel. It was to him a great advantage, that by the friendship of this man he was enabled to carry out the purposes of temperance and religion which he had formed, without coming in conflict with those who were in power. (2.) God was the author of the favour which was thus shown to Daniel. It was by a controlling influence which he exerted, that this result had been secured, and Daniel traced it directly to him. We may hence learn that the favour of others towards us is to be traced to the hand of God, and if we are prospered in the world, and are permitted to enjoy the friendship of those who have it in their power to benefit us, though it may be on account of our personal qualifications, we should learn to attribute it all to God. There

said unto Daniel, I fear my lord the king, who hath appointed your meat and your drink : for why should he see your faces [1] worse liking than

[1] *sadder.*

would have been great reason to apprehend beforehand, that the refusal of Daniel and his companions to partake of the food prepared for them would have been construed as an affront offered to the king, especially if it was understood to be on the ground that they regarded it as *defilement* or *pollution* to partake of it ; but God overruled it all so as to secure the favour of those in power.

10. *And the prince of the eunuchs said unto Daniel, I fear my lord the king.* He was apprehensive that if Daniel appeared less healthful, or cheerful, or beautiful, than it was supposed he would under the prescribed mode of life, it would be construed as disobedience of the commands of the king on his part, and that it would be inferred that the wan and emaciated appearance of Daniel was caused by the fact that the food which had been ordered had not been furnished, but had been embezzled' by the officer who had it in charge. We have only to remember the strict and arbitrary nature of Oriental monarchies to see that there were just grounds for the apprehensions here expressed. ¶ *For why should he see your faces worse liking.* Marg., *sadder.* The Hebrew word (זֹעֲפִים) means, properly, angry; and then morose, gloomy, sad. The primary idea seems to be, that of *any* painful, or unpleasant emotion of the mind which depicts itself on the countenance—whether anger, sorrow, envy, lowness of spirits, &c. Greek, σκυθρωπὰ—stern, gloomy, sad, Matt. vi. 16 ; Luke xxiv. 17. Here the reference is not to the expression of angry feelings in the countenance, but to the countenance as fallen away by fasting, or poor living. ¶ *Than the children.* The youths, or young men. The same word is here used which occurs in ver. 4. Comp. Notes on that verse. ¶ *Which are of your sort.* Marg., *term,* or *continuance.* The Hebrew word here used (גִּיל) means,

the children which *are* of your ¹ sort? then shall ye make *me* endanger my head to the king.

11 Then said Daniel to ² Melzar, whom the prince of the eunuchs

1 or, *term*, or *continuance*. 　 2 or, *the steward*.

properly, a circle, or circuit ; hence an age, and then the men of an age, a generation.—*Gesenius.* The word is not used, however, in the Scriptures elsewhere in this sense. Elsewhere it is rendered *joy*, or *rejoicing*, Job iii. 22 ; Psa. xliii. 4 ; xlv. 15 ; lxv. 12 ; Prov. xxiii. 24 ; Isa. xvi. 10 ; xxxv. 2 ; lxv. 18 ; Jer. xlviii. 33 ; Hos. ix. 1 ; Joel i. 16. This meaning it has from the usual sense of the verb גִּיל *to exult*, or *rejoice.* The verb properly means, to move in a circle ; then to *dance* in a circle ; and then to exult or rejoice. The word "*circle*," as often used now to denote those of a certain class, rank, or character, would accurately express the sense here. Thus we speak of those in the *religious* circles, in the *social* circles, &c. The reference here is to those of the same class with Daniel ; to wit, in the arrangements made for pre-senting them before the king. Greek, συνήλικα ὑμῶν, *of your own.* ¶ *Then shall ye make* me *endanger my head to the king.* As if he had disregarded the orders given him, or had embezzled what had been provided for these youths, and had furnished them with inferior fare. In the arbitrary courts of the East, nothing would be more natural than that such an apparent failure in the performance of what was enjoined would peril his life. The word here used, and rendered *make me endanger*— חוּב—occurs nowhere else in the Bible. It means, in Piel, to make guilty ; to cause to forfeit. Greek, καταδικάσητε —you will condemn, or cause me to be condemned.

11. *Then said Daniel to Melzar, whom the prince of the eunuchs had set over Daniel,* &c. Marg., or, *the steward.* It is not easy to determine whether the word here used (מֶלְצַר *Meltzar*) is to be regarded as a proper name, or the name of an office. It occurs nowhere else, except in ver. 16 of this chapter, applied to the same person. Gesenius regards

had set over Daniel, Hananiah Mishael, and Azariah,

12 Prove thy servants, I beseech thee, ten days ; and let them give us ³ pulse to eat, and water to drink.

3 *of pulse that we may eat.*

it as denoting the name of an office in the Babylonian court—master of the wine, chief butler. Others regard it as meaning a treasurer. The word is still in use in Persia. The Vulgate renders it as a proper name—*Malasar ;* and so the Syriac—*Meshitzar ;* and so the Greek—Ἀμελσὰδ, *Amelsad.* The use of the *article* in the word (הַמֶּלְצַר) would seem to imply that it denoted the name of an *office*, and nothing would be more probable than that the actual furnishing of the daily portion of food would be intrusted to a steward, or to some incumbent of an office inferior to that sustained by Ashpenaz, ver. 3.

12. *Prove thy servants, I beseech thee, ten days.* A period which would indicate the probable result of the entire experiment. If during that period there were no indications of diminished health, beauty, or vigour, it would not be unfair to presume that the experiment in behalf of temperance would be successful, and it would not be improper then to ask that it might be continued longer. ¶ *And let them give us pulse to eat.* Marg., *of pulse that we may eat.* Heb., "Let them give us of pulse, and we will eat." The word *pulse* with us means leguminous plants with thin seeds ; that is, plants with a pericarp, or seed-vessel, of two valves, having the seeds fixed to one suture only. In popular language the *legume* is called a *pod ;* as a *pea-pod*, or *bean-pod*, and the word is commonly applied to pease or beans. The Hebrew word (זֵרֹעִים) would properly have reference to seeds of any kind—from זָרַע *zără*, to disperse, to scatter seed, to sow. Then it would refer to plants that bear seed, of all kinds, and would be by no means limited to pulse—as pease or beans. It is rendered by Gesenius, "*seed-herbs, greens, vegetables; i. e.,* vegetable food, such as was eaten in a half-fast, opposed to meats and the more delicate kinds of food." The word

13 Then let our countenances be looked upon before thee, and the countenance of the children that eat of the portion of the king's meat; and as thou seest, deal with thy servants.

14 So he consented to them in this matter, and proved them ten days.

15 And at the end of ten days their countenances appeared fairer and fatter in flesh than all the chil-

---

occurs only here and in ver. 16. It is rendered in the Vulgate, *legumina ;* and in the Greek, ἀπὸ τῶν σπερμάτων— "from seeds." It is not a proper construction to limit this to *pulse*, or to suppose that Daniel desired to live solely on pease or beans ; but the fair interpretation is to apply it to that which grows up from *seeds*—such, probably, as would be sown in a garden, or, as we would now express it, *vegetable diet.* It was designed as an experiment—and was a very interesting one—to show the legitimate effect of such a diet in promoting beauty and health, and the result is worthy of special notice as contrasted with a more luxurious mode of life. ¶ *And water to drink.* This, also, was a most interesting and important experiment, to show that wine was not necessary to produce healthfulness of appearance, or manly strength and beauty. It was an experiment to illustrate the effect of *cold water* as a beverage, made by an interesting group of young men, when surrounded by great temptations, and is, therefore, worthy of particular attention.

13. *Then let our countenances be looked upon.* One of the *objects* to be secured by this whole trial was to promote their personal beauty, and their healthful appearance (vers. 4, 5), and Daniel was willing that the trial should be made with reference to that, and that a judgment should be formed from the observed effect of their temperate mode of life. The Hebrew word rendered *countenance* (מַרְאֵה) is not limited to *the face*, as the word countenance is with us. It refers to the whole appearance, the form, the "*looks ;*" and the expression here is equivalent to, "*Then look on us*, and see what the result has been, and deal with us accordingly." The Greek is, αἱ ἰδέαι ἡμῶν—*our appearance.* ¶ *Of the children.* Youths ; young men. Notes,

ver. 4. The reference is, probably, to the Chaldean youths who were trained up amidst the luxuries of the court. It is possible, however, that the reference is to Hebrew youths who were less scrupulous than Daniel and his companions. ¶ *And as thou seest, deal with thy servants.* As the result shall be. That is, let us be presented at court, and promoted or not, as the result of our mode of living shall be. What the effect would have been if there had been a failure, we are not informed. Whether it would have endangered their lives, or whether it would have been merely a forfeiture of the proffered honours and advantages, we have no means of determining. It is evident that Daniel had no apprehension as to the issue.

14. *So he consented to them in this matter.* Heb., "he *heard* them in this thing." The experiment was such, since it was to be for so short a time, that he ran little risk in the matter, as at the end of the ten days he supposed that it would be easy to change their mode of diet if the trial was unsuccessful.

15. *And at the end of ten days their countenances appeared fairer.* Heb., "*good ;*" that is, they appeared more beautiful and healthful. The experiment was successful. There was no diminution of beauty, of vigour, or of the usual indications of health. One of the results of a course of temperance appears in the countenance, and it is among the wise appointments of God that it should be so. He has so made us, that while the other parts of the body may be protected from the gaze of men, it is necessary that the *face* should be exposed. Hence he has made the countenance the principal seat of expression, for the chief muscles which indicate expression have their location there. See the valuable work of Sir Charles Bell on *the Anatomy of Expression*, London, 1844. Hence there are certain marks of guilt and

dren which did eat the portion of the king's meat.

16 Thus Melzar took away the portion of their meat, and the wine that they should drink, and gave them pulse.

---

vice which always are indicated in the countenance. God has so made us that the drunkard and the glutton must proclaim their own guilt and shame. The bloated face, the haggard aspect, the look of folly, the "heaviness of the eye, the disposition to squint, and to see double, and a forcible elevation of the eyebrow to counteract the dropping of the upper eyelid, and preserve the eyes from closing," are all marks which God has appointed to betray and expose the life of indulgence. "Arrangements are made for these expressions in the very anatomy of the face, and no art of man can prevent it."—Bell on the *Anatomy of Expression*, p. 106. God meant that if man *would* be intemperate he should himself proclaim it to the world, and that his fellow-men should be apprised of his guilt. This was intended to be one of the safeguards of virtue. The young man who will be intemperate *knows* what the result must be. He is apprised of it in the loathsome aspect of every drunkard whom he meets. He knows that if he yields himself to indulgence in intoxicating drink, he must soon proclaim it himself to the wide world. No matter how beautiful, or fresh, or blooming, or healthful, he may now be; no matter how bright the eye, or ruddy the cheek, or eloquent the tongue; the eye, and the cheek, and the tongue will soon become indices of his manner of life, and the loathsomeness and offensiveness of the once beautiful and blooming countenance must pay the penalty of his folly. And in like manner, and for the same reason, the countenance is an indication of temperance and purity. The bright and steady eye, the blooming cheek, the lips that eloquently or gracefully utter the sentiments of virtue, proclaim the purity of the life, and are the natural indices to our fellow-men that we live in accordance with the great and benevolent laws of our nature, and are among the rewards of temperance and virtue.*

* "In reviewing the disclosures made by the

16. *Thus Melzar took away the portion of their meat, &c.* Doubtless permanently. The experiment had been satisfactory, and it was inferred that if the course of temperance could be practised for ten days without unhappy results, there would be safety in suffering it to be continued. We may remark on this: I. That the experiment was a most important one, not only for the object then immediately in view, but for furnishing lessons of permanent instruction adapted to future times. It was worth one such trial, and it was desirable to have one such illustration of the effect of temperance recorded. There are so strong propensities in our nature to indulgence; there are so many temptations set before the young; there is so much that allures in a luxurious mode of life, and so much of conviviality and happiness is supposed to be connected with the social glass, that it was well to have a fair trial made, and that the result should be recorded for the instruction of future times. II. It was especially desirable that the experiment should be made of the effect of strict abstinence from the use of *wine*. Distilled liquors were indeed then unknown; but alcohol, the intoxicating principle in all ardent spirits, then

narrative contained in verses 12–17, it seems plain, that the writer meant to exhibit the thriving state of the lads upon their slender diet, as a special blessing of Providence upon their *pious resolution;* for so, in the view of the Mosaic prescriptions, it would seem that it ought to be called. Yet it is not certain that the writer intends their thrift to be regarded by his readers as strictly?*miraculous.* Certainly, in a climate so excessively hot as that of Babylon, a vegetable diet, for many months in the year, would be better adapted to occasion fairness of countenance and fulness of flesh than a luxurious diet of various highly-seasoned meats. That the God of heaven *rewarded* the pious resolution and the persevering abstinence of the Jewish lads, lies upon the face of the narrative; and this is a truth adapted to useful admonition, specially to the Jews who dwelt among the heathen, and were under strong temptations to transgress the Mosaic laws. The uncommon and extraordinary powers which were conferred upon these young Hebrews are placed in such a light, as to show that their peculiar gifts were the consequence of their pious resolution and firmness."—Stuart.

existed, as it does now, in wine, and was then, as it is now, of the same nature as when found in other substances. It was in the use of wine that the principal danger of intemperance then lay ; and it may be added, that in reference to a very large class of persons of both sexes, it is in the use of wine that the principal danger always lies. There are multitudes, especially of young men, who are in little or no danger of becoming intemperate from the use of the stronger kinds of intoxicating drinks. They would never *begin* with them. But the use of *wine* is so respectable in the view of the upper classes of society ; it is deemed so essential to the banquet ; it constitutes so much, apparently, a mark of distinction, from the fact that ordinarily only the rich can afford to indulge in it ; its use is regarded extensively as so proper for even refined and delicate females, and is so often sanctioned by their participating in it ; it is so difficult to frame an argument against it that will be decisive ; there is so much that is plausible that may be said in favour or in justification of its use, and it is so much sanctioned by the ministers of religion, and by those of influence in the churches, that one of the principal dangers of the young arises from the temptation to indulgence in wine, and it was well that there should be a fair trial of the comparative benefit of total abstinence. A trial could scarcely have been made under better circumstances than in the case before us. There was every inducement to indulgence which is ever likely to occur ; there was as much to make it a mere matter of *principle* to abstain from it as can be found now in any circumstances, and the experiment was as triumphant and satisfactory as could be desired. III. The result of the experiment. (*a*) It was complete and satisfactory. *More* was accomplished in the matter of the trial by abstinence than by indulgence. Those who abstained were more healthful, more beautiful, more vigorous than the others. And there was nothing miraculous— nothing that occurred in that case which does not occur in similar cases. Sir J. Chardin remarks, respecting

those whom he had seen in the East, "that the countenances of the kechicks [monks] are in fact more rosy and smooth than those of others ; and that those who fast much, I mean the Armenians and the Greeks, are, notwithstanding, very beautiful, sparkling with health, with a clear and lively countenance." He also takes notice of the very great abstemiousness of the Brahmins in the Indies, who lodge on the ground, abstain from music, from all sorts of agreeable smells, who go very meanly clothed, are almost always wet, either by going into water, or by rain ; "yet," says he, " I have seen also many of them very handsome and healthful."—Harmer's *Observa*. ii. pp. 112, 113. (*b*) The experiment has often been made, and with equal success, in modern times, and especially since the commencement of the temperance reformation, and an opportunity has been given of furnishing the most decisive proofs of the effects of temperance in contrast with indulgence in the use of wine and of other intoxicating drinks. This experiment has been made on a wide scale, and with the same result. It is demonstrated, as in the case of Daniel, that "MORE" will be secured of that which men are so anxious usually to obtain, and of that which it is desirable to obtain, than can be by indulgence. (1.) There will be " more " beauty of personal appearance. Indulgence in intoxicating drinks leaves its traces on the countenance— the skin, the eye, the nose, the whole expression—as God *meant* it should. See Notes on ver. 15. No one can hope to retain beauty of complexion or countenance who indulges freely in the use of intoxicating drinks. (2.) "More" clearness of mind and intellectual vigour can be secured by abstinence than by indulgence. It is true that, as was often the case with Byron and Burns, stimulating drinks may excite the mind to brilliant temporary efforts ; but the effect soon ceases, and the mind makes a compensation for its over-worked powers by sinking down below its proper level as it had been excited above. It will demand a penalty in the exhausted energies, and in the incapacity for even its usual efforts, and unless

17 ¶ As for these four children, God gave them knowledge and skill in all learning and wisdom : and

the exhausting stimulus be again applied, it cannot rise even to its usual level, and when often applied the mind is divested of *all* its elasticity and vigour ; the physical frame loses its power to endure the excitement ; and the light of genius is put out, and the body sinks to the grave. He who wishes to make the most of his mind *in the long run*, whatever genius he may be endowed with, will be a temperate man. His powers will be retained uniformly at a higher elevation, and they will maintain their balance and their vigour longer. (3.) The same is true in regard to everything which requires vigour of body. The Roman soldier, who carried his eagle around the world, and who braved the dangers of every clime—equally bold and vigorous, and hardy, and daring amidst polar snows, and the burning sands of the equator—was a stranger to intoxicating drinks. He was allowed only vinegar and water, and his extraordinary vigour was the result of the most abstemious fare. The wrestlers in the Olympic and Isthmian games, who did as much to give suppleness, vigour, and beauty to the body, as could be done by the most careful training, abstained from the use of wine and all that would enervate. Since the temperance reformation commenced in this land, the experiment has been made in every way possible, and it has been *settled* that a man will do more work, and do it better; that he can bear more fatigue, can travel farther, can better endure the severity of cold in the winter, and of toil in the heat of summer, by strict temperance, than he can if he indulges in the use of intoxicating drinks. Never was the result of an experiment more uniform than this has been ; never has there been a case where the testimony of those who have had an opportunity of witnessing it was more decided and harmonious ; never was there a question in regard to the effect of a certain course on health in which the testimony of physicians has been more uniform ; and never has there been a question in

1 Daniel had understanding in all visions and dreams.

1 or, *he made Daniel understand.*

regard to the amount of labour which a man could do, on which the testimony of respectable farmers, and master mechanics, and overseers of public works, could be more decided. (4.) The full force of these remarks about temperance in general, applies to the use of *wine.* It was in respect to *wine* that the experiment before us was made, and it is this which gives it, in a great degree, its value and importance. Distilled spirits were then unknown, but it was of importance that a fair experiment should be made of the effect of abstinence from wine. The great danger of intemperance, taking the world at large, has been, and is still, from the use of wine. This danger affects particularly the upper classes in society and young men. It is by the use of wine, in a great majority of instances, that the peril commences, and that the habit of drinking is formed. Let it be remembered, also, that the intoxicating principle is the same in wine as in any other drink that produces intemperance. It is *alcohol*— the same substance precisely, whether it be driven off by heat from wine, beer, or cider, and condensed by distillation, or whether it remain in these liquids without being distilled. It is neither more nor less intoxicating in one form than it is in the other. It is only more condensed and concentrated in one case than in the other ; better capable of preservation, and more convenient for purposes of commerce. Every *principle*, therefore, which applies to the temperance cause at all, applies to the use of wine ; and every consideration derived from health, beauty, vigour, length of days, reputation, property, or salvation, which should induce a young man to abstain from ardent spirits at all should induce him to abstain, as Daniel did, from the use of wine.

17. *As for these four children.* On the word *children*, see Notes on ver. 4. Comp. ver. 6. ¶ *God gave them knowledge and skill.* See Notes on ver. 9. There is no reason to suppose that in

18 Now at the end of the days | that the king had said he should

the "knowledge and skill" here referred to, it is meant to be implied that there was anything miraculous, or that there was any direct inspiration. Inspiration was evidently confined to Daniel, and pertained to what is spoken of under the head of "visions and dreams." The fact that all this was to be attributed to God as his gift, is in accordance with the common method of speaking in the Scriptures; and it is also in accordance with *fact*, that all knowledge is to be traced to God. See Exod. xxxi. 2, 3. God formed the intellect; he preserves the exercise of reason; he furnishes us instructors; he gives us clearness of perception; he enables us to take advantage of bright thoughts and happy suggestions which occur in our own minds, as much as he sends rain, and dew, and sunshine on the fields of the husbandman, and endows him with skill. Comp. Isa. xxviii. 26, "For his God doth instruct him." The knowledge and skill which we may acquire, therefore, should be as much attributed to God as the success of the farmer should. Comp. Job xxxii. 8, "For there is a spirit in man, and the inspiration of the Almighty giveth them understanding." In the case before us, there is no reason to doubt that the natural powers of these young men had been diligently applied during the three years of their trial (ver. 5), and under the advantages of a strict course of temperance; and that the knowledge here spoken of was the result of such an application to their studies. On the meaning of the words "knowledge" and "skill" here, see Notes on ver. 4. ¶ *In all learning and wisdom.* See also Notes on ver. 4. ¶ *And Daniel had understanding.* Showing that in that respect there was a special endowment in his case; a kind of knowledge imparted which could be communicated only by special inspiration. The margin is, *he made Daniel understand.* The margin is in accordance with the Hebrew, but the sense is the same. ¶ *In all visions.* On the word rendered *visions*—חזון—see Notes on Isa. i. 1, and Intro. to Isaiah, § VII.

(4). It is a term frequently employed in reference to prophecy, and designates the usual method by which future events were made known. The prophet was permitted to see those events *as if* they were made to pass before the eye, and to describe them *as if* they were objects of sight. Here the word seems to be used to denote all supernatural appearances; all that God permitted him to see that in any way shadowed forth the future. It would seem that men who were not inspired were permitted occasionally to behold such supernatural appearances, though they were not able to interpret them. Thus their attention would be particularly called to them, and they would be prepared to admit the truth of what the interpreter communicated to them. Comp. ch. iv.; ch. v. 5, 6; Ge. xl. 5; xli. 1–7. Daniel was so endowed that he could interpret the meaning of these mysterious appearances, and thus convey important messages to men. The same endowment had been conferred on Joseph when in Egypt. See the passages referred to in Genesis. ¶ *And dreams.* One of the ways by which the will of God was anciently communicated to men. See Intro. to Isaiah, § VII. (2), and Notes on Job xxxiii. 14–18. Daniel, like Joseph before him, was supernaturally endowed to explain these messages which God sent to men, or to unfold these preintimations of coming events. This was a kind of knowledge which the Chaldeans particularly sought, and on which they especially prided themselves; and it was important, in order to "stain the pride of all human glory," and to make "the wisdom of the wise" in Babylon to be seen to be comparative "folly," to endow one man from the land of the prophets in the most ample manner with this knowledge, as it was important to do the same thing at the court of Pharaoh by the superior endowments of Joseph (Gen. xli. 8).

18. *Now at the end of the days,* &c. After three years. See ver. 5. ¶ *The prince of the eunuchs brought them in.* Daniel, his three friends, and the others who had been selected and trained for the same purpose.

bring them in, then the prince of
the eunuchs brought them in before
Nebuchadnezzar.

19 And the king communed with
them ; and among them all was

a 1 Ki. 10. 1, 3 ; Ps. 119. 99.

found none like Daniel, Hananiah,
Mishael, and Azariah : therefore
stood they before the king.

20 And in *a* all matters of wisdom
1 *and* understanding, that the king

1 *of.*

19. *And the king communed with
them.* Heb., "spake with them." Probably he conversed with them on the
points which had constituted the principal subjects of their studies ; or he
examined them. It is easy to imagine
that this must have been to these young
men a severe ordeal. ¶ *And among
them all was found none like Daniel,*
&c. Daniel and his three friends had
pursued a course of strict temperance ;
they had come to their daily task with
clear heads and pure hearts—free from
the oppression and lethargy of surfeit,
and the excitement of wine ; they had
prosecuted their studies in the enjoyment of fine health, and with the buoy-
ousness and elasticity of spirit produced
by temperance, and they now showed
the result of such a course of training.
Young men of temperance, other things
being equal, will greatly surpass others
in their preparation for the duties of life
in any profession or calling. ¶ *Therefore stood they before the king.* It is
not said, indeed, that the others were
not permitted also to stand before the
monarch, but the object of the historian
is to trace the means by which *these
youths* rose to such eminence and virtue.
It is clear, however, that whatever may
have been the result on the others, the
historian means to say that these young
men rose to higher eminence than they
did, and were permitted to stand nearer
the throne. The phrase "stood before
the king," is one which denotes elevated
rank. They were employed in honourable offices at the court, and received
peculiar marks of the royal favour.

20. *And in all matters of wisdom*
and *understanding.* Marg., "*of.*"
The Hebrew is, "Everything of wisdom of understanding." The Greek,
"In all things of wisdom *and* knowledge." The meaning is, in everything
which required peculiar wisdom to understand and explain it. The points
submitted were such as would appropriately come before the minds of the

sages and magicians who were employed
as counsellors at court. ¶ *He found
them ten times better.* Better counsellors, better informed. Heb., "ten
hands above the magicians ;" that is,
ten *times,* or *many* times. In this
sense the word *ten* is used in Gen.
xxxi. 7, 41 ; Numb. xiv. 22 ; Neh. iv.
12 ; Job xix. 3. They greatly surpassed
them. ¶ *Than all the magicians.* Gr.,
τοὺς ἐπαοιδοὺς. The Greek word means,
those singing to; then those who propose to heal the sick by singing; then
those who practise magical arts or incantations—particularly with the idea
of charming with songs ; and then those
who accomplish anything surpassing
human power by mysterious and supernatural means.—Passow. The Hebrew
word (הַרְטֻמִּים *hhărtŭmmim*), occurs
only in the following places in the
Scriptures, in all of which it is rendered *magicians* :—Gen. xli. 8, 24 ;
Exod. vii. 11, 22 ; viii. 7 (3), 18 (14),
19 (15) ; ix. 11 ; Dan. i. 22 ; ii. 2. From
this it appears that it applied only to
the magicians in Egypt and in Babylon,
and doubtless substantially the same
class of persons is referred to. It is
found only in the plural number, *perhaps* implying that they formed com-
panies, or that they were always associated together, so that different persons performed different parts in their
incantations. The word is defined by
Gesenius to mean, "Sacred scribes,
skilled in the sacred writings or hiero-
glyphics—ἱερογραμματεῖς—a class of
Egyptian priests." It is, according to
him (*Lex.*), of Hebrew origin, and is
derived from חֶרֶט *hheret, stylus*—an instrument of writing, and ם—formative.
It is not improbable, he suggests, that
the Hebrews with these letters imitated
a similar Egyptian word. Prof. Stuart
(*in loc.*) says that the word would be
correctly translated *pen-men,* and supposes that it originally referred to those
who were "busied with books and writ-

inquired of them, he found them ing, and skilled in them." It is evident that the word is not of Persian origin, since it was used in Egypt long before it occurs in Daniel. A full and very interesting account of the Magians and their religion may be found in Creuzer, *Mythologie und Symbolik,* i. pp. 187– 234. Herodotus mentions the *Magi* as a distinct people, i. 101. The word *Mag* or *Mog* (whence the μάγοι—*magoi* —of the Greeks, and the *magi* of the Romans) means, properly, *a priest ;* and at a very early period the names *Chaldeans* and *Magi* were interchange- able, and both were regarded as of the same class.—Creuzer, i. 187, note. They were doubtless, at first, a class of priests among the Medes and Per- sians, who were employed, among other things, in the search for wisdom ; who were connected with heathen oracles ; who claimed acquaintance with the will of the gods, and who professed to have the power, therefore, of making known future events, by explaining dreams, visions, preternatural appearances, &c. The Magi formed one of the six tribes into which the Medes were formerly divided (Herodotus, i. 101), but on the downfall of the Median empire they continued to retain at the court of the conqueror a great degree of power and authority. "The learning of the Magi was connected with astrology and en- chantment, in which they were so cele- brated that their name was applied to all orders of magicians and enchanters." —Anthon, *Class. Dic.* These remarks may explain the reason why the word *magician* comes to be applied to this class of men, though we are not to sup- pose that the persons referred to in Genesis and Exodus, under the appel- lation of the Hebrew name there given to them (חַרְטֻמִּים), or those found in Babylon, referred to in the passage before us, to whom the same name is applied, were of that class of priests. The name *magi,* or *magician,* was so extended as to embrace *all* who made pretensions to the kind of knowledge for which the magi were distinguished, and hence came also to be synonymous with the *Chaldeans,* who were also cele- brated for this.   Compare Notes on

ten times better than all the magi- ch. ii. 2. In the passage before us it cannot be determined with certainty, that the persons were of *Magian* origin, though it is possible, as in ch. ii. 2, they are distinguished from the Chal- deans. All that is certainly meant is, that they were persons who laid claim to the power of diving into future events ; of explaining mysteries ; of interpreting dreams ; of working by en- chantments, &c.

[The subjoined figure represents a priest or magician with a gazelle, and is taken to be a diviner, one of the four orders of Chaldeans named in Dan. ii. 2, and the last of the three mentioned in v. 7. From these persons it was

the custom of the kings of Assyria to require the interpretation of dreams and the prediction of future events. This is the only perfect piece of sculpture found by Botta in one of the large courts of Khorsabad.]

¶ *And astrologers* — הָאַשָּׁפִים. This word is rendered by the LXX., μάγους, *magians.* So also in the Vulgate, *magos.* The English word *astrologer* denotes "one who professes to fore- tell future events by the aspects and situation of the stars." — Webster. The Hebrew word—אַשָּׁפִים—according to Gesenius, means *enchanters, magi- cians.* It is derived, probably, from the obsolete root אָשַׁף *to cover, to con-*

cians *and* astrologers that *were* in all his realm.

a ch. 6. 28; 10. 1. He lived to see that glorious time of the return of his people from the Baby-

ceal, and refers to those who were devoted to the practice of occult arts, and to the cultivation of recondite and cabalistic sciences. It is supposed by some philologists to have given rise, by dropping the initial א to the Greek σοφος, *wise, wise man*, and the Persian *sophi*, an epithet of equivalent import. See Gesenius on the word, and compare Bush on Dan. ii. 2. The word is found only in Daniel, ch. i. 20; ii. 2, 10, 27; iv. 7 (4); v. 7, 11, 15, in every instance rendered *astrologer* and *astrologers*. There is no evidence, however, that the science of astrology enters into the meaning of the word, or that the persons referred to attempted to practise divination by the aid of the stars. It is to be regretted that the term *astrologer* should have been employed in our translation, as it conveys an intimation which is not found in the original. It is, indeed, in the highest degree probable, that a part of their pretended wisdom consisted in their ability to cast the fates of men by the conjunctions and opposition of the stars, but this is not necessarily implied in the word. Prof. Stuart renders it *enchanters*. ¶ *In all his realm.* Not only in the capital, but throughout the kingdom. These arts were doubtless practised extensively elsewhere, but it is probable that the most skilful in them would be assembled at the capital.

21. *And Daniel continued* even *unto the first year of king Cyrus.* When the proclamation was issued by him to rebuild the temple at Jerusalem, Ezra i. 1. That is, he continued in influence and authority at different times during that period, and, of course, during the whole of the seventy years' captivity. It is not necessarily implied that he did not *live* longer, or even that he ceased then to have influence and authority at court, but the object of the writer is to show that, during that long and eventful period, he occupied a station of influence until the captivity was accomplished, and the royal order was issued for rebuilding the temple He was

21 And **Daniel** continued *ᵃeven* unto the first year of king Cyrus.

Ionian captivity, though he did not die then. So *till* is used, Ps. 110. 1; 112. 8.

among the first of the captives that were taken to Babylon, and he lived to see the end of the captivity—"the joyful day of Jewish freedom."—Prof. Stuart. It is commonly believed that, when the captives returned, he remained in Chaldea, probably detained by his high employments in the Persian empire, and that he died either at Babylon or at Shushan. Comp. the Intro. § I.

PRACTICAL REMARKS.

In view of the exposition given of this chapter, the following remarks may be made :—

(1.) There is in every period of the world, and in every place, much obscure and buried talent that might be cultivated and brought to light, as there are many gems in earth and ocean that are yet undiscovered. Notes on vers. 1–4. Among these captive youths—prisoners of war—in a foreign land, and as yet unknown, there was most rich and varied talent—talent that was destined yet to shine at the court of the most magnificent monarchy of the ancient world, and to be honoured as among the brightest that the world has seen. And so in all places and at all times, there is much rich and varied genius which might shine with great brilliancy, and perform important public services, if it were cultivated and allowed to develope itself on the great theatre of human affairs. Thus, in obscure rural retreats there may be bright gems of intellect ; in the low haunts of vice there may be talent that would charm the world by the beauty of song or the power of eloquence ; among slaves there may be mind which, if emancipated, would take its place in the brightest constellations of genius. The great endowments of Moses as a lawgiver, a prophet, a profound statesman, sprang from an enslaved people, as those of Daniel did; and it is not too much to say that the brightest talent of the earth has been found in places of great obscurity, and where, but for some remarkable dispensation of Providence, it might have remained for ever unknown. This thought has been immortalized by Gray :—

"Full many a gem of purest ray serene,
The dark unfathomed caves of ocean bear;
Full many a flower is born to blush unseen,
And waste its sweetness on the desert air.

"Some village Hampden, that with dauntless breast
The little tyrant of his fields withstood ;
Some mute inglorious Milton here may rest,
Some Cromwell, guiltless of his country's blood."

There is at any time on the earth talent enough created for all that there is to be done in any generation ; and there is always enough for talent to accomplish if it were employed in the purposes for which it was originally adapted. There need be at no time any wasted or unoccupied mind ; and there need be no great and good plan that should fail for the want of talent fitted to accomplish it, if that which actually exists on the earth were called into action.

(2.) He does a great service to the world who seeks out such talent, and gives it an opportunity to accomplish what it is fitted to, by furnishing it the means of an education, ver. 3. Nebuchadnezzar, unconsciously, and doubtless undesignedly, did a great service to mankind by his purpose to seek out the talent of the Hebrew captives, and giving it an opportunity to expand and to ripen into usefulness. Daniel has taken his place among the prophets and statesmen of the world as a man of rare endowments, and of equally rare integrity of character. He has, under the leading of the Divine Spirit, done more than most

other prophets to lift the mysterious veil which shrouds the future ; more than *could* have been done by the penetrating sagacity of all the Burkes, the Cannings, and the Metternichs of the world. So far as human appearances go, all this might have remained in obscurity, if it had not been for the purpose of the Chaldean monarch to bring forward into public notice the obscure talent which lay hid among the Hebrew captives. He always does a good service to mankind who seeks out bright and promising genius, and who gives it the opportunity of developing itself with advantage on the great theatre of human affairs.

(3.) We cannot but admire the arrangements of Providence by which this was done. Notes on vers. 1–4. This occurred in connection with the remarkable purpose of a heathen monarch—a man who, perhaps more than any other heathen ruler, has furnished an illustration of the truth that "the king's heart is in the hand of the Lord." *That purpose was, to raise to eminence and influence the talent that might be found among the Hebrew captives.* There can be no doubt that the hand of God was in this ; that there was a secret Divine influence on his mind, unknown to him, which secured this result ; and that, while he was aiming at one result, God was designing to secure another. There was thus a double influence on his mind : (1) that which arose from the purpose of the monarch himself, originated by considerations of policy, or contemplating the aggrandizement and increased splendour of his court ; and (2) the secret and silent influence of God, shaping the plans of the monarch to the ends which *He* had in view. Comp. Notes on Isa. x. 5, *seq.*

(4.) As it is reasonable to suppose that these young men had been trained up in the strict principles of religion and temperance (vers. 8–12), the case before us furnishes an interesting illustration of the temptations to which those who are early trained in the ways of piety are often exposed. Every effort seems to have been made to induce them to abandon the principles in which they had been educated, and there was a strong probability that those efforts would be successful. (a) They were among strangers, far away from the homes of their youth, and surrounded by the allurements of a great city. (b) Everything was done which could be done to induce them to *forget* their own land and the religion of their fathers. (c) They were suddenly brought into distinguished notice; they attracted the attention of the great, and had the prospect of associating with princes and nobles in the most magnificent court on earth. They had been selected on account of their personal beauty and their intellectual promise, and were approached, therefore, in a form of temptation to which youths are commonly most sensitive, and to which they are commonly most liable to yield. (d) They were far away from the religious institutions of their country; from the public services of the sanctuary; from the temple; and from all those influences which had been made to bear upon them in early life. It was a rare virtue which could, in these circumstances, withstand the power of such temptations.

(5.) Young men, trained in the ways of religion and in the habits of temperance, are often now exposed to similar temptations. They visit the cities of a foreign country, or the cities in their own land. They are surrounded by strangers. They are far away from the sanctuary to which in early life they were conducted by their parents, and in which they were taught the truths of religion. The eye of that unslumbering vigilance which was upon them in their own land, or in the country neighbourhood where their conduct was known to all, is now withdrawn. No one will know it if they visit the theatre; no one will see them who will make report if they are found in the gambling room, or the place of dissipation. In those new scenes new temptations are around them. They may be noticed, flattered, caressed. They may be invited to places by the refined and the fashionable, from which, when at home, they would have recoiled. Or, it may be, prospects of honour and affluence may open upon them, and in the whirl of business or pleasure, they may be under the strongest temptations to forget the lessons of early virtue, and to abandon the principles of the religion in which they were trained. Thousands of young men are ruined in circumstances similar to those in which these youths were placed in Babylon, and amidst temptations much less formidable than those which encompassed them; and it is a rare virtue which makes a young man safe amidst the temptations to which he is exposed in a great city, or in a distant land.

(6.) We have in this chapter an instructive instance of the value of early training in the principles of religion and temperance. There can be no doubt that these young men owed their safety and their future success wholly to this. Parents, therefore, should be encouraged to train their sons in the strictest principles of religion and virtue. Seed thus sown will not be lost. In a distant land, far away from home, from a parent's eye, from the sanctuary of God; in the midst of temptations, when surrounded by flatterers, by the gay and by the irreligious, such principles will be a safeguard to them which nothing else can secure, and will save them when otherwise they would be engulphed in the vortex of irreligion and dissipation. The best service which a parent can render to a son, is to imbue his mind thoroughly with the principles of temperance and religion.

(7.) We may see the value of a purpose of entire abstinence from the use of *wine*, ver. 8. Daniel resolved that he would not make use of it as a beverage. His purpose, it would seem, was decided, though he meant to accomplish it by mild and persuasive means if possible. There were good reasons for the formation of such a purpose then, and those reasons are not less weighty now. He never had occasion to regret the formation of such a purpose ; nor has any one who has formed a similar resolution ever had occasion to regret it. Among the reasons for the formation of such a resolution, the following may be suggested :—(1.) A fixed resolution in regard to the course which one will pursue ; to the kind of life which he will live ; to the principles on which he will act, is of inestimable value in a young man. Our confidence in a man is just in proportion as we have evidence that he has formed a steady purpose of virtue, and that he has sufficient strength of resolution to keep it. (2.) The same reasons exist for adopting a resolution of abstinence in regard to the use of wine, which exist for adopting it in relation to the use of ardent spirits ; for (*a*) the intoxicating principle in wine or other fermented liquors is precisely the same as in ardent spirits. It is the result of *fermentation*, not of *distillation*, and undergoes no change by distillation. The only effect of that chemical process is to drive it off by heat, condense, and collect it in a form better adapted to commerce or to preservation, but the alcoholic principle is precisely the same in wine as in distilled liquors. (*b*) Intoxication itself is the same thing, whether produced by fermented liquors or by distilled spirits. It produces the same effect on the body, on the mind, on the affections. A man who becomes intoxicated on wine—as he easily may —is in precisely the same condition, so far as intoxication is produced, as he who becomes intoxicated on distilled liquors. (*c*) There is the same kind of *danger* of becoming intemperate in the use of the one as of the other. The man who habitually uses wine is as certainly in danger of becoming a drunkard as he who indulges in the use of distilled liquors. The danger, too, arises from the same source. It arises from the fact that he who indulges once will feel induced to indulge again ; that a strong and peculiar craving is produced for stimulating liquors ; that the body is left in such a state that it demands a repetition of the stimulus ; that it is a law in regard to indulgence in this kind of drinks, that an increased *quantity* is demanded to meet the exhausted state of the system ; and that the demand goes on in this increased ratio until there is no power of control, and the man becomes a confirmed inebriate. All these laws operate in regard to the use of wine as really as to the use of any other intoxicating drinks ; and, therefore, there is the same reason for the adoption of a resolution to abstain from all alike. (*d*) The temptations are often *greater* in relation to wine than to any other kind of intoxicating drinks. There is a large class of persons in the community who are in comparatively little danger of becoming intemperate from any other cause than this. This remark applies particularly to young men of wealth ; to those who move in the more elevated circles ; to those who are in college, and to those who are preparing for the learned professions. They are in peculiar danger from this quarter, because it is regarded as genteel to drink a glass of wine ; because they are allured by the example of professed Christians, of ministers of the gospel, and of ladies ; and because they are often in circumstances in which it would not be regarded as respectable or respectful to decline it. (3.) A third reason for adopting such a resolution is, that it is the ONLY SECURITY that any one can have that he will not become a drunkard. No one who indulges at all in the use of intoxicating liquors can have any *certainty* that he will not yet become a confirmed inebriate. Of the great multitudes who have been, and who are drunkards, there are almost none who *meant* to sink themselves to that wretched condition. They have become intemperate by indulging in the social glass when they thought themselves safe, and they continued the indulgence until it was too late to recover themselves from ruin. He who is in the habit of drinking at all can have no *security* that he may not yet be all that the poor drunkard now is. But he *will* be certainly safe from this evil if he adopts the purpose of total abstinence, and steadfastly adheres to it. Whatever other dangers await him, he will be secure against this ; whatever other calamities he may experience, he is sure that he will escape all those that are caused by intemperance.

(8.) We have in this chapter a most interesting illustration of the *value* of temperance in *eating*, vers. 9–17. There are laws of our nature relating to the quantity and quality of food which can no more be violated with impunity than any other of the laws of God ; and yet those laws are probably more frequently violated than any other. There are more persons intemperate in the use of food than in the use of drink, and probably more diseases engendered, and more lives cut short, by improper indulgence in eating than in drinking. At the same time it is a more base, low, gross, and beastly passion. A drunkard is very often the wreck of a generous and noble-minded nature. He was large-hearted, open, free, liberal, and others took advantage of his generosity of disposition, and led him on to habits of intoxication. But there is nothing noble or generous in the gourmand. He approximates more nearly to the lowest forms of the brutal creation than any other human being ; and if there is any man who should be looked on with feelings of unutterable loathing, it is he who wastes his vigour, and destroys his health, by gross indulgence in eating. There is almost no sin that God speaks of in tones of more decided abhorrence than the sin of *gluttony.* Comp. Deut. xxi. 20, 21 ; Psal. cxli. 4 ; Prov. xxiii. 1–3, 20, 21 ; Luke xvi. 19 ; xxi. 34.

(9.) We have, in the close of the chapter before us, a most interesting illustration of the effect of an early course of strict temperance on the future character and success in life, vers. 17–21. The trial in the case of these young men was fairly made. It was continued through three years ; a period long enough for a *fair* trial ; a period long enough to make it an interesting example to young men who are pursuing a course of literary studies, who are preparing to enter one of the learned professions, or who are qualifying themselves for a life of mechanical or agricultural pursuits. In the case of these young men, they were strictly on *probation,* and the result of their probation was seen in the success which attended them when they passed the severe examination before the monarch (ver. 19), and in the honours which they reached at his court, vers. 19–21. To make this case applicable to other young men, and useful to them, we may notice two things : the fact that every young man is on probation ; and the effect of an early course of temperance in securing the object of that probation.

(*a*) Every young man is on probation ; that is, his future character and success are to be determined by what he is when a youth. (1.) All the great interests of the world are soon to pass into the hands of the young. They who now possess the property, and fill the offices of the land, will pass away. Whatever there is that is valuable in liberty, science, art, or religion, will pass into the hands of those who are now young. They will preside in the seminaries of learning ; will sit down on the benches of justice ; will take the vacated seats of senators ; will occupy the pulpits in the churches ; will be intrusted with all the offices of honour and emolument ; will be ambassadors to foreign courts ; and will dispense the charities of the land, and carry out and complete the designs of Christian benevolence. There is not an interest of liberty, religion, or law, which will not soon be committed to them. (2.) The world is favourably disposed towards young men, and they who are now intrusted with these great interests, and who are soon to leave them, are ready calmly to commit them to the guardianship of the rising generation, as soon as they have the assurance that they are qualified to receive the trust. They, therefore, watch with intense solicitude the conduct of those to whom so great interests are so soon to be committed (3.) Early virtue is indispensable to a favourable result of the probation of young men. A merchant demands evidence of integrity and industry in a young man before he will admit him to share his business, or will give him credit ; and the same thing is true respecting a farmer, mechanic, physician, lawyer, or clergyman. No young man can hope to have the confidence of others, or to succeed in his calling, who does not give evidence that he is qualified for success by a fair probation or trial. (4.) Of no young man is it *presumed* that he is qualified to be intrusted with these great and momentous interests until he has had a fair trial. There is no such confidence in the integrity of young men, or in their tendencies to virtue, or in their native endowments, that the world is *willing* to commit great interests to them without an appropriate probation. No advantage of birth or blood can secure this ; and no young man should presume that the world will be ready to confide in him until he has shown that he is qualified for the station to which he aspires. (5.) Into this probation, through which every young man is passing, the question of *temperance* enters perhaps more deeply than anything else respecting character. With reference to his habits on this point, every young man is watched with an eagle eye, and his character is well understood, when perhaps he least suspects it. The public cannot be deceived on this point, and every young man may be assured that there is an eye of unslumbering vigilance upon him.

(*b*) The effect of an early course of temperance on the issue of this probation. This is seen in the avoidance of a course of life which would certainly blast every hope ; and in its positive influence on the future destiny. 1. The avoidance of certain things which would blast every hope which a young man could cherish. There are certain evils which a young man will certainly avoid by a course of strict temperance, which would otherwise certainly come upon him. They are such as these : (a) Poverty, as arising from this source. He may, indeed, be poor if he is temperate. He may lose his health, or may meet with losses, or may be unsuccessful in business ; but he is certain that he will never be made poor from intemperance. Nine-tenths of the poverty in the community is caused by this vice ; nine-tenths of all who are in almshouses are sent there as the result of it ; but from all this he will be certain that *he* will be saved. There is a great difference, if a man *is* poor, between being such as the result of a loss of health, or other Providential dispensations, and being such as the result of intemperance. (b) He will be saved from committing *crime* from this cause. About nine-tenths of the crimes that are committed are the results of intoxicating drinks, and by a course of temperance a man is certain that he will be saved from the commission of all those crimes. Yet if *not* temperate, no man has any security that he will not commit any one of them. There is nothing in himself to save him from the very worst of them ; and every young man who indulges in the intoxicating cup should reflect that he has no security that he will not be led on to commit the most horrid crimes which ever disgrace humanity. (c) He will certainly be saved from the drunkard's death. He will indeed die. He may die young ; for, though temperate, he may be cut down in the vigour of his days. But there is all the difference imaginable between dying as a drunkard, and dying in the ordinary course of nature. It would be a sufficient inducement for any one to sign a temperance pledge, and to adhere to it, if there were no other, that he might avoid

the horrors of a death by *delirium tremens,* and be saved from the loathsomeness of a drunkard's grave. It is much for a young man to be able to say as he enters on life, and looks out on the future with solicitude as to what is to come, "Whatever may await me in the unknown future, of this one thing I am certain ; I shall never be poor, and haggard, and wretched, as the drunkard is. I shall never commit the crimes to which drunkenness prompts. I shall never experience the unutterable horrors of *delirium tremens.* I shall never die the death of unequalled wretchedness caused by a *mania a potu.* Come what may, I see, on the threshold of life, that I am to be free from the *worst* evils to which man is ever exposed. If I am poor, I will not be poor as the victim of intemperance is. If I die early, the world will not feel it is benefited by my removal, and my friends will not go forth to my grave with the unutterable anguish which a parent has who follows a drunken son to the tomb."

2. A course of temperance will have a direct and positive effect on the issue of such a probation. So it had in the case of the young men in the chapter before us ; and so it will have in every case. Its effect will be seen in the beauty, and healthfulness, and vigour of the bodily frame ; in the clearness of the intellect, and the purity of the heart ; in habits of industry, in general integrity of life, and in rendering it more probable that the soul will be saved. In no respect whatever will a steadfast adherence to the principles of temperance injure any young man ; in every respect, it may be the means of promoting his interests in the present life, and of securing his final happiness in the world to come. Why, then, should *any* young man hesitate about forming such a resolution as Daniel

did (ver. 8), and about expressing, in every proper way, in the most decided manner, his determined purpose to adhere through life to the strictest principles of temperance?

CHAPTER II.

§ I.—AUTHENTICITY OF THE CHAPTER.

The objections to the authenticity and credibility of this chapter are not numerous or important.

I. The first that is alleged, by Bertholdt (*Com.* pp. 192, 193), is substantially this : "that if the account here is true, the records of ancient times could not exhibit a more finished tyrant than Nebuchadnezzar was, if he doomed so many persons to death, on so slight and foolish an occasion, ver. 5. This cruelty, it is said, is wholly contrary to the general character of Nebuchadnezzar as it is reported to us, and wholly incredible. It is further said, that, though it was common in the East to trust in dreams, and though the office of interpreting them was an honourable office, yet no one was so unreasonable, or could be, as to require the interpreter to reveal the dream itself when it was forgotten. The proper office of the interpreter, it is said, was to interpret the dream, not to tell what the dream was."

To this objection, which seems to have considerable plausibility, it may be replied :—

(1.) Much reliance was placed on *dreams* in ancient times, alike among the Hebrews and in the heathen world. The case of Pharaoh will at once occur to the mind ; and it need not be said that men everywhere relied on dreams, and inquired earnestly respecting them, whether they *might* not be the appointed means of communication with the spiritual world, and of disclosing what was to occur in the future. There can

be no objection, therefore, to the supposition that this heathen monarch, Nebuchadnezzar, felt all the solicitude which he is reported to have done respecting the dream which he had. It may be further added, that in the dream itself there is nothing improbable as a dream, for it has all the characteristics of those mysterious operations of the mind ; and, if God ever communicated his will by a dream, or made known future events in this way, there is no absurdity in supposing that he would thus communicate what was to come, to him who was at that time at the head of the empires of the earth, and who was the king over the first of those kingdoms which were to embrace the world's history for so many ages.

(2.) There is no improbability in supposing that a dream would vanish from the distinct recollection, or that if it had vanished, the mind would be troubled by some vague recollection or impression in regard to it. This often occurs in our dreams now, as in the indistinct recollection that we have had a pleasant or a frightful dream, when we are wholly unable to recal the dream itself. This often occurs, too, when we would be *glad* to recover the dream if we could, but when no effort that we can make will recal its distinct features to our minds.

(3.) There was, really, nothing that was unreasonable, absurd, or tyrannical in the demand which Nebuchadnezzar made on the astrologers, that they should recal the dream itself, and then interpret it. Doubtless he could recollect it if they would suggest it, or at least he could so far recollect it as to prevent their imposing on him : for something like this constantly occurs in the operation of our own minds. When we have forgotten a story, or a piece of history, though we could not ourselves recal it, yet when it is repeated to us, we can then distinctly recollect it, and can perceive that that is the same narrative, for it agrees with all our impressions in regard to it. Furthermore, though it was not understood to be a part of the office of an interpreter of dreams to *recal* the dream if it had vanished from the mind, yet Nebuchadnezzar reasoned correctly, that if they could *interpret* the dream they ought to be presumed to be able to tell what it was. The one required no more sagacity than the other : and if they were, as they pretended to be, under the inspiration of the gods in interpreting a dream, it was fair to presume that, under the same inspiration, they could tell what it was. Comp. Notes on ver. 5. No objection, then, can lie against the authenticity of this chapter from any supposed absurdity in the demand of Nebuchadnezzar. It was not only strictly in accordance with all the just principles of reasoning in the case, but was in accordance with what might be expected from an arbitrary monarch who was accustomed to exact obedience in all things.

(4.) What is here said of the threatening of Nebuchadnezzar (ver. 5), accords with the general traits of his character as history has preserved them. He had in him the elements of cruelty and severity of the highest order, especially when his will was not immediately complied with. In proof of this, we need only refer to his cruel treatment of the king Zedekiah, when Jerusalem was taken : " So they took the king, and brought him to the king of Babylon to Riblah : and they gave judgment upon him. And they slew the sons of Zedekiah before his eyes, and put out the eyes of Zedekiah, and bound him with fetters of brass, and brought him to Babylon," 2 Ki. xxv. 6, 7 : compare also, in vers. 18–21 of the same chapter, the account of his slaying the large number of persons that were taken by Nebuzar-adan, captain of the guard, and brought by him to the king in Babylon. These were slain in cold blood by order of Nebuchadnezzar himself. These facts make it every way probable that, in a fit of passion, he would not hesitate to threaten the astrologers with death if they did not comply at once with his will. Comp. Jer. xxxix. 5, *seq.* ; lii. 9–11. The truth was, that though Nebuchadnezzar had some good qualities, and was religious *in his way*, yet he had all the usual characteristics of an Oriental despot. He was a man of strong passions, and was a man who would never hesitate in carrying out the purposes of an arbitrary, a determined, and a stubborn will.

II. A second objection made by Bertholdt, which may demand a moment's notice, is, substantially, that the account bears the mark of a later hand, for the purpose of conferring a higher honour on Daniel, and making what he did appear the more wonderful : pp. 62, 63, 193–196. The supposition of Bertholdt is, that the original account was merely that Nebuchadnezzar required of the interpreter to explain the sense of the dream, but that, in order to show the greatness of Daniel, the author of this book, long after the affair occurred, added the circumstance that Nebuchadnezzar required of them to make the *dream* known as well as the *interpretation*, and that the great superiority of Daniel was shown by his being able at once to do this.

As this objection, however, is not based on any historical grounds, and as it is throughout mere conjecture, it is not necessary to notice it further. Nothing is gained by the conjecture ; no difficulty is relieved by it ; nor is there any real difficulty *to be* relieved by any such supposition. The narrative, as we have it, has, as we have seen, no intrinsic improbability, nor is there anything in it which is contrary to the well-known character of Nebuchadnezzar.

III. A third objection to the authenticity of the chapter, which deserves to be noticed, is urged by Lüderwald, p. 40, *seq.*, and Bleek, p. 280, that this whole narrative has a strong resemblance to the account of the dreams of Pharaoh, and the promotion of Joseph at the court of Egypt, and was apparently made up from that, or copied from it.

But to this we may reply, (*a*) that, if either happened, there is no more improbability in supposing that it should happen to Daniel in Babylon than to Joseph in Egypt ; and, taken as separate and independent histories, neither of them is improbable. (*b*) There is so much diversity in the two cases as to show that the one is *not* copied from the other. They agree, indeed, in several circumstances :—in the fact that the king of Egypt and the king of Babylon had each a dream ; in the fact that Joseph and Daniel were enabled to interpret the dream ; in the fact that they both ascribed the ability to do this, not to themselves, but to God ; and in the fact that they were both raised to honour, as a consequence of their being able to interpret the dream. But in nothing else do they agree. The dreams themselves; the occasion; the explanation; the result ; the bearing on future events—in these, and in numerous other things, they differ entirely. It may be added, also, that *if* the one had been copied from the other, it is probable that there would have been some undesigned allusion by which it could be known that the writer of the one had the other before him, and that he was framing his

own narrative from that. But, as a matter of fact, there are no two records in history that have more the marks of being independent and original narratives of real transactions, than the account of Joseph in Egypt, and of Daniel in Babylon.

IV. A fourth objection to the account in this chapter arises from an alleged error in *chronology.* For a consideration of this, see Notes on ver. 1.

§ II.—ANALYSIS OF THE CHAPTER.

The subjects of this chapter are the following :—

I. The dream of Nebuchadnezzar, ver. 1. In accordance with the common belief among the ancients, he regarded this as a Divine message. The dream, too, was of such a character as to make a deep impression on his mind, though its distinct features and details had gone from him.

II. The demand of Nebuchadnezzar that the Chaldeans should recal the dream to his recollection, and expound its meaning, vers. 2–9. He ordered those whose business it was professedly to give such interpretations, to come into his presence, and to make known the dream and its meaning. But it would seem that their pretensions went no further than to explain a dream when it was known, and hence they asked respectfully that the king would state the dream in order that they might explain it. The king, in anger, threatened death, if they did not first recal the dream, and then make known the interpretation, promising at the same time ample rewards if they were able to do this. As all this, under Divine direction, was designed to communicate important information of future events, it was so ordered that the dream should be forgotten, thus entirely confounding the art of the Chaldeans, and giving an opportunity to Daniel to make the dream and its interpretation known, thus exalting a man from the land of the prophets, and showing that it was not by the skill of the pretended interpreters of dreams that future events could be made known, but that it was only by those who were inspired for that purpose by the true God.

III. The acknowledged failure of the power of the astrologers and Chaldeans, vers. 10, 11. They admitted that they could not do what was demanded of them. Whatever might be the consequence, they could not even *attempt* to recal a forgotten dream. And as, though we may be unable to recal such a dream distinctly ourselves, we could easily *recognize* it if it were stated to us ; and as we could not be imposed on by something else that any one should undertake to make us believe was the real dream, the magicians saw that it was hopeless to attempt to palm a story of their own invention on him, as if that were the real dream, and they therefore acknowledged their inability to comply with the demand of the king.

IV. The decree that they should die, vers. 12, 13. In this decree, Daniel and his three friends who had been trained with him at court (ch. i.) were involved, not because they had failed to comply with the demand of the king, for there is the fullest evidence that the subject had not been laid before them, but because they came under the general class of wise men, or counsellors, to whom the monarch looked to explain the prognostics of coming events.

V. Daniel, when apprised of the decree, and the cause of it, went to the king and requested a respite in the execution of the sentence, vers. 14–16. It would seem that he had the privilege of access to the king at pleasure. We may presume that he stated that the thing had not in fact been laid before him, though he had become involved in the general sentence, and it is no unreasonable supposition that the king was so much troubled with the dream, that he was so anxious to know its signification, and that he saw so clearly that if the decree was executed, involving Daniel and his friends, *all* hope of recalling and understanding it would be lost, that he was ready to grasp at *any* hope, however slender, of being made acquainted with the meaning of the vision. He was willing, therefore, that Daniel should be spared, and that the execution of the decree should be suspended.

VI. In these interesting and solemn circumstances, Daniel and his friends gave themselves to prayer, vers. 17, 18. Their lives were in danger, and the case was such that they could not be rescued but by a direct Divine interposition. There was no power which they had of ascertaining by any human means what was the dream of the monarch, and yet it was indispensable, in order to save their lives, that the dream should be made known. God only, they knew, could communicate it to them, and he only, therefore, could save them from death ; and in these circumstances of perplexity they availed themselves of the privilege which all the friends of God have—of carrying their cause at once before his throne.

VII. The secret was revealed to Daniel in a night vision, and he gave utterance to an appropriate song of praise, vers. 19–23. The occasion was one which demanded such an expression of thanksgiving, and that which Daniel addressed to God was every way worthy of the occasion.

VIII. The way was now prepared for Daniel to make known to the king the dream and the interpretation. Accordingly he was brought before the

CHAPTER II.

A ND in the second year of the reign of Nebuchadnezzar,

king, and he distinctly disclaimed any power of himself to recal the dream, or to make known its signification, vers. 24–30.

IX. The statement of the dream and the interpretation, vers. 31–45.

X. The effect on Nebuchadnezzar, vers. 46–49. He recognized the dream; acknowledged that it was only the true God who could have made it known ; and promoted Daniel to distinguished honour. In his own honours, Daniel did not forget the virtuous companions of his youth (ch. i.), and sought for them, now that he was elevated, posts of honourable employment also, ver. 49.

1. *And in the second year of the reign of Nebuchadnezzar.* There is an apparent chronological difficulty in this statement which has given some perplexity to expositors. It arises mainly from two sources. (1.) That in Jer. xxv. 1, it is said that the first year of the reign of Nebuchadnezzar corresponded with the fourth year of Jehoiakim, king of Judah, and as the captivity was in the third year of the reign of Jehoiakim (Dan. i. 1), the time here would be the *fourth* year of the reign of Nebuchadnezzar, instead of the second. (2.) That we learn from ch. i. 5, 18, that Daniel and his three friends had been in Babylon already three years, under a process of training preparatory to their being presented at court, and as the whole narrative leads us to suppose that it was *after* this that Daniel was regarded as enrolled among the wise men (comp. ch. ii. 13, 14), on the supposition that the captivity occurred in the first year of the reign of Nebuchadnezzar, this would bring the time of the dream into the fourth year of his reign. This difficulty is somewhat increased from the fact that when Nebuchadnezzar went up to besiege Jerusalem he is called "king," and it

Nebuchadnezzar dreamed dreams, wherewith *a* his spirit was troubled, and his sleep brake from him.

a ch. 4. 5; Gen. 41. 8; Job 33. 15-17.

is evident that he did not go as a lieutenant of the reigning monarch ; or as a general of the Chaldean forces under the direction of another. See 2 Ki. xxiv. 1, 11. Various solutions of this difficulty have been proposed, but the true one probably is, that Nebuchadnezzar reigned some time conjointly with his father, Nabopolassar, and, though the title *king* was given to him, yet the reckoning here is dated from the time when he began to reign alone, and that this was the year of his sole occupancy of the throne. Berosus states that his father, Nabopolassar, was aged and infirm, and that he gave up a part of his army to his son Nebuchadnezzar, who defeated the Egyptian host at Carchemish (Circesium) on the Euphrates, and drove Necho out of Asia. The victorious prince then marched directly to Jerusalem, and Jehoiakim surrendered to him ; and this was the beginning of the seventy years, captivity. See Jahn's *History of the Hebrew Commonwealth,* p. 134. Nabopolassar probably died about two years after that, and Nebuchadnezzar succeeded to the throne. The period of their reigning together was two years, and of course the second year of his single reign would be the fourth of his entire reign ; and a reckoning from either would be proper, and would not be misunderstood. Other modes of solution have been adopted, but as this meets the whole difficulty, and is founded on truth, it is unnecessary to refer to them. Comp. Prof. Stuart, on Daniel, Excursus I. and Excursus II. [See App. I. and II. to this Vol.] ¶ *Nebuchadnezzar dreamed dreams.* The plural is here used, though there is but one dream mentioned, and probably but one is referred to; for Nebuchadnezzar, when speaking of it himself (ver. 3), says, "I have dreamed *a dream.*" In the Latin Vulgate, and in the Greek, it is also in the singular. It is probable that this is a popular use of words, as if one should say, "I had strange dreams last night," though perhaps but a single dream was intended. — Prof. Bush.   Among the methods by which God made known future events in ancient times, that by *dreams* was one of the most common. See Notes on ch. i. 17; Intro. to Isaiah, § VII. (2); comp. Gen. xx. 3, 6; xxxi. 11; xxxvii. 5, 6; xl. 5; xli. 7, 25; 1 Ki. iii. 5; Numb. xii. 6; Joel ii. 28; Job xxxiii. 14–16.   The belief that the will of heaven was communicated to men by means of dreams, was prevalent throughout the world in ancient times. Hence the striking expression in Homer, *Il.* i. 63—*καὶ γάρ τ' ὄναρ ἐκ Διός ἐστιν, the dream is of Jove.*   So in the commencement of his second Iliad, he represents the will of Jupiter as conveyed to Agamemnon by *"Ονειρος, or the dream.*   So Diogenes Laertius makes mention of a dream of Socrates, by which he foretold his death as to happen in three days.   This method of communicating the Divine will was adopted, not only in reference to the prophets, but also to those who were strangers to religion, and even to wicked men, as in the case of Pharaoh, Abimelech, Nebuchadnezzar, the butler and baker in Egypt, &c.   In every such instance, however, it was necessary, as in the case before us, to call in the aid of a true prophet to interpret the dream; and it was only when thus interpreted that it took its place among the certain predictions of the future.   One *object* of communicating the Divine will in this manner, seems to have been to fix the attention of the person who had the dream on the subject, and to prepare him to receive the communication which God had chosen to make to him.   Thus it cannot be doubted that by the belief in dreams entertained by Pharaoh and Nebuchadnezzar, as disclosing future events, and by the anxiety of mind which they experienced in regard to the dreams, they were better prepared to receive the communications of Joseph and Daniel in reference to the future than they could have been by any other method of making known the Divine will.   They had no doubt that some important communication had been made to them respecting the future, and they were anxious to know what it was.   They were prepared, therefore, to welcome any explanation which commended itself to them as true, and in this way the servants of the true God had a means of access to their hearts which they could have found in no other way. By what laws it was so regulated that a dream should be *known* to be a preintimation of coming events, we have now no means of ascertaining.   That it is *possible* for God to have access to the mind in sleep, and to communicate his will in this manner, no one can doubt.   That it was, so far as employed for that purpose, a safe and certain way, is demonstrated by the results of the predictions thus made in the case of Abimelech, Gen. xx. 3, 6; of Joseph and his brethren, Gen. xxxvii. 5, 6; of Pharaoh, Gen. xli. 7, 25; and of the butler and baker, Gen. xl. 5.   It is not, however, to be inferred that the same reliance, or that any reliance, is now to be placed on dreams; for were there no other consideration against such reliance, it would be sufficient that there is no authorized interpreter of the wanderings of the mind in sleep. God now communicates his truth to the souls of men in other ways.   ¶ *Wherewith his spirit was troubled.*   Alike by the unusual nature of the dream, and by the impression which he undoubtedly had that it referred to some important truths pertaining to his kingdom and to future times.   See vers. 31–36   The Hebrew word here rendered *troubled* (פָּעַם) means, properly, *to strike, to beat, to pound;* then, in Niph., *to be moved,* or *agitated;* and also in Hithpa., *to be* agitated, or troubled.   The proper signification of the word is that of striking as on an anvil, and then it refers to any severe stroke, or anything which produces agitation.   The *verb* occurs only in the following places: Judg. xiii. 25, where it is rendered *move;* and Psa. lxvii. 4, (5); Gen. xli. 8; Dan. ii. 1, 3, where it is rendered *troubled.* The *noun* is of frequent occurrence.   ¶ *And his sleep brake from him.*   Heb. וְהִרְיָתֻה עָלָיו *שְׁנָתֻו.* Literally, "His sleep was upon him."   The Greek is, *his sleep was from him;* i.e. left him.   The Vulgate, *his sleep fled* (fugit) *from him.*   But it may be doubted whether the Hebrew will

2 Then the king commanded to call the magicians, and the astro-

logers, and the sorcerers, and the Chaldeans, for to show the king his

bear this construction. Probably the literal construction is the true one, by which the sense of the Hebrew—עַל *upon* —will be retained. The meaning then would be, that this remarkable representation occurred when he was *in* a profound sleep. It was *a dream*, and not *an open vision*. It was such a representation as passes before the mind when the senses are locked in repose, and not such as was made to pass before the minds of the prophets when they were permitted to see visions of the future, though awake. Comp. Numb. xxiv. 4, 16. There is nothing in the words which conveys the idea that there was anything preternatural in the sleep that had come upon Nebuchadnezzar, but the thought is, that all this occurred when he *was* sound asleep. Prof. Stuart, however, renders this, "his-sleep failed him," and so does also Gesenius. Winer renders it, "his sleep went away from him." But it seems to me that the more natural idea is that which occurs in the literal translation of the words, that this occurred as a dream, in a state of profound repose.

2. *Then the king commanded.* That is, when he awoke. The particle rendered *then*, does not imply that this occurred immediately. When he awoke, his mind was agitated ; he was impressed with the belief that he had had an important Divine communication ; but he could not even recal the dream distinctly, and he resolved to summon to his presence those whose business it was to interpret what were regarded as prognostics of the future. ¶ *The magicians, and the astrologers.* These are the same words which occur in ch. i. 20. See Notes on that place. ¶ *And the sorcerers.* Heb. מְכַשְּׁפִים. Vulgate, *malefici*—sorcerers. Gr., φαρμακούς. Syriac, *magician.* The Hebrew word is derived from כָּשַׁף *kâshăph*—meaning, in Piel, to practise magic ; to use magic formulas, or incantations ; to mutter ; and it refers to the various arts by which those who were addicted to magic practised their deceptions. The particular idea in this word would seem to be, that

on such occasions some forms of prayers were used, for the word in Syriac means to offer prayers, or to worship. Probably the aid of idol gods was invoked by such persons when they practised incantations. The word is found only in the following places : once as a *verb*, 2 Chron. xxxiii. 6, and rendered *used witchcraft ;* and as a *participle*, rendered *sorcerers*, in Exod. vii. 11 ; Dan. ii. 2 ; Mal. iii. 5 ; and *witch*, in Exod. xxii. 18 (17) ; Deut. xviii. 10. The *noun* (כֶּשֶׁף and כְּשָׁפִים) is used in the following places, always with reference to sorcery or witchcraft : Jer. xxvii. 9 ; 2 Kings ix. 22 ; Isa. xlvii. 9 ; Mic. v. 12 (11) ; Nah. iii. 4. It may not be easy to specify the exact sense in which this word is used as distinguished from the others which relate to the same general subject, but it would seem to be that some form of *prayer* or *invocation* was employed. The persons referred to did not profess to interpret the prognostics of future events by any original skill of their own, but by the aid of the gods. ¶ *And the Chaldeans.* See Notes on ch. i. 4. The Chaldeans appear to have been but one of the tribes or nations that made up the community at Babylon (comp. Notes on Isa. xxiii. 13), and it would seem that at this time they were particularly devoted to the practice of occult arts, and secret sciences. It is not probable that the other persons referred to in this enumeration were Chaldeans. The Magians, if any of these were employed, were Medians (Notes on ch. i. 20), and it is not improbable that the other classes of diviners might have been from other nations. The purpose of Nebuchadnezzar was to assemble at his court whatever was remarkable throughout the world for skill and knowledge (see analysis of ch. i.), and the wise men of the Chaldeans were employed in carrying out that design. The Chaldeans were so much devoted to these secret arts, and became so celebrated for them, that the name came, among the Greek and Roman writers, to be used to denote all those who laid claim to extraordinary powers in this department. Diodorus Siculus

dreams. So they came and stood before the king.

3 And the king said unto them, I have dreamed a dream, and my spirit was troubled to know the dream.

4 Then spake the Chaldeans to the king in Syriac, O king, live "for

a 1 Ki. 1. 31.

(lib. ii.) says of the Chaldeans in Babylon, that "they sustain the same office there that the priests do in Egypt; for being devoted to the worship of God through their whole lives, they give themselves to philosophy, and seek from astrology their highest glory." Cicero also remarks (*De Divin.*, p. 3), that "the Chaldeans, so named, not from their art, but their nation, are supposed, by a prolonged observation of the stars, to have wrought out a science by which could be predicted what was to happen to every individual, and to what fate he was born." Juvenal likewise (*Sat.* vi., vers. 552–554), has this passage : " Chaldaeis sed major erit fiducia ; quidquid dixerit astrologus, credent a fonte relatum Ammonis.—But their chief dependence is upon the Chaldeans ; whatever an astrologer declares, they will receive as a response of [Jupiter] Ammon." Horace refers to the *Babylonians* as distinguished in his time for the arts of magic, or divination :

"nec Babylonios,
Tentâris numeros."—*Car.* lib. i., xi.

It is not probable that the whole nation of Chaldeans was devoted to these arts, but as a people they became so celebrated in this kind of knowledge that it was their best known characteristic abroad. [See also appendix to this volume, No. III.] ¶ *For to show the king his dreams.* To show him what the dream was, and to explain its import. Comp. Gen. xli. 24 ; Judg. xiv. 12 ; 1 Kings x. 3. That it was common for kings to call in the aid of interpreters to explain the import of dreams, appears from Herodotus. When Astyages ascended the throne, he had a daughter whose name was Mandane. She had a dream which seemed to him so remarkable that he called in the "magi," whose interpretation, Herodotus remarks, was of such a nature that it "terrified him exceedingly." He was so much influenced by the dream and the interpretation, that it produced an entire change in his determination re-

specting the marriage of his daughter. —Book i., cvii. So again, after the marriage of his daughter, Herodotus says (book i., cviii.): "Astyages had another vision. A vine appeared to spring from his daughter which overspread all Asia. On this occasion, also, he consulted his interpreters ; the result was, that he sent for his daughter from Persia, when the time of her delivery approached. On her arrival, he kept a strict watch over her, intending to destroy her child. The magi had declared the vision to intimate that the child of his daughter should supplant him on the throne." Astyages, to guard against this, as soon as Cyrus was born, sent for Harpagus, a person in whom he had confidence, and commanded him to take the child to his own house, and put him to death. These passages in Herodotus show that what is here related of the king of Babylon, demanding the aid of magicians and astrologers to interpret his dreams, was by no means an uncommon occurrence.

3. *And the king said unto them, I have dreamed a dream, and my spirit was troubled to know the dream.* That is, clearly, to know all about it ; to recollect distinctly what it was, and to understand what it meant. He was agitated by so remarkable a dream ; he probably had, as Jerome remarks, a shadowy and floating impression of what the dream was—such as we often have of a dream that has agitated our minds, but of which we cannot recal the distinct and full image ; and he desired to recal that distinctly, and to know exactly what it meant. See ver. 1.

4. *Then spake the Chaldeans to the king.* The meaning is, either that the Chaldeans spoke in the name of the entire company of the soothsayers and magicians (Notes, ch. i. 20; ii. 2), because they were the most prominent among them, or the name is used to denote the collective body of sooth-

ever : tell thy servants the dream, | and we will show the interpretation.

sayers, meaning that this request was made by the entire company. ¶ *In Syriac.* In the original—אֲרָמִית—in *Aramean.* Gr., Συριστὶ — *in Syriac.* So the Vulgate. The Syriac retains the original word. The word means *Aramean,* and the reference is to that language which is known as East Aramean—a general term embracing the Chaldee, the Syriac, and the languages which were spoken in Mesopotamia. See Notes on ch. i. 4. This was the vernacular tongue of the king and of his subjects, and was that in which the Chaldeans would naturally address him. It is referred to here by the author of this book, perhaps to explain the reason why he himself makes use of this language in explaining the dream. The use of this, however, is not confined to the statement of what the magicians said, but is continued to the close of the seventh chapter. Comp. the Intro. § IV. III. The language used is that which is commonly called Chaldee. It is written in the same character as the Hebrew, and differs from that as one dialect differs from another. It was, doubtless, well understood by the Jews in their captivity, and was probably spoken by them after their return to their own land. ¶ *O king, live for ever.* This is a form of speech quite common in addressing monarchs. See 1 Sam. x. 24 ; 1 Kings i. 25 (margin) ; ch. iii. 9 ; v. 10. The expression is prevalent still, as in the phrases, " Long live the king," "*Vive l' empereur,*" "*Vive le roi,*" &c. It is founded on the idea that long life is to be regarded as a blessing, and that we can in no way express our good wishes for any one better than to wish him length of days. In this place, it was merely the usual expression of respect and homage, showing their earnest wish for the welfare of the monarch. They were willing to do anything to promote his happiness, and the continuance of his life and reign. It was especially proper for them to use this language, as they were about to make a rather unusual request, which *might* be construed as an act of disrespect, implying that the king had not

given them all the means which it was equitable for them to have in explaining the matter, by requiring them to interpret the dream when he had not told them what it was. ¶ *Tell thy servants the dream, and we will show the interpretation.* The claim which they set up in regard to the future was evidently only that of *explaining* what were regarded as the prognostics of future events. It was not that of being able to recal what is forgotten, or even to *originate* what might be regarded as pre-intimations of what is to happen. This was substantially the claim which was asserted by all the astrologers, augurs, and soothsayers of ancient times. Dreams, the flight of birds, the aspect of the entrails of animals slain for sacrifice, the positions of the stars, meteors, and uncommon appearances in the heavens, were supposed to be intimations made by the gods of what was to occur in future times, and the business of those who claimed the power of divining the future was merely to interpret these things. When the king, therefore, required that they should recal the dream itself to his own mind, it was a claim to something which was not involved in their profession, and which they regarded as unjust. To that power they made no pretensions. If it be asked why, as they were mere jugglers and pretenders, they did not *invent* something and state *that* as his dream, since he had forgotten what his dream actually was, we may reply, (1.) that there is no certain evidence that they were not sincere in what they professed themselves able to do—for we are not to suppose that all who claimed to be soothsayers and astrologers were hypocrites and intentional deceivers. It was not at that period of the world certainly determined that nothing could be ascertained respecting the future by dreams, and by the positions of the stars, &c. Dreams *were* among the methods by which the future was made known; and whether the knowledge of what is to come could be obtained from the positions of the stars, &c., was a question which was at that time unsettled. Even Lord Bacon maintained that the

5 The king answered and said to the Chaldeans, The thing is gone | from me: if ye will not make known unto me the dream, with the inter-

science of astrology was not to be *rejected*, but to be *reformed*. (2.) If the astrologers had been disposed to attempt to deceive the king, there is no probability that they could have succeeded in palming an invention of their own on him as his own dream. We may not be able distinctly to recollect a dream, but we have a sufficient impression of it—of its outlines—or of some striking, though disconnected, things in it, to know what it is *not*. We might instantly recognize it if stated to us; we should see at once, if any one should attempt to deceive us by palming an invented dream on us, that *that* was not what we had dreamed.

5. *The king answered and said to the Chaldeans, The thing is gone from me.* The Vulgate renders this, *Sermo recessit à me*—"The word is departed from me." So the Greek, 'Ο λόγος ἀπ' ἐμοῦ ἀπέστη. Luther, *Es ist mir entfallen*—"It has fallen away from me," or has departed from me. Coverdale, "It is gone from me." The Chaldee word rendered "the thing"—מִלְּתָה—means, properly, *a word, saying, discourse*—something which is *spoken*; then, like דָּבָר and the Greek ῥῆμα, a *thing*. The reference here is to the matter under consideration, to wit, the dream and its meaning. The fair interpretation is, that he had forgotten the dream, and that if he retained *any* recollection of it, it was only such an imperfect outline as to alarm him. The word rendered "is gone"—אַזְדָּא—which occurs only here and in ver. 8, is supposed to be the same as אֲזַל—*to go away, to depart*. Gesenius renders the whole phrase, "The word has gone out from me; *i.e.*, what I have said is ratified, and cannot be recalled;" and Prof. Bush (*in loc.*) contends that this is the true interpretation, and this also is the interpretation preferred by J. D. Michaelis, and Dathe. A construction somewhat similar is adopted by Aben Ezra, C. B. Michaelis, Winer, Hengstenberg, and Prof. Stuart, that it means, "My decree is firm, or steadfast;" to wit, that if they did not fur- | nish an interpretation of the dream, they should be cut off. The question as to the true interpretation, then, is between two constructions: whether it means, as in our version, that the dream had departed from him—that is, that he had forgotten it—or, that a decree or command had gone from him, that if they could not interpret the dream they should be destroyed. That the former is the correct interpretation seems to me to be evident. (1.) It is the natural construction, and accords best with the meaning of the original words. Thus no one can doubt that the word מִלָּה, and the words דָּבָר and ῥῆμα, are used in the sense of *thing*, and that the natural and proper meaning of the Chaldee verb אֲזַד is, *to go away, depart.* Comp. the Hebrew (אָזַל) in Deut. xxxii. 36, "He seeth that their power *is gone;*" 1 Sam. ix. 7, "The bread *is spent* in our vessels;" Job xiv. 11, "The waters *fail* from the sea;" and the Chaldee (אֲזַל) in Ezra iv. 23. "They *went up* in haste to Jerusalem;" v. 8, "We *went* into the province of Judea;" and Dan. ii. 17, 24; vi. 18 (19), 19 (20). (2.) This interpretation is sustained by the Vulgate of Jerome, and by the Greek. (3.) It does not appear that any such command had at that time gone forth from the king, and it was only when they came before him that he promulgated such an order. Even though the word, as Gesenius and Zickler (*Chaldaismus Dan. Proph.*) maintain, is a feminine participle present, instead of a verb in the preterit, still it would then as well apply to the *dream* departing from him, as the command or edict. We may suppose the king to say, "The thing leaves me; I cannot recal it." (4.) It was so understood by the magicians, and the king did not attempt to correct their apprehension of what he meant. Thus, in ver. 7, they say, "Let the king tell his servants the dream, and we will show the interpretation thereof." This shows that they understood that the dream had gone from him, and that they could not be

pretation thereof, ye shall be ¹cut

expected to interpret its meaning until they were apprised what it was. (5.) It is not necessary to suppose that the king retained the memory of the dream himself, and that he meant merely to try them; that is, that he told them a deliberate falsehood, in order to put their ability to the test. Nebuchadnezzar was a cruel and severe monarch, and such a thing would not have been entirely inconsistent with his character; but we should not needlessly charge cruelty and tyranny on any man, nor should we do it unless the evidence is so clear that we cannot avoid it. Besides, that such a test should be proposed is in the highest degree improbable. There was no need of it; and it was contrary to the established belief in such matters. These men were retained at court, among other reasons, for the very purpose of explaining the prognostics of the future. There was confidence in them; and they were retained *because* there was confidence in them. It does not appear that the Babylonian monarch had had any reason to distrust their ability as to what they professed; and why should he, therefore, on *this* occasion resolve to put them to so unusual, and obviously so unjust a trial? For these reasons, it seems clear to me that our common version has given the correct sense of this passage, and that the meaning is, that the dream had actually so far departed from him that he could not repeat it, though he retained such an impression of its portentous nature, and of its appalling outline, as to fill his mind with alarm. As to the objection derived from this view of the passage by Bertholdt to the authenticity of this chapter, that it is wholly improbable that any man would be so unreasonable as to doom others to punishment because they could not recal his dream, since it entered not into their profession to be able to do it (*Comm.* i. p. 192), it may be remarked, that the character of Nebuchadnezzar was such as to make what is stated here by Daniel by no means improbable. Thus it is said respecting him

in pieces, ᵃand your houses ᵇ shall be made a dunghill:

(2 Kings xxv. 7), "And they slew the sons of Zedekiah *before his eyes*, and put out the eyes of Zedekiah, and bound him with fetters of brass, and carried him to Babylon." Comp. 2 Kings xxv. 18–21; Jer. xxxix. 5, *seq.*; lii. 9–11. See also Dan. iv. 17, where he is called "the basest of men." Comp. Hengstenberg, *Die Authentie des Daniel*, pp. 79–81. On this objection, see Intro. to the chapter, § 1. I. ¶ *If ye will not make known unto me the dream, with the interpretation thereof.* Whatever may be thought as to the question whether he had actually forgotten the dream, there can be no doubt that he demanded that they should state what it was, and then explain it. This demand was probably as unusual as it was in one sense unreasonable, since it did not fall fairly within their profession. Yet it was not unreasonable in this sense, that if they really had communication with the gods, and were qualified to explain future events, it might be supposed that they would be enabled to recal this forgotten dream. If the gods gave them power to explain what was to *come*, they could as easily enable them to recal *the past*. ¶ *Ye shall be cut in pieces.* Marg., *made*. The Chaldee is, "Ye shall be made into pieces;" referring to a mode of punishment that was common to many ancient nations. Compare 1 Sam. xv. 33: "And Samuel hewed Agag in pieces before the Lord in Gilgal." Thus Orpheus is said to have been torn in pieces by the Thracian women; and Bessus was cut in pieces by order of Alexander the Great. ¶ *And your houses shall be made a dunghill.* Compare 2 Ki. x. 27. This is an expression denoting that their houses, instead of being elegant or comfortable mansions, should be devoted to the vilest cf uses, and subjected to all kinds of dishonour and defilement. The language here used is in accordance with that which is commonly employed by Orientals. They imprecate all sorts of indignities and abominations on the objects of their dislike, and it is not uncommon for them to smear over with filth what is

6 But *if ye show the dream, and the interpretation thereof ye shall receive of me gifts, and ¹ rewards,

a ch. 5. 16.   1 or. *fee*, ver. 48; ch. 5. 17.

the object of their contempt or abhorrence. Thus when the caliph Omar took Jerusalem, at the head of the Saracen army, after ravaging the greater part of the city, he caused dung to be spread over the site of the sanctuary, in token of the abhorrence of all Mussulmans, and of its being henceforth regarded as the refuse and offscouring of all things.—Prof. Bush. The Greek renders this, "And your houses shall be plundered;" the Vulgate, "And your houses shall be confiscated." But these renderings are entirely arbitrary. This may seem to be a harsh punishment which was threatened, and some may, perhaps, be disposed to say that it is improbable that a monarch would allow himself to use such intemperate language, and to make use of so severe a threatening, especially when the magicians had as yet shown no inability to interpret the dream, and had given no reasons to apprehend that they would be unable to do it. But we are to remember (1) the cruel and arbitrary character of the king (see the references above); (2) the nature of an Oriental despotism, in which a monarch is accustomed to require all his commands to be obeyed, and his wishes gratified promptly, on pain of death ; (3) the fact that his mind was greatly excited by the dream; and (4) that he was certain that something portentous to his kingdom had been prefigured by the dream, and that this was a case in which all the force of threatening, and all the prospect of splendid reward, should be used, that they might be induced to tax their powers to the utmost, and allay the tumults of his mind.

6. *But if ye show the dream.* If you show what the dream was. ¶ *And the interpretation thereof.* What it signifies. That is, they were so to state the dream that Nebuchadnezzar would recognise it ; and they were to give such an explanation of it as would commend itself to his mind as the true one. On this last point he would doubtless rely much on their supposed wisdom in per-

and great honour: therefore show me the dream and the interpretation thereof.

7 They answered again, and said

forming this duty, but it would seem clear, also, that it was necessary that the interpretation should be seen to be a *fair* interpretation, or such as would be *fairly* implied in the dream. Thus, when Daniel made known the interpretation, he saw at once that it met all the features of the dream, and he admitted it to be correct. So also when Daniel explained the handwriting on the wall to Belshazzar, he admitted the justness of it, and loaded him with honours, Dan. v. 29. So when Joseph explained the dreams of Pharaoh, he at once saw the appropriateness of the explanation, and admitted it to be correct (Gen. xli. 39–45) ; and so in the case above referred to (notes on ver. 2), of Astyages respecting the dreams of his daughter (Herod. 1, cvii., cviii.), he at once saw that the interpretation of the dreams proposed by the Magi accorded with the dreams, and took his measures accordingly. ¶ *Ye shall receive of me gifts, and rewards, and great honour.* Intending to appeal to their highest hopes to induce them, if possible, to disclose the meaning of the dream. He specifies no particular rewards, but makes the promise general ; and the evident meaning is, that, in such a case, he would bestow what it became a monarch like him to give. That the usual rewards in such a case were such as were adapted to stimulate to the most vigorous exertions of their powers, may be seen from the honour which he conferred on Daniel when he made known the dream (ver. 48), and from the rewards which Belshazzar conferred on Daniel for making known the interpretation of the writing on the wall (ch. v. 29): "Then commanded Belshazzar, and they clothed Daniel with scarlet, and put a chain of gold about his neck, and made a proclamation concerning him, that he should be the third ruler in the kingdom." Comp. Esth. v. 11 ; vi. 7–9.

7. *They answered again, and said, Let the king tell his servants the dream, and we will show the interpretation of*

Let the king tell his servants the dream, and we will show the interpretation of it.

8 The king answered and said, I know of certainty that ye would

gain [1] the time, because ye see the thing is gone from me.

9 But if ye will not make known unto me the dream, *there is but* one

1 or, *buy*, Ep. 5. 1.

---

it. Certainly not an unreasonable request, in any circumstances, and especially in theirs. They did not profess, evidently, to be able to recal a dream that was forgotten, but the extent of their profession on this subject appears to have been, that they were able to *explain* what was commonly regarded as a prognostic of a future event. 8. *The king answered and said, I know of certainty that ye would gain the time.* Marg., *buy.* The Chaldee word זְבִנִין (from זְבַן) means, to get for one's self, buy, gain, procure. Greek, ἐξαγοράζετε—"*that ye redeem* time;" and so the Vulgate—*quod tempus redimitis.* The idea is, that they saw that they could not comply with his requisition, and that their asking him (ver. 7) to state the dream was only a pretext for delay, in the hope that in the interval some device might be hit on by them to appease him, or to avert his threatened indignation. It would be natural to suppose that they might hope that on reflection he would become more calm, and that, although they *might* not be able to recal the dream and explain it, yet it would be seen to be unreasonable to expect or demand it. The king seems to have supposed that some such thoughts were passing through their minds, and he charges on them such a project. The argument of the king seems to have been something like this : "They who can explain a dream correctly can as well tell what it is as what its interpretation is, for the one is as much the result of Divine influence as the other ; and if men can hope for Divine help in the one case, why not in the other? As you cannot, therefore, recal the dream, it is plain that you cannot interpret it ; and your only object in demanding to know it is, that you may ward off as long as possible the execution of the threatened sentence, and, if practicable, escape it altogether." It is not improbable that what they said

was more than the simple request recorded in ver. 7. They would naturally enlarge on it, by attempting to show how unreasonable was the demand of the king in the case, and their arguments would give a fair pretext for what he here charges on them. ¶ *Because ye see the thing is gone from me.* According to the interpretation proposed in ver. 5, *the dream.* The meaning is, "You see that I have forgotten it. I have made a positive statement on that point. There can be no hope, therefore, that it *can* be recalled, and it is clear that your only object *must be* to gain time. Nothing can be gained by delay, and the matter may therefore be determined at once, and your conduct be construed as a confession that you cannot perform what is required, and the sentence proceed without delay." This makes better sense, it seems to me, than to suppose that he means that a sentence had gone forth from him that if they could not recal and interpret it they should be put to death.

9. *But if ye will not make known unto me the dream,* there is but *one decree for you.* That is, you shall share the same fate. You shall all be cut to pieces, and your houses reduced to ruin, ver. 5. There shall be no favour shown to any class of you, or to any individual among you. It seems to have been supposed that the responsibility rested on them individually as well as collectively, and that it would be right to hold each and every one of them bound to explain the matter. As no difference of obligation was recognized, there would be no difference of criminality. It should be said, however, that there is a difference of interpretation here. Gesenius, and some others, render the word translated *decree*—דָּת—*counsel, plan, purpose,* and suppose that it means, "this only is your counsel, or plan ;" that is, to prepare lying words, and to gain time. So Prof. Stuart renders the verse, "If ye will not make known to me the

decree for you; for ye have prepared lying and corrupt words to speak before me, till the time be changed: therefore tell me the dream, and I *a* shall know that ye can show me the interpretation thereof.

10 ¶ The Chaldeans answered

a Is. 41. 23.

dream, one thing is your purpose, both a false and deceitful word have ye agreed to utter before me, until the time shall have changed; therefore tell me the dream, and then I shall know that you can show me the interpretation thereof." The original word, however, is most commonly used in the sense of *law* or *decree.* See Deut. xxxiii. 2; Esth. i. 8, 13, 15, 19; ii. 8; iii. 8, 14, 15; iv. 3, 8, 11, 16; viii. 13, 14, 17; ix. 1, 13, 14; and there seems to be no necessity for departing from the common translation. It contains a sense according to the truth in the case, and is in accordance with the Greek, Latin, and Syriac versions. ¶ *For ye have prepared lying and corrupt words to speak before me.* That is, "You have done this in asking me to state the dream (vers. 4, 7), and in the demand that the dream should be made known to you, in order that you may interpret it. I shall know by your inability to recal the dream that you have been acting a false and deceitful part, and that your pretensions were all false. Your wish, therefore, to have me state the dream will be shown to be a mere pretence, an artifice for delay, that you might put off the execution of the sentence with the hope of escaping altogether." ¶ *Till the time be changed.* That is, till a new state of things shall occur; either until his purpose might change, and his anger should subside, or till there should be a change of government. It was natural for such thoughts to pass through the mind of the king, since, as matters could be no *worse* for them if the subject was delayed, there was a possibility that they might be *better*—for any change would be likely to be an advantage. There does not appear to have been any great confidence or affection on either side. The king suspected that they were influenced by bad motives, and they certainly had no strong reasons for attachment to him. Comp. notes on ver. 21, and ch. vii. 25.

10. *The Chaldeans answered before the king, and said.* Perhaps the *Chaldeans* answered because they were the highest in favour, and were those in whom most confidence was usually reposed in such matters. See Notes on ver. 2. On such an occasion, those would be likely to be put forward to announce their inability to do this who would be supposed to be able to interpret the dream, if any could, and on whom most reliance was usually placed. ¶ *There is not a man upon the earth that can show the king's matter.* Chald., אַרְעָא־בַל־עַ—"*upon the dry ground.*" Comp. Gen. i. 10. The meaning is, that the thing was utterly beyond the power of man. It was what none who practised the arts of divining laid claim to. They doubtless supposed that as great proficients in that art as the world could produce might be found among the wise men assembled at the court of Babylon, and if they failed, they inferred that all others would fail. This was, therefore, a decided confession of their inability in the matter; but they meant to break the force of that mortifying confession, and perhaps to appease the wrath of the king, by affirming that the thing was wholly beyond the human powers, and that no one could be expected to do what was demanded. ¶ *Therefore there is no king, lord, nor ruler, that asked such things.* No one has ever made a similar demand. The matter is so clear, the incompetency of man to make such a disclosure is so manifest, that no potentate of any rank ever made such a request. They designed, undoubtedly, to convince the king that the request was so unreasonable that he would not insist on it. They were urgent, for

before the king, and said, There is not a man upon the earth that can show the king's matter: therefore *there is* no king, lord, nor ruler, *that* asked such things at any magician, or astrologer, or Chaldean.

11 And *it is* a rare thing that

the king **requireth**: and there is | the king, except *a* the gods, whose
none other that can show it before | dwelling *b* is not with flesh.

|

their life depended on it, and they apprehended that they had justice on
their side.

11. *And it is a rare thing that the
king requireth.* Chald., רַקִּירָה—meaning, *choice, valuable, costly;* then,
heavy, hard, difficult. Greek, βαρὺς.
Vulgate, *gravis—heavy, weighty.* The
idea is not so much that the thing demanded by the king was *uncommon* or
rarely made—though that was true, as
that it was so difficult as to be beyond
the human powers. They would not
have been likely on such an occasion
to say that the requirement was absolutely unjust or unreasonable. The
term which they used was respectful,
and yet it implied that no man could
have any hope of solving the question
as it was proposed by him. ¶ *And
there is none other that can show it
before the king except the gods, whose
dwelling is not with flesh.* This was
clearly true, that a matter of that
kind could not be disclosed except by
Divine assistance. It would seem
from this that these persons did not
claim to be inspired, or to have communication with the gods; or, at least,
that they did not claim to be inspired
by the Supreme God, but that they
relied on their own natural sagacity,
and their careful and long study of the
meaning of those occurrences which
prefigured future events, and perhaps
on the mystic arts derived from their
acquaintance with science as then understood. The word *gods* here—אֱלָהִין
Elahin [the same as the Heb. *Elohim*]
—is in the plural number, but might
be applied to the true God, as the
Hebrew Elohim often is. It is by no
means certain that they meant to use
this in the plural, or to say that it was
an admitted truth that the gods worshipped in Babylon did not dwell with
men. It was, undoubtedly, the common opinion that they did; that the
temples were their abode; and that
they frequently appeared among men,
and took part in human affairs. But
it was a very early opinion that the
Supreme God was withdrawn from

human affairs, and had committed the
government of the world to intermediate beings—*internuncii*—demons, or
æons: beings of power far superior to
that of men, who constantly mingled in
human affairs. Their power, however,
though great, was limited; and may not
the Chaldeans here by the word אֱלָהִין—
Elahin—have meant to refer to the
Supreme God, and to say that *this* was
a case which pertained to him alone;
that no inferior divinity could be competent to do such a thing as he demanded; and that as the Supreme God
did *not* dwell among men it was hopeless to attempt to explain the matter?
Thus understood, the result will convey
a higher truth, and will show more im-
pressively the honour put on Daniel.
The phrase, *whose dwelling is not with
flesh,* means *with men — in human
bodies.* On the supposition that this
refers to the Supreme God, this undoubtedly accords with the prevailing
sentiment of those times, that however
often the inferior divinities might appear to men, and assume human forms,
yet the Supreme God was far removed,
and never thus took up his abode on the
earth. They could hope, therefore, for
no communication from Him who alone
would be competent to the solution of
such a secret as this. This may be regarded, therefore, as a frank confession
of their entire failure in the matter under consideration. They acknowledged
that *they* themselves were not competent to the solution of the question,
and they expressed the opinion that
the ability to do it could not be obtained from the help which the inferior
gods rendered to men, and that it was
hopeless to expect the Supreme God—
far withdrawn from human affairs—to
interpose. It was a public acknowledgment that their art failed on a most
important trial, and thus the way was
prepared to show that Daniel, under
the teaching of the true God, was able
to accomplish what was wholly beyond
all human power. The trial had been
fairly made. The wisest men of the
Chaldean realm had been applied to.

12 For this cause the king was angry and very furious, and com-manded to destroy all "the wise men of Babylon.

a Mat. 2. 16.

They on whom reliance had been placed in such emergencies; they who professed to be able to explain the prognostics of future events; they who had been assembled at the most important and magnificent court of the world—the very centre of Pagan power; they who had devoted their lives to investigations of this nature, and who might be supposed to be competent to such a work, if any on earth could, now openly acknowledged that their art failed them, and expressed the conviction that there was no resource in the case.

12. *For this cause the king was angry.* Because they failed in explaining the subject which had been referred to them. It is true that his anger was unjust, for their profession did not imply that they would undertake to explain what he de-manded, but his wrath was not unnatu-ral. His mind was alarmed, and he was troubled. He believed that what he had seen in his dream foreboded some im-portant events, and, as an arbitrary sovereign, unaccustomed to restrain his anger or to inquire into the exact jus-tice of matters which excited his indig-nation, it was not unnatural that he should resolve to wreak his vengeance on all who made any pretensions to the arts of divining. ¶ *And very furious.* Wrought up to the highest degree of passion. Chaldee, "Much enraged." It was not a calm and settled purpose to execute his threat, but a purpose at-tended with a high degree of excite-ment. ¶ *And commanded to destroy all the wise* men *of Babylon.* That is, all who made pretensions to this kind of wisdom; all who came under the well-known denomination of *wise men,* or *sages.* He had called that class be-fore him (ver. 2); he had demanded of them an explanation of his dream; he had been assured by the leading men among them, the Chaldeans (verses 10, 11), that they could not recall his dream; and, as he supposed that all who could be relied on in such a case had failed, he resolved to cut them off as impostors.

[The cruelty of Asiatic despots, and their in-

fliction of extreme and agonizing punishment on the most frivolous pretences, are proverbial. The fury and anger of Nebuchadnezzar would, no doubt, result in a sentence of death against

13 And the decree went forth that the wise *men* should be slain; and they sought Daniel and his fellows to be slain.

1 *returned.*

14 ¶ Then Daniel [1] answered with counsel and wisdom to Arioch the [2] captain of the king's guard,

2 *chief of the executioners,* or *slaughter-men,* or *chief marshal;* Ge. 37. 36; Jer. 52. 12, 14.

the wise men, accompanied by the most excruciating tortures. And we may probably learn its nature from the engraving, which represents the chief of the slayers commencing the operation of flaying alive, whilst the miserable culprit seems to be deprecating the monarch's wrath. This group forms part of the sculptures in the Hall of Judgment in the interior of the palace at Khorsabad.]

Where Daniel was at this time is not known. It would seem, however, that from some reason he had not been summoned before the king with the others, probably because, although he had shown himself to be eminently endowed with wisdom (ch. i. 20), he had not yet made any pretensions to this kind of knowledge, and was not numbered with the Magi, or Chaldeans. When, however, the decree went forth that *all* the " wise men of Babylon " should be slain, the exhibition of wisdom and knowledge made by him (chap. i. 18–20) was recollected, and the executioners of the sentence supposed that he and his companions were included in the general instructions. Whether the word *Babylon* here relates to the city of Babylon, or to the whole realm, there is no certain way of determining. Considering, however, the character of Oriental despotisms, and the cruelty to which absolute sovereigns have usually been transported in their passion, there would be no·improbability in supposing that the command included the whole realm, though it is probable that most of this class would be found in the capital.

13. *And the decree went forth that the wise* men *should be slain.* The original here will bear a somewhat different translation, meaning, "the decree went forth, *and* the wise men were slain;" that is, the execution of the sentence was actually commenced. So the Vulgate : *Et egressâ sententiâ, sapientes interficiebantur.* So also the Greek version : καὶ οἱ σοφοὶ ἀπεκτέννοντο —"and the wise men were slain." This seems to me to be the more probable inter-

pretation, and better to suit the connection. Then it would mean that they had actually begun to execute the decree, and that in the prosecution of their bloody work they sought out Daniel and his companions, and that by his influence with Arioch the execution of the sentence was arrested. ¶ *And they sought Daniel and his fellows to be slain.* His three companions (ch. i. 6), who probably had not been among those who were summoned to court to explain the matter. Had they been consulted at first, the issuing of the decree would have been prevented, but it seems to have been the design of Providence to give the fairest trial of the ability of these sages, and to allow matters to come to a crisis, in order to show that what was done was wholly beyond human power.

14. *Then Daniel answered.* Marg., *returned.* The original literally is, "returned counsel and wisdom," meaning, that he returned an answer which was replete with wisdom. It would seem probable that Arioch had communicated to Daniel the decree of the king, and had stated to him that he was involved in that decree, and must prepare to die. ¶ *Counsel and wisdom.* That is, *wise counsel.* He evinced great prudence and discretion in what he said. He made such a suggestion to Arioch as, if acted on, would stay the execution of the sentence against all the wise men, and would secure the object which the king had in view. What was the exact nature of this answer is not mentioned. It is probable, however, that it was that he might be enabled to disclose the dream, and that he made this so plausible to Arioch, that he was disposed to allow him to make the trial. It is evident that Arioch would not have consented to arrest the execution of the sentence, unless it had appeared to him to be in the highest degree probable that he would be able to relieve the anxiety of the king. Knowing that the *main* object of the king was to

which was gone forth to slay the wise *men* of Babylon :

obtain the interpretation of his dream, and seeing that this object was not any the more likely to be secured by the execution of this stern decree, and knowing the high favour with which Daniel had been received at court (ch. i. 19–21), he seems to have been willing to assume some measure of responsibility, and to allow Daniel to make his own representation to the king. ¶ *To Arioch the captain of the king's guard.* Marg., *" chief of the executioners,* or *slaughter-men,* or *chief marshal."* Greek, ἀρχιμαγείρῳ τοῦ βασιλέως —*chief cook of the king.* The Vulgate renders this, *"* Then Daniel inquired respecting the law and the sentence of Arioch, the commander of the royal army." The Chaldee word rendered *guard* is עַבָּחַיָא. It is derived from טַבָּח *tăbăhh,* to slaughter ; to kill animals ; and then to kill or slay men. The *noun,* then, means a slaughterer or slayer ; a cook ; an executioner, or one who kills men at the will of a sovereign, or by due sentence of law. There can be no doubt that the word here refers to Arioch, as sent out to execute this sentence ; yet we are not to regard him as a *mere* executioner, or as we would a hangman, for undoubtedly the king would entrust this sentence to one who was of respectable, if not of high rank. It is probable that one of the principal officers of his body-guard would be entrusted with the execution of such a sentence. In 1 Sam. viii. 13, the word is rendered *cooks.* It does not elsewhere occur. That he was not a *mere* executioner is apparent from the title given him in the next verse, where he is called "the king's *captain.*" ¶ *Which was gone forth to slay,* &c. He had gone to execute the decree, and its execution had already commenced.

15. *He answered and said to Arioch the king's captain.* The word *captain* —a different word from that which occurs in ver. 14, שַׁלִּיטָא—denotes one who has rule or dominion ; one who is powerful or mighty ; and it would be applied only to one who sustained a

15 He answered and said to Arioch the king's captain, Why *is*

post of honour and responsibility. See the use of the word שְׁלֵט, as meaning *to rule,* in Neh. v. 15 ; Eccles. ii. 19 ; vi. 2 ; viii. 9 ; Esth. ix. 1 ; Psa. cxix. 133. The word here used is the same which occurs in ver. 10, where it is rendered *ruler.* It doubtless denotes here an officer of rank, and designates one of more honourable employment than would be denoted by the word *executioner.* It should be said on these verses (14, 15), however, that the office of executioner in the East was by no means regarded as a dishonourable office. It was entrusted to those high in rank, and even nobles considered it an honour, and often boasted of it as such, that among their ancestors there were those who had in this way been entrusted with executing the commands of their sovereign. Hanway and Abdul-Kerim both say that this office conferred honour and rank. Tournefort says, that in Georgia " the executioners are very rich, and men of standing undertake this employment ; far different from what occurs in other parts of the world, in that country this gives to a family a title of honour. They boast that among their ancestors there were many who were executioners ; and this they base on the sentiment, that nothing is more desirable than justice, and that nothing can be more honourable than to be engaged in administering the laws." See Rosenmüller, *Morgenland,* 1079. ¶ *Why* is *the decree so hasty from the king?* Implying that all the effort had not been made which it was possible to make to solve the mystery. The idea is, that a decree of such a nature, involving so many in ruin, ought not to have proceeded from the king without having taken all possible precautions, and having made all possible efforts to find those who might be able to disclose what the king desired. It was to Daniel a just matter of surprise that, after the favour and honour with which he had been received at court (ch. i. 19, 20), and the confidence which had been reposed in him, a command like this should have been issued,

the decree *so* hasty from the king?
Then Arioch made the thing known
to Daniel.

16 Then Daniel went in, and
desired of the king that he would
give him time, and that he would
show the king the interpretation.

17 Then Daniel went to his
house, and made the thing known
to Hananiah, Mishael, and Azariah,
his companions;

18 That *a* they would desire
mercies 1 of the God of heaven

a ch. 3. 17; 1 Sa. 17. 37; 2 Ti. 4. 17, 18.

1 *from before.*

so comprehensive as to embrace him
and his friends, when they had done
nothing to deserve the displeasure of
the king. ¶ *Then Arioch made the
thing known to Daniel.* The statement
respecting the dream ; the trouble of
the king ; the consultation of the magicians ; their inability to explain the
dream, and the positive command to
put all the pretenders to wisdom to
death. It is clear that Daniel had not
before been informed of these things.

16. *Then Daniel went in,* &c. Either
by himself, or through the medium of
some friend. Perhaps all that is meant
is, not that he actually went into the
presence of the monarch, but that he
went into the palace, and through the
interposition of some high officer of
court who had access to the sovereign,
desired of him that he would give him
time, and that he would make it known.
It would rather appear, from vers. 24,
25, that the first direct audience which he
had with the king was after the thing was
made known to him in a night vision,
and it would scarcely accord with established Oriental usages that he should
go immediately and unceremoniously
into the royal presence. A petition,
presented through some one who had
access to the king, would meet all the
circumstances of the case. ¶ *That he
would give him time.* He did not specify *why* he desired time, though the
reason why he did it is plain enough.
He wished to lay the matter before
God, and to engage his friends in earnest prayer that the dream and the
interpretation might be made known
to him. This request was granted to
him. It may seem remarkable, as no
time was allowed to the Chaldeans that
they might make inquiry (ver. 8), that
such a favour should have been granted
to Daniel, especially after the execution
of the sentence had been commenced ;
but we are to remember (1) that the

king would recollect the favour which
he had already shown Daniel on good
grounds, and the fact that he regarded
him as endowed with great wisdom,
ch. i. 19, 20. (2.) Daniel did not ask,
as the Chaldeans did, that the king
should tell the dream before he undertook to explain it, but he proposed
evidently to unfold the whole matter.
(3.) It could not but occur to the king
that Daniel had not yet been consulted,
and that it was but reasonable that he
should have a fair trial now, since it
appeared that he was involved in the
general sentence. (4.) The anxiety of
the king to understand the dream was
so great that he was willing to grasp
at *any* hope in order that his perplexities might be relieved ; and (5) it is not
improper to suppose that there may
have been a Divine influence on the
mind of this monarch, making him
willing to do so simple an act of justice as this, in order that it might be
seen and acknowledged that the hand
of God was in the whole matter.

17. *Then Daniel went to his house.*
It is quite evident that he had obtained
the object of his request, though this is
not expressly mentioned. The king
was undoubtedly, for the reasons above
stated, willing that he should have a
fair opportunity to try his skill in disclosing the mysterious secret. ¶ *And
made the thing known to Hananiah,*
&c. Made the whole matter known
—the perplexity respecting the dream ;
the failure of the Chaldeans to interpret it ; the decree ; and his own petition to the king. They had a common
interest in knowing it, as their lives
were all endangered.

18. *That they would desire mercies
of the God of heaven concerning this
secret.* That they would implore of
God that he would show his mercy to
them in revealing this secret, that their
lives might be spared. In the margin,

concerning this secret, that [1] Daniel and his fellows should not perish with the rest of the wise *men* of Babylon.

19 ¶ Then was the secret revealed unto Daniel in a night

1 or, *they should not destroy Daniel.*

vision.[a] Then Daniel blessed the God of heaven.

20 Daniel answered and said, Blessed [b] be the name of God for ever and ever ; for wisdom [c] and might are his :

a Nu. 12. 6.　　*b* Ps. 50. 23.　　*c* Je. 32. 19.

as in the Chaldee, this is "*from before* the God of heaven." All depended now on God. It was clear that human skill was exhausted, and that no reliance could be placed on any ability which man possessed. The art of the Chaldeans had failed, and Daniel, as well by this failure as by the promptings of his own feelings, must now have perceived that the only hope was in God, and that his favour in the case was to be obtained only by prayer. As his three friends were equally interested in the issue, and as it was an early principle of religion, and one found in all dispensations (comp. Matt. xviii. 19), that *united* prayer has special power with God, it was natural and proper to call on his friends to join with him in asking this favour from Him who alone could grant it. It was the natural and the last resource of piety, furnishing an example of what all may do, and should do, in times of perplexity and danger. ¶ *That Daniel and his fellows should not perish.* Marg., "or, *they should not destroy Daniel.*" The leading in the margin is most in accordance with the Chaldee, though the sense is substantially the same. The word *fellows* is the same which is before rendered *companions*. ¶ *With the rest of the wise* men *of Babylon*. It seems to have been certain that the decree would be executed on the Chaldeans, soothsayers, &c. And, indeed, there was no reason *why* the decree should not be executed. They had confessed their inability to comply with the king's command, and whatever Daniel could now do could not be construed in their favour as furnishing any reason why the decree should not be executed on them. It was presumed, therefore, that the law, severe as it seemed to be, would be carried into effect on them, and we may suppose that this was probably done. The only hope of their escaping from the common lot was in the belief

that the God whom they served would now interpose in their behalf.

19. *Then was the secret revealed*, &c. To wit, the dream and the interpretation. The thing which had been *hidden* was disclosed. We may suppose that this occurred after a suitable time had been given to prayer. ¶ *In a night vision.* A representation made to him at night, but whether when he was asleep or awake does not appear. Comp. Notes on ch. i. 17 ; Isa. i. 1 ; Job iv. 13 ; xxxiii. 15. ¶ *Then Daniel blessed the God of heaven.* Nothing would be more natural than that he should burst forth in a song of grateful praise for disclosing a secret by means of which his life, and the lives of his companions, would be preserved, and by which such signal honour would redound to God himself, as alone able to reveal coming events.

20. *Daniel answered and said.* The word "answer," in the Scriptures, often occurs substantially in the sense of *speak* or *say.* It does not always denote a reply to something that has been said by another, as it does with us, but is often used when a speech is commenced, as if one were replying to something that *might* be said in the case, or as meaning that the circumstances in the case gave rise to the remark. Here the meaning is, that Daniel responded, as it were, to the goodness which God had manifested, and gave utterance to his feelings in appropriate expressions of praise. ¶ *Blessed be the name of God for ever and ever.* That is, blessed be God—the *name*, in the Scriptures, being often used to denote the person himself. It is common in the Bible to utter ascriptions of praise to God in view of important revelations, or in view of great mercies. Comp. the song of Moses after the passage of the Red Sea, Exod. xv. ; the song of Deborah after the overthrow of Sisera, Judg. v. ; Isa.

21 And he changeth the *a* times
and the seasons : he *b* removeth
a Ps. 31. 14, 15.   b Ps. 75. 6, 7.

kings, and setteth up kings: he
giveth *a* wisdom unto the wise, and
c Pr. 2. 6, 7.

xii. ¶ *For wisdom and might are
his.* Both these were manifested in a
remarkable manner in the circumstances of this case, and therefore these
were the beginnings of the song of
praise : *wisdom*, as now imparted to
Daniel, enabling him to disclose this
secret, when all human skill had failed ;
and *might*, as about to be evinced in
the changes of empire indicated by the
dream and the interpretation. Comp.
Jer. xxxii. 19, " Great in counsel, and
mighty in work."
21. *And he changeth the times and
the seasons.* The object of this is to
assert the general control of God in
reference to all changes which occur.
The assertion is made, undoubtedly, in
view of the revolutions in empire which
Daniel now saw, from the signification
of the dream, were to take place under
the Divine hand. Foreseeing now
these vast changes denoted by different parts of the image (vers. 36—45),
stretching into far-distant times, Daniel
was led to ascribe to God the control
over *all* the revolutions which occur
on earth. There is no essential difference between the words *times* and *seasons.* The words in Chaldee denote
stated or appointed seasons ; and the
idea of times *appointed, set, determined*, enters into both. Times and
seasons are not under the control of
chance, but are bounded by established
laws ; and yet God, who appointed
these laws, has power to change them,
and all the changes which occur under
those laws are produced by his agency.
Thus the changes which occur in regard
to day and night, spring and summer,
autumn and winter, clouds and sunshine, health and sickness, childhood
and youth, manhood and age, are under his control. Such changes, being
in accordance with certain laws, may
be regarded as *appointed*, or *set*, and
yet the laws and the revolutions consequent on them are all under his control. So in regard to the revolutions
of empire. By the arrangements of
his providence he secures such revolutions as he shall see it to be best should

occur, and in all of them his high hand
should be regarded. The words *seasons* and *times* are of frequent occurrence in Daniel, and are sometimes
used in a peculiar sense (see Notes on
ch. vii. 25), but here to
be employed in their usual and general signification, to denote that *all* the
revolutions which occur on earth are
under his control. ¶ *He removeth
kings, and setteth up kings.* He has
absolute control over all the sovereigns
of the earth, to place on the throne
whom he will, and to remove them
when he pleases. This was doubtless
suggested to Daniel, and was made the
foundation of this portion of his hymn
of praise, from what he was permitted
to see in the disclosures made to him
in the interpretation of the dream. He
then saw (compare vers. 37–45) that
there would be most important revolutions of kingdoms under the hand of
God, and being deeply impressed with
these great prospective changes, he
makes this general statement, that it
was the prerogative of God to do this
at pleasure. Nebuchadnezzar was
brought to feel this, and to recognize
it, when he said (ch. iv. 17), " The
Most High ruleth in the kingdom of
men, and giveth it to whomsoever he
will ;" " he doeth according to his will
in the army of heaven, and among the
inhabitants of the earth : none can stay
his hand, or say unto him, What doest
thou ?" ch. iv. 32, 35. This claim is
often asserted for God in the Scriptures as a proof of his supremacy and
greatness. " For promotion cometh
neither from the east, nor from the
west, nor from the south : but God is
the judge ; he putteth down one, and
setteth up another," Psa. lxxv. 6, 7.
Comp. 1 Sam. ii. 7, 8. Thus he claimed
absolute control over Sennacherib to
employ him at his pleasure in executing his purposes of punishment on the
Hebrew nation (Isa. x. 5–7), and thus
over Cyrus to execute his purposes on
Babylon, and to restore his people to
their land, Isa. xlv. 1, *seq.* See also
Isa. xlvi. 10, 11. In this manner, all

knowledge to them that know understanding.

22 He revealeth ^a the deep and

a Ps. 25. 14.   *b* Ps. 139. 11, 12; He. 4. 13.

the kings of the earth may be regarded as under his control ; and if the Divine plan were fully understood it would be found that each one has received his appointment under the Divine direction, to accomplish some important part in carrying forward the Divine plans to their fulfilment. A history of human affairs, showing the exact purpose of God in regard to each ruler who has occupied a throne, and the exact object which God designed to accomplish by placing *him* on the throne at the time when he did, would be a far more important and valuable history than any which has been written. Of many such rulers, like Cyrus, Sennacherib, Pilate, Henry VIII., Edward VI., and the Elector of Saxony, we can see the reason why they lived and reigned when they did ; and doubtless God has had some important end to accomplish in the development of his great plans in the case of every one who has ever occupied a throne.   ¶ *He giveth wisdom unto the wise*, &c. He is the source of all true wisdom and knowledge. This is often claimed for God in the Scriptures. Comp. Prov. ii. 6, 7 :

"For the Lord giveth wisdom ;
   Out of his mouth cometh knowledge and
      understanding.
   He layeth up sound wisdom for the righteous ;
   He is a buckler to them that walk uprightly."

See also 1 Kings iii. 9–12 ; Exod. xxxi. 3. God claims to be the source of all wisdom and knowledge. He originally formed each human intellect, and made it what it is ; he opens before it the paths of knowledge ; he gives to it clearness of perception ; he preserves its powers so that they do not become deranged ; he has power to make suggestions, to direct the laws of association, to fix the mind on important thoughts, and to open before it new and interesting views of truth. And as it would be found, if the history could be written, that God has placed each monarch on the throne with a distinct reference to some important purpose in the development of his great plans, so

secret things: he knoweth ^b what *is* in the darkness, and the light dwelleth ^c with him.

c 1 Ti. 6. 16; 1 Jn. 1. 5.

probably it would be seen that each important work of genius which has been written ; each invention in the arts ; and each discovery in science has been, for a similar purpose, under his control. He has created the great intellect just at the time when it was needful that such a discovery or invention should be made, and having prepared the world for it by the course of events, the discovery or invention has occurred just at the time when, on the whole, it was most desirable that it should.

22. *He revealeth the deep and secret things.* Things which are too profound for man to fathom by his own power, and which are concealed or hidden until he makes them known. What is said here is an advance on what was affirmed in the previous verse, and relates to another kind of knowledge. *That* related to such knowledge as was not properly beyond the grasp of the human intellect when unaided in any supernatural manner, and affirmed that even then all discoveries and inventions are to be traced to God ; *this* refers to a species of knowledge which lies beyond any natural compass of the human powers, and in which a supernatural influence is needed—such things as the Chaldeans and astrologers claimed the power of disclosing. The assertion here is, that when the highest human wisdom showed itself insufficient for the exigency, God was able to disclose those deep truths which it was desirable for man to understand. Applied generally, this refers to the truths made known by revelation—truths which man could never have discovered by his unaided powers.   ¶ *He knoweth what* is *in the darkness.* What appears to man to be involved in darkness, and on which no light seems to shine. This may refer not only to what is concealed from man in the literal darkness of night, but to all that is mysterious ; all that lies beyond the range of human inquiry ; all that pertains to unseen worlds. An immensely large portion of the universe

23 I thank thee, and praise thee, O thou God of my fathers, who hast given me wisdom and might, and hast made known unto me now what we desired of thee: for thou

lies wholly beyond the range of human investigation at present, and is, of course, dark to man. ¶ *And the light dwelleth with him.* The word rendered *dwelleth* (שְׁרֵא) means, properly, to loose, to unbind, to solve, as *e. g.* hard questions, Dan. v. 16; and is then applied to travellers who unbind the loads of their beasts to put up for the night, and then it comes to mean to put up for the night, to lodge, to dwell. Hence the meaning is, that the light abides with God; it is there as in its appropriate dwelling-place; he is in the midst of it: all is light about him; light when it is sent out goes from him; when it is gathered together, its appropriate place is with him. Comp. Job xxxviii. 19, 20 :—

'Where is the way where light dwelleth?
And as for darkness, where is the place thereof?
That thou shouldest take it to the bound thereof,
And that thou shouldest know the paths to the house thereof?"

See Notes on that passage. Comp. also 1 Tim. vi. 16: "Dwelling in the light which no man can approach unto." 1 John i. 5: "God is light, and in him is no darkness at all."

23. *I thank thee, and praise thee, O thou God of my fathers.* By his "fathers" here, Daniel refers doubtless to the Jewish people in general, and not to his own particular ancestors. The meaning of the phrase "God of my fathers" is, that he had been their protector; had regarded them as his people; had conferred on them great favours. The particular ground of thanksgiving here is, that the same God who had so often revealed himself to the Hebrew people by the prophets in their own land, had now condescended to do the same thing to one of their nation, though a captive in a strange country. The favour thus bestowed had an increased value, from the fact that it showed that the Hebrew people were not forgotten, though far from the land of their birth, and that, though in cap-

hast *now* made known unto us the king's matter.

24 ¶ Therefore Daniel went in unto Arioch, whom the king had ordained to destroy the wise *men*

tivity, they might still hope for the benign interposition of God. ¶ *Who hast given me wisdom and might.* The word "wisdom" here undoubtedly refers to the ability which had now been given him to declare the nature and purport of the dream, imparting to him a degree of wisdom far superior to those pretenders to whom the matter had been at first submitted. The word "might" (Chald., *strength*—גְּבוּרְתָא) does not probably differ materially from "wisdom." It means *ability* to interpret the dream —implying that it was a task beyond natural human ability. ¶ *For thou hast now made known unto us the king's matter.* That is, it had been made known to him and his friends. He joins himself with them; for, although it was particularly made known to *him,* yet, as they had united with him in prayer that the secret might be disclosed, and as they shared common dangers, he regarded it as in fact made known to them all.

24. *Therefore Daniel went in unto Arioch.* In view of the fact that the matter was now disclosed to him, he proposed to lay it before the king. This, of course, he did not do directly, but through Arioch, who was intrusted with the execution of the decree to slay the wise men of Babylon. That officer would naturally have access to the king, and it was proper that a proposal to arrest the execution of the sentence should be made through his instrumentality. The Chaldee (כָּל־קֳבֵל דְּנָה) is, properly, "on this whole account"— or, "on this whole account because" —in accordance with the usually full and pleonastic mode of writing particles, similar to the German *alldieweil,* or the compound English *forasmuch as.* The meaning is, that in view of the whole matter, he sought to lay the case before the king. ¶ *Destroy not the wise men of Babylon.* That is, "Stay the execution of the sentence on them. Though they have failed to furnish the

of Babylon : he went and said thus unto him, Destroy not the wise *men* of Babylon : bring me in before the king, and I will show unto the king the interpretation.

25 Then Arioch brought in Daniel before the king in haste, and said

1 *That I.*

thus unto him, [1] I have found a man of the [2] captives of Judah that will make known unto the king the interpretation.

26 The king answered, and said to Daniel, whose name *was* Belteshazzar, Art thou able to make

2 *children of the captivity.*

interpretation demanded, yet, as it *can* now be given, there is no occasion for the exercise of this severity." The ground of the sentence was that they could not interpret the dream. As the execution of the sentence involved Daniel and his friends, and as the reason why it was passed at all would now cease by his being able to furnish the required explanation, Daniel felt that it was a matter of mere justice that the execution of the sentence should cease altogether. ¶ *Bring me in before the king.* It would seem from this that Daniel did not regard himself as having free access to the king, and he would not unceremoniously intrude himself into his presence. This verse confirms the interpretation given of ver. 16, and makes it in the highest degree probable that this was the first occasion on which he was personally before the king in reference to this matter.

25. *Then Arioch brought in Daniel before the king in haste.* The Chaldee word used here implies *in tumultuous haste*, as of one who was violently excited, or in a state of trepidation, from בְּהַל—*to tremble, to be in trepidation.* The trepidation in this case may have arisen from one or both of two causes: (1) exultation, or joy, that the great secret was discovered ; or (2) joy that the effusion of blood might be stayed, and that there might be now no necessity to continue the execution of the sentence against the wise men. ¶ *I have found a man.* Marg., as in Chaldee, "That I have found a man." It is not to be supposed that Arioch had known anything of the application which Daniel had made to the king to delay the execution of the sentence (ver. 16), and, for anything that appears, he had suspended that execution on his own responsibility. Ignorant as he was, therefore, of any

DANIEL I.

such arrangement, and viewing only his own agency in the matter, it was natural for him to go in and announce this as something entirely new to the king, and without suggesting that the execution of the sentence had been at all delayed. It was a most remarkable circumstance, and one which looks like a Divine interposition, that he should have been disposed to delay the execution of the sentence at all, so that Daniel could have an opportunity of showing whether he could not divulge the secret. All the circumstances of the case seem to imply that Arioch was not a man of a cruel disposition, but was disposed, as far as possible, to prevent the effusion of blood. ¶ *Of the captives of Judah.* Marg., as in Chald., "of the children of the captivity." The word *Judah* here probably refers to the *country* rather than to the *people*, and means that he was among those who had been brought from the land of Judah. ¶ *That will make known unto the king the interpretation.* It is clear, from the whole narrative, that Arioch had great confidence in Daniel. All the *evidence* which he could have that he would be able to make this known. must have been from the fact that Daniel *professed* to be able to do it ; but such was his confidence in him that he had no doubt that he would be able to do it.

26. *The king answered, and said to Daniel, whose name was Belteshazzar.* Notes on ch. i. 7. The *king* may have addressed him by this name, and probably did during this interview. This was the name, it would seem, by which he was known in Babylon—a name which implied honour and respectability, as being conferred on one whom it was supposed the principal Babylonian divinity favoured. ¶ *Art thou able to make known unto me the dream?* One

K

known unto me the dream which I have seen, and the interpretation thereof?

27 Daniel answered in the presence of the king, and said, The secret which the king hath demanded,

a Is. 47. 13, 14.   *b* Ge. 40. 8 ; 41. 16.

cannot *a* the wise *men*, the astrologers, the magicians, the soothsayers show unto the king;

28 But *b* there is a God in heaven that revealeth secrets, and [1] maketh known to the king Nebuchadnez-

1 *hath made.*

---

of the first points in the difficulty was to recal *the dream itself,* and hence this was the first inquiry which the king presented. If he could not recal that, of course the matter was at an end, and the law would be suffered to take its course.

27. *Daniel answered in the presence of the king, and said, The secret which the king hath demanded, cannot the wise* men, &c., *show unto the king.* Daniel regarded it as a settled and indisputable point that the solution could not be hoped for from the Chaldean sages. The highest talent which the realm could furnish had been applied to, and had failed. It was clear, therefore, that there was no hope that the difficulty would be removed by human skill. Besides this, Daniel would seem also to intimate that the thing, from the necessity of the case, was beyond the compass of the human powers. Alike in reference to the question whether a forgotten dream could be *recalled,* and to the actual *signification* of a dream so remarkable as this, the whole matter was beyond the ability of man. ¶ *The wise* men, *the astrologers,* &c. On these words, see Notes on ch. i. 20. All these words occur in that verse, except גָּזְרִין *Gozrin*—rendered *soothsayers.* This is derived from גָּזַר—*to cut, to cut off;* and then *to decide, to determine;* and it is thus applied to those who decide or determine the fates or destiny of men ; that is, those who "by casting nativities from the place of the stars at one's birth, and by various arts of computing and divining, foretold the fortunes and destinies of individuals." See Gesenius, *Com. z. Isa.* ii. 349–356, § 4, Von den Chaldern und deren Astrologie. On p. 555, he has given a figure, showing how the heavens were *cut up,* or *divided,* by astrologers in the practice of their art. Comp. the phrase *numeri Babylonii,* in Hor. *Carm.* I. xi. 2. The Greek

is γαζαρηνῶν—the Chaldee word in Greek letters. This is one of the words—not very few in number—which the authors of the Greek version did not attempt to translate. Such words, however, are not useless, as they serve to throw light on the question how the Hebrew and Chaldee were pronounced before the vowel points were affixed to those languages.

28. *But there is a God in heaven that revealeth secrets.* One of the principal objects contemplated in all that occurred respecting this dream and its interpretation was, to direct the mind of the monarch to the true God, and to secure the acknowledgment of his supremacy. Hence it was so ordered that those who were most eminent for wisdom, and who were regarded as the favourites of heaven, were constrained to confess their entire inability to explain the mystery. The way was thus prepared to show that he who *could* do this must be the true God, and must be worthy of adoration and praise. Thus prepared, the mind of the monarch was now directed by this pious Hebrew youth, though a captive, to a truth so momentous and important. His whole training, his modesty and his piety, all were combined to lead him to attribute whatever skill he might evince in so difficult a matter to the true God alone : and we can scarcely conceive of a more sublime object of contemplation than this young man, in the most magnificent court of the world, directing the thoughts of the most mighty monarch that then occupied a throne, to the existence and the perfections of the true God. ¶ *And maketh known to the king Nebuchadnezzar.* Margin, *hath made.* The translation in the text is more correct, for it was not true that he had as yet actually made these things known to the king. He had furnished intimations of what was to occur, but he had not yet been permitted to under-

zar what shall be in the latter days. Thy dream, and the visions of thy head upon thy bed, are these;

29 As for thee, O king, thy thoughts [1] came *into thy mind* upon

1 *came up.*

thy bed, what should come to pass hereafter; and *a* he that revealeth secrets maketh known to thee what shall come to pass.

30 But as for me, this secret is

a Amos 4. 13.

---

stand their signification. ¶ *What shall be in the latter days.* Gr. ἐπ' ἐσχάτων τῶν ἡμερῶν—"in the last days." Vulg., *in novissimis temporibus*—"in the last times." Chald., בְּאַחֲרִית יוֹמַיָּא— "in the after days;" or, as Faber expresses it, *in the afterhood of days.* The phrase means what we should express by saying, *hereafter—in future times—in time to come.* This phrase often has special reference to the times of the Messiah, as the last dispensation of things on the earth, or as that under which the affairs of the world will be wound up. Comp. Notes on Isa. ii. 2. It does not appear, however, to be used in that sense here, but it denotes merely *future* times. The phrase "the latter days," therefore, does not exactly convey the sense of the original. It is *future* days rather than *latter* days. ¶ *Thy dream, and the visions of thy head upon thy bed.* The phrase "visions of thy head" means conceptions or notions formed by the brain. It would seem from this, that, even in the time of Daniel, the brain was regarded as, in some sense, the organ of thinking, or that *thought* had its seat in the head. We are not to suppose that by the use of these different expressions Daniel meant to describe two things, or to intimate that Nebuchadnezzar had had visions which were distinct. What he saw might be described as a dream or a vision; it, in fact, had the nature of both. ¶ *Are these.* "These which I now proceed to describe."

29. *As for thee, O king, thy thoughts came* into thy mind *upon thy bed.* Margin, *up;* that is, thy thoughts ascended. The Chaldee is, "thy thoughts ascended"—סְלִקוּ. So the Greek: "Thy thoughts ascended (ἀνέβησαν) upon thy couch." There is, evidently, some allusion to the thoughts *ascending,* or *going up;* and perhaps the idea is, that they were employed on important subjects—an idea which we now express

by saying that one's thoughts are *elevated,* as contrasted with those which are *low* and *grovelling.* ¶ *What should come to pass hereafter.* It would seem most probable from this, that the thoughts of Nebuchadnezzar were occupied with this subject in his waking moments on his bed, and that the dream was grafted on this train of thought when he fell asleep. Nothing is more probable than that his thoughts might be thus occupied. The question respecting his successor; the changes which might occur; the possibility of revolutions in other kingdoms, or in the provinces of his own vast empire, all were topics on which his mind would probably be employed. As God designed, too, to fix his thoughts particularly on that general subject—the changes which were to occur in his empire—such an occasion, when his attention was greatly engrossed with the subject, would be very suitable to impart the knowledge which he did by this vision. Daniel refers to this, probably, because it would do much to confirm the monarch in the belief of his inspiration, if he referred to the train of thought which had preceded the dream; as it is not improbable that the king would remember his *waking* thoughts on the subject, though his *dream* was forgotten.

30. *But as for me.* So far as I am concerned in this matter, or whatever skill or wisdom I may evince in the interpretation, it is not to be traced to myself. The previous verse commences with the expression "as for thee;" and in this verse, by the phrase "as for me," Daniel puts himself in strong contrast with the king. The way in which this was done was not such as to flatter the vanity of the king, and cannot be regarded as the art of the courtier, and yet it was such as would be universally adopted to conciliate his favour, and to give him an elevated idea of the modesty and piety of the youthful Daniel.

not revealed to me for *any* wisdom
a that I have more than any living,
but for ¹ *their* sakes that shall make

a Ac. 3. 12.
1 or, *the intent that the interpretation may
be made known.*

In the previous verse he says, that, as
to what pertained to the king, God had
greatly honoured him by giving him
important intimations of what was yet
to occur. Occupying the position which
he did, it might be supposed that it
would not be wholly unnatural that he
should be thus favoured, and Daniel
does not say, as in his own case, that
it was *not* on account of anything in
the character and rank of the king that
this had been communicated to him.
But when he comes to speak of himself
—a youth; a captive; a stranger in
Babylon; a native of another land—
nothing was more natural or proper
than that he should state distinctly that
it was not on account of anything in
him that this was done. ¶ *This secret
is not revealed to me for any wisdom
that I have more than any living.* That
is, "it is not *by* any wisdom which I
have above others, nor is it *on account
of* any previous wisdom which I have
possessed or manifested." There is an
absolute and total disclaimer of the idea
that it was in any sense, or in any way,
on account of his own superiority in
wisdom. All the knowledge which he
had in the case was to be traced entirely to God. ¶ *But for* their *sakes
that shall make known the interpretation
to the king.* Marg., " or, *the intent that
the interpretation may be made known.*"
The margin is the more correct rendering, and should have been admitted
into the text. The *literal* translation
is, " but (לְהֵן) on account of the thing
that they might make known the interpretation to the king." The word rendered "make known" is indeed in the
plural, but it is evidently used in an
impersonal sense, meaning that the interpretation would be made known.
"It was to the intent that they might
make it known;" that is, that some-
body might do it, or that it might be
done. Would not modesty and deli-
cacy lead to the choice of such an expression here, inclining Daniel to avoid,

known the interpretation to the
king, and that thou mightest know
the thoughts of thy heart.

31 ¶ Thou, O king, ² sawest, and,

as far as possible, all mention of himself? The main thought is, that the
grand object to be secured was not to
glorify Daniel, or any other human
being, but to communicate to this heathen monarch important truths respecting coming events, and through him to
the world. ¶ *And that thou mightest
know the thoughts of thy heart.* In
reference to this matter; that is, that
he might be able to recal the thoughts
which passed through his mind in the
dream. This (vers. 27–30) is the introduction to the important disclosure
which Daniel was about to make to the
king. This entire disclaimer of the
honour of having originated the interpretation by his own wisdom, and the
ascribing of it to God, are worthy here
of special attention. It is probable
that the magicians were accustomed to
ascribe to their own skill and sagacity
the ability to interpret dreams and the
other prognostics of the future, and to
claim special honour on that account.
In opposition to this, Daniel utterly
disclaims any such wisdom himself,
and attributes the skill which he has
entirely to God. This is a beautiful
illustration of the nature of modesty
and piety. It places before us a young
man, having now the prospect of being
elevated to great honours; under every
temptation to arrogate the possession
of extraordinary wisdom to himself;
suddenly exalted above all the sages of
the most splendid court on earth, dis-
claiming all merit, and declaring in the
most solemn manner that whatever
profound wisdom there might be in the
communication which he was about to
make, it was not in the slightest degree
to be traced to himself. See the remarks at the end of the chapter, (6.)

31. *Thou, O king, sawest.* Marg.,
wast seeing. The margin is in accordance with the Chaldee. The language
is properly that which denotes a prolonged or attentive observation. He
was in an attitude favourable to vision,
or was looking with intensity, and there

behold, a great image. This great image, whose brightness *was* excel-lent, stood before thee, and the form thereof *was* terrible.

appeared before him this remarkable image. Comp. ch. vii. 1, 2, 4, 6. It was not a thing which appeared for a moment, and then vanished, but which remained so long that he could contemplate it with accuracy. ¶ *And, behold, a great image.* Chald., *one image that was grand*—צְלֵם חַד שַׂגִּיא. So the Vulgate—*statua una grandis.* So the Greek —*εἰκὼν μία.* The object seems to be to fix the attention on the fact that there was but *one* image, though composed of so different materials, and of materials that seemed to be so little fitted to be worked together into the same statue. The idea, by its being represented as *one*, is, that it was, in some respects, *the same kingdom* that he saw symbolized: that is, that it would extend over the same countries, and could be, in some sense, regarded as a prolongation of the same empire. There was so much of *identity*, though different in many respects, that it could be represented as *one*. The word rendered *image* (צְלֵם) denotes properly a *shade*, or *shadow*, and then anything that *shadows forth*, or that represents anything. It is applied to man (Gen. i. 27) as shadowing forth, or representing God; that is, there was something in man when he was created which had so far a resemblance to God that he might be regarded as an *image* of him. The word is often used to denote idols—as supposed to be a *representation* of the gods, either in their forms, or as shadowing forth their character as majestic, stern, mild, severe, merciful, &c. Numb. xxxiii. 52; 1 Sam. vi. 5; 2 Kings xi. 18; 2 Chron. xxiii. 17; Ezek. vii. 20; xvi. 17; xxiii. 14; Amos, v. 26. This image is not represented as an idol to be worshipped, nor in the use of the word is it to be supposed that there is an allusion, as Prof. Bush supposes, to the fact that these kingdoms would be idolatrous, but the word is used in its proper and primitive sense, to denote something which would *represent*, or *shadow forth*, the kingdoms which would exist. The exact *size* of the image is not mentioned. It is only suggested that it was *great*—

a proper characteristic to represent the *greatness* of the kingdoms to which it referred. ¶ *This great image.* The word here rendered *great* (רַב) is different from that used in the previous clause, though it is not easy to determine the exact difference between the words. Both denote that the image was of gigantic dimensions. It is well remarked by Prof. Bush, that "the monuments of antiquity sufficiently evince that the humour prevailed throughout the East, and still more in Egypt, of constructing enormous statues, which were usually dedicated to some of their deities, and connected with their worship. The object, therefore, now presented in the monarch's dream was not, probably, entirely new to his thoughts." ¶ *Whose brightness was excellent.* "Whose brightness *excelled*, or was unusual and remarkable." The word rendered *brightness* (זִיו) is found only in Daniel. It is rendered *brightness* in ch. ii. 31, iv. 36, and in the margin in ch. v. 6, 9; and *countenance* in ch. v. 6 (*text*), and in vers. 9, 10, ch. vii. 28. From the places where it is found, particularly ch. iv. 36, it is clear that it is used to denote a certain beauty, or majesty, shining forth in the countenance, which was fitted to impress the beholder with awe. The term here is to be understood not merely of the face of the image, but of its entire aspect, as having something in it signally splendid and imposing. We have only to conceive of a colossal statue whose head was burnished gold, and a large part of whose frame was polished silver, to see the force of this language. ¶ *Stood before thee.* It stood over against him in full view. He had an opportunity of surveying it clearly and distinctly. ¶ *And the form thereof was terrible.* Vast, imposing, grand, fearful. The sudden appearance of such an object as this could not but fill the mind with terror. The design for which this representation was made to Nebuchadnezzar is clearly unfolded in the explanation which Daniel gives. It may be remarked here, in general, that such an appearance of a gigantic image

32 This image's head *was* of fine gold, his breast and his arms of sil- || ver, his belly and his ¹thighs of brass,

1 or, *sides.*

was well adapted to represent successive kingdoms, and that the representation was in accordance with the spirit of ancient times. "In ancient coins and medals," says the editor of the *Pictorial Bible,* "nothing is more common than to see cities and nations represented by human figures, male or female. According to the ideas which suggested such symbols, a vast image in the human figure was, therefore, a very fit emblem of sovereign power and dominion; while the materials of which it was composed did most significantly typify the character of the various empires, the succession of which was foreshown by this vision. This last idea, of expressing the condition of things by metallic symbols, was prevalent before the time of Daniel. Hesiod, who lived about two centuries before Daniel, characterizes the succession of ages (four) by the very same metals—gold, silver, brass, and iron."

32. *This image's head* was *of fine gold.* Chaldee, *good gold—*דְּהַב טָב*—* that is, fine, pure, unalloyed. The whole head of the figure, colossal as it was, appeared to be composed wholly of this. Had the *whole* image been made of gold, it would not have been so striking—for it was not uncommon to construct vast statues of this metal. Comp. ch. iii. 1. But the remarkable peculiarity of this image was, that it was composed of different materials, some of which were seldom or never used in such a structure, and all of which had a peculiar significancy. On the significancy of this part of the figure, and the resemblance between this head of gold and Nebuchadnezzar himself, see Notes on vers. 37, 38. ¶ *His breast and his arms of silver.* The word rendered *breast* (חֲדוֹהִי) is in the plural number, in accordance with a common usage in the Hebrew, by which several members of the human body are often expressed in the plural; as פָּנִים*—faces,* &c. There is a foundation for such a usage in nature, in the two-fold form of many of the por-

tions of the human body. The portion of the body which is here represented is obviously the upper portion of the front part—that which is prominently visible when we look at the human frame. Next to the head it is the most important part, as it embraces most of the vital organs. Some degree of inferiority, as well as the idea of succession, would be naturally represented by this. "The inferior value of silver as compared with gold will naturally suggest some degree of decline or degeneracy in the character of the subject represented by the metal; and so in other members, as we proceed downward, as the material becomes continually baser, we naturally infer that the subject deteriorates, in some sense, in the like manner."—Professor Bush, *in loc.* On the kingdom represented by this, and the propriety of this representation, see Notes on ver. 39. ¶ *His belly and his thighs of brass.* Marg., *sides.* It is not necessary to enter minutely into an examination of the words here used. The word *belly* denotes, unquestionably, the regions of the abdomen as externally visible. The word rendered *thighs* in the text is rendered *sides* in the margin. It is, like the word *breast* in the previous verse, in the plural number, and for the same reason. The Hebrew word (יָרֵךְ) is commonly rendered *thigh* in the Scriptures (Gen. xxiv. 2, 9 ; xxxii. 25 (26), 31, 32 (32, 33), *et al.*), though it is also frequently rendered *side,* Exod. xxxii. 27 ; xl. 22, 24 ; Lev. i. 11 ; Num. iii. 29, *et al.* According to Gesenius, it denotes "the thick and double fleshy member which commences at the bottom of the spine, and extends to the lower legs." It is that part on which the sword was formerly worn, Exod. xxxii. 27 ; Judg. iii. 16, 21 ; Psal. xlv. 3 (4). It is also that part which was smitten, as an expression of mourning or of indignation, Jer. xxxi. 19 ; Ezek. xxi. 12 (17). Comp. Hom. *Il.* xii. 162, xv. 397 ; *Od.* xiii. 198 ; Cic. cl. *Orat.* 80 : *Quinc.* xi. 3. It is not improperly

33 His legs of iron, his feet part of iron and part of clay.

1 or, *which was not in hands.*

34 Thou sawest till that a stone was cut out ¹ without ª hands, which

a Zec. 4. 6 ; Jn. 1. 13.

here rendered *thighs,* and the portion of the figure that was of brass was that between the breast and the lower legs, or extended from the breast to the knees. The word is elsewhere employed to denote the shaft or main trunk of the golden candlestick of the tabernacle, Exod. xxv. 31; xxxvii. 17 ; Num. viii. 4. ¶ *Of brass.* An inferior metal, and denoting a kingdom of inferior power or excellence. On the kingdom represented by this, see Notes on ver. 39.

33. *His legs of iron.* The portion of the lower limbs from the knees to the ankles. This is undoubtedly the usual meaning of the English word *legs,* and it as clearly appears to be the sense of the original word here. Iron was regarded as inferior to either of the other metals specified, and yet was well adapted to denote a kingdom of a particular kind—less noble in some respects, and yet hardy, powerful, and adapted to tread down the world by conquest. On the application of this, see Notes on ver. 40. ¶ *His feet part of iron and part of clay.* As to his feet ; or in respect to his feet, they were partly of iron and partly of clay —a mixture denoting great strength, united with that which is fragile and weak. The word rendered *clay* in this place (חֲסַף) is found nowhere else except in this chapter, and is always rendered *clay,* ch. ii. 33-35, 41 (twice), 42, 43 (twice), 45. In some instances (vers. 41, 43), the epithet *miry* is applied to it. This would seem to imply that it was *not* "burnt or baked clay," or "earthenware," as Professor Bush supposes, but clay in its natural state. The idea would seem to be, that the framework, so to speak, was iron, with clay worked in, or filling up the interstices, so as to furnish an image of strength combined with that which is weak. That it would be well adapted to represent a kingdom that had many elements of permanency in it, yet that was combined with things that made it weak—a mixture of that which was

powerful with that which was liable to be crushed ; capable of putting forth great efforts, and of sustaining great shocks, and yet having such elements of feebleness and decay as to make it liable to be overthrown. For the application of this, see Notes on vers. 41-43.

34. *Thou sawest.* Chaldee, "Thou wast seeing ;" that is, thou didst continue to behold, implying that the vision was of somewhat long continuance. It did not appear and then suddenly vanish, but it remained so long that he had an opportunity of careful observation. ¶ *Till that a stone was cut out without hands,* ver. 45. This idea is *expressed* in the Latin and the Greek version. The vision appears to have been that of a colossal image *standing on a plain* in the vicinity of a mountain, standing firm, until, by some unseen agency, and in an unaccountable manner, a stone became detached from the mountain, and was made to impinge against it. The margin here is, *which was not in his hands.* The more correct rendering of the Chaldee, however, is that in the text, literally, "a stone was cut out which was not by hands"—בִּידָין : or perhaps still more accurately, "a stone was cut out which was not *in* hands," so that the fact that it was not in or by *hands* refers rather to its not being projected by hands than to the manner of its being detached from the mountain. The essential idea is, that the agency of hands did not appear at all in the case. The stone seemed to be self-moved. It became detached from the mountain, and, as if instinct with life, struck the image and demolished it. The word rendered *stone* (אֶבֶן) determines nothing as to the *size* of the stone, but the whole statement would seem to imply that it was not of large dimensions. It struck upon *the feet* of the image, and it *became* itself a great mountain (ver. 35) —all which would seem to imply that it was at first not large. What increased

smote the image upon his feet *that
were* of iron and clay, and brake
them to pieces.

35 Then was the iron, the clay,
the brass, the silver, and the gold,
broken to pieces together, and be-

---

the astonishment of the monarch was,
that a stone of such dimensions should
have been adequate to overthrow so
gigantic a statue, and to grind it to
powder. The points on which it was
clearly intended to fix the attention
of the monarch, and which made the
vision so significant and remarkable,
were these : (*a*) the colossal size and
firmness of the image ; (*b*) the fact that
a stone, not of large size, should be
seen to be self-detached from the mountain, and to move against the image ;
(*c*) the fact that it should completely
demolish and pulverize the colossal
figure ; and (*d*) the fact that then this
stone of inconsiderable size should be
itself mysteriously augmented until it
filled the world. It should be added,
that the vision appears not to have
been that of a stone detached from the
side of a hill, and rolling *down* the
mountain by the force of gravitation,
but that of a stone detached, and then
moving off toward the image as if it
had been thrown from a hand, though
the hand was unseen. This would very
strikingly and appropriately express
the idea of something, apparently small
in its origin, that was impelled by a
cause that was unseen, and that bore
with mighty force upon an object of
colossal magnitude, by an agency that
could not be explained by the causes
that usually operate. For the application and pertinency of this, see Notes
on vers. 44, 45. ¶ *Which smote the
image upon his feet.* The word here
used (מְחָא) means, *to strike, to smite,*
without reference to the question whether it is a single blow, or whether the
blow is often repeated. The Hebrew
word (מָחָא) is uniformly used as referring to *the clapping of the hands ;* that
is, smiting them together, Ps. xcviii. 8 ;
Isa. lv. 12 ; Ezek. xxv. 6. The Chaldee word is used only here and in ver.
35, referring to the smiting of the
image, and in ch. iv. 35 (32), where it
is rendered "*stay*"—"none can *stay*
his hand." The connection here, and
the whole statement, would seem to

demand the sense of a continued or
prolonged smiting, or of repeated blows,
rather than a single concussion. The
great image was not only thrown down,
but there was a subsequent process
of *comminution,* independent of what
would have been produced by the fall.
A fall would only have broken it into
large blocks or fragments ; but this
continued smiting reduced it to powder. This would imply, therefore, not
only a single shock, or violent blow,
but some cause continuing to operate
until that which had been overthrown
was effectually destroyed, like a vast
image reduced to impalpable powder.
The *first concussion* on the feet made it
certain that the colossal frame would
fall ; but there was a longer process
necessary before the whole effect should
be accomplished. Compare Notes on
vers. 44, 45. ¶ *And brake them to
pieces.* In ver. 35, the idea is, "they
became like the chaff of the summer
threshing-floors." The meaning is not
that the image was broken to *fragments,* but that it was *beaten fine*—
reduced to powder—so that it might
be scattered by the wind. This is the
sense of the Chaldee word (דְּקַק), and
of the Hebrew word also (דָּקַק). See
Exod. xxxii. 20 : "And he took the
calf which they had made, and burned
it in the fire, *and ground it to powder.*"
Deut. ix. 21 : "And I took your sin,
the calf which ye had made, and burnt
it with fire, and stamped it, and ground
it very small, even until it was *as small*
as dust." Isa. xli. 15 : "Thou shalt
thresh the mountains and *beat them
small,* and shalt make the hills as
chaff." 2 Kings xxiii. 15 : "He burnt
the high place, and *stamped* it *small* to
powder." 2 Chron. xxxiv. 4 : "And
they brake down the altars, &c., and
made dust of them, and strewed it upon
the graves of them that had sacrificed
unto them." Compare Exod. xxx. 36 ;
2 Chron. xxxiv. 7 ; 2 Kings xxiii. 6.
From these passages it is clear that
the general meaning of the word is
that of reducing anything to fine dust

came like the [a] chaff of the summer threshing-floors; and the wind carried them away, that no [b] place was found for them: and the stone that smote the image became a great mountain, [c] and filled [d] the whole earth.

36 ¶ This *is* the dream; and we will tell the interpretation thereof before the king.

a Ps. 1. 4; Ho. 13. 3.　　*b* Ps. 37. 36.　　*c* Is. 2. 2, 3.　　*d* 1 Co. 15. 25.

or powder, so that it may be easily blown about by the wind.

35. *Then was the iron, the clay, the brass, the silver, and the gold broken to pieces together, and became like the chaff of the summer threshing-floor.* The word rendered *together* (כַּהֲדָה) our translators would seem to have understood as referring to *time;* to its being done simultaneously. The more literal interpretation, however, is, "*as one;*" that is, "they were beaten small *as one*," referring to *identity of condition.* They were all reduced to one indiscriminate mass; to such a mass that the original materials could no longer be distinguished, and would all be blown away together. The literal meaning of the word (חַד used and חֲדָה) is, *one*, or *first.* Ezra iv. 8, "wrote *a* letter;" v. 13, "in the *first* year of Cyrus;" vi. 2, "*a* roll;" Dan. ii. 9; "there is but *one* decree for you;" iii. 19, "heat the furnace *one* seven times hotter," &c. United with the conjunction (כ) it means *as one*, like the Heb. כְּאֶחָד.—Eccles. xi. 6; 2 Chron. v. 13; Ezra ii. 64; iii. 9; Isa. lxv. 25. The phrase "chaff of the summer threshing-floors" refers to the mode of winnowing grain in the East. This was done in the open air, usually on an elevated place, by throwing the grain, when thrashed, into the air with a shovel, and the wind thus drove away the chaff. Such chaff, therefore, naturally became an emblem of anything that was light, and that would be easily dissipated. See Notes on Isa. xxx. 24; Matt. iii. 12. ¶ *And the wind carried them away, that no place was found for them.* They were entirely dissipated like chaff. As that seems to have no longer any place, but is carried we know not where, so the figure here would denote an entire annihilation of the power to which it refers. ¶ *And the stone that smote the image became a great mountain, and filled the whole*

earth. The vision which was before the mind of the king as here represented was, that the stone which was cut out of the mountain was at first small, and that while he contemplated it, it swelled to larger dimensions, until it became an immense mountain—a mountain that filled the whole land. It was this which, perhaps more than anything else, excited his wonder, that a stone, at first of so small dimensions, should of itself so increase as to surpass the size of the mountain from which it was cut, until it occupied every place in view. Everything about it was so remarkable and unusual, that it was no wonder that he could not explain it. We have now gone over a description of the literal vision as it appeared to the mind of the monarch. Had it been left here, it is clear that it would have been of difficult interpretation, and possibly the true explanation might never have been suggested. We have, however, an exposition by Daniel, which leaves no doubt as to its design, and which was intended to carry the mind forward into some of the most important and remarkable events of history. A portion of his statement has been fulfilled; a part remains still unaccomplished; and a careful exposition of his account of the meaning of the vision will lead our thoughts to some of the most important historical events which have occurred in introducing the Christian dispensation, and to events still more important in the statement of what is yet to come.

36. *This* is *the dream; and we will tell the interpretation thereof before the king.* Daniel here speaks in his own name, and in the name of his companions. Hence he says, "*we* will tell the interpretation." It was in answer to their united supplications (ver. 18), that this meaning of the vision had been made known to him; and it would not only have been a violation of the

37 Thou, O King, *art* a king *a* of kings: for *b* the God of heaven hath

a Ezr. 7. 12; Is. 47. 5; Eze. 26. 7; Ho. 8. 10.
b Ezr. 1. 2.

rules of modesty, but an unjust assumption, if Daniel had claimed the whole credit of the revelation to himself. Though he was the only one who addressed the king, yet he seems to have desired that it might be understood that he was not alone in the honour which God had conferred, and that he wished that his companions should be had in just remembrance. Comp. ver. 49.

37. *Thou, O King,* art *a king of kings.* The phrase "king of kings" is a Hebraism, to denote a supreme monarch, or one who has other kings under him as tributary, Ezra vii. 12; Ezek. xxvi. 7. As such it is applied by way of eminence to the Son of God, in Rev. xvii. 14; xix. 16. As here used, it means that Nebuchadnezzar ruled over tributary kings and princes, or that he was the most eminent of the kings of the earth. The sceptre which he swayed was, in fact, extended over many nations that were once independent kingdoms, and the title here conferred on him was not one that was designed to flatter the monarch, but was a simple statement of what was an undoubted truth. Daniel would not withhold any title that was in accordance with reality, as he did not withhold any communication in accordance with reality that was adapted to humble the monarch. ¶ *For the God of heaven hath given thee a kingdom,* &c. At the same time that Daniel gave him a title which might in itself have ministered to the pride of the monarch, he is careful to remind him that he held this title in virtue of no wisdom or power of his own. It was the true God who had conferred on him the sovereignty of these extensive realms, and it was one of the designs of this vision to show him that he held his power at his will, and that at his pleasure he could cause it to pass away. It was the forgetfulness of this, and the pride resulting from that forgetfulness, which led to the melancholy calamity which befel this haughty monarch, as recorded in ch. iv.

38. *And wheresoever the children of*

given thee a kingdom, power, and strength, and glory.

38 And wheresoever the children of men dwell, the beasts of the field,

men dwell, the beasts of the field, and the fowls of the heaven, hath he given into thy hand. This is evidently general language, and is not to be pressed literally. It is designed to say that he ruled over the whole world; that is, the world as then known. This is common language applied in the Scriptures to the Babylonian, Persian, Grecian, and Roman kingdoms. Thus in ver. 39, the third of these kingdoms, the Grecian, was to "bear rule over all the earth." Comp. ch. viii. 5 : "And, as I was considering, behold, an he-goat came from the west on the face of the whole earth." So of the Roman empire, in ch. vii. 23 : "The fourth beast shall devour the whole earth." The declaration that his kingdom embraced the beasts of the field and the fowls of the air is a strong expression, meaning that he reigned over the whole world. A somewhat similar description of the extent of the empire of the king of Babylon occurs in Jer. xxvii. 4-8 : "And command them to say unto their masters, Thus saith the Lord of hosts, the God of Israel, Thus shall ye say unto your masters; I have made the earth, the man and the beast that are upon the ground, by my great power, and by my outstretched arm, and have given it unto whom it seemed meet unto me. And now I have given all these lands into the hand of Nebuchadnezzar, the king of Babylon, my servant ; and the beasts of the field I have given him also to serve him. And all nations shall serve him, and his son, and his son's son, until the very time of his land come : and then many nations and great kings shall serve themselves of him. And it shall come to pass, that the nation and kingdom which will not serve the same Nebuchadnezzar, the king of Babylon, and that will not put their neck under the yoke of the king of Babylon, that nation will I punish, saith the Lord, with the sword, and with the famine, and with the pestilence, until I have consumed them by his hand." At the time referred to by

and the fowls of the heaven, hath he given *a* into thine hand, and hath

a Je. 27. 6.

made thee ruler over them all Thou *art* this head of gold.

Daniel, the sceptre of Nebuchadnezzar extended over all these realms, and the world was, in fact, placed substantially under one head. "All the ancient Eastern histories," says Bishop Newton, "almost are lost; but there are some fragments even of heathen historians yet preserved, which speak of this mighty conqueror and his extended empire. Berosus, in Josephus (*Contra Apion*, l. i. § 19), says that he held in subjection Egypt, Syria, Phœnicia, Arabia, and by his exploits surpassed all the Chaldeans and Babylonians who reigned before him. Strabo asserts that this king among the Chaldeans was more celebrated than Hercules; that he proceeded as far as to the pillars of Hercules, and led his army out of Spain into Thrace and Pontus. But his empire, though of great extent, was not of long duration; for it ended in his grandson Belshazzar, not seventy years after the delivery of this prophecy, nor above twenty-three years after the death of Nebuchadnezzar." — Newton on the *Prophecies*, pp. 186, 187. ¶ *Thou art this head of gold.* The head of gold seen in the image represents thee as the sovereign of a vast empire. Compared with the other monarchs who are to succeed thee, thou art like gold compared with silver, and brass, and iron; or, compared with thy kingdom, theirs shall be as silver, brass, and iron compared with gold. It was common, at an early period, to speak of different ages of the world as resembling different metals. Comp. Notes on ver. 31. In reference to the expression before us, "*Thou* art this head of gold," it should be observed, that it is not probably to be confined to the monarch himself, but is rather spoken of him as the head of the empire; as representing the state; as an impersonation of that dynasty. The meaning is, that the Babylonian empire, as it existed under him, in its relation to the kingdoms which should succeed, was like the head of gold seen in the image as compared with the inferior metals that made up the remaining portions of the image. Daniel, as

an interpreter, did not state in what the resemblance consisted, nor in what respects his empire could be likened to gold as compared with those which should follow. In the scanty details which we now have of the life of that monarch, and of the events of his reign, it may not be possible to see as clearly as would be desirable in what that resemblance consisted, or the full propriety of the appellation given to him. So far as may now be seen, the resemblance appears to have been in the following things:—(I.) In respect to the empire itself of which he was the sovereign, as standing at the head of the others—the first in the line. This was not indeed the first kingdom, but the design here was not to give an account of *all* the empires on earth, but to take the world *as it was then,* and to trace the successive changes which would occur preparatory to the establishment of the kingdom which should finally spread over the earth. Viewed in reference to this design, it was undoubtedly proper to designate the empire of Babylon as *the head.* It not only stood before them in the order of time, but in such a relation that the others might be regarded as in some sort its successors; that is, *they would succeed it in swaying a general sceptre over the world.* In this respect they would resemble also the Babylonian. At the time here referred to, the dominion over which Nebuchadnezzar swayed his sceptre was at the head of the nations; was the central power of the Pagan world; was the only empire that could claim to be universal. For a long period the kingdom of Babylon had been dependent on that of Assyria; and while Nineveh was the capital of the Assyrian empire, Babylon was the head of a kingdom, in general subordinate to that of Assyria, until Nabopolassar, the immediate predecessor of Nebuchadnezzar, rendered the kingdom of Babylon independent of the Assyrians, and transferred the seat of empire to Babylon. This was about the year 626 before the Christian era. See *Universal History,* vol. iii.

pp. 412–415. Nebuchadnezzar, receiving this mighty kingdom, had carried his own arms to distant lands; had conquered India, Tyre, and Egypt; and, as would appear, all Northern Africa, as far as the pillars of Hercules, and, with quite unimportant exceptions, all the known world was subject to him. (II.) The appellation "head of gold" may have been given him on account of the splendour of his capital, and the magnificence of his court. In Isa. xiv. 4, Babylon is called "the golden city." See Notes on that place. In Isa. xiii. 19, it is called "the glory of kingdoms, the beauty of the Chaldees' excellency." In Isa. xlvii. 5, it is called "the lady of kingdoms." In Jer. li. 13, it is spoken of as "abundant in treasures," and in ver. 41, as "the praise of the whole earth." So in profane writers, Babylon has similar appellations. Thus in Æsch. *Per*. 51, mention is made of Βαβυλὼν ἡ πολύχρυσος—*Babylon abounding in gold.* The conquests of Nebuchadnezzar enabled him to bring to his capital the spoils of nations, and to enrich his capital above any other city on the earth. Accordingly, he gave himself to the work of adorning a city that should be worthy to be the head of universal empire, and succeeded in making it so splendid as to be regarded as one of the wonders of the world. His great work in adorning and strengthening his capital consisted, first, of the building of the immense walls of the city; second, of the tower of Belus; and third, of the hanging gardens. For a full description of these, see Prideaux's *Connexions*, vol. i. p. 232, *seq.* (III.) The appellation may have been given him by *comparison* with the kingdoms which were to succeed him. In *some* respects—in extent and power—some one or more of them, as the Roman, might surpass his; but the appellation which was appropriate to them was not *gold*, but they would be best denoted by the inferior metals. Thus the Medo-Persian kingdom was less splendid than that of Babylon, and would be better represented by silver; the Macedonian, though more distinguished by its conquests, was less magnificent, and would be better represented by brass; and the

Roman, though ultimately still more extensive in its conquests, and still more mighty in power, was less remarkable for splendour than strength, and would be better represented by iron. In magnificence, if not in power, the Babylonian surpassed them all; and hence the propriety of the appellation, "*head of gold.*" (IV.) It is possible that in this appellation there then may have been some reference to the character of the monarch himself. In Jer. xxvii. 6, he is spoken of as the "servant of God," and it is clear that it was designed that a splendid mission was to be accomplished by him as under the Divine control, and in the preparation of the world for the coming of the Messiah. Though he was proud and haughty as a monarch, yet his own personal character would compare favourably with that of many who succeeded him in these advancing kingdoms. Though his conquests were numerous, yet his career as a conqueror was not marked with cruelty, like that of many other warriors. He was not a mere conqueror. He loved also the arts of peace. He sought to embellish his capital, and to make it in outward magnificence and in the talent which he concentrated there, truly the capital of the world. Even Jerusalem he did not utterly destroy; but having secured a conquest over it, and removed from it what he desired should embellish his own capital, he still intended that it should be the subordinate head of an important province of his dominions, and placed on the throne one who was closely allied to the king who reigned there when he took the city. But the appellation here, and the reign of Nebuchadnezzar, are to be contemplated chiefly, like the kingdoms that succeeded, in their relation to redemption. It is in this aspect that the study of history becomes most interesting to a mind that regards all events as embraced in the eternal counsels of God, and it is undoubtedly with reference to this that the history of these kingdoms becomes in any way introduced into the inspired writings. All history may be contemplated under two aspects: in its secular bearing; and in its relation to the redemption of the world. In the

39 And after thee shall arise ano- | ther kingdom inferior [a] to thee, and

a ch. 5. 28.

former aspect, it has great and important uses. As furnishing lessons to statesmen ; as showing the progress of society ; as illustrating the effects of vice and immorality, and the evils of anarchy, ambition, and war ; as recording and preserving the inventions in the arts, and as showing what are the best methods of civil government, and what conduces most to the happiness of a people, its value cannot well be over-estimated. But it is in its relations to the work of redeeming man that it acquires its chief value, and hence the sacred volume is so much occupied with the histories of early nations. The rise and fall of every nation ; the conquests and defeats which have occurred in past times, may all have had, and perhaps may yet be seen to have had, an important connection with the redemption of man—as being designed to put the world in a proper position for the coming of the Prince of Peace, or in some way to prepare the way for the final triumph of the gospel. This view gives a new and important aspect to history. It becomes an object in which all on earth who love the race and desire its redemption, and all in heaven, feel a deep concern. Every monarch ; every warrior ; every statesman ; every man who, by his eloquence, bravery, or virtue, has contributed anything to the progress of the race, or who has in any way played an important part in the progress of the world's affairs, becomes a being on whom we can look with intense emotion ; and in reference to every man of this character, it would be an interesting inquiry what he has done that has contributed to prepare the way for the introduction of the Mediatorial scheme, or to facilitate its progress through the world. In reference to this point, the monarch whose character is now before us seems to have been raised up, under an over-ruling Providence, to accomplish the following things :—(1.) To inflict *punishment* on the revolted people of God for their numerous idolatries. See the book of Jeremiah, *passim.* Hence, he led his armies to the land of Palestine ;

he swept away the people, and bore them into captivity ; he burned the temple, destroyed the capital, and laid the land waste. (2.) He was the instrument, in the hand of God, of effectually purifying the Jewish nation from the sin of idolatry. It was for that sin eminently that they were carried away ; and never in this world have the ends of punishment been better secured than in this instance. The chastisement was effectual. The Jewish nation has never since sunk into idolatry. If there have been individuals of that nation—of which, however, there is no certain evidence—who have become idolaters, yet as a people they have been preserved from it. More than two thousand five hundred years have since passed away ; they have been wanderers and exiles in all lands ; they have been persecuted, ridiculed, and oppressed on account of their religion ; they have been placed under every possible inducement to conform to the religion around them, and yet, as professed worshippers of Jehovah, the God of their fathers, they have maintained their integrity, and neither promises nor threatenings, neither hopes nor fears, neither life nor death, have been sufficient to constrain the Hebrew people to bow the knee to an idol god. (3.) Another object that seems to have been designed to be accomplished by Nebuchadnezzar in relation to Redemption was, to gather the nations under one head preparatory to the coming of the Messiah. It will be seen in the remarks which will be made on the relation of the Roman empire to this work (Notes on vers. 40–43), that there were important reasons why this should be done. Preparatory to that, a succession of such kingdoms each swayed the sceptre over the whole world, and when the Messiah came, the way was prepared for the easy and rapid propagation of the new religion to the remotest parts of the earth.

39. *And after thee.* This must mean *subsequently* to the reign, but it does not mean that the kingdom here referred to would *immediately* succeed his own reign, for that would not be true. The

another third kingdom of brass, | which ^ashall bear rule over all the
earth.

a ch. 7. 6.

Medo-Persian empire did not come into the ascendency until many years after the death of Nebuchadnezzar. This occurred during the reign of Belshazzar, a grandson of Nebuchadnezzar, between whose reign and that of his grandfather there had intervened the reigns of Evil-merodach and Neriglissar ; besides, as the remainder of the prophecy relating to the image refers to *kingdoms*, and not to individual monarchs, it is clear that this also relates not primarily to Nebuchadnezzar as an individual, but as the head of a kingdom. The meaning is, that a kingdom would succeed that over which he reigned, so far inferior that it might be represented by silver as compared with gold. ¶ *Shall arise another kingdom.* Chaldee, "shall *stand up* (תְּקוּם) another kingdom." This is language which would denote something different from a succession in the same dynasty ; for that would be a mere *continuance of the same kingdom.* The reference is evidently to a change of empire ; and the language implies that there would be some revolution or conquest by which the existing kingdom would pass away, and another would succeed. Still there would be so much of sameness in respect to its occupying essentially the same territory, that it would be symbolized in the same image that appeared to Nebuchadnezzar. The kingdom here referred to was undoubtedly the Medo-Persian, established by Cyrus in the conquest of Babylon, which continued through the reigns of his successors until it was conquered by Alexander the Great. This kingdom succeeded that of Assyria or Babylon, 538 years B.C., to the overthrow of Darius Codomanus, 333 years B.C. It extended, of course, through the reigns of the Persian kings, who acted so important a part in the invasion of Greece, and whose defeats have given immortality to the names of Leonidas, Aristides, Miltiades, and Themistocles, and made the names of Salamis, Thermopylæ, Marathon, and Leuctra so celebrated. For a general account of Cyrus, and the founding of the Medo-Persian empire,

the reader is referred to the Notes on Isa. xli. 2. ¶ *Inferior to thee.* And therefore represented by silver as compared with gold. In what respects it would be inferior, Daniel does not specify, and this can only be learned from *the facts* which occurred in relation to that kingdom. All that is necessary to confirm the truth of the prophetic description is, that it was to be so far inferior as to make the appellation *silver* applicable to it in comparison with the kingdom of Babylon, represented by *gold.* The expression would denote that there was a general decline or degeneracy in the character of the monarchs, and the general condition of the empire. There have been different opinions as to the inferiority of this kingdom to the Babylonian. Calvin supposes that it refers to degeneracy. Geier supposes that it relates to the duration of the kingdom—this continuing not more than two hundred and forty years ; while the other, including the Assyrian, embraced a period of one thousand five hundred years. Polanus supposes that the meaning is, that the Babylonian had more rest and tranquillity ; while Junius, Willett, and others understand it of a milder and more humane treatment of the Jews by the Babylonians than the Persians. Perhaps, however, none of these opinions meet the circumstances of the case, for they do not furnish as full an account of the reasons of this inferiority as is desirable. In regard to this, it may be observed, (*a*) that it is not to be supposed that this kingdom was to be in *all respects* inferior to the Babylonian, but only that it would have certain characteristics which would make it more appropriate to describe it as *silver* than as *gold.* In certain *other* respects it might be far superior, as the Roman, though in the same general line of succession, was in extent and power superior to either, though there was still a reason why that should be represented by *iron* rather than by gold, by silver, or by brass. (*b*) The inferiority did not relate to the power, the riches, or the territorial extent of the Medo-Persian empire, for it embraced, so far as appears, all that was comprehended in the Babylonian empire, and all in addition which was added by the conquests of Cyrus. In his proclamation to rebuild the temple (Ezra i. 2), Cyrus speaks of the extent of his empire in language strongly resembling that which is applied to the kingdom of Nebuchadnezzar. "Thus saith Cyrus, king of Persia, The Lord God of heaven hath given me all the kingdoms of the earth." Thus also it is said of Ahasuerus or Astyages, king of Media—a kingdom that constituted a part of the Medo-Persian empire under Cyrus and his successors, that he "reigned from India even unto Ethiopia, over an hundred and twenty and seven provinces." To the kingdom of Babylon, as he found it when he conquered it, Cyrus of course added the kingdoms of Media and Persia, to the crowns of which he was the heir (see Notes on Isa. xli. 2), and also the various provinces which he had conquered before he came to the throne ; that is, Cappadocia, the kingdom of Lydia, and almost the whole of Asia Minor. (c) Nor can it be supposed that the kingdom was inferior in regard to *wealth*, for, in addition to all the wealth that Cyrus found in Babylon, he brought the spoils of his victories ; the treasures in the possession of the crowns of Persia and Media, and all the wealth of Croesus, the rich king of Lydia, of which he had become possessor by conquest. In considering the *inferiority* of this kingdom, which made it proper that it should be represented by silver rather than by gold, it is to be borne in mind that the representation should embrace *the whole kingdom* in all the successive reigns, and not merely the kingdom as it was under the administration of Cyrus. Thus regarded, it will comprehend the succession of Persian monarchs until the time of the invasion and conquest of the East by Alexander the Great. The reign of Cyrus was indeed splendid ; and if *he* alone, or if the kingdom during his administration, were contemplated, it would be difficult to assign a reason why an appellation should have been given to it implying any inferiority to that of Nebuchadnezzar. The *infe-*

riority of the kingdom, or that which made it proper to represent it by silver rather than by gold, as compared with the kingdom of Babylon, may have consisted in the following particulars :— (1.) In reference to the succession of kings who occupied the Persian throne. It is true that the character of Cyrus is worthy of the highest commendation, and that he was distinguished not only as a brave and successful conqueror, but as a mild, able, and upright civil ruler. Xenophon, who wished to draw the character of a model prince, made choice of Cyrus as the example ; and though he has not improbably embellished his character by ascribing to him virtues drawn from his own fancy in some degree, yet there can be no doubt that in the main his description was drawn from the life. "The true reason," says Prideaux (*Connexions*, vol. i. p. 252, Ed. Charlestown, 1815), "why he chose the life of Cyrus before all others for the purpose above mentioned " [that of giving a description of what a worthy and just prince ought to be] " seemeth to be no other but that he found the true history of that excellent and gallant prince to be, above all others, the fittest for those maxims of right policy and true princely virtue to correspond with, which he grafted upon it." But he was succeeded by a madman, Cambyses, and by a race of kings eminent among princes for folly and crime. "The kings of Persia," says Prideaux, "were the worst race of men that ever governed an empire." (2.) The kingdom was inferior in reference to the remarkable *defeats* in the military campaigns which were undertaken. The Assyrian or Babylonian empire was distinguished for the victories by which it carried its arms around the then known world. The Medo-Persian empire, after the reign of Cyrus, was almost as remarkable for the succession of defeats which have made the period of the world during which the empire continued, so well known in history. It is probable that no kingdom ever undertook so many foolish projects in reference to the conquests of other nations—projects so unwisely planned, and that resulted in so signal failures. The successor of Cyrus, Cambyses, invaded Egypt, and his conduct there in carrying on the war was such as to make him be regarded as a madman. Enraged against the Ethiopians for an answer which they gave him when, under pretence of friendship, he sent spies to examine their country, he resolved to invade their territory. Having come to Thebes, in Upper Egypt, he detached from his army fifty thousand men to go against the Hammonians, with orders to destroy their country, and to burn the temple of Jupiter Hammon that stood in it. After marching a few days in the desert, they were overwhelmed in the sands by a strong south wind, and all perished. Meantime Cambyses marched with the rest of his army against the Ethiopians, though he wanted all the means of subsistence for his army, until, having devoured all their beasts of burden, they were constrained to designate every tenth man of the army to be killed and eaten. In these deplorable circumstances, Cambyses returned to Thebes, having lost a great part of his army in this wild expedition.— Prideaux's *Con.* i. 328. It was also during the continuance of this kingdom, that the ill-starred expeditions to Greece occurred, when Mardonius and Xerxes poured the millions of Asia on the countries of Greece, and met such signal overthrows at Platea, Marathon, and Salamis. Such a series of disasters never before had occurred to invading armies, or made those who repelled invasion so illustrious. In this respect there was an evident propriety in speaking of this as an inferior or degenerate kingdom. (3.) It was inferior in respect to the growing degeneracy and effeminacy of character and morals. From the time of Xerxes (B.C. 479) "symptoms of decay and corruption were manifest in the empire; the national character gradually degenerated; the citizens were corrupted and enfeebled by luxury; and confided more in mercenary troops than in native valour and fidelity. The kings submitted to the control of their wives, or the creatures whom they raised to posts of distinction; and the satraps, from being civil functionaries, began to usurp military authority."—Lyman, *Hist. Chart.*

(4.) The kingdom was inferior by the gradual weakening of its power from internal causes. It was not only defeated in its attempts to invade others, and weakened by the degeneracy of the court and people, but, as a natural consequence, by the gradual lessening of the power of the central government, and the growing independence of the provinces. From the time of Darius Nothus (B.C. 423)—a weak, effeminate, and indolent prince—"the satraps of the distant provinces paid only a nominal obedience to the king. Many of them were, in fact, sovereigns over the countries over which they presided, and carried on wars against each other."— Lyman. It was from causes such as these that the power of the kingdom became gradually weakened, and that the way was prepared for the easy conquests of Alexander the Great. Their successive defeats, and this gradual degeneracy and weakening of the kingdom, show the propriety of the description given of the kingdom in the vision and the interpretation—that it would be an "inferior kingdom," a kingdom which, in comparison with that of Babylon, might be compared with silver as compared with gold. Still it sustained an important relation to the progress of events in regard to the history of religion in the world, and had an important bearing on the redemption of man. As this is the most important bearing of history, and as it was doubtless with reference to this that the mention of it is introduced into the sacred Scriptures, and as it is, in fact, often alluded to by Isaiah, and in the books of Ezra, Nehemiah, Esther, and some of the minor prophets, it may be proper, in the most summary way, to allude to some of those things which pertain to the bearing of this kingdom on the great events connected with redemption, or to what was done during the continuance of this kingdom for the promotion of the true religion. A full account may be found in Prideaux's *Connexions*, part 1, books iii. – vii. Compare Edwards' *History of Redemption*, Period I, part vi. The particular things which occurred in connection with this kingdom bearing on the progress of religion, and favourable to its advancement, were these: (a) The over-throw of Babylon, so long the formid-able enemy of the ancient people of God. (b) The restoration of the exiles to their own land under the auspices of Cyrus, Ezra i. 1. (c) The rebuilding of the temple under the same auspices, and with the favour of the successors of Cyrus. (d) The preparation of the world for the coming of the Messiah, in the agitations that took place during the continuance of the Persian monar-chy; the invasion of Greece; the de-feats there; the preparation by these defeats for the coming of Him who was so long promised as the "desire of all nations." Compare Hag. ii. 7: "And I will shake all nations, and the desire of all nations shall come; and I will fill this house" [the temple erected under the auspices of Cyrus and his succes-sors] "with glory, saith the Lord of hosts." There was a propriety, there-fore, that this kingdom should receive a distinct notice in the sacred Scrip-tures, for some of the most important events connected with the history of true religion in the world occurred un-der the auspices of Cyrus and his suc-cessors, and perhaps at no period has there been more occasion to recognize the hand of God than in the influences exerted on the minds of those heathen princes, disposing them to be favour-able to the long-oppressed children of God. ¶ And another third kingdom of brass. See notes on ver. 32. The parts of the image which were of brass were the belly and thighs, denoting inferio-rity not only to the head, but to the part which immediately preceded it— the breast and the arms of silver. It is not, indeed, specified, as in the for-mer case, that this kingdom would be inferior to the former, and it is only from the position assigned to it in the image, and the inferior quality of the metal by which it is represented, that it is implied that there would be any inferiority. There can be no reason-able doubt that by this third kingdom is denoted the empire founded by Alexander the Great—the Macedonian empire. It is known to all that he over-threw the Persian empire, and estab-lished a kingdom in the East, embrac-ing substantially the same territory

which had been occupied by the Medo-Persian and the Babylonian empire. While there can be no doubt that that kingdom is referred to, there can be as little that the reference is not merely to the empire during the reign of Alexan-der himself, but that it embraced the whole empire as founded and arranged by him, until it was succeeded by an-other universal empire—here denomi-nated the fourth kingdom. The reasons for supposing that the Macedonian em-pire is referred to here are almost too obvious to require that they should be specified. They are such as these: (1.) This kingdom actually succeeded that of Medo-Persia, covering the same territory, and, like that, was then un-derstood to be a universal monarchy. (2.) The empire of Alexander is else-where more than once referred to by Daniel in the same order, and in such a manner that the sense cannot be mis-taken. Thus, in ch. viii. 21: "And the rough goat is the king of Grecia: and the great horn that is between his eyes is the first king. Now that being broken, whereas four stood up for it, four kingdoms shall stand up out of the nation, but not in his power." Ch. x. 20: "And now," said the man that appeared in vision to Daniel (ver. 5), "will I re-turn to fight with the prince of Persia: and when I am gone forth, lo, the prince of Grecia shall come." Ch. xi. 2–4: "And now will I show thee the truth. Behold there shall stand up yet three kings in Persia; and the fourth shall be far richer than they all; and by his strength through his riches he shall stir up all against the realm of Grecia. And a mighty king shall stand up, that shall rule with great dominion, and do ac-cording to his will. And when he shall stand up, his kingdom shall be broken, and shall be divided toward the four winds of heaven; and not to his pos-terity, nor according to the kingdom that he ruled: for his kingdom shall be plucked up, even for others beside those." Since this kingdom is thus referred to elsewhere by Daniel in the same order, and as destined to act an important part in the affairs of the world, it is reasonable to suppose that there is a reference to it here. (3.) It is a circum-stance of some importance that the emblem here by which this kingdom is represented, *brass*, is one that is peculiarly appropriate to the Greeks, and one that could not be applied to any other nation with equal propriety. The Greeks were distinguished for their *brazen armour*, and the appellation, *the brazen-coated Greeks*—χαλκοχιτώνες 'Αχαιοὶ—is that by which they were designated most commonly by the ancients. — *Il.* i. 371; ii. 47; *Od.* i. 286. In accordance with this, Josephus says (*Ant.* b. x. c. 10, § 4), τὴν δὲ ἐκείνων ἕτερος τις ἀπὸ δύσεως καθαιρήσει χαλκὸν ἠμφιεσμένος —"*their empire another shall come from the West*, CLOTHED WITH BRASS, *shall destroy.*" These considerations leave no doubt that the kingdom here referred to was that Grecian or Macedonian, which, under Alexander, obtained dominion over all the East. ¶ *Which shall bear rule over all the earth.* In a sense similar to that of the Assyrian, the Babylonian, and the Medo-Persian empire. This is the common description of the empire of Alexander. He himself commanded that he should be called *the king of all the world*. *Accepto deinde imperio, regem se terrarum omnium ac mundi appellari jussit* (Justin. l. 12, c. 16, § 9)—"Having received the empire, he ordered himself to be called the king of all lands and of the world." Diodorus Siculus says that he received ambassadors from all countries; κατὰ δὲ τοῦτον τὸν χρόνον ἐξ ἁπάσης σχεδὸν τῆς οἰκουμένης ἧκον πρέσβεις, κ. τ. λ.—"At which time, legates came to him from almost the whole habitable world." —L. 17, c. 113. So Arrian (*Expedi. Alex.* l. 7, c. 15) remarks, that "Alexander then appeared to himself, and to those around him, *to be lord of all the earth and of the sea*—γῆς τε ἁπάσης καὶ θαλάσσης κύριον. The author of the book of Maccabees gives a similar account of the extent of this kingdom: "And it came to pass, after that Alexander, the son of Philip the Macedonian, who first reigned in Greece, had overthrown Darius, the king of the Persian and Medes, he fought many battles, and took the strongholds of all, and slew the kings of the earth; and he went through even to the ends of the earth; and took the spoil of many nations; and the earth was quiet before

him," 1 Macc. i. 1–3. The propriety of saying that this "kingdom bore rule over all the earth" is, therefore, apparent. It embraced, of course, all that was anciently included in the Assyrian and Babylonian empires; all that had been added to that empire by the conquests of Cyrus, and also all that Alexander had added to it by his hereditary dominions, and by his conquests in other places. Nearly or quite all the known world, except that which was then subject to the Romans, then just a rising power, was under the sway of Alexander. A question has been started whether this refers merely to the kingdom of Alexander during his own life, or whether it embraced also the succession of dynasties until the conquests of the Romans. That the latter is the correct opinion seems clear from the following considerations :— (1.) It was true, as we have seen, of the two previous kingdoms specified—the Babylonian and the Medo-Persian—that they embraced, not merely the kingdom under any one reigning monarch, but during its entire continuance until it was overthrown by one that had also pretensions to a universal empire — the former by the Medo-Persian, and the latter by the Macedonian. It is to be presumed that the same principles of interpretation are to be applied also to the Macedonian kingdom itself—especially as that was also actually succeeded by one that in a still higher sense laid claim to universal empire. (2.) This was, in fact, one kingdom. It is true that, on the death of Alexander, the empire which he founded was divided among four of his generals, and also that from that sprung the two reigns, the Seleucidæ in Syria, and of the Lagidæ who reigned in Egypt; but, as Newton has remarked, "their kingdom was no more a different kingdom from that of Alexander, than the parts differ from the whole. It was the same government still continued. Those who governed were still Macedonians. All ancient authors spoke of the kingdom of Alexander and of his successors as one and the same kingdom. The thing is implied in the very name by which they are usually called, *the successors of Alexander*. 'Alexander being dead,' says Josephus (*Ant.* b. xi. ch. 8, § 7), 'the empire was divided among his successors.' 'After the death of Alexander,' says Justin (lib. xli. c. 4, § 1), 'the kingdoms of the East were divided among his successors ;' and he still denominates them Macedonians, and their empire the Macedonian.''— Newton *on the Prophecies*, pp. 189, 190. In regard to the point before adverted to in reference to the kingdoms of Babylon and of Medo-Persia—the relation which they sustained to religion, or the methods in which they were made to contribute to its progress in the world, making it proper that they should be noticed in the volume of inspiration, it may be remarked that the Macedonian kingdom was also designed, undoubtedly, under an overruling Providence, to contribute to the progress of the great work of human redemption, and to prepare the way for the coming of the Messiah. A full statement of what was done under this reign in respect to religion—the most interesting aspect of history—may be seen in Edwards' *History of Redemption*, pp. 271–275, and in Prideaux's *Connexions*, vol. ii. p. 279, *seq.* The kingdom here referred to—the Macedonian, represented here by the portion of the image that was of brass, and in the vision of the four beasts (ch. vii.) by a leopard that had on its back the wings of a fowl, and in ch. viii. 21, by the rough goat—continued from the overthrow of Darius Codomanus by Alexander (B.C. 333), to the conquest of Syria, and the East, by the Romans under Pompey, about sixty-six years before the birth of the Saviour. The principal events during this period affecting the interests of religion, and preparing the way for the coming of the Messiah, were the following:—I. The extensive diffusion of the knowledge of the Greek language. The army of Alexander was mainly composed of Greeks. The Greek language was, of course, that which was spoken by the court, and in the cities which he founded ; the despatches were in Greek ; that language would be extensively cultivated to gratify those in power ; and the successors of Alexander were those who used the Greek tongue. The consequence was, that

the Greek language was extensively spread over the countries which were subdued by Alexander, and which were governed by his successors. That language became the popular tongue ; a sort of universal language understood by the great mass of the people, in a manner not unlike the French in Europe at the present day. The effect of this, in preparing for the introduction of the gospel, was seen in two respects : (*a*) In facilitating the *preaching* of the gospel. It is true that the apostles had the gift of tongues, and that there was, notwithstanding the prevalence of the Greek language, occasion for this. But there is no evidence that this was conferred on *all* the early preachers of the gospel, nor is it certain that those on whom it *was* conferred were able to make use of it on all occasions. It is not improbable that, in their ordinary labours, the apostles and others were left to rely on their natural endowments, and to use the language to which they had been most accustomed. As there was, therefore, a common language in most of the countries in which the gospel would be proclaimed, it is evident that the propagation of religion would be greatly facilitated by this, and there can be no doubt that it was *one* of the designs of Providence in permitting the Macedonian conquest thus to prepare the way for the more easy and rapid diffusion of the new religion. (*b*) In like manner, this conquest prepared the way *for the permanent record* of the history of the Saviour's life, and the doctrines of religion in the writings of the New Testament. It was evidently desirable, on many accounts, that the records should be made in one language rather than in many, and of all the languages then spoken on the earth, the *Greek* was the best adapted to such a purpose. It was not only the most polished and cultivated, but it was the most copious ; and it was the best fitted to express abstract ideas, and accurate distinctions. Probably with all the improvements since made in the copious Arabic language, and in the languages of modern times, there never has been one that was so well fitted for the purposes of a Divine revelation as the Greek. It may have been one design of Providence, in the extensive and accurate cultivation of that language in Greece itself, as well as in its diffusion over the world, that there should be at the time of the introduction of the Christian revelation a medium of permanent record that should be as free from imperfection as language could be ; a medium also in which there should be so much permanent and valuable literature that, even after it should cease to be a spoken language, it would be cultivated by the whole literary world, thus furnishing the means of an accurate knowledge of the meaning of the sacred writings. II. The translation of the Old Testament into the same language was another important event, which took place during the continuance of this kingdom, which greatly facilitated the introduction and spread of Christianity. The Hebrew language was understood by comparatively few. It ceased to be spoken in its purity after the time of the captivity. In that language the Scriptures of the Old Testament would have been but little diffused in the world. By their being translated, however, into Greek, they became extensively known, and furnished a ready and an intelligible ground of appeal to the preachers of the new religion when they referred to the prophecies of the Old Testament, and the recorded predictions of the Messiah. For a full account of the history of this version, the reader may consult Prideaux's *Connexions*, vol. iii. p. 53, *seq.* It was made according to Archbishop Usher, about 277 B.C. The probability is, that it was made at different periods, and by different hands, as it is executed with very various degrees of ability. See Intro. to Isaiah, § VIII. I. (1), for a more extended account of this version and its value. There can be no doubt that it contributed much to the diffusion of the knowledge of the Holy Scriptures, and was an important instrument in preparing the world for the reception of the revelation that should be made by the Messiah. III. Events of great importance occurred during the continuance of this kingdom in preserving the Jewish people in times of persecution, and saving their city and temple from ruin, and their nation from extinction.

(*a*) The destruction of Jerusalem and the temple was threatened by Alexander himself. After the siege and capture of Tyre, he became enraged at the Jews for refusing to furnish supplies for his army during the siege, under the plea that they were bound to show allegiance to Darius, and he marched to Jerusalem with an intention to take and destroy it. In order to appease him, it is said that Jaddua, the high-priest, went out to meet him in his pontifical robes, at the head of a procession of priests, and accompanied by the people in white garments. Alexander was so impressed with the scene that, to the surprise of all, he spared the city and temple ; and on being asked by Parmenio the reason of this clemency, said that he had seen this person in vision, who had directed him to lay aside all anxiety about his contemplated expedition to Asia, and that he had promised that God would give him the empire of the Persians. According to the story, Jaddua showed him the prophecies of Daniel, and confirmed him by those prophecies in the confident expectation of conquering the East ; and in view of this, Alexander offered sacrifices in the temple, and granted to the Hebrews the freedom of their country, and the exercise of their laws and religion. See Prideaux, vol. ii. p. 302, *seq.*; Josephus, *Ant.* b. xi. ch. 8. Whatever of fable there may be in this account, it is certain that this city and temple were not destroyed by Alexander, but that in his ravages in the East, he was led, by some cause, to deal with the capital of the Hebrew nation in a manner different from what he did with others. (*b*) A remarkable preservation of the Jewish people, of a somewhat similar character, and evincing the protection of God, occurred during the great persecution under Antiochus Epiphanes, one of the successors of Alexander, in the time of the Maccabees. See Prideaux, vol. iii. p. 230, and 2 Macc. v. 11–27. In the times of that celebrated persecution, multitudes of the Jews were slain by Antiochus himself ; the city was taken, and the temple defiled. Three years after it was taken by Antiochus (B.C. 168), Apollonius was directed by him to march against the city to vent his

40 And the fourth kingdom shall | be strong as iron: forasmuch as iron

wrath on the Jews; and when the people were assembled in their synagogues for worship, he let loose his forces on them, with a command to slay all the men, and to take all the women and children captives to be sold as slaves. After this, he plundered the city, demolished the houses, and pulled down the walls, and then with the ruins of the demolished city built a strong fortress on the top of an eminence in the city of David, in a place which overlooked the temple, and placed a strong garrison within. From this place attacks were made on all who went up to the temple to worship; and the temple was defiled with all manner of pollutions, until it was deserted, and the daily sacrifices ceased. From these calamities and persecutions, the city and the Jewish nation were delivered by the valour of Judas Maccabeus, in the manner detailed in the first book of Maccabees.

40. *And the fourth kingdom.* Represented in the image by the legs of iron, and the feet "part of iron, and part of clay," ver. 33. The first question which arises here is, what kingdom is referred to by this? In regard to this, there have been two leading opinions: one, that it refers to the Roman empire; the other, that it refers to the kingdoms or dynasties that immediately succeeded the reign of Alexander the Great; embracing the kingdoms of the Seleucidæ and Lagidæ, Syria, and Egypt—in the language of Prof. Stuart, who adopts this opinion, "that the legs and feet were symbols of that intermingled and confused empire which sprung up under the Grecian chiefs who finally succeeded him," [Alexander the Great].—*Com. on Daniel*, p. 173. For the reasoning by which this opinion is supported, see Prof. Stuart, pp. 173–193. The common opinion has been, that the reference is to the Roman empire, and in support of this opinion the following conditions may be suggested: (1.) The obvious design of the image was to symbolize the succession of great monarchies, which would precede the setting up of the kingdom of the Redeemer, and which would have an important agency in preparing the world for that.

The Roman empire was in itself too important, and performed too important an agency in preparing the world for that, to be omitted in such an enumeration. (2.) The kingdom here referred to was to be in existence at the time symbolized by the cutting of the stone out of the mountain; for, during the continuance of that kingdom, or under it, "the God of heaven was to set up a kingdom which should never be destroyed," ver. 44. But the kingdoms of the Seleucidæ and the Lagidæ—the "intermingled and confused empires that sprang up" after Alexander the Great—had ceased before that time, being superseded by the Roman. (3.) Unless the Roman power be represented, the symmetry of the image is destroyed; for it would make what was, in fact, one kingdom represented by two different metals—brass and iron. We have seen above that the Babylonian empire was represented appropriately by gold; the Medo-Persian by silver; and the Macedonian by brass. We have seen also, that in fact the empire founded by Alexander, and continued through his successors in Syria and Egypt, was in fact *one* kingdom, so spoken of by the ancients, and being in fact a *Greek* dynasty. If the appellation of *brass* belonged to that kingdom *as* a Greek kingdom, there is an obvious incongruity, and a departure from the method of interpreting the other portions of the image, in applying the term *iron* to any portion of that kingdom. (4.) By the application of the term *iron*, it is evidently implied that the kingdom thus referred to would be distinguished for *strength*—strength greater than its predecessors—as iron surpasses brass, and silver, and gold, in that quality. But this was *not* true of the confused reigns that immediately followed Alexander. They were unitedly weaker than the Babylonian and the Medo-Persian, and weaker than the empire of Alexander, out of which they arose. Comp. ch. viii. 21, 22. It *was* true, however, of the Roman power, that it was so much superior to all its predecessors in power, that it might well be represented by

breaketh in pieces and subdueth all | all these, shall it break in pieces and
things: and as iron that breaketh | bruise.

iron in comparison with brass, silver, and gold. (5.) The fourth monarchy represented in Nebuchadnezzar's dream is evidently the same which is represented by the fourth beast in Dan. vii. 7, 8, 23, 25. But it will appear, from the exposition of that chapter, that the reference there is to the Roman empire. See Notes on these passages. There can be no well-founded objection to this view on the ground that this kingdom was not properly a *succession* of the kingdom of Alexander, and did not occupy precisely the same territory. The same was true of each of the other kingdoms—the Medo-Persian and Macedonian. Yet while they were not, in the usual sense of the term, in the *succession,* they did, in fact, follow one after the other ; and with such accessions as were derived from conquest, and from the hereditary dominions of the conquerors, they did occupy the same territory. The design seems to have been to give a representation of a series of great monarchies, which would be, in an important sense, universal monarchies, and which should follow each other before the advent of the Saviour. The Roman, in addition to what it possessed in the West, actually occupied in the East substantially the same territory as the Babylonian, the Medo-Persian, and the Macedonian, and, like them, it had all the claims which any ancient sovereignty had to the title of a universal monarchy ; indeed no kingdom has ever existed to which this title could with more justice be applied. ¶ *Shall be strong as iron.* It is scarcely necessary to observe that this description is applicable to the Roman power. In nothing was it more remarkable than its *strength ;* for that irresistible power before which all other nations were perfectly weak. This characteristic of the Roman power is thus noticed by Mr. Gibbon : " The arms of the Republic, sometimes vanquished in battle, always victorious in war, advanced with rapid steps to the Euphrates, the Danube, the Rhine, and the ocean; and the images of gold, or silver, or brass, that might serve to represent

the nations and their kings, were successively broken by the *iron* monarchy of Rome."—*Dec. and Fall,* p. 642, Lond. ed. 1830, as quoted by Prof. Bush. ¶ *Forasmuch as iron breaketh in pieces and subdueth all* things. Iron is the metal which is used, and always has been used, for the purpose here suggested. In the form of hammers, sledges, and cannon-balls, and, in general, in reference to the accomplishment of any purpose, by beating or battering, this has been found to be the most valuable of the metals. It is heavy, is capable of being easily wrought into desired shapes; is abundant; is susceptible of being made hard so as not to be itself bruised, and has, therefore, all the properties which could be desired for purposes like this. ¶ *And as iron that breaketh all these.* That is, all these things ; to wit, everything. Nothing is able to stand before it ; there is nothing which it cannot reduce to powder. There is some repetition here, but it is for the sake of emphasis. ¶ *Shall it break in pieces and bruise.* Nothing could better characterize the Roman power than this. Everything was crushed before it. The nations which they conquered ceased to be kingdoms, and were reduced to provinces, and as kingdoms they were blotted out from the list of nations. This has been well described by Mr. Irving : "The Roman empire did beat down the constitution and establishment of all other kingdoms ; abolishing their independence, and bringing them into the most entire subjection ; humbling the pride, subjecting the will, using the property, and trampling upon the power and dignity of all other states. For by this was the Roman dominion distinguished from all the rest, that it was the work of almost as many centuries as those were of years ; the fruit of a thousand battles in which millions of men were slain. It made room for itself, as doth a battering-ram, by continual successive blows ; and it ceased not to beat and bruise all nations, so long as they continued to offer any resistance."—*Discourse on Daniel's Visions,* p. 180.

41 And whereas thou sawest the feet and toes, part of potters' clay and part of iron, the kingdom shall be divided; but there shall be in

41. *And whereas thou sawest the feet and toes, part of potters' clay and part of iron.* Ver. 33. The Chaldee is, "of them clay of the potter, and of them iron;" that is, part was composed of one material and part of the other. The sense is, not that the feet were composed entirely of one, and the toes of the other, but that they were intermingled. There was no homogeneousness of material; nothing in one that would coalesce with the other, or that could be permanently united to it, as two metals might be fused or welded together and form one solid compound. Iron and clay cannot be welded; and the idea here clearly is, that in the empire here referred to there would be two main elements which could never be made to blend. ¶ *The kingdom shall be divided.* That is, divided as the iron and clay were in the image. It does not necessarily mean that there would be an open rupture—an actual separation into two parts; but that there would be *such a diversity in the internal constitution* that, while there would be the element of great power, there would be also an element of weakness; there would be something which could never be blended with the element of strength, so as to produce one harmonious and homogeneous whole. ¶ *But there shall be in it of the strength of the iron, forasmuch as thou sawest the iron mixed with miry clay.* The principal idea in this part of the description is, that there would be great *power;* that whatever elements of weakness there might be, yet the *power* of the empire would be apparent. No one can fail to perceive how this applies to the Roman empire; a mighty power which, through all its long history, was distinguished for the vigour with which it carried forward its plans, and pressed on to universal dominion. As to the element of *weakness* symbolized too by the clay, it may not be possible to determine, with absolute certainty, what is referred to. *Any* internal source of weakness; anything in the constitution of the state, whether originally existing

it of the strength of the iron, forasmuch as thou sawest the iron mixed with miry clay.

42 And *as* the toes of the feet *were*

and constituting heterogeneous material, or whether springing up in the empire itself, or whether arising from the intermingling of foreign elements that never amalgamated themselves with the state, any one of these suppositions would meet all that is fairly implied in this language. From ver. 43, "they shall mingle themselves with the seed of men," it would seem, however, that the reference is to some *foreign* admixture—like the intermingling of nations of other languages, laws, and customs, which were never truly amalgamated with the original materials, and which constantly tended to weaken and divide the kingdom. It is to be remarked, in the exposition of the passage, that in the previous three kingdoms there was comparative homogeneousness. In the fourth kingdom, there was to be something of a peculiar character in this respect by which it should be distinguished from the others. As a matter of fact, the other three kingdoms were comparatively homogeneous in their character. The predominant feature was *Oriental;* and though there were different nations and people intermingled in the Babylonian, the Medo-Persian, and the Macedonian kingdoms, yet there was the same general prevailing character in each; there was not such an intermingling of foreign nations as to produce disturbing elements, or to mar the symmetry and strength of the whole. It was not thus with Rome. In that empire there was the intermingling of all nations and tongues, and though the essential element of the empire remained always—*the Roman*—yet there was an intermingling of other influences under the same general government, which could be appropriately compared with clay united with iron, and which ultimately contributed to its fall (see Notes on ver. 43).

42. *And* as *the toes of the feet* were *part of iron and part of clay, so the kingdom shall be partly strong, and partly broken.* Marg., *brittle.* The margin is the more correct rendering of the

part of iron and part of clay, *so the kingdom shall be partly strong, and partly* [1] *broken.*

> [1] *brittle.*

Chaldee word (הְבִירָה). It means *frail, fragile*—easily broken, but not necessarily that it was *actually* broken. That did not occur until the stone cut out of the mountain impinged on it. It has been commonly supposed (comp. Newton *on the Prophecies*), that the ten toes on the feet refer to the ten kingdoms into which the Roman empire was ultimately broken up, corresponding with the ten horns seen in the vision of Daniel, in ch. vii. 7. In regard to the *fact* that the Roman empire was ultimately broken up into *ten* such kingdoms, see the extended Notes on ch. vii. 24. The thing which struck the monarch in the vision, and Daniel in the interpretation, as remarkable, was that the feet and toes *were composed partly of iron and partly of clay.* In the upper portion of the image there had been uniformity in the different parts, and had been no intermingling of metals. Here a new feature was seen —not only that a new metal was employed, but that there was intermingled with that, in the same portion of the image, a different substance, and one that had no affinity with the iron, and that could never be made to blend with it. In the latter part of this verse, the original word for "*partly*" is not the same in each clause. In the former it is מִן־קְצָת—properly *from the end*, sc., of the kingdom. Comp. Dan. xii. 13, "*At the end* of the days ;" i. 15, "*At the end* of ten days ;" and vers. 5, 18. The word *might* be employed to denote the *end* or *extremity* of anything, *e.g.*, in respect to *time*, and some have supposed that there is a reference here to the later periods of the Roman empire. See Poole's *Synopsis*. But the word is also used to denote *the sum*, or *the whole number ;* and then the phrase is equivalent to *a part*—as *e.g.*, in the phrase מִקְצָת כְּלֵי בֵית הָאֱלֹהִים—*from the sum of the vessels of the house of God* (Dan. i. 2); that is, a portion of the whole number, or a part. Comp. Neh. vii. 70, "from the sum of the heads of the

---

43 And whereas thou sawest iron mixed with miry clay, they shall mingle themselves with the seed of

---

fathers ;" that is, a part of them. In the latter part of the clause it is מִנֵּה— *from it ;* that is, a part of it ; partly. The entire phrase means that one part of the whole would be strong, and one part would be fragile. The reference is not to the *time* when this would occur, but to the *fact* that it would be so. The idea in this verse does not vary materially from that in the former, except that in that, the prominent thought is, that there would be *strength* in the kingdom : in this, the idea is, that while there would be strength in the kingdom, there would be also the elements of weakness.

43. *And whereas thou sawest iron mixed with miry clay, they shall mingle themselves with the seed of men.* Various explanations have been given of this verse, and it certainly is not of easy interpretation. The phrase "seed of men," would properly denote something different from the original stock that was represented by iron ; some foreign admixture that would be so unlike that, and that would so little amalgamate with it, as to be properly represented by clay as compared with iron. Prof. Stuart interprets this of matrimonial alliances, and supposes that the idea expressed is, that, "while the object of such alliances was union, or at least a design to bring about a peaceable state of things, that object was, in a peculiar manner, defeated." The word rendered *men* (אֲנָשָׁא) is employed in Hebrew and in Chaldee to denote men of an inferior class—the lower orders, the common herd — in contradistinction from the more elevated and noble classes, represented by the word אִישׁ. See Isa. ii. 9 ; v. 15 ; Prov. viii. 4. The word here used also (from אָנַשׁ—to be sick, ill at ease, incurable), would properly denote feebleness or inferiority, and would be aptly represented by clay as contrasted with iron. The expression "seed of men," as here used, would therefore denote some intermingling of an inferior race

men: but they shall not cleave ¹ one to another, even as iron is not mixed with clay.

¹ *this with this.*

with the original stock; some union or alliance under the one sovereignty, which would greatly weaken it as a whole, though the original strength still was great. The language would represent a race of mighty and powerful men, constituting the stamina—the bone and the sinew of the empire—mixed up with another race or other races, with whom, though they were associated in the government, they could never be blended; could never assimilate. This foreign admixture in the empire would be a constant source of weakness, and would constantly tend to division and faction, for such elements could never harmonize. It is further to be remarked, that this would exist to a degree which would not be found in either of the three previous kingdoms. In fact, in these kingdoms there was no such intermingling with foreign nations as to destroy the homogeneousness of the empire. They were, in the main, Orientals; with the language, the manners, the customs, the habits of Orientals; and in respect to energy and power—the point here under consideration—there was no marked distinction between the subjected provinces and the original materials of the monarchy. By the act of subjection, they became substantially one people, and readily blended together. This remark will certainly apply to the two first of these monarchies—the Babylonian and the Medo-Persian; and though with less force to the Macedonian, yet it was not true of that that it became so intermingled with foreign people as to constitute heterogeneous elements as it was of the Roman. In that monarchy, the element of *strength* was *infused* by Alexander and his Greeks; all the elements of weakness were in the original materials of the empire. In the Roman, the element of strength—*the iron*—was in the original material of the empire; the weak, the heterogeneous element—*the clay*—was that which was introduced from the foreign nations. This consideration may perhaps do something to show that the

opinion of Grotius, Prof. Stuart, and others, that this fourth monarchy was that which immediately succeeded Alexander is not well founded. The only question then is, whether, in the constitution of the Roman empire, at the time when it became the successor of the other three as a universal monarchy, there was such an intermingling of a foreign element, as to be properly represented by clay as contrasted with the original and stronger material *iron.* I say, "at the time when it became the successor of the other three as a universal monarchy," because the only point of view in which Daniel contemplated it was that. He looked at this, as he did at the others, as already such a universal dominion, and not at what it was before, or at the steps by which it rose to power. Now, on looking at the Roman empire at that period, and during the time when it occupied the position of the universal monarchy, and during which the "stone cut out of the mountain" grew and filled the world, there is no difficulty in finding such an intermingling with other nations—"the seed of men"—as to be properly described by "iron and clay" in the same image that could never be blended. The allusion is, probably, to that intermingling with other nations which so remarkably characterized the Roman empire, and which arose partly from its conquests, and partly from the inroads of other people in the latter days of the empire, and in reference to both of which there was no proper amalgamation, leaving the original vigour of the empire substantially in its strength, but introducing other elements which never amalgamated with it, and which were like clay intermingled with iron. (1.) From their conquests. Tacitus says, "*Dominandi cupido cunctis affectibus flagrantior est*"—the lust of ruling is more ardent than all other desires; and this was eminently true of the Romans. They aspired at the dominion of the world; and, in their strides at universal conquest, they brought nations under their subjection, and admitted them to the rights of citizenship, which had no affinity with the original material which composed the Roman power, and which never really amalgamated with it, any more than clay does with iron. (2.) This was true, also, in respect to the hordes that poured into the empire from other countries, and particularly from the Scandinavian regions, in the latter periods of the empire, and with which the Romans were compelled to form alliances, while, at the same time, they could not amalgamate with them. "In the reign of the emperor Caracalla," says Mr. Gibbon, "an innumerable swarm of Suevi appeared on the banks of the Mein, and in the neighbourhood of the Roman provinces, in quest of food, or plunder, or glory. The hasty army of volunteers gradually coalesced into a great and permanent nation, and as it was composed of so many different tribes, assumed the name of Allemanni, or *allmen*, to denote their various lineage, and their common bravery." No reader of the Roman history can be ignorant of the invasions of the Goths, the Huns, and the Vandals, or of the effects of these invasions on the empire. No one can be ignorant of the manner in which they became intermingled with the ancient Roman people, or of the attempts to form alliances with them, by intermarriages and otherwise, which were always like attempts to unite iron and clay. "Placidia, daughter of Theodosius the Great, was given in marriage to Adolphus, king of the Goths; the two daughters of Stilicho, the Vandal, were successively married to Honorius; and Genseric, another Vandal, gave Eudocia, a captive imperial princess, to his son to wife." The effects of the intermingling of foreign people on the character and destiny of the empire cannot be stated perhaps in a more graphic manner than is done by Mr. Gibbon, in the summary review of the Roman history, with which he concludes his seventh chapter, and at the same time there could scarcely be a more clear or expressive commentary on this prophecy of Daniel. "During the four first ages," says he, "the Romans, in the laborious school of poverty, had acquired the virtues of war and government: by the vigorous exertion of those virtues, and by the assistance of fortune, they had obtained, in the course of the three succeeding centuries, an absolute empire over many countries of Europe, Asia, and Africa. The last three hundred years had been consumed in apparent prosperity and internal decline. The nation of soldiers, magistrates, and legislators, who composed the thirty-five tribes of the Roman people, was dissolved into the common mass of mankind, and confounded with the millions of servile provincials who had received the name without adopting the spirit of Romans. A mercenary army, levied among the subjects and barbarians of the frontier, was the only order of men who preserved and abused their independence. By their tumultuary election, a Syrian, a Goth, or an Arab was exalted to the throne of Rome, and invested with despotic power over the conquests and over the country of the Scipios. The limits of the Roman empire still extended from the Western Ocean to the Tigris, and from Mount Atlas to the Rhine and the Danube. To the undiscerning eye of the vulgar, Philip appeared a monarch no less powerful than Hadrian or Augustus had formerly been. The form was still the same, but the animating health and vigour were fled. The industry of the people was discouraged and exhausted by a long series of oppression. The discipline of the legions, which alone, after the extinction of every other virtue, had propped the greatness of the state, was corrupted by the ambition, or relaxed by the weakness of the emperors. The strength of the frontiers, which had always consisted in arms rather than in fortifications, was insensibly undermined, and the fairest provinces were left exposed to the rapaciousness or ambition of the barbarians, who soon discovered the decline of the Roman empire."—Vol. i. pp. 110, 111; Harper's Edit. (N. Y.) 1829. Comp. Notes on Rev. vi. 1–8. The agency of the Roman empire was so important in preparing the world for the advent of the Son of God, and in reference to the establishment of his kingdom, that there was an obvious propriety that it should be made a distinct subject of prophecy. We have seen that each of the other three kingdoms had an important influence in preparing the world for the introduction of Christianity, and was designed to accomplish an important part in the "History of Redemption." The agency of the Roman empire was more direct and important than any one or all of these; for (a) that was the empire which had the supremacy when the Son of God appeared; (b) that kingdom had performed a more direct and important work in preparing the world for his coming; (c) it was under authority derived from that sovereignty that the Son of God was put to death; and (d) it was by that that the ancient dispensation was brought to an end; and (e) it was under that that the new religion was spread through the world. It may be of use, therefore, in an exposition of this prophecy, to refer, with some particularity, to the things that were accomplished by this "fourth kingdom" in furthering the work of redemption, or in introducing and establishing the kingdom that was to be "set up, and which was never to be destroyed." That agency related to the following points:—(1.) The establishment of a universal dominion ; the fact that the world was brought under one sceptre greatly favoured the propagation of the Christian religion. We have seen, under the previous dynasties —the Babylonian, Persian, and Macedonian—that such an universal empire was important in earlier ages to *prepare* the world for the advent of the Messiah. This was still more important when he was about actually to appear, and his religion was to be spread over the world. It greatly favoured the diffusion of the new system that there was one empire ; that the means of communication from one part of the world to another had been so extended by the Romans ; and that one who was entitled to the privileges of citizenship could claim protection in nearly every part of the world. (2.) The prevalence of universal peace. The world had become subject to the Roman power, and conquest was at an end. The world at last, after so long agitations and strifes,

was at peace. The distant provinces quietly submitted to the Roman control; the civil dissensions which had reigned so long at the capital were hushed ; Augustus, having triumphed over all his rivals, quietly occupied the imperial throne, and, as a symbol of the universal peace, the temple of Janus was closed. Rarely in their history had that temple been closed before ;* and yet there was an obvious propriety that when the "Prince of Peace" should come, the world should be at rest, and that the clangour of arms should cease. It was a beautiful emblem of the nature of his reign. A world that had been always in conflict before rested on its arms ; the tumult of battle had died away ; the banners of war were furled ; the legions of Rome paused in their career of conquest, and the world tranquilly waited for the coming of the Son of God. (3.) The Roman power accomplished an important agency in the great transaction which the Son of God came to perform in his making an atonement for the sins of the world. It was so arranged, in the Divine counsels, that he should be put to death, not by the hands of his own kindred and countrymen, but by the hands of foreigners, and under their authority. The necessity and the certainty of this was early predicted by the Saviour (Matt. xx. 19 ; Mark x. 33 ; Luke xviii. 32), and it is clear that there were important reasons why it should be thus done ; and doubtless one design of bringing Judea and the rest of the world under the Roman yoke was, that it might be accomplished in this way. Among the *reasons* for this may be suggested such as the following: (a) The heathen world, as well as the Jewish community, thus had a part in the great transaction. He died for the whole world—Jews and Gentiles—and it was important that that fact should be referred to in the manner of his death, and that the two great

* This temple was built, or finished at least, by Numa. It was closed, first, in his reign; secondly, at the close of the first Punic war, B.C. 241; three times in the reign of Augustus, the last time near the epoch of the birth of the Saviour; and three times afterwards, once under Nero, once under Vespasian, and once under Constantius, A.D. 350.—Eschenburg, *Class. Lit.*, p. 18.

44 And in ¹ the days of these | kings shall the God ᵃ of heaven set

¹ *their.*

a Mi. 4. 7 ; Lu. 1. 32. 33.

divisions of the human family should be united in the great transaction. It thus became not a *Jewish* affair only ; not an event in which Judea alone was interested, but an affair of the world ; a transaction in which the representatives of the world took their part. (*b*) It was thus made a matter of publicity. The account of the death of the Saviour would thus, of course, be transmitted to the capital, and would demand the attention of those who were in power. When the gospel was preached at Rome, it would be proper to allege that it was a thing in which Rome itself had had an important agency, from the fact that under the Roman authority the Messiah had been put to death. (*c*) The agency of the Romans, therefore, established the certainty of the death of Jesus, and consequently the certainty of his having risen from the dead. In order to demonstrate the latter, it was indispensable that the former should be made certain, and that all questions in regard to the reality of his death should be placed beyond a doubt. This was done by the agency of Pilate, a Roman governor. His death was certified to him, and he was satisfied of it. It became a matter of record ; a point about which there could be no dispute. Accordingly, in all the questions that came up in reference to the religion of Christ, it was never made a matter of doubt that he had been really put to death under Pilate, the Roman governor, whatever question may have arisen about the fact of his resurrection. (*d*) Equally important was the agency of the Romans in establishing the *innocence* of the Saviour. After patient and repeated trials before himself, Pilate was constrained to say that he was innocent of the charges alleged against him, and that no fault could be found in him. In proclaiming the gospel, it was of immense importance to be able to affirm this throughout the world. It could never be alleged against the gospel that its Author had violated the laws ; that he deserved to be put to death as a malefactor, for the records of the Roman governor himself showed the con-

trary. The agency of the Romans, therefore, in the great work of the atonement, though undesigned on their part, was of inestimable importance in the establishment of the Christian religion ; and it may be presumed that it was for this, in part at least, that the world was placed under their control, and that it was so ordered that the Messiah suffered under authority derived from them. (4.) There was another important agency of the Romans in reference to the religion that was to fill the earth. It was in destroying the city of Jerusalem, and bringing to a final end the whole system of Hebrew rites and ceremonies. The ancient sacrifices lost their efficacy really when the atonement was made on the cross. Then there was no need of the temple, and the altar, and the ancient priesthood. It was necessary that the ancient rites should cease, and that, having now lost their efficacy, there should be no possibility of perpetuating them. Accordingly, within the space of about thirty years after the death of the Saviour, when there had been time to perceive the bearing of the atonement on their temple rites ; when it was plain that they were no longer efficacious, significant, or necessary, the Romans were suffered to destroy the city, the altar, and the temple, and to bring the whole system to a perpetual end. The place where the ancient worship had been celebrated was made a heap of ruins ; the altar was overturned, never to be built again ; and the pomp and splendour of the ancient ritual passèd away for ever. It was the design of God that that system should come to a perpetual end ; and hence, by his providence, it was so arranged, that ruin should spread over the city where the Lord was crucified, and that the Jewish people should never build an altar or a temple there again. To this day it has never been in their power to kindle the fire of sacrifice there, or to cause the smoke of incense to ascend in a temple consecrated to the worship of the God of their fathers. The agency of this fourth kingdom, therefore, was exceed-

up a kingdom which shall never be destroyed: and the ¹kingdom shall not be left to other people, *but* it

¹ *kingdom thereof.*

shall break ªin pieces and consume all these kingdoms, and it shall stand for ever.

ª Ps. 2. 9.

ingly important in the introduction and establishment of that kingdom which was to be perpetual, and which was to fill the earth, and hence the reference to it here, and the more extended reference in ch. vii.

44. *And in the days of these kings.* Marg., *their.* The reading in the text "*these* kings"—is the more correct. The Vulgate renders this, "in the days of these kingdoms." The natural and obvious sense of the passage is, that during the continuance of the kingdoms above-mentioned, or before they should finally pass away, that is, before the last one should become extinct, another kingdom would be established on the earth which would be perpetual. Before the succession of universal monarchies should have passed away, the new kingdom would be set up that would never be destroyed. Such language is not uncommon. "Thus, if we were to speak of anything taking place in the days of British kings, we should not of course understand it as running through all their reigns, but merely as occurring in some one of them."—Prof. Bush. So it is said in Ruth i. 1: "It came to pass *in the* days when the judges ruled, that there was a famine in the land;" that is, the famine occurred sometime under that general administration, or before it had passed away, evidently not meaning that there was a famine in the reign of each one. So it is said of Jephthah, that he was buried *in the cities of Gilead;* that is, some one of them. Josiah was buried *in the sepulchres of his fathers;* that is, in some one of them. ¶ *Shall the God of heaven.* The God, who rules in heaven; the true God. This is designed to show the Divine origin of this kingdom, and to distinguish it from all others. Though the others here referred to were under the Divine control, and were designed to act an important part in preparing the world for this, yet they are not represented as deriving their origin directly from heaven. They were

founded in the usual manner of earthly monarchies, but this was to have a heavenly origin. In accordance with this, the kingdom which the Messiah came to establish is often called, in the New Testament, "the kingdom of heaven," "the kingdom of God," &c. Compare Mic. iv. 7; Luke i. 32, 33. ¶ *Set up a kingdom.* "Shall cause to arise or stand up"—קרם. It shall not owe its origin to the usual causes by which empires are constituted on the earth—by conquests; by human policy; by powerful alliances; by transmitted hereditary possession—but shall exist because God shall *appoint* and *constitute* it. There can be no reasonable doubt as to what kingdom is here intended, and nearly all expositors have supposed that it refers to the kingdom of the Messiah. Grotius, indeed, who made the fourth kingdom refer to the Seleucidæ and Lagidæ, was constrained by consistency to make this refer to the Roman power; but in this interpretation he stands almost, if not entirely, alone. Yet even he supposes it to refer not to *heathen* Rome only, but to Rome as the perpetual seat of power —the permanent kingdom—the seat of the church: *Imperium Romanum perpetuò mansurum, quod sedes erit ecclesiæ.* And although he maintains that he refers to Rome primarily, yet he is constrained to acknowledge that what is here said is true in a higher sense of the kingdom of Christ: *Sensus sublimior, Christum finem impositurum omnibus imperiis terrestribus.* But there can be no real doubt as to what kingdom is intended. Its distinctly declared Divine origin; the declaration that it shall never be destroyed; the assurance that it would absorb all other kingdoms, and that it would stand for ever; and the entire accordance of these declarations with the account of the kingdom of the Messiah in the New Testament, show beyond a doubt that the kingdom of the Redeemer is intended. ¶ *Which shall never be destroyed.* The others would pass

away. The Babylonian would be succeeded by the Medo-Persian, that by
the Macedonian, that by the Roman,
and that in its turn by the one which
the God of heaven would set up.
This would be perpetual. Nothing
would have power to overthrow it. It
would live in the revolutions of all
other kingdoms, and would survive
them all. Compare Notes on ch. vii.
14 ; and the summary of the doctrines
taught here at the close of the Notes
on ver. 45. ¶ *And the kingdom shall
not be left to other people.* Marg.,
thereof. Literally, " *Its* kingdom shall
not be left to other people ;" that is,
the ruling power appropriate to this
kingdom or dominion shall never pass
away from its rightful possessor, and
be transferred to other hands. In
respect to other kingdoms, it often
happens that their sovereigns are deposed, and that their power passes into
the hands of usurpers. But this can
never occur in this kingdom. The
government will never change hands.
The administration will be perpetual.
No foreign power shall sway the sceptre
of this kingdom. There *may be* an
allusion here to the fact that, in respect to each of the other kingdoms
mentioned, the power over the same
territory *did* pass into the hands of
other people. Thus, on the same territory, the dominion passed from the
hands of the Babylonian princes to the
hands of Cyrus the Persian, and then
to the hands of Alexander the Macedonian, and then to the hands of the
Romans. But this would never occur
in regard to the kingdom which the
God of heaven would set up. In the
region of empire appropriate to it, it
would never change hands ; and this
promise of perpetuity made this kingdom wholly unlike all its predecessors.
¶ But *it shall break in pieces and consume all these kingdoms.* As represented by the stone cut out of the mountains without hands, impinging on the
image. See Notes on vers. 34, 35.

Two inquiries at once meet us here,
of somewhat difficult solution. The
first is, How, if this is designed to
apply to the kingdom of the Messiah,
can the description be true ? The language here would seem to imply some

violent action ; some positive crushing
force ; something like that which occurs
in conquests when nations are subdued.
Would it not appear from this that the
kingdom here represented was to make
its way by conquests in the same manner as the other kingdoms, rather than
by a silent and peaceful influence ? Is
this language, in fact, applicable to the
method in which the kingdom of Christ
is to supplant all others ? In reply to
these questions, it may be remarked,
(1) that the leading idea, as apparent in
the prophecy, is not so much that of
violence as that the kingdoms referred
to would be *utterly brought to an end ;*
that there would be, under this new
kingdom, ultimately an entire cessation
of the others ; or that they would be
removed or supplanted by this. This
is represented (ver. 35) by the fact that
the materials composing the other kingdoms are represented before this as becoming like " the chaff of the summer
threshing-floors ;" and as "being carried
away, so that no place was found for
them." The stone cut out of the mountain, small at first, was mysteriously
enlarged, so that it occupied the place
which they did, and ultimately filled
the earth. A process of gradual demolition, acting on them by constant at-
trition, removing portions of them, and
occupying their place until they should
disappear, and until there should be a
complete substitution of the new kingdom in their place, would seem to correspond with all that is essential in the
prophetic description. See Notes on
ver. 34, on the expression, " which
smote the image upon his feet." But
(2) this language is in accordance with
that which is commonly used in the
predictions respecting the kingdom of
the Messiah—language which is descriptive of the existence of *power* in
subduing the nations, and bringing the
opposing kingdoms of the world to an
end. Thus in Psal. ii. 9, " Thou shalt
break them with a rod of iron : thou shalt
dash them in pieces like a potter's vessel." Isa. lx. 12, " For the nation and
kingdom that will not serve thee shall
perish ; yea, those nations shall be
utterly wasted." So 1 Cor. xv. 24, 25,
" When he shall have put down all
rule, and all authority and power.

For he must reign till he hath put all enemies under his feet." These expressions denote that there will be an entire subjection of other kingdoms to that of the Messiah, called in the New Testament "the kingdom of God." They undoubtedly imply that there will be some kind of *force* employed—for this great work cannot be accomplished without the existence of *power;* but it may be remarked (*a*) that it does not necessarily mean that there will be *physical* force, or power like that by which kingdoms have been usually overturned. The kingdom of the Redeemer is a kingdom of *principles,* and those principles will subdue the nations, and bring them into subjection. (*b*) It does not necessarily mean that the effect here described will be accomplished *at once.* It may be by a gradual process, like a continual beating on the image, reducing it ultimately to powder.

The other question which arises here is, How can it be said that the new kingdom which was to be set up would "break in pieces and consume all these kingdoms?" How could the destruction of the image in the Roman period be in fact the destruction of the *three* previous kingdoms, represented by gold, and silver, and brass? Would they not in fact have passed away before the Roman power came into existence? And yet, is not the representation in ver. 35, that the iron, the clay, the brass, the silver, and the gold were broken in pieces together, and were all scattered like the chaff of the summer threshing-floor? Is it supposed that these kingdoms would be all in existence at the same time, and that the action of the symbolical "stone" was to be alike on all of them? To these questions, we may answer, (1.) That the meaning is, undoubtedly, that three of these kingdoms would have passed away at the time of the action of the "stone" referred to. They were to be a *succession* of kingdoms, occupying, to a great extent, the same territory, and not contemporary monarchies occupying distinct territories. (2.) The action of the "stone" was in fact, in a most important sense, to be on them all ; that is, it was to be on what *constituted* these successive kingdoms of gold, silver,

brass, and iron. Each was in its turn an universal monarchy. The same territory was substantially occupied by them all. The Medo-Persian sceptre extended over the region under the Babylonian ; the Macedonian over that ; the Roman over that. There were indeed *accessions* in each successive monarchy, but still anything which affected the Roman empire affected what had *in fact* been the Babylonian, the Medo-Persian, and the Macedonian. A demolition of the image in the time of the Roman empire would be, therefore, in fact, a demolition of the whole. (3.) This interpretation is necessary from the nature of the symbolical representation. The eye of the monarch in the dream was directed to the image as *a splendid whole.* It was necessary to the object in view that he should see it *all at a time,* that he might have a distinct conception of it. This purpose made it impossible to exhibit the kingdoms *in succession,* but they all stood up before him at once. No one can doubt that there *might* have been a different representation, and that the kingdoms might have been made to pass before him in their order, but the representation would have been less grand and imposing. But this design made it necessary that the image should be kept *entire* before the mind until its demolition. It would have been unseemly to have represented the head as removed, and then the shoulders and breast, and then the belly and thighs, until nothing remained but the feet and toes. It was necessary to keep up the representation of *the image of colossal majesty and strength,* until a new power should arise which *would demolish it all.* Nebuchadnezzar is not represented as seeing the parts of the image successively appear or disappear. He does not at first see the golden head rising above the earth, and then the other parts in succession ; nor the golden head disappearing, and then the other parts, until nothing was left but the feet and the toes. Such a representation would have destroyed the decorum and beauty of the whole figure ; and as it cannot be argued that because Nebuchadnezzar saw the whole image at the outset standing in its complete form, that *therefore* all

45 Forasmuch as thou sawest that the stone was cut out of the

mountain [1] without hands, and that it brake in pieces the iron, the

[1] *which was not in hands.*

these kingdoms must have been simultaneously in existence, so it cannot be argued because he saw the whole image standing when the stone smote upon it, that *therefore* all these kingdoms must have had an existence then. (4.) It may be added, that the destruction of the last was in fact the destruction of all the three predecessors. The whole power had become embodied in that, and the demolition affected the whole series.

45. *Forasmuch as thou sawest that the stone*, &c. On the meaning of the language employed here, see Notes on vers. 34, 35. The word *forasmuch* may be taken either in connection with what precedes, or with what follows. In the former method, there should be a period at the word *gold* in this verse ; and then the sense is, "In those days shall the God of heaven set up a kingdom, &c., *forasmuch*, or *because* thou sawest a stone," &c., that is, that was a certain indication of it. According to the other method, the meaning is, "Forasmuch as thou sawest the stone cut out and demolish the image, the great God has made known the certainty of it ;" that is, that is a certain indication that it will be done. The Vulgate is, "According to what thou sawest, that the stone was cut out without hands, and reduced the clay, &c., the great God has shown to the king what will be hereafter." The difference in the interpretation is not very material. ¶ *Cut out of the mountain.* This is not inserted in the statement in ver. 34. It seems, however, to be implied there, as there is mention of the stone as *"cut out."* The representation is evidently that of a stone disengaged from its native bed, the side of a mountain, without any human agency, and then rolling down the side of it and impinging on the image. ¶ *The great God hath made known to the king what shall come to pass hereafter.* Marg., the same as the Chaldee, *after this.* The meaning is simply, in time to come ; in some future period. Daniel claims none of the merit of this discovery to himself,

but ascribes it all to God. ¶ *And the dream is certain, and the interpretation thereof sure.* That is, it is no vain and airy phantom ; no mere working of the imagination. The dream was all that the monarch had supposed it to be—a representation of coming events, and his solicitude in regard to it was well-founded. Daniel speaks with the utmost assurance also as to its fulfilment. He knew that he had been led to this interpretation by no skill of his own ; and his representation of it was such as to satisfy the monarch of its correctness. Two circumstances probably made it appear certain to the monarch, as we learn from the next verse it did : one, that Daniel had recalled the dream to his own recollection, showing that he was under a Divine guidance ; and the other, the plausibility—the verisimilitude—the evident truthfulness of the representation. It was such a manifest *explanation* of the dream that Nebuchadnezzar, in the same manner as Pharaoh had done before him when his dreams were explained by Joseph, at once admitted the correctness of the representation.

Having now gone through with the *exposition* of this important passage respecting the stone cut from the mountain, it seems proper to make a few remarks in regard to the nature of the kingdom that would be set up, as represented by the stone which demolished the image, and which so marvellously increased as to fill the earth. That there is reference to the kingdom of the Messiah cannot be reasonably doubted. The points which are established in respect to that kingdom by the passage now under consideration are the following : —
1. Its superhuman origin. This is indicated in the representation of the stone cut out of the mountain "without hands ;" that is, clearly not by human agency, or in the ordinary course of events. There was to be a superhuman power exerted in detaching it from the mountain, as well as in its future growth. What appeared so marvellous was, that it was cut from its original

brass, the clay, the silver, and the gold ; the great God hath made known to the king what shall come to pass [1] hereafter: and the dream *is* certain, and the interpretation thereof sure.

[1] *after this.*

resting-place by some invisible power, and moved forward to the consummation of its work without any human agency. That this was designed to be significant of *something* there can be no reasonable doubt, for the result is made to turn on this. I do not see that any special significancy is to be attached to the idea of its being cut from "*a mountain,*" nor that it is required of us to attempt to refine on that expression, and to ascertain whether the mountain means the Roman kingdom, out of which the gospel church was taken, as many suppose ; or the Jewish nation, as Augustine supposed ; or that "the origin of Christ was sublime and superior to the whole world," as Calvin supposes ; or to the mountainous country of Judea in which the Messiah was born, as many others have maintained ; or to the tomb of Joseph, as a rock from which the Messiah sprang to life and victory, as others have imagined. All this belongs to a system of interpretation that is trifling in the extreme. The representation of the mountain here is merely for the sake of verisimilitude, like the circumstances in a parable. If a stone was "cut out without hands," it would be natural to speak of it as cut from the mountain or parent-rock to which it was attached. The eye is not here directed to the *mountain* as having anything significant or marvellous about it, but to the *stone* that so mysteriously left its bed, and rolled onward toward the image. The point of interest and of marvel, the mysterious thing that attracted the eye, was that there was no human agency employed : that no hands were seen at work ; that none of the ordinary instrumentalities were seen by which great effects are accomplished among men. Now this would properly represent the idea that the kingdom of the Messiah would have a supernatural origin. Its beginnings would be unlike what is usually seen among men. How appropriately this applies to the kingdom of the Messiah, as having its origin not in human power, need not here be stated. Nothing is more apparent ; nothing is more frequently dwelt on in the New Testament, than that it had a heavenly origin. It did not owe its beginning to human plans, counsels, or power.

II. Its feebleness in its beginning, compared with its ultimate growth and power. At first it was a stone comparatively small, and that seemed utterly inadequate to the work of demolishing and pulverizing a colossal statue of gold, silver, brass, and iron. Ultimately it grew to be itself of mountain-size, and to fill the land. Now this representation would undoubtedly convey the fair impression that this new power, represented by the stone, would at first be comparatively small and feeble ; that there would be comparative weakness in its origin as contrasted with what it would ultimately attain to ; and that it would seem to be utterly inadequate to the performance of what it finally accomplished. It is hardly necessary to say that this corresponds entirely with the origin of the Messiah's kingdom. Everywhere it is represented as of feeble beginnings, and, as a system, to human view, entirely inadequate to so great a work as that of bringing other kingdoms to an end, and subduing it to itself. The complete fulfilment of the prophetic statement would be found in such circumstances as the following : (1.) The humble origin of the head of this new power himself —the Messiah—the King of Sion. He was, in fact, of a decayed and dilapidated family ; was ranked among the poor ; was without powerful friends or political connections ; possessed no uncommon advantages of learning, and was regarded with contempt and scorn by the great mass of his countrymen. No one would have supposed that the religion originated by one of so humble an origin would have power to change the destiny of the kingdoms of the earth. (2.) The feebleness of the beginning of his kingdom. His few followers—the little band of fishermen ;

DANIEL I.   M

the slow progress at first made ; these were circumstances strikingly in accordance with the representation in Daniel. (3.) The absence in that band of all that seemed requisite to accomplish so great a work. They had no arms, no wealth, no political power. They had nothing of that which has commonly been employed to overthrow kingdoms, and the band of fishermen sent forth to this work seemed as little adequate to the undertaking as the stone cut from the mountain did to demolish the colossal image. (4.) All this feebleness in the beginning was wonderfully contrasted with the ultimate results, like the stone, when cut from the mountain, contrasted with its magnitude when it filled the earth. The Saviour himself often referred to the contrast between the feeble origin of his religion, and what it would grow to be. At first it was like a grain of mustard-seed, smallest among seeds ; then it grew to be a tree so large that the fowls of the air lodged in the branches. At first it was like leaven, hidden in meal ; ultimately it would diffuse itself through the mass, so that the whole would be leavened, Mat. xiii. 31–33.

III. It would supplant all other kingdoms. This was clearly indicated by the fact that the " stone " demolished the image, reducing it to powder, and filled the place which that occupied, and all the land. This has been explained (Notes on vers. 34, 35), as meaning that it would not be by sudden violence, but by a continued process of comminution. There would be such an action on the kingdoms of the earth represented by gold, and silver, and brass, and iron, that they would disappear, and the new power represented by the " stone " would finally take their place. As this new power was to be humble in its origin, and feeble to human view ; as it had nothing which, to outward appearance, would seem adequate to the result, the reference would seem to be to the *principles* which would characterize it, and which, as elements of power, would gradually but ultimately secure the changes represented by the demolition of the colossal statue. The only question then would be, whether the principles in the kingdom of the

Messiah had such originality and power as would gradually but certainly change the modes of government that existed in the world, and substitute another kind of reign ; or, what is the influence which it will exert on the nations, causing new methods of government, in accordance with its principles, to prevail on the earth. Though apparently feeble, without arms, or wealth, or civil alliances, it has elements of *power* about it which will ultimately subdue all other principles of government, and take their place. Its work was indeed to be a gradual work, and it is by no means accomplished, yet its effect has been mighty already on the principles that rule among the nations, and will still be more mighty until *the laws of the kingdom of the Messiah shall prevail in all the earth.* This seems to be the idea which it is designed to express by this prophetic image. If one were asked *in what respects* it is to be anticipated that these changes will be wrought, and *in what respects* we can discern the evidences of such changes already, we might say in such points as the following : (1.) In regard to the methods in which governments are founded. Governments were formerly mostly the result of civil or foreign wars. Nearly all the governments of antiquity were originally founded in the *power* of some military leader, and then held by power. Christianity originated new views about wars and conquests ; views that will ultimately prevail. In nothing are the opinions of mankind destined more entirely to be reversed than in regard to *war;* to its glory, its achievements, and the fame of those who have been most celebrated for bloody triumphs. (2.) In regard to the rights of the people. **A** mighty principle was originated by Christianity in respect to the *rights* of men ; the right of conscience ; the right to the avails of their own labour ; the right to life and liberty. (3.) In regard to oppression. The history of the world has been, to a great extent, a history of oppression. But all this is to be changed by the principles of the true religion ; and when the period shall arrive that there shall be no more occasion to use the word *oppression,* as descriptive of anything that shall have an actual existence on earth, this will be a different world. Then the time will have come, appropriately designated by the demolition of the colossal statue—symbolic of all governments of oppression, and the substitution in its place of that which was at first insignificant, but which had vital energy to supplant all that went before it.

IV. This kingdom will be perpetual. This is asserted in the unequivocal statements that it " shall never be destroyed," and that " it shall not be left to other people;" that is, shall never pass into other hands. There could not be a more positive declaration that the kingdom here referred to will continue through all coming time. Other kingdoms pass away, but this will not; and amidst all the revolutions of other empires this will remain. The lapse of eighteen hundred years since this kingdom was set up, has done not a little to confirm the truth of this prediction. Many other kingdoms during that time have disappeared from the earth, but this remains in its full vigour, and with extending power. It has, at this day, an extent of dominion which it never had before, and there are clearer indications that it will spread over all the earth than ever existed at any previous time. That this kingdom *will* be perpetual may be argued from the following considerations : (1.) From the promises of God. These are absolute; and they are attested by Him who has all power, and who can, with infinite ease, accomplish all that he has spoken. So in Dan. vii. 14, "His dominion is an everlasting dominion, which shall not pass away, and his kingdom that which shall not be destroyed." Luke i. 33, " and he'shall reign over the house of Jacob for ever : and of his kingdom there shall be no end." Psa. xlv. 6 (comp. Notes on Heb. i. 8), "Thy throne, O God, is for ever and ever." In Heb. i. 8, it is, "But unto the Son he saith, Thy throne, O God, is for ever and ever." Isa. ix. 7, " Of the increase of his government and peace there shall be no end, upon the throne of David, and upon his kingdom, to order it, and to establish it with judgment and with justice, from henceforth even for ever." (2.) It may be argued, from the fact that the efforts

which have been made to destroy it have shown that this cannot be done by any human power. Eighteen hundred years have now passed away—a period sufficiently long to test the question whether it can be destroyed by force and violence; by argument and ridicule. The experiment has been fairly made, and if it were possible that it should be destroyed by external force, it would have been done. It cannot be imagined that more favourable circumstances for such a purpose will ever occur. The church of Christ has met every form of opposition that we can conceive could be made against it, and has survived them all. Particularly it has survived the trial which has been made in the following respects :—(a) The Roman power, the whole might of the Roman arms, that had subdued and crushed the world, was brought to bear upon the kingdom of Christ to crush and destroy it, but wholly failed. It cannot be supposed that a new power will ever arise that will be more formidable to Christianity than the Roman was. (b) The power of persecution. That has been tried in every way, and has failed. The most ingenious forms of torture have been devised to extinguish this religion, and have all failed. It has always been found that persecution has only contributed ultimately to the triumph of the cause which it was hoped to crush. (c) The power of philosophy. The ancient philosophers opposed it, and attempted to destroy it by argument. This was early done by Celsus and Porphyry; but it soon became apparent that the ancient philosophy had nothing that could extinguish the rising religion, and not a few of the prominent philosophers themselves were converted, and became the advocates of the faith. (d) The power of science. Christianity had its origin in an age when science had made comparatively little progress, and in a country where it was almost unknown. The sciences since have made vast advances; and each one in its turn has been appealed to by the enemies of religion, to furnish an argument against Christianity. Astronomy, history, the discoveries in Egypt, the asserted antiquity of the Hindoos, and geology, have all been employed to overthrow the claims of the Christian religion, and have all been compelled to abandon the field. See this admirably demonstrated in Dr. Wiseman's *Lectures on the Connection between Science and Revealed Religion*. (*e*) The power of ridicule. At one time it was held that "ridicule is the test of truth," and this has been applied unsparingly to the Christian religion. But the religion still lives, and it cannot be supposed that there will be men endued with the power of sarcasm and wit superior to those who, with these weapons, have made war on Christianity, or that infidelity has any hope from that quarter. It may be inferred, therefore, that there is no *external* source of corruption and decay which will prevent its being perpetual. Other kingdoms usually have; and after a few centuries at most the internal corruption—the defect of the organization—developes itself, and the kingdom falls. But nothing of this kind occurs in the kingdom of Christ. It has lived now through eighteen hundred years, through periods of the world in which there have been constant changes in the arts, in the sciences, in manners, in philosophy, in forms of government. During that time many a system of philosophy has been superseded, and many a kingdom has fallen, but Christianity is as fresh and vigorous, as it meets each coming generation, as it ever was; and the past has demonstrated that the enemies of the gospel have no reason to hope that it will become weak by age, and will fall by its own decrepitude.

V. A fifth characteristic of this kingdom is, that it will universally prevail. This was symbolized by the stone that "became a great mountain, and that filled the whole earth," ver. 35. It is also implied, in the statement in ver. 44, that it "shall break in pieces, and consume all these kingdoms." They will cease, and this will occupy their places. The *principles* of the kingdom of the Messiah, whatever may be the external forms of government that shall exist on the earth, will everywhere prevail. That this will occur may be argued from the following considerations:—(1.) The promises recorded in the Bible. The passage before us is

one. Of the same nature are the following: Psa. ii. 8, "Ask of me, and I shall give thee the heathen for thine inheritance, and the uttermost parts of the earth for thy possession." Mal. i. 11, "For from the rising of the sun even unto the going down of the same, my name shall be great among the Gentiles; and in every place incense shall be offered to my name, and a pure offering." Isa. xi. 9, "The earth shall be full of the knowledge of the Lord, as the waters cover the sea." Comp. Hab. ii. 14; Isa. xlv. 22, and Isa. lx. (2.) The world in its progress *loses* nothing that is of value. Truth is eternal, and when once discovered, society will not let it go. It seizes upon great elements in human nature, and the world will not let it die. Thus it is with discoveries in science, inventions in the arts, and principles in morals. There is no evidence that anything that was known to the ancients which was of permanent value to mankind has been lost; and the few things that *were* lost have been succeeded by that which is better. All that was truly valuable in their science, their philosophy, their arts, their jurisprudence, their literature, we possess still, and the world will always retain it. And what can ever obliterate from the memory of man the printing-press, the steam-engine, the cotton-gin, the telescope, the blow-pipe, the magnetic telegraph! Society ACCUMULATES from age to age all that is truly valuable in inventions, morals, and the arts, and travels with them down to the period when the world shall have reached the highest point of perfectability. This remark is true also of Christianity—the kingdom of Christ. There are *principles* in regard to the happiness and rights of man in that system which cannot be *detached* from society, but which go into its permanent structure, and which "the world will not let die." (3.) Society is thus making constant *advances*. A position gained in human progress is never ultimately lost. "The principles thus accumulated and incorporated into society become permanent. Each age adds something in this respect to the treasures accumulated by all preceding ages, and each one is, in some respects,

46 ¶ Then the king Nebuchadnezzar fell upon his face, and worshipped Daniel, and commanded that they should offer an oblation and sweet odours unto him.

---

an advance on its predecessors, and makes the final triumph of the principles of truth, and liberty, and pure religion more sure." (4.) Christianity, or the kingdom of Christ, is *aggressive*. It makes a steady war on the evil customs, habits, and laws of the world. It is in accordance with its nature to diffuse itself. Nothing can prevent its propagation; and, according to the laws of society, nothing is so certain philosophically in regard to the future, as the final prevalence of the religion of the Redeemer. It may meet with temporary and formidable obstructions. It may be retarded, or extinguished, in certain places. But its general course is onward—like the current of the mighty river towards the ocean. The *only* thing certain in the future is, that the Christian religion will yet spread all over the world; and there is enough in this to gratify the highest wishes of philanthropy, and enough to stimulate to the highest effort to secure so desirable an end.

46. *Then the king Nebuchadnezzar fell upon his face*. This was the common method of signifying profound respect among the Orientals. Comp. Gen. xvii. 3; 1. 18; Lev. ix. 24; Numb. xiv. 5; Josh. v. 14; Judg. xiii. 20; Rev. xi. 16. ¶ *And worshipped Daniel*. The word rendered *worshipped* here (סְגִד), in the Chaldee portions of the Bible is uniformly rendered *worship*, Dan. ii. 26; iii. 5–7, 10–12, 14, 15, 18, 28. It occurs nowhere else, and in every instance, except in the one before us, is employed with reference to the homage paid to an idol, all the other cases occurring in the third chapter respecting the image that was set up by Nebuchadnezzar. The corresponding Hebrew word (סָגַד) occurs only in Isa. xliv. 15, 17, 19; xlvi. 6; and is, in every instance, rendered *fall down*, also with reference to idols. The proper idea, therefore, of the word here is, that the monarch meant to render *religious* homage to Daniel, or such adoration as was usually paid to idols. This is confirmed by what is immediately added, that he commanded that an oblation should be made to him. It is not, however, necessary to suppose that Daniel *received* or *approved* this religious homage of the king, or that he left the impression on his mind that he was *willing* to be honoured as a god. The prostration of the king before him, of course, he could not prevent. The views and feelings which the monarch had in doing it he could not prevent. The command to present an "oblation and sweet odours to him" he could not prevent. But it is not a fair inference that Daniel approved this, or that he did anything to countenance it, or even that he did not, in a proper manner, rebuke it: for (1) we are not to suppose that all that was said was recorded, and no one can prove that Daniel did not express his disapprobation of this religious honour shown to him. (2.) Daniel had in fact, expressed his views, in the clearest manner, on this very point before the monarch. He had, again and again, disclaimed all power to be able to reveal such secrets. He had directed his mind to the true God, as he who alone could disclose coming events, vers. 28, 30, 45. He had taken all possible precaution to prevent any such result, by declaring, in the most emphatic terms (ver. 30), that this secret was not revealed to him "on account of any wisdom which he had more than any living." If now, after all this precaution, and these disclaimers, the king should prostrate himself before him, and, for the moment, feel that he was in the presence of a God, Daniel was not responsible for it, and it should not be inferred that he encouraged or approved it. (3.) It would seem, from the narrative itself, more than probable that Daniel *did* refuse the homage, and direct the thoughts of the monarch to the true God. In the very next verse it is said, "The king *answered* unto Daniel, and said, Of a truth it is, that your God is a God of gods, and a Lord of kings, and a revealer of secrets." *Answered* what? Perhaps something that was said by Daniel. At all events,

47 The king answered unto
Daniel, and said, Of a truth *it is*,
that your God *is* a God of gods,

and a Lord of kings, and a revealer
of secrets, seeing thou couldest reveal this secret.

---

it is clear from this that whatever were
the momentary expressions of wonder,
gratitude, and adoration, on the part
of the king, his thoughts soon passed
to the proper object of worship—the
true God. *And commanded*, &c. The
fact that this was *commanded* does not
prove that it was *done*. The command
was probably given under the excitement of his admiration and wonder.
But it does not follow that Daniel received it, or that the command was not
recalled on reflection, or that the oblation and odours may not have been
presented to the true God. ¶ *That
they should offer an oblation*. That is,
his attendants, or perhaps the priests
to whom pertained the duty of making
offerings to the gods. The word rendered *oblation* (מִנְחָה) does not refer to
a *bloody* sacrifice, but means a gift or
present of any kind. It is applied in
the Scriptures to denote (1) *a gift*, or
present, Gen. xxxii. 13, 18, 20 (14, 19,
21); xliii. 11, 15, 25, 26 ; (2) *a tribute*,
such as was exacted from a subject
nation, under the notion of a present,
2 Sam. viii. 2, 6 ; 1 Kings iv. 21 (v. 1),
(3) *an offering* or sacrifice to God,
especially a bloodless offering, in opposition to (זֶבַח)—a bloody sacrifice, Lev.
ii. 1, 4–6 ; vi. 14 (7); vii. 9 ; Psa. xl.
6 (7) ; Jer. xvii. 26. See the word fully
explained in the Notes on Isa. i. 13.
There can be no doubt that Nebuchadnezzar *meant* · that such an offering
should be presented as was usually
made in idol worship. ¶ *And sweet
odours*. Incense was commonly used
in worship (see Notes on Isa. i. 13), and
it is not improbable that in the worship
of the gods it was accompanied with
other fragrant odours. Sweet odours,
or "savours," expressed by the same
word which is used here, were a part
of the prescribed worship in the Hebrew
ritual, Lev. i. 9, 13, 17 ; ii. 2, 9 ; iii.
5 ; vi. 21 (14); Numb. xv. 7.

47. *The king answered unto Daniel*.
Answered either what he had said in
the interpretation of the dream, or *possibly* something that he had said in

regard to the impropriety of offering
this homage to him. Comp. Notes on
ver. 46. It is certain that, for some
cause, whatever might have been the
homage which he was disposed to render to Daniel, his thoughts were soon
turned from him to the true God, and
to an acknowledgment of him as superior to all other beings. He seems, at
least, instantly to have reflected on
what Daniel had himself said (ver. 30),
and to have remembered that religious
homage was due, not to Daniel, but to
the God who had communicated the
secret to him. ¶ *Of a truth* it is. It
is truly so. This had been shown by
the manner in which this secret was
disclosed. ¶ *That your God* is *a God
of gods*. Is superior to all other gods;
is supreme over all. Comp. Rev. xvii.
14 ; 1 Tim. vi. 15. The idea is, that
whatever subordinate beings there may
be, *he* is supreme. ¶ *And a Lord of
kings*. Supreme over kings. They are
all inferior to him, and subject to his
control. ¶ *And a revealer of secrets*.
One of the attributes of divinity. See
Notes on ver. 28. ¶ *Seeing thou couldest reveal this secret*. A secret which
the wisest men of the realm had sought
in vain to disclose. The fact that a
professed servant of God had been able
to do this showed that God was himself
supreme, and worthy of adoration. We
have here, then, an instance in which
a proud and haughty heathen monarch
was brought to an acknowledgment of
the true God, and was constrained to
render him homage. This was a result
which it was evidently intended to reach
in the whole transaction ; in the dream
itself ; in the fact that the wise men of
Babylon could not interpret it ; and in
the fact that an acknowledged servant
of the Most High had been enabled to
make the disclosure. The instance is
instructive, as showing to what extent
a mind clearly not under the influence
of any genuine piety—for subsequent
events showed that no *permanent* effects
were produced on him, and that he was
still an idolater (ch. iii.), and a most
proud and haughty man (ch. iv.)—may

48 Then the king made Daniel a great man, and gave him many great gifts,*a* and made him ruler over the whole province of Babylon, and

a ver. 6.

chief of the *b* governors over all the wise *men* of Babylon.

49 Then Daniel requested of the king, and *c* he set Shadrach, Me-

b ch. 4. 9; 5. 11.   *c* ch. 3. 12.

---

be brought to acknowledge God. See the remarks at the end of the chapter (7).

48. *Then the king made Daniel a great man.* That is, he gave him an honourable appointment ; he so honoured him that he was regarded as a great man. He was really made great by the grace of God, and the extraordinary favour which God had bestowed upon him, but the estimate which the king had of his greatness was shown by the tokens of the royal favour. ¶ *And gave him many great gifts.* This is a common way of showing esteem in the East. The estimate in which one holds another is evinced by the variety and richness of the presents conferred on him. Hence all persons of distinction expect gifts of those who approach them as expressive of their regard for them, and of the esteem in which they are held. Comp. ver. 6 of this chapter. ¶ *And made him ruler over the whole province of Babylon.* Chald., הַשְׁלֵט—caused him to preside over, or to rule over, from the verb שְׁלֵט *shelat, to rule,* and commonly applied to one who rules as a prince, or in an elevated office. From this word the terms *sultan* and *sultana* are derived. ¶ *And chief of the governors over all the wise men of Babylon.* This would seem to be an appointment which did not pertain to him as governor of the province of Babylon, or as presiding in the capital, but was a separate appointment, and, therefore, an additional mark of favour. The phrase " chief of the governors " would seem to imply that the magi of Babylon were disposed in certain orders or classes, each of which had its appropriate head, like the head of a college or university. Daniel was placed over the whole as the president, principal, or chancellor. It had been the policy of Nebuchadnezzar to assemble at the capital the principal talent and learning of the realm. Compare Notes, ch. i. 18–20 ; ii. 2. Daniel thus, in both these sta-

tions of honour at an early period of life, though recently an unknown stranger, and a captive, was exalted to the highest honours which could be conferred on a subject, and raised to posts of distinction which would usually be regarded as the highest rewards which could be obtained by a long life of devotedness to the welfare of the country.

49. *Then Daniel requested of the king,* &c. In his own remarkable prosperity, and in the extraordinary honours conferred on him, he did not forget the companions of his humbler days. They were his countrymen ; they had been captives with him ; they had been selected with a view to stand with him before the king (ch. i. 3, 4); they had shared with him in his rules of abstinence (ch. i. 11–17); they had all passed an honourable examination before the king (ch. i. 18, 19) ; they had united with him in supplication to God that he would disclose the meaning of the vision (ch. ii. 17, 18) ; and now it was proper that they should be remembered by him who had been so signally honoured. ¶ *Over the affairs of the province of Babylon.* In what particular departments of business they were employed is not mentioned ; but it would seem that all that specially pertained to this province was intrusted to them. Daniel had the general superintendence, but the subordinate duties growing out of the office were intrusted to them. The fact that the king granted the request shows the influence that Daniel had at the court. The reasons which influenced the king in granting the request may have been, not only the favour with which he regarded Daniel, but the fact that the duties of the office conferred on him now were such as to require assistance, and the remembrance of the virtues of these youths when they stood before him. ¶ *But Daniel sat in the gate of the king.* The post of chief honour and dignity as a counsellor of the king. The *gate* of a city in the East, being a

shach, and Abed-nego, over the affairs of the province of Babylon:

but Daniel *sat* *d* in the gate of the king.

a Es. 2. 19; 3. 2.

chief place of concourse, was the place where courts were held, and public business was usually transacted. See Notes on Job xxix. 7. To say, therefore, that he "sat in the gate of the king," is merely to say that he occupied a place with the chief counsellors and dignitaries of the realm. The phrase "Sublime *Porte*," that is, "the Sublime *Gate*," is still employed at Constantinople to denote the government of the sultan; for, in the earlier days of Ottoman rule, the reigning sovereign, as is still the case in some parts of the East, held courts of justice and levees at the entrance of his residence. See Harper's *Magazine*, vol. iv. p. 333. The office of Daniel was, perhaps, not far different from that of the grand vizier of the Turkish government. See Murray's *Ency. Geog.* vol. ii. p. 202.

REMARKS.

Among the lessons of practical value suggested by this chapter, we may notice the following :—

(1.) We have an instance (ver. 1–3) of the methods which were resorted to in early periods of the world to ascertain what the future would be. This great monarch relied on a dream which greatly disturbed him, and on the power which he supposed was intrusted to men to interpret dreams. In common with the prevailing spirit of his times, and of all ancient times (Notes, ver. 1), he believed that dreams might be regarded as prognostics of future events; that they were under Divine direction; and that all that was necessary to make them safe guides in reference to what is to occur, was that they should be properly interpreted. In common, too, with all the people of ancient times, and with most of modern times, the king here referred to had an earnest desire to look into the future. There has been no desire in the human

bosom stronger than this. We are so made that we wish to lift the mysterious veil which shrouds the future; to penetrate the deep darkness which rests on the unseen world. Our great interests are there. The past is fixed, and cannot now affect us, except by the consequences of what we have done, and by teaching us lessons of value derived from our own observation, and that of others. But the future is not yet fixed. Man, so anxious to know what this is to be, finds himself in respect to it peculiarly unendowed. In relation to the past, he is endowed with the faculty of *memory*, but with nothing corresponding to this pertaining to *the future*. He can treasure up what *has* occurred, but he cannot in like manner make the future pass before his mind, that he may become wise by knowing what will take place in far distant times. There can be no doubt that God *could* have endowed the mind with one faculty as well as the other— for he has it himself—but there were obvious reasons why it should not be done. Destitute, then, as man was of this power, one great object of human inquiry has been to see whether the deficiency could be supplied, and whether something might not be found which would be to the future substantially what the memory is to the past. The efforts and results on this subject—one of which we have in the chapter before us—constitute one of the most instructive chapters of the history of our race, and show how effectually God has bounded the limits of human investigation in this respect. Among those methods of attempting to penetrate the future, and of laying open its deep mysteries, may be noticed the following :—

(*a*) Astrology. It was supposed that

the stars might exert an influence over the fates of men, and that by observing their positions, conjunctions, and oppositions, it might be ascertained what would be the destiny of individuals and nations. The belief of this has manifested itself more or less in every age; and in such instances as in the word *lunacy*, and in the common apprehensions about the influence of the moon on health and on vegetation, may be still seen traces of that belief. Even Lord Bacon held that "astrology was a science not to be *rejected*, but reformed;" and in the early periods of the world it was a *fair* subject of investigation whether the heavenly bodies actually exerted such an influence, and whether, if it were so, it was possible to ascertain the laws by which this was done. This was the so-called science of astrology.

(*b*) Necromancy. The belief of this also prevailed in nearly all ancient nations, and we find frequent reference to it in the Scriptures. This consisted in the belief that the dead must be acquainted with the world where they now dwell, so dark to the living, and that it might be possible to make a covenant or compact with them, by which they would be induced to disclose what they knew. It was extensively, if not universally, believed that they re-appeared to men, and that it was not an uncommon occurrence for them to leave their abodes, and to visit the earth again. It was, therefore, not an unnatural and not an unfair subject of inquiry, whether they would not disclose to the more favoured among mortals what they knew of the secrets of the invisible world, and what they knew of events which were to come. Comp. Notes on Isa. viii. 19.

(*c*) The arts of divination. These were founded mainly on the investigations of science. It was at first a fair question whether, amidst the wonders which science was unfolding to the view, it might not contribute to lift the veil from the future, and reveal what was yet to come. It took long to ascertain what *were* the legitimate aims of science, and what might be hoped for from it. Hence it was directed to the inquiry whether some substance might not be found which would transmute all things to gold; whether some elixir might not be discovered which would arrest all disease, and give immortality to man; and whether science would not disclose some means by which the future could be penetrated, and the mysteries of the invisible world be laid open to the view. It required centuries of investigation, a thousand failures, and the results of long and patient thought, to ascertain what *were* the true objects of science, and to convince the world that it was *not* its legitimate purpose to reveal the future to man.

(*d*) Heathen oracles. It was an early inquiry whether God would not, in some way, lift the veil from the future and disclose its secrets to man. The belief that this would be done seems to be natural to the mind of man; and in all ages, and in all countries, he has supposed that the future would be thus disclosed. Hence, among the heathen, certain persons claimed to be divinely inspired; hence such shrines as that at Delphi became celebrated; hence ambiguous responses were uttered, so expressed as to support the credit of the oracle, whatever might be the result; hence men were appointed to observe the flights of birds, to inspect the entrails of animals offered in sacrifice, to interpret any unusual phenomena in the clouds, to mark the direction of meteors, and, in general, to examine any unusual appearances in the heavens or the earth, which would seem to furnish any clew by which the future might be known. Much of all this undoubtedly became mere imposture, and justified the remark of Cicero, that he wondered that one augur could meet another without laughing; but there can be no doubt that by many these inquiries were honestly pursued, and that at first all this seemed to be a legitimate subject of inquiry. What forbade man to pursue it? And who could tell but that in some such ways the secrets of the mysterious future could be found out? It demanded long and patient inquiry and observation to show that this could *not* be so, and that whatever *might* be indicated by any of these things, it was never designed that they should be the means by which man could be made acquainted with the mysteries of the invisible world.

(*e*) Dreams. We have seen (Notes, ver. 1) that it was an early article of belief that through the medium of dreams the Divine will might be made known, and the secrets of the future disclosed. The *theory* on this subject seems to have been, that during sleep the ordinary laws of the mind are suspended; that the soul is abstracted from the visible world; that the thoughts which it has then must be originated by higher beings ; and that in this state it has converse with an invisible world, and may be permitted to see much of what is yet to occur. Comp. Intro. to Isaiah, § VII. (2).

(*f*) Visions. Men supposed that there might be representations made to certain favoured persons respecting the future, their senses being closed to surrounding objects,· and that while in an ecstasy, or trance, the mind might have a view of future events. Such were the visions of Balaam; such, in a remarkable manner, were the visions of the true prophets; and so deeply was

the conviction that this *might* occur engrafted in the human mind, that the belief of it seems to have had a place among the heathen nations. Comp. Intro. to Isaiah, § VII. (4).

Such were some of the ways by which it was supposed that the future might be penetrated by man, and its secrets disclosed. By allowing man to make trial of these methods, and to pursue them through a period of several thousand years, until he himself saw that they were fruitless, God was preparing the race to feel the necessity of direct communications from himself, and to welcome the true revelations which he would make respecting things to come.

(2.) We have in the chapter before us (vers. 4–11) an instance of *the acknowledged failure* of a class of the wisest of men, whose lives were devoted to this employment, in their attempts to disclose the future. This is a fair illustration of all the attempts of the heathen, and it was doubtless permitted in order that it might be seen that all such attempts *must* fail. The magicians, astrologers, and Chaldeans were foiled in a case which fairly came within the province of their art, and when pretenders to this kind of knowledge *ought* to have been able to solve the difficulties of the monarch. Regarding this as a fair illustration of all the attempts of the heathen to penetrate the future, and to discover the great truths which it is desirable for man to know, there are three observations which may be made in regard to it:—I. The trial has been a fair one. (*a*) There was *time* enough allowed for it. It was about four thousand years from the creation of man to the time when the canon of Scripture was completed, and promulgated to the whole world, and it could not be said that man required a longer time to test the question whether he needed a revelation. (b) The trial was a fair one, because it was one which men were at liberty to pursue to any extent, and which was conducted under the best advantages. It was confined to no country or favoured class of men. In all lands, and with every advantage of climate, government, and laws, man has been engaged in the great inquiry; and if it be remembered what immense *numbers* of minds have been employed in these investigations, it cannot be pretended that the utmost desirable freedom has not been allowed to man to test the question whether "by searching he can find out God," and disclose the future. (c) The same thing is true in respect to the *talent* which has been employed in this investigation. It is not too much to say, that the *highest* talent that the world has produced has been engaged in these inquiries, and that the rejecters of revelation cannot hope that higher powers can be brought to bear on it, or that the unaided human intellect can hope to accomplish more in this respect than has been done. The profoundest minds in Egypt and Chaldea were engaged in inquiries of this sort. The very highest talent which Greece produced in its best days was employed on questions of religion; in attempts to find out God, to ascertain the relations of man to him, and to determine what man was to be hereafter. What was true, also, of the ancient heathen, and of the modern heathen, that the best talent has been employed on these questions, is true also of the rejecters of revelation in Christian lands. Men of high powers of intellect have refused to acknowledge the Bible as a revelation, and have chosen to fall back on the unaided resources of their own minds. Aided with all that science and learning can do, they have inquired after a

system of religion that would commend itself to man as true, and as adapted to his wants; and it cannot be pretended that man in *this* respect has not had a fair opportunity to show what the human powers can do. (d) The trial has been a fair one in regard to the field of investigation. Astrology, necromancy, abstruse natural science, oracles, dreams, visions, the observation of the course of events—all these have been open before man, and in one and all of them he has been allowed to pursue his investigations at pleasure. II. There has been an entire *failure* in the attempt. The Chaldeans failed in Babylon, as the magicians had done in Egypt, to explain what was regarded as a prognostic of the future, and in both cases it was necessary to call in the aid of one who had a direct communication from heaven. The same has been the case in *all* attempts to explain the future, and to disclose what man was so desirous of knowing about the invisible world. (a) All reliance on astrology, necromancy, oracles, dreams, and the revelations of the abstruser sciences, has failed. Astrology has ceased to be a science, and the stars are studied for other purposes than to disclose future events; necromancy has ceased to be a science—for no one now hopes to be able to make a compact with the dead, in virtue of which they will disclose the secrets of the invisible world; no one now would consult a heathen oracle with the hope of receiving a response to his inquiries that might be relied on: the abstruser sciences are pursued for other purposes; and no one would repose on dreams to furnish a system of truth which would meet the wants of man. (b) The same thing has been true in regard to the various *systems of religion* on which men have relied. *It is true of the systems of the heathen.* They have been tried in the most ample manner, and have shown that they do not meet the wants of man. The experiment has been fairly made, and the system is becoming worse and worse. It is not adapted to elevate man in the scale of being in regard to the present life; it does not remove the evils which press now upon the race; it does not disclose a certain way by which a sinner may be prepared for the life to come. *It is true in regard to an atonement for sin.* The attempt has been made now for nearly six thousand years, to find some way in which an efficacious sacrifice may be made for sin. Blood has been poured on thousands of altars; animals have been offered, and thousands of human beings have been devoted to the gods, but still there has been no evidence that these bloody offerings have been accepted, or that they have availed to expiate transgression. The experiment has failed. There is no new sacrifice that can be offered now, and it is hopeless for man to attempt to make expiation for his own sins. *The same thing is true of the systems of religion proposed by infidelity.* They are all failures. One system after another is abandoned, and no one is such as the race needs. The best talent that infidelity can hope to produce has been exhausted in this undertaking; for how can it hope to produce men better fitted to propose a system of religion to mankind than Shaftesbury, or Hobbes, or Tindal, or Herbert, or Voltaire, or Hume? Yet, after all that has been done by infidelity in modern times, an intelligent man would prefer trusting his eternal interests to such a system as Socrates would propose, to one proposed by Hume; he would feel safer under the guidance of Cicero or Seneca than under the direction of Voltaire or Gibbon. III. The *reasons* why God has

permitted this trial to be made, in such a manner, and with such results, are obvious. In the cases which occurred in the time of Pharaoh in Egypt, and of Nebuchadnezzar in Babylon, the reason evidently was, that when there was an acknowledged failure of the power of the magicians, God might himself, through Joseph and Daniel, get honour to his own name. So the reasons why he has permitted this trial to be made on a large scale, and has suffered it everywhere to fail, are probably these two: (1) to show to man, in such a way as to admit of no doubt, his need of revelation; and (2) to induce him to prize the volume of revealed truth. We should value it the more, and adhere to it the more firmly, in view of the experiment which has been made in all lands. If *that* revelation be rejected, man has *no* resource; he is wholly unable to penetrate the future; he can devise no way of making atonement for sin; he can originate no system that shall alleviate the sorrows under which we groan, or disclose the prospect of happiness beyond the tomb. For if the Bible is taken away, on what shall we fall back to guide us? —on astrology; on necromancy; on heathen oracles and sacrifices; on dreams; on the ravings of priestesses at heathen shrines, or the speculations of infidelity in Christian lands? All these have been tried in vain. The Bible is the only guide on which man can rely to conduct him to heaven: if that fails, all fails, and man is in the midst of impenetrable night.

(3.) We may learn from this chapter (vers. 12–19), that in the perplexities and trials which arise in life, a good man may appeal to God for guidance and help. So Daniel felt, when all human power had failed in complying with the demands of a stern and arbitrary monarch, and when he and his friends, though innocent, were about to be involved in the sweeping sentence which had been issued against the wise men of Babylon. Then it was clear that nothing could save them but Divine interposition; nothing could avert the stroke but such a heavenly influence as would disclose the secret, and thus avert the wrath of the king. In this emergency Daniel felt that he *might* call upon God, and to this service he summoned also his three friends, who were equally interested with him in the issue. In view of this we may observe: I. That *all* good men are liable to meet with similar perplexities and embarrassments; to be placed in circumstances where nothing but the interposition of God can help them. This is true in such respects as the following: (*a*) In reference to the knowledge of the truth. The mind is often perplexed on the subject of religion: reason fails to disclose those truths which it is desirable to know; darkness and obscurity seem to envelope the whole subject; the soul, oppressed with a sense of conscious guilt, seeks to find some way of peace; the heart, entangled in the meshes of unbelief, struggles and pants to be free, and there is no human help—nothing this side the eternal throne on which reliance can be placed to impart the light which is needed. (*b*) In reference to duty. The mind is often perplexed to know what should be done. Though desirous of doing what is right, yet there may be so many conflicting views; there may be such doubt as to what is best and right, that none but God can direct in such an emergency. (*c*) In cases of peril. Daniel and his friends were in danger; and men are often now in such danger that they feel that none but God can save them. On a bed of pain, in a stranded vessel, in a burning house, men often feel that human help is powerless, and that aid can be found

in none but God. Thus the church, in the dark days of persecution, has often been so encompassed with dangers, that it could not but feel that none but God could avert the impending destruction. (*d*) In times when religion declines, and when iniquity abounds. Then the church often is led to feel that there is need of the aid of God, and that none but he can rouse it from its deathlike slumbers, and put back the swelling waves of iniquity. II. In such circumstances it is the privilege of a good man to appeal to God, with the hope that he will interpose. (1.) This was felt by Daniel, and it is an undoubted truth, as revealed in the Bible, that in such circumstances, if we will look to God, we may hope for his guidance and help. Comp. 2 Kings xix. 14, 15; Job xvi. 19–21; Psalm xxv. 9; xlvi. 1, *seq.*; lv. 22; James i. 5, 6. But (2) what kind of interposition and direction may *we* hope for in such perplexities? I answer: (*a*) We may expect the Divine direction by a careful study of the *principles* laid down in the Scriptures. The Bible indeed does not, for it could not, mention the names of individuals, or specify every case which would occur in which Divine direction would be needed, but it lays down great *principles* of truth, applicable to all the circumstances which will ever arise. In this respect there is a wonderful richness and fulness in the Word of God. There is many a rich vein of truth which seems never to have been worked until we are placed in some new and untried situation. When one is thrown into perplexing circumstances; when he is called to pass through trials; when he meets some powerful form of temptation, he is surprised to find how much there is in the Bible adapted to such circumstances that he never saw there before. It seems to be a new book, written to meet just such cases; nor in such circumstances does he ever consult its pages in vain. (b) We may expect direction by his providence. The sparrow falls not to the ground without his direction, and all events are under his control, and as these events occur they may be regarded as so many indications of his will. One of the most interesting and profitable employments in a man's life is to study the indications of Providence in regard to himself, and to endeavour to learn, from what is daily occurring to him, what is the will of God in regard to him. A careful and prayerful observer of the intimations of the Divine will is not in serious danger of error. (c) God guides those who are in perplexity by his Spirit. There is a secret and silent influence on the mind of him who is desirous of being led in the way of duty, suggesting what is true, delivering the mind from prejudice, overcoming opposition to the truth, disposing the heart to charity, peace, and love, prompting to the performance of duty, and gradually elevating the soul to God. If a man would pray when he feels an inward prompting to pray; would read the Bible when some inward voice seems to call him to do it; would do good when the inward monitor urges him to do it; would fix the eye and the heart on heaven when something within seems to lead him toward the skies, he would not be in much danger of error. Such are "spring-times of piety in the soul" —times when the soul may make rapid progress in the knowledge of the truth, and it is not enthusiasm to say that such states of mind are produced by an influence from above.

(4.) In view of this chapter (verses 17, 18), we may observe that it is a privilege to have praying friends— friends on whom we can call to unite with us in prayer in the time of trouble. So Daniel found it when *he* called on his friends to pray; so Esther found it when her whole people were in danger, and when all depended on her successful application to the sovereign (Esther iv. 16), and so the friends of God have found it in all ages. If prayer is heard at all, there are special reasons why it should prevail when many are united in the request. Comp. Matt. xviii. 19. Hence the propriety of worship in the family; hence the fitness of prayer-meetings; and hence the appropriateness of prayer offered in the great congregation.

(5.) God should be praised and acknowledged as having supremacy over all things, verses 20–23. Particularly he should be acknowledged (a) in the changes that occur on earth; in the changes from childhood to youth, and from youth to manhood, and to old age; in the beautiful changes of the seasons, and in all the variety which the seasons bring with them; in the changes from sickness to health, from poverty to affluence, from oppression and slavery to freedom, from an humble to an exalted condition; in all the revolutions of empire, and the changes of dynasties. (b) He should be acknowledged in his supremacy over the kings and rulers of the earth. Every monarch reigns by his permission, and every one is designed to accomplish some great purpose in the development of his plans. If a full and correct history of the world could be written, it would be found that God had *some* object to accomplish by the instrumentality of every one whom he has called to a throne, and that as we can now see a distinct design to be accomplished by the reign of Pharaoh, Sennacherib, Cyrus, and Augustus, so we could find some distinct design in reference to every one who has ever reigned. (c) He should be recognized as the source of all knowledge. Particularly (1) he originally endowed every mind, and gave it the capacity which it has for acquiring knowledge ; (2) he preserves the faculties of the mind, and gives them their just balance ; (3) he makes the intellect clear and bright, and when it applies itself to the investigation of truth he only can preserve it unclouded ; (4) he makes, under the operation of the regular laws of intellect, important *suggestions* to the mind—those pregnant HINTS containing so much "the seeds of things" on which all true progress in knowledge depends — those bright thoughts, those happy conceptions, which come into the soul, and which result in such happy inventions, and such advances in science, art, literature, and law ; and (5) he should be regarded as the original source of those *inventions* which contribute so much to the progress of the race. At the proper time, and the best time, when some new and wonderful discovery is to burst upon the world, he raises up the individual who is to make it, and the discovery takes its place as one of the fixed points of progress, and society, with that as a treasure never to be lost, moves forward on a higher elevation, with greatly accelerated progress. So it was with the invention of alphabetical writing ; the art of printing ; the application of steam to purposes of manufacture and navigation ; the telescope, and the telegraph ; and, in general, in respect to all those great inventions which have contributed to the progress of society. If the whole truth were known, it would be seen that the hand of God was in these things as really as in the "revelation of the deep and secret things to Daniel."

(6.) We may learn from this chapter, as was remarked in the Notes on ver. 30, that for all our attainments in knowledge and wisdom we should ascribe the praise to God alone. In illustration of this we may remark : I. That there is a strong native tendency in man to ascribe the honour of such attainments to himself. It is one of the most difficult of all things to induce man to attribute the praise of whatever excellence he may have, or whatever attainments he may make, to his Creator. This exists universally in regard to talent, rank, and scientific attainments ; and it is even hard for a heart that is endowed with true religion to free itself altogether from self-glorying, as if it were all to be traced to ourselves. II. Yet in our case, as in the case of Daniel, all the honour should be ascribed to God. For (1) it is to him we owe all our original endowments of mind and of body, whatever they may be. In this respect we are as he chose to make us. We have no natural endowment— whether of beauty, strength, genius, aptness for learning, or advantages for distinction in science which he did not confer on us, and which he could not as easily have withheld from us as he did from those less favoured. And why should we be proud of these things ? Shall the oak of Bashan be proud of its far-spreading arms, or its strength ? Shall the cedar of Lebanon be proud of its height, and its vastness, and its beauty ? Shall the rose be proud of its beauty or its sweetness, or shall the magnolia boast of its fragrance ? (2.) God has conferred on us all the means of education which we have enjoyed, and all to which the development of our natural powers can be traced. He has preserved our reason ; he has furnished us instructors ; he has provided the books which we have read ; he has continued to us the possession of the health which we have enjoyed. At any moment he could have driven reason from the throne ; he could have deprived us of health ; he could have summoned us away. (3.) It is equally owing to him that we have been favoured with any success in the prosecution of our calling in life. Let the merchant who has accumulated great property, apparently by his own industry, suppose that all Divine agency and influence in his case had been withheld, and whatever labour he may have expended, or with whatever skill he may be endowed, he could have met with no such success. Let him reflect how much he owes to favouring gales on the ocean ; to the seasons producing abundant harvests, and to what seems almost to be *chance* or *fortune*, and he will see at once that whatever success he may have been favoured with is to be traced, in an eminent sense, to God. The same thing is true of all the other successful departments of human effort. (4.) This is equally true of all the knowledge which we have of the way of salvation, and all our hopes of eternal life. It is a great principle of religion that we have nothing which we have not received, and that if we have received it, we should not glory as if we had not received it, for it is God who makes us to differ (see 1 Cor. iv. 7). It is God who originally gave us the volume of revealed truth—making us differ from the whole pagan world. It is God who awakened us to see our guilt and danger, making us to differ from the gay and careless world around us. It is God alone who has pardoned our sins, making us to differ from the multitude who are unpardoned in the world. It is God who has given us every hope that we cherish that is well-founded, and all the peace and joy which we have had in communion with himself. For these things, therefore, we should give all the praise to God ; and in our case, as in that of Daniel, it is one of the evidences of our piety when we are disposed to do so.

(7.) We have in this chapter (vers. 46, 47) an instructive instance of the extent to which an irreligious man may go in showing respect for God. It cannot be supposed that Nebuchadnezzar was a truly pious man. His characteristics and actions, both before and after this, were those of a heathen, and there is no evidence that he was truly converted to God. Yet he evinced the highest respect for one who was a servant and prophet of the Most High (ver. 46), and even for God himself (ver. 47). This was evinced in a still more remarkable manner at a subsequent period (ch. iv.) In this he showed how far it is possible for one to go who has no real piety, and as such cases are not uncommon, it may not be improper to consider them for a moment. I. This respect for God extends to the following things : (1.) An admiration of him, as great, and wise, and powerful. The evidences of his power and wisdom are traced in his works. The mind may be impressed with that which is wise, or overpowered with that which is vast, without there being any real religion, and all this admiration may terminate on God, and be expressed in language of respect for him, or for his ministers. (2.) This admiration of God may be extended to whatever is *beautiful* in religion. The beauty of the works of nature, of the sky, of a landscape, of the ocean, of the setting sun, of the changing clouds, of the flowers of the field, may lead the thoughts up to God, and produce a certain admiration of a Being who has clothed the world with so much loveliness. There is a religion of sentiment as well as of principle ; a religion that terminates on the *beautiful* as well as a religion that terminates on the *holy*. The Greeks, natural admirers of beauty, carried this kind of religion to the highest possible degree ; for their religion was, in all its forms, characterized by the love of the beautiful. So also there is much that is beautiful in

Christianity, as well as in the works of God, and it is possible to be charmed with that without ever having felt any compunction for sin. or any love for pure religion itself. It is possible for one who has a natural admiration for that which is lovely in character, to see a high degree of moral beauty in the character of the Redeemer; for one whose heart is easily moved by sympathy to be affected in view of the sufferings of the injured Saviour. The same eyes that would weep over a well-told tale, or over a tragic representation on the stage, or over a scene of real distress, might weep over the wrongs and woes of Him who was crucified, and yet there might be nothing more than the religion of sentiment—the religion springing from mere natural feeling. (3.) There is much *poetic* religion in the world. It is possible for the imagination to form such a view of the Divine character that it shall *seem* to be lovely, while perhaps there may be scarcely a feature of that character that shall be correct. Not a little of the religion of the world is of this description—where such a God is conceived of as the mind chooses, and the affections are fixed on that imaginary being, while there is not a particle of love to the true God in the soul. So there is a poetic view of man, of his character, of his destiny, while the *real* character of the heart has never been seen. So there is a poetic view of heaven—strongly resembling the views which the ancients had of the Elysian fields. But heaven as a place of holiness has never been thought of, and would not be loved. Men look forward to a place where the refined and the intelligent; the amiable and the lovely; the accomplished and the upright; where poets, orators, warriors, and philosophers will be assembled together. This is the kind of religion which is often manifested in

eulogies, and epitaphs, and in conversation, where those who never had any better religion, and never pretended to any serious piety, are represented as having gone to heaven when they die. There are few who, under the influence of such a religion, are not looking forward to some kind of a heaven; and few persons die, whatever may be their character, unless they are openly and grossly abandoned, for whom the hope is not expressed that they have gone safe to a better world. If we may credit epitaphs, and obituary notices, and funeral eulogiums, and biographies, there are few poets, warriors, statesmen, or philosophers, about whose happiness in the future world we should have any apprehension. II. But in all this there may be no real religion. There is no evidence that there was any in the case of Nebuchadnezzar, and as little is there in the instances now referred to. Such persons may have a kind of reverence for God as great, and powerful, and wise; they may have even a kind of pleasure in looking on the evidence of his existence and perfections in his works; they may have a glow of pleasurable emotion in the mere *poetry* of religion; they may be restrained from doing many things by their consciences; they may erect temples, and build altars, and contribute to the support of religion, and even be zealous for religion, as they understand it, and still have no just views of God, and no true piety whatever. (1.) The mind that is truly religious is not insensible to all this, and may have as exalted notions of God as a great and glorious being, and be as much impressed with the beauty evinced in his works as in the cases supposed. True religion does not destroy the sense of the sublime and beautiful, but rather cultivates this in a higher degree. But (2) there is much besides this that enters into true religion, and without which all these things are vain. (*a*) True religion always arises from just views of God as he is; not from him as an imaginary being. (*b*) True religion must regard God as having *moral* attributes; as benevolent, and just, and true, and holy, and not merely as powerful and great. (*c*) In all these things referred to, there is not necessarily any moral excellence on the part of those who thus admire God and his works. The mere admiration of power implies in us no moral excellence. The admiration of the wisdom which made the worlds and keeps them in their place; of the beauties of poetry, or of a flower, or landscape, though made by God, implies no moral excellence in us, and, therefore, no true religion. There is no more religion in admiring *God* as an architect or painter, than there is in admiring Sir Christopher Wren, or Michael Angelo; and the mere admiration of the works of God as such, implies no more moral excellence in us than it does to admire St. Paul's or St. Peter's. In religion, the heart does not merely admire the beautiful and the grand; it loves that which is pure, and just, and good, and holy. It delights in God as a holy being rather than as a powerful being; it finds pleasure in his moral character, and not merely in his greatness.

(8.) We may learn from this chapter (ver. 49), that when we are favoured with prosperity and honour we should not neglect, or be ashamed of, the companions of our earlier days, and the partakers of our fortune when we were poor and unknown. Joseph, when exalted to the premiership of Egypt, was not ashamed of his aged father, but, though he had been an humble shepherd, presented him, with the deepest feelings of respect towards an aged parent, to Pharaoh; nor was he ashamed of his brethren, though they had done him so much wrong. Daniel, when in a similar manner advanced to the most honourable post which one could reach, in the most magnificent monarchy of the world, was not ashamed of the youthful friends with whom he had shared the humble and severe lot of bondage. So we, if we are made rich; if we are raised to honour; if we become distinguished for learning or talent; if our names are known abroad, or we are intrusted with a high and honourable office, should not forget the friends and companions of our earlier years.

CHAPTER III.

§ I.—AUTHENTICITY OF THE CHAPTER.

The objections which have been urged against the authenticity of this chapter are much more numerous than those which have been alleged against the two previous chapters.

I. The first which deserves to be noticed is stated by De Wette (p. 383, under the general head of *improbabilities* in the chapter), and Bleek, p. 268, as quoted by Hengstenberg, *die Authentie des Daniel*, p. 83. The objection is, substantially, that if the account in this chapter is true, it would prove that the Chaldeans were inclined to persecution on account of religious opinions, which, it is said, is contrary to their whole character as elsewhere shown. So far as we have any information in regard to them, it is alleged, they were far from having this character, and it is not probable, therefore, that Nebuchadnezzar would make a law which would compel the worship of an idol under severe pains and penalties.

To this objection the following reply may be made:—

(1.) Little is known, on any supposition, of the Chaldeans in general, and little of the character of Nebuchadnezzar in particular, beyond what we find in the book of Daniel. So far, however, as we have any knowledge of either from any source, there is no inconsistency between that and what is said in this chapter to have occurred. It is probable that no one ever perceived any incongruity of this kind in the book itself, nor, if this were all, should we suppose that there was any improbability in the account in this chapter.

(2.) There is properly no account of *persecution* in this narrative, nor any reason to suppose that Nebuchadnezzar designed any such thing. This is admitted by Bertholdt himself (p. 261), and is manifest on the face of the whole narrative. It is indeed stated that Nebuchadnezzar demanded, on severe penalties, a recognition of the god that he worshipped, and required that the reverence should be shown to that god which he thought to be his due. It is true, also, that the monarch intended to be obeyed in what seems to us to be a very arbitrary and unreasonable command, that they should assemble and fall down and worship the image which he had set up. But this does not imply any disposition to persecute on account of religion, or to prevent in others the free exercise of their own religious opinions, or the worship of their own gods. It is well known that it was a doctrine of all ancient idolaters, that respect might be shown to foreign gods—to the gods of other people—without in the least degree implying a want of respect for their own gods, or violating any of their obligations to them. The universal maxim was, that the gods of all nations were to be respected, and hence foreign gods might be introduced for worship, and respect paid to them without in any degree detracting from the honour which was due to their own. Nebuchadnezzar,

therefore, simply demanded that homage should be shown to the idol that *he* had erected; that the god whom *he* worshipped should be acknowledged as *a* god; and that respect should thus be shown to himself, and to the laws of his empire, by acknowledging *his* god, and rendering to that god the degree of homage which was his due. But it is nowhere intimated that he regarded his idol as the *only* true god, or that he demanded that he should be recognized as such, or that he was not willing that all other gods, in their place, should be honoured. There is no intimation, therefore, that he meant to *persecute* any other men for worshipping their own gods, nor is there any reason to suppose that he apprehended that there would be any scruples on religious grounds about acknowledging the image that he set up to be worthy of adoration and praise.

(3.) There is no reason to think that he was so well acquainted with the peculiar character of the Hebrew religion as to suppose that its votaries would have any difficulty on this subject, or would hesitate to unite with others in adoring his image. He knew, indeed, that they were worshippers of Jehovah; that they had reared a magnificent temple to his honour in Jerusalem, and that they professed to keep his laws. But there is no reason to believe that he was very intimately acquainted with the laws and institutions of the Hebrews, or that he supposed that they would have any difficulty in doing what was universally understood to be proper—to show due respect to the gods of other nations. Certainly, if he had intimately known the history of a considerable portion of the Hebrew people, and been acquainted with their proneness to fall into idolatry, he would have seen little to make him doubt that they would readily comply with a command to show respect to the gods worshipped in other lands. There is no reason, therefore, to suppose that he anticipated that the Hebrew exiles, any more than any other people, would hesitate to show to his image the homage which he required.

(4.) The whole account agrees well with the character of Nebuchadnezzar. He was an arbitrary monarch. He was accustomed to implicit obedience. He was determined in his character, and resolute in his purposes. Having once formed the resolution to erect such a magnificent image of his god—one that would correspond with the greatness of his capital, and, at the same time, show his respect for the god that he worshipped—nothing was more natural than that he should issue such a proclamation that homage should be shown to it by all his subjects, and that, in order to secure this, he should issue this decree, that whoever did *not* do it should be punished in the severest manner. There is no reason to suppose that he had any particular class of persons in his eye, or, indeed, that he anticipated that the order would be disobeyed by *any* class of persons. In fact, we see in this whole transaction just one illustration of what usually occurred under the arbitrary despotisms of the East, where, *whatever* is the order that is issued from the throne, universal and absolute submission is demanded, under the threatening of a speedy and fearful punishment. The order of Nebuchadnezzar was not more arbitrary and unreasonable than those which have been frequently issued by the Turkish sultan.

II. A second objection to the chapter is the account of the musical instruments in ver. 5. The objection is, that to some of these instruments *Grecian* names are given, and that this proves that the transaction must have a later date than is attributed to it, or that the account must have been written by one of later times. The objection is, that the whole statement seems to have been derived from the account of some Greek procession in honour of the gods of Greece. See Bleek, p. 259.

To this objection, it may be replied (*a*) that such processions in honour of the gods, or such assemblages, accompanied with musical instruments, were, and are, common among all people. They occur constantly in the East, and it cannot, with any propriety, be said that one is borrowed from another. (*b*) A large part of these instruments have undoubtedly Chaldee names given to them, and the names are such as we may suppose that one living in the times of Nebuchadnezzar would give them. See Notes on ver. 5. (*c*) As to those which are alleged to indicate a Greek origin, it may be observed, that it is quite uncertain whether the origin of the name was Greek or Chaldee. That such names *are* found given to instruments of music by the Greeks is certain; but it is not certain whence they obtained the name. For anything that can be proved to the contrary, the name may have had an Eastern origin. It is altogether probable that many of the names of things among the Greeks had such an origin; and if the instrument of music itself—as no one can prove it did not—came in from the East, the *name* came also from the East. (*d*) It may be further stated, that, even on the supposition that the name had its origin in Greece, there is no absolute certainty that the name and the instrument were unknown to the Chaldeans. Who can prove that some Chaldean may not have been in Greece, and may not have borne back to his own country some instrument of music that he found there different from those which he had been accustomed to at home, or that he may not have constructed an instrument resembling one which he had seen there, and given it the same name? Or who can prove that some strolling Greek musician may not have travelled as far as Babylon—for the Greeks travelled everywhere—and carried with him some instrument of music before unknown to the Chaldeans, and imparted to them at the same time the knowledge of the instrument and the name? But until this is shown the objection has no force.

III. A third objection is, that the statement in ver. 22, that the persons appointed to execute the orders of the king died from the heat of the furnace, or that the king issued an order, to execute which perilled the lives of the innocent who were intrusted with its execution, is improbable.

To this it may be said (a) that there is no evidence or affirmation that the king contemplated *their* danger, or designed to peril their lives; but it is undoubtedly a fact that he was intent on the execution of his own order, and that he little regarded the peril of those who executed it. And nothing is more probable than this; and, indeed, nothing more common. A general who orders a company of men to silence or take a battery has no malice against them, and no design on their lives; but he is intent on the accomplishment of the object, whatever may be the peril of the men, or however large a portion of them may fall. In fact, the objection which is here made to the credibility of this narrative is an objection which would lie with equal force against most of the orders issued in battle, and not a few of the commands issued by arbitrary monarchs in time of peace. The fact in this case was, the king was intent on the execution of his purpose— the punishment of the refractory and stubborn men who had resisted his commands, and there is no probability

that, in the excitements of wrath, he would pause to inquire whether the execution of his purpose would endanger the lives of those who were intrusted with the execution of the order or not. (b) There is every probability that the heat *would be* so great as to peril the lives of those who should approach it. It is said to have been made seven times hotter than usual (ver. 19); that is, as hot as it could be made, and, if this were so, it is by no means an unreasonable supposition that those who were compelled to approach it so near as to cast others in should be in danger.

IV. A fourth objection, urged by Griesinger, p. 41, as quoted by Hengstenberg, *Authentie des Daniel,* p. 92, is, that "as Nebuchadnezzar had the furnace already prepared ready to throw these men in, he must have known beforehand that they would not comply with his demand, and so must have designed to punish them; or that this representation is a mere fiction of the writer, to make the delivery of these men appear more marvellous."

To this it may be replied, (a) that there is not the slightest evidence, from the account in Daniel, that Nebuchadnezzar had the furnace prepared beforehand, as if it were expected that some would disobey, and as if he meant to show his wrath. He indeed (ver. 6) threatens this punishment, but it is clear, from ver. 19, that the furnace was not yet heated up, and that the occasion of its being heated in such a manner was the unexpected refusal of these three men to obey him. (b) But if it should be admitted that there was a furnace thus glowing—heated with a view to punish offenders—it would not be contrary to what sometimes occurs in the East under a despotism. Sir John Chardin (*Voy. en Perse.* iv. p. 276) mentions in his time (in the seventeenth century) a case similar to this.

He says that during a whole month, in a time of great scarcity, an oven was kept heated to throw in all persons who had failed to comply with the laws in regard to taxation, and had thus defrauded the government. This was, in fact, strictly in accordance with the character of Oriental despotism. We know, moreover, from Jer. xxix. 22, that this mode of punishment was not unknown in Babylon, and it would seem probable that it was not uncommon in the time of Nebuchadnezzar. Thus Jeremiah says, "And of them shall be taken up a curse by all the captivity of Judah which are in Babylon, saying, The Lord make thee like Zedekiah and like Ahab, whom the king of Babylon roasted in the fire."

V. A fifth objection is stated thus by Bertholdt : "Why did the wonders recorded in this chapter take place ? It was only for this purpose that Nebuchadnezzar might be made to appear to give praise to God, that he is represented as giving commandment that no one should reproach him. But this object is too small to justify such an array of means." To this it may be replied, (a) that it does not appear from the chapter that this was the *object* aimed at. (b) There were other designs in the narrative beside this. They were to show the firmness of the men who refused to worship an idol-god ; to illustrate their conscientious adherence to their religion ; to show their confidence in the Divine protection ; to prove that God will defend those who put their trust in him, and that he can deliver them even in the midst of the flames. These things were worthy of record.

VI. It has been objected that "the expression in which Nebuchadnezzar (ver. 28) is represented as breaking out, after the rescue of the three men, is altogether contrary to his dignity, and to the respect for the religion of his fathers and of his country, which he was bound to defend."—Bertholdt, p. 253. But to this it may be replied, (a) that if this scene actually occurred before the eyes of the king—if God had thus miraculously interposed in delivering his servants in this wonderful manner from the heated furnace, nothing would be more natural than this. It was a manifest miracle, a direct interposition of God, a deliverance of the professed friends of Jehovah by a power that was above all that was human, and an expression of surprise and admiration was in every way proper on such an occasion. (b) It accorded with all the prevailing notions of religion, and of the respect due to the gods, to say this. As above remarked, it was a principle recognized among the heathen to honour the gods of other nations, and if they had interposed to defend their own votaries, it was no more than was admitted in all the nations of idolatry. If, therefore, Jehovah had interposed to save his own friends and worshippers, every principle which Nebuchadnezzar held on the subject would make it proper for him to acknowledge the fact, and to say that honour was due to him for his interposition. In this, moreover, Nebuchadnezzar would be understood as saying nothing derogatory to the gods that he himself worshipped, or to those adored in his own land. All that is *necessary* to be supposed in what he said is, that he now felt that Jehovah, the God whom the Hebrews adored, had shown that he was worthy to be ranked among the gods, and that in common with others, he had power to protect his own friends. To this it may be added (c) that, in his way, Nebuchadnezzar everywhere showed that he was a *religious* man : that is, that he recognized the gods, and was ever ready to acknowledge their interference in human affairs, and to render them the honour which was their due. Indeed, this whole affair grew out of his respect for *religion*, and what here occurred was only in accordance with his general principle, that when any God had shown that he had power to deliver his people, he should be acknowledged, and that no words of reproach should be uttered against him, ver. 29.

VII. A more plausible objection than those which have just been noticed is urged by Lüderwald, Jahn, Dereser, in regard to the account which is given of the image which Nebuchadnezzar is said to have erected. This objection has reference to the *size* of the image, to its proportions, and to the material of which it is said to have been composed. This objection, as stated by Bertholdt (p. 256), is substantially the following :—" That the image had probably a human form, and yet that the proportions of the human figure are by no means observed—the height being represented to have been sixty cubits, and its breadth six cubits—or its height being to its breadth as ten to one, whereas the proportion of a man is only six to one ; that the amount of gold in such an image is incredible, being beyond any means which the king of Babylon could have possessed ; and that probably the image here referred to was one that Herodotus says he saw in the temple of Belus at Babylon (I. 183), and which Diodorus Siculus describes (II. 9), and which was only forty feet in height." See Notes on ver. 1. In regard to this objection, we may observe, then—

(*a*) That there is no certainty that this was the same image which is referred to by Herodotus and Diodorus Siculus. That image was *in* the temple ; this was erected on the "plain of Dura." See Notes on ver. 1. But, so far as appears, this may have been erected for a temporary purpose, and the materials may then have been employed for other purposes ; that in the temple was permanent.

(*b*) As to the amount of gold in the image—it is not said or implied that it was of *solid* gold. It is well known that the images of the gods were made of wood or clay, and overlaid with gold or silver, and this is all that is necessarily implied here. See Notes on ver. 1.

(*c*) The *height* of the alleged image can be no real objection to the statement. It is not necessary to assume that it had the human form—though that is probable—but if that be admitted, there can be no objection to the supposition that, either standing by itself, or raised on a pedestal, it may have been as lofty as the statement here implies. The colossal figure at Rhodes was an hundred and five Grecian feet in height, and being made to stride the mouth of the harbour, was a work of much more difficult construction than this figure would have been.

(*d*) As to the alleged *disproportion* in the figure of the image, see Notes on ver. 1. To what is there said may be added : (1.) It is not *necessary* to suppose that it had the human form. Nothing of this kind is affirmed, though it may be regarded as probable. But if it had not, of course the objection would have no force. (2.) If it had the human form, it is by no means clear whether it had a sitting or a standing posture. Nothing is said on this point in regard to the image or statue, and until *this* is determined, nothing can be said properly respecting the proportions. (3.) It is not said whether it stood by itself, or whether it rested on a basis or pediment—and until *this* is determined, no objections can be valid as to the proportion of the statue. It is every way probable that the image was reared on a lofty pedestal, and for anything that appears, the proportions of the *image itself*, whether sitting or standing, may have been well preserved. (4.) But in addition to this it should be said, that if the account here is to be taken literally as stating that the image was ten times as high as it was broad—thus failing to observe the proper human proportions—the account would not be incredible. It is admitted by Gesenius (*Ency. von Ersch und Gruber*, art. *Babylon*, *Th.* vii. p. 24), that the Babylonians had no correct taste in these matters. "The ruins," says he, "are imposing by their colossal greatness, not by their beauty; all the ornaments are rough and barbarian." The Babylonians, indeed, possessed a taste for the colossal, the grand, the imposing, but they also had a taste for the monstrous and the prodigious, and a mere want of *proportion* is not a sufficient argument to prove that what is stated here did not occur.

VIII. But one other objection remains to be noticed. It is one which is noticed by Bertholdt (pp. 251, 252), that, if this is a true account, it is strange that *Daniel* himself is not referred to; that if he was, according to the representation in the last chapter, a high officer at court, it is unaccountable that he is not mentioned as concerned in these affairs, and especially that he did not interpose in behalf of his three friends to save them. To this objection it is sufficient to reply (*a*) that, as Bertholdt himself (p. 287) suggests, Daniel may have been absent from the capital at this time on some business of state, and consequently the question whether *he* would worship the image may not have been tested. It is probable, from the nature of the case, that he would be employed on such embas-

sies, or be sent to some other part of the empire from time to time, to arrange the affairs of the provinces, and no one can demonstrate that he was not absent on this occasion. Indeed, the fact that he is not mentioned at all in the transaction would serve to imply this; since, if he were at court, it is to be presumed that he himself would have been implicated as well as his three friends. Comp. ch. vi. He was not a man to shrink from duty, or to decline any proper method of showing his attachment to the religion of his fathers, or any proper interest in the welfare of his friends. But (*b*) it is possible that even if Daniel were at court at that time, and did not unite in the worship of the image, he might have escaped the danger. There were undoubtedly many more Jews in the province of Babylon who did not worship this image, but no formal accusation was brought against them, and their case did not come before the king. For some reason, the accusation was made specific against these three men —*for they were rulers in the province* (ch. ii. 49), and being foreigners, the people under them may have gladly seized the occasion to complain of them to the king. But so little is known of the circumstances, that it is not possible to determine the matter with certainty. All that needs to be said is, that the fact that Daniel was *not* implicated in the affair is no proof that the three persons referred to were not; that it is no evidence that what is said of *them* is not true because nothing is said of *Daniel*.

§ II.—ANALYSIS OF THE CHAPTER.

This chapter, which is complete in itself, or which embraces the entire narrative relating to an important transaction, contains the account of a magnificent brazen image erected by Nebuchadnezzar, and the result of at-

CHAPTER III.

NEBUCHADNEZZAR the king made *a* an image of gold,

a 2 Ki. 19. 17, 18; Ps. 115. 4, &c.; Is. 40. 19, &c.; Je. 16. 20; Ac. 19. 26.

whose height *was* threescore cubits, *and* the breadth thereof six cubits: he set it up in the plain of Dura, in the province of Babylon.

tempting to constrain the conscientious Hebrews to worship it. The narrative comprises the following points:—

I. The erection of the great image in the plain of Dura, ver. 1.

II. The dedication of the image in the presence of the great princes and governors of the provinces, the high officers of state, and an immense multitude of the people, accompanied with solemn music, vers. 2–7.

III. The complaint of certain Chaldeans respecting the Jews, that they refused to render homage 'to the image, reminding the king that he had solemnly enjoined this on all persons, on penalty of being cast into a burning furnace in case of disobedience, vers. 8–12. This charge was brought particularly against Shadrach, Meshach, and Abed-nego. Daniel escaped the accusation, for reasons which will be stated in the Notes on ver. 12. The common people of the Jews also escaped, as the command extended particularly to the rulers.

IV. The manner in which Nebuchadnezzar received this accusation, vers. 13–15. He was filled with rage; he summoned the accused into his presence; he commanded them to prostrate themselves before the image on penalty of being cast at once into the fiery furnace.

V. The noble answer of the accused, vers. 16–18. They stated to the king that his threat did not alarm them, and that they felt no solicitude to answer him in regard to the matter (ver. 16); that they were assured that the God whom they served was able to deliver them from the furnace, and from the wrath of the king (ver. 17); but that even if he did not, whatever might be

the issue, they could not serve the gods of the Chaldeans, nor worship the image which the king had set up.

VI. The infliction of the threatened punishment, vers. 19–23. The furnace was commanded to be heated seven times hotter than usual; they were bound and thrown in with their usual apparel on; and the hot blast of the furnace destroyed the men who were employed to perform this service.

VII. Their protection and preservation, vers. 24–27. The astonished monarch who had commanded *three* men to be cast in *bound,* saw *four* men walking in the midst of the flames *loose;* and satisfied now they had a Divine Protector, awed by the miracle, and doubtless dreading the wrath of the Divine Being that had become their protector, he commanded them suddenly to come out. The princes, and governors, and captains were gathered together, and these men, thus remarkably preserved, appeared before them uninjured.

VIII. The effect on the king, vers. 28–30. As in the case when Daniel had interpreted his dream (ch. ii.), he acknowledged that this was the act of the true God, ver. 28. He issued a solemn command that the God who had done this should be honoured, for that no other God could deliver in this manner, ver. 29. He again restored them to their honourable command over the provinces, ver. 30.

1. *Nebuchadnezzar the king made an image of gold.* The time when he did this is not mentioned; nor is it stated in whose honour, or for what design, this colossal image was erected. In the Greek and Arabic translations, this

is said to have occurred in the eighteenth year of Nebuchadnezzar. This is not, however, in the original text, nor is it known on what authority it is asserted. Dean Prideaux (*Connex.* I. 222) supposes that it was at first some marginal comment on the Greek version that at last crept into the text, and that there was probably some good authority for it. If this is the correct account of the time, the event here recorded occurred B.C. 587, or, according to the chronology of Prideaux, about nineteen years after the transaction recorded in the previous chapter. Hales makes the chronology somewhat different, though not essentially. According to him, Daniel was carried to Babylon B.C. 586, and the image was set up B.C. 569, making an interval from the time that he was carried to Babylon of seventeen years ; and if the dream (ch. ii.) was explained within three or four years after Daniel was taken to Babylon, the interval between that and this occurrence would be some thirteen or fourteen years. Calmet makes the captivity of Daniel 602 years before Christ ; the interpretation of the dream 598 ; and the setting up of the image 556—thus making an interval of more than forty years. It is impossible to determine the time with certainty ; but allowing the shortest-mentioned period as the interval between the interpretation of the dream (ch. ii.) and the erection of this statue, the time would be sufficient to account for the fact that the impression made by that event on the mind of Nebuchadnezzar, in favour of the claims of the true God (ch. ii. 46, 47), seems to have been entirely effaced. The two chapters, in order that the right impression may be received on this point, should be read with the recollection that such an interval had elapsed. At the time when the event here recorded is supposed by Prideaux to have occurred, Nebuchadnezzar had just returned from finishing the Jewish war. From the spoils which he had taken in that expedition in Syria and Palestine, he had the means in abundance of rearing such a colossal statue ; and at the close of these conquests, nothing would be more natural than that he should wish to rear in his capital

some splendid work of art that would signalize his reign, record the memory of his conquests, and add to the magnificence of the city. The word which is here rendered *image* (Chald. צְלֵם —

Greek *εἰκόνα*), in the usual form in the Hebrew, means a shade, shadow ; then that which shadows forth anything ; then an image of anything, and then an *idol*, as representing the deity worshipped. It is not necessary to suppose that it was of solid gold, for the amount required for such a structure would have been immense, and probably beyond the means even of Nebuchadnezzar. The presumption is, that it was merely covered over with plates of gold, for this was the usual manner in which statues erected in honour of the gods were made. See Isa. xl. 19. It is not known in honour of whom this statue was erected. Grotius supposed that it was reared to the memory of Nabopolassar, the father of Nebuchadnezzar, and observes that it was customary to erect statues in this manner in honour of parents. Prideaux, Hales, the editor of the *Pict. Bible,* and most others, suppose that it was in honour of Bel, the principal deity worshipped in Babylon. See Notes on Isa. xlvi. 1. Some have supposed that it was in honour of Nebuchadnezzar himself, and that he purposed by it to be worshipped as a god. But this opinion has little probability in its favour. The opinion that it was in honour of Bel, the principal deity of the place, is every way the most probable, and this derives some confirmation from the well-known fact that a magnificent image of this kind was, at some period of his reign, erected by Nebuchadnezzar in honour of this god, in a style to correspond with the magnificence of the city. The account of this given by Herodotus is the following :—"The temple of Jupiter Belus, whose huge gates of brass may still be seen, is a square building, each side of which is two furlongs. In the midst rises a tower, of the solid depth and height of one furlong ; upon which, resting as upon a base, seven other lesser towers are built in regular succession. The ascent is on the outside ; which, winding from the ground, is continued to the highest tower; and in the middle of the whole structure there is a convenient resting-place. In the last tower is a large chapel, in which is placed a couch, magnificently adorned, and near it a table of solid gold; but there is no statue in the place. In this temple there is also a small chapel, lower in the building, which contains a figure of Jupiter, in a sitting posture, with a large table before him; these, with the base of the table, and the seat of the throne, are all of the purest gold, and are estimated by the Chaldeans to be worth eight hundred talents. On the outside of this chapel there are two altars; one is gold, the other is of immense size, and appropriated to the sacrifice of full-grown animals; those only which have not yet left their dams may be offered on the golden altar. On the larger altar, at the anniversary festival in honour of their god, the Chaldeans regularly consume incense to the amount of a thousand talents. There was formerly in this temple a statue of solid gold twelve cubits high; this, however, I mention from the information of the Chaldeans, and not from my own knowledge."—*Clio*, 183. Diodorus Siculus, a much later writer, speaks to this effect: " Of the tower of Jupiter Belus, the historians who have spoken have given different descriptions; and this temple being now entirely destroyed, we cannot speak accurately respecting it. It was excessively high; constructed throughout with great care; built of brick and bitumen. Semiramis placed on the top of it three statues of massy gold, of Jupiter, Juno, and Rhea. Jupiter was erect, in the

Colossal Figures on the Plain of Thebes, near the Memnonium.
The nearer of the two is known by the name of the Vocal Memnon.

attitude of a man walking; he was forty feet in height; and weighed a thousand Babylonian talents: Rhea, who sat in a chariot of gold, was of the same weight. Juno, who stood upright, weighed eight hundred talents."—B. ii.

The temple of Bel or Belus, in Babylon, stood until the time of Xerxes; but on his return from the Grecian expedition, he demolished the whole of it, and laid it in rubbish, having first plundered it of its immense riches. Among the spoils which he took from the temple, are mentioned several images and statues of massive gold, and among them the one mentioned by Diodorus Siculus, as being forty feet high. See Strabo, lib. 16, p. 738; Herodotus, lib. 1; Arrian *de Expe. Alex.* lib. 7, quoted by Prideaux I. 240. It is not very probable that the image which Xerxes removed was the same which Nebuchadnezzar reared in the plain of Dura—comp. the Intro. to this chapter, § I. VII. (*a*); but the fact that such a colossal statue was found in Babylon may be adduced as one incidental corroboration of the probability of the statement here. It is not impossible that Nebuchadnezzar was led, as the editor of Calmet's *Dictionary* has remarked (Taylor, vol. iii. p. 194), to the construction of this image by what he had seen in Egypt. He had conquered and ravaged Egypt but a few years before this, and had doubtless been struck with the wonders of art which he had seen there. Colossal statues in honour of the gods abounded, and nothing would be more natural than that Nebuchadnezzar should wish to make his capital rival everything which he had seen in Thebes. Nor is it improbable that, while he sought to make his image more magnificent and costly than even those in Egypt were, the views of sculpture would be about the same, and the *figure* of the statue might be borrowed from what had been seen in Egypt. An illustration of the subject before us is furnished by the preceding engraving, from a photograph, of the two celebrated colossal figures of Amunoph III. standing in the plains of Goorneh, Thebes, one of which is known as the Vocal Memnon. These colossi, exclusive of the pedestals (partially buried), are forty-seven feet high, and eighteen feet three inches wide across the shoulders, and according to Wilkinson are each of one single block, and contain about 11,500 cubic feet of stone. They are made of a

stone not known within several days' journey of the place where they are erected. Calmet refers to these statues, quoting from Norden. ¶ *Whose height was threescore cubits.* Prideaux and others have been greatly perplexed at the *proportions* of the image here represented. Prideaux says on the subject (*Connex.* I. 240, 241), "Nebuchadnezzar's golden image is said indeed in Scripture to have been sixty cubits, that is, ninety feet high; but this must be understood of the image and pedestal both together; for that image being said to be but six cubits broad or thick, it is impossible that the image would have been sixty cubits high; for that makes its height to be ten times its breadth or thickness, which exceeds all the proportions of a man, no man's height being above six times his thickness, measuring the slenderest man living at the waist. But where the breadth of this image was measured is not said; perchance it was from shoulder to shoulder; and then the proportion of six cubits breadth will bring down the height exactly to the measure which Diodorus has mentioned; for the usual height of a man being four and a half of his breadth between the shoulders, if the image were six cubits broad between the shoulders, it must, according to this proportion, have been twenty-seven cubits high, which is forty and a half feet." The statue itself, therefore, according to Prideaux, was forty feet high; the pedestal fifty feet. But this, says Taylor, the editor of Calmet, is a disproportion of parts which, if not absolutely impossible, is utterly contradictory to every principle of art, even of the rudest sort. To meet the difficulty, Taylor himself supposes that the height referred to in the description was rather *proportional* than *actual* height; that is, if it had stood upright it would have been sixty cubits, though the actual elevation in a sitting posture may have been but little more than thirty cubits, or fifty feet. The breadth, he supposes, was rather the depth or thickness measured from the breast to the back, than the breadth measured from shoulder to shoulder. His argument and illustration may be seen in Calmet, vol. iii. Frag. 156. It is not absolutely

2 Then Nebuchadnezzar the king sent to gather together the princes, the governors, and the captains, the judges, the treasurers, the counsel-

certain, however, that the image was in a sitting posture, and the *natural* construction of the passage is, that the statue was actually sixty cubits in height. No one can doubt that an image of that height could be erected; and when we remember the one at Rhodes, which was 105 Grecian feet in height (see art. "Colossus," in Anthon's *Class. Dict.*), and the desire of Nebuchadnezzar to adorn his capital in the most magnificent manner, it is not to be regarded as improbable that an image of this height was erected. What was the height of the pedestal, if it stood on any, as it probably did, it is impossible now to tell. The length of the *cubit* was not the same in every place. The length originally was the distance between the elbow and the extremity of the middle finger, about eighteen inches. The Hebrew cubit, according to Bishop Cumberland and M. Pelletier, was twenty-one inches ; but others fix it at eighteen. — Calmet. The Talmudists say that the Hebrew cubit was larger by one quarter than the Roman. Herodotus says that the cubit in Babylon was three fingers longer than the usual one. — Clio, 178. Still, there is not absolute certainty on that subject. The usual and probable measurement of the cubit would make the image in Babylon about ninety feet high. ¶ And *the breadth thereof six cubits.* About nine feet. This would, of course, make the height ten times the breadth, which Prideaux says is entirely contrary to the usual proportions of a man. It is not known on what *part* of the image this measurement was made, or whether it was the thickness from the breast to the back, or the width from shoulder to shoulder. If the *thickness* of the image here is referred to by the word *"breadth,"* the proportion would be well preserved. "The thickness of a well-proportioned man," says Scheuchzer (*Knupfer Bibel, in loc.*), "measured from the breast to the back is one-tenth of his height." This was understood to be the proportion by Augustine, *Civi. Dei,* l. xv. c. 26. The word which is here rendered *breadth* (פְּתָי) occurs nowhere else in the Chaldean of the Scriptures, except in Ezra vi. 3 : "Let the house be builded, the height thereof threescore cubits, and the *breadth* thereof threescore cubits." Perhaps this refers rather to the *depth* of the temple from front to rear, as Taylor has remarked, than to the breadth from one side to another. If it does, it would correspond with the measurement of Solomon's temple, and it is not probable that Cyrus would vary from that plan in his instructions to build a new temple. If that be the true construction, then the meaning here may be, as remarked above, that the image was of that *thickness,* and the breadth from shoulder to shoulder may not be referred to. ¶ *He set it up in the plain of Dura.* It would seem from this that it was set up in an open plain, and not in a temple; perhaps not near a temple. It was not unusual to erect images in this manner, as the colossal figure at Rhodes shows. Where this plain was, it is of course impossible now to determine. The Greek translation of the word is Δειρᾳ —*Deeira.* Jerome says that the translation of Theodotion is *Deira ;* of Symmachus, *Doraum ;* and of the LXX. περίβολον —which he says may be rendered *vivarium* vel *conclusum locum.* "Interpreters commonly," says Gesenius, "compare Dura, a city mentioned by Ammian. Marcel. 25. 6, situated on the Tigris ; and another of like name in Polyb. 5, 48, on the Euphrates, near the mouth of the Chaboras." It is not necessary to suppose that this was in the *city* of Babylon ; and, indeed, it is probable that it was not, as the "province of Babylon" doubtless embraced more than the city, and an extensive plain seems to have been selected, perhaps near the city, as a place where the monument would be more conspicuous, and where larger numbers could convene for the homage which was proposed to be shown to it. ¶ *In the province of Babylon.* One of the provinces, or departments, embracing the capital, into which the empire was divided, ch. ii. 48.

2. *Then Nebuchadnezzar the king sent to gather together the princes.* It is difficult now, if not impossible, to

lors, the sheriffs, and all the rulers of the provinces, to come to the de-

determine the exact meaning of the words used here with reference to the various officers designated; and it is not material that it should be done. The general sense is, that he assembled the great officers of the realm to do honour to the image. The object was doubtless to make the occasion as magnificent as possible. Of course, if these high officers were assembled, an immense multitude of the people would congregate also. That this was contemplated, and that it in fact occurred, is apparent from verses 4, 7. The word rendered *princes* (אֲחַשְׁדַּרְפְּנַיָּא) occurs only in Daniel, in Ezra, and in Esther. In Dan. iii. 2, 3, 27, vi. 1–4, 6, 7, it is uniformly rendered *princes;* in Ezra viii. 36, Esther iii. 12, viii. 9, ix. 3, it is uniformly rendered *lieutenants.* The word means, according to Gesenius (*Lex.*), "*satraps*, the governors or viceroys of the large provinces among the ancient Persians, possessing both civil and military power, and being in the provinces the representatives of the sovereign, whose state and splendour they also rivalled." The etymology of the word is not certainly known. The Persian word *satrap* seems to have been the foundation of this word, with some slight modifications adapting it to the Chaldee mode of pronunciation. ¶ *The governors.* סִגְנַיָּא. This word is rendered *governors* in ch. ii. 48 (see Notes on that place), and in chap. iii. 3, 27; vi. 7. It does not elsewhere occur. The Hebrew word corresponding to this —סְגָנִים—occurs frequently, and is rendered *rulers* in every place except Isa. xli. 25, where it is rendered *princes:* Ezra ix. 2; Neh. ii. 16; iv. 14 (7); v. 7,.17; vii. 5; Jer. li. 23, 28, 57; Ezek. xxiii. 6, 12, 23, *et al.* The office was evidently one that was inferior to that of the *satrap*, or governor of a whole province. ¶ *And the captains.* פַּחֲוָתָא. This word, wherever it occurs in Daniel, is rendered *captains*, ch. iii. 2, 3, 27; vi. 7; wherever else it occurs it is rendered *governor*, Ezra v. 3, 6, 14; vi. 6, 7, 13. The Hebrew word corres-

dication of the image which Nebuchadnezzar the king had set up.

ponding to this (פֶּחָה) occurs frequently, and is also rendered indifferently, *governor* or *captain:* 1 Kings x. 15; 2 Chron. ix. 14; Ezra viii. 36; 1 Kings xx. 24; Jer. li. 23, 28, 57, *et al.* It refers to the governor of a province less than a satrapy, and is applied to officers in the Assyrian empire, 2 Kings xviii. 24; Isa. xxxvi. 9; in the Chaldean, Ezek. xxiii. 6, 23; Jer. li. 23; and in the Persian, Esth. viii. 9; ix. 3. The word *captains* does not now very accurately express the sense. The office was not exclusively military, and was of a higher grade than would be denoted by the word *captain* with us. ¶ *The judges.* אֲדַרְגָּזְרַיָּא. This word occurs only here, and in ver. 3. It means properly *great* or *chief judges*—compounded of two words signifying *greatness*, and *judges.* See Gesenius, (*Lex.*) ¶ *The treasurers.* גְּדָבְרַיָּא. This word occurs nowhere else. The word גִּזְבָּר *Gisbâr*, however, the same word with a slight change in the pronunciation, occurs in Ezra i. 8, vii. 21, and denotes *treasurer.* It is derived from a word (גָּנַז) which means to hide, to hoard, to lay up in store. ¶ *The counsellors.* דְּתָבְרַיָּא. This word occurs nowhere else, except in ver. 3. It means one skilled in the law; a judge. The office was evidently inferior to the one denoted by the word *judges.* ¶ *The sheriffs.* A sheriff with us is a county officer, to whom is intrusted the administration of the laws. In England the office is judicial as well as ministerial. With us it is merely ministerial. The duty of the sheriff is to execute the civil and criminal processes throughout the county. He has charge of the jail and prisoners, and attends courts, and keeps the peace. It is not to be supposed that the officer here referred to in Daniel corresponds precisely with this. The word used (תִּפְתָּיֵא) occurs nowhere else. It means, according to Gesenius, persons learned in the law; lawyers. The office had a close relation to that of *Mufti* among the Arabs, the term being derived from the same word, and properly means "a

3 Then the princes, the governors, and captains, the judges, the treasurers, the counsellors, the sheriffs, and all the rulers of the provinces, were gathered together unto the dedication of the image that Nebuchadnezzar the king had set up:

and they stood before the image that Nebuchadnezzar had set up.

4 Then an herald cried [1] aloud, To you [2] it is commanded, O *a* people, nations, and languages.

5 *That* at what time ye hear the sound of the cornet, flute, harp,

1 *with might*, ch. 4. 14.   2 *they command.*

a ch. 4. 1; 6. 25.

wise man; one whose response is equivalent to law." ¶ *And all the rulers of the provinces.* The term here used is a general term, and would apply to any kind of officers or rulers, and is probably designed to embrace all which had not been specified. The object was to assemble the chief officers of the realm. Jacchiades has compared the officers here enumerated with the principal officers of the Turkish empire, and supposes that a counterpart to them may be found in that empire. See the comparison in Grotius, *in loc.* He supposes that the officers last denoted under the title of "rulers of the provinces" were similar to the Turkish *Zangiahos* or *viziers.* Grotius supposes that the term refers to the rulers of cities and places adjacent to cities—a dominion of less extent and importance than that of the rulers of provinces. ¶ *To come to the dedication of the image,* &c. The public setting it apart to the purposes for which it was erected. This was to be done with solemn music, and in the presence of the principal officers of the kingdom. Until it was dedicated to the god in whose honour it was erected, it would not be regarded as an object of worship. It is easy to conceive that such an occasion would bring together an immense concourse of people, and that it would be one of peculiar magnificence.

3. *And they stood before the image.* In the presence of the image. They were drawn up, doubtless, so as at the same time to have the best view of the statue, and to make the most imposing appearance.

4. *Then an herald cried aloud.* Marg., as in Chald., *with might.* He made a loud proclamation. A *herald* here means a public crier. ¶ *To you it is commanded.* Margin, *they commanded.* Literally, "to you command-

ing" (plural); that is, the king has commanded. ¶ *O people, nations, and languages.* The empire of Babylon was made up of different nations, speaking quite different languages. The representatives of these nations were assembled on this occasion, and the command would extend to all. There was evidently no exception made in favour of the scruples of any, and the order would include the Hebrews as well as others. It should be observed, however, that no others *but* the Hebrews would have any scruples on the subject. They were all accustomed to worship idols, and the worship of one god did not prevent their doing homage also to another. It accorded with the prevailing views of idolaters that there were many gods; that there were tutelary divinities presiding over particular people; and that it was not improper to render homage to the god of any people or country. Though, therefore, they might themselves worship other gods in their own countries, they would have no scruples about worshipping also the one that Nebuchadnezzar had set up. In this respect the Jews were an exception. They acknowledged but one God; they believed that all others were false gods, and it was a violation of the fundamental principles of their religion to render homage to any other.

5. That *at what time ye hear the sound of the cornet.* It would not be practicable to determine with precision what kind of instruments of music are denoted by the words used in this verse. They were, doubtless, in many respects different from those which are in use now, though they may have belonged to the same general class, and may have been constructed on substantially the same principles. A full inquiry into the kinds of musical instruments in use

sackbut, psaltery, ¹ dulcimer, and all kinds of music, ye fall down and worship the golden image that Nebuchadnezzar the king hath set up:

¹ *symphony, or, singing.*

among the Hebrews may be found in the various treatises on the subject in Ugolin's *Thesau. Ant. Sacra.* tom. xxxii. Comp.' also the Notes on Isa. v. 12. The Chaldee word rendered *cornet*—קַרְנָא—the same as the Hebrew word קֶרֶן *keren*—means a *horn*, as *e.g.*, of an ox, stag, ram. Then it means a wind instrument of music resembling a horn, or perhaps horns were at first literally used. Similar instruments are now used, as the *French horn*, &c. ¶ *Flute.* מַשְׁרוֹקִיתָא *mashrokitha.* Gr., σύριγγός. Vulg., *fistula, pipe.* The Chaldee words occurs nowhere else but in this chapter, ver. 5, 7, 10, 15, and is in each instance rendered *flute.* It probably denoted all the instruments of the pipe or flute class in use among the Babylonians. The corresponding Hebrew word is חָלִיל *hhâlil.* See this explained in the Notes on Isa. v. 12. The following remarks of the Editor of the *Pictorial Bible* will explain the usual construction of the ancient pipes or flutes : "The ancient flutes were cylindrical tubes, sometimes of equal diameter throughout, but often wider at the off than the near end, and sometimes widened at that end into a funnel shape, resembling a clarionet. They were always blown, like pipes, at one end, never transversely; they had mouthpieces, and sometimes plugs or stopples, but no keys to open or close the holes beyond the reach of the hands. The holes varied in number in the different varieties of the flute. In their origin they were doubtless made of simple reeds or canes, but in the progress of improvement they came to be made of wood, ivory, bone, and even metal. They were sometimes made in joints, but connected by an interior nozzle which was generally of wood. The flutes were sometimes double, that is, a person played on two instruments at once, either connected or detached; and among the classical ancients the

Sacred Musicians.—Instruments of Music.

player on the double-flute often had a leathern bandage over his mouth to prevent the escape of his breath at the corners. The ancient Egyptians used the double-flute." Illustrations of the flute or pipe may be seen in the Notes on Isa. v. 12. Very full and interesting descriptions of the musical instruments which were used among the Egyptians may be found in Wilkinson's *Manners and Customs of the Ancient Egyptians*, vol. ii. pp. 222–327. The preceding engraving will furnish an illustration of the usual form of this instrument among the ancients. ¶ *Harp.* On the form of the *harp*, see Notes on Isa. v. 12. Comp. Wilkinson, as above quoted. The harp was one of the earliest instruments of music that was invented, Gen. iv. 21. The Chaldee word here used is not the common Hebrew word to denote the harp (כִּנּוֹר *kinnor*), but is a word which does not occur in Hebrew—קִיתָרֹס *kathros*. This occurs nowhere else in the Chaldee, and it is manifestly the same as the Greek κιθάρα, and the Latin *cithara*, denoting a harp. Whether the Chaldees derived it from the Greeks, or the Greeks from the Chaldees, however, cannot be determined with certainty. It has been made an objection to the genuineness of the book of Daniel, that the instruments here referred to were instruments bearing Greek names. See Intro. to ch. § II. IV. (*c*) (5). ¶ *Sackbut.* Vulg., *Sambuca.* Gr., like the Vulg., σαμβύκη. These words are merely different forms of writing the Chaldee word סַבְּכָא *sabbecha.* The word occurs nowhere else except in this chapter. It seems to have denoted a stringed instrument similar to the lyre or harp. Strabo affirms that the Greek word σαμβύκη, *sambykē*, is of barbarian, that is, of Oriental origin. The Hebrew word from which this word is not improperly derived—כָּבַךְ *sabach*—means, *to interweave, to entwine, to plait,* as *e.g.*, branches; and it is possible that this instrument may have derived its name from the *intertwining* of the strings. Comp. Gesenius on the word. Passow defines the Greek word σαμβύκη, *sambuca* (*Lat.*), to mean a triangular-stringed instrument that made the highest notes, or had the highest key; but as an instrument which, on account of the shortness of the strings, was not esteemed as very valuable, and had little power. Porphyry and Suidas describe it as a triangular instrument, furnished with cords of unequal length and thickness.

DANIEL I.

The classical writers mention it as very ancient, and ascribe its invention to the Syrians. Musonius describes it as having a sharp sound; and we are also told that it was often used to accompany the voice in singing Iambic verses. *Pict. Bib.* It seems to have been a species of triangular lyre or harp. ¶ *Psaltery.* The Chaldee is פְּסַנְתֵּרִין *pĕsantērin.* Gr., ψαλτήριον; Vulg., *psalterium.* All these words manifestly have the same origin, and it has been on the ground that this word, among others, is of Greek origin, that the genuineness of this book has been called in question. The word occurs nowhere else but in this chapter, vers. 5, 7, 10, 15. The Greek translators often use the word ψαλτήριον, *psaltery,* for נֶבֶל *nēbhĕl,* and כִּנּוֹר *kinnor;* and the instrument here referred to was doubtless of the harp kind. For the kind of instrument denoted by the נֶבֶל *nēbhĕl,* see Notes on Isa. v. 12. Comp. the illustrations in the *Pict. Bible* on Psa. xcii. 3. It has been alleged that this word is of Greek origin, and hence an objection has been urged against the genuineness of the book of Daniel on the presumption that, at the early period when this book is supposed to have been written, Greek musical instruments had not been introduced into Chaldea. For a general reply to this, see the Intro. § I. II. (*d*). It may be remarked further, in regard to this objection, (1.) that it is not absolutely certain that the word is derived from the Greek. See Pareau, l. c. p. 424, as quoted in Hengstenberg, *Authentie des Daniel,* p. 16. (2.) It cannot be demonstrated that there were no Greeks in the regions of Chaldea as early as this. Indeed, it is more than probable that there were. See Hengstenberg, p. 16, *seq.* Nebuchadnezzar summoned to this celebration the principal personages throughout the realm, and it is probable that there would be collected on such an occasion all the forms of music that were known, whether of domestic or foreign origin. ¶ *Dulcimer.* סוּמְפֹּנְיָה *sumponya.* This word occurs only here, and in vers. 10 and 15 of this chapter. In the margin it is rendered *symphony* or *singing.* It is the same as the Greek word συμφωνία, symphony, and in Italy the same instrument of music is now called by a name of the same origin, zampogna, and in Asia Minor zambonja. It answered probably to the Hebrew עוּגָב, rendered organ, in Gen. iv. 21; Job xxi. 12; xxx. 31; Ps. cl. 4. See Notes on Job xxi. 12. Comp. the tracts on Hebrew musical instruments inscribed schilte haggibborim in Ugolin, Thesau. vol. xxxii. The word seems to have had a Greek origin, and is one of those on which an objection has been founded against the genuineness of the book. Comp. the Intro. § i. II. (c). The word dulcimer means sweet, and would denote some instrument of music that was characterized by the sweetness of its tones. Johnson (Dict.) describes the instrument as one that is "played by striking brass wires with little sticks." The Greek word would denote properly a concert or harmony of many instruments; but the word here is evidently used to denote a single instrument. Gesenius describes it as a double pipe with a sack ; a bagpipe. Servius (on Virg. Æn. xi. 27) describes the symphonia as a bagpipe : and the Hebrew writers speak of it as a bagpipe consisting of two pipes thrust through a leathern bag, and affording a mournful sound. It may be added, that this is the same name which the bagpipe bore among the Moors in Spain; and all these circumstances concur to show that this was probably the instrument intended here. "The modern Oriental bagpipe is composed of a goatskin, usually with the hair on, and in the natural form, but deprived of the head, the tail, and the feet; being thus of the same shape as that used by the water-carriers. The pipes are usually of reeds, terminating in the tips of cows' horns slightly curved; the whole instrument being most primitively simple in its materials and construction."— Pict. Bible. ¶ And all kinds of music. All other kinds. It is not probable that all the instruments employed on that occasion were actually enumerated. Only the principal instruments are mentioned, and among them those which showed that such as were of foreign origin were employed on the occasion. From the

following extract from Chardin, it will be seen that the account here is not an improbable one, and that such things were not uncommon in the East:—"At the coronation of Soliman, king of Persia, the general of the musqueteers having whispered some moments in the king's ear, among several other things of lesser importance gave out, that both the loud and soft music should play in the two balconies upon the top of the great building which stands at one end of the palace royal, called kaisarie, or palace imperial. No nation was dispensed with, whether Persians, Indians, Turks, Muscovites, Europeans, or others ; which was immediately done. And this same tintamarre, or confusion of instruments, which sounded more like the noise of war than music, lasted twenty days together, without intermission, or the interruption of night; which number of twenty days was observed to answer to the number of the young monarch's years, who was then twenty years of age," p. 51; quoted in Taylor's Fragments to Calmet's Dict. No. 485. It may be observed, also, that in such an assemblage of instruments, nothing would be more probable than that there would be some having names of foreign origin, perhaps names whose origin was to be found in nations not represented there. But if this should occur, it would not be proper to set the fact down as an argument against the authenticity of the history of Sir John Chardin, and as little should the similar fact revealed here be regarded as an argument against the genuineness of the book of Daniel.

[The annexed illustration is a copy of part of the bass-reliefs discovered by Layard at Kouyunjik, and which, in their entire series, represent the triumphal procession of an Assyrian king, returning from conquest with spoils and captives, and accompanied by all the pomp and circumstance of Eastern ceremony. The portion here shown has an especial value in its relation to the Scriptural text, giving, as it does, the form of the harp and other instruments of music from veritable relics, coeval with Biblical events. "We find," says Layard, "from various passages in the Scriptures, that the instruments of music chiefly used on triumphal occasions were the harp, one with ten strings (rendered

viol or lyre in some versions, but probably a kind of dulcimer, the tabor, and the pipe, precisely those represented in the bass-reliefs. First came five men; three carried harps of many strings, which they struck with both hands, dancing at the same time to the measure; a fourth played on the double pipes, such as are seen on the monuments of Egypt, and were used by the Greeks and Romans. They were blown at the end, like the flutes of the modern Yezidis, which they probably resembled in tone and form. The fifth musician carried an instrument not unlike the modern *santour* of the East, consisting of a number of strings stretched over a hollow case or sounding-board. The strings, pressed with the left hand to produce the notes, were struck with a small wand or hammer held in the right. The men were followed by six female musicians, four playing on harps, one on the double pipes, and the sixth on a kind of drum, beaten with both hands, resembling the *tubbul* still used by Eastern dancing-girls. The musicians were accompanied by six women, and nine boys and girls of different ages, singing and clapping their hands to the measure. Some wore their hair in long ringlets, some platted or braided, and others confined in a net. One held her hands to her throat, as the Arab and Persian women still do when they make those shrill and vibrating sounds peculiar to the vocal music of the East." He adds, "it is scarcely possible to determine what these instruments (those named in Daniel) really

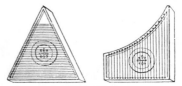

Ancient Musical Instruments.

were: they probably resembled those represented in the bass-reliefs." The sackbut, from its Hebrew name, *Sabca*, has been thought of similar form and character with the Greek *Sambuka*, a triangular instrument, with strings of unequal length and thickness, and which emitted shrill sounds.]

¶ *Ye shall fall down and worship.* That is, you shall render *religious homage.* See these words explained in the Notes on ch. ii. 46. This shows, that whether this image was erected in honour of Belus, or of Nabopolassar, it was designed that he in whose honour

6 And whoso ^afalleth not down and worshippeth, shall the same

a Rev. 13. 15.

hour be cast into the midst of a burning fiery ^bfurnace.

b Jer. 29. 22.

---

it was erected should be worshipped as a god.

6. *And whoso falleth not down and worshippeth.* The order in this verse seems to be tyrannical, and it is contrary to all our notions of freedom of religious opinion and worship. But it was much in the spirit of that age, and indeed of almost every age. It was an act to enforce uniformity in religion by the authority of the civil magistrate, and to secure it by threatened penalties. It should be observed, however, that the command at that time would not be regarded as harsh and oppressive by *heathen* worshippers, and might be complied with consistently with their views, without infringing on their notions of religious liberty. The homage rendered to one god did not, according to their views, conflict with any honour that was due to another, and though they were required to worship this divinity, that would not be a prohibition against worshipping any other. It was also in accordance with all the views of heathenism that all proper honour should be rendered to the particular god or gods which any people adored. The nations assembled here would regard it as no dishonour shown to the particular deity whom they worshipped to render homage to the god worshipped by Nebuchadnezzar, as this command implied no prohibition against worshipping any other god. It was only in respect to those who held that there is but one God, and that all homage rendered to any other is morally wrong, that this command would be oppressive. Accordingly, the contemplated vengeance fell only on the Jews—all, of every other nation, who were assembled, complying with the command without hesitation. It violated *no* principle which they held to render the homage which was claimed, for though they had their own tutelary gods whom they worshipped, they supposed the same was true of every other people, and that *their* gods were equally entitled to respect; but it violated *every* principle on which the Jew acted—

for he believed that there was but one God ruling over all nations, and that homage rendered to any other was morally wrong. Comp. Hengstenberg, *Authentic des Daniel*, pp. 83, 84. ¶ *Shall the same hour.* This accords with the general character of an Oriental despot accustomed to enjoin implicit obedience by the most summary process, and it is entirely conformable to the whole character of Nebuchadnezzar. It would seem from this, that there was an apprehension that some among the multitudes assembled would refuse to obey the command. Whether there was any *design* to make this bear hard on the Jews, it is impossible now to determine. The word which is here rendered *hour* (שַׁעְתָּא) is probably from שְׁעָה—*to look;* and properly denotes a look, a glance of the eye, and then the *time* of such a glance—a moment, an instant. It does not refer to *an hour,* as understood by us, but means *instantly, immediately*—as quick as the glance of an eye. The word is not found in Hebrew, and occurs in Chaldee only in Dan. iii. 6, 15; iv. (16, 30), 19, 33; v. 5, in each case rendered *hour.* Nothing can be inferred from it, however, in regard to the division of time among the Chaldeans into *hours*—though Herodotus says that the Greeks received the division of the day into twelve parts from them.—Lib. ii., c. 109. ¶ *Be cast into the midst of a burning fiery furnace.* The word here rendered *furnace* (אַתּוּן *attun*) is derived from תֵּן *tenan, to smoke;* and may be applied to any species of furnace, or large oven. It does not denote the use to which the furnace was commonly applied, or the form of its construction. Any furnace for burning lime—if lime was then burned—or for burning bricks, if they were burned, or for smelting ore, would correspond with the meaning of the word. Nor is it said whether the furnace referred to would be one that would be constructed for the occasion, or one in common use for some other purpose. The editor of Calmet (Taylor) supposes

7 Therefore at that time, when all the people heard the sound of the cornet, flute, harp, sackbut, psaltery, and all kinds of music, all the people, the nations, and the languages, fell down *and* worshipped the golden image that Nebuchadnezzar the king had set up.

8 ¶ Wherefore at that time certain Chaldeans came near, and accused the Jews.

9 They spake and said to the king Nebuchadnezzar, O king, live for *a* ever.

10 Thou, O king, hast made a decree, that every man that shall hear the sound of the cornet, flute,

a ch. 2. 4; 6. 21; Rom. 13. 7.

---

that the "furnace" here referred to was rather a fire kindled in the open court of a temple, like a place set apart for burning martyrs, than a closed furnace of brick. See Cal. *Dict.* vol. iv. p. 330, *seq.* The more obvious representation, however, is, that it was a closed place, in which the intensity of the fire could be greatly increased. Such a mode of punishment is not uncommon in the East. Chardin (vi. p. 118), after speaking of the common modes of inflicting the punishment of death in Persia, remarks that "there are other modes of inflicting the punishment of death on those who have violated the police laws, especially those who have contributed to produce scarcity of food, or who have used false weights, or who have disregarded the laws respecting taxes. The cooks," says he, "were fixed on spits, and roasted over a gentle fire (comp. Jer. xxix. 22), and the bakers were cast into a burning oven. In the year 1668, when the famine was raging, I saw in the royal residence in Ispahan one of these ovens burning to terrify the bakers, and to prevent their taking advantage of the scarcity to increase their gains." See Rosenmüller, *Alte u. neue Morgenland, in loc.*

7. *All the people, the nations, and the languages fell down,* &c. All excepting the Jews. An express exception is made in regard to them in the following verses, and it does not appear that any of them were present on this occasion. It would seem that only the *officers* had been summoned to be present, and it is not improbable that all the rest of the Jewish nation absented themselves.

8. *Wherefore at that time certain Chaldeans came near, and accused the Jews.* It does not appear that they accused the Jews in general, but par-

ticularly Shadrach, Meshach, and Abednego, ver. 12. They were present on the occasion, being summoned with the other officers of the realm (ver. 2), but they could not unite in the idolatrous worship. It has been frequently said that the whole thing was arranged, either by the king of his own accord, or by the instigation of their enemies, with a view to involve the Jews in difficulty, knowing that they could not conscientiously comply with the command to worship the image. But nothing of this kind appears in the narrative itself. It does not appear that the Jews were unpopular, or that there was any less disposition to show favour to them than to any other foreigners. They had been raised indeed to high offices, but there is no evidence that any office was conferred on them which it was not regarded as proper to confer on foreigners ; nor is there any evidence that in the discharge of the duties of the office they had given occasion for a just accusation. The plain account is, that the king set up the image for other purposes, and with no malicious design towards them ; that when summoned to be present with the other officers of the realm at the dedication of the image they obeyed the command ; but that when the order was issued that they should render *religious homage* to the idol, every principle of their religion revolted at it, and they refused. For the probable reasons why Daniel was not included in the number, see Note on ver. 12.

9. *O king, live for ever.* A customary form of address to a monarch, implying that long life was regarded as an eminent blessing. See Notes on ch. ii. 4.

10, 11. *Thou, O king, hast made a decree,* &c. See vers. 4, 5. As the harp, sackbut, psaltery, and dulcimer, and all kinds of music, shall fall down and worship the golden image:

11 And whoso falleth not down and worshippeth, *that* he should be cast into the midst of a burning fiery furnace.

12 There are certain Jews, whom thou hast set *a* over the affairs of

a ch. 2. 49.

the province of Babylon, Shadrach, Meshach, and Abed-nego; these men, O king, have [1] not regarded *b* thee; they serve not thy gods, nor worship the golden image which thou hast set up.

13 ¶ Then Nebuchadnezzar, in *his c* rage and fury, commanded to bring Shadrach, Meshach, and

1 *set no regard upon.* *b* ch. 6. 13.
c ver. 19.

---

decree included "every man" who heard the sound of the music, it of course embraced the Jews, whatever religious scruples they might have. Whether their scruples, however, were known at the time is not certain; or whether they would have been regarded if known, is no more certain.

12. *There are certain Jews whom thou hast set over the affairs of the province of Babylon, Shadrach, Meshach, and Abed-nego.* Ch. ii. 49. It is quite remarkable that the name of Daniel does not occur in the record of this transaction, and that he does not appear to have been involved in the difficulty. *Why* he was not cannot now be certainly known. We may be sure that he would not join in the worship of the idol, and yet it would seem, as Nebuchadnezzar had summoned all the high officers of the realm to be present (ver. 2), that he must have been summoned also. The conjecture of Prideaux (*Con.* I. 222) is not improbable, that he occupied a place of so much influence and authority, and enjoyed in so high degree the favour of the king, that they did not think it prudent to begin with him, but rather preferred at first to bring the accusation against subordinate officers. If *they* were condemned and punished, consistency might require that he should be punished also. If he had been involved at first in the accusation, his high rank, and his favour with the king, might have screened them all from punishment. It is possible, however, that Daniel was absent on the occasion of the dedication of the image. It should be remembered that perhaps some eighteen years had elapsed since the transaction referred to in ch. ii. occurred

(see Notes on ch. iii. 1), and Daniel *may* have been employed in some remote part of the empire on public business. Comp. Intro. to the chapter, § I. VIII. ¶ *These men, O king, have not regarded thee.* Marg., *set no regard upon.* Literally, "they have not placed towards thee the decree;" that is, they have not made any account of it; they have paid no attention to it. ¶ *They serve not thy gods.* Perhaps it was inferred from the fact that they would not pay religious homage to *this* idol, that they did not serve the gods at all that were acknowledged by the king; or possibly this may have been known from what had occurred before. It may have been well understood in Babylon, that the Hebrews worshipped Jehovah only. Now, however, a case had occurred which was a *test* case, whether they would on any account render homage to the idols that were worshipped in Babylon. In their refusal to worship the idol, it seemed much to aggravate the offence, and made the charge much more serious, that they did not acknowledge *any* of the gods that were worshipped in Babylon. It was easy, therefore, to persuade the king that they had arrayed themselves against the fundamental laws of the realm.

13. *Then Nebuchadnezzar, in his rage and fury.* The word rendered *fury* means *wrath.* Everything that we learn of this monarch shows that he was a man of violent passions, and that he was easily excited, though he was susceptible also of deep impressions on religious subjects. There was much here to rouse his rage. His command to worship the image was positive. It extended to all who were summoned to

Abed-nego. Then they brought these men before the king.

14 Nebuchadnezzar spake, and

its dedication. Their refusal was an act of positive disobedience, and it seemed necessary that the laws should be vindicated. As a man and a monarch, therefore, it was not unnatural that the anger of the sovereign should be thus enkindled. ¶ *Commanded to bring Shadrach,* &c. It is remarkable that he did not order them at once to be slain, as he did the magicians who could not interpret his dream, ch. ii. 12. This shows that he had some respect still for these men, and that he was willing to hear what they could say in their defence. It is proper, also, to recognize the providence of God in inclining him to this course, that their noble reply to his question might be put on record, and that the full power of religious principle might be developed.

14. *Nebuchadnezzar spake and said unto them,* Is it *true.* Marg., "*of purpose;*" that is, have you done this intentionally? Wintle renders this, "Is it insultingly?" Jacchiades says that the word is used to denote admiration or wonder, as if the king could not believe that it was possible that they could disregard so plain a command, when disobedience was accompanied with such a threat. De Dieu renders it, "Is it a joke?" That is, can you possibly be serious or in earnest that you disobey so positive a command?

said unto them, *Is it* ¹ true, O Shadrach, Meshach, and Abed-nego, do

1 or, *of purpose,* as Ex. 21. 13.

Aben Ezra, Theodotion, and Saadias render it as it is in margin, "Have you done this of set purpose and design?" as if the king had regarded it as possible that there had been a misunderstanding, and as if he was not unwilling to find that they could make an apology for their conduct. The Chaldee word (צְדָא) occurs nowhere else. It is rendered by Gesenius, *purpose, design.* That is, "Is it on purpose?" The corresponding Hebrew word (צָדָה) means, *to lie in wait, to waylay,* Exod. xxi. 13; 1 Sam. xxiv. 11, (12). Comp. Numb. xxxv. 20, 22. The true meaning seems to be, "Is it your *determined purpose* not to worship my gods? Have you deliberately made up your minds to this, and do you mean to abide by this resolution?" That this is the meaning is apparent from the fact that he immediately proposes to try them on the point, giving them still an opportunity to comply with his command to worship the image if they would, or to show whether they were finally resolved not to do it. ¶ *Do not ye serve my gods?* It was one of the charges against them that they did not do it, ver. 12.

[A group from Nimroud represents the king and divinities before Baal and the symbolic tree, and illustrates, in part, the service of these gods. At either end is one of the winged divinities,

with the pine, cone, and basket, and in the centre the conventional form of the sacred tree, surmounted by the emblem of Baal. A king stands on each side of the tree, apparently in

not ye serve my gods, nor worship the golden image which I have set up?

15 Now, if ye be ready, that at what time ye hear the sound of the cornet, flute, harp, sackbut, psaltery, and dulcimer, and all kinds of music, ye fall down *a* and worship the image which I have made, *well:* *b* but if ye worship

a Luke 4. 7, 8.　　*b* Exod. 32. 32; Luke 13. 9.

converse, or in treaty, under the auspices of the god.]

15. *Now, if ye be ready, that at what time,* &c. At the very time; on the very instant. It would seem probable from this that the ceremonies of the consecration of the image were prolonged for a considerable period, so that there was still an opportunity for them to unite in the service if they would. The supposition that such services would be continued through several days is altogether probable, and accords with what was usual on festival occasions. It is remarkable that the king was willing to give them another trial, to see whether they were disposed or not to worship the golden image. To this he might have been led by the apprehension that they had not understood the order, or that they had not duly considered the subject; and possibly by respect for them as faithful officers, and for their countryman Daniel. There seems, moreover, to have been in the bosom of this monarch, with all his pride and passion, a readiness to do justice, and to furnish an opportunity of a fair trial before he proceeded to extremities. See ch. ii. 16, 26, 46, 47. ¶ *And who is that God that shall deliver you out of, my hands?* That is, he either supposed that the God whom they worshipped would not be *able* to deliver them, or that he would not be *disposed* to do it. It was a boast of Sennacherib, when he warred against the Jews, that none of the gods of the nations which he had conquered had been able to rescue the lands over which they presided, and he argued from these premises that the God whom the Hebrews worshipped would not be able to defend their country: "Hath any of

not, ye shall be cast the same hour into the midst of a burning fiery furnace; and *c* who *is* that God that shall deliver you out of my hands?

16 Shadrach, Meshach, and Abed-nego answered and said to the king, O Nebuchadnezzar, we *are* not careful *d* to answer thee in this matter.

c Exod. 5. 2; 2 Kings 18. 35.　　*d* Matt. 10. 19.

the gods of the nations delivered his land out of the hand of the king of Assyria? Where are the gods of Hamath, and of Arphad? where are the gods of Sepharvaim? and have they delivered Samaria out of my hand? Who are they among all the gods of these lands, that have delivered their land out of my hand, that the Lord should deliver Jerusalem out of my hand?" Isa. xxxvi. 18–20. Nebuchadnezzar seems to have reasoned in a similar manner, and with a degree of vain boasting that strongly resembled this, calling their attention to the certain destruction which awaited them if they did not comply with his demand.

16. *Shadrach, Meshach, and Abed-nego answered and said to the king.* They appear to have answered promptly, and without hesitation, showing that they had carefully considered the subject, and that with them it was a matter of settled and intelligent principle. But they did it in a respectful manner, though they were firm. They neither reviled the monarch nor his gods. They used no reproachful words respecting the image which he had set up, or any of the idols which he worshipped. Nor did they complain of his injustice or severity. They calmly looked at their own duty, and resolved to do it, leaving the consequences with the God whom they worshipped. ¶ *We are not careful to answer thee in this matter.* The word rendered *careful* (חַשְׁחִין) means, according to Gesenius, *to be needed* or *necessary;* then, *to have need.* The Vulgate renders it, *non oportet nos*—it does not behove us; it is not needful for us. So the Greek, οὐ χρείαν ἔχομεν —we have no need. So Luther, *Es ist Nicht noth*—there is no necessity. The

17 If it be *so*, our God, whom *a* we serve, is able to deliver us from the burning fiery furnace; and he will deliver *us* out of thy hand, O king.

a Psa. 121. 5, 7; Acts 27. 23, 25.

18 But if not,*b* be it known unto thee, O king, that we will not serve thy *c* gods, nor worship the golden image which thou hast set up.

b Job 13. 15; Acts 4. 19.
c Ex. 20. 3–5; Lev. 19. 4

meaning therefore is, that it was not *necessary* that they should reply to the king on that point; they would not give themselves trouble or solicitude to do it. They had made up their minds, and, whatever was the result, they could not worship the image which he had set up, or the gods whom he adored. They felt that there was no necessity for stating the reasons why they could not do this. Perhaps they thought that argument in their case was improper. It became them to do their duty, and to leave the event with God. They had no need to go into an extended vindication of their conduct, for it might be presumed that their principles of conduct were well known. The *state of mind*, therefore, which is indicated by this passage, is that their minds were made up; that their principles were settled and well understood; that they had come to the deliberate determination, as a matter of conscience, not to yield obedience to the command; that the result could not be modified by any statement which they could make, or by any argument in the case; and that, therefore, they were not anxious about the result, but calmly committed the whole cause to God.

17. *If it be* so. Chald., אֵזְרַי הֵן — *so it is*. That is, "this is true, that the God whom we serve can save us." The idea is not, as would seem in our translation, "if we are to be cast into the furnace," but the mind is turned on the fact that the God whom they served could save them. Coverdale renders this whole passage, "O Nebuchadnezzar, we ought not to consent unto thee in this matter, for why? our God whom we serve is able to keep us," &c. ¶ *Our God, whom we serve*. Gr., "our God in the heavens, whom we serve." This was a distinct avowal that they were the servants of the true God, and they were not ashamed to avow it, whatever might be the consequences.

¶ *Is able to deliver us from the burning fiery furnace*. This was evidently said in reply to the question asked by the king (ver. 15), "Who is that God that shall deliver you out of my hands?" They were sure that the God whom they worshipped was able, if he should choose to do it, to save them from death. In what way they supposed he could save them is not expressed. Probably it did not occur to them that he would save them in the manner in which he actually did, but they felt that it was entirely within his power to keep them from so horrid a death if he pleased. The state of mind indicated in this verse is that of *entire confidence in God*. Their answer showed (*a*) that they had no doubt of his *ability* to save them if he pleased; (*b*) that they believed he would do what was best in the case; and (*c*) that they were entirely willing to commit the whole case into his hands to dispose of it as he chose. Comp. Isa. xliii. 2.

18. *But if not*. That is, "if he should *not* deliver us; if it should *not* occur that he would protect us, and save us from that heated oven: whatever may be the result in regard to us, our determination is settled." ¶ *Be it known unto thee, O king, that we will not serve thy gods*, &c. This answer is firm and noble. It showed that their minds were made up, and that it was with them a matter of *principle* not to worship false gods. The state of mind which is denoted by this verse is that of a determination to do their duty, whatever might be the consequences. The attention was fixed on what was *right*, not on what would be the result. The sole question which was asked was, what *ought* to be done in the case; and they had no concern about what would follow. True religion is a determined purpose to do right, and not to do wrong, whatever may be the consequences in either case. It matters not what follows—wealth or poverty;

19 ¶ Then was Nebuchadnezzar full [1] of fury, [a] and the form of his visage was changed against Shadrach, Meshach, and Abed-nego: *therefore* he spake, and commanded [b] that they should heat the furnace

[1] *filled.*　　*a* Isa. 51. 13 ; Luke 12. 4, 5.
b Prov. 16. 14; 21. 24; 27. 3, 4.

one seven times more than it was wont to be heated.

20 And he commanded the [1] most mighty men that *were* in his army to bind Shadrach, Meshach, and Abed-nego, *and* to cast *them* into the burning fiery furnace.

[1] *mighty of strength.*

---

honour or dishonour; good report or evil report; life or death; the mind is firmly fixed on doing right, and not on doing wrong. This is *the religion of principle;* and when we consider the circumstances of those who made this reply; when we remember their comparative youth, and the few opportunities which they had for instruction in the nature of religion, and that they were captives in a distant land, and that they stood before the most absolute monarch of the earth, with no powerful friends to support them, and with the most horrid kind of death threatening them, we may well admire the grace of that God who could so amply furnish them for such a trial, and love that religion which enabled them to take a stand so noble and so bold.

19. *Then was Nebuchadnezzar full of fury.* Marg., *filled.* He was exceedingly enraged. He evidently was not prepared for a stand so firm and determined on their part, and he did not appreciate their motives, nor was he disposed to yield to them the privilege and right of following their honest convictions. He was deeply excited with anger when the complaint was made that they would not worship his gods (ver. 13), but he had hoped that possibly they had not understood his command, and that what they had done had not been by deliberate purpose (Notes on ver. 14); and he had therefore given them an opportunity to reconsider the subject, and, by complying with his will, to save themselves from the threatened punishment. He now saw, however, that what they had done was done deliberately. He saw that they firmly and intelligently refused to obey, and supposing now that they not only rebelled against his *commands,* but that they disregarded and despised even his *forbearance* (ver. 15), it is not won-

derful that he was filled with wrath. What was with them fixed *principle,* he probably regarded as mere *obstinacy,* and he determined to punish them accordingly. ¶ *And the form of his visage was changed.* As the face usually is when men become excited with anger. We may suppose that up to this point he had evinced self-control; *possibly* he may have shown something like tenderness or compassion. He was indisposed to punish them, and he hoped that they would save him from the necessity of it by complying with his commands. Now he saw that all hope of this was vain, and he gave unrestrained vent to his angry feelings. ¶ *He spake and commanded that they should heat the furnace one seven times more than it was wont to be heated.* Chald., "Than it was *seen* to be heated ;" that is, than it was ever seen. The word *seven* here is a perfect number, and the meaning is, that they should make it as hot as possible. He did not reflect probably that by this command he was contributing to shorten and abridge their sufferings. Wicked men, who are violently opposed to religion, often overdo the matter, and by their haste and impetuosity defeat the very end which they have in view, and even promote the very cause which they wish to destroy.

20. *And he commanded the most mighty men that* were *in his army.* Marg., *mighty of strength.* Chald., "And to mighty men, mighty men of strength who were in his army, he said." He employed the strongest men that could be found for this purpose.

[The two right-hand figures in the annexed sculpture, from Khorsabad, bearing a heavy chariot—a portion of spoil or tribute brought to the Assyrian monarch—represent the *mighty* or strong men who were always in attendance on the person of the king, or in the courts of

21 Then these men were bound in their ¹ coats, their hosen, and their ² hats, and their *other* gar- | ments, and were cast into the midst of the burning fiery furnace.

1 or, *mantles.*   2 or. *turbans.*

the palace, to execute the royal commands. At the present day, and especially in the East, men of gigantic proportions are selected for attendants on kings and nobles.]

¶ *To bind Shadrach,* &c. Gill supposes that they were probably bound together, as the king afterwards was astonished to see them walking separately in the furnace. But there is no certain evidence of this, and in itself it is not very probable. It is well remarked by Gill, however, that there was no need of binding them at all. They would have made no resistance, and there was no danger that they would make any effort to escape.

21. *Then these men were bound in their coats.* They were seized just as they were. No time was given them for preparation; no change was made in their dress. In *autos-da-fé* of later times, it has been usual to array those who were to suffer in a peculiar dress, indicative of the fact that they were heretics, and that they deserved the flame. Here, however, the anger of the king was so great, that no delay was allowed for any such purpose, and they proceeded to execute the sentence upon them just as they were. The fact that they were thus thrown into the furnace, however, only made the miracle the more conspicuous, since not even their garments were affected by the fire. The word rendered *coats,* is in the margin rendered *mantles.* The Chaldee word (כַּרְבְּלָן) means, according to Gesenius, the long and wide pantaloons which are worn by the Orientals, from כַּרְבֵּל *sarbel,*

to cover. The Greek word used in the translation is derived from this—σαράβαρα—and the word σαρβαρίδες is still used in modern Greek. The Chaldee word is used only in this chapter. The Vulgate renders this, *cum braccis suis* —hence the word *breeches,* and *brogues.* The garment referred to, therefore, seems rather to be that which covered the lower part of their person than either a coat or mantle. ¶ *Their hosen.* This word was evidently designed by our translators to denote drawers, or trousers—not stockings, for that was the common meaning of the word when the translation was made. It is not probable that the word is designed to denote *stockings,* as they are not commonly worn in the East. Harmer supposes that the word here used means properly *a hammer,* and that the reference is to a hammer that was carried as a symbol of office, and he refers in illustration of this to the plates of Sir John Chardin of carvings found in the ruins of Persepolis, among which a man is represented with a hammer or mallet in each hand. He supposes that this was some symbol of office. The more common and just representation, however, is to regard this as referring to an article of dress. The Chaldee word (פַּטִּישׁ *pattish*) is from פַּטַשׁ *patash,* to break, to hammer (πατάσσω); to spread out, to expand; and the noun means (1) a ham-

22 Therefore because the king's commandment [1] was urgent, and the furnace exceeding hot, the flame [2] of the fire slew those *a* men

23 And these three men, Shadrach, Meshach, and Abed-nego, that took up Shadrach, Meshach, and Abed-nego.

1 *word.*   2 *or, spark.*   *a* ch. 6. 24.

mer; Isa. xli. 7; Jer. xxiii. 29; l. 23; and (2) a garment, probably with the idea of its being *spread out*, and perhaps referring to a tunic or under-garment. Compare Gesenius on the word. The Greek is, τιάραις, and so the Latin Vulgate, *tiaris:* the *tiara*, or covering for the head, turban. The probable reference, however, is to the under-garment worn by the Orientals; the tunic, not a little resembling a shirt with us. ¶ *And their hats.* Marg., or *turbans.* The Chaldee word (כַּרְבְּלָא) is rendered by Gesenius *mantle, pallium.* So the version called the "Breeches" Bible, renders it *clokes.* Coverdale renders it *shoes,* and so the Vulgate, *calceamentis, sandals;* and the Greek, περικνημίσιν, greaves, or a garment inclosing the lower limbs; pantaloons. There is

certainly no reason for rendering the word *hats*—as hats were then unknown; nor is there any evidence that it refers to a turban. Buxtorf (*Chald. Lex.*) regards it as meaning a garment, particularly an outer garment, a cloak, and this is probably the correct idea. We should then have in these three words the principal articles of dress in which the Orientals appear, as is shown by the preceding engraving, and from the ruins of Persepolis—the large and loose trou-

sers; the tunic, or inner garment; and the outer garment, or cloak, that was commonly thrown over all. ¶ *And their other garments.* Whatever they had on, whether turban, belt, sandals, &c.

22. *Therefore because the king's commandment was urgent.* Marg., as in Chald., *word.* The meaning is, that the king would admit of no delay; he urged on the execution of his will, even at the imminent peril of those who were intrusted with the execution of his command. ¶ *And the furnace exceeding hot.* Probably so as to send out the flame so far as to render the approach to it dangerous. The urgency of the king would not admit of any arrangements, even if there could have been any, by which the approach to it would be safe. ¶ *The flame of the fire slew those men.* Marg., as in Chald., *spark.* The meaning is, what the fire threw out—the blaze, the heat. Nothing can be more probable than this. It was necessary to approach to the very mouth of the furnace in order to cast them in, and it is very conceivable that a heated furnace would belch forth such flames, or throw out such an amount of heat, that this could not be done but at the peril of life. The Chaldee word rendered *slew* here, means *killed.* It does not mean merely that they were overcome with the heat, but that they actually died. To expose these men thus to death was an act of great cruelty, but we are to remember how absolute is the character of an Oriental despot, and how much enraged this king was, and how regardless such a man would be of any effects on others in the execution of his own will.

23. *And these three men—fell down bound,* &c. That is, the flame did not loosen the cords by which they had been fastened. The fact that they were seen to fall into the furnace *bound,* made the miracle the more remarkable that they should be seen walking loose in the midst of the fire.

In the Septuagint, Syriac, Arabic,

fell down bound into the midst of the burning fiery furnace.

24 Then Nebuchadnezzar the king was astonied, and rose up in haste, *and* spake, and said unto his counsellors, [1] Did not we cast three

1 or, *governors.*

men bound into the midst of the fire? They answered and said unto the king, True, O king.

25 He answered and said, Lo, I see four men loose, walking *a* in the midst of the fire, and [2] they have

a Isa. 43. 2.   2 *there is no hurt in them.*

and Latin Vulgate, there follow in this place sixty - eight verses, containing "The Song of the Three Holy Children." This is not in the Chaldee, and its origin is unknown. It is with entire propriety placed in the Apocrypha, as being no part of the inspired canon. With some things that are improbable and absurd, the "song" contains many things that are beautiful, and that would be highly appropriate if a song had been uttered at all in the furnace.

24. *Then Nebuchadnezzar the king was astonied.* The word *astonied,* which occurs several times in our translation (Ezra ix. 3; Job xvii. 8; xviii. 20; Ezek. iv. 17; Dan. iii. 24; iv. 19; v. 9), is but another form for *astonished,* and expresses wonder or amazement. The reasons of the wonder here were that the men who were bound when cast into the furnace were seen alive, and walking unbound; that to them a fourth person was added, walking with them; and that the fourth had the appearance of a Divine personage. It would seem from this, that the furnace was so made that one could conveniently see into it, and also that the king remained near to it to witness the result of the execution of his own order. ¶ *And rose up in haste.* He would naturally express his surprise to his counsellors, and ask an explanation of the remarkable occurrence which he witnessed. ¶ *And spake, and said unto his counsellors.* Marg., *governors.* The word used (הַדָּבְרִין) occurs only here and in ver. 27; ch. iv. 36; vi. 7. It is rendered *counsellors* in each case. The Vulgate renders it *optimatibus;* the LXX. μεγιστᾶσιν — his nobles, or distinguished men. The word would seem to mean those who were authorized to *speak* (from דָּבַר); that is, those authorized to give counsel; ministers of state, viziers, cabinet counsellors. ¶ *Did not we cast three men bound,* &c.

The emphasis here is on the words *three,* and *bound.* It was now a matter of astonishment that there were *four,* and that they were all *loose.* It is not to be supposed that Nebuchadnezzar had any doubt on this subject, or that his recollection had so soon failed him, but this manner of introducing the subject is adopted in order to fix the attention strongly on the fact to which he was about to call their attention, and which was to him so much a matter of surprise.

25. *He answered and said, Lo, I see four men loose.* From the fact that he saw these men now loose, and that this filled him with so much surprise, it may be presumed that they had been bound with something that was not combustible—with some sort of fetters or chains. In that case it would be a matter of surprise that they should be *loose,* even though they could survive the action of the fire. The *fourth* personage now so mysteriously added to their number, it is evident, assumed the appearance of *a man,* and not the appearance of a celestial being, though it was the aspect of a man so noble and majestic that he deserved to be called a son of God. ¶ *Walking in the midst of the fire.* The furnace, therefore, was large, so that those who were in it could walk about. The vision must have been sublime; and it is a beautiful image of the children of God often walking unhurt amidst dangers, safe beneath the Divine protection. ¶ *And they have no hurt.* Marg., *There is no hurt in them.* They walk unharmed amidst the flames. Of course the king judged in this only from appearances, but the result (ver. 27) showed that it was really so. ¶ *And the form of the fourth.* Chaldee, רֵוֵהּ—*his appearance* (from רָאָה —*to see*); that is, he *seemed* to be a son of God; he *looked* like a son of God. The word does not refer to anything

no hurt; and the form of the fourth is like the son *a* of God.

special or peculiar in his *form* or *figure*, but it may be supposed to denote something that was noble or majestic in his mien; something in his countenance and demeanour that declared him to be of heavenly origin. ¶ *Like the son of God.* There are two inquiries which arise in regard to this expression: one is, what was the idea denoted by the phrase as used by the king, or who did he take this personage to be? the other, who he actually was? In regard to the former inquiry, it may be observed, that there is no evidence that the king referred to him to whom this title is so frequently applied in the New Testament, the Lord Jesus Christ. This is clear (1) because there is no reason to believe that the king had *any* knowledge whatever that there would be on earth one to whom this title might be appropriately given; (2) there is no evidence that the title was then commonly given to the Messiah by the Jews, or, if it was, that the king of Babylon was so versed in Jewish theology as to be acquainted with it; and (3) the language which he uses does not necessarily imply that, even *if* he were acquainted with the fact that there was a prevailing expectation that such a being would appear on the earth, he designed so to use it. The insertion of the article "*the*," which is not in the Chaldee, gives a different impression from what the original would if literally interpreted. There is nothing in the Chaldee to limit it to *any* "son of God," or to designate any one to whom that term could be applied as peculiarly intended. It would seem probable that our translators meant to convey the idea that "*the* Son of God" peculiarly was intended, and doubtless they regarded this as one of his appearances to men before his incarnation; but it is clear that no such conception entered into the mind of the king of Babylon. The Chaldee is simply, דָּמֵה לְבַר־אֱלָהִין —"like to *a* son of God," or to a son of the *gods*—as the word אֱלָהִין *Elohin* (Chald.), or *Elohim* (Heb.), though often, and indeed usually applied to the true God, is in the plural number, and in the mouth of a heathen would properly be used to denote the gods that he worshipped. The article is not prefixed to the word "son," and the language would apply to any one who might properly be called *a* son of God. The Vulgate has literally rendered it, "like to *a* son of God"—*similis filio Dei;* the Greek in the same way — ὁμοία υἱῷ θεοῦ; the Syriac is like the Chaldee; Castellio renders it, *quartus formam habet Deo nati similem*—"the fourth has a form resembling one born of God;" Coverdale "the fourth is like an angel to look upon;" Luther, more definitely, und der vierte ist gleich, als wäre er *ein* Sohn der Götter—"and the fourth as if he might be *a* son of the gods." It is clear that the authors of none of the other versions had the idea which our translators supposed to be conveyed by the text, and which implies that the Babylonian monarch *supposed* that the person whom he saw was the one who afterwards became incarnate for our redemption. In accordance with the common well-known usage of the word *son* in the Hebrew and Chaldee languages, it would denote any one who had *a resemblance* to another, and would be applied to any being who was of a majestic or dignified appearance, and who seemed worthy to be ranked among the gods. It was usual among the heathen to suppose that the gods often appeared in a human form, and probably Nebuchadnezzar regarded this as some such celestial appearance. If it be supposed that he regarded it as some manifestation connected with the *Hebrew* form of religion, the most that would probably occur to him would be, that it was some *angelic* being appearing now for the protection of these worshippers of Jehovah. But a second inquiry, and one that is not so easily answered, in regard to this mysterious personage, arises. Who in fact *was* this being that appeared in the furnace for the protection of these three persecuted men? Was it an angel, or was it the second person of the Trinity, *the* Son of God? That this was the Son of

God—the second person of the Trinity, who afterwards became incarnate, has been quite a common opinion of expositors. So it was held by Tertullian, by Augustine, and by Hilary, among the fathers; and so it has been held by Gill, Clarius, and others, among the moderns. Of those who have maintained that it was Christ, some have supposed that Nebuchadnezzar had been made acquainted with the belief of the Hebrews in regard to the Messiah; others, that he spoke under the influence of the Holy Spirit, without being fully aware of what his words imported, as Caiaphas, Saul, Pilate, and others have done.—Poole's *Synopsis.* The Jewish writers Jarchi, Saadias, and Jacchiades suppose that it was an angel, called a son of God, in accordance with the usual custom in the Scriptures. That this latter is the correct opinion, will appear evident, though there cannot be exact certainty, from the following considerations: (1.) The language used implies necessarily nothing more. Though it *might* indeed be applicable to the Messiah—the second person of the Trinity, if it could be determined from other sources that it was he, yet there is nothing in the language which necessarily suggests this. (2.) In the explanation of the matter by Nebuchadnezzar himself (ver. 28), he understood it to be an angel—"Blessed be the God of Shadrach, &c., *who hath sent his angel,*" &c. This shows that he had had no other view of the subject, and that he had no higher knowledge in the case than to suppose that he was an angel of God. The knowledge of the existence of angels was so common among the ancients, that there is no improbability in supposing that Nebuchadnezzar was sufficiently instructed on this point to know that they were sent for the protection of the good. (3.) The belief that it was an angel accords with what we find elsewhere in this book (comp. ch. vi. 22; vii. 10; ix. 21), and in other places in the sacred Scriptures, respecting their being employed to protect and defend the children of God. Compare Psa. xxxiv. 7; xci. 11, 12; Matth. xviii. 10; Luke xvi. 22; Heb. i. 14. (4.) It may be added, that it should not be supposed that it was the Son of God in the peculiar sense of that term without positive evidence, and such evidence does not exist. Indeed there is scarcely a probability that it was so. If the Redeemer appeared on this occasion, it cannot be explained why, in a case equally important and perilous, he did not appear to Daniel when cast into the lions' den (ch. vi. 22); and as Daniel then attributed his deliverance to the intervention of an angel, there is every reason why the same explanation should be given of this passage. As to the probability that an angel would be employed on an occasion like this, it may be observed, that it is in accordance with the uniform representation of the Scriptures, and with what we know to be a great law of the universe. The weak, the feeble, and those who are in danger are protected by those who are strong; and there is, in itself, no more improbability in the supposition that an *angel* would be employed to work a miracle than there is that a *man* would be. We are not to suppose that the angel was able to prevent the usual effect of fire by any natural strength of his own. The miracle in this case, like all other miracles, was wrought by the power of God. At the same time, the presence of the angel would be a pledge of the Divine protection; would be an assurance that the effect produced was not from any natural cause; would furnish an easy explanation of so remarkable an occurrence; and, perhaps more than all, would impress the Babylonian monarch and his court with some just views of the Divine nature, and with the truth of the religion which was professed by those whom he had cast into the flames. As to the probability that a miracle would be wrought on an occasion like this, it may be remarked that a more appropriate occasion for working a miracle could scarcely be conceived. At a time when the true religion was persecuted; at the court of the most powerful heathen monarch in the world; when the temple at Jerusalem was destroyed, and the fires on the altars had been put out, and the people of God were exiles in a distant land, nothing was more probable than that God would give to his people some

26 ¶ Then Nebuchadnezzar came near to the [1] mouth of the burning fiery furnace, *and* spake, and said, Shadrach, Meshach, and Abednego, ye *a* servants of the most high *b* God, come forth, and come *hither.* Then Shadrach, Meshach, and Abed-nego, came forth of the midst of the fire.

1 *door.*　　*a* Gal. 1. 10.　　*b* Gen. 14. 18.

27 And the princes, governors, and captains, and the king's counsellors, being gathered together, saw these men, upon whose bodies the fire had *c* no power, nor was a hair of their head singed, neither were their coats changed, nor the smell of fire had passed on them.

28 *Then* Nebuchadnezzar spake,

c Isa. 43. 2; Heb. 11. 34.

---

manifest tokens of his presence, and some striking confirmation of the truth of his religion. There has perhaps never been an occasion when we should more certainly expect the evidences of the Divine interposition than during the exile of his people in Babylon; and during their long captivity there is it not easy to conceive of an occasion on which such an interposition would be more likely to occur than when, in the very presence of the monarch and his court, three youths of eminent devotedness to the cause of God were cast into a burning furnace, *because* they steadfastly refused to dishonour him.

26. *Then Nebuchadnezzar came near to the mouth,* &c. Marg., door. The Chaldee word means door, gate, entrance. The *form* of the furnace is unknown. There was a place, however, through which the fuel was cast into it, and this is doubtless intended by the word *door* or *mouth* here used. ¶ *Ye servants of the most high God.* They had professed to be his servants; he now saw that they were acknowledged as such. The phrase "most high God" implies that he regarded him as supreme over all other gods, though it is probable that he still retained his belief in the existence of inferior divinities. It was much, however, to secure the acknowledgment of the monarch of the capital of the heathen world, that the God whom they adored was supreme. The phrase "most high God" is not often employed in the Scriptures, but in every instance it is used as an appellation of the true God. ¶ *Come forth, and come* hither. The *reasons* which seem to have influenced this singular monarch to recal the sentence passed on them, and to attempt to punish them no further, seem to have been, that he

had some remains of conscience; that he was accustomed to pay respect to what *he* regarded as God; and that he now saw evidence that a *true* God was there.

27. *And the princes, governors, and captains.* Notes, verse 3. ¶ *And the king's counsellors.* Notes, verse 24. ¶ *Being gathered together, saw these men.* There could be no mistake about the reality of the miracle. They came out as they were cast in. There could have been no trick, no art, no legerdemain, by which they could have been preserved and restored. If the *facts* occurred as they are stated here, then there can be no doubt that this was a real miracle. ¶ *Upon whose bodies the fire had no power.* That is, the usual power of fire on the human body was prevented. ¶ *Nor was a hair of their head singed.* That which would be most likely to have burned. The design is to show that the fire had produced absolutely no effect on them. ¶ *Neither were their coats changed.* On the word coats, see Notes on ver. 21. The word *changed* means that there was no change caused by the fire either in their colour or their texture. ¶ *Nor the smell of fire had passed on them.* Not the slightest effect had been produced by the fire; not even so much as to occasion the smell caused by fire when cloth is singed or burned. Perhaps, however, sulphur or pitch had been used in heating the furnace; and the idea may be, that their preservation had been · so entire, that not even the smell of the smoke caused by those combustibles could be perceived.

28. Then *Nebuchadnezzar spake, and said, Blessed* be *the God of Shadrach,* &c. On the characteristic of mind thus evinced by this monarch, see the Notes and practical remarks on ch. ii. 46, 47.

and said, Blessed *be* the God of Shadrach, Meshach, and Abednego, who hath sent his angel, *ᵃ* and delivered his servants that trusted in *ᵇ* him, and have changed the king's word, and yielded their *ᶜ*

a Gen. 19. 15,16; Ps. 34. 7, 8; 103. 20; Heb. 1.14.
　　b ch. 6. 22, 23; Jer. 17. 7.
　c Rom. 12. 1; Heb. 11. 37.

¶ *Who hath sent his angel.* This proves that the king regarded this mysterious fourth personage as an angel, and that he used the phrase (ver. 25) " is like the son of God " only in that sense. That an angel should be employed on an embassage of this kind, we have seen, is in accordance with the current statements of the Scriptures. Comp. *Excursus I.* to Prof. Stuart *on the Apocalypse.* See also Luke i. 11–20, 26–38 ; Matt. i. 20, 21 : ii. 13, 19, 20 ; iv. 11 ; xviii. 10 ; Acts xii. 7–15 ; Gen. xxxii. 1, 2 ; 2 Ki. vi. 17 ; Ex. xiv. 19 ; xxiii. 20 ; xxxiii. 2 ; Numb. xx. 16; Josh. v. 13 ; Is. lxiii. 9; Dan. x. 5–13, 20, 21 ; xii. 1. ¶ *And have changed the king's word.* That is, his purpose or command. Their conduct, and the Divine protection in consequence of their conduct, had had the effect wholly to change his purpose towards them. He had resolved to destroy them ; he now resolved to honour them. This is referred to by the monarch himself as a remarkable result, as indeed it was—that an Eastern despot, who had resolved on the signal punishment of any of his subjects, should be so entirely changed in his purposes towards them. ¶ *And yielded their bodies.* The Greek adds here **ἐις πυρ**—" to the fire." So the Arabic. This is doubtless the sense of the passage. The meaning is, that rather than bow down to worship gods which they regarded as no gods ; rather than violate their consciences, and do wrong, they had preferred to be cast into the flames, committing themselves to the protection of God. It is implied here that they had done this voluntarily, and that they might easily have avoided it if they had chosen to obey the king. He had given them time to deliberate on the subject (vers.14, 15), and he knew that they had resolved to pursue the course which they did from principle, no matter what might be the

DANIEL.

bodies, that they might not serve nor worship any god, except their own God.

29 Therefore ¹I make a decree, That *ᵈ* every people, nation, and language, which speak any ²thing

1 *a decree is made by me.*　*d* ch. 6. 26, 27.
2 *error.*

results (vers. 16–18). This strength of principle—this obedience to the dictates of conscience—this determination not to do wrong at any hazard—he could not but respect; and this is a remarkable instance to show that a firm and steady course in doing what is right *will* command the respect of even wicked men. This monarch, with all his pride, and haughtiness, and tyranny, had not a few generous qualities, and some of the finest illustrations of human nature were furnished by him. ¶ *That they might not serve nor worship any god, except their own God.* They gave up their bodies to the flame rather than do this.

29. *Therefore I make a decree.* Marg., *A decree is made by me.* Chald., " And from me a decree is laid down," or enacted. This Chaldee word (טְעֵם) means, properly, *taste, flavour;* then *judgment,* the power of *discerning*—apparently as of one who can judge of *wine,* &c., by the taste ; then the sentence, the decree which is consequent on an act of judging—always retaining the idea that the determination or decree is based on a conception of the true merits of the case. The decree in this case was not designed to be regarded as arbitrary, but as being founded on what was right and proper. He had seen evidence that the God whom these three youths worshipped was a true God, and was able to protect those who trusted in him; and regarding him as a real God, he made this proclamation, that respect should be shown to him throughout his extended realm. ¶ *That every people, nation, and language.* This decree is in accordance with the usual style of an Oriental monarch. It was, however, a fact that the empire of Nebuchadnezzar extended over nearly all of the then known world. ¶ *Which speak any thing amiss.* Marg., *error.* The Chaldee word

P

amiss against the God of Shadrach, Meshach, and Abed-nego, shall be cut [1] in pieces, [a] and their houses shall be made a dunghill: because

1 *made.*   *a* ch. 2. 5.

there is no other god that can deliver after this sort.

30 Then the king [2] promoted Shadrach, Meshach, and Abed-nego, in the province of Babylon.

2 *made to prosper.*

(שָׁלוּ) means *error, wrong*, and it refers here to anything that would be fitted to lead the minds of men astray in regard to the true character of the God whom these persons worshipped. The Vulgate renders it *blasphemy.* So also it is rendered in the Greek, βλασφημίαν. The intention was, that their God was to be acknowledged as a God of eminent power and rank. It does not appear that Nebuchadnezzar meant that he should be regarded as the *only* true God, but he was willing, in accordance with the prevailing notions of idolatry, that he should take his place among *the* gods, and a most honoured place. ¶*Shall*

be cut in pieces. Marg., *made.* This was a species of punishment that was common in many ancient nations. — Gesenius.

[Death by strokes with the sword, or, literally, by hewing in pieces, is still in use in China and in Abyssinia, as we learn from Bruce. The sculpture shown in the engraving is supposed by some to refer only to the breaking up of an idol, but the balance of probabilities is in favour of its being an Assyrian execution. The mutilated figure has none of the attributes of a god, and differs not greatly in costume and appearance from the others. This is one of the sculptures from Khorsabad.]

¶*And their houses shall be made a dunghill.* Comp. 2 Kings x. 27. The idea is, that the utmost possible dishonour and contempt should be placed on their houses, by devoting them to the most vile and offensive uses. ¶*Because there is no other god that can deliver after this sort.* He does not say that there was no other god at all, for his mind had not yet reached this conclusion, but there was no other one who had equal power with the God of the Hebrews. He had seen a manifestation of his power in the preservation of the three Hebrews, such as no other god had ever exhibited, and he was willing to admit that in this respect he surpassed all other divinities.

30. *Then the king promoted Shadrach,*

&c. Marg., *made to prosper.* The Chaldee means no more than *made to prosper.* Whether he restored them to their former places, or to higher honours, does not appear. There would be, however, nothing inconsistent with his usual course in supposing that he raised them to more exalted stations. ¶*In the province of Babylon.* See Notes on ch. ii. 49. The Greek and the Arabic add here, "And he counted them worthy to preside over all the Jews that were in his kingdom." But nothing of this is found in the Chaldee, and it is not known by whom this addition was made.

In the Vulgate and the Greek versions, and in some of the critical editions of the Hebrew Scriptures (Walton, Hahn, &c.), the three first verses of the following chapter are subjoined to this. It is well known that the divisions of the chapters are of no authority, but it is clear that these verses belong more appropriately to the following chapter than to this, as the reason there assigned by the monarch for the proclamation is what occurred to himself (ver. 2), rather than what he had witnessed in others. The division, therefore, which is made in our common version of the Bible, and in the Syriac and the Arabic, is the correct one.

PRACTICAL REMARKS.

I. The instance recorded in this chapter (vers. 1–7) is not improbably the first case which ever occurred in the world of an attempt to produce *conformity* in idolatrous worship by penal statute. It has, however, been abundantly imitated since, alike in the heathen and in the nominally Christian world. There are no portions of history more interesting than those which describe the progress of religious liberty ; the various steps which have been taken to reach the result which has now been arrived at, and to settle the principles which are now regarded as the true ones. Between the views which were formerly entertained, and which are still entertained in many countries, and those which constitute the Protestant notions on the subject, there is a greater difference than there is, in regard to civil rights, between the views which prevail under an Oriental despotism, and the most enlarged and enlightened notions of civil freedom. The views which have prevailed on the subject are the following :—1. The *general* doctrine among the heathen has been, that there were many gods in heaven and earth, and that all were entitled to reverence. One nation was supposed to have as good a right to worship its own gods as another, and it was regarded as at least an act of courtesy to show respect to the gods that any nation adored, in the same way as respect would be shown to

the sovereigns who presided over them. Hence the gods of all nations could be consistently introduced into the Pantheon at Rome ; hence there were few attempts to *proselyte* among the heathen ; and hence it was not common to *persecute* those who worshipped other gods. Persecution of idolaters *by* those who were idolaters was, therefore, rarely known among the heathen, and *toleration* was not contrary to the views which prevailed, provided the gods of the country were recognized. In ancient Chaldea, Assyria, Greece, and Rome, in the earliest ages, persecution was rare, and the toleration of other forms of religion was usual. 2. The views which have prevailed leading to persecution, and which are a violation, as we suppose, of all just notions of liberty on the subject of religion, are the following : (*a*) Those among the heathen which, as in the case of Nebuchadnezzar, require *all* to worship a particular god that should be set up. In such a case, it is clear that while all who were *idolaters*, and who supposed that *all* the gods worshipped by others should be respected, could render homage ; it is also clear that those who regarded *all* idols as false gods, and believed that *none* of them ought to be worshipped, could *not* comply with the command. Such was the case with the Jews who were in Babylon (vers. 8–18) ; for supposing that there was but *one* God, it was plain that they could not render homage to any other. While, therefore, every idolater could render homage to *any* idol, the Hebrew could render homage to *none*. (*b*) The views among the heathen *prohibiting* the exercise of a certain kind of religion. According to the prevailing views, no mode of religion could be tolerated which would maintain that *all* the gods that were worshipped were false. Religion was supposed to be identified with the best interests of the state, and was recognized by the laws, and protected by the laws. To deny the claim, therefore, of any and of all the gods that were worshipped; to maintain that all were false alike; to call on men to forsake their idols, and to embrace a new religion—all this was regarded as an attack on the state. This was the attitude which Christianity assumed towards the religions of the Roman empire, and it was this which led to the fiery persecutions which prevailed there. While Rome could consistently tolerate any form of idolatry that would recognize the religion established by the state, it could not tolerate a system which maintained that *all* idolatry was wrong. It would allow another god to be placed in the Pantheon, but it could not recognize a system which would remove every god from that temple. Christianity, then, made war on the system of idolatry that prevailed in the Roman empire in two respects: in proclaiming a *purer* religion, denouncing all the corruptions which idolatry had engendered, and which it countenanced; and in denying altogether that the gods which were worshipped were true gods—thus arraying itself against the laws, the priesthood, the venerable institutions, and all the passions and prejudices of the people. These views may be thus summed up: (*a*) all the gods worshipped by others were to be recognized; (*b*) new ones might be introduced by authority of the state; (*c*) the gods which the state approved and acknowledged were to be honoured by all; (*d*) if any persons denied their existence, and their claims to homage, they were to be treated as enemies of the state. It was on this last principle that persecutions ever arose under the heathen forms of religion. Infidels, indeed, have been accustomed to charge Christianity with all the persecutions on account of religion, and to

speak in high terms of "the mild tolerance of the ancient heathens;" of "the universal toleration of polytheism;" of "the Roman princes beholding without concern a thousand forms of religion subsisting in peace under their gentle sway."—Gibbon. But it should be remembered that pagan nations required of every citizen conformity to their national idolatries. When this was refused, persecution arose as a matter of course. Stilpo was banished from Athens for affirming that the statue of Minerva in the citadel was no divinity, but only the work of the chisel of Phidias. Protagoras received a similar punishment for this sentence: "Whether there be gods or not, I have nothing to offer." Prodicus, and his pupil Socrates, suffered death for opinions at variance with the established idolatry of Athens. Alcibiades and Æschylus narrowly escaped a like end for a similar cause. Cicero lays it down as a principle of legislation entirely conformable to the laws of the Roman state, that "no man shall have separate gods for himself; and no man shall worship by himself new or foreign gods, unless they have been publicly acknowledged by the laws of the state."—*De Legibus*, ii. 8. Julius Paulus, the Roman civilian, gives the following as a leading feature of the Roman law: "Those who introduced new religions, or such as were unknown in their tendency and nature, by which the minds of men might be agitated, were degraded, if they belonged to the higher ranks, and if they were in a lower state, were punished with death." See M'Ilvaine's *Lectures on the Evidences of Christianity*, pp. 427–429. (*c*) The attempts made to produce conformity in countries where the *Christian* system has prevailed. In such countries, as among the heathen, it has been supposed that religion is an important auxiliary to the purposes of the state, and that it is proper that the state should not only *protect* it, but *regulate* it. It has claimed the right, therefore, to prescribe the form of religion which shall prevail; to require conformity to that, and to punish all who did not conform to the established mode of worship. This attempt to produce conformity has led to most of the persecutions of modern times. 3. The principles which have been settled by the discussions and agitations of past times, and which are recognized in all countries where there are any just views of religious liberty, and which are destined yet to be universally recognized, are the following: (*a*) There is to be, on the subject of religion, perfect liberty to worship God in the manner that shall be most in accordance with the views of the individual himself, provided in doing it he does not interfere with the rights or disturb the worship of others. It is not merely that men are to be *tolerated* in the exercise of their religion—for the word *tolerate* would seem to imply that the state had some right of control in the matter—but the true word to express the idea is *liberty.* (*b*) The state is to *protect* all in the enjoyment of these equal rights. Its *authority* does not go beyond this; its *duty* demands this. These two principles comprise all that is required on the subject of religious liberty. They have been in our world, however, principles of slow growth. They were unknown in Greece—for Socrates died because they were not understood; they were unknown in Rome—for the state claimed the power to determine what gods should be admitted into the Pantheon; they were unknown even in Judea—for a national or state religion was established there; they were unknown in Babylon—for the monarch there claimed the right of enforcing conformity to the national religion; they were unknown in Europe in the middle ages—for all the horrors of the Inquisition grew out of the fact that they were not understood; they are unknown in Turkey, and China, and Persia—for the state regards religion as under its control. The doctrine of entire freedom in religion, of perfect liberty to worship God according to our own views of right, is *the last point which society is to reach in this direction.* It is impossible to conceive that there is to be anything *beyond* this which mankind are to desire in the progress towards the perfection of the social organization; and when this shall be everywhere reached, the affairs of the world will be placed on a permanent footing.

II. In the spirit evinced by the three young men, and the answer which they gave, when accused of not worshipping the image, and when threatened with a horrid death, we have a beautiful illustration of the nature and value *of the religion of principle,* vers. 12–18. To enable us to see the force of this example, and to appreciate its value, we are to remember that these were yet comparatively young men; that they were captives in a distant land; that they had no powerful friends at court; that they had had, compared with what we now have, few advantages of instruction; that they were threatened with a most horrid death; and that they had nothing of a worldly nature to hope for by refusing compliance with the king's commands. This instance is of value to us, because it is not only important *to have religion,* but *to have the best kind of religion;* and it is doubtless in order that we *may* have this, that such examples are set before us in the Scriptures. In regard to this kind of religion, there are three inquiries which would present themselves: On what is it founded? what will it lead us to do? and what is its value? (1.) It is founded mainly on two things—an intelligent view of duty, and fixed principle. (*a*) An intelligent view of duty; an acquaintance with what is right, and what is wrong. These young men had made up their minds intelligently, that it was right to worship God, and that it was wrong to render homage to an idol. This was not *obstinacy.* Obstinacy exists where a man has made up his mind, and resolves to act, without any good reason, or without an intelligent view of what is right or wrong, and where he adheres to his purpose not because it is right, but from the influence of mere *will.* The religion of principle is always found where there is an intelligent view of what is right, and a man can give *a reason* for what he does. (*b*) This religion is founded on a determination to *do* what is right, and *not* to do what is wrong. The question is not what is expedient, or popular, or honourable, or lucrative, or pleasant, but what is right. (2.) What will such a religion lead us to do ? This question may be answered by a reference to the case before us, and it will be found that it will lead us to do three things : (*a*) To do our *duty* without being solicitous or anxious about the results, ver. 16. (*b*) To put confidence in God, feeling that if he pleases he *can* protect us from danger, ver. 17. (*c*) To do our duty, *whatever may be the consequences—whether he protects us or not*, ver. 18. (3.) What is the *value* of this kind of religion ? (*a*) It is the only kind in which there is any fixed and certain standard. If a man regulates his opinions and conduct from expediency, or from respect to the opinions of others, or from feeling, or from popular impulses, there is no standard; there is nothing settled or definite. Now one thing is popular, now another; to-day the feelings may prompt to one thing, to-morrow to another; at one time ex-

pediency will suggest one course, at another a different course. (*b*) It is the only kind of religion on which reliance can be placed. In endeavouring to spread the gospel; to meet the evils which are in the world; to promote the cause of temperance, chastity, liberty, truth, and peace, the only thing on which permanent reliance can be placed is the religion of principle. And (*c*) it is the only religion which is *certainly* genuine. A man may see much poetic beauty in religion; he may have much of the religion of sentiment; he may admire God in the grandeur of his works; he may have warm feelings; easily enkindled on the subject of religion, and may even weep at the foot of the cross in view of the wrongs and woes that the Saviour endured ; he may be impressed with the forms, and pomp, and splendour of gorgeous worship, and still have no genuine repentance for his sins, no saving faith in the Redeemer, no real love to God.

III. We have in this chapter (vers. 19–23) an affecting case of an attempt to *punish* men for holding certain opinions, and for acting in conformity with them. When we read of an instance of persecution like this, it occurs to us to ask the following questions :— What is persecution ? why has it been permitted by God ? and what effects have followed from it ? (1.) What is persecution ? It is pain inflicted, or some loss, or disadvantage in person, family, or office, on account of holding certain opinions. It has had *two* objects : one to *punish* men for holding certain opinions, as if the persecutor had a right to regard this as an offence against the state; and the other a professed view to reclaim those who are made to suffer, and to save their souls. In regard to the *pain* or *suffering* involved in persecution, it is not material what *kind* of pain is inflicted in order to constitute persecution. *Any* bodily suffering; any deprivation of comfort; any exclusion from office; any holding up of one to public reproach; or any form of ridicule, constitutes the essence of persecution. It may be added, that not a few of the inventions most distinguished for inflicting pain, and known as refinements of cruelty, have been originated in times of persecution, and would probably have been unknown if it had not been for the purpose of restraining men from the free exercise of religious opinions. The Inquisition has been most eminent in this; and within the walls of that dreaded institution it is probable that human ingenuity has been exhausted in devising the most refined modes of inflicting torture on the human frame. (2.) Why has this been permitted? Among the reasons why it has been permitted may be the following: (*a*) To show the power and reality of religion. It seemed desirable to subject it to *all kinds* of trial, in order to show that its existence could not be accounted for except on the supposition that it is from God. If men had never been called on to *suffer* on account of religion, it would have been easy for the enemies of religion to allege that there was little evidence that it was genuine, or was of value, for it had never been tried. Comp. Job i. 9–11. As it is, it has been subjected to *every form* of trial which wicked men could devise, and has shown itself to be adapted to meet them all. The work of the martyrs has been well done; and religion in the times of martyrdom has shown itself to be all that it is desirable it should be. (*b*) In order to promote its spread in the world. "The blood of the martyrs" has been "the seed of the church;" and it is probable that religion in past times has owed much of its purity, and of its diffusion, to the fact that it has been persecuted. (*c*) To fit the sufferers for an exalted place in heaven. They who have suffered persecution needed trials as well as others, for *all* Christians need them—and *theirs* came in this form. Some of the most lovely traits of Christian character have been brought out in connection with persecution, and some of the most triumphant exhibitions of preparation for heaven have been made at the stake. (3.) What have been the effects of persecution? (*a*) It has been the *settled* point that the Christian religion cannot be destroyed by persecution. There is no power to be brought against it more mighty than, for example, was that of the Roman empire; and it is impossible to conceive that there should be greater refinements of cruelty than have been employed. (*b*) The effect has been to diffuse the religion which has been persecuted. The manner in which the sufferings inflicted have been endured has shown that there is reality and power in it. It is also a law of human nature to *sympathize* with the wronged and the oppressed, and we insensibly learn to transfer the sympathy which we have for these *persons* to their *opinions*. When we see one who is *wronged*, we soon find our hearts beating in unison with his, and soon find ourselves taking sides with him in everything.

IV. We have in this chapter (vers. 24–27) an instructive illustration of the *protection* which God affords his people in times of trial. These men were thrown into the furnace on account of their obedience to God, and their refusal to do that which they knew he would not approve. The result showed, by a most manifest miracle, that they were right in the course which they took, and their conduct was the occasion of furnishing a most striking proof of the wisdom of trusting in God in the faithful performance of duty, irrespective of consequences. Similar illustrations were furnished in the case of Daniel in the lions' den (ch. vi. 16-22), and of Peter (Acts xii. 1-10). But a question of much interest arises here, which is, What kind of protection may *we* look for now ? (1.) There are numerous *promises* made to the righteous of every age and country. They are not promises indeed of *miraculous* interference, but they are promises of *an* interposition of some kind in their behalf, which will show that "it is not a vain thing to serve God." Among them are those recorded in the following places :—2 Chron. xvi. 9 ; Psa. iv. 3 ; v. 12 ; xv. 1-5 ; xxxvii. 3-10, 17-26, 34-40 ; lviii. 11 ; lxxxiv. 11 ; xcii. 12-15 ; xcvii. 11 ; cxii. 1-5 ; Prov. iii. 3, 4, 31-35 ; x. 2, 3, 6-9, 25-30 ; xiii. 6, 21, 22 ; xiv. 30-34 ; xvi. 7 ; xx. 7 ; xxi. 21 ; Isa. xxxii. 17 ; xxxiii. 15, 16 ; Matt. vi. 33 ; 1 Tim. iv. 8, 9 ; vi. 6 ; 1 Pet. iii. 10-13 ; John xii. 26 ; Exod. xx. 5, 6 ; Psal. ix. 9, 10 ; xxiii. 4 ; xlvi. 1 ; lv. 22 ; Isa. liv. 7, 8 ; Matt. v. 4 ; Job v. 19. (2.) In regard to the *kind* of interposition that we may look for now, or the *nature* of the favours implied in these promises, it may be observed : (*a*) That we are not to look for any *miraculous* interpositions in our favour. (*b*) We are not to expect that there will be on earth an *exact adjustment* of the Divine dealings according to the deserts of all persons, or according to the principles of a *completed* moral government, when there will be a perfect system of rewards and punishments. (*c*) We are not to expect that there will be such manifest and open rewards of obedience, and such direct and constant benefits resulting from religion in this world, as to lead men *merely* from these to serve and worship God. If religion were *always* attended with prosperity ; if the righteous were never persecuted, were never

poor, or were never bereaved, multitudes would be induced to become religious, as many followed the Saviour, not because they saw the miracles, but because they did eat of the loaves and fishes, and were filled : John vi. 26. While, therefore, in the Divine administration here it is proper that there should be so many and so marked interpositions in favour of the good as to show that God is the friend of his people, it is *not* proper that there should be so many that men would be induced to engage in his service for the love of the reward rather than for the sake of the service itself ; because they are to be happy, rather than because they love virtue. It may be expected, therefore, that while the general course of the Divine administration will be in favour of virtue, there may be much intermingled with this that will appear to be of a contrary kind ; much that will be fitted to *test* the faith of the people of God, and to show that they *love* his service for its own sake.

V. We have, in vers. 28-30, a striking instance of the effect which an adherence to principle will produce on the minds of worldly and wicked men. Such men have no *love* for religion, but they can see that a certain course accords with the views which are professedly held, and that it indicates high integrity. They can see that firmness and consistency are worthy of commendation and reward. They can see, as Nebuchadnezzar did in this case, that such a course will secure the Divine favour, and they will be disposed to honour it on that account. For a time, a tortuous course may seem to prosper, but in the end, solid fame, high rewards, honourable offices, and a grateful remembrance after death, follow in the path of strict integrity and unbending virtue.

CHAPTER IV.

§ I.—AUTHENTICITY OF THE CHAPTER.

To the authenticity of this chapter, as to the preceding, objections and difficulties have been urged, sufficient, in the view of the objectors, to destroy its credibility as a historical narrative. Those objections, which may be seen at length in Bertholdt (pp. 70–72, 285–309), Bleek (*Theol. Zeitscrift, Drittes Heft*, 268, *seq.*), and Eichhorn (*Einlei.* iv. 471, *seq.*), relate mainly to two points—those derived from the want of historical proofs to confirm the narrative, and those derived from its alleged intrinsic improbability.

I. The former of these, derived from the want of historic confirmation of the truth of the narrative, are summarily the following:—(1.) That the historical books of the Old Testament give no intimation that these remarkable things happened to Nebuchadnezzar, that he was deranged and driven from his throne, and made to dwell under the open heaven with the beasts of the field—an omission which, it is said, we cannot suppose would have occurred if these things had happened, since the Hebrew writers, on account of the wrongs which Nebuchadnezzar had done to their nation, would have certainly seized on such facts as a demonstration of the Divine displeasure against him. (2.) There is no record of these events among the heathen writers of antiquity; no writer among the Greeks, or other nations, ever having mentioned them. (3.) It is equally remarkable that Josephus, in his narrative of the sickness of Nebuchadnezzar, makes no allusion to any knowledge of this among other nations, and shows that he derived his information only from the sacred books of his own people. (4.) It is acknowledged by Origen and Jerome that they could find no historical grounds for the truth of this account. (5.) If these things had occurred, as here related, they would not have been thus concealed, for the king himself took all possible measures, by the edict referred to in this chapter, to make them known, and to make a permanent record of them. How could it have happened that all knowledge would have been lost if they had thus occurred? (6.) If the edict was lost, how was it ever recovered again? When, and where, and by whom, was it found? If actually issued, it was designed to make the case known throughout the empire. Why did it fail of producing that effect so as not to have been forgotten? If it was lost, how was the event known? And if it was lost, how could it have been recovered and recorded by the author of this book? Comp. Bertholdt, p. 298.

To these objections, it may be replied, (1) that the silence of the historical books of the Old Testament furnishes no well-founded objection to what is said in this chapter, for none of them pretend to bring down the history of Nebuchadnezzar to the close of his life, or to this period of his life. The books of Kings and of Chronicles mention his invasion of the land of Palestine and of Egypt; they record the fact of his carrying away the children of Israel to Babylon, but they do not profess to make any record of what occurred to *him* after that, nor of the close of his life. The second book of Chronicles closes with an account of the removal of the Jews to Babylon, and the carrying away of the sacred vessels of the temple, and the burning of the temple, and the destruction of the city, but does not relate the history of Nebuchadnezzar any farther, 2 Chron. xxxvi. The silence of the book cannot, therefore, be alleged as an argument against anything that may be said to have occurred after that. As the history closes there; as the design was to give a record of Jewish affairs to the carrying away to Babylon, and not a history of Nebuchadnezzar as such, there is no ground of objection furnished by this silence in regard to anything that might be said to have occurred to Nebuchadnezzar subsequently to this in his own kingdom.

(2) In regard to profane writers, also, nothing can be argued as to the improbability of the account mentioned here from their silence on the subject. It is not remarkable that in the few fragments which are found in their writings respecting the kings and empires of the East, an occurrence of this kind should have been omitted. The general worthlessness or want of value of the historical writings of the Greeks in respect to foreign nations, from which we derive most of our knowledge of those nations, is now generally admitted, and is expressly maintained by Niebuhr, and by Schlosser (see Hengstenberg, *Die Authentie des Daniel*, p. 101), and most of these writers make no allusion at all to Nebuchadnezzar. Even Herodotus, who travelled into the East, and who collected all he could of the history of the world, makes no mention whatever of a conqueror so illustrious as Nebuchadnezzar. How could it be expected that when they have omitted all notice of his conquests, of the great events under him, which exerted so important an effect on the world, there should have been a record of an occurrence like that referred to in this chapter —an occurrence that seems to have exerted no influence whatever on the foreign relations of the empire? It is remarkable that Josephus, who searched for all that he could find to illustrate the literature and history of the Chaldees, says (*Ant.* b. x. ch. xi. § 1) that

he could find only the following "histories as all that he had met with concerning this king: Berosus, in the third book of his Chaldaic history; Philostratus, in the history of Judea and of the Phœnicians, who only mentions him in respect to his siege of Tyre; the Indian history of Megasthenes—'Ινδικά—in which the only fact which is mentioned of him is that he plundered Libya and Iberia; and the Persian history of Diocles, in which there occurs but one solitary reference to Nebuchadnezzar." To these he adds, in his work *against Apion* (b. i. 20), a reference to the "Archives of the Phœnicians," in which it is said that "he conquered Syria and Phœnicia." Berosus is the only one who pretends to give any extended account of him. See *Ant.* b. x. ch. xi. § 1. All those authorities mentioned by Josephus, therefore, except Berosus, may be set aside, since they have made no allusion to many undeniable facts in the life of Nebuchadnezzar, and, therefore, the events referred to in this chapter may have occurred, though they have not related them. There remain two authors who have noticed Nebuchadnezzar at greater length, Abydenus and Berosus. Abydenus was a Greek who lived 268 B.C. He wrote, in Greek, a historical account of the Chaldeans, Babylonians, and Assyrians, only a few fragments of which have been preserved by Eusebius, Cyrill, and Syncellus. Berosus was a Chaldean, and was a priest in the temple of Belus, in the time of Alexander, and having learned of the Macedonians the Greek language, he went to Greece, and opened a school of astronomy and astrology in the island of Cos, where his productions acquired for him great fame with the Athenians. Abydenus was his pupil. Berosus wrote three books relative to the history of the Chaldeans, of which only some fragments are preserved in Josephus and Eusebius. As a priest of Belus he possessed every advantage which could be desired for obtaining a knowledge of the Chaldeans, and if his work had been preserved it would doubtless be of great value. Both these writers professedly derived their knowledge from the traditions of the Chaldeans, and both should be regarded as good authority.

Berosus is adduced by Josephus to confirm the truth of the historical records in the Old Testament. He mentions, according to Josephus, the deluge in the time of Noah, and the account of the resting of the ark on one of the mountains of Armenia. He gives a catalogue of the descendants of Noah, and "at length comes down to Nabolassar, who was king of Babylon and of the Chaldeans." He then mentions the expedition of his son, Nabuchodonosor (Nebuchadnezzar), against the Egyptians; the capture of Jerusalem; the burning of the temple; and the removal of the Jews to Babylon. He then mentions the manner in which Nebuchadnezzar succeeded to the throne; the way in which he distributed his captives in various parts of Babylonia; his adorning of the temple of Belus; his re-building the old city of Babylon, and the building of another city on the other side of the river; his adding a new palace to that which his father had built; and the fact that this palace was finished in fifteen days. After these statements respecting his conquests and the magnificence of his capital, Berosus gives the following narrative:—"Nabuchodonosor, after he had begun to build the forementioned wall, fell sick—*ἐμπεσὼν εἰς ἀῤῥωστίαν*—and departed this life—*μετηλλάξατο τὸν βίον*"—[a phrase meaning to die, see Passow on the word *μετάλλασσω*] "when he had reigned forty-three years, whereupon his son,

Evil-Merodach, obtained the kingdom." Josephus *against Apion*, b. i. § 20.

Now this narrative is remarkable, and goes in fact to confirm the statement in Daniel in two respects: (a) It is manifest that Berosus here refers to some sickness in the case of Nebuchadnezzar that was unusual, and that probably preceded, for a considerable time, his death. This appears from the fact, that in the case of the other monarchs whom he mentions in immediate connection with this narrative, no sickness is alluded to as preceding their death. This is the case with respect to Neriglissar and Nabonnedus—successors of Nebuchadnezzar. See Jos. *against Ap.* i. 20. There is no improbability in supposing, that what Berosus here calls *sickness* is the same which is referred to in the chapter before us. Berosus, himself a Chaldean, might not be desirous of stating all the facts about a monarch of his own country so distinguished, and might not be willing to state all that he knew about his being deprived of reason, and about the manner in which he was treated, and yet what occurred to him was so remarkable, and was so well known, that there seemed to be a necessity of alluding to it in some way; and this he did in the most general manner possible. If this were his object, also, he would not be likely to mention the fact that he was restored again to the throne. He would endeavour to make it appear as an ordinary event—a sickness which preceded death—as it *may* have been the fact that he never was wholly restored so far as to be in perfect health. (b) This statement of Berosus accords, in respect to *time*, remarkably with that in Daniel. Both accounts agree that the sickness occurred after he had built Babylon, and towards the close of his reign.

The other author which is referred

to is Abydenus. The record which he makes is preserved by Eusebius, *præp. Evang.* ix. 41, and *Chronicon Armeno-latinum*, I. p. 59, and is in the following words: μετὰ ταῦτα δὲ, λέγεται πρὸς Χαλδαίων, ὡς ἀναβὰς ἐπὶ τὰ βασιλήια, κατασχεθείη θεῷ ὅτεῳ δὴ, φθεγξάμενος δὲ εἶπεν· οὗτος ἐγὼ Ναβουκοδρόσορος, ὦ Βαβυλώνιοι, τὴν μέλλουσαν ὑμῖν προαγγέλλω συμφορὴν, τὴν ὅτε Βῆλος ἐμὸς πρόγονος, ἤ τε βασίλεια Βῆλτις ἀποτρέψαι Μοίρας πεῖσαι ἀσθενοῦσιν· ἥξει Πέρσης ἡμίονος, τοῖσιν ὑμετέροισι δαίμοσι χρεώμενος συμμάχοισιν· ἐπάξει δὲ δουλοσύνην· οὗ δὴ συναίτιος ἔσται Μήδης, τὸ Ἀσσύριον αὔχημα· ὡς εἴθε μιν πρόσθεν ἢ δοῦναι τοὺς πολιήτας, Χάρυβδίν τινα, ἢ θάλασσαν εἰσδεξαμένην, ἀϊστῶσαι πρόρριζον· ἤ μιν ἄλλας ὁδοὺς στραφέντα φέρεσθαι διὰ τῆς ἐρήμου, ἵνα οὔτε ἄστεα, οὔτε πάτος ἀνθρώπων, θῆρες δὲ νόμον ἔχουσι, καὶ ὄρνιθες πλάζονται, ἔν τε πέτρῃσι καὶ χαράδρῃσι μοῦνον ἀλώμενον· ἐμέ τε, πρὶν εἰς νόον βαλίσθαι ταῦτα, τέλεος ἀμείνονος κυρῆσαι. Ὁ μὲν θεσπίσας παραχρῆμα ἠφάνιστο. This passage is so remarkable, that I annex a translation of it, as I find it in Prof. Stuart's work on Daniel, p. 122 : "After these things" [his conquests which the writer had before referred to], "as. it is said by the Chaldeans, having ascended his palace, he was seized by some god, and speaking aloud, he said : 'I, Nebuchadnezzar, O Babylonians, foretell your future calamity, which neither Belus, my ancestor, nor queen Beltis, can persuade the destinies to avert. A *Persian mule* will come, employing your own divinities as his auxiliaries ; and he will impose servitude [upon you]. His coadjutor will be the *Mede*, who is the boast of the Assyrians. Would that, before he places my citizens in such a condition, some Charybdis or gulf might swallow him up with utter destruction ! Or that, turned in a different direction, he might roam in the desert (where are neither cities, nor

footsteps of man, but wild beasts find pasturage, and the birds wander), being there hemmed in by rocks and ravines! May it be my lot to attain to a better end, before such things come into his mind !' Having uttered this prediction, he forthwith disappeared." This passage so strongly resembles the account in Daniel iv., that even Bertholdt (p. 296) admits that it is identical (*identisch*) with it, though he still maintains, that although it refers to mental derangement, it does nothing to confirm the account of his being made to live with wild beasts, eating grass, and being restored again to his throne. The points of *agreement* in the account of Abydenus and that of Daniel are the following : — (1.) The account of Abydenus as Bertholdt admits, refers to mental derangement. Such a mental derangement, and the power of prophecy, were in the view of the ancients closely connected, or were identical, and were believed to be produced by the overpowering influence of the gods on the soul. The rational powers of the soul were supposed to be suspended, and the god took entire possession of the body, and through that communicated the knowledge of future events. Compare Dale, *de Oraculis Ethnicorum*, p. 172. Eusebius, *Chron. Arm.-lat.*, p. 61. In itself considered, moreover, nothing would be more natural than that Nebuchadnezzar, in the malady that came upon him, or when it was coming upon him, would express himself in the manner affirmed by Abydenus respecting the coming of the Persian, and the change that would occur to his own kingdom. If the account in Daniel is true respecting the predictions which he is said to have uttered concerning coming events (ch. ii.), nothing would be more natural than that the mind of the monarch would be filled with the anticipation of these events, and that he would give utterance to his anticipations in a time of mental excitement. (2.) There is a remarkable agreement between Abydenus and Daniel in regard to the *time* and the *place* in which what is said of the king occurred. According to Abydenus, the prophetic ecstasy into which he fell was at the close of all his military expeditions, and occurred in the same place, and in the same circumstances, which are mentioned in the book of Daniel—upon his palace—apparently as he walked upon the roof, or upon some place where he had a clear view of the surrounding city which he had built—*ἀναβὰς ἐπὶ τὰ βασιλήϊα.* (3.) The accounts in Abydenus and in Daniel harmonize so far as they relate to the God by whom what occurred was produced. In Daniel it is attributed to the true God, and not to any of the objects of Chaldean worship. It is remarkable that in Abydenus it is not ascribed to an idol, or to any god worshipped by the Chaldees, but to *God* simply, as to a God that was not known—*κατασχεθείη θεῷ ὅτεῳ δή.* It would seem from this that even the Chaldee tradition did not attribute what was said by Nebuchadnezzar, or what occurred to him, to any of the gods worshipped in Babylon, but to a foreign god, or to one whom they were not accustomed to worship. (4.) In the language which Nebuchadnezzar is reported by Abydenus to have used respecting the return of the Persian king after his conquest, there is a remarkable resemblance to what is said in Daniel, showing that, though the language is applied to different things in Daniel and in Abydenus, it had a common origin. Thus, in the prophecy of Nebuchadnezzar, as reported by Abydenus, it is said, "may he, returning through other ways, be borne through the desert where there are no cities, where

there is no path for men, where wild beasts graze, and the fowls live, wandering about in the midst of rocks and caves." These considerations show that the Chaldean traditions strongly corroborate the account here; or, that there are things in these traditions which cannot be accounted for except on the supposition of the truth of some such occurrence as that which is here stated in Daniel. The sum of the evidence from history is (*a*) that very few things are known of this monarch from profane history; (*b*) that there is nothing in what *is* known of him which makes what is here stated improbable; (*c*) that there *are* things related of him which harmonize with what is here affirmed; and (*d*) that there are traditions which can be best explained by some such supposition as that the record in this chapter is true.

As to the objection that if the edict was promulgated it would not be likely to be lost, or the memory of it fade away, it is sufficient to observe that almost *all* of the edicts, the laws, and the statutes of the Assyrian and Chaldean princes have perished with all the other records of their history, and almost all the facts pertaining to the personal or the public history of these monarchs are now unknown. It cannot be believed that the few fragments which we now have of their writings are all that were ever composed, and in the thing itself there is no more improbability that *this* edict should be lost than any other, or that though it may have been kept by a Hebrew residing among them, it should not have been retained by the Chaldeans themselves. As to the question which has been asked, if this were lost how it could have been recovered again, it is sufficient to remark that, for anything that appears, it never *was* lost in the sense that no one had it in his possession. It would undoubtedly come into the hands of Daniel if he were, according to the account in his book, then in Babylon ; and it is not probable that so remarkable a document would be suffered by *him* to be lost. The fact that it was preserved by him is all that is needful to answer the questions on that point. It *may* have been swept away with other matters in the ruin that came upon the Chaldean records in their own country ; it has been preserved where it was most important that it should be preserved—in a book where it would be to all ages, and in all lands, a signal proof that God reigns over kings, and that he has power to humble and abase the proud.

II. There is a second class of objections to the credibility of the account in this chapter quite distinct from that just noticed. They are based on what is alleged to be the intrinsic *improbability* that the things which are said to have occurred to Nebuchadnezzar should have happened. It cannot be alleged, indeed, that it is incredible that a monarch should become a maniac —for the kings of the earth are no more exempt from this terrible malady than their subjects ; but the objections here referred to relate to the statements respecting the manner in which it is said that this monarch was treated, and that he lived during this long period. These objections may be briefly noticed. (1.) It has been objected, that it is wholly improbable that a monarch at the head of such an empire would, if he became incapable of administering the affairs of government, be so utterly neglected as the representation here would imply :—that he would be suffered to wander from his palace to live with beasts ; to fare as they fared, and to become in his whole appearance so *like* a beast. It is indeed admitted by those who make this objection, that there is no improbability that the cala-

mity would befall a king as well as other men ; and Michaelis has remarked that it is even more probable that a monarch would be thus afflicted than others (*Anm. Z. Dan.* p. 41 ; comp. Bertholdt, p. 304), but it is alleged that it is wholly improbable that one so high in office and in power would be treated with the utter neglect which is stated here. "Is it credible," says Bertholdt (p. 300–303), "that the royal family, and the royal counsellors, should have shown so little care or concern for a monarch who had come into a state so perfectly helpless ? Would no one have sought him out, and brought him back, if he had wandered so far away ? Could he anywhere in the open plains, and the regions about Babylon, destitute of forests, have concealed himself so that no one could have found him ? It could only have been by a miracle, that one could have wandered about for so long a time, amidst the dangers which must have befallen him, without having been destroyed by wild beasts, or falling into some form of irrecoverable ruin. What an unwise policy in a government to exhibit to a newly-conquered people so dishonourable a spectacle !"

To this objection it may be replied, (*a*) that its force, as it was formerly urged, may be somewhat removed by a correct interpretation of the chapter, and a more accurate knowledge of the disease which came upon the king, and of the manner in which he was actually treated. According to some views formerly entertained respecting the nature of the malady, it would have been impossible, I admit, to have defended the narrative. In respect to these views, see Notes on ver. 25. It *may* appear, from the fair interpretation of the whole narrative, that nothing more occurred than was natural in the circumstances. (*b*) The supposition that he was left to wander without any kind of oversight or guardianship is entirely gratuitous, and is unauthorized by the account which Nebuchadnezzar gives of what occurred. This opinion has been partly formed from a false interpretation of the phrase in ver. 36—"and my counsellors and my lords *sought unto me*"—as if they had sought him when he was wandering, with a view to find out where he was ; whereas the true meaning of that passage is, that *after* his restoration they sought unto him, or applied to him as the head of the empire, as they had formerly done. (*c*) There is some probability from the passage in ver. 15—"leave the stump of his roots in the earth, *even with a band of iron and brass*"—that Nebuchadnezzar was secured in the manner in which maniacs often have been, and that in his rage he was carefully guarded from all danger of injuring himself. See Notes on ver. 15. (*d*) On the supposition that he was not, still there might have been all proper *care* taken to guard him. All that may be implied when it is said that he "was driven from men, and did eat grass as oxen," &c., may have been that this was his *propensity* in that state ; that he had this roving disposition, and was disposed rather to wander in fields and groves than to dwell in the abodes of men ; and that he was driven *by this propensity*, not *by men*, to leave his palace, and to take up his residence in parks or groves—anywhere rather than in human habitations. This has been not an uncommon propensity with maniacs, and there is no improbability in supposing that this was permitted by those who had the care of him, as far as was consistent with his safety, and with what was due to him as a monarch, though his reason was driven from its throne. In the parks attached to the palace ; in the large pleasure-grounds, that were not improbably stocked with various kinds of animals, as a sort of royal menagerie, there is no improbability in supposing that he may have been allowed at proper times, and with suitable guards, to roam, nor that the fallen and humbled monarch may have found, in comparatively lucid intervals, a degree of pleasant amusement in such grounds, nor even that it might be supposed that this would contribute to his restoration to health. Nor, on *any* supposition in regard to these statements, even admitting that there was a great degree of criminal inattention on the part of his friends, would his treatment have been worse than what has usually occurred in respect to the insane. Up to quite a recent period, and even now in many civilized lands, the insane have been treated with the most gross neglect, and with the severest cruelty, even by their friends. Left to wander where they chose without a protector ; unshaven and unwashed ; the sport of the idle and the vicious ; thrown into common jails among felons ; bound with heavy chains to the cold walls of dungeons ; confined in cellars or garrets with no fire in the coldest weather ; with insufficient clothing, perhaps entirely naked, and in the midst of the most disgusting filth—such treatment, even in Christian lands, and by Christian people, may show that in a heathen land, five hundred years before the light of Christianity dawned upon the world, it is not *wholly* incredible that an insane monarch *might* have been treated in the manner described in this chapter. If the best friends now may so neglect, or treat with such severity, an insane son or daughter, there is no improbability in supposing that in an age of comparative barbarism there may have been as *little* humanity as is implied in this chapter. The following extracts from the Second Annual Report of the Prison Discipline Society (*Boston*) will show what has occurred in the nineteenth century, in this Christian land, and in the old commonwealth of Massachusetts — a commonwealth distinguished for morals, and for humane feeling—and will demonstrate at the same time that what is here stated about the monarch of heathen Babylon is not unworthy of belief. They refer to the treatment of lunatics in that commonwealth before the establishment of the hospital for the insane at Worcester. "In Massachusetts, by an examination made with care, about thirty lunatics have been found in prison. In one prison were found three; in another five; in another six; and in another ten. It is a source of great complaint with the sheriffs and jailers that they must receive such persons, because they have no suitable accommodations for them. Of those last mentioned, one was found in an apartment in which he had been nine years. He had a wreath of rags around his body, and another around his neck. This was all his clothing. He had no bed, chair, or bench. Two or three rough planks were strewed around the room; a heap of filthy straw, like the nest of swine, was in the corner. He had built a bird's nest of mud in the iron grate of his den. Connected with his wretched apartment was a dark dungeon, having no orifice for the admission of light, heat, or air, except the iron door, about two and a half feet square, opening into it from the prison. The other lunatics in the same prison were scattered about in different apartments, with thieves and murderers, and persons under arrest, but not yet convicted of guilt. In the prison of five lunatics, they were confined in separate cells, which were almost dark dungeons. It was difficult after the door was open to see them distinctly.

The ventilation was so incomplete that more than one person on entering them has found the air so fetid as to produce nausea, and almost vomiting. The old straw on which they were laid, and their filthy garments, were such as to make their insanity more hopeless; and at one time it was not considered within the province of the physician to examine particularly the condition of the lunatics. In these circumstances any improvement of their minds could hardly be expected. Instead of having three out of four restored to reason, as is the fact in some of the favoured lunatic asylums, it is to be feared that in these circumstances some who might otherwise be restored would become incurable, and that others might lose their lives, to say nothing of present suffering. In the prison in which were six lunatics their condition was less wretched. But they were sometimes an annoyance, and sometimes a sport to the convicts; and even the apartment in which the females were confined opened into the yard of the men; there was an injurious interchange of obscenity and profanity between them, which was not restrained by the presence of the keeper. In the prison, or house of correction, so called, in which were ten lunatics, two were found about seventy years of age, a male and female, in the same apartment of an upper story. The female was lying upon a heap of straw under a broken window. The snow in a severe storm was beating through the window, and lay upon the straw around her withered body, which was partially covered with a few filthy and tattered garments. The man was lying in the corner of the room in a similar situation, except that he was less exposed to the storm. The former had been in this apartment six, and the latter twenty-one years. Another lunatic in the same prison was found in a plank apartment of the first story, where he had been eight years. During this time he had never left the room but twice. The door of this apartment had not been opened in eighteen months. The food was furnished through a small orifice in the door. The room was warmed by no fire ; and still the woman of the house said '*he had never froze.*' As he was seen through the orifice of the door, the first question was, ' Is that a human being ?' The hair was gone from one side of his head, and his eyes were like balls of fire. In the cellar of the same prison were five lunatics. The windows of this cellar were no defence against the storm, and, as might be supposed, the woman of the house said, 'We have a sight to do to keep them from freezing.' There was no fire in this cellar which could be felt by four of these lunatics. One of the five had a little fire of turf in an apartment of the cellar by herself. She was, however, infuriate, if any one came near her. The woman was committed to this cellar seventeen years ago. The apartments are about six feet by eight. They are made of coarse plank, and have an orifice in the door for the admission of light and air, about six inches by four. The darkness was such in two of these apartments that nothing could be seen by looking through the orifice in the door. At the same time there was a poor lunatic in each. A man who has grown old was committed to one of them in 1810, and had lived in it seventeen years. An emaciated female was found in a similar apartment, in the dark, without fire, almost without covering, where she had been nearly two years. A coloured woman in another, in which she had been six years ; and a miserable man in another, in which he had been four years."

(2.) It is asked by Bertholdt, as an DANIEL I.

objection (p. 301), whether " it is credible that one who had been for so long a time a maniac would be restored again to the throne ; and whether the government would be again placed in his hands, without any apprehension that he would relapse into the same state ? Or whether it can be believed that the lives and fortunes of so many millions would be again intrusted to his will and power?" To these questions it may be replied : (*a*) That if he was restored to his reason he had a *right* to the throne, and it might not have been a doubtful point whether he should be restored to it or not. (*b*) It is probable that during that time a *regency* was appointed, and that there would be a hope entertained that he would be restored. Undoubtedly, during the continuation of this malady, the government would be, as was the case during the somewhat similar malady of George III. of Great Britain, placed in the hands of others, and unless there was a revolution, or an usurpation, he would be, of course, restored to his throne on the recovery of his reason. (*c*) To this it may be added, that he was a monarch who had been eminently successful in his conquests ; who had done much to enlarge the limits of the empire, and to adorn the capital ; and that much was to be apprehended from the character of his legal successor, Evil-Merodach (Hengstenberg, p. 113) ; and that if he were displaced, they who were then the chief officers of the nation had reason to suppose that, in accordance with Oriental usage on the accession of a new sovereign, they would lose their places.

(3.) It has been asked also, as an objection, whether " it is not to be presumed that Nebuchadnezzar, on the supposition that he was restored from so fearful a malady, would have employed all the means in his power to suppress the knowledge of it ; or whether, if any communication was made in regard to it, pains would not have been taken to give a colouring to the account by suppressing the real truth, and by attributing the affliction to some other cause?"—Bertholdt, p. 301. To this it may be replied: (a) That if the representation here made of the cause of his malady is correct, that it was a Divine judgment on him for his pride, and that God's design in bringing it on him was that he himself might be made known, it is reasonable to presume that, on his restoration, there would be such a Divine influence on the mind of the monarch, as to lead him to make this proclamation, or this public recognition of the Most High ; (b) that the edict seems to have been made, not as a matter of policy, but under the fresh recollection of a restoration from so terrible a calamity; (c) that Nebuchadnezzar seems to have been a man who had *a conscience* that prompted him to a decided acknowledgment of Divine interposition; (d) that he had a strong religious propensity (comp. ch. iii.), and was ready to make any public acknowledgment of that which he regarded as Divine ; and (e) that perhaps he supposed that, by stating the truth as it actually occurred, a better impression might be made than already existed in regard to the nature of the malady. It *may* have been an object, also, with him to convince his subjects that, although he had been deprived of his reason, he was now, in fact, restored to a sound mind.

(4.) Another ground of objection has been urged by Eichhorn, Bertholdt, and others, derived from the character of the edict. It is said that "the narrative represents Nebuchadnezzar at one time as an orthodox Jew, setting forth his views almost in the very words used in the writings of the Jews, and which only a Jew would employ (see vers.

2, 3, 34–37), and then again as a mere idolater, using the language which an idolater would employ, and still acknowledging the reality of idol gods, vers. 8, 9, 18." To this it may be replied, that this very circumstance is rather a confirmation of the truth of the account than otherwise. It is just such an account as we should suppose that a monarch, trained up in idolatry, and practising it all his life, and yet suddenly, and in this impressive man-ner, made acquainted with the true God, would be likely to give. In an edict published by such a monarch, under such circumstances, it would be strange if there should be no betrayal of the fact that he had been a worshipper of heathen gods, nor would it be strange that when he disclosed his dream to Daniel, asking him to interpret it, and professing to believe that he was under the influence of inspiration from above, he should trace it to the gods in general, vers. 8, 9, 18. And, in like manner, if the thing actually occurred, as is related, it would be certain that he *would* use such language in describing it as an "orthodox Jew" might use. It is to be remembered that he is represented as obtaining his view of what was meant by the vision from Daniel, and nothing is more probable than that he would use such language as Daniel would have suggested. It could not be supposed that one who had been an idolater all his life would soon efface from his mind all the impressions made by the habit of idolatry, so that no traces of it would appear in a proclamation on an occa-sion like this ; nor could it be supposed that there would be no recognition of God as the true God. Nothing would be more natural than such an inter-mingling of false notions with the true. Indeed, there is in fact scarcely any circumstance in regard to this chapter that has more the air of authenticity, nor could there well be anything more probable in itself, than what is here stated. It is just such an intermingling of truth with falsehood as we should expect in a mind trained in heathenism; and yet this is a circumstance which would not be *very* likely to occur to one who attempted a forgery, or who endeavoured to draw the character of a heathen monarch in such circumstances without authentic materials. If the edict was the work of a Jew, he would have been likely to represent its author without any remains of heathenism in his mind: if it were the work of a heathen, there would have been no such recognition of the true God. If it is a mere fiction, the artifice is too refined to have been likely to occur, to attempt to draw him in this state of mind, where there was an intermingling of falsehood with truth; of the remains of all his old habits of thinking, with new and momentous truths that had just begun to dawn on his mind. The supposition that will best suit all the circumstances of the case, and be liable to the fewest objections, is, that the account is an unvarnished statement of what actually occurred. On the whole subject of the objections to this chapter, the reader may consult Hengstenberg, *Die Authentie des Daniel,* pp. 100–119. For many of the remarks here made, I am indebted to that work. Comp. further the Notes on ver. 25, *seq.* of the chap.

§ II.—ANALYSIS OF THE CHAPTER.

THE chapter professes to be an edict published by Nebuchadnezzar after his recovery from a long period of insanity, which was brought upon him for his pride. The edict was promulgated with a view to lead men to acknowledge the true God. It states, in general, that the approach of his calamity was made known to him in a dream, which was interpreted by Daniel; that his own heart had been lifted up with pride in view of the splendid city which he had built; that the predicted malady came suddenly upon him, even while he was indulging in these proud reflections; that he was driven away from the abodes of men, a poor neglected maniac; that he again recovered his reason, and then his throne; and that the God who had thus humbled him, and again restored him, was the true God, and was worthy of universal adoration and praise. The edict, therefore, embraces the following parts:—

I. The reason why it was promulgated—to show to all people, dwelling in all parts of the earth, the great things which the high God had done towards him, vers. 1–3.

II. The statement of the fact that he had had a dream which greatly alarmed him, and which none of the Chaldean soothsayers had been able to interpret, vers. 4–7.

III. The statement of the dream in full to Daniel, vers. 8–18.

IV. The interpretation of the dream by Daniel—predicting the fact that he would become a maniac, and would be driven from his throne and kingdom, and compelled to take up his abode with the beasts of the field—a poor neglected outcast, vers. 19–26.

V. The solemn and faithful counsel of Daniel to him to break off his sins, and to become a righteous man, if possibly the terrible calamity might be averted, ver. 27.

VI. The fulfilment of the prediction of Daniel. Nebuchadnezzar was walking on his palace, and, in the pride of his heart, surveying the great city which he had built, and suddenly a voice from heaven addressed him, announcing that his kingdom had departed, and his reason left him, vers. 28–33.

CHAPTER IV.

NEBUCHADNEZZAR the king, unto *a* all people, nations, and languages, that dwell

a ch. 3. 4; 6. 25-27.

VII. At the end of the appointed time, his reason was restored, and he gratefully acknowledged the Divine sovereignty, and was again reinstated on his throne, vers. 34–36.

VIII. For all this, he says that he praised the God of heaven, for he had learned that all his works are truth, and his ways judgment, and that those who walk in pride he is able to abase, ver. 37.

1. *Nebuchadnezzar the king, unto all people,* &c. The Syriac here has, "Nebuchadnezzar the king *wrote* to all people," &c. Many manuscripts in the Chaldee have שְׁלַח *sent,* and some have כְּתַב *wrote;* but neither of these readings are probably genuine, nor are they necessary. The passage is rather a part of the edict of the king than a narrative of the author of the book, and in such an edict the comparatively abrupt style of the present reading would be that which would be adopted. The Septuagint has inserted here a historical statement of the fact that Nebuchadnezzar did actually issue such an edict: "And Nebuchadnezzar the king wrote an encyclical epistle—ἐπιστολὴν ἐγκύκλιον—to all those nations in every place, and to the regions, and to all the tongues that dwell in all countries, generations and generations: 'Nebuchadnezzar the king,'" &c. But nothing of this is in the original. ¶ *Unto all people, nations, and languages that dwell in all the earth.* That is, people speaking all the languages of the earth. Many nations were under the sceptre of the king of Babylon; but it would seem that he designed this as a general proclamation, not only to those who were embraced in his empire, but to all the people of the world. Such a proclamation would be much in accordance with the Oriental style. Comp. Notes on ch. iii. 4. ¶ *Peace be multiplied unto*

in all the earth; Peace *b* be multiplied unto you.

2 I [1] thought it good to show the signs and wonders that the

b 1 Pet. 1. 2.   [1] *it was seemly before me.*

you. This is in accordance with the usual Oriental salutation. Comp. Gen. xliii. 23; Judg. vi. 23; 1 Sam. xxv. 6; Psa. cxxii. 7; Luke x. 5; Eph. vi. 23; 1 Pet. i. 2. This is the salutation with which one meets another now in the Oriental world—the same word still being retained, *Shalom,* or *Salam.* The idea seemed to be, that every blessing was found in peace, and every evil in conflict and war. The expression included the wish that they might be preserved from all that would disturb them; that they might be contented, quiet, prosperous, and happy. When it is said "peace be *multiplied,*" the wish is that it might *abound,* or that they might be blessed with the numberless mercies which peace produces.

2. *I thought it good.* Marg., *it was seemly before me.* The marginal reading is more in accordance with the original (שְׁפַר קֳדָמַי). The proper meaning of the Chaldee word (שְׁפַר) is, to be fair or beautiful; and the sense here is, that it seemed to him to be appropriate or becoming to make this public proclamation. It was fit and right that what God had done to him should be proclaimed to all nations. ¶ *To show the signs and wonders.* Signs and wonders, as denoting mighty miracles, are not unfrequently connected in the Scriptures. See Exod. vii. 3; Deut. iv. 34; xiii. 1; xxxiv. 11; Isa. viii. 18; Jer. xxxii. 20. The word rendered *signs* (Heb. אוֹת—Chald. אָת) means, properly, a *sign,* as something significant, or something that points out or designates anything; as Gen. i. 14, "shall be for *signs* and for seasons;" that is, signs of seasons. Then the word denotes an ensign, a military flag, Numb. ii. 2; then a sign of something past, a token or remembrancer, Exod. xiii. 9, 16; Deut. vi. 8; then a sign of something future, a portent, an omen, Isa. viii. 18; then a sign or token of what is visible, as circumcision, Gen. xvii. 11, or the rainbow in the cloud, as a

high *a* God hath wrought toward me.

a ch. 3. 26.

token of the covenant which God made with man, Gen. ix. 12; then anything which serves as a sign or proof of the fulfilment of prophecy, Exod. iii. 12; 1 Sam. ii. 34; and then it refers to anything which is a sign or proof of Divine power, Deut. iv. 34; vi. 22; vii. 19, *et al.* The Hebrew word is commonly rendered *signs,* but it is also rendered *token, ensign, miracles.* As applied to what God does, it seems to be used in the sense of anything that is significant of his presence and power; anything that shall manifestly show that what occurs is done by him; anything that is beyond human ability, and that makes known the being and the perfections of God by a direct and extraordinary manifestation. Here the meaning is, that what was done in so remarkable a manner was *significant* of the agency of God; it was that which demonstrated that he exists, and that showed his greatness. The word rendered *wonders* (תִּמְהָה) means, properly, that which is fitted to produce astonishment, or to lead one to wonder, and is applied to miracles as adapted to produce that effect. It refers to that state of mind which exists where anything occurs out of the ordinary course of nature, or which indicates supernatural power. The Hebrew word rendered *wonders* is often used to denote miracles, Exod. iii. 20; vii. 3; xi. 9; Deut. vi. 22, *et al.* The meaning here is, that what had occurred was fitted to excite amazement, and to lead men to wonder at the mighty works of God. ¶ *That the high God.* The God who is exalted, or lifted up; that is, the God who is above all. See ch. iii. 26. It is an appellation which would be given to God as the Supreme Being. The Greek translation of this verse is, "And now I show unto you the deeds—πράξις—which the great God has done unto me, for it seemed good to me to show to you and your wise men"—τοῖς σοφισταῖς ὑμῶν.

3. *How great* are *his signs!* How great and wonderful are the things by

3 How great *are* his signs! *b* and how mighty *are* his wonders! *c* his

b Deut. 4. 34; Ps. 105. 27; Heb. 2. 4.
c Ps. 72. 18; 86. 10; Isa. 25. 1; 28. 29.

which he makes himself known in this manner! The allusion is doubtless to what had occurred to himself—the event by which a monarch of such state and power had been reduced to a condition so humble. With propriety he would regard this as a signal instance of the Divine interposition, and as adapted to give him an exalted view of the supremacy of the true God. ¶ *And how mighty* are *his wonders!* The wonderful events which he does; the things fitted to produce admiration and astonishment. Comp. Psal. lxxii. 18; lxxxvi. 10; Isa. xxv. 1. ¶ *His kingdom is an everlasting kingdom.* Nebuchadnezzar was doubtless led to this reflection by what had occurred to him. He, the most mighty monarch then on earth, had seen that *his* throne had no stability; he had seen that God had power at his will to bring him down from his lofty seat, and to transfer his authority to other hands; and he was naturally led to reflect that the throne of God was the only one that was stable and permanent. He could not but be convinced that God reigned over all, and that his kingdom was not subject to the vicissitudes which occur in the kingdoms of this world. There have been few occurrences on the earth better adapted to teach this lesson than this. ¶ *And his dominion* is *from generation to generation.* That is, it is perpetual. It is not liable to be arrested as that of man is, by death; it does not pass over from one family to another as an earthly sceptre often does. The same sceptre; the same system of laws; the same providential arrangements; the same methods of reward and punishment, have always existed under his government, and will continue to do so to the end of time. There is, perhaps, no more sublime view that can be taken of the government of God than this. All earthly princes die; all authority lodged in the hands of an earthly monarch is soon withdrawn. No one is so mighty that he can prolong his own reign; and no one can make his own

kingdom *is* an everlasting *a* kingdom, and his dominion *b is* from
generation to generation.

a ch. 2. 44; Rev. 11.15.   *b* Job 25.2; 1 Pet. 4.11.

4 ¶ I Nebuchadnezzar was at
rest in mine house, and flourishing
in my palace:

5 I saw a dream which made me

---

authority extend to the next generation.
Earthly governments, therefore, however mighty, are of short duration ; and
history is made up of the records of a
great number of such administrations,
many of them exceedingly brief, and of
very various character. The sceptre
falls from the hand of the monarch,
never to be resumed by him again ;
another grasps it to retain it also but a
little time, and then he passes away.
But the dominion of God is in all generations the same. This generation is
under the government of the same
Sovereign who reigned when Semiramis or Numa lived ; and though the
sceptre has long since fallen from the
hands of Alexander and the Cæsars,
yet the same God who ruled in their
age is still on the throne.

4. *I Nebuchadnezzar was at rest.*
Some manuscripts in the Greek add
here, "In the eighteenth year of his
reign Nebuchadnezzar said." These
words, however, are not in the Hebrew,
and are of no authority. The word
rendered *"at rest"* (שְׁלֵה) means, to be
secure ; to be free from apprehension
or alarm. He designs to describe a
state of tranquillity and security. Gr.,
at peace—εἰρηνεύων : enjoying peace, or
in a condition to enjoy peace. His
wars were over ; his kingdom was tranquil ; he had built a magnificent capital ; he had gathered around him the
wealth and the luxuries of the world,
and he was now in a condition to pass
away the remainder of his life in ease
and happiness. ¶ *In mine house.* In
his royal residence. It is possible that
the two words here—*house* and *palace*—
may refer to somewhat different things :
the former—*house*—more particularly
to his own private family—his domestic
relations as a man ; and the latter—
palace—to those connected with the
government who resided in his palace.
If this is so, then the passage would
mean that all around him was peaceful,
and that from no source had he any
cause of disquiet. In his own private

family—embracing his wife and children ; and in the arrangements of the
palace — embracing those who had
charge of public affairs, he had no cause
of uneasiness. ¶ *And flourishing in
my palace.* Gr., εὐθηνῶν ἐπὶ τοῦ θρόνου
μου — literally, "abundant upon my
throne ;" that is, he was tranquil, calm,
prosperous on his throne. The Chaldee
word (רַעֲנָן) means, properly, *green ;*
as, for example, of leaves or foliage.
Comp. the Hebrew word in Jer. xvii.
8 ; "He shall be as a tree planted by
the waters—her leaf shall be *green.*"
Deut. xii. 2, "Under every *green* tree,"
2 Kings xvi. 4. A green and flourishing tree becomes thus the emblem of
prosperity. See Psal. i. 3 ; xxxvii. 35 ;
xcii. 12–14. The general meaning
here is, that he was enjoying abundant
prosperity. His kingdom was at peace,
and in his own home he had every
means of tranquil enjoyment.

5. *I saw a dream.* That is, he saw
a representation made to him in a dream.
There is something incongruous in our
language in saying of one that he *saw*
a dream. ¶ *Which made me afraid.*
The fear evidently arose from the apprehension that it was designed to disclose some important and solemn event.
This was in accordance with a prevalent belief then (comp. ch. ii. 1), and it
may be added that it is in accordance
with a prevalent belief now. There are
few persons, whatever may be their abstract belief, who are not more or less
disturbed by fearful and solemn representations passing before the mind in
the visions of the night. Comp. Job
iv. 12–17 ; xxxiii. 14, 15. So Virgil
(*Æn.* iv. 9):—

"Anna soror, quæ me suspensam insomnia
terrent!"

¶ *And the thoughts upon my bed.* The
thoughts which I had upon my bed ;
to wit, in my dream. ¶ *And the visions of my head.* What I seemed to
see. The vision seemed to be floating
around his head. ¶ *Troubled me.* Disturbed me ; produced apprehension of

afraid, and the thoughts upon my bed and the visions of my head troubled me.

6 Therefore made I a decree to bring in all the wise *men* of Babylon before me, that they might make known unto me the interpretation of the dream.

7 Then *a* came in the magicians, the astrologers, the Chaldeans, and the soothsayers: and I told the dream before them; but they did not make known unto me the interpretation thereof.

8 ¶ But at the last Daniel came

a ch. 2. 1, 2.

what was to come; of some great and important event.

6. *Therefore made I a decree.* The word here rendered *decree* (טְעֵם) means, commonly, *taste, flavour*, as of wine; then *judgment, discernment, reason;* and then a judgment of a king, a mandate, edict. Comp. chap. iii. 10. The primary notion seems to be that of a delicate *taste* enabling one to determine the qualities of wines, viands, &c.; and then a delicate and nice discrimination in regard to the qualities of actions. The word thus expresses a sound and accurate judgment, and is applied to a decree or edict, as declared by one who had the qualifications to express such a judgment. Here it means, that he issued a royal order to summon into his presence all who could be supposed to be qualified to explain the dream. The Greek (Cod. Chisian.) omits vers. 6, 7, 8, and 9. ¶ *To bring in all the wise* men, &c. Particularly such as are enumerated in the following verse. Comp. chap. ii. 12. It was in accordance with his habit thus to call in the wise men who were retained at court to give counsel, and to explain those things which seemed to be an intimation of the Divine will. See Notes on ch. ii. 2. Comp. also Gen. xli. 8.

7. *Then came in the magicians*, &c. All the words occurring here are found in ch. ii. 2, and are explained in the Notes on that verse, except the word rendered *soothsayers*. This occurs in chap. ii. 27. See it explained in the Notes on that verse. All these words refer to the same general class of persons—those who were regarded as endued with eminent wisdom; who were supposed to be qualified to explain remarkable occurrences, to foretell the future, and to declare the will of heaven from portents and wonders. At a time

when there was yet a limited revelation; when the boundaries of science were not determined with accuracy; when it was not certain but that some way *might* be ascertained of lifting the mysterious veil from the future, and when it was an open question whether that might not be by dreams or by communication with departed spirits, or by some undisclosed secrets of nature, it was not unnatural that persons should be found who claimed that this knowledge was under their control. Such claimants to preternatural knowledge are found indeed in every age; and though a large portion of them are undoubted deceivers, yet the existence of such an order of persons should be regarded as merely the *exponent* of the deep and earnest desire existing in the human bosom to penetrate the mysterious future; to find *something* that shall disclose to man, all whose great interests lie *in* the future, what is yet to be. Comp. the remarks at the close of ch. ii. ¶ *And I told the dream before them*, &c. In their presence. In this instance he did not lay on them so hard a requisition as he did on a former occasion, when he required them not only to interpret the dream, but to tell him what it was, ch. ii. But their pretended power here was equally vain. Whether they *attempted* an interpretation of this dream does not appear; but if they did, it was wholly unsatisfactory to the king himself. It would seem more probable that they supposed that the dream might have some reference to the proud monarch himself, and that, as it indicated some awful calamity, they did not dare to hazard a conjecture in regard to its meaning.

8. *But at the last.* After the others had shown that they could not interpret the dream. Why Daniel was not called with the others does not appear;

in before me, whose name *a was* Belteshazzar, according to the name of my god, and in whom *is* the spirit *b* of the holy gods: and

a ch. 1. 7.   *b* Num. 11. 17, &c.; Isa. 63. 11.

nor is it said in what manner he was at last summoned into the presence of the king. It is probable that his skill on a former occasion (ch. ii.) was remembered, and that when all the others showed that they had no power to interpret the dream, he was called in by Nebuchadnezzar. The Latin Vulgate renders this, Donec collega ingressus est—"until a colleague entered." The Greek, *ἕως, until.* Aquila and Symmachus render it, "until another entered before me, Daniel." The common version expresses the sense of the Chaldee with sufficient accuracy, though a more literal translation would be, "until afterwards." ¶ *Whose name* was *Belteshazzar.* That is, this was the name which he bore at court, or which had been given him by the Chaldeans. See Notes on ch. i. 7. ¶ *According to the name of my god.* That is, the name of my god Bel, or Belus, is incorporated in the name given to him. This is referred to here, probably, to show the propriety of thus invoking his aid; because he bore the name of the god whom the monarch had adored. There would seem to be a special fitness in summoning him before him, to explain what was supposed to be an intimation of the will of the god whom he worshipped. There is a singular, though not unnatural, mixture of the sentiments of heathenism and of the true religion in the expressions which this monarch uses in this chapter. He had been a heathen all his life; yet he had had some knowledge of the true God, and had been made to feel that he was worthy of universal adoration and praise, ch. ii. That, in this state of mind, he should alternately express such sentiments as were originated by heathenism, and those which spring from just views of God, is not unnatural or improbable. ¶ *And in whom* is *the spirit of the holy gods.* It is not easy to determine whom he meant by *the holy gods.* It would seem probable that *this* was such language as was dic-

before him I told the dream, *saying,*

9 O Belteshazzar, master of the magicians, because I know that the spirit of the holy gods *is* in thee,

tated by the fact that he had been an idolater. He had been brought to feel that the God whom Daniel worshipped, and by whose aid he had been enabled to interpret the dream, was a true God, and was worthy of universal homage; but perhaps his ideas were still much confused, and he only regarded him as superior to all others, though he did not intend to deny the real existence of others. It might be true, in his apprehension, that there were other gods, though the God of Daniel was supreme, and perhaps he meant to say that the spirit of *all* the gods was in Daniel; that *in* an eminent degree he was the favourite of heaven, and that he was able to interpret *any* communication which came from the invisible world. It is perhaps unnecessary to observe here that the word *spirit* has no intended reference to the Holy Spirit. It is probably used with reference to the belief that the gods were accustomed to impart wisdom and knowledge to certain men, and may mean that the very spirit of wisdom and knowledge which dwelt in the gods themselves seemed to dwell in the bosom of Daniel. ¶ *And before him I told the dream.* Not requiring him, as he did before (ch. ii.), to state both the dream and its meaning.

9. *O Belteshazzar, master of the magicians.* "Master," in the sense that he was first among them, or was superior to them all. Or, perhaps, he still retained office at the head of this class of men—the office to which he had been appointed when he interpreted the former dream, ch. ii. 48. The word rendered *master* (רַב *Rab*) is that which was applied to a teacher, a chief, or a great man among the Jews — from whence came the title *Rabbi.* Comp. ch. ii. 48; v. 11. ¶ *Because I know that the spirit of the holy gods is in thee.* This he had learned by the skill which he had shown in interpreting his dream on a former occasion, ch. ii.

and no secret troubleth *a* thee, tell me the visions of my dream that I have seen, and the interpretation thereof.

10 Thus *were* the visions of my head in my bed: I [1] saw, and, behold,

a Isa. 33. 18; 54. 14.   1 *was seeing.*

a *b* tree in the midst of the earth, and the height thereof *was* great.

11 The tree grew, and was strong, and the height thereof reached unto heaven, and the sight thereof to the end of all the earth.

b Ezek. 31. 3, &c.

¶ *And no secret troubleth thee.* That is, so troubles you that you cannot explain it; it is not beyond your power to disclose its signification. The word rendered *secret* (רָז) occurs in ch. ii. 18, 19, 27–30, 47. It is not elsewhere found. It means that which is *hidden*, and has reference here to the concealed truth or intimation of the Divine will couched under a dream. The word rendered *"troubleth thee"* (אָנֵס) means, to urge, to press, to compel; and the idea here is, that it did not so *press* upon him as to give him anxiety. It was an easy matter for him to disclose its meaning. Gr., "No mystery is beyond your power"—ἐυκ ἀδυνατεῖ σε. ¶ *Tell me the visions of my dream.* The nature of the vision, or the purport of what I have seen. He seems to have desired to know *what sort* of a vision he should regard this to be, as well as its interpretation—whether as an intimation of the Divine will, or as an ordinary dream. The Greek and Arabic render this, *"Hear* the vision of my dream, and tell me the interpretation thereof." This accords better with the probable meaning of the passage, though the word *hear* is not in the Chaldee. 10. *Thus* were *the visions of my head in my bed.* These are the things which I saw upon my bed. When he says that they were the "visions of his *head,"* he states a doctrine which was then doubtless regarded as the truth, that the head is the seat of thought. ¶ *I saw.* Marg., *was seeing.* Chald., "seeing I saw." The phrase would imply attentive and calm contemplation. It was not a flitting vision; it was an object which he contemplated deliberately so as to retain a distinct remembrance of its form and appearance. ¶ *And, behold, a tree in the*

midst of the earth. Occupying a central position on the earth. It seems to have been by itself—remote from any forest: to have stood alone. Its central position, no less than its size and proportions, attracted his attention. Such a tree, thus towering to the heavens, and sending out its branches afar, and affording a shade to the beasts of the field, and a home to the fowls of heaven (ver. 12), was a striking emblem of a great and mighty monarch, and it undoubtedly occurred to Nebuchadnezzar at once that the vision had some reference to himself. Thus in Ezek. xxxi. 3, the Assyrian king is compared with a magnificent cedar: "Behold, the Assyrian was a cedar in Lebanon, with fair branches, and with a shadowing shroud, and of a high stature, and his top was among the thick boughs." Comp. also Ezek. xvii. 22–24, where "the high tree and the green tree" refer probably to Nebuchadnezzar. See Notes on Isa. ii. 13. Comp. Is. x. 18, 19; Jer. xxii. 7, 23. Homer often compares his heroes to trees. Hector, felled by a stone, is compared with an oak overthrown by a thunderbolt. The fall of Simoisius is compared by him to that of a poplar, and that of Euphorbus to the fall of a beautiful olive. Nothing is more obvious than the comparison of a hero with a lofty tree of the forest, and hence it was natural for Nebuchadnezzar to suppose that this vision had a reference to himself. ¶ *And the height thereof* was *great.* In the next verse it is said to have reached to heaven.

[The symbolic or sacred tree occupies a prominent place in the Assyrian mythology. It is here represented under some variation of its conventional form; and on either side of it is a figure of Nisroch, with the usual attributes. The tree of Nebuchadnezzar's vision may have

12 The leaves thereof *were* fair, and the fruit thereof much, and in it *was* meat for all: the beasts *a* of the field had shadow *b* under it, and the fowls of the heaven dwelt in the boughs thereof, and all flesh was fed of it.

a Ezek. 17. 23.   *b* Lam. 4. 20.

been generally suggested to the monarch's mind by the religious emblem with which he was familiar, in the temple of his gods. The sculpture is from the Hall of Nisroch, at Nimroud.]

11. *The tree grew.* Or the tree was *great*—רְבָה. It does not mean that the tree *grew* while he was looking at it so as to reach to the heaven, but that it stood before him in all its glory, its top reaching to the sky, and its branches extending afar. ¶ *And was strong.* It was well-proportioned, with a trunk adapted to its height, and to the mass of boughs and foliage which it bore. The strength here refers to its trunk, and to the fact that it seemed fixed firmly in the earth. ¶ *And the height thereof reached unto heaven.* To the sky; to the region of the clouds. The comparison of trees reaching to heaven is common in Greek and Latin authors. —Grotius. Comp. Virgil's description of Fame.

"Mox sese attollit in auras,
Ingrediturque solo, et caput inter nubila condit."—*Æn.* iv. 176.

¶ *And the sight thereof to the end of all the earth.* It could be seen, or was visible in all parts of the earth. The Greek here for *sight* is κῦτος, *breadth, capaciousness.* Herodotus (*Polymnia*) describes a vision remarkably similar to this, as indicative of a wide and universal monarchy, respecting Xerxes:

"After these things there was a third vision in his sleep, which the magicians (μάγοι) hearing of, said that it pertained to all the earth, and denoted that all men would be subject to him. The vision was this: Xerxes seemed to be crowned with a branch of laurel, and the branches of laurel seemed to extend through all the earth." The vision which Nebuchadnezzar had here, of a tree so conspicuous as to be seen from any part of the world, was one that would be naturally applied to a sovereign having a universal sway.

12. *The leaves thereof* were *fair.* Were beautiful. That is, they were abundant, and green, and there were no signs of decay. Everything indicated a vigorous and healthy growth— a tree in its full beauty and majesty— a striking emblem of a monarch in his glory. ¶ *And the fruit thereof much.* It was loaded with fruit—showing that the tree was in its full vigour. ¶ *And in it* was *meat for all.* Food for all, for so the word *meat* was formerly used. This would indicate the dependence of the multitudes on him whom the tree represented, and would also denote that he was a liberal dispenser of his favours. ¶ *The beasts of the field*

13 I saw in the visions of my head upon my bed, and, behold, a

a vers. 17, 23.

watcher *a* and an holy *b* one came down from heaven.

b Matt. 25. 31; Rev. 14. 10.

---

had shadow under it. Found a grateful shade under it in the burning heat of noon—a striking emblem of the blessings of a monarchy affording protection, and giving peace to all under it. ¶ *And the fowls of the heaven dwelt in the boughs thereof.* The fowls of the air. They built their nests and reared their young there undisturbed, another striking emblem of the protection afforded under the great monarchy designed to be represented. ¶ *And all flesh was fed of it.* All animals; all that lived. It furnished protection, a home, and food for all. Bertholdt renders this, "all men." In the Greek *Codex Chisian.* there is the following version or paraphrase given of this passage : " Its vision was great, its top reached to the heaven, and its breadth (κῦτος) to the clouds—they filled the things (τὰ) under the heaven—there was a sun and moon, they dwelt in it, and enlightened all the earth."

13. *I saw in the visions of my head upon my bed.* In the visions that passed before me as I lay upon my bed, ver. 10. ¶ *And, behold, a watcher and an holy one.* Or rather, perhaps, " even a holy one ; " or, " who was a holy one." He evidently does not intend to refer to *two* beings, a " watcher," *and* " one who was holy ;" but he means to designate the character of the watcher, that he was holy, or that he was one of the class of " watchers " who were ranked as holy—as if there were others to whom the name " watcher " might be applied who were *not* holy. So Bertholdt, " not two, but only one, who was both a watcher, and was holy ; one of those known as watchers and as holy ones." The copulative (ו) *and* may be so used as to denote not an additional one or thing, but to specify something in addition to, or in explanation of, what the name applied would indicate. Comp. 1 Sam. xxviii. 3 : " In Ramah, *even* (ו) in his own city." 1 Sam. xvii. 40 : " And put them in a shepherd's bag which he had, *even* (ו) in a scrip." Comp. Psa. lxviii. 9 (10) ; Amos iii. 11 ; iv. 10 ; Jer. xv. 13 ;

Isa. i. 13 ; xiii. 14 ; lvii. 11 ; Eccles. viii. 2.—Gesenius, *Lex.* The word rendered *watcher* (עִיר) is rendered in the Vulgate *vigil ;* in the Greek of Theodotion the word is retained without an attempt to translate it—εἲρ ; the Codex Chisianus has ἄγγελος— " an angel was sent in his strength from heaven." The original word (עִיר) means, properly, *a watcher,* from עִיר, to be hot and ardent ; then to be lively, or active, and then to awake, to be awake, to be awake at night, to watch. Comp. Cant. v. 2 ; Mal. ii. 12. The word used here is employed to denote one who watches, only in this chapter of Daniel, vers. 13, 17, 23. It is in these places evidently applied to the angels, but *why* this term is used is unknown. Gesenius (*Lex.*) supposes that it is given to them as watching over the souls of men. Jerome (*in loc.*) says that the reason why the name is given is because they always *watch,* and are prepared to do the will of God. According to Jerome, the Greek ἴρις— Iris—as applied to the rainbow, and which seems to be a heavenly being sent down to the earth, is derived from this word. Comp. the *Iliad,* ii. 27. Theodoret says that the name is given to an angel, to denote that the angel is without a body—ἀσώματον—" for he that is encompassed with a body is the servant of sleep, but he that is free from a body is superior to the necessity of sleep." The term *watchers,* as applied to the celestial beings, is of Eastern origin, and not improbably was derived from Persia. " The seven Amhaspands received their name on account of their great, holy eyes, and so, generally, all the heavenly Izeds watch in the high heaven over the world and the souls of men, and on this account are called the watchers of the world."— Zendavesta, as quoted by Bertholdt, *in loc.* " The Bun-Dehesh, a commentary on the Zendavesta, contains an extract from it, which shows clearly the name and object of the *watchers* in the ancient system of Zoroaster. It runs thus :

14 He cried [1] aloud, and said thus, Hew [a] down the tree, and cut off his branches, shake off his

1 *with might*, ch. 3. 4.
a Matt. 3. 10; Luke 13. 7.

leaves, and scatter his fruit: let the beasts get away from under it, and the fowls get from his branches.

15 Nevertheless, leave the [b] stump

b Job 14. 7–9.

"Ormuzd has set four *watchers* in the four parts of the heavens, to keep their eye upon the host of the stars. They are bound to keep watch over the hosts of the celestial stars. One stands here as the watcher of his circle ; the other there. He has placed them at such and such posts, as watchers over such and such a circle of the heavenly regions ; and this by his own power and might. Tashter guards the east, Statevis watches the west, Venant the south, and Haftorang the north."— Rhode, Die heilige Sage des Zendvolks, p. 267, as quoted by Prof. Stuart, *in loc*. "The epithet *good* is probably added here to distinguish this class of *watchers* from the *bad* ones ; for Ahriman, the evil genius, had *Archdeves* and *Deves*, who corresponded in rank with the Amhaspands and Izeds of the Zendavesta, and who *watched* to do evil as anxiously as the others did to do good."—Prof. Stuart. It is not improbable that these terms, as applicable to celestial beings, would be known in the kingdom of Babylon, and nothing is more natural than that it should be so used in this book. It is not found in any of the books of pure Hebrew.

14. *He cried aloud.* Marg., as in the Chaldee, *with might.* That is, he cried with a strong voice. ¶ *Hew down the tree.* This command does not appear to have been addressed to any particular ones who were to execute the commission, but it is a strong and significant way of saying that it would certainly be done. Or possibly the command may be understood as addressed to his fellow-watchers (ver. 17), or to orders of angels over whom this one presided. ¶ *And cut off his branches,* &c. The idea here, and in the subsequent part of the verse, is, that the tree was to be utterly cut up, and all its glory and beauty destroyed. It was first to be felled, and then its limbs chopped off, and then these were to be stripped of their foliage, and then the

fruit which it bore was to be scattered. All this was strikingly significant, as applied to the monarch, of some awful calamity that was to occur to him *after* he should have been brought down from his throne. A process of humiliation and desolation was to continue, as if the tree, when cut down, were not suffered to lie quietly in its grandeur upon the earth. ¶ *Let the beasts get away,* &c. That is, it shall cease to afford a shade to the beasts and a home to the fowls. The purposes which it had answered in the days of its glory will come to an end.

15. *Nevertheless, leave the stump of his roots in the earth.* As of a tree that is not wholly dead, but which may send up suckers and shoots again. See Notes on Isa. xi. 1. In Theodotion this is, τὴν φυήν τῶν ῥιξῶν—the nature, germ. Schleusner renders the Greek, "the *trunk* of its roots." The Vulgate is, germen radicum ejus, "the germ of his roots." The *Codex Chis.* has, ῥίξαν μίαν ἄφετε αὐτοῦ ἐν τῇ γῇ—"leave one of his roots in the earth." The original Chaldee word (עִקַּר) means a *stump, trunk* (Gesenius) ; the Hebrew — עֵקֶר —the same word with different pointing, means a shrub, or shoot. It occurs only once in Hebrew (Lev. xxv. 47), where it is applied to the stock of a family, or to a person sprung from a foreign family resident in the Hebrew territory: "the *stock* of the stranger's family." The Chaldee form of the word occurs only in Dan. iv. 15, 23, 26, rendered in each place *stump*, yet not meaning *stump* in the sense in which that word is now commonly employed. The word *stump* now means the stub of a tree ; the part of the tree remaining in the earth, or projecting above it after the tree is cut down, without any reference to the question whether it be alive or dead. The word here used implies that it was still alive, or that there was a germ which would send up a new shoot,

of his roots in the earth, even with a band of iron and brass, in the tender grass of the field; and let it

be wet with the dew of heaven, and let his portion be with the beasts in the grass of the earth:

---

so that the tree would live again. The idea is, that though the mighty tree would fall, yet there would remain vitality in the root, or the portion that would remain in the earth after the tree was cut down, and that this would spring up again—a most striking image of what would occur to Nebuchadnezzar after he should be cast down from his lofty throne, and be again restored to his reason and to power. ¶ *Even with a band of iron and brass.* This expression may be regarded as applicable either to the cut-down tree, or to the humbled monarch. If applied to the former, it would seem that the idea is, that the stump or root of a tree, deemed so valuable, would be carefully secured by an inclosure of iron or brass, either in the form of a hoop placed round the top of the stump, to preserve it from being opened or cracked by the heat of the sun, so as to admit moisture, which would rot it; or around the roots, to bind it together, with the hope that it would grow again; or it may refer to a railing or inclosure of iron or brass, to keep it from being ploughed or dug up as worthless. In either case, it would be guarded with the hope that a tree so valuable might spring up again. If applied to the monarch—an explanation not inconsistent with the proper interpretation of the passage—it would seem to refer to some method of securing the royal maniac in bonds of iron and brass, as with the hope that his reason might still be restored, or with a view to keep him from inflicting fatal injury on himself. That the thing here referred to might be practised in regard to a valuable tree cut down, or broken down, is by no means improbable; that it might be practised in reference to the monarch is in accordance with the manner in which the insane have been treated in all ages and countries. ¶ *In the tender grass of the field.* Out of doors; under no shelter; exposed to dews and rains. The stump would remain in the open field where the grass grew, until it should shoot up again; and in a condition strongly resembling that, the

monarch would be excluded from his palace and from the abodes of men. For the meaning of this, as applied to Nebuchadnezzar, see Notes on ver. 25. The word which is rendered *tender grass*, means simply young grass or herbage. No emphasis should be put on the word *tender*. It simply means that he would be abroad where the grass springs up and grows. ¶ *And let it be wet with the dew of heaven.* As applied to the tree, meaning that the dew would fall on it and continually moisten it. The falling of the dew upon it would contribute to preserve it alive and secure its growth again. In a dry soil, or if there were no rain or dew, the germ would die. It cannot be supposed that, in regard to the monarch, it could be meant that his remaining under the dew of heaven would in any way contribute to restore his reason, but all that is implied in regard to him is *the fact* that he would thus be an outcast. The word rendered "*let it be wet*"— יִצְטַבַּע from צְבַע—means, to dip in, to immerse; to tinge; to dye; though the word is not found in the latter senses in the Chaldee. In the Targums it is often used for "to dye, to colour." The word occurs only in this chapter of Daniel (vers. 15, 23, 33), and is in each place rendered in the same way. It is not used in the Hebrew scripture in the sense of to dye or tinge, except in the form of a noun—צֶבַע—in Judg. v. 30: "To Sisera a prey of *divers colours*, a prey of *divers colours* of needlework, of *divers colours* of needlework." In the passage before us, of course, there is no allusion of this kind, but the word means merely that the stump of the tree would be kept moist with the dew; as applicable to the tree that it might be more likely to sprout up again. ¶ *And let his portion be with the beasts in the grass of the earth.* Here is a change evidently from the *tree* to something represented by the tree. We could not say of a *tree* that its "portion was with the beasts in the grass," though in the confused and in-

16 Let his heart be *a*changed from man's, and let a beast's heart

a Isa. 6. 10.

congruous images of a dream, nothing would be more natural than such a change from a tree to some object represented by it, or having some resemblance to it. It is probable that it was this circumstance that particularly attracted the attention of the monarch ; for though the dream began with a *tree,* it ended with reference to a *person,* and evidently some one whose station would be well represented by such a magnificent and solitary tree. The sense here is, "let him share the lot of beasts ; let him live as they do :" that is, let him live on grass. Comp. ver. 25.

16. *Let his heart be changed from man's, and let a beast's heart be given unto him.* Here the same thing occurs in a more marked form, showing that some *man* was represented by the vision, and indicating some change which was fitted to attract the deepest attention —as if the person referred to should cease to be a man, and become a beast. The word *heart* here seems to refer to *nature*—"let his nature or propensity cease to be that of a man, and become like that of a beast ; let him cease to act as a man, and act as the beasts do —evincing as little mind, and living in the same manner." ¶ *And let seven times pass over him.* In this condition, or until he is restored. It is not indeed *said* that he would be restored, but this is implied (*a*) in the very expression "*until* seven times shall pass over him," as if he would then be restored in some way, or as if this condition would then terminate ; and (*b*) in the statement that "the stump of the roots" would be left in the earth as if it might still germinate again. Everything, however, in the dream was fitted to produce perplexity as to what it could mean. The word rendered *times* (עִדָּנִין—sing. עִדָּן) is an important word in the interpretation of Daniel. It is of the same class of words as the Hebrew יָעַד—to point out, to appoint, to fix ; and would refer properly to time considered as *appointed* or *designated;* then it may mean any stated or designated period, as a year.

be given unto him ; and let seven times *b* pass over him.

b ch. 12. 7.

The idea is that of time considered as designated or fixed by periods, and the word may refer to *any* such period, however long or short—a day, a month, a year, or any other measure of duration. What measurement or portion is intended in any particular case must be determined from the connection in which the word is found. The word used here does not occur in the Hebrew scripture, and is found only in the book of Daniel, where it is uniformly rendered *time* and *times.* It is found only in the following places: Dan. ii. 8, "that ye would gain *the time;*" ii. 9, "till *the time* be changed;*" ii. 21, "and he changeth *the times;*" iii. 5, 15, "at what *time* ye shall hear;*" iv. 16, 23, "and let seven *times* pass over him," 25, 32, "seven *times* shall pass over him;*" vii. 12, "for a season and *time;*" vii. 25, "until a *time* and *times* and the dividing of *time.*" In the place before us, so far as the meaning of the *word* is concerned, it might mean a day, a week, a month, or a year. The more common interpretation is that which supposes that it was a year, and this will agree better with all the circumstances of the case than any other period. The Greek of Theodotion here is, καὶ ἑπτὰ καιροὶ ἀλλαγήσονται ἐπ᾿ αὐτόν —"And seven times shall change upon him ;" that is, until seven seasons revolve over him. The most natural construction of this Greek phrase would be to refer it to years. The Latin Vulgate interprets it in a similar way—*et septem tempora mutentur super eum*— "And let seven times be changed " or revolve "over him." In the *Cod. Chis.* it is, καὶ ἑπτὰ ἔτη βοσκηθῇ σὺν αὐτοῖς— "and let him feed with them seven years." Luther renders it *times.* Josephus understands it for "*seven years.*" — *Ant.* b. x. ch. x. § 6. While the Chaldee word is indeterminate in respect to the length of time, the most natural and obvious construction here and elsewhere, in the use of the word, is to refer it to years. Days or weeks would be obviously too short, and though in this place the word *months*

17 This matter *is* by the [a]decree of the watchers, and the demand by the word of the holy ones: to the intent that the living may know [b] that the Most High [c] ruleth in the kingdom of men, and giveth it to whomsoever [d] he will, and setteth up over it the basest [e] of men.

[a] vers. 13, 14. [b] Ps. 9. 16, 20. [c] vers. 25, 32, 35.

[d] Ps. 75. 6, 7.   [e] Exod. 9. 16; 1 Kings 21. 25; 2 Kings 21. 6, &c.; 2 Chr. 28. 22.

would perhaps embrace all that would be necessary, yet in the other places where the word occurs in Daniel it undoubtedly refers to years, and there is, therefore, a propriety in understanding it in the same manner here.

17. *This matter* is *by the decree of the watchers.* Notes on ver. 13. They are described here not only as watching over the affairs of men, but as intrusted with the execution of high and important designs of God. The representation is, that one of these heavenly beings was seen by Nebuchadnezzar in his visions, and that this one stated to him that he had come to execute what had been determined on by his associates, or in counsel with others. The idea would seem to be, that the affairs of the kingdom of Nebuchadnezzar had been in important respects placed under the administration of these beings, and that in solemn council they had resolved on this measure. It is not said that this was not in accordance with, and under the direction of, a higher power —that of God; and that is rather implied when it is said that the great design of this was to show to the living that "the *Most High* ruleth in the kingdom of men." In itself considered, there is no improbability in supposing that the affairs of this lower world are in some respects placed under the administration of beings superior to man, nor that events may occur as the result of their deliberation, or, as it is here expressed, by their "decree." If, in any respect, the affairs of the world are subject to their jurisdiction, there is every reason to suppose that there would be harmony of counsel and of action, and an event of this kind might be so represented. ¶ *And the demand.* Or, the matter; the affair; the business. The Chaldee word properly means a question, a petition; then a subject of inquiry, a matter of business. Here it means, that this matter, or this busi-

ness, was in accordance with the direction of the holy ones. ¶ *The holy ones.* Synonymous with the *watchers*, and referring to the same. See Notes on ver. 13. ¶ *To the intent that the living may know.* With the design that those who live on the earth may understand this. That is, the design was to furnish a proof of this, so impressive and striking, that it could not be doubted by any. No more effectual way of doing this could occur than by showing the absolute power of the Most High over such a monarch as Nebuchadnezzar. ¶ *That the Most High.* He who is exalted above all men; all angels; all that pretend to be gods. The phrase here is designed to refer to the true God, and the object was to show that he was the most exalted of all beings, and had absolute control over all. ¶ *Ruleth in the kingdom of men.* Whoever reigns, he reigns over them. ¶ *And giveth it to whomsoever he will.* That is, he gives dominion over men to whomsoever he chooses. It is not by human ordering, or by arrangements among men. It is not by hereditary right; not by succession; not by conquest; not by usurpation; not by election, that this matter is finally determined; it is by the decree and purpose of God. He can remove the hereditary prince by death; he can cause him to be set aside by granting success to a usurper; he can dispose of a crown by conquest; he can cut off the conqueror by death, and transfer the crown to an inferior officer; he can remove one who was the united choice of a people by death, and put another in his place. So the apostle Paul says, "There is no power but of God: the powers that be are ordained of God" (Rom. xiii. 1). ¶ *And setteth up over it the basest of men.* That is, he appoints over the kingdom of men, at his pleasure, those who are of the humblest or lowest rank. The allusion here is not to Nebuchadnezzar as if he

18 This dream I king Nebuchadnezzar have seen. Now thou, O Belteshazzar, declare the interpretation thereof, forasmuch *a* as all the wise *men* of my kingdom are not able to make known unto me the interpretation : but thou *art* able ; for the spirit of the holy gods *is* in thee.

19 ¶ Then Daniel, whose name

a ver. 7.

was Belteshazzar, was astonied for one hour, and his thoughts troubled him. *b* The king spake and said, Belteshazzar, let not the dream, or the interpretation thereof, trouble thee. Belteshazzar answered and said, My lord, the dream *be* to them *c* that hate thee, and the interpretation thereof to thine enemies.

b ver. 9.   c 2 Sam. 18. 32; Jer. 29. 7.

were the *basest* or the *vilest* of men, but the statement is a general truth, that God, at his pleasure, sets aside those of exalted rank, and elevates those of the lowest rank in their place. There is an idea now attached commonly to the word *basest*, which the word used here by no means conveys. It does not denote the mean, the vile, the worthless, the illiberal, but those of humble or lowly rank. This is the proper meaning of the Chaldee word שְׁפַל—and so it is rendered in the Vulgate, *humillimum hominem.* The Greek of Theodotion, however, is, *"that which is disesteemed among men"*—ἐξουδένωμα ἀνθρώπων. In the latter part of the dream (vers. 15, 16) we have an illustration of what often occurs in dreams—their singular incongruity. In the early part of the dream, the vision is that of a *tree*, and the idea is consistently carried out for a considerable part of it—the height of the tree, the branches, the leaves, the fruit, the shade, the stump ; then suddenly there is a *change* to something that is living and human—the change of the *heart* to that of a beast ; the being exposed to the dew of heaven ; the portion with the beasts of the earth, &c. Such changes and incongruities, as every one knows, are common in dreams. So Shakespeare—

> "True, I talk of dreams,
> Which are the children of an idle brain,
> Begot of nothing but vain fantasy;
> Which is as thin of substance as the air,
> And more inconstant than the wind, who woos
> Even now the frozen bosom of the North,
> And, being anger'd, puffs away from thence,
> Turning his face to the dew-dropping South."
> *Romeo and Juliet.*

18. *This dream I king Nebuchadnezzar have seen.* This is the dream which I saw. He had detailed it at

length as it appeared to him, without pretending to be able to explain it. ¶ *Forasmuch as all the wise men of my kingdom,* &c. Ver. 7. ¶ *But thou art able,* &c. Notes on ver. 9.

19. *Then Daniel, whose name* was *Belteshazzar.* Ver. 8. It has been objected that the mention in this edict of *both* the names by which Daniel was known is an improbable circumstance ; that a heathen monarch would only have referred to him by the name by which he was known in Babylon—the name which he had himself conferred on him in honour of the god (*Belus*) after whom he was called. See Notes on ch. i. 7. To this it may be replied, that although in ordinary intercourse with him in Babylon, in addressing him as an officer of state under the Chaldean government, he would undoubtedly be mentioned only by that name ; yet, in a proclamation like this, *both* the names by which he was known would be used—the one to identify him among his own countrymen, the other among the Chaldeans. This proclamation was designed for people of all classes, and ranks, and tongues (ver. 1); it was intended to make known the supremacy of the God worshipped by the Hebrews. Nebuchadnezzar had derived the knowledge of the meaning of his dream from one who was a Hebrew, and it was natural, therefore, in order that it might be known by whom the dream had been interpreted, that he should so designate him that it would be understood by all. ¶ *Was astonied.* Was astonished. The word *astonied*, now gone out of use, several times occurs in the common version ; Ezra ix. 3 ; Job xvii. 8 ; xviii. 20 ; Ezek. iv. 17 ; Dan. iii. 24 ; iv. 19 ; v. 9. Daniel was

20 The tree *a* that thou sawest, which grew, and was strong, whose height reached unto the heaven, and the sight thereof to all the earth;

a vers. 10-12.

21 Whose leaves *were* fair, and the fruit thereof much, and in it *was* meat for all; under which the beasts of the field dwelt, and upon whose branches the fowls of the heaven had their habitation:

amazed and *overwhelmed* at what was manifestly the fearful import of the dream. ¶ *For one hour.* It is not possible to designate the exact time denoted by the word *hour*—שָׁעָה. According to Gesenius (*Lex.*), it means a moment of time; properly, a look, a glance, a wink of the eye—German, *augenblick*. In Arabic the word means both a moment and an hour. In Dan. iii. 6, 15, it evidently means *immediately*. Here it would seem to mean *a short time.* That is, Daniel was fixed in thought, and maintained a profound silence until the king addressed him. We are not to suppose that this continued during the space of time which we call an hour, but he was silent until Nebuchadnezzar addressed him. He would not seem to be willing even to speak of so fearful calamities as he saw were coming upon the king. ¶ *And his thoughts troubled him.* The thoughts which passed through his mind respecting the fearful import of the dream. ¶ *The king spake and said,* &c. Perceiving that the dream had, as he had probably apprehended, a fearful significancy, and that Daniel hesitated about explaining its meaning. Perhaps he supposed that he hesitated because he apprehended danger to himself if he should express his thoughts, and the king therefore assured him of safety, and encouraged him to declare the full meaning of the vision, whatever that might be. ¶ *Belteshazzar answered and said, My lord, the dream be to them that hate thee.* Let such things as are foreboded by the dream happen to your enemies rather than to you. This merely implies that he did not desire that these things should come upon *him.* It was the language of courtesy and of respect; it showed that he had no desire that any calamity should befall the monarch, and that he had no wish for the success of his enemies. There is not, in this, anything necessarily implying a hatred of the

enemies of the king, or any wish that calamity should come upon them; it is the expression of an earnest desire that such an affliction might not come upon *him.* If it must come on any, such was his respect for the sovereign, and such his desire for his welfare and prosperity, that he preferred that it should fall upon those who were his enemies, and who hated him. This language, however, should not be rigidly interpreted. It is the language of an Oriental; language uttered at a court, where only the words of respect were heard. Expressions similar to this occur not unfrequently in ancient writings. Thus Horace, b. iii. ode 27 :—

"Hostium uxores puerique cæcos
Sentiant motus orientis Austri."

And Virgil, *Georg.* iii. 513 :—

"Di meliora piis, erroremque hostibus illum."

"Such rhetorical embellishments are pointed at no individuals, have nothing in them of malice or ill-will, are used as marks of respect to the ruling powers, and may be presumed to be free from any imputation of a want of charity." —Wintle, *in loc.*

20, 21. *The tree that thou sawest,* &c. In these two verses Daniel refers to the leading circumstances respecting the tree as it appeared in the dream, without any allusion as yet to the order to cut it down. He probably designed to show that he had clearly understood what had been said, or that he had attended to the most minute circumstances as narrated. It was important to do this in order to show clearly that it referred to the king; a fact which probably Nebuchadnezzar himself apprehended, but still it was important that this should be so firmly fixed in his mind that he would not revolt from it when Daniel came to disclose the fearful import of the remainder of the dream.

22. *It* is *thou, O king.* It is a representation of thyself. Comp. ch. ii. 38. ¶ *That art grown and become*

DANIEL I.　　　　　　　R

22 It *is* thou, ^a O king, that art grown and become strong: for thy greatness is grown, and reacheth unto heaven, and thy dominion ^b to the end of the earth.

23 And whereas ^c the king saw a watcher and an holy one coming down from heaven, and saying, Hew the tree down, and destroy it; yet leave the stump of the roots thereof in the earth, even with a band of iron and brass, in the ten-

a ch. 2. 38.   b Jer. 27. 6–8.   c vers. 13, 14.

der grass of the field; and let it be wet with the dew of heaven, and *let* his portion *be* with the beasts of the field, till seven times pass over him;

24 This *is* the interpretation, O king, and this *is* the decree of the Most High, which is come upon my lord the king:

25 That they shall drive ^d thee from men, and thy dwelling shall be with the beasts of the field, and

d ver. 33.

strong. Referring to the limited extent of his dominion when he came to the throne, and the increase of his power by a wise administration and by conquest. ¶ *For thy greatness is grown.* The majesty and glory of the monarch had increased by all his conquests, and by the magnificence which he had thrown around his court. ¶ *And reacheth unto heaven.* An expression merely denoting the greatness of his authority. The tree is said to have reached unto heaven (ver. 11), and the stateliness and grandeur of so great a monarch might be represented by language which seemed to imply that he had control over all things. ¶ *And thy dominion to the end of the earth.* To the extent of the world as then known. This was almost literally true.

23. *And whereas the king saw a watcher,* &c. See Notes on ver. 13. The recapitulation in this verse is slightly varied from the statement in vers. 14–16, still so as not materially to affect the sense. Daniel seems to have designed to recal the *principal* circumstances in the dream, so as to identify it in the king's mind, and so as to prepare him for the statement of the fearful events which were to happen to him.

24. *This* is *the decree of the Most High.* Daniel here designs evidently to direct the attention of the monarch to the one living and true God, and to show him that he presides over all. The purpose of the vision was, in a most impressive way, to convince the king of his existence and sovereignty. Hence Daniel says that all this was in accordance with his "decree." It was

not a thing of chance; it was not ordered by idol gods; it was not an event that occurred by the mere force of circumstances, or as the result of the operation of secondary laws: it was a direct Divine interposition—the solemn purpose of the living God that it should be so. Nebuchadnezzar had represented this, in accordance with the prevailing views of religion in his land, as a "decree of the *Watchers*" (ver. 17); Daniel, in accordance with his views of religion, and with *truth*, represents it as the decree of the true God. ¶ *Which is come upon my Lord the king.* The decree had been previously formed; its execution had now come upon the king.

25. *That they shall drive thee from men.* That is, thou shalt be driven from the habitations of men; from the place which thou hast occupied among men. The prophet does not say *who* would do this, but he says that it *would* be done. The language is such as would be used of one who should become a maniac, and be thrust out of the ordinary society in which he had moved. The Greek of Theodotion here is, καὶ σὲ ἐκδιώξουσιν. The *Codex Chisian.* has, "And the Most High and his angels shall run upon thee—κατατρέχουσιν — leading thee into prison," or into detention—εἰς φυλακὴν—"and shall thrust thee into a desert place." The general sense is, that he would be in such a state as to be treated like a beast rather than a man; that he would be removed from his ordinary abodes, and be a miserable and neglected outcast. This commences the account of the calamity that was to come upon Nebuchadnezzar, and as there have

they shall make thee to eat [a]grass as oxen, and they shall wet thee with the dew of heaven, and seven times shall pass over thee, till thou

know that the Most High [b] ruleth in the kingdom of men, and giveth it to whomsoever he will.

a Ps. 106. 20.   b Ps. 83. 18.

been many opinions entertained as to the nature of this malady, it may be proper to notice some of them. Comp. Bertholdt, pp. 286–292. Some have held that there was a real metamorphosis into some form of an animal, though his rational soul remained, so that he was able to acknowledge God and give praise to him. Cedrenus held that he was transformed into a beast, half lion and half ox. An unknown author, mentioned by Justin, maintained that the transformation was into an animal resembling what was seen in the visions of Ezekiel—the Cherubim—composed of an eagle, a lion, an ox, and a man. In support of the opinion that there was a real transformation, an appeal has been made to the common belief among ancient nations, that such metamorphoses had actually occurred, and especially to what Herodotus (iv. 105) says of the *Neuri* (Νευροι): " It is said by the Scythians, as well as by the Greeks who dwell in Scythia, that once in every year they are all of them changed into wolves, and that after remaining in that state for the space of a few days, they resume their former shape." Herodotus adds, however, " This I do not believe, although they swear that it is true." An appeal is also made to an assertion of Apuleius, who says of himself that he was changed into an ass ; and also to the *Metamorphoses* of Ovid. This supposed transformation of Nebuchadnezzar some have ascribed to Satan.—Joh. Wier *de Præstigiis Dæmonum*, I. 26, iv. 1. Others have attributed it to the arts of magic or incantation, and suppose that it was a change in appearance only. Augustine (*de Civit. Dei.* lib. xviii. cap. 17), referring to what is said of Diomed and his followers on their return from Troy, that they were changed into birds, says that Varro, in proof of the truth of this, appeals to the fact that Circe changed Ulysses and his companions into beasts ; and to the Arcadians, who, by swimming over a certain lake, were changed into wolves,

and that " if they ate no man's flesh, at the end of nine years they swam over the same lake and became men again." Varro farther mentions the case of a man by the name of Dæmonetus, who, tasting of the sacrifices which the Arcadians offered (a child), was turned into a wolf, and became a man again at the end of two years. Augustine himself says, that when he was in Italy, he heard a report that there were women there, who, by giving one a little drug in cheese, had the power of turning him into an ass. See the curious discussion of Augustine how far this could be true, in his work *de Civit. Dei*, lib. xviii. cap. 18. *He* supposes that under the influence of drugs men might be made to *suppose* they were thus transformed, or to have a recollection of what passed in such a state *as if* it were so. Cornelius à Lapide supposes that the transformation in the case of Nebuchadnezzar went only so far that his knees were bent in the other direction, like those of animals, and that he walked like animals. Origen, and many of those who have coincided with him in his allegorical mode of interpreting the Scriptures, supposed that the whole of this account is an allegory, designed to represent the fall of Satan, and his restoration again to the favour of God—in accordance with his belief of the doctrine of universal salvation. Others suppose that the statement here means merely that there was a formidable conspiracy against him; that he was dethroned and bound with fetters ; that he was then expelled from the court, and driven into exile ; and that, as such, he lived a miserable life, finding a precarious subsistence in woods and wilds, among the beasts of the forest, until, by another revolution, he was restored again to the throne. It is not necessary to examine these various opinions, and to show their absurdity, their puerility, or their falsehood. Some of them are simply ridiculous, and none of them are demanded by any fair interpretation of the chapter. It may seem, perhaps, to be undignified even to *refer* to such opinions now; but this may serve to illustrate the method in which the Bible has been interpreted in former times, and the steps which have been taken before men arrived at a clear and rational interpretation of the sacred volume. It is indeed painful to reflect that such absurdities and puerilities have been in any way connected with the interpretation of the Word of God; sad to reflect that so many persons, in consequence of them, have discarded the Bible and the interpretations together as equally ridiculous and absurd. The *true* account in regard to the calamity of Nebuchadnezzar is undoubtedly the following: (1.) He was a maniac—made such by a direct Divine judgment on account of his pride, vers. 30, 31. The essential thing in the statement is, that he was deprived of his reason, and that he was treated *as* a maniac. Comp. Intro. to the chapter, II. (1). (2.) The particular *form* of the insanity with which he was afflicted seems to have been that he imagined himself to be a beast; and, this idea having taken possession of his mind, he acted accordingly. It may be remarked in regard to this, (*a*) that such a fancy is no uncommon thing among maniacs. Numerous instances of this may be seen in the various works on insanity—or indeed may be seen by merely visiting a lunatic asylum. One imagines that he is a king, and decks himself out with a sceptre and a diadem; another that he is glass, and is filled with excessive anxiety lest he should be broken; others have regarded themselves as deprived of their proper nature as human beings; others as having been once dead, and restored to life again; others as having been dead and sent back into life without a heart; others as existing in a manner unlike any other mortals; others as having no rational soul. See Arnold *on Insanity*, I. pp. 176–195. In all these cases, when such a fancy takes possession of the mind, there will be an effort on the part of the patient to act in exact conformity to this view of himself, and his whole conduct will be adapted to it. Nothing can convince him that it is

not so; and there is no absurdity in supposing that, if the thought had taken possession of the mind of Nebuchadnezzar that he was a beast, he would live and act *as* a wild beast— just as it is said that he did. (*b*) In itself considered, *if* Nebuchadnezzar was deprived of his reason, and for the cause assigned—his pride, nothing is more probable than that he would be left to imagine himself a beast, and to act like a beast. This would furnish the most striking contrast to his former state; would do most to bring down his pride; and would most effectually show the supremacy of the Most High. (3.) In this state of mind, fancying himself a wild beast, and endeavouring to act in conformity with this view, it is probable that he would be indulged as far as was consistent with his safety. Perhaps the regency would be induced to allow this partly from their long habits of deference to the will of an arbitrary monarch; partly because by this indulgence he would be less troublesome; and partly because a painful spectacle would thus be removed from the palace. We are not to suppose that he was permitted to roam in forests at large without any restraint, and without any supervision whatever. In Babylon, attached to the palace, there were doubtless, as there are all over the East, royal parks or gardens; there is every probability that in these parks there may have been assembled rare and strange animals as a royal menagerie; and it was doubtless in these parks, and among *these* animals that he was allowed to range. Painful as such a spectacle would be, yet it is not improbable that to *such* a maniac this would be allowed, as contributing to his gratification, or as a means of restoring him to his right mind. (4.) A king, however wide his empire, or magnificent his court, would be as *likely* to be subject to mental derangement as any other man. No situation in life can save the human mind from the liability to so overwhelming a calamity, nor should we deem it strange that it should come on a king as well as other men. The condition of Nebuchadnezzar, as represented by himself in this edict, was scarcely more pitiable than that of

George III. of England, though it is not surprising that in the eighteenth century of the Christian era, and in a Christian land, the treatment of the sovereign in such circumstances was different from that which a monarch received in heathen Babylon. (5.) It cannot be shown that this did *not* come upon Nebuchadnezzar, as stated in this chapter (vers. 30, 31), on account of his pride. That he *was* a proud and haughty monarch is apparent from all his history; that God would take some effectual means to humble him is in accordance with his dealings with mankind; that this would be a most effectual means of doing it cannot be doubted. No one can prove, in respect to *any* judgment that comes upon mankind, that it is *not* on account of some sin reigning in the heart; and when it is affirmed in a book claiming to be inspired, that a particular calamity is brought upon men on account of their transgressions, it cannot be demonstrated that the statement is not true. If these remarks are correct, then no well-founded objection can lie against the account here respecting the calamity that came upon this monarch in Babylon. This opinion in regard to the nature of the affliction which came upon Nebuchadnezzar, is probably that which is now generally entertained, and it certainly meets all the circumstances of the case, and frees the narrative from material objection. As a confirmation of its truth, I will copy here the opinion of Dr. Mead, as it is found in his *Medica Sacra:* "All the circumstances of Nebuchadnezzar's case agree so well with a hypochondriacal madness, that to me it appears evident that Nebuchadnezzar was seized with this distemper, and under its influence ran wild into the fields; and that, fancying himself transformed into an ox, he fed on grass after the manner of cattle. For every sort of madness is the result of a disturbed imagination; which this unhappy man laboured under for full seven years. And through neglect of taking proper care of himself, his hair and nails grew to an uncommon length; whereby the latter, growing thicker and crooked, resembled the claws of birds. Now the an-

cients called people affected with this kind of madness, λυκάνθρωποι, *wolf-men* —or κυνάνθρωποι, *dog-men*—because they went abroad in the night imitating wolves or dogs; particularly intent upon opening the sepulchres of the dead, and had their legs much ulcerated, either from frequent falls or the bites of dogs. In like manner are the daughters of Prœtus related to have been mad, who, as Virgil says, *Ecl.* vi. 48,

' —— implerunt falsis mugitibus agros.'
'With mimic howlings filled the fields.'

For, as Servius observes, Juno possessed their minds with such a species of fury, that, fancying themselves cows, they ran into the fields, bellowed often, and dreaded the plough. Nor was this disorder unknown to the moderns, for Schneckius records a remarkable instance of a husbandman in Padua, who, imagining himself a wolf, attacked and even killed several people in the fields; and when at length he was taken, he persevered in declaring himself a real wolf, and that the only difference consisted in the inversion of his skin and hair." The same opinion as to the nature of the disease is expressed by Dr. J. M. Good, in his *Study of Medicine.* So also Burton (*Anatomy of Melancholy,* Part I. § I. Memb. i. Subs. 4). Burton refers to several cases which would illustrate the opinion. "Wierus," says he, "tells a story of such a one in Padua, 1541, that would not believe the contrary but that he was a wolf. He hath another instance of a Spaniard, who thought himself a bear. Such, belike, or little better, were king Prœtus' daughters, that thought themselves *kine*"—an instance strikingly resembling this case of Nebuchadnezzar, who seems to have imagined himself some kind of beast. Pliny, perhaps referring to diseases of this kind, says, "Some men were turned into wolves in my time, and from wolves to men again," lib. viii. c. 22. See Burton as above. ¶ *And thy dwelling shall be with the beasts of the field.* That is, as above explained, thou wilt imagine thyself to be a beast, and wilt act like a beast. Indulgence will be given to this propensity so as to allow you to range with the beasts in the park, or

26 And whereas they com-
manded to leave the stump of the
tree roots; thy kingdom shall be
sure unto thee, after that thou shalt

have known that the *a* heavens do
rule.
27 Wherefore, O king, let my

a Matt. 5. 34; Luke 15. 18, 21.

the royal menagerie. ¶ *And they shall
make thee to eat grass as oxen.* That
is, this shall be thy propensity, and
thou shalt be indulged in it. Fancying himself a beast of some kind—probably, as appears from this expression,
an ox—nothing would be more natural
than that he should attempt to live as
oxen do, on grass, that he should be so
far indulged that his food would consist of vegetables. Nothing is more
common among maniacs than some
such freak about food; and it is just
as likely that a king would manifest
this as any other man. The word
grass here (עֲשַׂב Heb. עֵשֶׂב) means,
properly, *herbs; green herbs; vegetables*
—represented commonly, as furnishing
food for man, Gen. i. 11,'12; ii. 5;
iii. 18; Exod. x. 12, 15; Ps. civ. 14.
The word *grass*, in our language, conveys an idea which is not *strictly* in
accordance with the original. That
word would denote only the vegetable
productions which cattle eat; the Hebrew word is of a more general signification, embracing all kinds of vegetables
—those which man eats, as well as
those which animals eat; and the
meaning here is, that he would live on
vegetable food—a propensity in which
they would doubtless indulge a man in
such circumstances, painful and humiliating as it would be. The phrase
"they shall *make* thee eat grass,"
rather means, "they shall *permit* thee
to do it," or they shall treat thee so
that thou wilt do it. It would be his
inclination; and they would allow him
to be gratified in it. ¶ *And they shall
wet thee with the dew of heaven.* Or,
shall suffer you to be wet with the dew
of heaven; that is, to be out in the
open air—no improbable treatment of
a maniac, and especially likely to occur
in a climate where it was no uncommon thing for all classes of persons to
pass the night under the sky. ¶ *And
seven times shall pass over thee.* Notes
on ver. 16. ¶ *Till thou know,* &c.
Until thou shalt effectually learn that

the true God rules; that he gives authority to whom he pleases; and that
he takes it away when he pleases.
Notes on ver. 17. Nothing could be
better fitted to teach this lesson than
to deprive, by a manifest judgment of
heaven, such a monarch of the exercise
of reason, and reduce him to the pitiable condition here described.

26. *And whereas they commanded.*
The watchers, ver. 15. Comp. ver. 17.
¶ *To leave the stump of the tree roots.*
Or, to leave roots to the stump of the
tree; that is, it was not to be dug up,
or wholly destroyed, but vitality was
to be left in the ground. The Chaldee
here is the same as in ver. 15, "leave
the stump of his roots." ¶ *Thy kingdom shall be sure unto thee.* That is,
thou shalt not die under this calamity,
but after it has passed away shalt be
restored to authority. It *might* have
been supposed that this meant that the
authority would survive in his family,
and that those who were to succeed
him would reign—as shoots spring up
after the parent tree has fallen; but
Daniel was directed to an interpretation
which is not less in accordance with the
fair meaning of the dream than this
would have been. ¶ *After that thou
shalt have known that the heavens do
rule.* That God rules. This was the
great lesson which the event was designed to teach, and when that should
have been learned, there would be a
propriety that he should be restored to
his throne, and should proclaim this to
the world.

27. *Wherefore, O king, let my counsel
be acceptable unto thee.* Daniel was
permitted to see not only the fact that
this calamity impended over the king,
but the cause of it, and as that cause
was his proud and sinful heart, he supposed that the judgment might be
averted if the king would reform his
life. If the *cause* were removed, he
inferred, not unreasonably, that there
was a hope that the calamity might be
avoided. We cannot but admire here

counsel be acceptable unto thee, and break off *a* thy sins by righteousness, and thine iniquities by

showing mercy to the poor; if *b* it may be [1] a lengthening of thy tranquillity.

---

a Isa. 55. 7.

b Ps. 41. 1, 2.   1 or, *a healing of thine error.*

---

the boldness and fidelity of Daniel, who not only gave a fair interpretation of the dream, in the case submitted to him, but who went beyond that in a faithful representation to the most mighty monarch of the age, that this was in consequence of his wicked life. ¶ *And break off thy sins by righteousness.* By acts of righteousness or justice ; by abandoning a wicked course of life. It is fairly to be inferred from this that the life of the monarch had been wicked— a fact which is confirmed everywhere in his history. He had, indeed, some good qualities as a man, but he was proud ; he was ambitious ; he was arbitrary in his government ; he was passionate and revengeful ; and he was, doubtless, addicted to such pleasures of life as were commonly found among those of his station. He had a certain kind of respect for religion, whatever was the object of worship, but this was not inconsistent with a wicked life. The word translated *break off* (פְּרֻק) is rendered in the Vulgate *redime,* "*redeem,*" and so in the Greek of Theodotion, λύτρωσαι, and in the *Codex Chis.* From this use of the word in some of the versions, and from the fact that the word rendered *righteousness* is often employed in the later Hebrew to denote almsgiving (comp. the margin in Matt. vi. 1, and the Greek text in Tittmann and Hahn where the word δικαιοσύνην is used to denote *alms*), the passage here has been adduced in favour of the doctrine of expiatory merits, and the purchase of absolution by almsgiving—a favourite doctrine in the Roman Catholic communion. But the ordinary and common meaning of the word is not to redeem, but to break, to break off, to abandon. It is the word from which our English word *break* is derived — Germ., *brechen.* Comp. Gen. xxvii. 40, "that thou shalt *break* his yoke ;" Exod. xxxii. 2, "*Break off* the golden ear-rings ;" Exod. xxxii. 3, " And all the people *brake off*

the golden ear-rings ;" Exod. xxxii. 24, " Whosoever hath any gold let them *break it off;*" 1 Kings xix. 11, " A great and strong wind *rent* the mountains ;" Zech. xi. 16, " And *tear* their claws in *pieces;*" Ezek. xix. 12, " her strong rods were *broken.*" The word is rendered in our common version, *redeem* once (Psa. cxxxvi. 24), "And hath *redeemed* us from our enemies." It is translated *rending* in Psa. vii. 2, and *deliver* in Lam. v. 8. It does not elsewhere occur in the Scriptures. The fair meaning of the word is, as in our version, *to break off,* and the idea of redeeming the soul by acts of charity or almsgiving is not in the passage, and cannot be derived from it. This passage, therefore, cannot be adduced to defend the doctrine that the soul may be redeemed, or that sins may be expiated by acts of charity and almsgiving. It means that the king was to break off his sins by acts of righteousness ; or, in other words, he was to show by a righteous life that he had abandoned his evil course. The exhortation is, that he would practise those great duties of justice and charity towards mankind in which he had been so deficient, if, perhaps, God might show mercy, and avert the impending calamity. ¶ *And thine iniquities by showing mercy to the poor.* The peculiar "iniquity" of Nebuchadnezzar may have consisted in his oppressing the poor of his realm in the exorbitant exactions imposed on them in carrying on his public works, and building and beautifying his capital. Life, under an Oriental despot, is regarded as of little value. Sixty thousand men were employed by Mohammed Ali in digging the canal from Cairo to Alexandria, in which work almost no tools were furnished them but their hands. A large portion of them died, and were buried by their fellow-labourers in the earth excavated in digging the canal. Who can estimate the number of men that were recklessly employed under the arbitrary monarch of

Egypt on the useless work of building the pyramids? Those structures, doubtless, cost millions of lives, and there is no improbability in supposing that Nebuchadnezzar had employed hundreds of thousands of persons without any adequate compensation, and in a hard and oppressive service, in rearing the walls and the palaces of Babylon, and in excavating the canals to water the city and the adjacent country. No counsel, therefore, could be more appropriate than that he should relieve the poor from those burdens, and do justice to them. There is no intimation that he was to attempt to *purchase* release from the judgments of God by such acts; but the meaning is, that if he would cease from his acts of oppression, it might be hoped that God would avert the threatened calamity. The duty here enjoined of showing mercy to the poor, is one that is everywhere commanded in the Scriptures, Psa. xli. 1; Matt. xix. 21; Gal. ii. 10, *et sæpe*. Its influence in obtaining the Divine favour, or in averting calamity, is also stated. Comp. Psa. xli. 1, "Blessed is he that considereth the poor; the Lord will deliver him in time of trouble." It is a sentiment which occurs frequently in the books of the Apocrypha, and in these books there can be found the progress of the opinion to the point which it reached in the later periods of the Jewish history, and which it has obtained in the Roman Catholic communion, that almsgiving or charity to the poor would be an expiation for sin, and would commend men to God as a ground of righteousness; or, in other words, the progress of the doctrine towards that which teaches that works of supererogation may be performed. Thus in the book of Tobit iv. 8–10, "If thou hast abundance, give alms accordingly; if thou have little, be not afraid to give according to that little: for thou layest up a good treasure for thyself against the day of necessity. *Because that alms do deliver from death*, and suffereth not to come into darkness." Tobit xii. 9, 10, "For alms *doth deliver from death, and shall purge away all sin*. Those that exercise righteousness and alms shall be filled with life; but they that sin are enemies

to their own life." Tobit xiv. 10, 11, "Manasses gave alms, and escaped the snares of death which they had set for him; but Aman fell into the snare and perished. Wherefore now, my son, consider what alms doeth, and how righteousness doth deliver." Ecclesiasticus xxix. 12, 13, "Shut up alms in thy storehouses; it shall deliver thee from all affliction. It shall fight for thee against thine enemies better than a mighty shield and a strong spear." Ecclesiasticus xl. 24, "Brethren and help are against time of trouble; but alms shall deliver more than them both." In these passages there is evidence of the progress of the sentiment towards the doctrine of supererogation; but there is none whatever that Daniel attributed any *such* efficacy to alms, or that he meant to teach anything more than the common doctrine of religion, that when a man breaks off from his sins it may be hoped that the judgments which impended over him may be averted, and that doing good will meet the smiles and approbation of God. Compare in reference to this sentiment the case of the Ninevites, when the threatening against them was averted by their repentance and humiliation, Jonah iii. 10; the case of Hezekiah, when his predicted death was averted by his tears and prayers, Isa. xxxviii. 1–5; and Jer. xviii. 7, 8, where this principle of the Divine government is fully asserted. ¶ *If it may be a lengthening of thy tranquillity.* Marg., "or, *a healing of thine error.*" The Greek of Theodotion here is, "Perhaps God will be long-suffering toward thy offences." The Greek of the *Codex Chisianus* is, "And thou mayest remain a long time (πολυήμερος γίνῃ) upon the throne of thy kingdom." The Vulgate, "Perhaps he will pardon thy faults." The Syriac, "Until he may remove from thee thy follies." The original word rendered *lengthening* (אַרְכָא) means, properly, as translated here, a prolongation; a drawing out; a lengthening; and the word is here correctly rendered. It has not the meaning assigned to it in the margin of *healing*. It would apply properly to a prolongation of anything—as of life, peace,

28 ¶ All this came upon the king Nebuchadnezzar.

29 At the end of twelve months

he walked [1] in the palace of the kingdom of Babylon.

1 or, *upon*.

health, prosperity. The word rendered *tranquillity* (שְׁלֵוָה) means, properly, security, safety, quiet; and the reference here is to his calm possession of the throne; to his quietness in his palace, and peace in his kingdom. There is nothing in the text to justify the version in the margin.

28. *All this came upon the king Nebuchadnezzar.* That is, the threatened judgment came upon him in the form in which it was predicted. He did not repent and reform his life as he was exhorted to, and, having given him sufficient time to show whether he was disposed to follow the counsel of Daniel, God suddenly brought the heavy judgment upon him. Why he did *not* follow the counsel of Daniel is not stated, and cannot be known. It may have been that he was so addicted to a life of wickedness that he would not break off from it, even while he admitted the fact that he was exposed on account of it to so awful a judgment—as multitudes do who pursue a course of iniquity, even while they admit that it will be followed by poverty, disgrace, disease and death here, and by the wrath of God hereafter; or it may be, that he did not credit the representation which Daniel made, and refused to follow his counsel on that account; or it may be, that though he purposed to repent, yet, as thousands of others do, he suffered the time to pass on until the forbearance of God was exhausted, and the calamity came suddenly upon him. A full year, it would seem (ver. 29), was given him to see what the effect of the admonition would be, and then all that had been predicted was fulfilled. His conduct furnishes a remarkable illustration of the conduct of sinners under threatened wrath; of the fact that they continue to live in sin when exposed to certain destruction, and when warned in the plainest manner of what will come upon them.

29. *At the end of twelve months.* After the dream, and the interpretation—giving him ample opportunity to re-

pent, and to reform his life, and to avoid the calamity. ¶ *He walked in the palace.* Marg., *upon.* The margin is the more correct rendering. The roofs of houses in the East are made flat, and furnish a common place of promenade, especially in the cool of the evening. See Notes on Mat. ix. 2. The *Codex Chis.* has here, "The king walked upon the walls of the city with all his glory, and went around the towers, and answering, said." The place, however, upon which he walked, appears to have been the roof of his own palace—doubtless reared so high that he could have a good view of the city from it. ¶ *Of the kingdom of Babylon.* Appertaining to that kingdom; the royal residence. As it is to be supposed that this "palace of the kingdom," on the roof of which the king walked, was that which he had himself reared, and as this contributed much to the splendour of the capital of his empire, and doubtless was the occasion, in a considerable degree, of his vainglorious boasting when the judgment of heaven fell upon him (vers. 30, 31), a brief description of that palace seems to be not inappropriate. The description is copied from an article on Babylon in Kitto's *Cyclopædia of Bibli cal Literature*, vol. i. pp. 270, 271: "The new palace built by Nebuchadnezzar was prodigious in size, and superb in embellishments. Its outer wall embraced six miles; within that circumference were two other embattled walls, besides a great tower. Three brazen gates led into the grand area, and every gate of consequence throughout the city was of brass. The palace was splendidly decorated with statues of men and animals, with vessels of gold and silver, and furnished with luxuries of all kinds brought thither from conquests in Egypt, Palestine, and Tyre. Its greatest boast were the hanging gardens, which acquired, even from Grecian writers, the appellation of one of the wonders of the world. They are attributed to the gallantry of Nebuchadnezzar, who constructed them

30 The king spake *a* and said, Is not this great Babylon, that I have built for the house of the kingdom,

a Luke 12. 19, 20.

in compliance with a wish of his queen Amytis to possess elevated groves, such as she had enjoyed on the hills around her native Ecbatana. Babylon was all flat, and to accomplish so extravagant a desire, an artificial mountain was reared, four hundred feet on each side, while terraces, one above another, rose to a height that overtopped the walls of the city, that is, above three hundred feet in elevation. The ascent from terrace to terrace was made by corresponding flights of steps, while the terraces themselves were reared to their various stages on ranges of regular piers, which, forming a kind of vaulting, rose in succession one over the other to the required height of each terrace, the whole being bound together by a wall twenty-two feet in thickness. The level of each terrace or garden was then formed in the following manner: the tops of the piers were first laid over with flat stones, sixteen feet in length, and four in width; on these stones were spread beds of matting, then a thick layer of bitumen, after which came two courses of bricks, which were covered with sheets of solid lead. The earth was heaped on this platform, and in order to admit the roots of large trees, prodigious hollow piers were built and filled with mould. From the Euphrates, which flowed close to the foundation, water was drawn up by machinery. The whole, says Q. Curtius (v. 5), had, to those who saw it from a distance, the appearance of woods overhanging mountains. The remains of this palace are found in the vast mound or hill called by the natives *Kasr*. It is of irregular form, eight hundred yards in length, and six hundred yards in breadth. Its appearance is constantly undergoing change from the continual digging which takes place in its inexhaustible quarries for brick of the strongest and finest material. Hence the mass is furrowed into deep ravines, crossing and recrossing each other in every direction."

by the might of my power, and for the honour of my majesty?

31 While *b* the word *was* in the

b 1 Thess. 5. 3.

30. *The king spake and said.* The Chaldee, and the Greek of Theodotion and of the *Codex Chis.*, here is, "the king *answered* and said:" perhaps he replied to some remark made by his attendants in regard to the magnitude of the city; or perhaps the word *answered* is used, as it often seems to be in the Scriptures, to denote a reply to something passing in the mind that is not uttered; to some question or inquiry that the mind starts. He might merely have been thinking of the magnitude of this city, and he gave response to those thoughts in the language which follows. ¶ *Is not this great Babylon, that I have built.* In regard to the situation and the magnitude of Babylon, and the agency of Nebuchadnezzar in beautifying and enlarging it, see the analysis prefixed to the Notes on the thirteenth chapter of Isaiah. He greatly enlarged the city; built a new city on the west side of the river; reared a magnificent palace; and constructed the celebrated hanging gardens; and, in fact, made the city so different from what it was, and so greatly increased its splendour, that he could say without impropriety that he had "built" it. ¶ *For the house of the kingdom.* To be considered altogether—embracing the whole city—as a sort of palace of the kingdom. He seems to have looked upon the whole city as one vast palace fitted to be an appropriate residence of the sovereign of so vast an empire. ¶ *And for the honour of my majesty.* To ennoble or glorify my reign; or where one of so much majesty as I am may find an appropriate home.

31. *While the word was in the king's mouth.* In the very act of his speaking—thus showing that there could be no doubt as to the connection between the crime and the punishment. ¶ *There fell a voice from heaven.* There came a voice; or, perhaps, it seemed to *fall* as a thunderbolt. It was uttered above him, and appeared to come from heaven.

king's mouth, there fell a voice from heaven, *saying*, O king Nebuchadnezzar, to thee it is spoken: The kingdom is departed from thee:

32 And ^a they shall drive thee from men, and thy dwelling *shall be* with the beasts of the field:

a vers. 25, 26.

they shall make thee to eat grass as oxen, and seven times shall pass over thee, until thou know that the Most High ruleth in the kingdom of men, and giveth it to whomsoever he will.

33 The same hour was the thing fulfilled upon Nebuchadnezzar: and he was driven from men, and

---

There was an important sense in which it *did* fall from heaven; for it was the voice of God. ¶ Saying, *O king Nebuchadnezzar, to thee it is spoken.* For you it is particularly intended; or what is predicted is now spoken to thee. ¶ *The kingdom is departed from thee.* Thou art about to cease to reign. Up to this time he retained his reason, that he might distinctly understand the source from whence the judgment was to come, and why it was brought upon him, and that he might be prepared, when he should be recovered from his insanity, to testify clearly to the origin and the nature of the judgment. The *Codex Chis.* has an important *addition* to what is said here, which, though of no authority, as having nothing corresponding to it in the original text, yet states what is in itself not improbable. It is as follows: "And at the end of what he was saying, he heard a voice from heaven, To thee it is spoken, O king Nebuchadnezzar, the kingdom of Babylon shall be taken away from thee, and shall be given to another, a man despised or of no rank—ἐξουθενημένῳ ἀνθρώπῳ—in thy house. Behold, I will place him over thy kingdom, and thy power, and thy glory, and thy luxury—τὴν τρυφήν—he shall receive, until thou shalt know that the God of heaven has authority over the kingdom of men, and gives it to whomsoever he will: but until the rising of the sun another king shall rejoice in thy house, and shall possess thy power, and thy strength, and thine authority, and the angels shall drive thee away for seven years, and thou shalt not be seen, and shalt not speak with any man, but they shall feed thee with grass as oxen, and from the herb of the field shall be thy support."

32. *And they shall drive thee from men,* &c. See Notes on ver. 25. 33. *The same hour was the thing fulfilled.* On the word *hour*, see Notes on ver. 19. The use of the word here would seem to confirm the suggestion there made that it means a brief period of time. The idea is clearly that it was done instantly. The event came suddenly upon him, without any interval, as he was speaking. ¶ *Till his hairs were grown like eagles'* feathers. By long neglect and inattention. The Greek version of Theodotion has in this place the word *lions* instead of *eagles:* "till his hairs were grown long like that of lions;" and the passage is paraphrased by Jackson thus, "till his hair was grown long and shagged like the mane of a lion." This would make good sense, but it is not the reading of the Chaldee. The *Codex Chis.* reads it, "and my hairs were like the wings of an eagle, and my nails like those of a lion." The correct idea is, that his hair was neglected until in appearance it resembled the feathers of a bird. ¶ *And his nails like birds'* claws. No unnatural thing, if he was driven out and neglected as the insane have been in much later times, and in much more civilized parts of the world. In regard to the probability of the statement here made respecting the treatment of Nebuchadnezzar, and the objection derived from it against the authenticity of the book of Daniel, see Introduction to the chapter, II. (1). In addition to what is said there, the following cases may be referred to as showing that there is no improbability in supposing that what is here stated actually occurred. The extracts are taken from the *Second Annual Report of the Prison Discipline Society*, and they describe the condition of some

did eat grass as oxen, and his body was wet with the dew of heaven, till his hairs were grown like eagles' *feathers*, and his nails like birds' *claws*.

of the patients before they were admitted into the insane asylum at Worcester. If these things occurred in the commonwealth of Massachusetts, and in the nineteenth century of the Christian era, there is nothing incredible in supposing that a similar thing may have occurred in ancient heathen Babylon. "No. 1. Had been in prison twenty-eight years when he was brought to the Institution. During seven years he had not felt the influence of fire, and many nights he had not lain down for fear of freezing. He had not been shaved for twenty-eight years, and had been provoked and excited by the introduction of hundreds to see the exhibition of his raving. No. 2. Had been in one prison fourteen years: he was naked—his hair and beard grown long—and his skin so entirely filled with the dust of charcoal as to render it impossible, from its appearance, to discover what nation he was of. He was in the habit of screaming so loud as to annoy the whole neighbourhood, and was considered a most dangerous and desperate man. No. 3. An old man of seventy years of age or more; had been *chained for twenty-five years*, and had his chain taken off but once in that time. No. 4. A female: had so long been confined with a *short chain* as wholly to lose the use of her lower limbs. Her health had been materially impaired by confinement, and she was unable to stand, and had not walked for years. No. 8. Had been ten years without clothes: a most inconceivably filthy and degraded being: exceedingly violent and outrageous. No. 9. Another female, exceedingly filthy in her habits, had not worn clothes for two years, during which time she had been confined in a filthy cell, destitute of everything like comfort, tearing everything in pieces that was given her. No. 10. Had been insane eight years: almost the whole of the time in jail and in a cage."

34. *And at the end of the days.* That is, the time designated; to wit, the

34 And at the end of the days I Nebuchadnezzar lifted up mine eyes unto heaven, and mine understanding returned unto me; and I blessed the Most High; and I

"seven times" that were to pass over him. ¶ *I Nebuchadnezzar lifted up mine eyes unto heaven.* Probably the first thing that indicated returning reason. It would not be unnatural, on the supposition that he was deprived of reason *at the very instant* that a voice seemed to speak to him from heaven, and that he continued wholly insane or idiotic during the long interval of seven years, that the first indication of returning reason would be his looking up to the place from whence that voice seemed to come, as if it were still speaking to him. In some forms of mental derangement, when it comes suddenly upon a man, the effect is wholly to *annihilate* the interval, so that, when reason is restored, the individual connects in his recollection the last thing which occurred when reason ceased with the moment when it is restored. A patient had been long an inmate of an insane apartment in Providence, Rhode Island. He was a seaman, and had been injured on the head when his vessel was in a naval engagement, and it was supposed that his brain had been permanently affected. For many years he was idiotic, and no hopes were entertained of his recovery. It was at length suggested that the operation of trepanning should be performed, and the very instant that the bone was raised from its pressure on the brain, he exclaimed, "Has she struck?" The whole interval of time was obliterated from his memory. Similar instances are mentioned by Dr. Abercrombie (*Intellectual Powers*, pp. 252, 253). A man had been employed for a day with a beetle and wedges in splitting pieces of wood for erecting a fence. At night, before going home, he put the beetle and wedges into the hollow of an old tree, and directed his sons, who had been at work in an adjoining field, to accompany him next morning to assist in making the fence. In the night he became maniacal, and continued in a state of insanity for several years, during which time his

praised and honoured him [a] that liveth for ever, whose dominion *is* an everlasting [b] dominion, and his

a ch. 12. 7; Rev. 4. 10.　　b ch. 2. 44; 7. 14;
Ps. 10. 16; Jer. 10. 10; Mic. 4. 7; Luke 1. 33.

mind was not occupied with any of the subjects with which he had been conversant when in health. After several years his reason returned suddenly, and the first question he asked was, whether his sons had brought home the beetle and wedges. A lady had been intensely engaged for some time in a piece of needlework. Before she had completed it she became insane, and continued in that state for seven years; after which her reason returned suddenly. One of the first questions she asked related to her needlework, though she had never alluded to it, so far as was recollected, during her illness. Another lady was liable to periodical paroxysms of delirium, which often attacked her so suddenly that in conversation she would stop in the middle of a story, or even of a sentence, and branch off into the subject of hallucination. On the return of her reason, she would resume the subject of her conversation on which she was engaged at the time of the attack, beginning exactly where she had left off, though she had never alluded to it during her delirium; and on the next attack of delirium she would resume the subject of hallucination with which she had been occupied at the conclusion of the former paroxysm. A similar thing may have occurred to Nebuchadnezzar. He was deprived of reason by a sudden voice from heaven. Nothing was more natural, or would be more in accordance with the laws respecting insanity, than that *at the very instant* when reason returned he should look up to the place whence the voice had seemed to come. ¶ *And mine understanding returned unto me.* This shows that he regarded himself as having been a maniac, though doubtless he was ignorant of the manner in which he had been treated. It would seem from the narrative, and from the probabilities of the case, that he found himself driven out from his palace, herding with cattle, and in the deplorable condition in regard to personal

kingdom *is* from generation [c] to generation:

35 And [d] all the inhabitants of

c Ps. 90. 1.　　　　d Isa. 40. 15, 17.

appearance which he here describes. Seeing this in fact, and recollecting the prediction, he could not doubt that this was the way in which he had been treated during the period of his distressing malady. ¶ *And I blessed the Most High.* For his recovery, and in an humble acknowledgment of his dependence. "The acts of praise here referred to are the suitable returns of a mind truly penitent, and deeply sensible of its faults and of its mercies."— Winkle. ¶ *And I praised and honoured him.* That is, I *honoured* him by rendering thanks for his restoring mercy, by recognizing him as the true God, and by the acknowledging of the truth that he has a right to reign, and that his kingdom is over all. ¶ *That liveth for ever.* He is the *living* God, as he is often styled, in contradistinction from all false gods—who have no life; and he lives *for ever* in contradistinction to his creatures on earth, all of whom are destined to die. He will live when all on earth shall have died; he will live for ever in the future, as he has lived for ever in the past. ¶ *Whose dominion is an everlasting dominion.* His empire extends through all time, and will continue while eternal ages roll away. ¶ *And his kingdom is from generation to generation.* The generations of men pass away. One succeeds another, and there is no permanency. Dynasties change, and monarchs die. No human sovereign can extend his own power over the next generation, nor can he secure his authority in the person of his successors. But the dominion of God is unchanged, while the generations of men pass away; and when one disappears from the earth, he meets the next with the same claim to the right of sovereignty, with the same principles of government—carrying forward, through that and successive ages, the fulfilment of his great and glorious purposes.

35. *And all the inhabitants of the earth* are *reputed as nothing.* Are re-

the earth *are* reputed as nothing: and he *a* doeth according to his will in the army of heaven, and *among*

a Ps. 115. 3; 135. 6.   *b* Isa. 43. 13.

garded as nothing in comparison with him. Comp. Notes on Isa. xl. 15, 17. Precisely the same sentiment occurs in Isaiah which is expressed here : "All nations before him are as nothing; and they are accounted unto him less than nothing and vanity." ¶ *And he doeth according to his will in the army of heaven.* In the host of heaven—בְּחֵיל —Gr., *in the power of heaven,* ἐν τῇ, δυνάμει. The Chaldee word means properly strength, might, valour ; and it is then applied to an army as possessing strength, or valour, or force. It is here applied to the inhabitants of heaven, probably considered as an army or host, of which God is the head, and which he leads forth or marshals to execute his purposes. In ch. iii. 20, the word is rendered *army.* The sentiment here is, that in respect to the inhabitants of heaven, represented as organized or marshalled, God does his own pleasure. An intimation of his will is all that is needful to control them. This sentiment is in accordance with all the statements in the Scripture, and is a point of theology which must enter into every just view of God. Thus in the Lord's prayer it is implied : "Thy will be done in earth as it is in heaven." So Eph. i. 11—"Who worketh all things after the counsel of his own will." In heaven the will of God is accomplished in the most strict and absolute sense, for his will is law, and the only law to all the dwellers there. The obedience is as entire as if the will of each one of the dwellers there were but a form or manifestation of the will of God itself. ¶ *And* among *the inhabitants of the earth.* This cannot mean, even as understood by Nebuchadnezzar, that the will of God is actually done among the inhabitants of the earth in the same sense, and to the same extent, as among those who dwell in heaven. His design was, undoubtedly, to assert the supremacy and absolute control of God; a fact that had been so strikingly illustrated in his own case. The sentiment

the inhabitants of the earth : and none can stay *b* his hand, or say unto him, What *c* doest thou ?

c Job 9. 12; Isa. 45. 9; Rom. 9. 20.

expressed by Nebuchadnezzar is *true* in the following respects :—(1.) That man has no power to prevent the fulfilment of the Divine purposes. (2.) That God will accomplish his design in all things, whatever opposition man may make. (3.) That he has absolute control over every human being, and over all that pertains to any one and every one. (4.) That he will overrule all things so as to make them subservient to his own plans. (5.) That he will make use of men to accomplish his own purposes. Comp. Notes on Isa. x. 7. (6.) That there is a great and glorious scheme of administration which God is carrying out by the instrumentality of men. ¶ *And none can stay his hand.* Literally, "none can smite upon his hand" (Gesenius, *Lex.*) ; that is, none can restrain his hand. The language is taken, says Bertholdt, from the custom of striking children upon the hand when about to do anything wrong, in order to restrain them. The phrase is common in the Targums for *to restrain, to hinder.* The Arabs have a similar expression in common use. See numerous instances of the use of the word מְחָא in the sense of *restrain* or *prohibit,* in Buxtorf.—*Lex. Chal.* The truth taught here is, that no one has power to keep back the hand of God when it is put forth to accomplish the purposes which he intends to execute; that is, he will certainly accomplish his own pleasure. ¶ *Or say unto him, What doest thou ?* A similar expression occurs in 2 Sam. xvi. 10: "So let him curse, because the Lord hath said unto him, Curse David. Who shall then say, Wherefore hast thou done so ?" Also in Job ix. 12: "Behold, he taketh away : Who can hinder him ? Who will say unto him, What doest thou ?" See Notes on that passage. The meaning here is plain. God is supreme, and will do his pleasure in heaven and in earth. The *security* that all will be done right is founded on the perfection of his nature ; and that is ample. Mys-

36 At the same time my reason returned unto me ; and for the glory of my kingdom, mine honour and brightness returned unto me ; and my counsellors and my lords sought

unto me ; and I was established in my kingdom, and excellent majesty was added *a* unto me.

37 Now I Nebuchadnezzar praise

a Job 42. 12.

---

terious though his ways may seem to us, yet in that perfection of his nature we have the fullest assurance that no wrong will be done to any of his creatures. Our duty, therefore, is calm submission to his holy will, with the deep conviction that whatever God does will yet be seen to be right.

36. *At the same time my reason returned unto me.* Showing that he regarded himself as having been insane. ¶ *And for the glory of my kingdom.* That is, his restoration to the exercise of his reason contributed to the glory of his kingdom, either by the acts of justice and beneficence which he intended should characterize the remainder of his reign, or by his purpose to reform the abuses which had crept into the government while he was deprived of his reason, or by his determination to complete public works which had been purposed or commenced before his affliction. ¶ *Mine honour and brightness returned unto me.* Evidently referring to his intellect. He was again restored to that strength and clearness of understanding by which, before his affliction, he had been able to do so much for the glory of his kingdom. ¶ *And my counsellors and my lords sought unto me.* As they had done formerly. During his state of mental alienation, of course, the great lords of the empire would not resort to him for counsel. ¶ *And excellent majesty was added unto me.* Majesty and honour appropriate to my state, instead of the treatment incident to the condition of a maniac. Theodotion renders this, "and greater majesty was added to me." It is by no means improbable that additional honour would be conferred on the recovered monarch.

37. *Now I Nebuchadnezzar praise and extol and honour the King of Heaven.* Comp. ch. ii. 47, and vers. 1–3 of this chapter. He felt himself called on, in this public manner, to acknowledge the true God, with whose supremacy he had

been made acquainted in so affecting a manner ; to *praise* him that he had preserved him, and restored him to his reason and his throne ; to *extol* or exalt him, by recognizing his sovereignty over the mighty kings of the earth, and the power to rule over all ; and to *honour* him by making his name and attributes known abroad, and by using all his influence as a monarch to have him reverenced throughout his extended empire. ¶ *All whose works are truth.* See Deut. xxxii. 4; Psal. xxxiii. 4; Rev. xv. 3. The meaning is, that all that he does is done in accordance with the true nature of things, or with justice and propriety. It is not based on a false estimate of things, as what is done by man often is. How often are the plans and acts of man, even where there are the best intentions, based on some false estimate of things ; on some views which are shown by the result to have been erroneous ! But God sees things precisely as they are, and accurately knows what should be done in every case. ¶ *And those that walk in pride he is able to abase.* What had occurred to Nebuchadnezzar might occur to others, and as God had shown that he could reduce the most exalted sovereign of the earth to the lowest condition in which a human being can be, he inferred that he could do the same to all, and that there was no one so exalted in rank, so vigorous in health, and so mighty in intellect, that he could not effectually humble and subdue him. This is indeed an affecting truth which is constantly illustrated in the world. The reverses occurring among men, the sick-bed, the loss of reason, the grave, show how easily God can bring down rank, and beauty, and talent and all that the world calls great, to the dust.

In the Greek *Codex Chis.* there is at the close of this chapter a beautiful ascription of praise to God, which has nothing to correspond with it in the Chaldee, and the origin of which is un-

and extol and honour the King of
heaven, all whose works *a are* truth,
and his ways judgment: and those

that walk in pride *b* he is able to
abase.

a Deut. 32. 4; Ps. 33. 4; Rev. 15. 3.
b Exod. 18. 11; Job 40. 11, 12; ch. 5. 20.

known. I will translate it, because,
although it is not of Divine authority,
and is no part of the sacred writings,
it contains sentiments not inappropriate
to the close of this remarkable chapter.
It is as follows :—" To the Most High
I make confession, and render praise
to Him who made the heaven, and the
earth, and the seas, and the rivers, and
all things in them ; I acknowledge him
and praise him because he is the God
of gods, and Lord of lords, and King
of kings, for he does signs and wonders,
and changes times and seasons, taking
away the kingdoms of kings, and placing others in their stead. From this
time I will serve him, and from the fear
of him trembling has seized me, and I
praise all his saints; for the gods of the
heathen have not in themselves power
to transfer the kingdom of a king to
another king, and to kill and to make
alive, and to do signs, and great and
fearful wonders, and to change mighty
deeds, as the God of heaven has done
to me, and has brought upon me great
changes. I, during all the days of my
reign, on account of my life, will bring
to the Most High sacrifices for an odour
of sweet savour to the Lord, and I and
my people will do that which will be
acceptable before him—my nation, and
the countries which are under my power.
And whosoever shall speak against the
God of heaven, and whosoever shall
countenance those who speak anything,
I will condemn to death. Praise the
Lord God of heaven, and bring sacrifice
and offering to him gloriously. I, king
of kings, confess Him gloriously, for so
he has done with me ; in the very day
he set me upon my throne, and my
power, and my kingdom; among my
people I have power, and my majesty
has been restored to me. , And he sent
letters concerning all things that were
done unto him in his kingdom, to all
the nations that were under him."
Nebuchadnezzar is supposed to have
lived but about one year after this
(Wintle), but nothing is known of his
subsequent deeds. It may be hoped

that he continued steadfast in his faith
in that God whom he had thus been
brought to acknowledge, and that he
died in that belief. But of this nothing
is known. After so solemn an admonition, however, of his own pride, and
after being brought in this public manner to acknowledge the true God, it is
to be regarded as not improbable that
he looked on the Babylon that he had
reared, and over his extended realms,
with other feelings than those which
he had before this terrible calamity
came upon him. " Nebuchadnezzar
was succeeded in his kingdom by his
son Iloarudam, according to Ptolemy,
who is the Evil-Merodach of Jeremiah.
After the death of Evil-Merodach, who
reigned two years, Niricassolassar, or
Neriglissar, who seems to have been
the chief of the conspirators against
the last king, succeeded him. He had
married a daughter of Nebuchadnezzar,
and in the course of his reign made a
great stand against the growing power
of the Medes and Persians; but at
length, after a reign of four years, was
killed in a battle with them under the
command of Cyrus. His son Laboro-
soarchod succeeded him, and having
reigned only nine months, and not
reaching a Thoth, or beginning of an
Egyptian year, he is not mentioned by
Ptolemy; but he is said to have been
quite the reverse of his father, and to
have exercised many acts of wanton
cruelty, and was murdered by his own
subjects, and succeeded by his son Nabonadius, or Belshazzar."—Wintle.

REMARKS.

(1.) The narrative in this chapter furnishes an illustration of the disposition
among men to make arrangements for
their own ease and comfort, especially
in view of advancing years, ver. 4.
Nebuchadnezzar had drawn around him
all that it is possible, perhaps, for man
to accumulate with this view. He was
at the head of the heathen world—the

mighty monarch of the mightiest kingdom on the earth. He was at peace—having finished his wars, and having been satiated with the glory of battle and conquest. He had enlarged and beautified his capital, so that it was one of the "wonders of the world." He had built for himself a palace, which surpassed in richness, and elegance, and luxury, all the habitations of man in that age. He had accumulated vast wealth, and there was not a production of any clime which he could not command, nor was there anything that is supposed to be necessary to make man happy in this life which he had not in his possession. All this was the result of arrangement and purpose. He *designed* evidently to reach the point where he might feel that he was "at ease, and flourishing in his palace."

What was true in his case on a large scale is true of others in general, though on a much smaller scale. Most men would be glad to do the same thing; and most men seek to make such an arrangement according to their ability. They look to the time when they may retire from the toils and cares of life, with a competence for their old age, and when they may enjoy life, perhaps, many years, in the tranquillity of honourable and happy retirement. The merchant does not expect always to be a merchant; the man in office to be always burdened with the cares of state. The soldier does not expect always to be in the camp, or the mariner on the sea. The warrior hopes to repose on his laurels; the sailor to find a quiet haven; the merchant to have enough to be permitted to sit down in the evening of life free from care; and the lawyer, the physician, the clergyman, the farmer, each one hopes, after the toils and conflicts of life are over, to be permitted to spend the remainder of his days in comfort, if not in affluence.

This seems to be based on some law of our nature; and it is not to be spoken of harshly, or despised as if it had no foundation in that which is great and noble in our being. I see in this a high and noble truth. It is that our nature looks forward to *rest;* that we are so made as to pant for *repose*—for calm repose when the work of life is over. As our Maker formed us, the law was that we should seek this in the world to come—in that blessed abode where we may be free from all care, and where there shall be everlasting rest. But man, naturally unwilling to look to that world, has abused this law of his being, and seeks to find the rest for which the soul pants, in that interval, usually *very* short, and quite unfitted for tranquil enjoyment, between the period when he toils, and lies down in the grave. The true law of his being would lead him to look onward to everlasting happiness; he abuses and perverts the law, and seeks to satisfy it by making provision for a brief and temporary rest at the close of the present life.

(2.) There is a process often going on in the case of these individuals to *disturb* or *prevent* that state of ease. Thus there was in the case of Nebuchadnezzar, as intimated by the dream. Even then, in his highest state of grandeur, there was a *tendency* to the sad result which followed when he was driven from his throne, and treated as a poor and neglected maniac. This was intimated to him by the dream; and to one who could see all the future, it would be apparent that things were *tending* to this result. The very excitements and agitations of his life, the intoxication of his pride, and the circumstances of ease and grandeur in which he was now placed, all tended by a natural course of things to produce what followed.

And so, in other cases, there is often a process going on, if it could be seen, destined to disappoint all those hopes, and to prevent all that anticipated ease and tranquillity. It is not always visible to men, but could we see things as God sees them, we should perceive that there are causes at work which will blast all those hopes of ease, and disappoint all those expectations of tranquillity. There *may be* (*a*) the loss of all that we possess : for we hold it by an uncertain tenure, and "riches often take to themselves wings." There *may be* (*b*) the loss of a wife, or a child—and all our anticipated comforts shall be tasteless, for there shall be none with whom to share them. There *may be* (*c*) the loss of reason, as in the case of Nebuchadnezzar, for no human precaution can guard against that. There *may be* (*d*) the loss of health—a loss against which no one can defend himself—which shall render all his preparations for comfort of no value. Or (*e*) death itself *may* come—for no one has any basis of calculation in regard to his own life, and no one, therefore, who builds for himself a palace can have any security that he will ever enjoy it. Men who build splendid houses for themselves may yet experience sad scenes in their dwellings ; and if they could foresee all that will occur in them, it would so throw a gloom over all the future as to lead them to abandon the undertaking. Who could engage cheerfully in such an enterprise if he saw that he was constructing a house in which a daughter was to lie down and die, or from which his wife and children were soon to be borne forth to the grave ? In this chamber your child may be long sick ; in that one you or your wife may lie down on a bed from which you will never rise; from those doors yourself, your wife, your child, will be borne forth to the grave; and if you *saw* all this now, how could you engage with so much zeal in constructing your magnificent habitation ?

(3.) Our plans of life should be formed with the feeling that this is *possible:* 1 say not with the gloomy apprehension that these calamities will certainly come, or with no anticipation or hope that there will be different scenes—for then life would be nothing else but gloom ; but that we should allow the *possibility* that these things may occur to enter, as an element, into our calculations respecting the future. Such a feeling will give us sober and just views of life ; will break the force of trouble and disappointment when they come ; and will give us just apprehensions of our dependence on Him in whose hand are all our comforts.

(4.) The dealings of God in our world are such as are eminently fitted to keep up the recognition of these truths. What occurred to Nebuchadnezzar, in the humbling of his pride, and the blighting of his anticipated pleasures, is just an illustration of what is constantly occurring on the earth. What house is there into which trouble, disappointment, and sorrow never come ? What scheme of pride is there in respect to which something does not occur to produce mortification ? What habitation is there into which sickness, bereavement, and death never find their way ? And what abode of man on earth can be made secure from the intrusion of these things ? The most splendid mansion must soon be left by its owner, and never be visited by him again. The most magnificent banqueting-hall will be forsaken by its possessor, and never will he return to it again ; never go into the chamber where he sought repose ; never sit down at the table where he joined with others in revelry.

(5.) The counsel given by Daniel to Nebuchadnezzar (ver. 27), to break off his sins by righteousness, that there might be a lengthening out of his tranquillity, is counsel that may now be given to all sinners, with equal propriety. (I.) For, as in his case, there are certain consequences of sin to which we must look forward, and on which the eye of a sinner should rest. Those consequences are (1) such as spring up in the course of nature, or which are the regular results of sin in the course of events. They are such as can be foreseen, and can be made the basis of calculation, or which a man can know beforehand *will* come upon him if he perseveres in a certain course. Thus he who is intemperate can look upon certain results which will inevitably follow if he perseveres in that course of life. As he looks upon the poverty, and babbling, and woe, and sorrow, and misery, and death of an inebriate, he can see that that lot will be *certainly* his own if he perseveres in his present course, and this can be made with him a matter of definite calculation or anticipation. Or (2) there are all those consequences of sin which are made known in the sacred Scriptures as sure to come upon transgressors. This, too, is a large class; but these consequences are as *certain* as those which occur in the regular course of events. The principal difference between the two is, that revelation has designated *more* sins that will involve the sinner in calamity than can be ascertained in the ordinary course of events, and that it has carried the mind forward, and discloses what will take place in the *future* world as well as what will occur in *this*. But the one is more certain than the other; and alike in reference to what is *sure* to occur in the present life, and what we are *told* will occur in the future state, the sinner should allow himself to be influenced by the anticipation of what is to come. II. Repentance, reformation, and a holy life would, in many cases, go far to arrest these calamities— or, in the language of Daniel, "lengthen out tranquillity." This is true in the following respects : (1.) That impending *temporal* calamities may be often partially or wholly turned away by reformation. An illustration of this thought occurred in the case of Nineveh; and the same thing now occurs. A young man who is in danger of becoming intemperate, and who has already contracted some of the habits that lead to intemperance, could avert a large class of impending ills by so simple a thing as signing the temperance pledge, and adhering to it. *All* the evils of poverty, tears, crime, disease, and an early death, that intemperance produces, he would *certainly* avert; that is, he would make it certain that the large class of ills that intemperance engenders would *never* come upon him. He might experience *other* ills, but he would never suffer those. So it is of the sufferings produced by licentiousness, by gluttony, by the spirit of revenge; and so it is of all the woes that follow the violation of human laws. A man may indeed be poor; he may be sick; he may be bereaved; he may lose his reason, but *these* ills he will never experience. But what Daniel here affirms is true in another sense in regard to temporal calamities. A man may, by repentance, and by breaking off from his sins, do much to stay the progress of woe, and to avert the results which he has already begun to experience. Thus the drunkard may reform, and may have restored health, vigour, and prosperity; and thus the licentious may turn from the evil of his ways, and enjoy health and happiness still. On this subject, see Notes on Job xxxiii. 14–25, particularly the Notes on ver. 25. (2.) But by repentance and holy living a man may turn away *all* the results of sin in the future world, and may make it certain that he will never experience a pang beyond the grave. All the woe that sin would cause in the future state may be thus averted, and he who has been deeply guilty may enter the eternal world with the assurance that he will never suffer beyond the grave. Whether, then, we look to the future in the present life, or to the future beyond the grave, we have the highest conceivable motives to abandon the ways of sin, and to lead lives of holiness. If a man were to live *only* on the earth, it would be for his welfare to break off from the ways of transgression ; how much higher is this motive when it is remembered that he must exist for ever !

(6.) We have an illustration in the account in this chapter of the evil of *pride*, vers. 29–31. The pride which we may have on account of beauty, or strength, or learning, or accomplishments ; which we feel when we look over our lands that we have cultivated, or the houses that we have built, or the reputation which we have acquired, is no less offensive in the sight of a holy God than was the pride of the magnificent monarch who looked out on the towers, and domes, and walls, and palaces of a vast city, and said, "Is not this great Babylon that I have builded?"

(7.) And in view of the calamity that came upon Nebuchadnezzar, and the treatment which he received in his malady, we may make the following remarks : (*a*) We should be thankful for the continuance of *reason*. When we look on such a case as this, or when we go into a lunatic asylum, and see the wretchedness that the loss of reason causes, we should thank God *daily* that we are not deprived of this inestimable blessing. (*b*) We should be thankful for science, and for the Christian religion, and for all that they have done to give comfort to the maniac, or to restore him to a sound mind. When we compare the treatment which the insane

now receive in the lunatic asylums with that which they everywhere meet with in the heathen world, and with that which they have, up to a very recent period, received in Christian lands, there is almost nothing in which we see more marked proof of the interposition of God than in the great change which has been produced. There are few persons who have not, or may not have, some friend or relative who is insane, and there is no one who is not, or may not be, personally interested in the improvement which religion and science have made in the treatment of this class of unfortunate beings. In no one thing, so far as I know, has there been so decided progress in the views and conduct of men ; and on no one subject has there been so evident an improvement in modern times, as in the treatment of the insane. (*c*) The possibility of the loss of reason should be an element in our calculations about the future. On this point we can have no security. There is no such vigour of intellect, or clearness of mind, or cultivation of the habits of virtue, and even no such influence of religion, as to make it certain that *we* may not yet be reckoned among the insane ; and the *possibility* that this may be so should be admitted as an element in our calculations in regard to the future. We should not jeopard any valuable interest by leaving that undone which *ought* to be done, on the supposition that we may at a future period of life enjoy the exercise of reason. Let us remember that there *may be* in our case, even in youth or middle life, the loss of this faculty ; that there *will be*, if we reach old age, in all probability, such a weakening of our mental powers as to unfit us for making any preparation for the life to come, and that on the bed of death, *whenever* that occurs, there is often an entire loss of the mental powers, and commonly so much pain, distress, or prostration, as to unfit the dying man for calm and deliberate thought ; and let us, therefore, while we *have* reason and health, do all that we know we *ought* to do to make preparation for our eternal state. For what is our reason more certainly given us than to prepare for another world ?

CHAPTER V.

§ I.—AUTHENTICITY OF THE CHAPTER.

Much fewer objections have been made to the authenticity of this chapter, and much fewer difficulties started, than in regard to chapter iv. Those which have been urged may be classed under the following heads :—

I. The first is substantially stated in this manner by Bertholdt, that "Daniel is represented as speaking to the king in such a tone, that if it had actually occurred, he would have been cut to pieces by an arbitrary Babylonian despot; but instead of that, he is not only unpunished, but is suffered to announce to the king the certain destruction of his kingdom by the Medes and Persians ; and not only this, but he is immediately promoted to be a minister or officer of a state of exalted rank," p. 345.

To this it may be replied, (1.) That the way in which Daniel addressed him was entirely in accordance with the manner in which he addressed Nebuchadnezzar, in which Nathan addressed David, in which Isaiah addressed Ahaz, and Jeremiah the kings in his time. (2.) Belshazzar was overpowered with the remarkable vision of the handwriting on the wall ; his conscience smote him, and he was in deep alarm. He sought the meaning of this extraordinary revelation, and could not but regard it as a communication from heaven. In this state of mind, painful as was the announcement, he would naturally receive it as a Divine communication, and he might fear to treat with indig-

nity one who showed that he had the power of disclosing the meaning of words so mysterious.   (3.) It was in accordance with the custom of those times to honour those who showed that they had the power of penetrating the Divine mysteries, and of disclosing the meaning of dreams, prodigies, and omens.   (4.) It is not impossible, as Hengstenberg *Authentie des Dan.* 120, suggests, that, smitten with the consciousness of guilt, and knowing that he deserved punishment, he may have hoped to turn away the wrath of God by some act of piety ; and that he resolved, therefore, to honour Daniel, who showed that he was a favourite of heaven.   The main security of Daniel, however, in these bold and fearful announcements, was undoubtedly to be found in the *smitten conscience* of the trembling monarch, and in the belief that he was a favourite of heaven.

II. The improbability that all this should occur in one night—that so many scenes should have been crowded into so short a time—embracing the feast, the writing, the calling in of the magicians, the investing of Daniel with his new office, the taking of the city, &c. "Why," says Bertholdt, "was not the proclamation in regard to the new minister deferred to the following day ? Why did all this occur in the midst of the scenes of revelry which were then taking place ?" pp. 345, 346.

To this it may be replied, (1.) That there is, indeed, every appearance of haste and confusion in the transactions. This was natural. But there was assuredly no want of *time* to accomplish all that it is said was accomplished. If it was true that Cyrus broke into the city in the latter part of the night, or if, as historians say was the fact, he had entered the city, and made considerable progress in it before the tidings were communicated to Belshazzar, there is no improbability in supposing that all that is said of the feast, and of the handwriting, and of the calling in of the magicians, and of their failure to decipher the meaning of the writing, and of the summoning of Daniel, and of the interpretation which he gave, actually occurred, for there was time enough to accomplish all this. (2.) As to the other part of the objection, that it is improbable that Daniel would be so soon invested with office, and that a proclamation would be made in the night to this effect, it may be replied, that all that is fairly meant in the chapter (ver. 29) may be that *an order* was made to that effect, with a purpose to carry it into execution on the following day. Bertholdt himself translates the passage (ver. 29), "Then Belshazzar gave command that they should clothe Daniel with scarlet, and put a chain of gold around his neck," &c. Hierauf *gab Belschazar den Befehl* dem Daniel den purpurmantel und den goldenen Halsschmuck umzuhängen, &c. On the one hand, nothing forbids the supposition that the execution of this order might have been deferred; or, on the other, that the order *was* executed at once. But little time would have been necessary to do it. See however, Notes on ver. 29.

III. A third objection or difficulty arises from the writing itself. It is, that it is wholly improbable that Daniel could have had sufficient knowledge to enable him to interpret these words when no one of the Chaldean sages could do it. Where, it is asked, could he have obtained this knowledge? His instruction in reading languages he must have received in Babylon itself, and it is wholly improbable that among so many sages and wise men who were accustomed to the languages spoken in Babylon and in other countries, no one should have been found who was as

able to interpret the words as he.— Bertholdt, p. 346.

To this it is obvious to reply, that the whole narrative supposes that Daniel owed his ability to interpret these words, not to any natural skill, or to any superior advantages of genius or education, but to the fact that he was directly endowed from on high. In other cases, in the times of Nebuchadnezzar, he always disclaimed any power of his own of revealing the meaning of dreams and visions (ch. ii. 27–30), nor did he set up any claim to an ability to do it of himself on this occasion. If he received his knowledge directly from God, all the difficulty in this objection vanishes at once; but the whole book turns on the supposition that he *was* under Divine teaching.

IV. It has been objected that there was no object to be accomplished worthy of such a miracle as that of writing in this mysterious manner on the wall. It is asked by Bertholdt (p. 347), "Is the miracle credible? What purpose was it designed to serve? What end would it accomplish? Was the design to show to Belshazzar that the city was soon to be destroyed? But of what use could this be but a couple of hours before it should occur? Or was it the design to make Belshazzar acquainted with the power of Jehovah, and to punish him for desecrating the vessels of the temple service? But who could attribute to the all-perfect Being such a weakness that he could be angry, and take this method to express his anger, for an act that could not be regarded as so heinous as to be worthy of such an interposition?"

To this it may be replied, (1.) That the objection here made would lie in some degree against almost any single miracle that is recorded in the Scriptures. (2.) That it may have been the intention to warn the king of the impending danger, not so much with a view that the danger should be averted, as to show that it came from God. (3.) Or it may have been the intention to show him the enormity of his sins, and even then to bring him to repentance. (4.) Or it may have been the intention to connect quite distinctly, in the apprehension of all present, and in the view of all future ages, the destruction of Babylon with the crimes of the monarchs, and especially their crimes in connection with the destruction of the city of Jerusalem, the burning of the temple, and the carrying away of the people into a long captivity. There can be no doubt, from many parts of the prophetic writings, that the overthrow of Babylon, and the subversion of the Chaldean power, was in consequence of their treatment of the Hebrew people; and nothing was better fitted to show this than to make the destruction of the city coincident with the desecration of the sacred vessels of the temple. (5.) Or it may have been the intention to recal Daniel into notice, and to give him authority and influence again preparatory to the restoration of his countrymen to their own land. It would seem from the whole narrative that, in accordance with a custom which still prevails in Persia (Chardin, as referred to by Hengstenberg, *Authentie des Daniel*, p. 123), all the magicians and astrologers had been dismissed from court on the death of Nebuchadnezzar, and that Daniel with the others had retired from his place. Yet it may have been important, in order to the restoration of the Hebrew people to their land at the appointed time, that there should be one of their own nation occupying an influential station at court, and Daniel was thus, in consequence of his ability to interpret this mysterious language, restored to his place, and was permitted to keep it until the time of the return of the Hebrews to their country arrived. See ch. vi. 2, 3, 28. (6.) And it may have been the intention to furnish an impressive demonstration that Jehovah is the true God. Other objections it will be more convenient to notice in the course of the exposition of the chapter.

§ II.—BELSHAZZAR.

Of Belshazzar, the closing scene of whose reign is described in this chapter, little more is known than is recorded here. He is mentioned by Daniel as the last king of the Chaldees, under whom Babylon was taken by the Medes and Persians. Herodotus (i. 188) calls this king, and also his father, *Labynetus*, which is undoubtedly a corruption of Nabonnedus, the name by which he was known to Berosus.—Josephus *against Apion*, i. 20. Josephus himself (*Ant.* x. ch. xi. § 2) says that the name of this king, whom he calls Baltasar, among the Babylonians, was Nabandelus. Nabonadius in the canon of Ptolemy, Nabonedus in Eusebius (*Chron. Armen.* i. p. 60), and Nabonnidochus in Eusebius (*Prep. Evang.* ix. 41), are remarked by Winer as only varieties of his name. Winer conjectures that in the name Belshazzar, the element *shazzar* means "the principle of fire." See Kitto's *Cyclopædia*.

The accounts which we have of this king are very meagre, and yet, meagre as they are, they are by no means uniform, and it is difficult to reconcile them. That which is given by Josephus as his own account of the successors of Nebuchadnezzar is in the following language:—"After the death of Nebuchadnezzar Evil-Merodach, his son, succeeded in the kingdom, who immediately set Jeconiah at liberty, and esteemed him among his most intimate friends. When Evil-Merodach was dead, after a reign of eighteen years,

Neglissar, his son, took the government, and retained it forty years, and then ended his life; and after him the succession came to his son, Labosordacus, who continued it in all but nine months; and when he was dead, it came to Baltasar, who by the Babylonians was called Naboandelus; against him did Cyrus the king of Persia, and Darius the king of Media, make war; and when he was besieged in Babylon there happened a wonderful and prodigious vision. He was sat down at supper in a large room, and there were a great many vessels of silver, such as were made for royal entertainments, and he had with him his concubines and his friends; whereupon he came to a resolution, and commanded that those vessels of God which Nebuchadnezzar had plundered out of Jerusalem, and had not made use of, but had put them into his own temple, should be brought out of that temple."—*Ant.* b. x. ch. xi.

§ 2. Josephus then proceeds to give an account of the appearance of the hand, and of the writing, and of the result in the taking of Babylon, substantially the same as that which is found in this chapter of Daniel.

The account which Berosus gives as preserved by Josephus (*against Apion,* b. i. § 20) varies from this in some important particulars. For an account of Berosus, see the Introduction to ch. iv.

§ I. I. He says, "Nabuchodonosor (Nebuchadnezzar), after he had begun to build the forementioned wall, fell sick and departed this life, when he had reigned forty-three years; whereupon his son, Evil-Merodach, obtained the kingdom. He governed public affairs after an illegal and impure manner, and had a plot laid against him by Neriglissar, his sister's husband, and was slain by him when he had reigned but two years. After he was slain, Neriglissar, the person who plotted against him, succeeded him in the kingdom, and reigned four years; but his son Laborosoarchad obtained the kingdom, though he was but a child, and kept it nine months; but by reason of the very ill temper, and the ill practices he exhibited to the world, a plot was laid against him also by his friends, and he was tormented to death. After his death the conspirators got together, and by common consent put the crown upon the head of Nabonnedus, a man of Babylon, and one who belonged to that insurrection. In his reign it was that the walls of the city of Babylon were curiously built with burnt brick and bitumen; but when he was come to the seventeenth year of his reign, Cyrus came out of Persia with a great army, and having already conquered the rest of Asia, he came hastily to Babylonia. When Nabonnedus perceived he was coming to attack him, he met him with his forces, and joining battle with him, was beaten, and fled away with a few of his troops with him, and was shut up in the city of Borsippus. Hereupon Cyrus took Babylon, and gave orders that the outer walls of the city should be demolished, because the city had proved very troublesome to him, and cost him a great deal of pains to take it. He then marched away to Borsippus to besiege Nabonnedus; but as Nabonnedus did not sustain the siege, but delivered himself into his hands, he was at first kindly used by Cyrus, who gave him Carmania as a place for him to inhabit in, but sent him out of Babylonia. Accordingly, Nabonnedus spent the rest of his time in that country, and there died."

Roos (*Exposition of Daniel,* p. 65) supposes that Evil-Merodach, who succeeded Nebuchadnezzar, did not reign more than one year, and that this accounts for the reason why he was not mentioned by Daniel; and that Bel-

shazzar was a grandson of Nebuchadnezzar, though, according to the idiom
of Scripture, he is called his son, and
Nebuchadnezzar his father, Dan. v. 11,
22. Belshazzar, he supposes, must have
reigned more than twenty years.

The succession in the Babylonian
Chaldean kingdom, according to Dr.
Hales, was as follows: "Nabonassar
reigned 14 years, from 747 B.C.; Nadius,
2, 733; Chinzirus, 5, 731; Jugaus, 5,
726; Mardok Empad, or Merodach
Baladan, 12, 721; Arcianus, 5, 709;
first interregnum, 2, 704; Belibus, 3,
702; Aphronadius, 6, 699; Regibelus,
1, 693; Mesessemordach, 4, 692; second
interregnum, 8, 688; Asaradin, or
Esar-haddon, 13, 680; Saosduchin, 20,
667; Chyneladon, 22, 647; Nabopolassar, or Labynetus I., 21, 625;
Nineveh taken by the Babylonians
and Medes, 604 B.C. Then follows
the Babylonian dynasty, to wit, Nabopolassar, Labynetus I., Boktanser, or,
Nebuchadnezzar, who reigned 43 years
from 604 B.C.; Ilverodam, or Evil-
Merodach, 3, 561 B.C.; Nericassolassar,
Neriglissar, or Belshazzar, 5, 558 B.C.;
Nabonadius, or Labynetus II., appointed by Darius the Mede, 17, 553
B.C.; Babylon taken by Cyrus, 536 B.C."

Dr. Hales remarks in connection with
this, "Nothing can exceed the various
and perplexed accounts of the names
and reigns of the princes of this dynasty
(the Babylonian) in sacred and profane
history."

Jahn, following Ptolemy chiefly, thus
enumerates the kings of Babylon from
the reign of Nebuchadnezzar: "Nabo-
cholassar, or Nebuchadnezzar, 43, 605
B.C.; Iluarodamus, or Evil-Merodach,
2, 562 B.C.; Nerichassolassar, or
Neriglissar, 4, 560 B.C; Laborasoar-
chad, 9 months, 556 B.C.; Nabounned,
17 years, 556 B.C.; Babylon taken by
the Medes and Persians, 540 B.C."

In this confusion and discord respecting the chronology of these princes, the
following remarks may be made in regard to the credibility of the statements
in the book of Daniel: (1.) It is clear
that it was not uncommon for the same
prince to have more names than one.
This has not been unusual, especially
among Oriental princes, who seem to
have often prided themselves on the
number of epithets which they could
use as designating their royal state.
Since this was the case, it would not
be strange if the names of the same
kings should be so used by writers, or
in tradition, as to leave the impression
that there were several; or if one writer
should designate a king by one name,
and another by another. (2.) It would
seem probable, from all the accounts,
that Belshazzar was the grandson of
Nebuchadnezzar, but little is known of
the king or kings whose reign intervened between that of Nebuchadnezzar
and Belshazzar. (3.) The testimony of
Daniel in the book before us should
not be set aside by the statement of
Berosus, or by the other confused accounts which have come down to us.
For anything that appears to the contrary, the authority of Daniel is as
good as that of Berosus, and he is as
worthy of belief. Living in Babylon,
and through a great part of the reigns
of this dynasty; present at the taking
of Babylon, and intimate at court;
honoured by some of these princes more
than any other man in the realm, there
is no reason why he should not have
had access to the means of information
on the subject, and no reason why it
should not be supposed that he has
given a fair record of what actually
occurred. Though the account in regard to the last days of Belshazzar, as
given by Berosus, does not agree with
that of Daniel, it should not be *assumed*
that that of Berosus is correct, and that
of Daniel false. The account in Daniel

CHAPTER V.

BELSHAZZAR the king made a great feast *a* to a thousand of his lords, and drank wine before the thousand.

a Esth. 1. 3.

is, to say the least, as probable as that of Berosus, and there are no means of proving that it is false except by the testimony of Berosus. (4.) The statement in Daniel of the manner in which Babylon was taken, and of the death of Belshazzar, is confirmed by Xenophon (*Cyrop.* vii.)—an authority quite equal, at least, to that of Berosus. See Notes on ver. 30 of the chapter. In the record in Daniel of the close of the life of Belshazzar, there is nothing that might not have been supposed to occur, for nothing is more probable than that a king *might* have been celebrating a feast in the manner described, or that the city might be surprised in such a night of revelry, or that, being surprised, the monarch might be slain.

ANALYSIS OF THE CHAPTER.

The chapter comprises a record of the series of events that occurred in Babylon on the night in which it was taken by the Medes and Persians. The scene may be supposed to open in the early evening, at a time when a festival would probably be celebrated, and to continue through a considerable part of the night. It is not known precisely at what time the city was taken, yet it may be supposed that Cyrus was making his approaches while the revel was going on in the palace, and that even while Daniel was interpreting the handwriting on the wall, he was conducting his armies along the channel of the river, and through the open gate on the banks of the river, toward the palace. The order of the events referred to is as follows : (1.) The feast given by Belshazzar in his palace, vers. 1–4 ; (2.) the mysterious appearance of the part of the hand on the wall, ver. 5 ; (3.) the summoning of the soothsayers to interpret the handwriting, and their inability to do it, vers. 6–9 ; (4.) the entrance of the queen into the banqueting-hall on account of the trouble of the king, and her reference to Daniel as one qualified to interpret the vision, vers. 10–12 ; (5.) the summoning of Daniel by the king, and his address to him, vers. 13–16 ; (6.) the answer of Daniel, declining any rewards for his service, and his solemn address to the king, reminding him of what had occurred to Nebuchadnezzar, and of the fact that he had forgotten the lessons which the Divine dealings with Nebuchadnezzar were adapted to teach, and that his own heart had been lifted up with pride, and that his conduct had been eminently wicked, vers. 17–23 ; (7.) the interpretation of the words by Daniel, vers. 24–28 ; (8.) the order to clothe Daniel in a manner appropriate to one of high rank, and the appointment to the third office in the kingdom, ver. 29 ; and (9.) the taking of the city, and the death of Belshazzar, vers. 30, 31.

1. *Belshazzar the king.* See Intro. to the chapter, § II. In the Introduction to the chapter here referred to, I have stated what seemed to be necessary in order to illustrate the history of Belshazzar, so far as that can be now known. The statements in regard to this monarch, it is well understood, are exceedingly confused, and the task of reconciling them is now hopeless. Little depends, however, in the interpretation of this book, on the attempt to reconcile them, for the narrative here given is equally credible, whichever of the accounts is taken, unless that of Berosus is followed. But it may not be improper to exhibit here the two principal accounts of the successors of Nebuchadnezzar, that the discrepancy may be distinctly seen. I copy from the *Pictorial Bible.* "The common account

we shall collect from *L'Art de Verifier les Dates*, and the other from Hales's *Analysis*, disposing them in opposite columns for the sake of comparison:—

From *L'Art de Verifier*.	From Hales's *Analysis*.
B.C.	B.C.
605 Nebuchadnezzar, who was succeeded by his son	604 Nebuchadnezzar was succeeded by his son
562 Evil-Merodach, who, having provoked general indignation by his tyranny and atrocities, was, after a short reign of about two years, assassinated by his brother-in-law	561 Evil-Merodach, or Ilverodam, who was slain in a battle against the Medes and Persians, and was succeeded by his son
560 Nerigilassar, or Nericassolassar, who was regarded as a deliverer, and succeeded by the choice of the nation. He perished in a battle by Cyrus, and was succeeded by his son	558 Neriglissar, Niricassolassar, or Belshazzar, the common accounts of whom seem to combine what is said both of Neriglissar, and his son, opposite. He was killed by conspirators on the night of the 'impious feast,' leaving a son (a boy),
555 Laborosoarchod, notorious for his cruelty and oppression, and who was assassinated by two nobles, Gobryas and Gadatas, whose sons he had slain. The vacant throne was then ascended by	553 Laborosoarchod, on whose death, nine months after, the dynasty became extinct, and the kingdom came peaceably to 'Darius the Mede,' or Cyaxares who, on the well-known policy of the Medes and Persians, appointed a Babylonian nobleman, named Nabonadius, or Labynetus, to be king, or viceroy. This person revolted against Cyrus, who had succeeded to the united empire of the Medes and Persians. Cyrus could not immediately attend to him, but at last marched to Babylon, took the city, B.C. 536, as foretold by the prophets.
554 Nabonadius, the Labynetus of Herodotus, the Naboandel of Josephus, and the Belshazzar of Daniel, who was the son of Evil-Merodach, and who now succeeded to the throne of his	
538 father. After a voluptuous reign, his city was taken by the Persians under Cyrus, on which occasion he lost his life.	

It will be observed that the principal point of difference in these accounts is, that Hales contends that the succession of Darius the Mede to the Babylonian throne was not attended with war; that Belshazzar was not the king in whose time the city was taken by Cyrus; and, consequently, that the events which took place this night were quite distinct from and anterior to that siege and capture of the city by the Persian king which Isaiah and Jeremiah so remarkably foretold. ¶ *Made a great feast.* On what occasion this feast was made is not stated, but it was not improbably an annual festival in honour of some of the Babylonian deities. This opinion seems to be countenanced by the words of the *Codex Chis.*, "Belshazzar the king made a great festival (ἐν ἡμέρᾳ ἐγκαινισμοῦ τῶν βασιλείων) on the day of the dedication of his kingdom;" and in ver. 4 it is said that "they praised the gods of gold, of silver, and of brass," &c. ¶ *To a thousand of his lords.* The word *thousand* here is doubtless used as a general term to denote a very large number. It is not improbable, however, that this full number was assembled on such an occasion. "Ctesias says, that the king of Persia furnished provisions daily for fifteen thousand men. Quintus Curtius says that ten thousand men were present at a festival of Alexander the Great; and Statius says of Domitian, that he ordered, on a certain occasion, his guests 'to sit down at a thousand tables.'"—Prof. Stuart, *in loc.* ¶ *And drank wine before the thousand.* The Latin Vulgate here is, "And each one drank according to his age." The Greek of Theodotion, the Arabic, and the Coptic is, "and wine was before the thousand."

The Chaldee, however, is, as in our version, "he drank wine before the thousand." As he was the lord of the feast, and as all that occurred pertained primarily to him, the design is undoubtedly to describe *his* conduct, and to show the effect which the drinking of wine had on him. He drank it in the most public manner, setting an example to his lords, and evidently drinking it to great excess.

[The industrious researches of Layard and Botta have made us familiar with the details of Assyrian life; and we have here sculptured representations of attendants supplying wine to the guests, and of the guests themselves seated at table. For convenience in filling and carrying, the cups have handles; but they are held by the guests in a different manner. The toast is being given, to which all are responding. These remains are from Khorsabad.

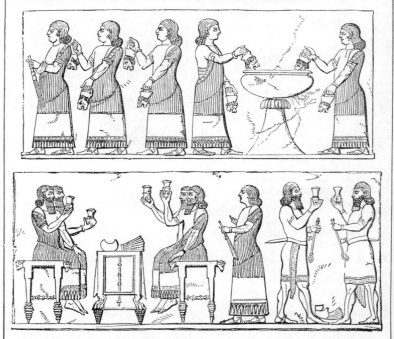

"The drinking cups and vessels used on festive occasions (by the Assyrians) were probably of gold, like those of Solomon, or of silver.

When Ahasuerus feasted all the people, both great and small, for seven days, in Shushan the palace, wine was given to them in vessels of

2 Belshazzar, while he tasted
the wine, commanded to bring the
golden and silver vessels *a* which

a ch. 1. 2; Jer. 52. 19.

his [1] father Nebuchadnezzar had
taken[2] out of the temple which *was*

1 or, *grandfather*, as Jer. 27. 7; 2 Sam. 9. 7.;
    vers. 11, 18.   2 *brought forth.*

gold, each one differing from the other. The
drinking vases of the Assyrians were frequently
wrought into the shape
of the head and neck of
an animal, such as a lion
or a bull, and resembled
those afterwards in use
amongst the Greeks, and
found in the tombs of
Etruria." The form of
cup referred to in the preceding extract is shown
in the engraving, copied
from the Assyrian re-
mains discovered at Khor-
sabad.]

2, 3. *Belshazzar,
while he tasted the
wine.* As the effect
of tasting the wine
—stating a fact which is illustrated in
every age and land, that men, under
the influence of intoxicating drinks,
will do what they would not do when
sober. In his sober moments it would
seem probable that he would have respected the vessels consecrated to the
service of religion, and would not have
treated them with dishonour by introducing them for purposes of revelry.
¶ *Commanded to bring the golden and
silver vessels.* These vessels had been
carefully deposited in some place as

the spoils of victory (see ch. **i.** 2), and
it would appear that they had not before been desecrated for purposes of
feasting. Belshazzar did what other
men would have done in the same condition. He wished to make a display;
to do something unusually surprising;
and, though it had not been contemplated when the festival was appointed
to make use of these vessels, yet, under
the excitement of wine, nothing was
too sacred to be introduced to the scenes
of intoxication; nothing too foolish to
be done. In regard to the vessels taken
from the temple at Jerusalem, see Notes
on ch. i. 2. ¶ *Which his father Nebuchadnezzar had taken.*

[The recent discoveries by Layard and Botta
at Nimroud and Khorsabad have revealed to us
all the details of Assyrian life, and more particularly all the circumstances attendant on the
warlike expeditions and conquests. In the annexed engraving, we have a portion of a bass-
relief, in which the spoils of a conquered people
are brought together, and an inventory or account taken of them. Amongst other things, a
number of vessels are seen of different shapes
and capacities; and, from the lavish use of the
precious metals in the luxurious East, there
can be no doubt that "the golden vessels,"
whether secular or sacred, would form an important part of the spoils.]

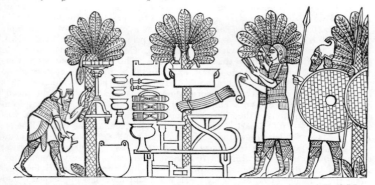

Marg., *grandfather.* According to the
best account which we have of Bel-

shazzar, he was the son of Evil-Mero
dach, who was the son of Nebuchad-

in Jerusalem; that the king, and his princes, his wives, and his concubines, might drink therein.

3 Then they brought the golden vessels that were taken out of the

temple of the house of God which *was* at Jerusalem; and the king, and his princes, his wives, and his concubines, drank in them.

4 They drank wine, and praised

---

nezzar (see the Intro. to the chapter, § II.), and therefore the word is used here, as in the margin, to denote grandfather. Compare Jer. xxvii. 7. See Notes on Isa. xiv. 22. The word *father* is often used in a large signification. See 2 Sam ix. 7; also Notes on Matt. i. 1. There is no improbability in supposing that this word would be used to denote a grandfather, when applied to one of the family or dynasty of Nebuchadnezzar. The fact that Belshazzar is here called *the son* of Nebuchadnezzar has been made a ground of objection to the credibility of the book of Daniel, by Lengerke, p. 204. The objection is, that the "last king of Babylon was *not* the son of Nebuchadnezzar." But, in reply to this, in addition to the remarks above made, it may be observed that it is not necessary, in vindicating the assertion in the text, to suppose that he was the *immediate* descendant of Nebuchadnezzar, in the first degree. "The Semitic use of the word in question goes far beyond the first degree of descent, and extends the appellation of *son* to the designation *grandson*, and even of the most remote posterity. In Ezra vi. 14, the prophet Zechariah is called *the son of Iddo;* in Zech. i. 1, 7, the same person is called *the son of Berechiah, the son of Iddo.* So Isaiah threatens Hezekiah (xxxix. 7) that *the sons whom he shall beget* shall be conducted as exiles to Babylon; in which case, however, four generations intervened before this happened. So in Matt. i. 1, ' Jesus Christ, the son of David, the son of Abraham.' And so we speak every day: 'The sons of Adam, the sons of Abraham, the sons of Israel, the sons of the Pilgrims,' and the like.ᵛ—Prof. Stuart, *Com. on Dan.* p. 144. ¶ *That the king and his princes, his wives, and his concubines, might drink therein.* Nothing is too sacred to be profaned when men are under the influence of wine. They do not hesitate to desecrate the holiest things, and vessels taken from the altar

of God are regarded with as little reverence as any other. It would seem that Nebuchadnezzar *had* some respect for these vessels, as having been employed in the purposes of religion; at least so much respect as to lay them up as trophies of victory, and that this respect had been shown for them under the reign of his successors, until the exciting scenes of this "impious feast" occurred, when all veneration for them vanished. It was not very common for females in the East to be present at such festivals as this, but it would seem that all the usual restraints of propriety and decency came to be disregarded as the feast advanced. The "wives and concubines" were probably not present when the feast began, for it was made for "his *lords*" (ver. 1); but when the scenes of revelry had advanced so far that it was proposed to introduce the sacred vessels of the temple, it would not be unnatural to propose also to introduce the females of the court. A similar instance is related in the book of Esther. In the feast which Ahasuerus gave, it is said that "on the seventh day, when the heart of the king was merry with wine, he commanded Mehuman, Biztha, &c., the seven chamberlains that served in the presence of Ahasuerus the king, to bring Vashti the queen before the king with the crown royal, to show the people and the princes her beauty," &c. Esth. i.10, 11. Comp. Joseph. *Ant.* b. xi. ch. vi. § 1. The females that were thus introduced to the banquet were those of the harem, yet it would seem that she who was usually called "the queen" by way of eminence, or the queen-mother (comp. Notes on ver. 10), was not among them at this time. The females in the court of an Oriental monarch were divided into two classes; those who were properly concubines, and who had none of the privileges of a wife; and those of a higher class, and who were spoken of as wives, and to whom appertained the privileges of that

the gods of gold, *a* and of silver, of brass, of iron, of wood, and of stone.

5 ¶ In the same hour *b* came forth fingers of a man's hand, and wrote over against the candle-

relation. Among the latter, also, in the court of a king, it would seem that there was one to whom properly belonged the appellation of *queen;* that is, probably, a favourite wife whose children were heirs to the crown. See Bertholdt, *in loc.* Comp. 2 Sam. v. 13; 1 Kings xi. 3; Cant. vi. 8.

4. *They drank wine, and praised the gods of gold, and of silver,* &c. Comp. Notes on ver. 1. Idols were made among the heathen of all the materials here mentioned. The word *praised* here means that they spake in praise of these gods; of their history, of their attributes, of what they had done. Nothing can well be conceived more senseless and stupid than what it is said they did at this feast, and yet it is a fair illustration of what occurs in all the festivals of idolatry. And is that which occurs in more civilized Christian lands, in the scenes of carousal and festivity, more rational than this? It was not much worse to lavish praises on idol gods in a scene of revelry than it is to lavish praises on idol men now; not much less rational to "toast" *gods* than it is to "toast" *men.*

[These various gods are represented in general by the annexed engravings. The three grotesque figures, of which the one to the right hand is shown in front and profile, are copied from remains discovered at Khorsabad; and if

these may be taken as part of the gods in whose honour Belshazzar and his lords drank wine and gave praise, the preceding remarks of our author on their senseless and stupid conduct derive additional force. It is probable that the homage was rather directed to the false divinities which were customarily borne on men's shoulders, on festal occasions, with much pomp and ceremony. Two of these are given, from a bass-relief in the south west palace at Nimroud; the one to the left is sufficiently identified with the description of Belus or Baal, by Herodotus; and the seated figure has the attributes of the Assyrian Venus, Astarta. In the Epistle of Jeremy, which concludes the apocryphal book of Baruch, there is a remarkable allusion to these idols, which goes far to establish its authenticity.

In the 6th chapter of Baruch, forming Jeremy's Epistle, we read:—

stick upon the plaster of the wall
of the king's palace ; and the king

> 4 v. Now shall ye see in Babylon gods of sil-
> ver, and of gold, *borne upon shoulders,*
> which cause the nations to fear.
> 15 v. He hath also in his right hand a dagger,
> *and an axe.*

The writer, beyond a doubt, must have witnessed the Assyrian processions, and been familiar with the forms and attributes of the idols
borne in them.

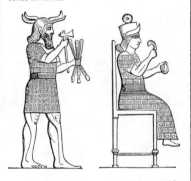

The seated figure, a conventional image of
Astarta, comes with peculiar force as an illustration of the character and purpose of Belshazzar's feast. The voluptuous and sensual
monarch would naturally direct his homage to
a deity in whose service he delighted; and, indeed, it is a very allowable surmise that this
feast was made expressly in honour of her: and
the impious profanation of the sacred vessels,
" taken out of the temple which was in Jerusalem," strengthens this supposition.]

5. *In the same hour.* On the word
hour, see Notes on ch. iv. 19. ¶ *Came
forth fingers of a man's hand.* Not
the whole hand, but only the parts usually employed in writing. Not a man
writing ; not even an arm, but *fingers*
that seemed to move themselves. They
appeared to come forth from the walls,
and were seen before they began to
write. It was this that made it so impressive and alarming. It could not be
supposed that it was the work of man,
or that it was devised by man for the
purpose of producing consternation. It
was perfectly manifest to all who were
there that this was the work of some

saw the part of the hand that
wrote.

one superior to man ; that it was designed as a Divine intimation of some
kind in regard to the scene that was
then occurring. But whether as a rebuke for the sin of revelry and dissipation, or for sacrilege in drinking out of
the consecrated vessels, or whether it
was an intimation of some approaching
fearful calamity, would not at once be
apparent. It is easy to imagine that it
would produce a sudden pause in their
revelry, and diffuse seriousness over
their minds. The suddenness of the
appearance ; the fingers, unguided by
the hand of man, slowly writing in
mysterious characters on the wall ; the
conviction which must have flashed
across the mind that this must be
either to rebuke them for their sin, or
to announce some fearful calamity, all
these things must have combined to
produce an overwhelming effect on the
revellers. Perhaps, from the prevalent
views in the heathen world in regard
to the crime of sacrilege, they may
have connected this mysterious appearance with the profane act which they
were then committing—that of desecrating the vessels of the temple of God.
How natural would it be to suppose—
recognizing as they did the gods of
other nations as *real,* as truly as those
which they worshipped—that the God
of the Hebrews, seeing the vessels of
his worship profaned, had come forth
to express his displeasure, and to intimate that there was impending wrath
for such an act. The crime of sacrilege was regarded among the heathen
as one of the most awful which could
be committed, and there was no state
of mind in which men would be more
likely to be alarmed than when they
were, even in the midst of scenes of
drunken revelry, engaged in such an
act. "The heathen," says Grotius,
"thought it a great impiety to convert
sacred things to common uses." Numerous instances are on record of the
sentiments entertained among the heathen on the subject of sacrilege, and of
the calamities which were believed to
come upon men as a punishment for it.
Among them we may refer to the miser-

6 Then *a* the king's ¹ countenance was changed, ² and his
thoughts troubled him, so that the

joints³ of his loins were loosed, and
his knees *b* smote one against
another.

a Isa. 21. 2–4.   1 *brightnesses*, ver. 9.
　　　　2 *changed it.*

3 *bindings ;* or, *knots ;* or, *girdles,* Isa. 5. 27.
　　　　b Nah. 2. 10.

able end of the Phocians, who robbed
the temple of Delphos, and whose act
was the occasion of that war which
was called the Holy War ; the destruction of the Gauls in their attempt upon
the same temple ; and of Crassus, who
plundered the temple of Jerusalem, and
that of the Syrian goddess.—See Lowth,
in loc. That a conviction of the sin of
sacrilege, according to the prevalent
belief on the subject, may have contributed to produce consternation when
the fingers of the hand appeared at Belshazzar's feast, there is no good reason
to doubt, and we may suppose that the
minds of the revellers were at once
turned to the insult which they had
thus offered to the God of the Hebrews.
¶ *And wrote over against the candlestick.* The candlestick, or lamp-bearer,
perhaps, which had been taken from the
temple at Jerusalem, and which was,
as well as the sacred vessels, introduced
into this scene of revelry.   It is probable that as they brought out the vessels of the temple to drink in, they
would also bring out all that had been
taken from the temple in Jerusalem.
Two objects may have been contemplated in the fact that the writing was
" over against the candlestick ; " one
was that it might be clearly visible, the
other that it might be more directly intimated that the writing was a rebuke
for the act of sacrilege.   On the probable situation where this miracle occurred, the reader may consult Taylor's
Fragments to Calmet's Dictionary, No.
205.   He supposes that it was one of
the large inner courts of the palace—
that part of the palace which was prohibited to persons not sent for.   See
Notes on ver. 10.   ¶ *Upon the plaster
of the wall.* The Chaldee word means
lime, not inappropriately rendered here
plaster. The *manner* of the writing is
not specified.   All that is necessary to
suppose is, that the letters were traced
along on the wall so as to be distinctly
visible.   Whether they seemed to be
DANIEL. I.

cut into the plaster, or to be traced in
black lines, or lines of light, is not
mentioned, and is immaterial.   They
were such as could be seen distinctly
by the king and the guests.   Compare,
however, the remarks of Taylor in the
Fragment just referred to.   ¶ *And the
king saw the part of the hand that wrote.*
It is not necessary to suppose that the
others did not see it also, but the king
was the most important personage there,
and the miracle was intended particularly for him.   Perhaps his eyes were
first attracted to it.
　6. *Then the king's countenance was
changed.* The word rendered *countenance* is, in the margin, as in ver. 9,
brightnesses. The Chaldee word means
brightness, splendour (זִיו), and the
meaning here is *bright looks, cheerful-
ness, hilarity.* The word rendered *was
changed,* is in the margin *changed it;*
and the meaning is, that it changed itself : probably from a jocund, cheerful,
and happy expression, it assumed suddenly a deadly paleness.   ¶ *And his
thoughts troubled him.* Whether from
the recollection of guilt, or the dread
of wrath, is not said.   He would, doubtless, regard this as some supernatural
intimation, and his soul would be
troubled.   ¶ *So that the joints of his
loins were loosed.*   Marg., *bindings,* or
knots, or *girdles.* The Chaldee word
rendered *joints* (קְטַר) means, properly,
knots ; then joints of the bones, as resembling knots, or apparently answering the purposes of knots in the human
frame, as binding it together.   The
word *loins* in the Scriptures refers to
the part of the body around which the
girdle was passed, the lower part of the
back ; and Gesenius supposes that the
meaning here is, that the joints of his
back, that is, the vertebræ, are referred
to.   This part of the body is spoken of
as the seat of strength.   When this is
weak the body has no power to stand,
to walk, to labour.   The simple idea

T

7 The king cried [1] aloud to bring in the astrologers, [a] the Chaldeans, and the soothsayers. *And* the king spake, and said to the wise *men* of Babylon, Whosoever shall read this

1 *with might.*   *a* ch. 2. 2; Isa. 47. 13.

writing, and show me the interpretation thereof, shall be clothed with scarlet,[2] and *have* a chain of gold about his neck, and shall be the third ruler [b] in the kingdom.

1 or, *purple.*   *b* ch. 6. 2.

is, that he was greatly terrified, and that under the influence of fear his strength departed. ¶ *And his knees smote one against another.* A common effect of fear (Nah. ii. 10). So Horace, *Et corde et genibus tremit.* And so Virgil, *Tarda trementi genua labant.* " Belshazzar had as much of power, and of drink withal to lead him to bid defiance to God as any ruffian under heaven ; and yet when God, as it were, lifted but up his finger against him, how poorly did he crouch and shiver. How did his joints loose, and his knees knock together ! " — South's *Sermons,* vol. iv. p. 60.

7. *And the king cried aloud.* Marg., as in the Chaldee, *with might.* This indicates a sudden and an alarming cry. The king was deeply terrified ; and, unable himself to divine the meaning of the mysterious appearance of the hand, he naturally turned at once to those whose office it was to explain dreams and supernatural appearances. ¶ *To bring in the astrologers,* &c. See Notes on ch. ii. 2 ; iv. 7. ¶ *And said to the wise* men *of Babylon.* Those just referred to—the astrologers, &c. Having the power, as was supposed, of interpreting the indications of coming events, they were esteemed as eminently wise. ¶ *Whosoever shall read this writing.* It would seem from this that even the *characters* were not familiar to the king and to those who were with him. Evidently the letters were not in the ordinary Chaldee form, but in some form which to them was strange and unknown. Thus there was a double mystery hanging over the writing—a mystery in regard to the language in which the words were written, and to the meaning of the words. Many conjectures have been formed as to the language employed in this writing (comp. Notes on ver. 24), but such conjectures are useless, since it is impossible now to ascertain what it was.

As the writing, however, had a primary reference to the sacrilege committed in regard to the sacred vessels of the temple, and as Daniel was able to read the letters at once, it would seem not improbable that the words were in the Hebrew character then used—a character such as that found now in the Samaritan Pentateuch—for the Chaldee character now found in the Bible has not improbably been substituted for the more ancient and less elegant character now found in the Samaritan Pentateuch alone. There is no improbability in supposing that even the astrologers and the soothsayers were not familiar with that character, and could not readily read it. ¶ *And show me the interpretation thereof.* The meaning of the words. ¶ *Shall be clothed with scarlet.* The colour worn usually by princes and by persons of rank. The margin is *purple.* So the Greek of Theodotion—*πορφύραν.* So also the Latin Vulgate—*purpurâ.* On the nature and uses of this colour, see Notes on Isa. i. 18. ¶ *And have a chain of gold about his neck.* Also indicative of rank and authority. Comp. Gen. xli. 42. When Joseph was placed over the land of Egypt, the king honoured him in a similar manner, by putting "a gold chain about his neck." This was common in Persia. See Xen. *Cyrop.* I. 3, 2, II. 4, 6, VIII. 5, 18 ; *Anab.* I. 5, 8. Upon most of the figures in the ruins of Persepolis the same ornament is now found. Prof. Stuart renders this, "a collar of gold." ¶ *And shall be the third ruler in the kingdom.* Of course, the king was first. Who the second was, or why the one who could disclose the meaning of the words should not be raised to the second rank, is not stated. It may be, that the office of prime minister was so fixed, or was held by one whose services were so important to the king, that he could not be at once displaced.

8 Then came in all the king's wise *men:* but they could not read the writing, nor make known to the king the interpretation thereof.

9 Then was king Belshazzar greatly troubled, and his countenance [1] was changed in him, and his lords were astonied.

10 ¶ *Now* the queen, by reason of the words of the king and his lords, came into the banquet-house; *and* the queen spake and said, O king, live for ever; let not thy thoughts trouble thee, nor let thy countenance be changed:

1 *brightnesses,* ver. 6.

Or the meaning may be, that the favoured person who could interpret this would be raised to the third *rank* of dignity, or placed in the third *class* of those who held offices in the realm. The Chaldee is, "and shall rule third in the kingdom," and the idea would seem rather to be that he should be of the third rank or grade in office. So Bertholdt understands it. Grotius understands it as the third person in rank. He says the first was the king; the second, the son of the king; the third, the prince of the Satraps.

8. *Then came in all the king's wise* men. The classes above referred to, ver. 7. ¶ *But they could not read the writing.* The character was an unknown character to them. It *may* have been a character which was not found in *any* language, and which made the power of Daniel to read it the more remarkable, or it may have been, as suggested in the Notes on ver. 7, a *foreign character* with which they had no acquaintance, though familiar to Daniel.

9. *Then was king Belshazzar greatly troubled.* Not doubting that this was a Divine intimation of some fearful event, and yet unable to understand its meaning. We are quite as likely to be troubled by what is merely *mysterious* in regard to the future—by anything that gives us some undefined foreboding—as we are by that which is really formidable when we know what it is. In the latter case, we know the worst; we can make some preparation for it; we can feel assured that when *that* is past, *all* is past that we fear—but who can guard himself, or prepare himself, when that which is dreaded is undefined as well as awful; when we know not how to meet it, or how long it may endure, or how terrific and wide may be the sweep of its

desolation? ¶ *And his countenance was changed in him.* Marg., *brightnesses.* See Notes on ver. 6. ¶ *And his lords were astonied.* Amazed. The Chaldee word means to perplex, disturb, trouble. They were doubtless as much perplexed and troubled as the king himself.

10. Now *the queen.* "Probably the queen-mother, the Nitocris of Herodotus, as the king's wives were at the entertainment."—Wintle. Comp. vers. 2, 3. So Prof. Stuart. The editor of the *Pictorial Bible* also supposes that this was the queen-mother, and thinks that this circumstance will explain her familiarity with the occurrences in the reign of Nebuchadnezzar. He says, "We are informed above, that the 'wives and concubines' of the king were present at the banquet. It therefore seems probable that the 'queen' who now first appears was the *queen-mother;* and this probability is strengthened by the intimate acquaintance which she exhibits with the affairs of Nebuchadnezzar's reign; at the latter end of which she, as the wife of Evil-Merodach, who was regent during his father's alienation of mind, took an active part in the internal policy of the kingdom, and in the completion of the great works which Nebuchadnezzar had begun in Babylon. This she continued during the reigns of her husband and son, the present king Belshazzar. This famous queen, Nitocris, therefore, could not but be well acquainted with the character and services of Daniel." On the place and influence of the queen-mother in the Oriental courts, see Taylor's *Fragments to Calmet's Dictionary,* No. 16. From the extracts which Taylor has collected, it would seem that she held an exalted place at court, and that it is every way probable that she would be called in, or would come in, on such

11 There *a* is a man in thy kingdom, in whom *is* the spirit of the holy gods: and, in the days of thy father,[1] light, and understanding, and wisdom, like the wisdom of the gods, was found in him; whom the king Nebuchadnezzar thy father,[1] the king, *I say*, thy [1] father, made master of the magicians, astrologers, Chaldeans, *and* soothsayers;

a ch. 4. 8, 9.

[1] or, *grandfather*, ver. 2.

an occasion. See also Knolles's *History of the Turks*, as quoted by Taylor, *Fragments*, No. 50. ¶ *By reason of the words of the king and his lords.* Their words of amazement and astonishment. These would doubtless be conveyed to her, as there was so much alarm in the palace, and as there was a summons to bring in the wise men of Babylon. If her residence was in some part of the palace itself, nothing would be more natural than that she should be made acquainted with the unusual occurrence; or if her residence was, as Taylor supposes, detached from the palace, it is every way probable that she would be made acquainted with the consternation that prevailed, and that, recollecting the case of Nebuchadnezzar, and the forgotten services of Daniel, she would feel that the information which was sought respecting the mysterious writing could be obtained from him. ¶ And *the queen spake and said, O king, live for ever.* A common salutation in addressing a king, expressive of a desire of his happiness and prosperity. ¶ *Let not thy thoughts trouble thee,* &c. That is, there is a way by which the mystery may be solved, and you need not, therefore, be alarmed.

11. *There is a man in thy kingdom.* To wit, Daniel. As the queen-mother had lived in the time of Nebuchadnezzar, and recollected the important service which he had rendered in interpreting the dream of the king, it was natural that her mind should at once recur to him. It would seem, also, that though Daniel was no longer employed at court, yet that she still had an acquaintance with him, so far at least as to know that he was accessible, and might be called in on this occasion. It may be asked, perhaps, how it was Belshazzar was so ignorant of all this as to need this information? For it is clear from the question which the king asks in ver. 13, "Art thou that

Daniel?" that he *was* ignorant of him personally, and probably even of his services as an officer in the court of Nebuchadnezzar. An ingenious and not improbable solution of this difficulty has been proposed as founded on a remark of Sir John Chardin: "As mentioned by the queen, Daniel had been made by Nebuchadnezzar 'master of the magicians, astrologers, Chaldeans, and soothsayers.' Of this employment Chardin conjectures that he had been deprived on the death of that king, and obtains this conclusion from the fact that when a Persian king dies, both his astrologers and physicians are driven from court—the former for not having predicted, and the latter for not having prevented, his death. If such was the etiquette of the ancient Babylonian, as it is of the modern Persian court, we have certainly a most satisfactory solution of the present difficulty, as Daniel must then be supposed to have relinquished his public employments, and to have lived retired in private life during the eight years occupied by the reigns of Evil-Merodach and Belshazzar."—Harmer, as quoted by Rosenmüller (*Morgenland*, on Dan. v. 13). ¶ *In whom* is *the spirit of the holy gods.* This is language such as a heathen would be likely to use when speaking of one who had showed extraordinary knowledge of Divine things. See Notes on ch. iv. 9. ¶ *And, in the days of thy father.* Marg., *grandfather.* See Notes on vers. 1, 2. ¶ *Light, and understanding, and wisdom.* Light is the emblem of knowledge, as it makes all things clear. The meaning here is, that he had showed extraordinary wisdom in interpreting the dream of Nebuchadnezzar. ¶ *Like the wisdom of the gods.* Such as the gods only could possess. ¶ *Whom the king Nebuchadnezzar thy father, the king,* I say, *thy father, made master of the magicians,* &c. See ch. ii. 48. This is repeated

12 Forasmuch as an *a* excellent spirit, and knowledge, and understanding, interpreting 1 of dreams, and showing of hard sentences, and dissolving 2 of doubts,3 were found in the same Daniel, whom the king named Belteshazzar : now let Daniel be called, and he will show the interpretation.

13 Then was Daniel brought in before the king. *And* the king spake and said unto Daniel, *Art*

a ch. 6. 3.   1 or, *of an interpreter.*
2 or, *of a dissolver.*   3 *knots.*

thou that Daniel, which *art* of the children of the captivity of Judah, whom the king my father 4 brought out of Jewry?

14 I have even heard of thee, that the spirit of the gods *is* in thee, and *that* light, and understanding, and excellent wisdom, is found in thee.

15 And now the wise *men*, the astrologers, have been brought in before me, that they should read

4 or, *grandfather*, ver 2.

---

here, and dwelt on, in order to call the attention of the king to the fact that Daniel was worthy to be consulted. Though now living in obscurity, there was a propriety that one who had been placed at the very head of the wise men of Babylon by a prince so distinguished as Nebuchadnezzar, should be consulted on the present occasion.

12. *Forasmuch as an excellent spirit.* Not an excellent spirit in the sense in which that phrase is sometimes used now, as denoting a good and pious spirit, but a spirit or mind that *excels;* that is, that is *distinguished* for wisdom and knowledge.   ¶ *Interpreting of dreams.* Marg., " or, *of an interpreter.*" This was regarded as a great attainment, and was supposed to prove that one who could do it was inspired by the gods.   ¶ *And showing of hard sentences.* The meaning of enigmatical or obscure sentences.   To be able to do this was supposed to indicate great attainments, and was a knowledge that was much coveted.   Comp. Prov. i. 6: " To understand a proverb, and the interpretation ; the words of the wise, and their dark sayings."   ¶ *And dissolving of doubts.* Marg., " or, *a dissolver of knots.*" So the Chaldee. This language is still common in the East, to denote one who has skill in explaining difficult subjects. " In the copy of a patent given to Sir John Chardin in Persia, we find it is addressed ' to the Lords of lords, who have the presence of a lion, the aspect of Deston ; the princes who have the stature of Tahemten-ten, who seem to be in the time of Ardevon, the regents who carry

the majesty of Ferribours. The conquerors of kingdoms. Superintendents *that unloose all manner of knots,* and who are under the ascendant of Mercury,'" &c.—Taylor's *Fragments to Calmet's Dict.*, No. 174. The language used here would be applicable to the explanation of any difficult and perplexing subject.   ¶ *Whom the king named Belteshazzar.* That is, the name was given to him by his authority (see Notes on ch. i. 7), and it was by this name that he called him when he addressed him, ch. iv. 9.

13. *Then was Daniel brought in before the king.* From this it is clear that he lived in Babylon, though in comparative obscurity. It would seem to be not improbable that he was still known to the queen-mother, who, perhaps, kept up an acquaintance with him on account of his former services. ¶ *Art thou that Daniel.* This is a clear proof that Belshazzar was not acquainted personally with him. See Notes on ver. 11.   ¶ *Which* art *of the children of the captivity of Judah.* Belonging to those of Judah, or those Jews who were made captives, and who reside in Babylon. See Notes on ch. i. 3. He could not be ignorant that there were Jews in his kingdom, though he was not personally acquainted with Daniel.   ¶ *Whom the king my father.* Marg., as in vers. 2, 11, *grandfather.*   ¶ *Brought out of Jewry?* Out of Judea. See ch. i. 1-3.

14. *I have even heard of thee,* &c. Ver. 11.

15. *And now the wise* men, &c. Vers. 7, 8.

this writing, and make known unto me the interpretation thereof: but they could not show the interpretation of the thing:

16 And I have heard of thee, that thou canst make ¹ interpretations, and dissolve doubts: now, if thou canst read the writing, and make known to me the interpretation thereof, thou shalt be clothed with scarlet, and *have* a chain of gold about thy neck, and shalt be the third ruler in the kingdom.

1 *interpret.*

17 ¶ Then Daniel answered and said before the king, Let *a* thy gifts be to thyself, and give thy rewards ² to another; yet I will read the writing *b* unto the king, and make known to him the interpretation.

18 O thou king, the most high God gave Nebuchadnezzar thy father a kingdom, and majesty, and glory, and honour:

a Gen. 14. 23.   2 or, *fee, as* ch. 2 6.

b Psa. 119. 46.

---

16. *And I have heard of thee,* &c. Ver. 11. ¶ *Canst make interpretations.* Marg., *interpret.* Chald., "interpret interpretations." The meaning is, that he was skilled in interpreting or explaining dreams, omens, &c. ¶ *And dissolve doubts.* Notes on ver. 12. ¶ *Now, if thou canst read the writing,* &c., *thou shalt be clothed with scarlet,* &c. This was the reward which at the first he had promised to any one that was able to do it, and as all others had failed, he was willing that it should be offered to a Jew.

17. *Then Daniel answered and said before the king, Let thy gifts be to thyself.* That is, "I do not desire them; I do not act from a hope of reward." Daniel means undoubtedly to intimate that what he would do would be done from a higher motive than a desire of office or honour. The answer is one that is eminently dignified. Yet he says he would read the writing, implying that he was ready to do anything that would be gratifying to the monarch. It may seem somewhat strange that Daniel, who here disclaimed all desire of office or reward, should so soon (ver. 29) have submitted to be clothed in this manner, and to receive the insignia of office. But, it may be remarked, that when the offer was proposed to him he stated his wishes, and declared that he did not *desire* to be honoured in that way; when he had performed the duty, however, of making known the writing, he could scarcely feel at liberty to resist a command of the king to be clothed in that manner, and to be regarded as an officer in the

kingdom. His intention, in the verse before us, was modestly to decline the honours proposed, and to intimate that he was not influenced by a desire of such honours in what he would do; yet to the king's command afterwards that he should be clothed in robes of office, he could not with propriety make resistance. There is no evidence that he took these honours voluntarily, or that he would not have continued to decline them if he could have done it with propriety. ¶ *And give thy rewards to another.* Marg., "or *fee,* as in ch. ii. 6." Gesenius supposes that the word used here (נְבִזְבָּה) is of Persian origin. It means a *gift,* and, if of Persian origin, is derived from a verb, meaning to load with gifts and praises, as a prince does an ambassador. The sense here seems to be, that Daniel was not disposed to interfere with the will of the monarch if he chose to confer gifts and rewards on others, or to question the propriety of his doing so; but that, so far as he was concerned, he had no desire of them for himself, and could not be influenced by them in what he was about to do. ¶ *Yet I will read the writing,* &c. Expressing no doubt that he could do it without difficulty. Probably the *language* of the writing was familiar to him, and he at once saw that there was no difficulty, in the circumstances, in determining its meaning.

18. *O thou king, the most high God gave Nebuchadnezzar thy father a kingdom,* &c. This reference to Nebuchadnezzar is evidently designed to show to Belshazzar the wickedness of his

19 And, for the majesty that he gave him, all *a* people, nations, and languages, trembled and feared before him : whom he would he slew, and whom he would he kept alive, and whom he would he set up, and whom he would he put down.

20 But when his heart was lifted up, and his mind hardened [1] in pride, he was deposed [2] from his kingly throne, and they took his glory from him :

a ch. 4. 22, &c.; Jer. 27. 7.
1 or, *to deal proudly*, Exod. 18. 11.
2 *made to come down.*

21 And he was driven from the sons of men : and his [3] heart was made like the beasts, and his dwelling *was* with the wild asses : they fed him with grass like oxen, and his body was wet with the dew of heaven ; till he knew that the most high God ruled in the kingdom of men, and *that* he appointeth over it whomsoever he will.

22 And thou his son, O Belshazzar, hast not humbled *b* thine

3 or, *he made his heart equal.*
b 2 Chron. 33. 23; 36. 12; Jam. 4. 6.

own course, and the reason which he had to apprehend the Divine vengeance, because he had not learned to avoid the sins which brought so great calamities upon his predecessor. As he was acquainted with what had occurred to Nebuchadnezzar ; as he had doubtless seen the proclamation which he had made on his recovery from the dreadful malady which God had brought upon him for his pride ; and as he had not humbled himself, but had pursued the same course which Nebuchadnezzar did, he had the greater reason to apprehend the judgment of Heaven. See vers. 22, 23. Daniel here traces all the glory which Nebuchadnezzar had to "the most high God," reminding the king that whatever honour and majesty he had he was equally indebted for it to the same source, and that he must expect a similar treatment from him.

19. *And, for the majesty that he gave him.* That is, on account of his greatness, referring to the talents which God had conferred on him, and the power which he had put in his hands. It was so great that all people and nations trembled before him. ¶ *All people, nations, and languages trembled and feared before him.* Stood in awe of him. On the extent of his empire, see Notes on ch. iii. 4 ; iv. 1, 22. ¶ *Whom he would he slew,* &c. That is, he was an arbitrary—an absolute sovereign. This is exactly descriptive of the power which Oriental despotic monarchs have. ¶ *Whom he would he kept alive.* Whether they had, or had not, been guilty of crime. He had the absolute power of life and death over them.

There was no such instrument as we call a "constitution" to control · the sovereign as well as the people ; there was no tribunal to which he was responsible, and no law by which he was bound ; there were no judges to determine on the question of life and death in regard to those who were accused of crime, whom he did not appoint, and whom he might not remove, and whose judgments he might not set aside if he pleased ; there were no "juries" of "peers" to determine on the question of fact whether an accused man was guilty or not. There were none of those safeguards which have been originated to protect the accused in modern times, and which enter so essentially into the notions of liberty now. In an absolute despotism all power is in the hands of one man, and this was in fact the case in Babylon. ¶ *Whom he would he set up.* That is, in places of trust, of office, of rank, &c. ¶ *And whom he would he put down.* No matter what their rank or office.

20. *But when his heart was lifted up.* See ch. iv. 30. ¶ *And his mind hardened in pride.* Marg., *to deal proudly.* The state of mind indicated here is that in which there is no sense of dependence, but where one feels that he has all resources in himself, and need only look to himself. ¶ *He was deposed from his kingly throne.* Marg., *made to come down.* That is, he was so deposed by the providence of God, not by the acts of his own subjects.

21. *And he was driven,* &c. See this fully explained in ch. iv. 25–33.

22. *And thou his son, O Belshazzar,*

heart, though thou knewest all this;

23 But ^a hast lifted up thyself against the Lord of heaven; and they have brought the vessels of his house before thee, and thou, and thy lords, thy wives, and thy concubines, have drunk wine in them;

_a vers.3,4. _b Judg.16.23. _c Ps.115.5–8; Is.37.19.

and thou hast praised ^b the gods of silver, and gold, of brass, iron, wood, and stone, which ^c see not, nor hear, nor know : and the God in whose hand thy breath ^d is, and whose are all thy ways, ^e hast thou not glorified : ^f

24 Then was the part of the

_d Acts 17. 28, 29. _e Jer. 10. 23. _f Rom. 1. 21.

hast not humbled thine heart, &c. As thou shouldst have done in remembrance of these events. The idea is, that we ought to derive valuable lessons from what has taken place in past times; that, from the events which have occurred in history, we should learn what God approves and what he disapproves; that we should avoid the course which has subjected others to his displeasure, and which has brought his judgments upon them. The course, however, which Belshazzar pursued has been that of kings and princes commonly in the world, and indeed of mankind at large. How little do men profit by the record of the calamities which have come upon others for their crimes! How little are the intemperate of one generation admonished by the calamities which have come upon those of another; how little are the devotees of pleasure; how little are those in places of power!

23. *But hast lifted up thyself against the Lord of heaven.* The God who had so signally rebuked and humbled Nebuchadnezzar. The monarch had done this, it would seem, during the whole of his reign, and now by a crowning act of impiety he had evinced special disregard of him, and contempt for him, by profaning the sacred vessels of his temple. ¶ *And they have brought the vessels of his house before thee,* &c. See Notes on vers. 2–4. ¶ *And the God in whose hand thy breath* is. Under whose power, and at whose disposal, is thy life. While you have been celebrating the praises of idol gods, who can do you neither good nor evil, you have been showing special contempt for that great Being who keeps you in existence, and who has power to take away your life at any moment. What is here said of Belshazzar is true of all men—

high and low, rich and poor, bond and free, princes and people. It is a deeply affecting consideration, that the breath, on which our life depends, and which is itself so frail a thing, is in the "hand" of a Being who is invisible to us, over whom we can have no control; who can arrest it when he pleases; who has given us no intimation when he will do it, and who often does it so suddenly as to defy all previous calculation and hope. Nothing is more absolute than the power which God holds over the breath of men, yet there is nothing which is less recognized than that power, and nothing which men are less disposed to acknowledge than their dependence on him for it. ¶ *And whose* are *all thy ways.* That is, he has power to control thee in all thy ways. You can go nowhere without his permission; you can never, when abroad, return to your home without the direction of his providence. What is here said, also, is as true of all others as it was of the Chaldean prince. "It is not in man that walketh to direct his steps." "A man's heart deviseth his way, but the Lord directeth his steps." None of us can take a step without his permission; none can go forth on a journey to a distant land without his constant superintending care; none can return without his favour. And yet how little is *this* recognized! How few feel it when they go out and come in; when they go forth to their daily employments; when they start on a voyage or journey; when they propose to return to their homes ! ¶ *Hast thou not glorified.* That is, thou hast not honoured him by a suitable acknowledgment of dependence on him.

24. *Then was the part of the hand sent from him.* To wit, the fingers. See ver. 5. The sense is, that when it

hand sent from him; and this writing was written.

25 And this *is* the writing that was written, MENE, MENE, TEKEL, UPHARSIN.

26 This *is* the interpretation of

was fully perceived that Belshazzar was not disposed to learn that there was a God in heaven; when he refused to profit by the solemn dispensations which had occurred in respect to his predecessor; when his own heart was lifted up with pride, and when he had gone even farther than his predecessors had done by the sacrilegious use of the vessels of the temple, thus showing especial contempt for the God of heaven, then appeared the mysterious handwriting on the wall. It was then an appropriate time for the Most High God, who had been thus contemned and insulted, to come forth and rebuke the proud and impious monarch.

25. *And this* is *the writing that was written.* The Babylonians, it would seem, were unacquainted with the *characters* that were used, and of course unable to understand the meaning. See ver. 8. The first thing, therefore, for Daniel to do was to read the writing, and this he was able to do without difficulty, probably, as already remarked, because it was in the ancient Hebrew character—a character quite familiar to him, though not known to the Babylonians, whom Belshazzar consulted. It is every way probable that that character *would be* used on an occasion like this, for (*a*) it is manifest that it was intended that the true God, the God of the Hebrews, should be made known, and this was the character in which his communications had been made to men; (*b*) it was clearly the design to honour his own religion, and it is morally certain that there would be something which would show the connection between this occurrence and his own agency, and nothing would do this better than to make use of such a character; and (*c*) it was the Divine intention to put honour on Daniel, and this would be well done by making use of a character which he understood. There have been, indeed, many conjectures respecting the characters which were employed on this occasion, and the reasons of the difficulty of interpreting the words used, but it is most probable that the above is the true statement, and this will relieve all the difficulties in regard to the account. Prideaux supposes that the characters employed were the ancient Phœnician characters, that were used by the Hebrews, and that are found now in the Samaritan Pentateuch; and that, as above suggested, these might be unknown to the Babylonians, though familiar to Daniel. Others have supposed that the characters were those in common use in Babylon, and that the reason why the Babylonians could not read them was, that they were smitten with a sudden blindness, like the inhabitants of Sodom, Gen. xix. 11. The Talmudists suppose that the words were written in a cabalistic manner, in which certain letters were used to stand for other letters, on the principle referred to by Buxtorf (*Lex. Chal. Rabb. et Talm.* p. 248), and known as אתבש—that is, where the alphabet is reversed, and א (A) is used for ת (T), ב (B) for ש (S), &c., and that on account of this cabalistic transmutation the Babylonians could not read it, though Daniel might have been familiar with that mode of writing. Rabbi Jochanan supposed that there was a change of the order in which the letters of the words were written; other Rabbins, that there was a change merely in the order of the first and second letters; others, that the words were written backwards; others that the words were written, not in the usual horizontal manner, but perpendicularly; and others, that the words were not written in full, but that only the first letters of each were written. See Bertholdt, pp. 349, 350. All these are mere conjectures, and most of them are childish and improbable suppositions. There is no real difficulty in the case if we suppose that the words were written in a character familiar to Daniel, but not familiar to the Babylonians. Or, if this is not admitted, then we may suppose that some mere marks were employed whose signification was made known to Daniel in a miraculous manner.

the thing: MENE; God hath numbered thy kingdom, and finished it.

a Job 31. 6; Ps. 62. 9.

27 TEKEL; Thou art *a* weighed in the balances, and art found wanting.*b*

b Matt. 22. 11, 12; 1 Cor. 3. 13.

26. *This* is *the interpretation of the thing.* It may seem not to have been difficult to interpret the meaning of the communication, when one was able to read the words, or when the sense of the words was understood. But, if the words are placed together, and considered in their abstract form, the whole communication would be so enigmatical that the interpretation would not be likely to occur to any one without a Divine guidance. This will appear more clearly by arranging the words together, as has been done by Hales :—

| MENE, | MENE, | TEKEL, | [PERES] | UPHARSIN. |
| NUMBER, | NUMBER, | WEIGHT, | [DIVISION] | DIVISIONS; |

or, as it is explained more accurately by Bertholdt and Gesenius:—

| *Mene,* | *Mene,* | *Tekel,* | *Upharsin.* |
| *Numbered,* | *Numbered,* | *Weighed,* | *Divided.* |

From this arrangement it will be at once seen that the interpretation proposed by Daniel was not one that would have been likely to have occurred to any one. ¶ *Mene.* מְנֵא. This word is a participle passive from מְנָה—*to number, to review.*—Gesenius, *Lex.* The verb is also written מְנָא.—Buxtorf, *Lex.* It would be literally translated *numbered,* and would apply to that of which an estimate was taken by counting. We use now an expression which would convey a similar idea, when we say of one that " his days are *numbered;*" that is, he has not long to live, or is about to die. The idea seems to be taken from the fact, that the duration of a man's life cannot usually be known, and in the general uncertainty we can form no correct estimate of it, but when he is old, or when he is dangerously sick, we feel that we can with some degree of probability *number* his days, since he cannot now live long. Such is the idea here, as explained by Daniel. All uncertainty about the duration of the kingdom was now removed, for, since the evil had come, an exact estimate of its whole duration—of the number of the years of its continuance —could be made. In the Greek of Theodotion there is no attempt to translate this word, and it is retained in Greek letters—Μανὴ. So also in the *Codex Chis.,* and in the Latin Vulgate. ¶ *God hath numbered thy kingdom.* The word which is used here, and ren-

dered *numbered*—מְנָה—is the verb of which the previous word is the participle. Daniel applies it to the *kingdom* or *reign* of the monarch, as being a thing of more importance than the life of the king himself. It is evident, if, according to the common interpretation of ver. 30, Belshazzar was slain that very night, it *might* have been applied to the king himself, meaning that *his* days were numbered, and that he was about to die. But this interpretation (see Notes) is not absolutely certain, and perhaps the fact that Daniel did *not* so apply the word may be properly regarded as one circumstance showing that such an interpretation is not necessary, though probably it is the correct one. ¶ *And finished it.* This is not the meaning of the word *Mene,* but is the explanation by Daniel of the thing intended. The word in its interpretation fairly implied that; or that might be understood from it. The fact that the " kingdom " in its duration was "*numbered,*" properly expressed the idea that it was now to come to an end. It did actually then come to an end by being merged in that of the Medes and Persians.

27. *Tekel.* This word (תְּקֵל) is also, according to Gesenius, a passive participle (from תְּקַל—*to poise, to weigh*), and means *weighed.* It would be used with reference to anything placed in a balance to ascertain its weight; and hence, like the word *measure,* would

denote that the extent, dimensions, true worth, or character of anything was ascertained. As by the use of scales the weight of anything is known, so the word is applied to any estimate of character or of actions, and a balance becomes the emblem of justice. Thus God, in his judgments of men, is represented as *weighing* their actions. 1 Sam. ii. 3, "The Lord is a God of knowledge, and by him actions are weighed." Comp. Job vi. 2:—

"O that my grief were thoroughly weighed,
And my calamity laid in the balances together."

Job xxxi. 6:—

"Let me be weighed in an even balance,
That God may know mine integrity."

The balance thus used to denote judgment in this life became also the emblem of judgment in the future state, when the conduct of men will be accurately estimated, and justice dealt out to them according to the strict rules of equity. To illustrate this, I will insert a copy of an Egyptian "Death Judgment," with the remarks of the editor of the *Pictorial Bible* in regard to it:—

"The Egyptians entertained the belief that the actions of the dead were so-

lemnly weighed in balances before Osiris, and that the condition of the departed was determined according to the preponderance of good or evil. Such judgment scenes are very frequently represented in the paintings and papyri of ancient Egypt, and one of them we have copied as a suitable illustration of the present subject. One of these scenes, as represented on the walls of a small temple at Dayr-el-Medeeneh, has been so well explained by Mr. Wilkinson, that we shall avail ourselves of his description; for although that to which it refers is somewhat different from the one which we have engraved, his account affords an adequate elucidation of all that ours contains. 'Osiris, seated on his throne, awaits the arrival of those souls that are ushered into Amenti. The four genii stand before him on a lotus-blossom [ours has the lotus without the genii], the female Cerberus sits behind them, and Harpocrates on the crook of Osiris. Thoth, the god of letters, arrives in the presence of Osiris, bearing in his hand a tablet, on which the actions of the deceased are noted down, while Horus and Aroeris are employed in weighing the good deeds * of the judged against

* "This M. Champollion supposes to be the

the ostrich feather, the symbol of truth and justice. A cynocephalus, the emblem of truth, is seated on the top of the balance. At length arrives the deceased, who appears between two figures of the goddess, and bears in his hand the symbol of truth,† indicating his meritorious actions, and his fitness for admission to the presence of Osiris.'

"If the Babylonians entertained a similar notion, the declaration of the prophet, 'Thou art weighed in the balances, and art found wanting!' must have appeared exceedingly awful to them. But again, there are allusions in this declaration to some such custom of literally weighing the royal person, as is described in the following passage in the account of Sir Thomas Roe's embassy to the great Mogul:—'The first of September (which was the late Mogul's birthday), he, retaining an ancient yearly custom, was, in the presence of his chief grandees, weighed in a balance: the ceremony was performed

heart. I still incline to the construction I have put upon it—a type of the good actions of the deceased.

† "Sometimes, instead of the ostrich feather, the deceased bears a vase (which is placed in the other scale), and it has then a similar import."

within his house, or tent, in a fair spacious room, whereinto none were admitted but by special leave. The scales in which he was thus weighed were plated with gold : and so was the beam, on which they hung by great chains, made likewise of that most precious metal. The king, sitting in one of them, was weighed first against silver coin, which immediately afterwards was distributed among the poor ; then was he weighed against gold ; after that against jewels (as they say), but I observed (being there present with my ambassador) that he was weighed against three several things, laid in silken bags in the contrary scale. When I saw him in the balance, I thought on Belshazzar, who was found too light. By his weight (of which his physicians yearly keep an exact account), they presume to guess of the present state of his body, of which they speak flatteringly, however they think it to be.'"

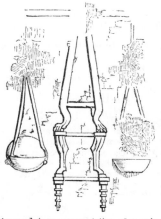

[Annexed is a representation of a pair of scales in the sculptures at Khorsabad. "The Assyrian warriors are seen in the sculptures bearing away in triumph the idols of the conquered nations, or breaking them into pieces, weighing them in scales, and dividing the fragments." The declaration, "Thou art weighed in the balances," takes part of its force from this custom of warfare, intimating, as it does, the entire ruin and overthrow of the monarch. "Lepsius has recently published a bass-relief

from an Egyptian tomb, representing a man weighing rings of gold or silver, with weights in the form of a bull's head, and of a seated lion with a ring on its back, precisely similar to those from Nineveh now in the British Museum."]

The engraving, on the next page, from the sarcophagus of Alexander, will further show how commonly this opinion prevailed, and how natural is the representation here. If the Babylonians entertained such notions in regard to the dead as are here represented, the declaration made by the prophet must have been exceedingly solemn. But whether this were so or not, the language of Daniel in interpreting the word must have been overwhelming to the monarch. It could be understood by him as denoting nothing less than that a solemn sentence had been passed upon his character and conduct by the great Judge of all, and that he was found to have failed in the requirements which had been made of him, and was now condemned. He had no righteousness when his actions came to be estimated as in a balance, and nothing awaited him but an awful condemnation. Who is there now who would not tremble at seeing the word *Tekel*—*weighed*—written on the wall of his chamber at midnight ? ¶ *Thou art weighed in the balances.* That is, this, in the circumstances, is the proper interpretation of this word. It would apply to anything whose value was ascertained by weighing it; but as the reference here was to the king of Babylon, and as the whole representation

28 PERES ; Thy kingdom is divided, and given [a] to the [b] Medes and Persians.[c]

a Foretold, Isa. 21. 2.   *b* ver. 31.   *c* ch. 6. 28.

was designed for him, Daniel distinctly applies it to him: "*thou* art weighed." On the use and application of this language, see 1 Sam. ii. 3: "The Lord is a God of knowledge, and by him ac-tions are weighed." Comp. also Job xxxi. 6; Prov. xvi. 2, 11. ¶ *And art found wanting.* This is added, like the previous phrase, as an explanation. Even if the *word* could have been read

by the Chaldeans, yet its meaning could not have been understood without a Divine communication, for though it were supposed to be applicable to the monarch, it would still be a question what the result of the weighing or trial would be. That could have been known to Daniel only by a communication from on high.

28. *Peres.* In ver. 25 this is *Uphar-sin.* These are but different forms of the same word—the word in ver. 25 being in the plural, and here in the singular. The verb (פְּרַס) means, *to divide;* and in this form, as in the previous cases, it is, according to Gesenius, a participle meaning *divided.* As it stands here, it would be applicable to anything that was *divided* or *sundered* —whether a kingdom, a palace, a house, a territory, &c. *What* was divided could be known only by Divine revelation. If the *word* had been understood by Belshazzar, undoubtedly it would have suggested the idea that there was to be some sort of division or sundering, but what that was to be would not be indicated by the mere use of the word. Perhaps to an affrighted imagination there might have been conveyed the idea that there would be a revolt in some of the provinces of the empire, and that a part would be rent away, but it would not have occurred that it would be so rent that the whole would pass under the dominion of a foreign power. Josephus (*Ant.* b. x. ch. xi. § 3) says, that the word "Phares in the Greek tongue means a *fragment,* κλασμα —God will, therefore, break thy kingdom in pieces, and divide it among the Medes and Persians." ¶ *Thy kingdom is divided.* That is, the pro-per interpretation of this communica-tion is, that the kingdom is about to be rent asunder, or broken into frag-ments. It is to be separated or torn from the dynasty that has ruled over it, and to be given to another. ¶ *And*

29 Then commanded Belshazzar,
and they clothed Daniel with scarlet, and *put* a chain of gold about
his neck, and made a proclamation concerning him, that *a* he

should be the third ruler in the
kingdom.

30 ¶ In that night *b* was Belshazzar the king of the Chaldeans
slain.

a ver. 7.

b Jer. 51. 31, 39.

given to the Medes and Persians. On
this united kingdom, see Notes on Isa.
xiii. 17. It was *given* to the Medes
and Persians when it was taken by
Cyrus, and when the kingdom of Babylon became extinct, and thencefor-
ward became a part of the Medo-Persian empire. See Notes on Isa. xiii.
17, 19.

29. *Then commanded Belshazzar.* In
compliance with his promise, ver. 16.
Though the interpretation had been so
fearful in its import, and though Daniel
had been so plain and faithful with him,
yet he did not hesitate to fulfil his promise. It is a remarkable instance of
the result of fidelity, that a proud monarch should have received such a re-
proof, and such a prediction in this
manner, and it is an encouragement to
us to do our duty, and to state the truth
plainly to wicked men. Their own consciences testify to them that it is the
truth, and they will see the truth so

clearly that they cannot deny it. ¶ *And
they clothed Daniel with scarlet,* &c.
All this, it would seem, was transacted
in a single night, and it has been made
an objection, as above remarked, to
the authenticity of the book, that such
events are said to have occurred in so
short a space of time, and that Daniel
should have been so soon clothed with
the robes of office. On this objection,
see Intro. to the chapter, § I. II. In
respect to the latter part of the objection, it may be here further remarked,
that it was not necessary to *fit* him
with a suit of clothes made expressly
for the occasion, for the loose, flowing
robes of the Orientals were as well
adapted to one person as another, and
in the palaces of kings such garments
were always on hand. See Harmer's
Observations on the East, vol. ii. 392,
seq. Comp. Rosenmüller, *Morgenland,
in loc.* ¶ *That he should be the third
ruler,* &c. See Notes on ver. 7.

[The engraving, copied from one of the tab-
lets at Khorsabad, represents a eunuch holding
distinguished rank in the Assyrian court; and
the chain and other neck ornaments are most
probably honorary adornments bestowed upon
the wearer by the king, as the rewards of fidelity, or important services rendered.]

30. *In that night was Belshazzar the
king of the Chaldeans slain.* On the
taking of Babylon, and the consequences, see Notes on Isa. xiii. 17–22,
and ch. xlv. 1, 2. The account which
Xenophon (*Cyrop.* vii. 5.) gives of the
taking of Babylon, and of the death of

31 And Darius *a* the Median took

a ch. 9. 1.   1 *he as the son of.*   2 or, *now.*

the king—though without mentioning his name, agrees so well with the statement here, that it may be regarded as a strong confirmation of its correctness. After describing the preparation made to take the city by draining off the waters of the Euphrates, so as to leave the channel dry beneath the walls for the army of Cyrus, and after recording the charge which Cyrus gave to his generals Gadatas and Gobryas, he adds, "And indeed those who were with Gobryas said that it would not be wonderful if the gates of the palace should be found open, *as the whole city that night seemed to be given up to revelry*"—ὡς ἐν κώμῳ γὰρ δοκεῖ ἡ πόλις πᾶσα εἶναι τῇδε τῇ νυκτί. He then says that as they passed on, after entering the city, "of those whom they encountered, part being smitten died, part fled again back, and part raised a clamour. But those who were with Gobryas also raised a clamour as if they also joined in the revelry, and going as fast as they could, they came soon to the palace of the king. But those who were with Gobryas and Gadatas being arrayed, found the gates of the palace closed, but those who were appointed to go against the guard of the palace fell upon them when drinking before a great light, and were quickly engaged with them in hostile combat. Then a cry arose, and they who were within having asked the cause of the tumult, the king commanded them to see what the affair was, and some of them rushing out opened the gates. As they who were with Gadatas saw the gates open, they rushed in, and pursuing those who attempted to return, and smiting them, they came to the king, and they found him standing with a drawn sabre—ἀκινάκην. And those who were with Gadatas and Gobryas overpowered him, ἐχειροῦντο—and those who were with him were slain—one opposing, and one fleeing, and one seeking his safety in the best way he could. And Cyrus sent certain of his horsemen away, and commanded that they should put to death those whom they found out of their dwellings, but that those who were in their houses,

the kingdom, 1 *being* 2 about threescore and two years old.

and could speak the Syriac language, should be suffered to remain, but that whosoever should be found without should be put to death. "These things they did. But Gadatas and Gobryas came up; and first they rendered thanks to the gods because they had taken vengeance on the impious king—ὅτι τετιμωρημένοι ἦσαν τὸν ἀνόσιον βασιλέα. Then they kissed the hands and feet of Cyrus, weeping with joy and rejoicing. When it was day, and they who had the watch over the towers learned that the city was taken, and *that the king was dead*—τὸν βασιλέα τεθνηκότα—they also surrendered the towers." These extracts from Xenophon abundantly confirm what is here said in Daniel respecting the death of the king, and will more than neutralize what is said by Berosus. See Intro. to the chapter, § II.

31. *And Darius the Median took the kingdom.* The city and kingdom were actually taken by Cyrus, though acting in the name and by the authority of Darius, or Cyaxares, who was his uncle. For a full explanation of the conquests of Cyrus, and of the reason why the city is said to have been taken by Darius, see Notes on Isa. xli. 2. In regard to the question who Darius the Median was, see the Intro. to ch. vi. § II. The name Darius — דָּרְיָוֶשׁ, or *Darjavesh* — is the name under which the three Medo-Persian kings are mentioned in the Old Testament. There is some difference of opinion as to its meaning. Herodotus (vi. 98) says, that it is equivalent to ἐρξίης, *one who restrains,* but Hesychius says that it is the same as φρόνιμος— *prudent.* Grotefend, who has found it in the cuneiform inscriptions at Persepolis, as Darheush, or Darjeush (*Heeren's Ideen,* i. 2, p. 350), makes it to be a compound word, the first part being an abbreviation of *Dara,* " *Lord,*" and the latter portion coming from *kshah,* " *king.*" St. Martin reads the name *Dareiousch Vyschtasponca* on the Persepolitan inscriptions; that is, *Darius,* son of *Vishtaspo.* Lassen, however, gives *Darhawus Vistaspaha,* the latter word

being equivalent to the *Gustasp* of the modern Persian, and meaning "one whose employment is about horses." See Anthon's *Class. Dict.*, and Kitto's *Cyclo.*, art. "Darius." Comp. Niehbuhr, *Reisebeschr.*, Part II. Tab. 24, G. and B. Gesenius, *Lex.* This Darius is supposed to be Cyaxares II. (Intro. to ch. vi. § II.), the son and successor of Astyages, the uncle and father-in-law of Cyrus, who held the empire of Media between Astyages and Cyrus, B.C. 569–536. ¶ *Being.* Marg., "He as *son of.*" The marginal reading is in accordance with the Chaldee—קבְּרֵ. It is not unusual in the language of the Orientals to denote the age of any one by saying that he is the son of so many years. ¶ *About.* Marg., "or, *now.*" The word, both in the text and the margin, is designed to express the supposed sense of his "being the son of sixty years." The language of the original would, however, be accurately expressed by saying that he was then sixty years old. Though Cyrus was the active agent in taking Babylon, yet it was done in the name and by the authority of Cyaxares or Darius; and as he was the actual sovereign, the name of his general—Cyrus—is not mentioned here, though he was in fact the most important agent in taking the city, and became ultimately much more celebrated than Darius was.

This portion of history, the closing scene in the reign of a mighty monarch, and the closing scene in the independent existence of one of the most powerful kingdoms that has ever existed on the earth, is full of instructive lessons; and in view of the chapter as thus explained, we may make the following

REMARKS.

(1.) We have here an impressive illustration of the sin of sacrilege (vers. 2, 3). In all ages, and among all people, this has been regarded as a sin of peculiar enormity, and it is quite evident that God in tnis solemn scene meant to confirm the general judgment of mankind on the subject. Among all people, where any kind of religion has prevailed, there are places and objects which are regarded as set apart to sacred use, and which are not to be employed for common and profane purposes. Though in themselves—in the gold and silver, the wood and stone of which they are made — there is no essential holiness, yet they derive a sacredness from being set apart to Divine purposes, and it has always been held to be a high crime to treat them with indignity or contempt—to rob altars, or to desecrate holy places. This general impression of mankind it was clearly the design of God to confirm in the case before us, when the sacred vessels of the temple—vessels consecrated in the most solemn manner to the worship of Jehovah—were profanely employed for the purposes of carousal. God had borne it patiently when those vessels had been removed from the temple at Jerusalem, and when they had been laid up among the spoils of victory in the temples of Babylon; but when they were profaned for purposes of revelry — when they were brought forth to grace a heathen festival, and to be employed in the midst of scenes of riot and dissipation, it was time for him to interpose, and to show to these profane revellers that there is a God in heaven.

(2.) We may see the peril of such festivals as that celebrated by Belshazzar and his lords, ver. 1, *seq.* It is by no means probable that when the feast was contemplated and arranged, anything was designed like that which occurred in the progress of the affair. It was not a matter of set purpose to introduce the females of the harem to this scene of carousal, and still less to make use of the sacred vessels dedicated to the worship of Jehovah, to grace the midnight revelry. It is not improbable that they would have been at first shocked at such an outrage on what was regarded as propriety, or what would have been deemed sacred by all people. It was only when the king had "tasted the wine" that these things were proposed; and none who attend on such a banquet as this, none who come together for purposes of drinking and feasting, can foretell what they may be led to do under the influence of wine and strong drink. No man is certain of *not* doing foolish and wicked things who gives himself up to such indulgences; no man knows what he may do that may be the cause of bitter regret and painful mortification in the recollection.

(3.) God has the means of access to the consciences of men (ver. 5). In this case it was by writing on the wall with his own fingers certain mysterious words which none could interpret, but which no one doubted were of fearful import. No one present, it would appear, had any doubt that somehow what was written was connected with some awful judgment, and the fearfulness of what they dreaded arose manifestly from the consciousness of their own guilt. It is not often that God comes forth in this way to alarm the guilty; but he has a thousand methods of doing it, and no one can be sure that in an instant he will not summon all the sins of his past life to remembrance. He *could* write our guilt in letters of light before us— in the chamber where we sleep; in the hall where we engage in revelry; on the face of the sky at night; or he can make it as plain to our minds *as if* it were thus written out. To Belshazzar, in his palace, surrounded by his lords, he showed this; to us in society or solitude he can do the same thing. No sinner can have any security that he may not in a moment be overwhelmed with the conviction of his own depravity, and with dreadful apprehension of the wrath to come.

DANIEL I.

(4.) We have in this chapter (ver. 6) a striking illustration of the effects of a sudden alarm to the guilty. The countenance of the monarch was changed; his thoughts troubled him; the joints of his loins were loosed, and his knees smote together. Such effects are not uncommon when a sinner is made to feel that he is in the presence of God, and when his thoughts are led along to the future world. The human frame is so made that these changes occur as indicative of the troubles which the mind experiences, and the fact that it is thus agitated shows the power which God has over us. No guilty man can be secure that he will *not* thus be alarmed when he comes to contemplate the possibility that he may soon be called before his Maker, and the fact that he *may* thus be alarmed should be one of the considerations bearing on his mind to lead him to a course of virtue and religion. Such terror is proof of conscious guilt, for the innocent have nothing to dread; and if a man is sure that he is prepared to appear before God, he is *not* alarmed at the prospect. They who live in sin; they who indulge in revelry; they who are profane and sacrilegious; they who abuse the mercies of God, and live to deride sacred things, can never be certain that in a moment, by the revelation of their guilt to their own souls, and by a sudden message from the eternal world, they may not be overwhelmed with the deepest consternation. Their countenances may become deadly pale, their joints may be loosed, and their limbs tremble. It is only the righteous who can look calmly at the judgment.

(5.) We may see from this chapter one of the effects of the terror of a guilty conscience. It is not said, indeed, that the mysterious fingers on the wall recorded the *guilt* of the mon-

U

arch. But they recorded *something;* they were making some record that manifestly pertained to him. How natural was it to suppose that it was a record of his guilt! And who is there that could bear a record made in that manner of his own thoughts and purposes; of his desires and feelings; of what he is conscious is passing within the chambers of his own soul? There is no one who would not turn pale if he saw a mysterious hand writing all his thoughts and purposes — all the deeds of his past life—on the wall of his chamber at night, and bringing at once all his concealed thoughts and all his forgotten deeds before his mind. And if this is so, how will the sinner bear the disclosures that will be made at the day of judgment?

APPENDIX.

I.

EXCURSUS I.

ON THE ALLEGED DISCREPANCY BE-TWEEN DANIEL I. 1, AND JER. XXV. 1, AND SOME OTHER PASSAGES.

THE charge of *historical incorrectness* against the writer of the book of Daniel, rests partly upon some *dates of time*, and partly upon some *historical occurrences*. I shall first examine the allegation of error in respect to the designation of TIME.

In Dan. i. 1, it is said, that Nebuchadnezzar king of Babylon came up against Jerusalem, besieged it, took Jehoiakim captive, and rifled the temple of a part of its furniture, *in the third year of Jehoiakim*. In Jer. xxv. 1, it is explicitly said, that the *first* year of Nebuchadnezzar's reign was the *fourth* year of Jehoiakim's. Moreover, in Jer. xlvi. 2, it is said that king Nebuchadnezzar smote Carchemish on the Euphrates, then in possession of Pharaoh-Necho king of Egypt, in the same *fourth* year of Jehoiakim. Taking all these passages into view, it is alleged that the writer of the book of Daniel could not have lived in the time of Nebuchadnezzar, when the true date of the invasion of Palestine by that king must necessarily have been well known; but at a subsequent period, when the chronology of these events was more obscure, and when he might be misled by erring tradition. That period is placed, by most of the recent critics belonging to the so-called *liberal* school, near to the close of the Maccabean times, with the history of which, as they aver, the book of Daniel concludes.

As this has been, of late, an almost uniform assertion among critics of the new school, and has been placed in the front rank of objections against the genuineness of the book of Daniel, it becomes necessary to give it an attentive examination. Lengerke says of it, in his recent *Commentary* on this book, that "all attempts to remove this objection have to the present hour been frustrated. . . . Not only is the *date* wrong, but the *deportation* [of captives] under Jehoiakim remains at least unproved," p. 2, *seq.*

The documents which must guide our inquiries, are a fragment of Berosus (preserved by Josephus), and several brief passages in the Hebrew Scriptures. These are all the historical data on which we can place any reliance. All subsequent testimony is either a mere repetition of these, or a constructive exegesis of them, or if not, it is mere conjecture. In respect to the original documents, we have evidently the same right of interpretation as Abydenus, Megasthenes, Josephus, Eusebius, and others had. The native Greek historians, whose works are now extant, make no mention at all of Nebuchadnezzar; consequently, Josephus's quotations from the Oriental writers, and the historical notices comprised in the Hebrew Scriptures, are all on which we can place any dependence as legitimate sources of testimony. These consist of the following particulars:—

No. I.—The king of Egypt, Pharaoh-Necho, after having slain Josiah, and deposed his successor, Jehoahaz, made Eliakim (surnamed *Jehoiakim*), the son of Josiah, king over the Hebrews, and treated him as a tributary

vassal; 2 Kings xxiii. 29–37. The
sacred writer then proceeds thus, in
2 Kings xxiv. 1: "In his days came
up Nebuchadnezzar king of Babylon;
and Jehoiakim became his servant
three years; then he turned and rebelled against him. (2) And Jehovah
sent against him bands of the Chaldees, and bands of Syria, and bands of
Moab, and bands of the sons of Ammon; yea, he sent them against Judah
to destroy him; according to the word
of the Lord which he spoke by his
servants the prophets."

No. II.—After relating events previous to Jehoiakim's reign, as in the
book of Kings, the writer thus proceeds in 2 Chron. xxxvi. 6: "Against
him came up Nebuchadnezzar king of
Babylon, and he bound him in fetters
to convey him to Babylon. (7) And
a part of the vessels of the house of
the Lord did Nebuchadnezzar take to
Babylon, and he put them in his
temple at Babylon."

No. III.—Jer. xxv. 1: "The message which was to Jeremiah, concerning all the people of Judah, in the
fourth year of Jehoiakim the son of
Josiah king of Judah; the same was
the first year of Nebuchadnezzar king
of Babylon."

No. IV.—Jer. xlvi. 1, 2: "The
word of the Lord . . . against Egypt,
against the army of Pharaoh-Necho
king of Egypt, which was by the
river Euphrates in Carchemish, which
Nebuchadnezzar king of Babylon
smote, in the fourth year of Jehoiakim
king of Judah."

No. V.—Dan. i. 1, 2: "In the
third year of the reign of Jehoiakim
king of Judah came Nebuchadnezzar
king of Babylon to Jerusalem, and
besieged it. And the Lord gave into
his hand Jehoiakim king of Judah,
and a part of the vessels of the house of
God; and he brought them to the land
of Shinar, to the house of his God,
and the vessels did he bring into the
treasure-house of his God."

No. VI.—Berosus, as quoted by
Josephus, Antiq. X. 11. 1, also Contra
Ap. I. 19: "When his father Nabopolassar had heard that the satrap,
who had been appointed over Egypt
and the regions around Coelo-Syria

and Phœnicia, had rebelled, not being
able himself to endure hardships, he
committed to his son Nebuchadnezzar,
then in the vigour of life, certain portions of his forces, and sent them
against him. And Nebuchadnezzar,
falling in with the rebel, and putting
his forces in order, gained a victory
over him, and the country belonging
to his control he brought under his
own dominion. Now it came to pass,
that Nabopolassar fell sick at that
period, and died, having reigned twenty-
one years. Not long after, having
learned the death of his father, he arranged his affairs in Egypt and the
other regions, and committed the captives of the Jews, the Phœnicians, the
Syrians, and the nations in Egypt, to
certain of his friends, to conduct them
to Babylon, with the most weighty
part of his forces, and the remainder
of his booty. He himself, accompanied by very few, went to Babylon
through the desert. Then taking
upon him the affairs which had been
managed by the Chaldees, and the
kingdom which had been preserved for
him by their leader, becoming master
of the whole (ὁλοκλήρου) of his father's
dominion (ἀρχῆς), he assigned to the
captives who had arrived, colonial
dwelling-places in the most suitable
regions of Babylon," &c. The passage goes on to show how Nebuchadnezzar used a part of the spoils as
ἀναθήματα, i.e., votive offerings, in
the temples of his gods, and the rest
in building and adorning the city of
Babylon.

Preceding this passage, as quoted
from Berosus (Cont. Apion. I. 19), Josephus gives a summary of the history
of Nebuchadnezzar, as exhibited by
the Chaldean historian. In this summary he says, that Berosus has related,
"how Nabopolassar sent his son, Nebuchadnezzar, against Egypt and against
our land [Palestine], with a large force
(μετὰ πολλῆς δυνάμεως), who subdued
them, burned the temple at Jerusalem,
and, transplanting the great mass of
the people, carried them away to Babylon." In a part of this summary,
he seems to quote the words of Berosus,
and represents him as saying, that "the
Babylonian conquered Egypt, Syria,

Phœnicia, and Arabia, and exceeded in achievements all of the Chaldean and Babylonian kings, who had reigned before him." We have now before us all the documents on which any reliance can be safely placed. On these I would make a few remarks which may assist our further inquiries. (*a*) From a survey of these documents it is plain, at first sight, that no one of them is anything more than a mere *summary* sketch of Jehoiakim's reign ; and so of Nebuchadnezzar's. The particulars of events, and even the order of them, in some respects, are not specified at all. Thus in No. I., *two* invasions of Nebuchadnezzar are made certain ; but no particular time of either is specified. In No. II. only one (probably the final) invasion appears to be mentioned. In Berosus, there is a still more rapid *coup d'œil* of events, without any effort to narrate particulars, much less to make out dates. (*b*) We are, therefore, at liberty to supply the omissions of one account, by that which another has furnished. An argument against more than one invasion, in the time of Jehoiakim, drawn from the fact that no more than one is mentioned in 2 Chronicles, would amount to nothing ; for it need not be again proved, that the *argumentum a silentio* is in such cases of no value. So an argument drawn from the silence of Berosus as to more than one invasion of Palestine by Nebuchadnezzar, would prove nothing against the united testimony of Kings, Jeremiah, and Daniel, that there was more than one. (*c*) It follows, that we are at liberty to make out probabilities of time and order of succession in respect to events, from *circumstances* that are narrated, where the writers have omitted formally to make out these in their narrations. This, however, should always be done with caution, and we should keep strictly within the bounds of probability.

In respect to the main subject now before us I would remark, that there are some points so well settled, and of such controlling influence, that nothing can be safely admitted which is inconsistent with them. (1.) It is now a matter of nearly universal agreement, that Nabopolassar, the father of Nebuchadnezzar, in union with the Median king Astyages, destroyed the Assyrian empire, and began his independent reign in Babylon, in 625 B.C. (2.) It seems to be certain, from the testimony of Berosus (No. VI. above) and Syncellus, that he reigned *twenty-one* years. Of course his death was near the close of 605 B.C., or at the beginning of 604. At this period, then, Nebuchadnezzar by inheritance became sole king of Babylon. (3.) *Previously* to this period, Nebuchadnezzar had invaded and subdued Carchemish, and overrun and brought under subjection to himself Syria, Palestine, Moab, the country of the Ammonites, Phœnicia, and Lower Egypt. This is clear from a comparison of No. I. and No. VI. with its sequel above. When these achievements and conquests were completed, Nebuchadnezzar received tidings of his father's death, hastened to Babylon, and left the captives and the booty to be forwarded by his subordinate officers ; No. VI. above. These are *facts* which we must either admit, or else renounce the credit of historical testimony which we are unable fairly to impeach.

The question, then, whether Nebuchadnezzar came into the regions of Hither Asia *before* 604 B.C., is settled. But—how long before? Long enough, at any rate, to overrun and subdue all these countries. Less than some two years for such achievements, no one who looks at the extent of those countries, and knows the slowness with which armies formerly moved in the East, will venture to fix upon. The book of Daniel (i. 1, 2) says, that Nebuchadnezzar came up and besieged Jerusalem in the *third* year of Jehoiakim, *i.e.*, in 607. That this was near the close of that third year, would seem probable from two circumstances ; first, the fast kept by Jehoiakim and his people, on the *ninth* month of the fifth year of this king, *i.e.*, Dec. 605. This was no legal or ritual fast (for none belonged to this period), but one either commemorative of some great evil, *e.g.*, the capture of the city by Nebuchadnezzar (comp. Zech. viii. 19, where four fasts of a like kind are specified) ; or anticipative of some great and dangerous struggle, *e.g.*,

Jehoiakim's rebellion against Nebuchadnezzar. Moreover, as Nebuchadnezzar is called *king*, while on this expedition, both in Daniel, Kings and Chronicles, and Jeremiah, and as we know (see Nos. III. IV.), that Jehoiakim's *fourth* year corresponded with the *first* year of Nebuchadnezzar, as viewed by the Hebrews, it would seem to follow of course, allowing the historical verity of Daniel, that the invasion by Nebuchadnezzar must have been late in 607. If so, then of course the greater part of his *first* year, as counted by the Hebrews, corresponded to the *fourth* year of Jehoiakim, as Nos. III. IV. declare. Later than the time which Daniel designates, Nebuchadnezzar's expedition could not well have been, if we admit the great extent of his conquests already made at, or a little before, the beginning of 604. Cyrus and Cyaxares were about ten years in subduing Asia Minor; could Nebuchadnezzar have overrun all Hither Asia and Egypt in less than *two?* All those then, who, like Lengerke, Winer, &c., make the fourth year of Nebuchadnezzar and the eighth of Jehoiakim, *i.e.*, 602 or 601, to be the time when the king of Babylon first invaded Palestine, are obliged to dishonour the credit of Berosus, who (No. VI.) says, in so many words, that "when Nebuchadnezzar heard of his father's death, he left the spoil and the captive *Jews*, Syrians, Phœnicians, and Egyptians, to be conducted to Babylon by his officers." The same is also asserted by Alexander Polyhistor, Euseb. *Chron. Arm.* I. p. 45. All agree that this must have been in 604; and scarcely a doubt can remain, that it was near the *commencement* of this year. Lengerke says, in respect to what Berosus asserts, that "it may appear to be doubtful;" p. 6. He refers to Jer. xxix. 10, comp. ver. 2, for proof that the exile of Jeconiah was the *first* deportation of Jews by Nebuchadnezzar. But I can find no proof of such a nature here. The simple truth is, that events are everywhere related, in respect to Jehoiakim's reign, *without any dates* of time, with the exception of Dan. i. 1, 2. But still, these events are plainly such as to show the entire probability of what is declared by Daniel.

"But Nebuchadnezzar took Carchemish in the *fourth* year of Jehoiakim (No. IV. above); how could he do this, and yet send Daniel and his compeers into exile, in the *third* year of the same Jehoiakim?"

One may well reply, that there is no impossibility, or even improbability in this. Where is the passage of history to show that Nebuchadnezzar did not besiege and take Jerusalem, *before* he went against Carchemish? Babylon, Carchemish, and Jerusalem, are at the extreme points of a triangle, the shortest side of which is indeed the distance from Babylon to Carchemish? Why then did not Nebuchadnezzar go directly from Babylon to Carchemish? The probable answer seems to me not to be difficult. Jehoiakim was placed on the throne by Pharaoh-Necho, and consequently was his hearty ally and tributary. Nebuchadnezzar, by marching first against him, and then subduing all the countries under Egyptian sway, through which he passed on his march to Carchemish, avoided the possibility of aid from Egypt being given to the city in question, or from the allies of Egypt. Carchemish was the strongest place in all that region; and such a plan showed the expertness of Nebuchadnezzar as a warrior. The whole course of events, in this case, certainly looks as if the assertion in Dan. i. 1, 2, were true.

"But how could Jeremiah, then, in the *fourth* year of Jehoiakim (xxv. 1, *seq.*), threaten an invasion of the Chaldees, and seventy years of exile? The exile, according to this view, had already begun." But to this question one may reply, that Nebuchadnezzar's first work, viz., the subjection of Jehoiakim and the making of him a tributary, had indeed already been done; but all of the work which Nebuchadnezzar was to perform, was not yet completed. In his victorious march from Carchemish, where he had been successful, through all the countries of Hither Asia and Lower Egypt, and of course through Palestine, he was still to collect more booty, and to carry away such and so many captives as he thought would effectually prevent insurrection after his departure. It is not probable that he sent away many captives to Babylon, immediately on his first capture of Jerusalem. He could not then spare the troops necessary for such an escort as was required to do this. In all probability, therefore, he contented himself with sending away a sufficient number of *hostages,* belonging to the princes and nobles, to secure the fidelity of Jehoiakim. The book of Daniel (i. 1–3), merely avers, that in the *third* year of Jehoiakim, a part of the vessels of the temple, and *some of the king's seed and of the princes,* were sent to Babylon. Nothing could be more natural or probable than this, under such circumstances. One has only to call to mind, that *hostages,* and those of princely descent, were usually demanded by conquerors, where want of fidelity in the subdued was suspected ; and also, that the booty of gold and silver was one main object, in all such expeditions as that of Nebuchadnezzar's. Hence, in Jer. lii. 27–30, no mention is made of those first hostages as exiles ; first, because they were few in number, and secondly, because their condition was different from that of ordinary exiles. When we find Jeremiah, therefore, in xxv. 1–11, in the *fourth* year of Jehoiakim, threatening subjugation and exile to the Jews, it cannot reasonably be doubted that he did so, because Jehoiakim, the former ally of Egypt, and who moreover had been set on his throne by the Egyptian king, was meditating revolt. Nebuchadnezzar's success at Carchemish was probably as yet unknown in Judea. Jehoiakim, therefore, hoped for a different result, and was ready to join his former master, in case of his success. To prevent this catastrophe, Jeremiah uttered the comminations of chap. xxv. 1–11. And that Jehoiakim's intentions were known to Nebuchadnezzar, seems quite probable from the treatment which, according to Berosus, the Jews experienced at the close of Nebuchadnezzar's expedition, viz., the deportation of Hebrew captives. Still, as this class of exiles is not particularized in Jer. lii. 27–30, they probably consisted mostly of such as might come under the denomination of hostages, *i.e.*, they belonged to the more wealthy and influential families.

That all which has been said of the disposition of Jehoiakim to rebel, is true, seems to be confirmed by the fact, that not long after this period, as soon as Nebuchadnezzar had gone to Babylon and become stationary there, *i.e.*, probably about the end of 604, Jehoiakim did actually rebel, and throw off his allegiance to Babylon. The king of Babylon, however, was so intent on beautifying his capital and his temples, and thus expending the immense wealth which he had collected in his predatory incursions (Berosus in Jos. *Cont. Ap.* i. 19), that he did not immediately undertake to chastise the Jewish king. But at the close of 600 B.C., or early in 599; he again marched up to Jerusalem, and inflicted the penalty that was usual in cases of revolt.

Lengerke and others assert, that Nebuchadnezzar did not invade Judea again, during the life of Jehoiakim, and that this king died and was buried in peace, contrary to the threats of Jeremiah, xxii. 19, and xxxvi. 30, viz., that he should be destroyed by violence, and his dead body be cast out unburied. The appeal for proof of this is to 2 Ki. xxiv. 6, which states, that "Jehoiakim *slept with his fathers,* and that Jehoiachin his son reigned in his stead." Lengerke (p. 7) avers, that the expression *slept* or *rested with his fathers,* means, always and only, that "the person in question descended in quiet to the common grave of his fathers." Surely an entire mistake ! That שָׁכַב of itself merely designates the *death* of an individual, without determining the fact whether it was *peaceful* or *violent,* is clear enough from Hebrew usage. In almost every narration respecting the death of a king, either in the book of Kings or Chronicles, it is said of him, that *he slept with his fathers.* But that this has no concern with indicating his *peaceful burial,* is quite certain from the fact, that in nearly every case of this nature, the burial of the king is the subject of a separate mention, showing of course that this is not involved or implied in the first expression. Nor does שָׁכַב (*slept*) even involve the idea of a *peaceful death;* for it is said of Ahab, who perished of wounds received in battle, that "he slept with his fathers" (1 Ki. xxiv. 40). In ver. 36 is the equivalent expression : *So the king died ;* and it is then added : "They buried him in Samaria." In the same way עָצַב alone is used for death, and mostly for the designation of violent death, in Isa. xiv. 8, 17, 43 ; xvii ; Job iii. 13 ; xx. 11, 21 ; xxvi. Not a word is said in 2 Ki. xxiv. 6, of Jehoiakim's *burial;* and of course there is nothing there to show that Jeremiah, in declaring that he should perish *unburied,* had predicted what proved to be untrue. On the other hand ; what are we to make of לְהַאֲבִידוֹ, to *destroy him (i.e.,* Jehoiakim, as Lengerke himself (p. 6) concedes), in 2 Ki. xxiv. 2 ? And what of 2 Chron. xxxvi. 6, which says that the king of Babylon *bound Jehoiakim in fetters to carry him to Babylon,* but makes no mention at all of his being actually sent thither ? That Jeremiah has not given an account of the fulfilment of his own prediction respecting Jehoiakim, is not strange, unless the principle is to be assumed, that prophets are obligated to write full and regular *history,* as well as prediction. I might even argue in favour of the fulfilment of the prediction, from the silence of the prophet. It was an event so well known, one might say with probability, that a special record of it was not needed on his part. Yet I think the books of Chronicles and of Kings, as cited above, have *impliedly* recorded the event in question. Still more express do I find, with Grotius, the recognition of it in Ezek. xix. 9. Here, the preceding context describes the reign and fate of Jehoahaz or Shallum ; comp. 2 Ki. xxiii. 31–33. Then the prophet comes, in his parable, to the *successor* of Shallum, viz., Jehoiakim (in case he means the *immediate* successor), and he says of him, that "the nations set against him . . . . and he was taken in their pit, and they put him in ward *in chains,* and brought him to the king of Babylon ; they brought him into holds, that his voice should no more be heard upon the mountains

of Israel." To interpret all this of Jechoniah, as Rosenmüller, Lengerke, and others have done, seems to me very incongruous. The prophet says of this *lion,* that "he went up and down among the lions . . . . learned to catch prey, and devoured men ; and he knew their desolate places, and laid waste their cities, and the land was desolate, and the fulness thereof, by reason of his roaring." All this now, of a boy *eight* years old, according to 2 Chron. xxxvi. 9, and according to 2 Ki. xxiv. 8, only *eighteen ;* and of a child, moreover, who as both records aver, reigned only about *three months !* A most extravagant parable would Ezekiel seem to have written, if all this is to be predicated of such a child, whether aged eight or eighteen, and of only a three months' reign.

There is indeed a difficulty, arising from the extreme brevity of the sacred writers, in finding out the *particulars* in the history of the closing part of Jehoiakim's reign. But certain it is, that nothing against the supposition that he died a violent death, and was left unburied, can be made out from what is recorded. Would Jeremiah have left his predictions standing as they do in his prophecy, if they had not been fulfilled ? Lengerke intimates, that the peaceful accession of Jehoiachin to his father's throne, shows that Nebuchadnezzar was not in Palestine at the time of Jehoiakim's death. But if Nebuchadnezzar had already chastised Jehoiakim on account of his rebellion, and put him into fetters, in which he died through hard usage or violence, may he not have ceded to Jehoiachin the throne of Judea, in consequence of renewed and solemn stipulations to become his vassal ? And specially as he was so young, that little was to be feared from him ? I see nothing of the impossible, or even of the improbable, in all this. The fact that Nebuchadnezzar was very suspicious of Jehoiachin, is clear from the circumstance, that after only three months he returned with his army, and carried off that king and many of his subjects, into exile at Babylon. The phrase לִתְשׁוּבַת הַשָּׁנָה, in 2 Chron. xxxvi. 10, indicates something more, in my apprehension, than has been usually noticed by commentators. In all probability, this *return* or *turning of the year* means the spring of the year, when kings were wont to go out on military expeditions. But still the word *year* here plainly stands related to some other period of time, from which it is reckoned. And what can this be, except the antecedent period when Jehoiakim was deposed and slain? If this were done in the autumn, and Jehoiachin made king either by Nebuchadnezzar himself, or by the people rebelling against Babylon after his departure, he might reign during the three winter months, and in the spring of the year be attacked and carried into exile by Nebuchadnezzar. No doubt this conqueror had large standing garrisons, in all the conquered countries, ready to act at short warning. Hence the shortness of the time, between the first and second invasion at this period, according to the statement made above.

That I have reasoned correctly in regard to the mere *summary* or generic accounts of Jehoiakim's reign, both in the sacred records and in Berosus, I must believe no one will deny who takes due pains minutely to examine them. It follows of course, unless the credibility of these historians can be reasonably impeached, that the omission of particulars by any one of them, is no argument against the verity of another who does state some particulars. This is notably illustrated by Jer. lii. 28, 29. In ver. 28 it is stated, that Nebuchadnezzar carried away captive, in his *seventh* year, 3023 persons. In 2 Ki. xxiv. 12, it is stated, that Jehoiachin and his court gave themselves up to Nebuchadnezzar in the *eighth* year of his reign, who carried him away to Babylon, with 10,000 captives and all the craftsmen and smiths, ver. 14. In Jeremiah, then, the statement refers to what was done one year (*i.e.*, in 599) before that took place which is related in the book of Kings. Both the time and the number of exiles mentioned in the two passages, are discrepant; and consequently we may regard this circumstance as heightening the probability of two invasions, as stated

above, which took place within a small period of time. Again, in Jer. lii. 29 it is stated, that Nebuchadnezzar, in his *eighteenth* year, carried away captive 832 persons. In 2 Ki. xxv. 3–10, it is declared that Nebuchadnezzar, in his *nineteenth* year, took Jerusalem, burned the temple, and carried away captive all except the poor of the land, ver. 12. How many were the captives, is not stated; but there must have been a great many thousands. The same thing is repeated in Jer. lii. 12–16. Here then (in lii. 29) is a statement of deportation, in a different year and in very different numbers from what is stated or implied in the book of Kings. Jer. lii. 29 seems evidently to relate to captives sent away *one year before the siege was completed;* for it lasted some twenty months. Then, again, there is a third deportation mentioned in Jer. lii. 30, in the twenty-third year of Nebuchadnezzar; of which we have no other account. Who will venture now to say, that the books of Jeremiah and of Kings are at variance; or rather, that they are contradictory, in regard to the deportation of exiles? Both may be regarded as true, without doing the least violence to probability.

"But both Daniel and Jeremiah call Nebuchadnezzar *king*, some two or more years before he was king. How can such a mistake be accounted for?"

Easily, I would say; or rather, I would deny that there is any real error in the Jewish historians or prophets, with regard to this matter. Of the father of Nebuchadnezzar, viz., Nabopolassar, the Hebrew Scriptures know nothing. Nebuchadnezzar was generalissimo of the Chaldean invading army. Before he left the country of Palestine, in order to return to Babylon, his father had died, and he had become actual and sole king. The books of Daniel and Jeremiah, written some years afterwards, and also the books of Kings and Chronicles, call him by the name which he had long and universally borne. In the narrations of Jeremiah and Daniel, and also of the other books named, the writers all give him the title of *king*, which was so familiar to them all. The same thing is every day practised, even at the present time.

We speak of Alexander the Great, of the Emperor Augustus, of the Emperor Napoleon, &c., as having done or said this and that, even when we are relating, in a popular way, the things which took place before the sovereignty of these men actually existed. The object of the sacred historians is mainly to designate the leading individual who achieved this or that, not to show in particular how and when he entered on his highest office. The Hebrews, who knew Nebuchadnezzar as the *leader* of the Chaldean army, and also as *king*, before he had actually ended the expedition against them in which he was first engaged, would very naturally of course speak of him as a *king*, when he first invaded Judea. We may easily concede, that he is *anticipatively* so called; for the usage is too common to be either a matter of offence or of stumbling. It cannot fairly be put to the account of error or mistake.

I do not feel, therefore, that we need to resort, as many writers have done, to the expedient of showing that Nebuchadnezzar was constituted by his father a *joint partner* with him of the throne of Babylon, before he set out on the celebrated expedition against Hither Asia, which established an extensive Babylonish empire. Yet this *partnership* is, after all, far from being improbable. Nabopolassar was so enfeebled as to be unable to lead the invading army. Berosus says of him: συστήσας τῷ υἱῷ Ναβουχοδνοσόρῳ, ὄντι ἔτι ἐν ἡλικίᾳ, μέρη τινὰ τῆς δυνάμεως, ἐξέπεμψεν ἐπʼ αὐτόν, κ. τ. λ. Jos. *Cont. Ap.* 1. 19. But δυνάμεως does not here mean *regal power* (as has been maintained), but *military force*. This seems plain from a preceding declaration, in which Berosus states that "Nabopolassar sent his son (Nebuchadnezzar) ἐπὶ τήν ἡμετέραν γῆν—(against Palestine) . . . μετὰ πολλῆς δυνάμεως, i.e., with a large military force." But there is another passage in Berosus, which seems more probably to favour the idea of *copartnership* in the throne, at the time of Nebuchadnezzar's expedition. After the war is finished, Nebuchadnezzar returns, and is formally installed by the Magi as sole and supreme king. Berosus says of him: "Κυριεύσας ἐξ ὁλοκλήρου

τῆς πατρικῆς ἀρχῆς, i.e., becoming supreme over *the whole* of his father's domain." Is there not a natural implication here, that before this he was in part a κύριος? So Hitzig concedes, (*Begriff der Kritik*, p. 186), and states expressly that Nebuchadnezzar's father made him *co-regent*, before the battle at Carchemish. Knobel (*Prophetism*. II. p. 226) also states this as probable. The like do many others; but I deem it unnecessary to make this a point of any moment. The various sacred writers can be harmonized with each other, and with probable facts, independently of this circumstance. But still, it would be an additional reason for the Hebrew usage, in regard to the appellative *king*, as applied to Nebuchadnezzar previously to his father's death, that he was *co-regent* with his father, from the time that he entered on his first Palestine expedition. The contrary of this cannot be shown. That *Berosus*, a Babylonian, should count dominion as belonging to Nabopolassar until his death, seems to be a matter of course, for such dominion was matter of fact. That Nebuchadnezzar, the appointed heir, then obtained his father's *domain* or *dominion* (ἀρχῆς), was also a matter of course; but that he then obtained it ἐξ ὁλοκλήρου, would seem to imply what has been stated above. Be all this, however, as it may, it seems that all the Hebrew writers, in Kings, Chronicles, Jeremiah, and Daniel, are uniform in regard to the appellative in question. Whatever may have been the state of actual facts, it is a sufficient vindication of the Hebrew historians and prophets, that they have followed the usage of their country in regard to this matter. If they had been writing the particular history of Nebuchadnezzar's life and reign, the matter might then be viewed in a different light, in case a *co-regency* never actually took place.

But we are met, in regard to our views of the *time* of Nebuchadnezzar's *first* invasion, by the allegation of Lengerke, Winer, and others, that in that expedition Nebuchadnezzar did not overrun Judea, nor send away any captives from that country. To confirm this, they appeal to Josephus,

Ant. X. 6. 1, who, after describing the capture of Carchemish, says, that "Nebuchadnezzar then passed over the Euphrates, and took all Syria even to Pelusium, παρἰξ τῆς 'Ιουδαίας, *i.e.*, *excepting Judea.*" One is led to wonder, at first view, how Josephus could make this exception; and this wonder is much increased by comparing the declaration in question with what he says in *Cont. Ap.* I. 19. Beyond any reasonable doubt, the two passages are at variance. In the latter passage, he quotes Berosus as saying, that Nebuchadnezzar's father "sent him with an army against Egypt, and against τὴν ἡμετέραν γῆν, *i.e.*, against Judea." And in the sequel he quotes Berosus as also saying, that, at the close of this expedition, Nebuchadnezzar "sent to Babylon τοὺς αἰχμαλώτους 'Ιουδαίων, *the captives of the Jews*, as well as of the Syrians, Phœnicians, and Egyptians." Yet Berosus and the Hebrew Scriptures were, beyond all reasonable question, the only authorities which Josephus had, or at least which he employed, in respect to the history of Nebuchadnezzar. But the source of Josephus's mistake in *Antiq.* X. 6. 1, is in all probability to be found in a passage from Berosus in *Cont. Ap.* I. 19, where, in making a summary in a single sentence of the achievements of Nebuchadnezzar, the Chaldee historian says : "The Babylonian [king] conquered Egypt, Syria, Phœnicia, Arabia, and in his achievements far exceeded all the kings who had before reigned over the Chaldeans and Babylonians." In this mere summary sentence, Berosus omits *Judea*, *i.e.*, the small country of the two tribes, (for this was Judea, at that period); as he also omits Moab, the country of the Ammonites, &c.—omits them evidently because of their comparative smallness. Josephus has unwittingly overlooked this, and so he has *excepted* Judea, in *Antiq.* X. 6. 1, because Berosus has not mentioned it in the passage just quoted. It does not, indeed, much commend his careful accuracy to us, when we find him so doing, because Berosus, as quoted by him, both before and after the sentence in question, has explicitly averred that Nebuchadnezzar came up, in that very first

expedition, to attack *Judea*, and that he carried away captives from that country. But negligences of this kind are somewhat frequent, in this otherwise very valuable historian ; *e.g.*, in respect to this same portion of history, Josephus states (*Antiq.* X. 7. 1), that when Nebuchadnezzar took Jehoiachin captive, he carried away with him 10,832 others into exile. Now this statement is palpably made out from combining together 2 Ki. xxiv. 14, and Jer. lii. 29 ; Josephus having added together the numbers in both passages, without noticing that one deportation is in the *seventh*, and the other in the *eighth* year of Nebuchadnezzar. This discrepancy he does not even notice, much less pretend to reconcile. And so he has not unfrequently done elsewhere. He needs to be closely watched in such matters. Haste, and carelessness of such a kind, may not unfrequently be charged upon him. I cannot think, however, that he meant to make any wrong statements. It is impossible for me, after having carefully examined all that Berosus or Josephus has to say on these matters, to attach any historical value to the παρἰξ τῆς 'Ιουδαίας, which has been quoted above and examined. All things being duly compared and considered, I cannot but think that the evidence of a Babylonian invasion, commencing in the latter part of the third year or Jehoiakim, repeated in 599 at the close of his reign ; renewed against Jehoiachin in 598 ; and then, lastly, at the close of Zedekiah's reign ; are facts as well made out, and as probable, as most facts of such a nature in ancient history. Had there been no gain to be made out of this matter, by warmly enlisted partizans, I do not believe that it would have ever been seriously controverted.

I do not see, then, why Lengerke should be so liberal of his *exclamation points*, when speaking of the intimation of Hengstenberg and Hävernick, that the book of Daniel, by assigning the invasion of Palestine to the *third* year of Jehoiakim, has shown an unusually minute and accurate acquaintance with the history of the Hebrews. Is it not certain, that Nebuchadnezzar's father began his reign, as independent king, in 625 B.C. ? Is it not well established that he died near the end of 605, or at the beginning of 604? Is it not sufficiently established by historical testimony, that Nebuchadnezzar had reduced Carchemish, and overrun all Syria, Phoenicia, Moab, Northern Arabia, Palestine, and Egypt, *before* the death of his father? Was it possible to accomplish all this in less than some *two* years? If not, then Dan. i. 1, 2, seems plainly to be in the right, which assigns Nebuchadnezzar's first invasion of Palestine to the *third* year of Jehoiakim. It could not have been later. Exclamation points, it would be well for Lengerke, and sometimes for his opponents too, to remember, are not arguments, either ratiocinative or historical. The book of Daniel must, as it would seem, be in the right as to the main point in question. Nor does it contradict at all the other books.

The appeal made to Jer. xxxv. 11, in order to show that Nebuchadnezzar had not yet invaded Palestine, in the fourth year of Jehoiakim, is not valid, because there is no note of time in ch. xxxv., and because, as Nebuchadnezzar probably passed through Judea several times during his first invasion, there are no data in this chapter to decide which of his transitions occasioned the flight of the Rechabites to Jerusalem. The fact that Jehoiakim was the known ally and vassal of Pharaoh-Necho, would of itself show that the attitude of Nebuchadnezzar toward Palestine must have been one of hostility. The probability seems to be (comparing this chapter with the following one), that the Rechabites fled from Nebuchadnezzar when he was on his return from Carchemish ; for then he was accompanied by troops from the conquered nations mentioned in Jer. xxxv. 11.

I would merely observe, at the close of this difficult and perhaps too long protracted investigation, that no one who has experience in these matters will think of arguing against the actual occurrence of certain particular events, merely because they are not stated in this book of Scripture or in that, since nearly all of the Jewish history in later times is given to us in professed and acknowledged *summaries* only. One writer sometimes sees fit to insert some special particular, which the rest have passed by. *E.g.*, Jer. li. 59, *seq.*, mentions a journey of Zedekiah, with some of his courtiers, to Babylon, in the fourth year of his reign. In 2 Chron. xxxiii. 11, *seq.*, we have an account of Manasseh as having been carried to Babylon, and of his penitence, and his return to Jerusalem. Nowhere else is either of these events even alluded to, so far as I can find. Yet after the recent investigations respecting the books of Chronicles by Movers, Keil, and others, I think no sober critic will be disposed to call in question the position that neither of these accounts is improbable, and that neither can, on any grounds worthy of credit, be fairly controverted. And I would again suggest, that when leading events as to time and place are certain, an assumption of particular circumstances and events attending them, which is built upon the common course of things and supported by probability, is surely neither uncritical nor unsafe. When we suppose, for example, that Daniel and his associates were sent to Babylon as *hostages*, at the time when Jehoiakim first became a vassal to Nebuchadnezzar, and combine this supposition with the declaration in Dan. i. 1, *seq.*, we suppose what seems to be altogether probable, although we cannot establish this particular by any direct testimony, but merely by implication.

It may not be useless to add, that as the Jews evidently called Nebuchadnezzar *king*, from the time that he invaded Palestine, so by a comparison of Dan. i. 1, *seq.*; Jer. xxv. 1; 2 Ki. xxv. 27, we make out forty-five years (inclusively) as the period of Nebuchadnezzar's reign, according to the Hebrew method of reckoning. At the same time, Berosus and others make out only forty-three years. Still, there is no real disagreement in the case. The Jews began to reckon two years earlier than Berosus, who counts only upon the *sole* reign of Nebuchadnezzar after the death of his father.

II.

EXCURSUS II.

A second charge of *chronological* error against the book of Daniel is, that it makes an evident mistake in respect to the period when Nebuchadnezzar's dream took place, and Daniel interpreted it. The dream was in the *second* year of Nebuchadnezzar's reign (Dan. ii. 1). Previously to this, Daniel and his fellows had been subjected to a *three* years' discipline, as preparatory to waiting upon the king (Dan. i. 5). That period had passed before Daniel was presented to the king (Dan. i. 18). How, it is asked, could Nebuchadnezzar, as *king*, appoint to Daniel *three* years of discipline, and yet bring in the same Daniel, in the *second* year of his actual reign, to interpret his dream, when it is evident, from the author's own showing, that this Daniel had already completed his three years' course of discipline, and taken his place among the Magi before he was called to interpret the dream? Dan. i. 20; ii. 2, 13.

If the result of the preceding investigation be admitted, then is the solution of this seemingly difficult problem rendered quite easy. Nebuchadnezzar is called king in Dan. i. 1., after the usual manner of the Hebrews (comp. 2 Kin. xxiv. 1; 2 Chron. xxxvi. 6), and in the way of anticipation. In fact he became sole king before that expedition had ended. But when a Jewish writer in Babylon (Daniel) comes to the transactions of his actual reign as reckoned of course in Babylon (for of course the date of his reign there would be from the period when he became *sole* king), the writer dates the events that happened under that reign, in accordance with the Babylonish reckoning. So it seems to be in Dan. ii. 1. According to the result of the preceding examination, Daniel was sent to Babylon in the latter part of 607, or the beginning of 606. Nebuchadnezzar became actual king, by the death of his father, near the end of 605, or at the beginning of 604. Ne-

buchadnezzar's *second* year of actual and sole reign would then be in 603. If we suppose the latter part of this year to be the time when the dream occurred, then we have a period of nearly four years between Daniel's exile and his call to interpret the king's dream. Any part of 603 saves the accuracy of the book of Daniel in respect to this matter. In fact it lies on the very face of this statement in the book of Daniel, that it is scrupulously conformed to historical truth; for how could the writer, after having announced Daniel's deportation as belonging to the *third* year of Jehoiakim, and his discipline as having been completed in *three* years, then declare that Daniel was called upon as one of the Magi, to interpret dreams in the *second* year of Nebuchadnezzar? If Nebuchadnezzar was actual king in the third year of Jehoiakim, he was so when Daniel was carried away to Babylon; and plain enough is it, that Daniel's course of discipline was not complete until the *fourth*, or at least the end of the *third* year of Nebuchadnezzar. The error would, in such a case, be so palpable, that no writer of any intelligence or consistency could fail to notice and correct it. We are constrained to believe, then, that Nebuchadnezzar is named *king* merely in the way of *anticipation*, in Dan. i. 1 (and so in 2 Kings xxiv., 2 Chron. xxxvi., Jer. xxv.); and that the date of his sole and actual reign is referred to in Dan. ii. 1, as the Babylonians reckoned it. Thus understood, all is consistent and probable. We need not resort, as Rosenmüller and others have done, to a *long series* of dreams on the part of Nebuchadnezzar, in which the same thing was repeated; nor to the improbable subterfuge, that, although he dreamed in the *second* year of his reign, he did not concern himself to find out an interpreter of his nocturnal visions, until some considerable time afterwards. Both of these representations seem to me to be contrary to the plain and evident tenor of the whole narration. The agitation was immediate, and the stronger because it was immediate. Procrastination of the matter might, and probably would, have liberated him from his fears, and blunted the edge of his curiosity. That Jeremiah reckons in the Palestine Jewish way, *i.e.*, *anticipatively*, is certain from Jer. xxv. 1; xlvi. 2. That he did not this by mistake, but only in compliance with the usage of the Jews in Palestine seems altogether

probable. On the other hand, the state of facts as to Nebuchadnezzar's conquests, as exhibited above, shows that his invasion of Judea must have begun as early as Dan. i. 1 asserts. In truth, facts and events vouch for the writer's minute historical accuracy in this matter, in case it be conceded that Nebuchadnezzar is called king in Dan. i. 1, in the way of *anticipation*, and in accordance with the common Hebrew usage.

III.

EXCURSUS III.

ON THE CHALDEES.

Some Greek writers frequently apply the word *Chaldees* (Χαλδαῖοι) to a fierce people, in the mountainous country bordering on Armenia. Xenophon met with such on his retreat, and he has often made mention of them; *e.g.*, *Anab.* IV. 3, 4; V. 5, 17; VII. 8, 25. Comp. Hab. i. 6, *seq.;* Job i. 17. Strabo notices tribes of the same name, in the country of Pontus, XII. c. 3, p. 26, 27, 36, Tom. III. edit. Lip. From the Armenian [Assyrian] Chaldees many writers have of late supposed the Babylonian Chaldees to have come; which Isa. xxiii. 13, as interpreted by them, seems to favour: "See! the country of the Chaldeans, this people was not; Assyria assigned it [the country] to the dwellers of the desert; they [the Chaldees] erect their watch-towers, they set in commotion the palaces of it [Tyre], they make it a heap of ruins." As Assyria anciently extended her dominion over all middle Asia, and of course over the Armenian Chaldees, the latter might, under their permission, have emigrated to the plains, and being a courageous and warlike people, they might have obtained pre-eminence wherever they settled, over the feeble inhabitants of the plains. But if the Nomades of Chaldean Armenia were indeed the *predominant* portion of the Babylonish people, so that the country was early named from them, those Nomades must at least have emigrated at

an early period of the Assyrian dynasty, *i.e.*, during the one which preceded the invasion of Arbaces, and (according to Ctesias) ended with Sardanapalus, B. C. 747.

The deductions from Isa. xxiii. 13, by Gesenius, Hitzig, Knobel, and others, viz., that the Chaldean power and even name in southern Mesopotamia and Babylon are of *recent* origin, must depend mainly on the correctness of their exegesis of the text in question. But this is far from being made out. On the other hand, substantially with Hupfeld (*Exercitt.*), and Leo (*Allgem. Geschichte*, s. 106), we may with much more probability translate thus: "Behold, the country of the Chaldeans—this people was not [a people]; Assyria—it has assigned it to the beasts of the desert; they erected their towers, they watched her palaces; [but] it has made her a heap of ruins."

In this way we have one main agent, viz., the Chaldean people. The "heap of ruins" is Nineveh, and the "desert" made by invasion, is the Assyrian domain. The prophet is threatening Tyre, and bids her look to what the Chaldeans, their invaders, have already achieved in Assyria. It were easy to vindicate the interpretation just given, but Hupfeld (*Exercitt. Herod.*) has sufficiently done it, and it would be out of place here. The reason why I have now introduced the subject is, because this text is the main dependence of many recent critics for establishing a favourite position of theirs, to which I have already adverted, viz., that the Chaldean power, and even name, in southern Mesopotamia and Babylon, is comparatively recent, and that Chaldea was unknown to the biblical writers before the time of Jehoiakim, at least as a national and independent country. *Facts*, strong and (as it seems to me) irresistible, make against this. Schleyer, in his *Würdigung der Einwürfe*, s. 48, *seq.*, 138, *seq.*, has made objections to it which cannot well be met. *Shinar* was the older name of Babylonia, Gen. xi. 2. This had a king (Amraphel) in the days of Abraham, Gen. xiv. 1, 9. That Babylon justly claims a very high antiquity, cannot be denied. Ctesias, Herodotus, Berosus, the Jewish SS., all agree in this. The latter make Nimrod its founder, who was a grandson of Noah (B.C. 2218), Gen. x. 8. Its walls, towers, palaces, bridges, dykes, and architecture of every kind, most of which was on a gigantic scale that rivalled or exceeded that of Egypt, prove incontestably an advanced state of knowledge in Babylon at a very early period, and indicate a metropolis of the highest grandeur. Other facts of much importance are in accordance with this. Simplicius (*Comm. ad Aristot. de Coelo*, p. 123) tells us, that Calisthenes, who accompanied Alexander the Great to Babylon, found astronomical observations there which reached back to 1903 years before that period, and which he sent to Aristotle; and also that the Magi claimed to be in possession of much older ones still. Ptolemy, in his famous *Canon*, plainly allows their astronomical observations to be correct as far back as Nabonassar (about 747 B.C.), and there begins his era from which he dates events. Larcher, and above all Ideler (on the Astronomy of the Chaldees), have shown that the period of 1903 years is neither impossible nor improbable; as Gesenius himself appears to concede, *Comm. in Es.* III. p. 350. But be this as it may, Diodorus Sic. (II. 29) says expressly, that the Chaldean priests (whom, like Daniel, he calls *Chaldeans*), are of *the most ancient Babylonians*, Χαλδαῖοι τοίνυν τῶν ἀρχαιοτάτων ὄντες Βαβυλωνίων. All this seems to show, that the *Chaldees* (both na-

tion and priests) are of the highest antiquity, and that an emigration from the northern mountains, if it ever took place so as to give a name to the country, must have been at a very remote period. Whenever it was, priests and people appear to have come to Babylonia together. There they amalgamated with the population; and the *Magi* (the priests of the fire-worshippers, such as are described by Zoroaster in the Zendavesta), probably engaged in the studies, and united in some of the pursuits, of the native priests in Babylon; the conquerors thus assimilating to the conquered, their superiors in knowledge, like the Goths and Vandals assimilating to the Romans. Hence the mixture of Parsism and gross Polytheism in the religion of Babylon; for plainly the latter contains both elements. In this way, moreover, can we account for that mixture of the Zend and Pehlvi languages with the Semitic, in the composition of many names and offices in Babylon, in the time of Daniel. *Mag* (מַג Jer. xxxix. 3) is the same as the Sanscrit *maha*, Pers. *mogh*, Zend, *meh*, and is equivalent to the Hebrew רַב; and the הַבְּרִימוֹן in Daniel are the same as the מָעִים and רַבִּים. But although many, or perhaps even most, of the proper names of men and of *civil* offices among the Chaldeans are best explained from the Zend, or the old Persian, yet the names of their gods and of their *religious* offices are mostly of a *Semitic* origin; *e.g.*, *Belus* = בֵּעֵל or בְּעֵל; Mylitta = מוּלֶדֶת (genetrix); הַרְטֻמִּים from חֶרֶט, Daniel i. 20; ii. 2; and also in Gen. xli. 8; Exod. vii. 11, 22; viii. 3, 14, 15; ix. 11; אַשָּׁף, Dan. i. 20; ii. 2 (Chald.), x. 27; iv. 4; v. 7, 11, 15, = Syr. (incantator), מְכַשֵּׁף, Dan. ii. 2; also Ex. vii. 11; xxii. 17; Deut. xviii. 10; Mal. iii. 5; and so the generic Chaldee word הַכִּים (= *Magus*), Dan. ii. 12, 21; iv. 3; v. 7, 8, is notoriously the same as the Hebrew הָכָם. But many of the names of kings, and of the higher civil officers, seem to be compounds of Semitic with the Parsi, Pehlvi, or Zend; such as Nebuchadnezzar, Belshazzar, &c. (See *Lex.*) The internal evidence, therefore, of a *mixture* of inhabitants in Chaldea, from some quarter or other, appears to be inscribed in high relief upon the language of the Chaldeans, in the time of Nebuchadnezzar. The religion of the Babylonians (as exhibited best of all by Münter in his essay on this subject, and by Gesenius in his Excursus at the end of his *Comm. on Isaiah*), affords striking evidence of Parsism and Polytheism commingled by the union of different nations who retained some of their respective rites, and by the natural progress of the attractive sensual parts of those rites, as the metropolis progressed in riches, and luxury, and debauchery.

This general view of the subject seems necessary, in order to place the reader of the book of Daniel in a position in which he may rightly estimate the various phenomena of the book. There is a mixture throughout of the Assyro-Median and Semitic, both in the names of men and offices, and also in the rites, customs, and opinions of the inhabitants. That the *Assyro*-Chaldean at the time when Daniel lived, was the common spoken language of the court and king, seems to be plainly *negatived*, by Dan. ii. 4, *seq.* The Magi address the king אֲרָמִית *i.e.*, in the *Aramean*, which is substantially the same that we now name *East Aramean* or *Chaldee*. In this language, more than half of the book of Daniel is composed. Doubtless the Jews who lived in that quarter when Daniel wrote the book, could read and understand it; and indeed to the younger part of them, at that period, it must have been vernacular, or nearly so. It is even quite probable, that the history contained in the book of Daniel would thus be more easily read by the younger portion of the Hebrew community in that region than if it had been in the Hebrew; and this, perhaps, might have been the inducement to write it in Aramean.

But to return to the הַכַּשְׂדִּים of our text; I have only to add, that this name, employed to designate a *literary order of men* (equivalent to חַכָמִים, Chald. הַכִּימִין, and *Magi*), passed into very common

use among the Greeks and Romans. So Strabo XV. Tom. III. p. 326, ed. Lips. Diod. Sic. 2. 29, *seq.* Cic. Div. 1. 1, 2. Ammian. Marc. 23. 6. Arrian Alex. 3. 16. In still later times, fortune-tellers and magicians from the East were called *Chaldeans* by European nations. The progress of meaning in regard to the appellation is obvious. First, the Chaldees are conquerors, and offices, or whatever else is eminent, are called Chaldean *par excellence*. Then, as Chaldea abounded in astrologers and soothsayers, it was natural for Greeks and Romans to call these classes of men by the name of *Chaldeans*. Last of all, among the western nations, soothsayers and magicians were called by the same name, without any special regard to the country from which they sprung. One meets, not unfrequently in the classics, with the appellation employed in this manner.

Several questions, of some importance in regard to the genuineness of the book of Daniel, have been recently made, first in regard to the *number* of classes specified in the verse before us, and then in respect to the employment of כַּשְׂדִּים, as designating only one portion of the Magi.

To begin with the latter; Gesenius (*Comm. in Es.* II. s. 355) seems to call in question the limited meaning of the word, and Bleek (on Dan. in *Schleiermacher,* &c., *Zeitschrift,* s. 225) even doubts whether there was any such thing as different classes. Both doubt against the evidence of usage widely extended. Daniel plainly uses the word to denote a *class* of the Magi, in ii. 2, 10; iv. 4 (Engl. Vers. iv. 7); v. 7, 11. And when Gesenius and Hitzig suggest, that in Dan. ii. 4, 10, the name *Chaldeans* is generically employed, Lengerke himself (sufficiently inclined to all which can make against the genuineness of the book), avers very justly that this is only in the way of breviloquence, where one class that is pre-eminent is named instead of recapitulating or particularizing all (*Comm.* s. 50). Decisive, as to the usage of such a method of expression by the writer, is Dan. iii. 24, where only the

הַדָּבְרִין (state-counsellors) are addressed, while ver. 27 shows that they are only one class of the state-officers then and there assembled, to witness the spectacle which is described. Such methods of breviloquence are quite common; and besides all this, we have heathen usage of the same kind as that under discussion; e. g., Herodotus, 1. 181, οἱ Χαλδαῖοι, ἐόντες ἱερέες τούτου τοῦ Θεοῦ [i.e.. βήλου], compare I. 183, where Χαλδαῖοι occurs three times in the same sense; Diod. Sic. II. 24, τῶν ἱερέων, οὓς Βαβυλώνιοι καλοῦσι Χαλδαίους, and again in c. 29, Χαλδαῖοι τοίνυν τῶν ἀρχαιοτάτων Βαβυλωνίων . . . παραπλησίαν ἔχουσι τάξιν τοῖς κατ' Αἴγυπτον ἱερεῦσι; and so Hesychius, Χαλδαῖοι, γένος Μάγων. Ctesias (edit. Bähr, p. 68) seems, indeed, to use Chaldeans and Magi as synonymes; and so, as we have seen above, later usage among Greeks and Romans often employed the words. But even in Ctesias, the context shows that by Chaldeans is there meant the higher order of the Magi. So in Dan. ii. 4, 10.

Thus much for the limited use of the name Chaldeans, which is sufficiently clear and certain. As to the number of the classes, with respect to which Lengerke (s. 49 f.) thinks he detects the error of a later writer who was not intimately acquainted with Chaldean matters, the question seems not to be one of any great difficulty. He admits, as do nearly all others, that there were divisions or classes among the Magi. This was notoriously the case as to the priests in Egypt, Ex. vii. 11. Herod. II. 36. 58. Jablonsky, Panth. Egypt. Prol. c. 3. The division of priests in India, from the remotest period, is well known. The Medes and Persians admitted the like divisions among their Magi. The author of Daniel, in ii. 2, iv. 4, (Eng. iv. 7), v. 7, 12, appears to name five classes of Magi (if indeed the מְכַשְּׁפִים of ii. 2 be not merely another name for the גָּזְרִין of the other passages); on account of which Lengerke accuses him of mistake; and he declares (p. 47), that "all other ancient writers everywhere acknowledge only three classes," and concludes from this DANIEL I.

that the writer of the book was some person of a later age and of a remote country, where tradition gave an indistinct and uncertain report. His authorities as to the "united report of all antiquity," are Jerome (Contra Jovin. I. p. 55), and Porphyry (de Abstin. 4. 16). These are somewhat late writers as to the matter of testifying, "for all antiquity," to a particular usage in Babylon about a thousand years before their time. But in fact neither of these give their own testimony. They both appeal to Eubulus. If Eubulus the philosopher is meant, he lived about 200 B.C. If either the comedian or the orator of the same name be meant (which seems not probable), they lived about 376 B.C. In his history of Mithra, Eubulus asserts, that "the Magi were divided into three classes." When? In his time, or at an earlier period? Among the Persians, or among the Babylonians of Nebuchadnezzar's time? Unquestionably he refers to the Persians, inasmuch as the history of Mithra concerns them. But even admitting the correctness of the testimony at the time when it was given, it proves nothing in respect to the custom or usage at Babylonia, in the seventh century B.C. Magi indeed there were at Babylonia; for among the military chieftains of Nebuchadnezzar, at the siege of Jerusalem in Zedekiah's time, was Nergal Sharezer רַב־מָג, chief Magian. The priesthood, so far from excluding men from civil or military office in those times, was a leading recommendation of them to appointments of this nature, because it implied an unusual degree of knowledge. Thus Ctesias represents Belesys, the leader of the Chaldeans when Nineveh was destroyed, as "the most distinguished of the priests, οὓς Βαβυλώνιοι καλοῦσι Χαλδαίους," Diod. Sic. II. 24. So a Magian was elevated to the throne of Persia, after the death of Cambyses; Ctes. Persica, c. 13, seq. So, after the death of Nebuchadnezzar's father, while the former was carrying on the war in Judea, the affairs of government, before the return of the prince to Babylon, were administered by priests [ὑπὸ Χαλδαίων], and the supremacy was

x

vested in the *archimagus*, who gave it up, in due time, to Nebuchadnezzar, according to Berosus in Joseph. *Antiq.* X. 11. 1. In fact the Oriental and Egyptian kings, as well as some of the Cæsars, paid the homage to the priesthood of becoming members of their body, if they were not already so when they became kings. It may, I readily concede, have been the usual fact, that the leading divisions of the *Persian* Magi were *three* in number.* But this would be of little avail in showing that such was the custom of the Babylonians, among whom, although the priesthood retained, as it would seem, the honorary name of *Magi*, yet their religion differed in the most striking manner, in many respects, from that of the Parsis. In the rites of the latter there was no temple, no altar, no sacrifice of human victims, no consumption by fire even of any victims, no images of gods, no prostitution-worship of Mylitta ; in a word none of the impurity, cruelty, ridiculous prodigality of expenditure, and abominable rites of the Babylonians. All matters of religion had been changed, by the commingling of the (Assyro-) Chaldean conquerors with the grosser and more sensual heathen of Babylonia, if indeed we concede such an intermixture. How then can testimony about the Magi in a country where pure Parsism prevailed, be applicable to the case of the Babylonian priests and literati, as described by Daniel ? But if we must resort, in

the present case, to the testimony of Greek writers, the position of Lengerke is far enough from being confirmed. Diodorus Sic., in speaking περὶ τῶν ἐν Βαβυλῶνι καλουμίνων Χαλδαίων, represents them as practising astrology, soothsaying, magic, incantations, augury from the flight of birds, and the interpretation of dreams and remarkable occurrences, II. 29 ; all of which plainly betokens different classes.† Strabo, most of all among the Greeks to be relied on in such matters, says (XVI. 1. § 6), "There are, among the Chaldean astronomers, γίνη πλεία *many kinds* or *classes*, some are called *Orcheni*, and some *Borsippeni*, besides *many others* (ἄλλοι πλείους), who affirm different things in respect to their doctrines, according to their respective sects." Here then is abundance of room for the four or five classes of Daniel ; and it is indeed quite probable that the subdivisions must have amounted to many more, although it was not to his purpose to name any more than the leading ones. At all events, the testimony of Daniel stands high above any fair

* But this is not established by the *Zendavesta*, as cited by Heeren (*Ideen* I. s. 480, ed. 3d); for in Kleuker's edition, II. 261, only *two* classes are spoken of; viz., *Herbeds* and *Mobeds*. But in *Yesht Sades* (LXXXIII. *ad fin.* II. p. 194), the *Avesta* speaks of the *three* orders of the *Athorne* = priests ; again (*ib.* p. 276), the same thing is mentioned ; once more (p. 156), "the *threefold*, like the Athorne." But in another passage *four* orders of priests seem to be designated. So in *Zendavesta*, III., p. 225, we find *Herbed* (= candidate for the priesthood), *Mobed* (priest), *Destur-Mobed* (teacher-priest), and *Destur Desturan* = (archbishop), a provincial superior. Probably the case is the same in the *Zendavesta* as in Daniel ; *i.e.*, sometimes the leading class only is noted, as in ii. 4, 10; then again we have four classes, in ii. 2 ; in v. 7 are three classes (one a new one); four classes in iv. 4; three in v. 7; and four in v. 11. To insist, now, that any one of these passages exhibits the full and exclusive designation of all the classes of the Magi, would be entirely nugatory.

† Certainly this assertion seems very probable, if we turn our attention, for a moment, to the divisions of the priesthood among the Greeks, in relation to such matters. With them every god and goddess had a separate order of priests; and even the same orders differed from each other in different places. Again, each of these orders had a *high-priest* ; in some places, two; the Delphians, five. Then there were *assistants* of the sacred order; viz., the *Parasiti*, or those who provided materials for the celebration of religious rites, and then the Κήρυκες, or criers, who also acted the part of cooks and butchers. Besides these classes, there were the νεωκόροι, who kept clean and adorned the temples; then the ναοφύλακες, who guarded those temples; and lastly, the προπόλοι, or general waiters; Potter's *Gr. Antiq.* 1. p. 222, *seq.* Beyond these general divisions, were subordinate ones almost without end; *e. g.*, as to diviners, μάντεις, χρησμολόγοι, θεομάντεις, of three kinds; interpreters of dreams, ὀνειροκρίται, ὀνειροσκόποι, ὀνειροπόλοι ; divination by sacrifices employed at least six classes; by birds, at least as many more; by lots, at least three; by ominous words and things, many classes; by magic and incantation, at least nineteen; Potter, *ib.* pp. 327, *seq.* We must add to all this, that the priesthood among the Romans was arranged in quite a similar way. I do not aver that the Chaldeans made all of these subdivisions, which are almost endless; but I may well say, that the offices which Diodorus ascribes to their Magi, involves, from the very nature of the case, something not unlike to this.

exception, in regard to the classification of the Magi. Certainly he has named no improbable class. Nearly all of the classes named, indeed, appertain to the priesthood of the heathen, as elsewhere exhibited in the Scriptures; and if there be a class *sui generis* in Daniel, there can be no good reason to charge him with error; for how can we reasonably suppose, that there was not some one class or more of the priesthood that was peculiar to Babylon? The suggestion of Gesenius (*Comm.* II. p. 355), that the writer in all probability merely brought together the various designations of such classes of persons as are mentioned elsewhere in the Heb. Scriptures; and the assertion of Lengerke (p. 47), that "he undoubtedly did thus;" seem to have no other basis than an inclination to throw discredit upon the book, and industriously to collect and reckon up everything which may help to show that the writer was lacking as to accurate knowledge. Something more than this, however, seems necessary in order to discredit the book in question.

Equally nugatory seems to be the assertion of Bleek (*Schleierm*, &c., *Zeits. s.* 225), that "it is altogether wonderful, that Nebuchadnezzar should summon all classes of the Magi to interpret his dream, instead of summoning the appropriate class, viz., the ὀνειροσκόποι." It is enough to say in reply, that as Nebuchadnezzar had forgotten all the particulars of his dream, and these were required to be disclosed as well as the interpretation to be given; and moreover, since he knew, as the Magi assert (Da. ii. 10), that "no king or ruler was wont to make such a demand;" the very difficulty and extraordinary nature of the case would naturally induce him to summon all classes of his חַכִּימִין, so that what one class could not accomplish, another perhaps might be able to do. Nothing was more common among the Greeks and Romans, than, where one method of divination failed, to resort to another. Probability, therefore, and consistency are stamped upon the very face of the narrative, in regard to this matter.

One other objection against the pro-

bability of the narration in Dan. ii., has been strongly urged, viz., "the improbability that a *foreigner* should be admitted among the Magi; and above all, that a most rigid Jew could at all be promoted to *supremacy* over the whole order, as it is related of Daniel (ii. 48), that he became כָּל־חַכִּימֵי בָבֶל רַב־סִגְנִין עַל; or if he was promoted, that such a man as Daniel could accept the office, and discharge its duties."

That the Magi had a *supreme head*, is plain from Jer. xxxix. 3, where Nergal Sharezer, a military chieftain of Nebuchadnezzar, is named רַב מָג, *i.e.*, *arch-Magian.* So Sozomen (*Hist. Ecc.* II. 13) speaks of μέγας ἀρχίμαγος. Berosus, as cited by Athenæus (*Deipnos.* XIV. 44), in speaking of the Sakea (*i.e.*, Saturnalian feast) of the Babylonians, mentions the *overseer* as being arrayed in king-like robes, and as called Ζωγάνης (= סָגָן), which means *præfect.* Diodorus Sic. says of the priest Belesys, who led the Babylonians in revolt against Sardanapalus, that he was τῶν ἱερέων ἐπισημότατος. Every large town, province, and kingdom, had an ἀρχίμαγος, *Zendav.* III. p. 226.

That a foreigner, by special favour of the king, could be introduced among the Magi, seems quite probable from the usage of the Persians, who, although they excluded foreigners in general from that order, did this, as Philostratus (in *Protagora*) asserts, ἦν μὴ ὁ βασιλεύς ἐφῆ, *i.e.*, only in cases where the king did not demand his admission. The Magi, and all others, were at the disposal of the absolute monarch, either in Persia or in Babylon. So Brissonius, *de Regno Pers.* II. § 67, 68. So, likewise, Moses is said to have been "learned in all the wisdom of the Egyptians," being the adopted child of Pharaoh's daughter (Acts vii. 22). Lengerke, however, says: "We know nothing of his being admitted into the order of the priests." But we do at least know, that the Egyptian kings and princes, as a matter of honour and respect, were admitted to this order; nor is there any probability of Moses' being thus instructed, unless he had been admitted into that order.

That Daniel was a *Jew*, would, so far as we know, be no more objection to his promotion, in the eyes of Nebuchadnezzar, than if he had been a foreigner of any other country. This king does not seem to have used the Jews more roughly, than he did all his conquered subjects. That Daniel, as one of the Magi, was made a civil ruler, *i.e.*, Satrap of Babylonia (Dan. ii. 48), as well as Chief Magian, is perfectly in accordance with Oriental usage in general, and with that of Babylon in particular (Jer. xxxix. 3).

"But it must awaken great doubt," it is said, "when Daniel is described as holding the office of chief overseer, over priests who worshipped Bel and Mylitta." (Leng. p. 50). It might, I am ready to concede, if the acceptance of such an office obliged him to the personal performance of heathen rites. But it should be remembered, that *priests* were only a portion of the Magi. I do not say that Daniel's office was a *sinecure;* but I may say, that there was little or no probability, that as *chief* Magian he was subjected to perform the details of priestly rites. He decided cases of appeal; prescribed general rules of order; participated in the studies of the Literati ; and (which seems to have been the king's special object in promoting him), received the honours and emoluments attached to his high station. Was it not quite possible for an intelligent man, so situated, to avoid participating in the details of heathen worship ? The whole book of Daniel shows him to be both conscientious and fearless. His station must have sub-

jected him, indeed, to severe trials; but it also afforded him great opportunity to aid his exiled countrymen, and to mitigate the severity of their captive state. Reasonably may we suppose, that this was his motive for accepting the office.

Lengerke represents the author of the book of Daniel (who in his view belonged to the period of the Maccabees), as "evidently introducing Daniel among the Magi, that he might, by his interpretation of dreams, elevate the God of Israel above the vanities which the heathen worshipped " (p. 51). That the narration has such a purpose in view, I would readily concede; but that the whole matter is a mere figment of a sagacious writer in the second century B.C., in order to accomplish such an end, is an assertion which needs some proof. The *ultima ratio*, in all such cases, of this writer, and of others who sympathize in feeling with him, is plain enough. It is simply the denial of all supernatural interposition and occurrences. Against such views, the present volume would not be an appropriate place for argument. The New Testament has given its clear and decided testimony in favour of the truthfulness of this book. A consistent man who renounces the book of Daniel as a record of true history, must also renounce the New Testament. My own belief is, that the God who made the world, *governs* it; and that he can interpose, and has interposed, in respect to the regular and established order of things, where special purposes were or are to be accomplished that cannot well be brought about in another way.